Church and State in Modern Britain 1700–1850

In this, the second part of his history of the Industrial Revolution, Richard Brown examines the political and religious developments that took place between the 1780s and the 1840s in terms of the aristocratic elite and through the expression of alternative radical ideologies. Opening with a discussion of the nature of History and Britain in 1700, the book ends with an examination of Britain's foreign policy, the emergence of the modern state and the mid-century 'crisis' of the 1840s. Unlike many previous works it emphasises *British* not just English history. It is this emphasis on the diversity of experience and the focus on continuity as well as change, women as well as men that makes this a distinctive text. Students will also find the theoretical foundations of historical narrative and analysis clearly explained.

Society and Economy in Modern Britain 1700–1850, completes Richard Brown's two-part study of British history 1700–1850.

Richard Brown, co-editor of *Teaching History* is currently SCIL co-ordinator at Manshead School, Bedfordshire.

Church and State in Modern Britain 1700–1850

Richard Brown

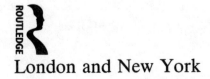

London and New York

First published 1991 by Routledge
11 New Fetter Lane, London EC4P 4EE

Simultaneously published in the USA and Canada by Routledge
a division of Routledge, Chapman and Hall, Inc.
29 West 35th Street, New York, NY 10001

Typeset in 10/12 pt Times Linotron 300
by Input Typesetting Ltd, London
Printed in England by Richard Clay

British Library Cataloguing in Publication Data
Brown, Richard
   Church and state in modern Britain: a political and
   religious history.
   1. Great Britain 1714–1837
   I. Title
   941.07

Library of Congress Cataloging-in-Publication Data
Brown, Richard
    Church and state in modern Britain: a political and religious history,
    1700–1850 / Richard Brown
        p. cm.
    Includes bibliographical references.
        1. Church and state—Great Britain—History—18th century.
    2. Church and state—Great Britain—History—19th century. 3. Great
    Britain—Church history—18th century. 4. Great Britain—Politics
    and government—18th century. 5. Great Britain—Politics and
    government—19th century. 6. Great Britain—Church history—19th
    century. I. Title.
    BR758.B76 1991
    941.07—dc20   91–31958
                                                                   CIP

ISBN 0–415–01122–1

To Margaret, without whose constant support
I could not have written these volumes

Contents

Figures and tables

Preface

'What is history?', asked Robert Lowell in his *Notebooks 1967–68*, and with the wisdom of the poet he responded: 'What you cannot touch.' Into the fabric of our own existence we incorporate the records and the multifarious expressions of thought and action of past peoples and social groups. They put us in touch with human history and yet they do not enable us to touch that history alive. They compel us to listen and yet their sound alone cannot bring us fully within hearing presence of the word of history. Intangible and inaudible though it is, this historical reality, this sense of 'pastness' is nevertheless formatively present in our lives and reflections. Lowell's question remains to incite us to improve our understanding of that past and his answer also stands as a caution against any belief that we can fully discover what happened and why.

People study history for many reasons but all have in common a need to explain and understand past societies. We ask questions, many of which have their origins in our own present-day experience, like how did individuals react to rapid change, why did society change so slowly, what was it like to live then, have people's needs changed, what was the nature of belief or power and how did people register their protest against the action or inaction of those in government? In attempting to answer questions like these it seems to me perfectly legitimate to use ideas and methodologies from disciplines other than history. We may begin to understand people in the past by examining, for example, the social sciences, geography, technology, science and philosophy. We may develop 'models' which can be applied to past events and people. But they must always be grounded in the available sources of information, the raw data from which historians draw their conclusions.

Church and state in modern Britain is the second of two volumes covering the economic, social and political history of Britain from the beginning of the eighteenth century until 1850. Two further volumes will bring the story up to date. It is aimed at students studying A or AS Level examinations and first-year students at university or college. This book covers the political and religious history of Britain from the beginning of the eighteenth century through to the mid-nineteenth century. It provides an explanation of what actually happened and why, since narrative and description form the basis for historical studies at all levels. It examines how historians have interpreted the past and provides a conceptual framework through which the past can be illuminated. Each chapter has references to both contemporary and secondary sources. The book divides into two parts, corresponding to the political and religious dimensions of past experience. Chapters 1 and 2 set the scene, outlining the nature of history and what Britain was like around 1700. Chapters 5 and 14 cover the major religious themes of the period. The remaining chapters cover the main political questions. The final chapter of the book covers the mid-nineteenth century 'crisis' which, I maintain, set the agenda for the next half century.

It is a history of Britain in which the histories of Wales, Scotland and Ireland are given an emphasis in their own right not simply mentioned when their experience had some impact on England. Recent trends in historical writing have led to a growing awareness of the role of women in the past and particularly their marginalization in a male-dominated and male-focused society. Historians have also become aware of the place of ethnic minorities within the dominant cultural hegemony. Both these issues receive particular emphasis. The past was, like the present, lived, and if we are to understand that fully it is fundamental that we should aim to achieve some 'totality' of past experience.

My debt to others in writing this volume will be obvious from the references to each chapter. I hope I have not misrepresented their views. I am particularly grateful to Bedfordshire County Council for giving me two years' secondment to do research in education at Cambridge University between 1985 and 1987. This gave me time to think out my ideas in a less hectic atmosphere than that of a school. I have been fortunate to teach in an authority and at two schools, Houghton Regis Upper School and Manshead School, Dunstable, in which students have been both stimulating and unwilling to accept my views as 'tablets from Sinai'. My thanks to Anna Fedden who originated the project, Nancy Marten who kept me going over the writing period, and Claire L'Enfant, Julia Hall and Antonia Pledger who saw it to its conclusion. Above all I must thank my wife and children whose forbearance, patience and willingness to leave me in peace created the right atmosphere in which to write. This book is dedicated to them.

Richard Brown
1 January 1990

1 The nature of history

'A SOCIAL NECESSITY'

Much has been written about the uses of history.[1] Understanding of the present and the potential of the future is impossible without a temporal perspective. History is to society what remembered experience is to an individual. Marwick sees it as 'a social necessity'. There are three practical advantages to society from the study of the past. First, it alerts people to the sheer variety of human mentality and achievement and thus to the range of possibilities people have now. History provides imaginative range but is also an inventory of assets whose value may only be realized by later generations. Second it is a source of precedent and prediction. Though this is primarily a justification for contemporary history, the drawing of historical analogies, often half-consciously, is a habitual and unavoidable dimension of human reasoning. Comparisons across time can illuminate the present by highlighting both what is recurrent and what is new, what is durable, transient and contingent on our present conditions. Finally history provides a critique of the myths that pervade society. It has a crucial corrective function in that by removing myths, it can act as the conscience of society.

HISTORY – A DEFINITION

History is about people in society, their actions and interactions, their beliefs and prejudices, their pasts and presents. 'People in society' means people as individuals, communities, groups, institutions, states and nations. Individuals can be simultaneously members of a community (the village where they live), an institution (the church they attend), a group (the occupational group they belong to), a nation (Wales, Scotland, Ireland or England) as well as a member of the United Kingdom. 'Actions and interactions' mean the ways in which people behave as individuals and communities and the ways they react to each other. 'Beliefs and prejudices' mean the ways in which individuals and communities perceive(d) 'their worlds', the values upon which 'their worlds' are based and the consequences of this in terms of their own perceptions of others and others' perceptions of them. 'Past and presents' provide people in society with an individual and collective memory, a storehouse of experience through which to develop their sense of social identity, to judge present actions and assess future prospects.

HISTORIANS ON HISTORY – DIFFERING METHODOLOGIES

History is also about how historians examine and interpret the past.[2] Although there are more than 'two kinds of history' the recent debate between Fogel and Elton brings out some of the different ways in which historians approach their study. Fogel sees 'traditional historians' as aspiring

> to portray the entire range of human experience, to capture all of the essential features of the civilizations they were studying, and to do so in a way that would clearly have relevance to the present. They were continually searching for 'synthesising principles' that would allow them to relate in a meaningful way the myriad of facts that they were uncovering.[3]

In their analysis, he maintains, historians turn to the social sciences for insights into behaviour. But they recoil from its analytical methods because these threaten history's intrinsic qualities: 'its literary art, its personal voice and its concern with the countless subtle questions that are involved in the notion of individuality'.[4]

Fogel believes that this is the result of the way 'traditional' historians evaluate evidence. They use a 'legal model' which is well suited to examining specific events and individuals but which is suspicious of statistical evidence and scientific method.

So how do 'cliometricians' like Fogel approach their study of the past? First, they want it to be based on explicit models of human behaviour. Secondly, they believe that all historians use behavioural models in relating the facts of history to each other. The difference is that for traditional historians these are implicit, vague and incomplete whereas for the cliometrician they are explicit, specific and complete. They allow historians to cut through the diversity of experience and behaviour that characterize human activity and to make judgements as to why people are likely to have behaved as they did. Thirdly, this approach often leads cliometricians to represent behaviour in mathematical equations which are then verified or refuted with quantitative evidence. However, quantification is not the universal characteristic of this approach. The crux of the difference between these two methods is that

> many traditional historians tend to be highly focused on specific individuals, on particular institutions, on particular ideas, and on nonrepeti-

tive occurrences . . . they make only limited use of explicit behavioural models and usually rely on literary models. Cliometricians tend to be highly focused on collections of individuals, on categories of institutions and on repetitive occurrences . . . These involve explicit behavioural models and . . . quantitative evidence.[5]

The traditional historian may want to explain why Thomas Edwards of Risby, Suffolk stole four hen's eggs in 1864 whereas the cliometrician would wish to understand why egg-stealing expanded in the nineteenth century. Both types of history are concerned with explaining the past. Both search for meaning using evidence that is often incomplete, inconsistent and ambiguous. Historians can and should use any method, concept, or model which help them to do this.

HISTORY AND ITS CONCEPTS

Historians examine the past through a number of methodological concepts. First, historians need to have an understanding of historical context, a sense of time and chronology. Secondly, the nature of events, their causation and consequences needs to be made clear. Piecing together what happened in the past will, thirdly, result in narrative, analysis and synthesis. Fourthly, historians examine the past in terms of change and continuity, progression, regression, evolution or revolution and discreet phenomena as 'agents' or 'inhibitors' of change. It is now fashionable to emphasize the continuities in historical experience and to play down the importance and effects of change and discontinuities in the past.[6] Finally, history is less about truth than about possible and tentative interpretations on the basis of the available evidence.

What concepts can historians use to examine people in the past? These can be divided into –

  (i) understanding people in the past as individuals and social groups.
 (ii) understanding the role of specific individuals and social groups.
(iii) understanding the actions, values, beliefs, attitudes and decisions of individuals.
 (iv) understanding people in their local, regional, national and global context.
  (v) understanding the various choices open to individuals and groups at particular times and why they opted for one direction rather than another.
 (vi) understanding the different dimensions of life which people in the past have experienced and the relationship between them – I will highlight economic, social, political, cultural (including religious), technological and scientific and environmental experiences.
(vii) understanding that people live different lives within the same time-scales – the diversity of contemporary experience.

(viii) understanding that the historical process is one of development, that, despite appearances, it is not static and that development may be resisted.

 (ix) understanding the relationships, tensions and conflicts that exist between individuals and social groups.

Through the use of these concepts, and the available evidence historians can attempt to explain what happened in the past.

PEOPLE IN HISTORY

Individuals in the eighteenth and nineteenth centuries lived in various types of association. There were quite definite forms of the family, marriage, religious worship, property and inheritance, economic organization, governmental procedures and so on and these formed something more than the individuals who lived and behaved within their contexts.

These associational forms were interconnected. Together they made up a total social system and it is important that they are examined as part of that system. Three points make this clear. First, a social system came into being and regulated the activities and experiences of people who shared the same collective conditions of life – who worked out a particular pattern of life in relation to the same ecological constraints, economic resources and historical experiences. In eighteenth-century Britain this was evident not just in the collective conditions of Ireland, Wales, Scotland and England but in different regional experiences and expectations. Secondly, associational forms were essentially forms of regulation. Each association had its own set of rules – some implicit, others formalized – by which some individuals exercised authority which others were obliged to obey; by which different tasks were defined; through which satisfactory work or behaviour was rewarded and the unsatisfactory punished. Finally, the place of a particular association within the social system was made even more clear by the existence of institutions which actually linked and inter-penetrated them all. 'Marriage', for example, was not just a familial one but was also a religious, legal, political and economic institution.

Associations and social systems are essentially characterized by meanings and values. Every social institution contains a set of values at its core: it forbids certain things and requires, upholds and encourages others. Although not all individuals agreed or abided by all the values embodied within social institutions, the network of regulation was a moral condition.

Individuals born within a particular social system with particular associational forms have a multi-dimensional private experience from birth to death quite different from those born within another. The experience of a Welsh farmer was different from a Scottish one. These different private experiences are articulated, understood and expressed in terms of the language with which they are familiar. The collective conditions and social systems shared by individuals have played a large part in making private experience and in shaping the nature of individuals. This view does not negate the role of individuals in the past but places them in a context that did influence, though did not determine, their responses to particular circumstances. For example, in periods of high food prices those whose standard of living was directly affected were likely to riot for the restoration of the 'moral economy'. But similar circumstances did not always bring about the same individual response.

Associations and the social system will be inherited by generation after generation. Although certain aspects will be sustained and continued, others will be gradually, or in some cases radically, altered. This 'heritage' plays an important part in the way that individuals perceive their presents. It establishes systems of culture based upon inherited symbols, meanings, sentiments, values, ideologies and sanctions. Through cultural hegemony, control over values and beliefs, the governing association in eighteenth- and early nineteenth-century Britain was able to maintain its dominant economic and political position. Inherited experience underpins existing cultural values.

HISTORY AND CHANGE

This can help historians understand features of importance in a society at a particular point in time. But it does not explain the dynamics of change within that society. There is a surprising amount of agreement between social theorists about how societies change. First, the contemporary social experience (at any point in history) was, they maintain, the result of social evolution. Secondly, they agree on the central importance of the transition from a predominantly 'traditional' to a predominantly 'rational and contractual' social order. Thirdly, the promise and threat of this transformation is recognized, as is the necessity for the deliberate reconstruction of associations and institutions. These theories have a direct relevance in explaining the development from a pre-industrial society (though whether it was a 'traditional' society is a separate question) to an industrial society in Britain. The development of industrial and particularly urban society led to existing forms of association and institutions being brought into question. Parliamentary reform, in 1832 and particularly in 1867 and 1885, was the result of the increasing difficulty in defending a demonstrably irrational system of suffrage. Developments in women's rights were part of the same process. Resistance to logical change, the defence of the indefensible, however, also played an important part in the chronology of these developments.

Richard Wilkinson

These sociological theories identify progress as the driving force behind change. Marx, for example, saw the creation of a more humane, non-exploiting society as the end of social development. But this is not the only possible explanation. Richard Wilkinson[7] argues that development is the result of a society outgrowing its resources and productive system. As the established economic system proved inadequate and subsistence problems became more severe, he maintains, a society is driven to change its methods

> Development comes out of poverty, not out of plenty as many economic theories would lead one to suppose. Poverty stimulates the search for additional sources of income and makes people willing to do things they may previously have avoided.[8]

He identifies the ending of constraints upon population growth as the major cause of change.[9] This led to growing resource scarcities. In England and Wales rising cost of living, falling real wages and population growth coincided before 1800: 'In English history there can be no mistaking the intimate connection between the periodic appearance of population pressure and economic development.'[10]

Wilkinson then goes on to analyse the English industrial revolution:

> The ecological roots of the English industrial revolution are not difficult to find. The initial stimulus to change came directly from resource shortages and other ecological effects of an economic system expanding to meet the needs of a population growing within a limited area.[11]

Population growth from the 1740s put pressure on land resources and Britain changed from the 1760s from being a net exporter of wheat to a net importer. Initially, change in industry did not involve the establishment of new industries but technical innovation in existing industries. Stimulus came from the limitations which land shortage imposed on the supply of industrial raw materials. Three examples illustrate his argument. First, the substitution of coal for wood. From the early sixteenth century there was a consistent increase in firewood prices. By the 1630s it was about two and a half times as expensive in relation to other prices as it had been in 1500. Rising cost and growing scarcity put pressure upon both industrial and domestic consumers with the result that during the seventeenth century there was a shift from wood to coal. Iron-smelting was the only major industry not to make this change by 1700. It took ironmasters longer to work out a solution because of the complexity of smelting iron with coal. The move to coal, Wilkinson argues, was followed by other innovations: 'The invention of the steam-engine was a direct result of the new technical problems posed by deep mines.'[12]

Using coal meant that woodlands could be converted to arable farming and the pressure of feeding a growing population eased. Second, the introduction of canals and then railways had the same effect. They released land which had previously been used to provide horse feed. In 1800 a canal engineer wrote that

> as one horse on an average consumes the produce of four acres of land, and there are 1,350,000 in this island that pay the horse-tax, of course there must be 5,400,000 acres of land occupied in providing provender for them. How desirable any improvement that will lessen the keep of horses. . . . [13]

Wilkinson states that

> Undoubtedly one of the most important reasons for the commercial success of canals was the high price of horse feed. Only when competition for land had forced the price of horse feed sufficiently high was it worth expending labour on the construction of canals which allowed larger loads to be drawn by fewer horses.

Finally the growth of the cotton industry meant that the manufacture of clothing could be expanded without threatening the production of food.

Wilkinson admits that his analysis is based upon the cultural imperative of 'survival' and that it is neutral towards the place of progress in development.[14] But his ecological model is, he believes, based on the reality of living people not on some idealized form. Development is the response to actual and perceived 'needs' and 'wants' rather than some notion of human perfectibility.

Other models

There are alternative models: W. W. Rostow put forward his 'stages of economic growth' in 1960 and E. E. Hagen his 'theory of social change' in 1962. In 1965 the historian R. M. Hartwell proposed an approach to the industrial revolution based upon the techniques of developmental economics and as early as 1955 W. A. Lewis had recognized the social influences on economic development. Historians specialize in both time and place. This is the result of their need to reduce the volume of primary evidence to manageable proportions. This often leads them to ignore the interaction between the various themes.

Interactions

In attempting to explain or understand any problem historians are struggling with a number of interactions. It is possible to see one element as a 'prime mover', in the sense of being something from which all others follow. This is an attractive approach but it imposes an order on the past which was not obvious to contemporaries. At its extreme the 'prime mover' attitude can become Whiggish history, an approach which examines the past in relation to the present. A second approach is one that sees a particular factor as the stimulus to change – for example population growth stimulated agricultural change. This too is inadequate. It is clear that, important as the connection between population and agriculture was, their relationship must be explained in a wider context, of interaction between a number of social, economic and intellectual variables. It is in the mutual interaction of the various elements that make up a particular past that the best means of understanding that past is to be found.

CONCLUSIONS

To understand fully the development of Britain between 1700 and 1850 it is important that the mutual interaction between the main themes is established. One of the reasons why social and economic change appeals to many historians is that it allows them to get to grips with the historical experience of whole societies rather than with restricted elites or parliamentary sessions. This has led to a move towards 'total' history or *histoire intégrale*, examining the life of a total society in an integrated way. This has proved immensely difficult for a single country and has resulted in the geographical limits of the enquiry being narrowed down to a particular locality. 'Total' history may therefore mean local history. W. G. Hoskins maintains that 'The local historian is in a way like the old-fashioned G. P. of English medical history, now a fading memory confined to the more elderly among us, who treated Man as a whole.'[15]

History concerns both events and structures, individuals and groups, ideas and perceptions, reality and myth. Historians need to combine narrative with analytical skills. They need to re-create and give meaning as well as provide valid explanations and interpretations based on an objective analysis of primary and secondary evidence. But as Antonio Gramsci wrote, though he neglects the role of women, it is more than that

> I think you must like history, as I liked it when I was your age, because it deals with living men, and everything that concerns men, as many men as possible, all the men in the world in so far as they united together in society, and work and struggle and make a bid for a better life, all that can't fail to please you more than anything else. Isn't that right?[16]

NOTES

1 The most convenient recent statements are to be found in J. Tosh *The Pursuit of History*, Longman, 1984, pp. 1–26 and A. Marwick *The Nature of History*, 3rd edn, Macmillan, 1989.
2 On the question of historical method and writing see J. Cannon (ed.) *The Historian at Work*, Allen & Unwin, 1980; G. Kitson Clark *The Critical His-*

torian, Heinemann, 1967 and R. W. Fogel and G. R. Elton *Which Road to the Past?*, Yale, 1983. P. Veyne *Writing History*, Wesleyan University Press, 1984 provides a valuable theoretical perspective. D. N. McCloskey *Econometric History*, Macmillan, 1987, summarizes the issues. C. Parker, *English Historical Tradition since 1850*, John Donald, 1990 is a critical account of the empiricist approach.

3 Fogel and Elton op. cit. p. 19.
4 Ibid. p. 21.
5 Ibid. p. 29.
6 D. Cannadine 'Change and Continuity in British History', *History Today*, April 1985, pp. 4–5 is a straightforward examination of the issues involved.
7 The following discussion is based upon R. Wilkinson *Poverty and Plenty – an Ecological Model of Economic Development*, Methuen, 1973.
8 Ibid. p. 5.
9 Ibid. pp. 57–89.
10 Ibid. p. 81.
11 Ibid. p. 112.
12 Ibid. pp. 123–4.
13 Ibid. p. 124.
14 Ibid. pp. 217–18.
15 W. G. Hoskins *English Local History: the Past and the Future*, Leicester University Press, 1966, p. 21.
16 From a letter to his son written shortly before Gramsci's death in 1937, quoted in H. J. Kaye *The British Marxist Historians*, Polity Press, 1984, p. 222.

2 Britain in the early eighteenth century

In 1749 the philosopher Montesquieu made the distinction in his *The Spirit of the Laws* between the internal (social and psychological) and external (physical or environmental) aspects of human life suggesting that the link between them was to be found in legal structures which institutionalized a society's relationship with its environment.[1] He explained that different physical environments gave rise to different needs which in turn produced different modes of life. This chapter is concerned with outlining the contrasting experiences that existed in the early eighteenth century in the four parts which made up the British Isles.

GEOGRAPHY – STRUCTURE AND CLIMATE

Although the geological structure of the British Isles is extremely complex when looked at in detail, in broad outline it is quite simple.[2] The basic division is between the Highland zone of the west and north and the Lowland zone of the south and east and Ireland. The Highland zone consists of very old rocks eroded and shaped by glaciation in some areas leaving nothing but a thin covering of soil. But the glaciers also dumped heavy boulder clays and finely sifted sands and gravels. The human response to these differences in soil type, drainage and structure in the early eighteenth century was diversity of meadow, heath, pasture, arable field and bog. Oats were the main corn crop. Hunting and fishing took on a central importance in supplying basic needs. Defoe wrote in the 1720s of north-west Scotland that

> the people [live] dispersed among the hills without any settled towns. Their employment is chiefly hunting, which is, as we may say, their food; though they do also breed large quantities of black cattle, with which they pay their lairds or leaders for the rent of the lands . . . these cattle . . . are driven annually to England to be sold, and are even brought up to London. . . . [3]

The prevailing western winds bring high rainfall. Annual rainfall is rarely below 40 inches and in some areas of Wales, the Lake District, the

Western Isles and north-west Scotland it exceeds 100 inches. This too has influenced what people could do. Drainage is poor, the rain has washed out many of the nutrients leaving a soil capable of sustaining only poor vegetation. Altitude has the greatest impact on human activity. In the 1760s the Duke of Hamilton determined rent for his farms by height above sea-level – the higher the farm, the lower the rent. There was variation of human response to these different conditions. In Scotland, for example, there were differences in farming techniques between the wetter West Highlands and the East Highlands. In parts of Wales and Cornwall animals were driven up to the summer pastures and brought down to the shelter of their byres at the beginning of winter. In or around the Highland zone lie most of Britain's mineral resources: coal in Wales, Lancashire, Yorkshire, Durham and Scotland; tin, copper and kaolin in Cornwall; lead in the Mendips and Derbyshire; iron in the Forest of Dean, the Cleveland Hills and central Scotland.

Lowland Britain and Ireland contains as much diversity as the Highland zone (see Figure 2.1). The underlying rocks are softer and have weathered more quickly than those in the Highland zone to produce deeper and more fertile soils. There is less rain and the climate is generally less harsh. In Lowland Britain the type of soil also determines what sort of farming is possible. In the early eighteenth century the heavy clay soils were difficult to drain and plough. Lighter sandy soils were easier to till. In Ireland, for example, woodland was strongest below 500 feet and had been largely cleared so that the rich alluvial valleys could be used for pastoral or arable use. Flooding was a problem in the river valleys after heavy rain. The coastal area between the Humber estuary and the mid-east coast was turned to swampy fens by the sluggish estuarine rivers. Some advance had been made in the Fens proper in the seventeenth century as the result of the imported Dutch drainage methods associated with Cornelius Vermuyden.

PEOPLE AND PLACES

In 1700 there were about 4.9 million people living in England, 406,000 in Wales, about a million in Scotland and about 2.5 million in Ireland. In Ireland there were concentrations of population on the coastal plain from Belfast to Dublin and around Limerick and Cork in the west. In Scotland there were three sharp regional divisions: the greatest concentration was in the Central Lowlands with Edinburgh containing about 40,000 people and Glasgow 12,000. The Southern Uplands, with their better soils and climate, were more densely populated than the Highlands with its settled population concentrated on the coasts and islands. The population of Wales was evenly distributed though some concentration had already begun in the Vale of Glamorgan. Towns were small. Wrexham was the largest, with only about 3,000 people. In England there was a marked

Figure 2.1 Physical divisions and resources in Britain

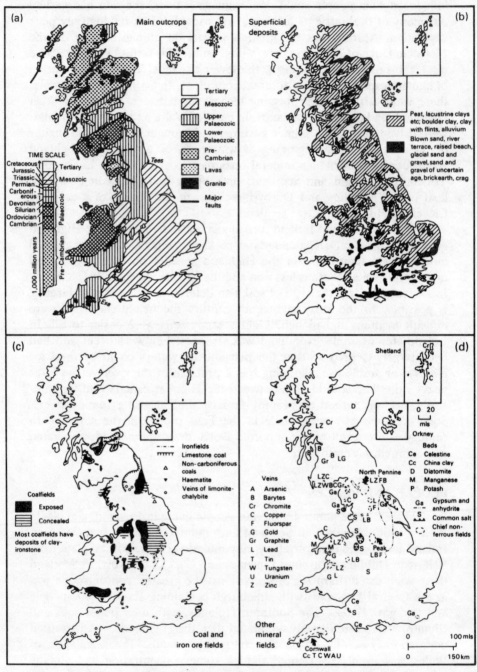

Source: J. Langton and R. J. Morris (eds) *Atlas of Industrializing Britain
1780–1914*, Methuen, 1986, p. 3.

contrast between the heavily populated areas of south and eastern England, the mining areas of Northumberland and Durham and the textile manufacturing West Riding of Yorkshire and the rest of the west and north, where people were thinly scattered. London and its suburbs, containing about 600,000 people, was the densest concentration of people in Europe. Its influence on almost every aspect of national life is difficult to exaggerate at this time. This dominance can be seen by comparing it with the other major cities: Norwich, the second city, had just 30,000 people, as did Bristol, but Birmingham had only 12,000, Newcastle 15,000 and Manchester and Leeds 10,000 each.

IRELAND

In 1700 Britain had a largely rural economy and society. Ireland was separate from mainland Britain physically and was not constitutionally assimilated until the Act of Union in 1800. During the seventeenth century it emerged from a woodland economy with hides as the only major export to a substantial agricultural country based on exporting cattle, beef, sheep and dairy produce.[4] Much of this went either to the continually growing London or to the expanding textile areas of North Wales and England. Growing trade led to concentration of traffic in Cork, Belfast and particularly Dublin, which had a population of about 60,000 in 1700. This marked the beginning of the distinction between a 'maritime' economy based on a cash economy which looked outwards and a 'subsistence' peasant economy.

In 1700 the Anglo-Irish Protestant landowners, who ruled through their control of 80 per cent of the land, were a beleaguered minority. They accounted for about a quarter of the Irish population, were often absentees and were bitterly resented by the Catholic tenant majority on religious and national grounds. This position was worsened by the nature of their settlement. Theirs was a gentry plantation without the buffer of yeomanry and small freeholders which characterized England. Landlord control was limited by the terms of the lease. Roman Catholics, who were excluded from public office, could not hold a lease for longer than thirty-one years as a result of an act of 1704. But it was in the landlord's interest to give Protestants life-leases. This effectively made the tenant a freeholder with the right to vote in parliamentary elections and the landlords' influence depended on how many votes they could muster. Leaseholders were reasonably secure and many were well off by 1700. But other sections of society were less comfortable. Some leaseholders sub-let all or part of their land at a substantially higher rent than they themselves paid. Worse off still was the large body of labourers or 'cottiers' which made up about half of Ireland's population and lived on or below subsistence level. This was largely the result of underemployment since Irish farming did not require high levels of labour. Wages were low, about 4d. per day, and were inadequate even though prices were lower than those in England. An agrarian economy cannot easily absorb an expanding population and it was the cottiers who suffered most and came to depend most heavily on the potato by 1800. By comparison with England they may have appeared backward but, compared to much of the rest of Europe, their conditions were perhaps less wretched. Domestic production of woollen cloth provided both additional employment and the basis for expanding woollen exports after 1660. Low land prices in Ulster led to an influx of Scottish and English immigrants in the 1680s, whose Presbyterianism was as suspect to the Anglo-Irish as was Catholicism. Ulster was transformed from being the most backward of Ireland's four provinces to being the centre of linen production, with Belfast as the fourth port in the country.

The relationship between the Anglo-Irish and England was based upon survival for the former and security for the latter. The Anglo-Irish could not survive in Ireland's hostile environment without England's permanent military presence and they provided a secure base through which the country was governed. In England the relationship between landlord and tenant was based on a shared religious tradition. In Ireland the landlords were almost all Protestant while most of their tenants, with the exception of those in Ulster, were Catholic. Little wonder that contemporaries and later historians have seen Ireland as a 'colonial possession'. For the Catholic Irish majority the memory of war, conquest and dispossession survived and was maintained through Gaelic, the everyday language of the peasantry, which kept alive a sense of cultural distinctiveness. This 'colonial' status was reflected in the constitutional machinery through which Ireland was ruled.[5] Power was exercised in theory from Dublin Castle by the Lord Lieutenant or, in his absence, a commission of Lords Justices. The Lord Lieutenant was appointed from England and was responsible to English ministers. The English Crown enjoyed substantial 'hereditary revenues' and the Irish Parliament was only called to vote for additional supplies to top them up. Right to prepare legislation lay with the Irish Privy Council, but approval had to be obtained from England. The Irish Parliament could either accept or reject these bills but could not amend them and, if necessary, the Westminster Parliament had the power to legislate directly for Ireland.

In practice the situation was somewhat different. The early eighteenth century saw the Irish Parliament develop a power of the purse and its Commons began to question legislation presented to it. These constitutional debates coincided with the increase in restrictive English economic legislation, especially the Woollen Act of 1699, and came to a head in the 1720s. The 1720 Declaratory Act reasserted Westminster's authority 'to make laws and statutes of sufficient force and validity to bind the kingdom and people of Ireland'.

The prolonged struggle over 'Wood's Halfpence', between 1723 and 1725 raised greater issues than that of copper coinage. William Wood, a

Figure 2.2 Counties of Ireland

COUNTIES OF IRELAND

1 – Antrim
2 – Armagh
3 – Carlow
4 – Cavon
5 – Clare
6 – Cork
7 – Donegal
8 – Down
9 – Dublin
10 – Fermanagh
11 – Galway
12 – Kerry
13 – Kildare
14 – Kilkenny
15 – Laoighis
16 – Leitrim
17 – Limerick
18 – Londonderry
19 – Longford
20 – Louth
21 – Mayo
22 – Meath
23 – Monaghan
24 – Offaly
25 – Roscommon
26 – Sligo
27 – Tipperary
28 – Tyrone
29 – Waterford
30 – Westmeath
31 – Wexford
32 – Wicklow

Source: Based on R. K. Webb, *Modern England*, Allen and Unwin, 1969, pp. 4–5.

Wolverhampton ironmaster, obtained a patent in July 1722 to mint copper coins for Ireland. This project was viewed in Ireland both as a symbol of English oppression and as a real threat to the Irish economy. It roused Irish patriotism against what was seen as a government-inspired financial scheme and Walpole proved incapable of dampening opposition both in England and Ireland. In 1725 he recalled the patent. Walpole had yet to develop an effective system of managing government. During the next decade he built up a more effective way of managing the Irish Commons through several leading MPs known as the 'undertakers' who guaranteed to put through government business in return for a considerable share of Crown patronage. This reinforced the strength of the Protestant minority.

Mainland Britain had been brought under the control of the Westminster Parliament by 1710. Wales was assimilated into England by two acts of Parliament: the 1536 Act divided it up into counties on the English model and gave it representation in the English Parliament and in 1543 an act provided for the appointment of justices of the peace and the replacement of Welsh land law with English common law. Although the crowns of England and Scotland were united on the death of Elizabeth I in 1603 a more tangible union between the two countries was delayed until the Act of Union of 1707. In the early eighteenth century the kingdom of Great Britain was of recent origin.

SCOTLAND

Scotland retained much of its own character after 1707.[6] The Act of Union abolished the Scottish Parliament. It added 45 new members to the English Commons, made up of thirty county representatives and fifteen from royal 'burghs' and added sixteen 'representative peers' to the House of Lords. The twenty-seven largest counties received one member while the remaining six (Nairn and Cromerty, Clackmannanshire and Kinross, Bute and Caithness) were paired with one seat each. The county electorate was confined to 'freeholders of the old extent' or to owners of land rated at £400 Scots (£35 sterling), one that was much smaller than in England and open to fraud. The burghs[7] were arranged into fourteen groups each of which had one seat, with Edinburgh taking the fifteenth. Each burgh council elected a representative which met with the other representatives in its group and these individuals then proceeded to choose the MP.

The abolition of the Scottish Privy Council in 1708 effectively removed central government in Scotland. There was a Secretary of State between 1708 and 1725 and again from 1742 to 1746 but Scotland was 'managed' by London-appointed Scottish whigs – Jacobites being excluded because they did not acknowledge the Hanoverian succession. Scotland was largely governed from local level for much of the century and the Scottish aristocracy totally dominated political and social life. Administration lay in the hands of the burghs and the parishes. The burghs fell into two types: royal burghs established by the Crown and burghs of barony established by the aristocracy. In both cases they were completely dominated by the landed interest. Theoretically the sixty-six royal burghs had a monopoly of trade, domestic or foreign, and their Convention, an annual assembly of delegates, did attempt to maintain this monopoly. But burghs in general were essential to rural society as markets or market-places and it was impossible to enforce this against growing burghs of barony like Kilmarnock, Greenock and Hawick.

The parishes

The 938 Scottish parishes were governed by kirk sessions, the Scottish equivalent of the English vestry, which used money raised by church-door collections and fines to finance poor relief. In Scotland levying a poor rate was discretionary rather than mandatory, with the result that less than

Figure 2.3 Counties of Scotland

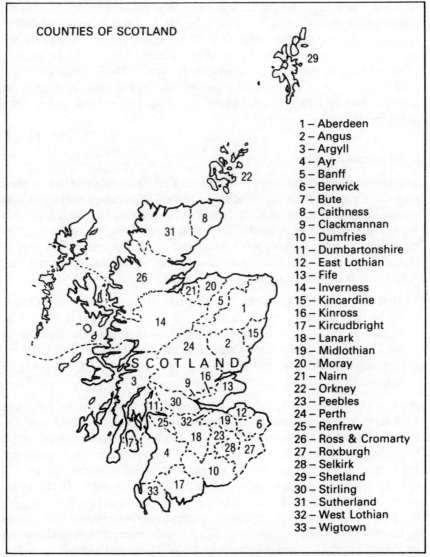

COUNTIES OF SCOTLAND

1 – Aberdeen
2 – Angus
3 – Argyll
4 – Ayr
5 – Banff
6 – Berwick
7 – Bute
8 – Caithness
9 – Clackmannan
10 – Dumfries
11 – Dumbartonshire
12 – East Lothian
13 – Fife
14 – Inverness
15 – Kincardine
16 – Kinross
17 – Kircudbright
18 – Lanark
19 – Midlothian
20 – Moray
21 – Nairn
22 – Orkney
23 – Peebles
24 – Perth
25 – Renfrew
26 – Ross & Cromarty
27 – Roxburgh
28 – Selkirk
29 – Shetland
30 – Stirling
31 – Sutherland
32 – West Lothian
33 – Wigtown

Source: Based on R. K. Webb, *Modern England*, Allen and Unwin, 1969, pp. 4–5.

one in ten parishes chose to do so. But since Acts of 1616 and 1633 each parish was required to establish a school, provide a schoolhouse and pay for a schoolmaster. In the 1696 Act for Settling Schools landowners were rated for this system, though they could and did pass half of the burden on to their tenantry. By 1700 most Lowland parishes had a school but in the Highlands their establishment came more slowly, particularly because of the difficulty in getting Gaelic-speaking teachers.

The parish was also a system of ecclesiastical administration. In 1690 episcopal church government was replaced by Presbyterianism ruled by a General Assembly. The parish minister had considerable power over his congregation on moral, education, religious and other issues. Ministers received a regular stipend which in 1633 was laid down as a minimum 800 Scottish merks or just over £44 sterling. Tithes were less of an issue in Scotland than in England. In 1633 they became a fixed charge or 'teind' paid in cash or meal by each estate in the parish. Provision was made for commutation of teinds at nine years' purchase. Glebe land was of little importance.

Legal system

The most radical differences between Scotland and England lay in their respective legal systems. England had a unified and centralized jurisdiction under the Crown but in Scotland heritable jurisdiction and offices, notably the sheriffs, were widespread. The baron courts were the basic units of rural society dealing with petty crimes and community rules. The Act of Union guaranteed the survival of the Courts of Session, Justiciary and Admiralty in their existing form and in article 20

> That all heritable Offices, Superiorities, heritable Jurisdictions, Offices for life and Jurisdictions for life, be reserved to the Owners thereof, as Rights of Property, in the same manner as they are now enjoyed by the Laws of Scotland, notwithstanding of this Treaty and an independent legal profession was to become the 'bearers and defenders of nationality'.

Justices of the Peace had been introduced by legislation in 1587 and 1609 though they were never as important as in England. Their role was complemented by the commissioners of supply who were responsible for collecting the land tax introduced in 1667. The difficulty in collecting this led to the commissioners becoming more involved in parish affairs and helping the justices keep Scotland's roads in working order. In the eighteenth century their work was made easier, for two reasons. First, in 1748 heritable jurisdiction was abolished. Secondly, commissioner and justice were often the same person and also a local landlord with much wider and more clearly defined powers over tenants than in England.

Scotland – an agrarian society

Scotland was a largely agrarian society. There were three main farming regions, with many smaller sub-regions further complicating the picture. Good soils were largely concentrated in the Central Lowlands, the corridor sandwiched between the poorer soils of the Highlands and the Southern Uplands. Both these areas were better suited to pastoral than arable farming. By 1700 the Border region was geared to rearing sheep for marketing both wool and meat, usually in England. In Galloway, in the south-west, the rise of large-scale cattle production for the English market produced large enclosed cattle parks of up to 2,000 acres. Arable farming was based on common grazing with an infield and outfield round the settlement. The settlement was a cluster of houses known as a 'ferm toun' in the Lowlands and a 'clachan' in the Highlands. The infield, the land under continuous cultivation, was divided into 'breaks'. The land of individual farmers was distributed 'runrig' and lay dispersed throughout the infield in strips (rigs). Each 'break' was sown with oats and barley and, sometimes in the Lothians, with wheat. Sometimes a break was allowed to lie fallow for a year but generally the only time it was not under cultivation was in the winter:

> In place of a chequerboard of separate fields one must imagine the ground everywhere lying as open as moorland . . . seldom divided in any way by hedge, wall or dyke . . . The pastoral land . . . was all more or less rough brown waste: there was no question of grass being cultivated as a crop. The ploughed land within was in a series of undulating strips or rigs.[8]

In 1700 there were about 10,000 landowners in Scotland. Eighty per cent of these were the 'bonnet lairds', who owned small farms and were more akin to English yeoman than landowners living on rents. But there were still 1,500 more substantial landowners. In the Highlands power and authority lay with the clan chiefs and society was organized for war. Extensive areas were leased by the clan chief to 'tacksmen' who in turn sub-leased, generally on an annual verbal basis, to as many tenants as possible. Payment was often in terms of goods and particularly military service. The nature of rural society in the Lowlands and Southern Uplands, with some 'middling groups', in many areas holding direct from the Crown or by virtual ownership known as 'feuing', was rather more complex. By 1700 most tenant farmers in the Lowlands had written leases for up to twenty years. The older system of joint tenancies, where tenants held a specific fraction of a farm, gave way to single tenancies starting in the Lowlands. Tenants sub-let to people variously called acremen, crofters (who held infield but not outfield), cottars (who held small amounts of land to supplement their main works as hired labourers), grassmen (who had rights of pasture on the outfields but no arable land), mailers and pendiclers.

Urban society

The small burghs were completely dominated by the landed interest and were not cut off from agriculture. They used their common grazing, took peat from the hills and had arable lands to which their own labour force was restricted in harvest time. Towns were important centres of specialist services, craft activity and mercantile capital. But they were generally small because the centres of industrial activity – soap and salt production, the linen industry and the cattle trade – did not need towns to process their products. The larger cities gained support from international trade – Glasgow, for example, was growing as a centre of the tobacco trade – and also made specialized goods for the aristocracy.[9]

The Scottish economy at the beginning of the eighteenth century had a dual nature. There was a basic agricultural sector which was weak in its market aspects though capable of producing a surplus to sustain an aristocratic elite. There was also a more sophisticated sector supplying that elite with imported luxury goods though increasing amounts were home-made. But Scotland was an insecure society. It was split culturally between the Gaelic-speaking world and the Scots speech of the Lowlanders. It was split politically between those who had Jacobite sympathies and those who looked to the Hanoverians. The Highland society was based on clan kinship and personal loyalty whereas in the Lowlands a commercial relationship between landlord and tenant was beginning to develop. The reality of 1707 was that England absorbed Scotland. The 45 Scottish MPs only just exceeded the 44 returned by the county of Cornwall.

WALES[10]

Wales returned MPs from twenty-seven constituencies to the House of Commons. Wales only had half the representation given to England – one county member (except for Monmouthsire) and one borough member. In 1700 between 1.8 and 4 per cent of the county population could vote. The voting qualification for the twelve county MPs was the 40-shilling freehold, and the size of the county electorate reflected the restricted number of freeholders, which was a result of the smallness of the farming units. The term 'freeholder' was interpreted flexibly and, as in Ireland, often admitted people with long leases or copyholds to the vote. Borough MPs were elected by a group of boroughs consisting of the county borough and a number of 'out-boroughs'. In the case of Glamorgan seven out-boroughs shared with Cardiff, the county borough, the right of election. In some boroughs, like Beaumaris, the franchise was vested in the corporation. In others, like Brecon, only resident freemen could vote, while non-resident freemen could vote in Cardigan. More people voted in Welsh boroughs than in the counties. In England there was a growing number of people who converted wealth into land but they were not sufficiently numerous in Wales to affect the political monopoly of established landed interest.

Physically Wales can be divided into three regions: the highland areas; the coastal areas around these and the areas adjacent to England. Pastoral farming was the dominant feature in the first two regions, with some elements of it apparent in the third. In the highland areas farms consisted mainly of rough grazing with some meadowland around the farmhouse.

In the second area upland farms with little arable land were common in 1700 though in the lowlands arable land made up about a third of the land used and mixed farming dominated. Cattle rearing, for consumption in the massive English market, was still more important than sheep rearing and was dominated by the 'porthmon' or cattle dealer. By 1700 much of the lowland was already gathered into compact farms but strip farming existed in the Vale of Glamorgan, Vale of Clwyd and Pembrokeshire. However, the traditional Welsh pattern was more diffuse with dispersed small farming units together with an occasional hamlet. Even in lowland Wales the response to farming was intensely local, reflecting differences in soil, slope, altitude and drainage.

Welsh society and economy

Welsh society was traditionally divided into *bonedd a gwreng* which broadly represented an upper and lower class. *Bonedd* related to lineage which was accepted as the basis for authority and lay with the gentry. The aristocratic element was not prominent though some Welsh land formed part of English aristocratic estates. Social and economic changes in the seventeenth century depressed the conditions of the lesser gentry, who lost their traditional position in the Inns of Court and the universities, in politics and Parliament. Just as in England it was those people with larger estates who capitalized on new techniques and sources of income who prospered. There were between thirty and forty families in Wales with incomes in excess of £3,000 a year: families like the Bulkeleys in Angelsy, the Mostyns in Flint, the Vaughans of Transcoed in Cardiganshire, the Vaughans of Golden Grove in Carmarthanshire and the Morgans of Monmouthshire monopolized Commons seats and the patronage which went with them. Each county contained between twenty-five and fifty families with incomes between £500 and £1,000 a year, who served as JPs and ran their counties through the quarter sessions. Recent work on Glamorgan[11] has spotlighted the diverse nature of this broad description. In 1700 there were ten families with incomes over £1,500 per year and forty-seven men owned 80 per cent of the county. But in the next fifty years many of the older families died out and their heiresses were married off. Glamorgan's ruling elite became Anglicized, creating a language barrier with those they ruled. By the late eighteenth century such names as Corbet, Pennant, Assheton-Smith, Cawdor and Bute testified to the extent of English and Scottish penetration. They were increasingly marked off from the community by a growing gulf of language and religious and political affiliation. Smaller landowners switched their enterprise into fields which brought them into contact with the growing 'middling order'. This process of modernization can also be detected in Denbighshire and Flintshire under the pervasive influence of Watkin William Wynn of Wynnstay in the north-east and in Monmouthshire. These men rented their land out to tenant farmers who in turn employed farm labourers, hired for the year or half year. Single labourers usually lived in as did women servants on the larger farms. Though workers were hired for a specific job there was no strict division of labour and in the winter hired men often did the weaving.

The woollen industry was next in importance to the cattle trade in the Welsh rural economy. The cloth trade had been moved to North and mid-Wales in the sixteenth century and was subjected to the Drapers' Company of Shrewsbury. Its farm-based production was concentrated in the area running from Machynlleth on the west coast through Merioneth, Montgomery and Denbigh to the borderlands. Output was small in comparison with England: the four counties of Merioneth, Montgomery, Monmouth and Pembroke in 1747 was estimated at £100,000 compared to Yorkshire's £2,371,940. The whole of the south and north had a scattering of industries. Copper, tinplate and related industries had existed in Swansea-Neath and Pontypool since the sixteenth century. By 1700 most British production was concentrated there and was yoked to the mines of Anglesey. By 1720 a sixth of British pig-iron production was from the scattered charcoal furnaces of South Wales. Slate production in north-west Wales was already a major exporting industry to England and Ireland – a million slates were exported in 1688.

The economies of Wales and England were closely linked. The cattle industry was based on English needs. North Wales was under the control of Shrewsbury and this was to Pass to Liverpool after 1770. South Wales was enmeshed by Bristol. It has been argued that

> Generally, this core of the British imperial economy was itself colonial. . . . Many of the Welsh, on their upland farms and at their treadmill of loom and spinning wheel and domestic drudgery, were trapped in a back-breaking poverty and an unremitting colonial dependence which sent great droves of skinny cattle and skinny people seasonally tramping into England to be fattened.[12]

POLITICAL, SOCIAL AND ECONOMIC STRUCTURES

Who could vote

The economies, societies and politics of Ireland, Scotland and Wales were dominated by England. In Ireland, a dual system of administration between Westminster and Dublin testified to the separate role of Ireland in public policy. In Wales, the Home Office and Court of Chancery made no distinction between Welsh and English problems. No Welsh-speaking bishop was consecrated in the eighteenth century after 1714. But in Scotland, the Presbyterian Kirk remained a representative assembly of a Scots community. Parliament at Westminster legislated for all four countries and after 1707 only Ireland had its own legislative assembly. The House

Figure 2.4 Counties of England and Wales

COUNTIES OF
ENGLAND AND WALES

1 – Anglesey	19 – Flintshire	37 – Northumberland
2 – Bedfordshire	20 – Glamorganshire	38 – Nottinghamshire
3 – Berkshire	21 – Gloucestershire	39 – Oxfordshire
4 – Brecknockshire	22 – Hampshire	40 – Pembrokeshire
5 – Buckinghamshire	23 – Herefordshire	41 – Radnorshire
6 – Caernarvonshire	24 – Hertfordshire	42 – Rutland
7 – Cambridgeshire	25 – Huntingdonshire	43 – Shropshire
8 – Cardiganshire	26 – Kent	44 – Somersetshire
9 – Carmarthenshire	27 – Lancashire	45 – Staffordshire
10 – Cheshire	28 – Leicestershire	46 – Suffolk
11 – Cornwall	29 – Lincolnshire	47 – Surrey
12 – Cumberland	30 – London	48 – Sussex
13 – Denbighshire	31 – Meirionethshire	49 – Warwickshire
14 – Derbyshire	32 – Middlesex	50 – Westmorland
15 – Devonshire	33 – Monmouthshire	51 – Wiltshire
16 – Dorsetshire	34 – Montgomeryshire	52 – Worcestershire
17 – Durham	35 – Norfolk	53 – Yorkshire
18 – Essex	36 – Northamptonshire	

Source: Based on R. K. Webb, *Modern England*, Allen and Unwin, 1969, pp. 4–5

of Lords was composed of some 220 Peers in the early eighteenth century, of whom 26 were bishops and 16 'representative' Scottish Peers. These were the wealthy landowners whose vast territorial possessions gave them social standing and political influence through their control of nomination to many seats in the House of Commons. They were a relatively homogeneous group united by interest, blood and marriage. The House of Commons was made up of 489 English members: 80 county MPs, 405 borough members and 2 MPs each for the universities of Oxford and Cambridge. The county MPs were elected by the 40-shilling freeholders. There were about 200,000 of these in 1700 but (if there was an election), they could generally be influenced to vote, in accordance with the wishes of the dominant landowners. The cost of county elections meant that it was usual practice to try to get agreement between the rival groupings without the need for an electoral contest. Of the 203 English boroughs, 196 returned two members, the City of London and Weymouth returned four members each, and five boroughs one member. Voting qualifications were far more varied. In 1700 the total electorate was probably no more than 85,000. In the 12 'potwalloper' boroughs all residents who had a house or hearth and did not receive poor relief could vote – in Preston this meant a large electorate but in St Germans, Devon only twenty. The 37 'scot and lot' boroughs saw the franchise given to those who paid this medieval poor rate – again the size varied, from 9,000 for Westminster down to two for Gatton. There were 27 'corporation' boroughs where the mayor and members of the corporation had the right of election and 92 'freeman' boroughs. In some boroughs the right to vote was attached to certain freeholds – in 29 'burgage' boroughs it was vested in tenancy of land and in 6 'freehold' boroughs in the ownership of land. The scale of the borough electorate gave far greater scope for influence and intimidation. Well over a hundred constituencies belonged to the category of 'close', 'rotten' or pocket boroughs. This was aided by the public nature of voting on the 'hustings'. The 1716 Septennial Act lengthened the life of a parliament from three to seven years, cutting down on the expense of electoral contests.

Parliament – functions

Parliament made laws, largely of a local nature, voted monies and discussed grievances. It was dominated by ministers who, with the Crown, determined policy. Though the House of Commons was increasingly the focus for political power the House of Lords retained its importance, if only because most ministers were peers. Successful ministers like Robert Walpole were able to 'manage' both the Commons and the Crown, and political success depended on being acceptable to both. Government was very much a co-operative venture between Commons, ministers and the Crown, and was concerned with external security, promoting and protecting commercial interests, and maintaining law and order at home. Government gave ministers access to Crown patronage and offices, many of which were sinecures carrying a good salary without involving duties, through which they could 'manage' affairs.[13] This was an administrative conception of government, concerned with maintaining the existing system rather than changing it.

Local administration – county and parish

At local level power was wielded by institutions working within the fixed and known boundaries of the county, parish and borough. At the head of the county stood the Lord Lieutenant, a royal appointment. Below him were the JPs, usually from among the gentry and were required by acts of 1732 and 1744 to possess land worth at least £100 per year, who exercised their judicial and administrative powers through the quarter sessions but also had increasing powers of summary justice. The only real check on their actions was that they had to act within the law though there was some supervision in Wales through the Courts of Great Session, for which Wales was divided into four circuits, each of three countries.

There were some 9,000 parishes in England and Wales in 1700 which were governed by the vestry, composed of the most important inhabitants often with an Anglican clergyman as chairman. It dealt with nearly all aspects of parish life: it appointed churchwardens and received the accounts of the surveyors of highways and overseers of the poor though these were appointed by the JPs. The vestry was the only institution in the country other than Parliament that could levy taxes or rates. Parishes were also ecclesiastical units of the Established Church. Parishes were arranged into dioceses controlled by bishops and the dioceses in turn were grouped into two provinces under the control of the archbishops of York and Canterbury. The close proximity of manor house and church reflected the lay patronage in the church. The right of appointment or advowson to a benefice generally lay with the landed gentry – this applied in Scotland as well. The parson drew his income from fees, from his glebe land and from tithes. Tithes were paid by all, whether members of the Anglican Church or not and were bitterly resented.

Local administration – town and city

Urban local government was less uniform. There were about 800 towns in England and Wales. About 200 were boroughs and were governed by a corporation composed of mayor, aldermen and burgesses. Corporations had extensive powers – the right to have civil courts of law and their own Sessions of the Peace, to have markets and make their own by-laws for the regulation of trade and manufacture. The Corporation Act of 1661 and the Test Act of 1678 excluded Nonconformists and Catholics from public office locally as well as nationally, though Nonconformists could get round this by annually attending the Anglican church. The position of the non-corporate towns, including some of the most rapidly growing areas like Manchester and Birmingham, was different: these relied on increasingly ineffective parish and manorial organizations for their government.

A rural society

English economy and society too was largely rural. What marked England off from continental Europe, except for Holland, was that during the eighteenth century it became increasingly less rural in outlook. The open field system of farming was widespread in much of central, midland and southern England at the beginning of the eighteenth century. Although there had already been substantial enclosure since the sixteenth century much of this had been piecemeal, affecting some parishes completely, others partially whilst some were unaffected. In spite of the basic unity of practice the operation of the common field system varied considerably. Farming on the heavy clay soil was different from that on chalklands and lighter soils. It is a gross oversimplification to imply that northern and western England were given over entirely to animal farming. In these areas there were small areas of intensely farmed arable land and large expanses of unenclosed pastures.

England was both diverse and remarkably united. It was a close-knit country partly because, despite regional differences, its economy was interlocking. London lay at the centre of this economy and one in eight people in England lived there. Defoe commented in the 1720s that 'The neighbourhood of London sucks the vitals of trade in this trade to itself.'

British farming fed London: cattle from Wales and from the Scottish Borders; vegetables from the market gardens that grew up in Kent and Berkshire; fish from East Anglia, Sussex and Devon. Yet England had a market economy with each region specializing in particular commodities. It is possible to identify certain regional differences which were profoundly important.[14] There was the divide between the south-east and the north-west, broadly the contrast between the richer and poorer counties, and the greater and less urbanized parts of the country. The area south of the Bristol-Humber line was both heavily industrialized and farmed. Iron-founding was still concentrated in the Weald and the Forest of Dean. Textile production was largely in the West Country and East Anglia, though the West Riding was fast gaining in importance. Luxury trades were concentrated in London. A second divide was between coastal and inland areas or, more importantly, between those places which had access to navigable water and those which did not. Sea and river transport was the cheapest and safest way of carrying people and goods before the development of canals. The most important English towns were either ports or had easy access to the sea. A third contrast was between 'lowland' and 'upland', which usually meant the difference between open and wooded country, arable and pasture, nucleated villages and dispersed settlement and between densely and thinly populated areas.

Town and country

The close interrelationship of country and town and of farming and manufacturing meant that there was considerable social understanding within this segregated economy. The aristocratic elite's authority and power was based on their possession of land. The flexible way in which they exploited their industrial as well as their agrarian advantages contrasts with the myopic attitude of some continental nobilities towards their economic role. The Court never took on the same symbolic importance to the English aristocracy as it did to the French. Despite the differences in religion, occupation, gender role and status there was a remarkable unity in English society. At the top of the social hierarchy stood a numerically small aristocratic elite whose control of both the economic and political systems made it a 'ruling class'. Aristocratic status came from owning property. From a peer like the Duke of Newcastle, whose income in 1710 was over £30,000, down to the poorest yeoman with an income of £100 there was a community of interest based on the ownership of land. They may have done other things – held government or local office, engaged in trade, commerce or manufacture – but rank in society was a consequence of land. At a local level it was the gentry who were the real rulers of the countryside monopolizing political and economic power through their ownership of land, position as MPs and as employers of labour. Many people rented land as tenant farmers and large-scale farmers could outrank smaller owner-occupiers. Below them were the labourers who worked the land and who received wages in either cash or kind. In 1700 up to three-quarters of the English population as directly dependent on the land. Its social fabric was intricate and this complexity was mirrored in a deep-rooted division of labour and by the moral force of custom and tradition. The remaining quarter of the population looked to other sources of income. But no rigid distinction can be made, since landowners invested in industry and commerce and many smaller farmers and tenants relied on their rural industry for survival. The successful merchant or financier used his profits to buy land to give him the status which money alone did not provide.

BRITAIN – A DEVELOPED COUNTRY?

In 1700 Britain was not, in the modern sense of the term, an underdeveloped country.[15] However, there were marked variations in the level of development of its constituent parts. Much of England was productive farmland with regional economies served by a web of market towns with London exerting a powerful economic influence. There were loose concentrations of industrial activity. Wales, Scotland and Ireland were considerably different. Urban development was less advanced than in England though Edinburgh, Dublin, Glasgow and Belfast were beginning to advance. Agriculture in all three areas was largely geared to subsistence in grain and capitalism in animals which could be exported to England. But even if Britain had achieved a fair level of development by 1700 it still showed many of the characteristics of underdevelopment. Its economy was relatively unspecialized, based upon agriculture and the production of very basic goods. Economic activity was dominated by London with no provincial towns to rival it in size or influence. Fortunately London was a wealthy market and source of enterprise and a future focus for economic changes. Finally, people were still subject to the vagaries of nature. Famine and disease were still widespread. Scotland, for example, was hit by famines in the 1690s. The death rate was high and life expectancy low. Demographically Britain was an insecure society. In 1700 therefore the British economy was quite advanced in some respects and relatively underdeveloped in others. It was only its market economy, in which a high proportion of the population participated, that prevents Britain in 1700 from being labelled as an underdeveloped country in a Third World sense.

NOTES

1 For a fuller discussion of Montesquieu see D. Thomson (ed.) *Political Ideas*, Penguin, 1978, chapter 6. J. N. Shklar *Montesquieu*, Oxford, 1987 is a recent, brief study.

2 For landscape history the seminal work is W. G. Hoskins *The Making of the English Landscape*, Penguin 1964. Hodder and Stoughton have published a series of books dealing with the making of the English landscape covering counties while Longman has adopted a regional approach. On Wales see M. Williams *The Making of the South Wales Landscape*, Hodder & Stoughton, 1975 and on Scotland M. L. Parry and T. R. Slater (eds) *The Making of the Scottish Landscape*, 1980. M. Reed *The Georgian Triumph 1700–1830*, Methuen, 1983 is an excellent brief synopsis.

3 D. Defoe *A Tour Through the Whole Island of Great Britain*, ed. P. Rogers, Penguin, 1971, p. 664.

4 On the state of the Irish economy and society in 1700 see L. M. Cullen *An Economic History of Ireland since 1660*, Batsford, 1972, chapters 1 and 2, E. M. Johnston *Ireland in the Eighteenth Century*, Gill & Macmillan, 1974.

5 A convenient summary of the problems of early eighteenth-century Irish politics can be found in D. Hayton 'Walpole and Ireland', in J. Black (ed.) *Britain in the Age of Walpole*, Macmillan 1985, pp. 95–119, and R. Foster *Modern Ireland 1600–1972*, Allen Lane, 1988.

6 On Scotland R. Mitchison *Lordship to Patronage: Scotland 1603–1745*, Edward Arnold, 1983 and T. C. Smout *A History of the Scottish People 1560–1830*, Collins, 1969 provide excellent background while B. P. Lenman 'A Client Society: Scotland between the '15 and the '45', in J. Black (ed.) op. cit., pp. 69–93 is the most recent account. Two recent collections are essential: T. M.

Devine and R. M. Mitchison (eds) *People and Society in Scotland*, volume I 1760–1830, John Donald, 1988 and R. A. Houston and I. D. Whyte (eds) *Scottish Society* 1500–1800, Cambridge University Press, 1989.

7 See M. Lynch 'The Scottish Early Modern Burgh', *History Today*, February 1985, pp. 10–15.

8 T. C. Smout, op. cit. p. 120.

9 On trade see A. J. G. Cummings 'Scotland's Links with Europe 1600–1800', *History Today*, April 1985, pp. 45–9.

10 For Wales convenient starting points are D. Williams *A History of Modern Wales*, John Murray 1977, E. D. Evans *A History of Wales 1660–1815*, University of Wales Press, 1976 and the infuriating and eminently readable G. A. Williams *When Was Wales?*, Penguin, 1985.

11 P. Jenkins, *The Making of a Ruling Class: the Glamorgan Gentry 1640–1790*, Cambridge University Press, 1983.

12 G. A. Williams op. cit. p. 145.

13 W. A. Speck *Stability and Strife: England 1714–1760*, Edward Arnold, 1977, chapter 1 and D. Marshall *Eighteenth Century England*, Longman 1974, chapter 2 are good starting points.

14 R. Porter *English Society in the Eighteenth Century*, Penguin 1982, rev. edn 1990, pp. 56–61 discusses this more fully.

15 E. Pawson *The Early Industrial Revolution*, Batsford, 1979, pp. 13–22 examines these issues.

3 Politics in the eighteenth century I

The next two chapters are concerned with British politics in the eighteenth century. They aim to highlight the ways in which people, particularly within the upper section of society, thought about their constitution and political system, how the system worked in practice and how historians have looked at this period. They are consequently selective.[1] This chapter concentrates on the problem of historiography, politics in theory – the constitution and political ideas, politics in practice and the relationship between the king and his ministers. The following chapter looks at the issue of Jacobitism, popular politics, foreign and colonial policy and political issues in Wales, Scotland and Ireland.

HISTORIANS' VIEWS: NAMIER AND AFTER

Namier

The 1960s and 1970s saw a dramatic expansion in the scale and breadth of work on eighteenth-century British history. This was, in part, a reaction against the interpretation of the period, associated with the work of Sir Lewis Namier and his school.[2] From the publication of *The Structure of Politics at the Accession of George III* in 1929 until his death in 1960 Namier dominated the field. 'Namierism' meant a rigorous substitution of accurate detail for the generalizations that had contented earlier historians. Namier went back to the the world of 'high' politics and the actions of a small number of politicians, arguing that this was essential if historians were to understand 'political man' in his historical environment. In attempting to understand groups as well as individuals he began a process of parliamentary 'collective biography' suggesting that history is mastering 'the past immanent both in his [the historian's] person and in his social setting [in order to] induce in him a fuller understanding of the present'. Namier's approach was concerned with structure. Ideas, principles, prejudice and passion had little to offer in his view of politics and he has been criticized for 'taking the mind out of history'. This must, however, be approached with some caution. Namier was fully aware of the complex psychological forces which influenced people's actions. What he distrusted was the over-readiness of historians to accept that people were governed by rational ideas, though his own emphasis on the importance of self-interest as a motivating force in politics lays him open to the charge of oversimplifying the complex problem of explaining political actions. The title of John Brewer's *Party Ideology and Popular Politics at the Accession of George III*, published in 1976, was an implicit challenge to Namier's view that ideas had little or no part to play in eighteenth-century politics.

Reaction and 'revisionism'

The reaction against Namier was an overt one.[3] His view of politics ignored the role of extra-parliamentary groups and critics of the governing elite, the political views and actions of the lower orders and the impact of political writers and the press. The political structure of eighteenth-century Britain could only be fully appreciated if the politicization of society was fully accepted. Popular politics was of importance and Brewer discerns an alternative political structure, one exploited by John Wilkes. Newspapers, addresses to MPs and petitions linked Whitehall and Westminster with the localities. Elections might be corrupt, as Namier had shown, but the powerful had to take the views of the wider society into account as well as the emergent and as yet nebulous notion of 'public opinion'.

Namier's narrow view of politics was replaced by a perspective stressing ideology, issues, the broadening of the scope of the political world and a 'political nation' increasingly impatient with aristocratic hegemony rather than corruption and self-interest. This viewpoint was essentially urban, secular and radical, the result of economic change, and laid the foundations of calls for social and political reform from the 1760s. Historians have concentrated on different aspects of this response. Some have argued for the decline of religion as a means of social control and its replacement by the 'spectacle' of the law and the spectacle of trial and punishment. Others have stressed the importance of the bourgeoisie, particularly the expansion of the urban population and the professions who set the 'radical' pace, a view rejected by E. P. Thompson who sees a society polarized between patricians and plebians. The overall emphasis is upon a dynamic, expansive and confident society preparing to dismantle Britain's *ancien régime* and upon episodes like the Wilkesite agitations in the 1760s where it flexed its muscles. In recent years, however, several works have implicitly or explicitly rejected or revised this interpretation.

J. C. D. Clark and 'Tory' approaches

The most radical has been the work of J. C. D. Clark in two books *English Society 1688–1832* and his broader *Revolution and Rebellion: State and*

Society in England in the Seventeenth and Eighteenth Centuries, published in 1985 and 1986 respectively. Clark is an unashamedly 'revisionist' historian and in these two well-written books he is both challenging and infuriating. His work emphasizes the stability of the eighteenth century in both social and ideological terms. The power of the monarchy, Church and aristocracy and the limited impact of social change are considered in relation to popular radicalism. His thesis is that England was a 'confessional state', in which Anglicanism was a vital force, until the rapid collapse of its political position between 1828 and 1832. He criticizes those historians who interpret the later eighteenth century in terms of the triumph of secularism over religion and of radicalism leading to reform. For him it is the aristocracy not the middle class who formed the cutting edge of social change. His critique focuses attention on those interpretations which exaggerated the importance of elements in English society which looked to the future and minimized those which were to be eclipsed. In this interpretation the principal threat to stability in the first half of the century comes from the Jacobite challenge to the legitimacy of the Hanoverians rather than from political radicals. The crucial date is not the Glorious Revolution of 1688–9 but the final defeat of the Jacobites at Culloden in 1746. This ended the general challenge to the Hanoverian position and the more specific 'mid-century' crisis which began in 1731 with the collapse of the Anglo–French alliance of 1716–31: the combination of a significant domestic challenge with the threat of a major foreign state. For Clark the early eighteenth century cannot simply be interpreted in terms of the growth of a Whig oligarchy ruling Britain as a 'one-party state', reinforced by a compliant electorate and monarchy, and the demise of the Tory party. The constitutional significance of 1688 is seen as of limited importance. The political as opposed to the constitutional power of monarchy survived 1688, particularly in terms of foreign policy and the choice of ministers.

Continuity reasserted and questions posed

The importance of Clark's thesis lies in his resurrection of the strength of continuity in eighteenth-century England. Attention is displaced from Methodism to Anglicanism, from urban radicalism to rural conservatism and to the vitality of traditional society and its values. But it provides little explanation for change and tension. What he has done in his two books is to set the agenda for future historians through his critique of progressive interpretations and his own more conservative perspective. Clark's thesis is drawn on a large canvas; undoubtedly the picture is far more complex.

This brief examination of recent historiography of the eighteenth century poses certain broad questions which will be examined in more detail in the following chapters: how stable was eighteenth-century society?

What was the character and impact of popular politics? Can historians talk about a Whig ascendancy? What about the Tories? How important was 1688 in defining the political as opposed to the constitutional powers of monarchy? What were the dominant ideologies and how were they criticized? How can historians link political change and continuity?

THE CONSTITUTION – THEORY AND PRACTICE

There was an overwhelming impression by the mid-eighteenth century that the British constitution, though not without its critics, should be as near to perfection as possible.[4] This belief was based upon the stability created by the Glorious Revolution of 1688–9 and the peaceful succession of the Hanoverians in 1714. Englishmen – though not perhaps Welshmen, Irishmen and Scots or women generally – were under the impression that they enjoyed religious and civil liberty under the freest constitution on earth. Contemporary European intellectuals agreed. Voltaire wrote in 1728 of 'This happy blend in the Government of England, this harmony between the Commons, the Lords and the King . . .'. and

> The English nation is the only one on earth which has succeeded in controlling the power of kings by resisting them, which by effort after effort has at last established this wise system of government in which the prince, all-powerful for doing good, has his hands tied for doing evil, in which the aristocrats are great without arrogance, and in which the people share in the government without confusion. The House of Lords and the Commons are the arbiters of the nation, the king is the super-arbiter.[5]

And Montesquieu said in 1748 that Britain was 'the one nation in the world which has as the direct object of its constitution political liberty'.[6]

According to Norman Gash: 'To the Europe of the Enlightenment England presented a spectacle of intellectual and personal liberty all the more enviable because it was combined with economic wealth and naval strength.'[7]

The 'Revolution Settlement'

Between 1688 and 1714, it has generally been argued, the central tenets of the English constitutional structure were established. The power of monarchy was circumscribed by the Bill of Rights of 1689 which ended the royal prerogative of suspending the operation of laws and its 'dispensing powers' (the right to remit penalties under the law in special circumstances). The right to maintain a standing army in peacetime was also abolished in 1689. This now depended on the passage of annual Mutiny Acts, thus necessitating annual parliamentary sessions and preventing periods of non-parliamentary rule like those of 1629–40 and 1681–5. The 1694

Triennial Act prevented parliaments being continued indefinitely, like that of Charles II between 1661 and 1679, by calling general elections every three years. The Act of Settlement in 1701 limited the power of monarchy to dismiss judges, who now retained their offices not at the pleasure of the king but as long as they maintained 'good behaviour' and settled the succession on the Protestant House of Hanover when Anne died.

The theoretical picture is one of a mixed constitution of three 'balanced' and independent parts: King, Parliament and the Judiciary. The King represented the monarchical element in the state, the Lords the aristocratic and the Commons the popular. It was believed that this mixture prevented degeneration into either autocracy or anarchy: Lords and Commons prevented the King from acting tyranically; King and Commons prevented the Lords from becoming oligarchic and King and Lords checked the Commons' tendency towards anarchy. This constitutional structure is shown in Figure 3.1.

Norman Gash has commented that

> The more the eighteenth century is studied, in fact, the more apparent do certain features become: the absence of any overwhelming authority in any of its branches; the practical recognition of limitations; the readiness to work together.[8]

The power of monarchy

It is, however, important to get this statutory limitation of royal power into a proper perspective. It has been translated by historians into a view of the first two Georges as uninterested in English politics and as failing to understand how the system worked. This is linked to the fact that neither was fluent in English and both preferred their German home. George III, supposedly stupid, obstinate and under his mother's influence, tried to reverse constitutional evolution by his assumption of obsolete monarchical powers and sacrificed the American colonies. This perspective, unlikely to be put forward by any reputable historian today, neglected the real power exercised by the first two Georges, the general contemporary support George III had in his attempts to uphold rather than subvert the constitution and the importance of dialogue between Crown and legislature if political actions were to be successful. The Court was throughout much of the eighteenth century the principal arena for intrigue and manoeuvre, the place where real power, royal favour and nomination for office and patronage were fought for, won and lost.

There has been a consistent underestimation of the strength of monarchy from 1688 to 1760, a consequence of problems with evidence. William III's role was minimized by historians who could not read Dutch and the roles of George I and II can only fully be appreciated through a working knowledge of German.[9] In this revisionist perspective the only

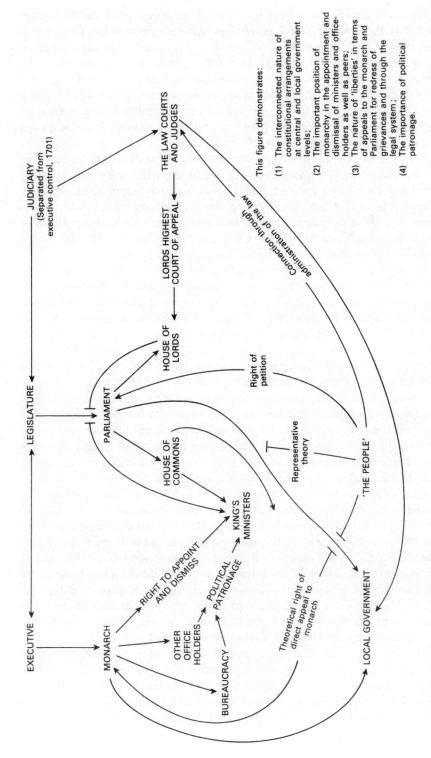

This figure demonstrates:

(1) The interconnected nature of constitutional arrangements at central and local government levels;
(2) The important position of monarchy in the appointment and dismissal of ministers and office-holders as well as peers;
(3) The nature of 'liberties' in terms of appeals to the monarch and Parliament for redress of grievances and through the legal system;
(4) The importance of political patronage.

EXECUTIVE

LEGISLATURE

JUDICIARY
(Separated from executive control, 1701)

THE LAW COURTS AND JUDGES

LORDS HIGHEST COURT OF APPEAL

Connection through administration of the law

HOUSE OF LORDS

PARLIAMENT

Right of petition

HOUSE OF COMMONS

Representative theory

KING'S MINISTERS

'THE PEOPLE'

RIGHT TO APPOINT AND DISMISS

POLITICAL PATRONAGE

Theoretical right of direct appeal to monarch

LOCAL GOVERNMENT

MONARCH

OTHER OFFICE HOLDERS

BUREAUCRACY

Figure 3.1 A model of the constitution

thing 1688 decided was that the English monarch must be Protestant and that there was no real revolution in relations between Crown and Parliament, only a gradual evolutionary modification. The independence of the Crown has always varied to some extent with the health of its finances. The 1698 Civil List Act removed certain problems by transferring to Parliament responsibility for many areas of expenditure while leaving the king with revenues for the purpose of government including ministerial salaries, the royal household, pensions and secret service. These revenues were the most sensitive areas of expenditure, particularly as they were often used for political manipulation and were not really made accountable to the House of Commons until the 1780s. Parliamentary provision for the Civil List was improved under successive monarchs until, in 1760, George III undid the system by accepting a fixed, annual sum which soon proved to be inadequate. This led to a gradual erosion in the position of the Crown, culminating in the Civil Establishment Act of 1782 which brought offices and pensions under parliamentary scrutiny.

How effective was the Revolutionary Settlement in limiting the power and influence of monarchy during the eighteenth century? Dunning's proposition in 1780 that 'The influence of the Crown has increased, is increasing and ought to be diminished.'[10] was not simply parliamentary rhetoric but was based on the well-founded belief that the Crown could and did interfere in the operations of the political system. The formal provisions contained in the Revolutionary Settlement which limited the Crown had proved to be only paper safeguards. The Bill of Rights had established the principle of parliamentary control over taxation, but efficient political management of the legislature and the expansion of the national debt ensured that the Crown always had sufficient money to wage war in the eighteenth century. It also prohibited keeping a standing army without parliamentary consent but it was only the existence of such an army, rubber-stamped by successive Whig majorities, that protected Britain from a successful Jacobite restoration until the 1750s. The holding of regular parliamentary elections, enshrined in the 1694 Triennial Act, was altered in the 1716 Septennial Act and George I even contemplated putting the Westminster Parliament on the same footing as that in Dublin, which was dissolved only on the death of the monarch until 1768. The 1701 Act of Succession also failed in its attempts to limit the Crown. Despite its provisions George I, at least until 1719, relied on foreign ministers for advice. The Privy Council declined as an effective institution and was replaced by the more secret Cabinet Council. Attempts to exclude placemen and pensioners from the Commons were modified in 1706, 1708 and 1716. The provision that the monarch had to seek parliamentary permission to leave the country was repealed in 1716. The early Hanoverians had far greater powers of manipulation over the House of Commons than their Stuart predecessors. This was reinforced by monarchical influence in the House of Lords which went virtually unchallenged but a resolute

House of Lords could and did reject unwelcome bills. For example, George III used his influence there to ensure the defeat of the Fox–North coalition in 1783, and into the 1820s the Lords stonewalled successive attempts by the Commons to pass contentious bills, like those on Catholic Emancipation.

It is no longer sufficient to see the decline of the Crown simply in constitutional terms. The non-use of the royal veto after 1708 was a reflection not of the ineffectiveness of the Crown but of Parliament ensuring that it did not demand what the King was unwilling to give. It was recognized that a stronger state meant not only a stronger monarch but a stronger parliament in which both parties could get their way. The Whig historians' assumption that a powerful minister meant a weakened monarchy was, at least between 1714 and 1760, unjustified. After 1760 it was perhaps less clear, but successful and stable government was still based on co-operation between king and ministers rather than conflict. Both diplomacy and military affairs – major aspects of government business in a period of endemic warfare – continued to be controlled by royal prerogative in terms of personnel and daily decision-making. In neither sphere was there parliamentary control over spending, though incompetence or failure occasionally led to censure. Both George I and George II kept tight control on the army and on foreign policy, though this was undermined by George III. The authoritarian tone of the Hanoverians was acceptable because there was no doubting their support for Protestantism and the Established Church.

If, as some historians argue, English monarchy reached its apogee of power under the first two Georges, can the case that George III attempted to introduce a 'new absolutism' any longer be sustained? Did he break with constitutional conventions in the 1760s in respect of his role in government, or in the 1770s in respect of American liberties? There is no evidence that he deliberately perverted constitutional forms and, after his youthful ideals wore off, George III can be seen in a similar way to his two predecessors. In this light Dunning's proposition marked the beginning of the erosion of royal power. That erosion continued after the 1780s was a result of a combination of things: increasingly inadequate royal income, for which George III must bear the blame; the expansion in volume and complexity of government; the ill-health of George from the 1790s and the poor public image of the Prince Regent. The resignation of William Pitt in 1801 over the king's refusal to grant Catholic emancipation demonstrated how little monarchical power had been transformed during the eighteenth century.

Clark again

J. C. D. Clark has also criticized historians who interpret the early eighteenth century largely in terms of the growth of a Whig oligarchy which ruled a stable Britain as a 'one-party state'. This thesis, he argues, was supported by psephological arguments which claimed that the electorate was no longer volatile or acted independently and that the Tories were not serious contestants for power.[11] Several major questions need addressing. Just how independent was the electorate? How was the Commons managed? Was Britain a 'one-party state'? What role did ideology play? What political issues were important? How politically stable was Britain between 1714 and the 1780s.

How independent was the electorate?

First, how independent was the electorate? Who could vote in the early eighteenth century has already been examined.[12] The representative nature of the Commons was justified by contemporaries, despite the limited nature of the franchise. Edmund Burke argued towards the end of the century that, if a state is governed well with due regard to its different interests, people are represented even if they lack the franchise. If not represented actually, he claimed, they were represented 'virtually'.

The notion of the eighteenth-century electorate acting 'independently' can be interpreted in several ways. It could mean that it was volatile and unpredictable or, from a governmental point of view, that its support could not be relied upon or that the electorate increased in number. It is important not to impose twentieth-century notions of electoral action on an electorate which was different both quantitively and qualitatively. If 'independence' is to be found anywhere in the eighteenth century, historians need to examine county elections. The size of their electorate varied from under 1,000 in Rutland to about 20,000 in Yorkshire. On average in the mid-eighteenth century counties had about 4,000 electors. This was no guarantee of independence. Counties were either too big to bribe or too expensive to canvass. Contested county elections were few – in 1747, for example, there were only three – and only occurred when the leading landowners could not reach agreement over who should be elected. D. Marshall sums up the position of the county elector as follows: 'It is misleading to speak of the independence of the 40/- freeholder; in practice such manoeuvring meant that he had been disfranchised.'[13]

Borough electorates were more volatile since their small size made them more open to bribery and influence. About half of the boroughs had less than 100 electors and only 22 had more than a thousand. However, electoral independence was limited since many boroughs can be categorized as 'close', 'rotten', 'proprietory' or 'pocket' where nomination to the seat was in the hands of either a local magnate or commoner. In 1818 some 300 borough seats were open to the nomination of 91 peers and 81 commoners. Few people had influence over more than four seats – 4 peers and 18 commoners in 1818. The number of borough contests was also small and certainly diminished after mid-century (see Table 3.1).

Table 3.1 Borough contests 1715–84

Year	Contests	% 204 English boroughs contested
1715	119	58
1722	154	75
1727	114	56
1734	133	65
1741	94	46
1747	62	30
1754	62	30
1761	53	26
1768	83	41
1774	94	46
1784	83	41

Source: Table derived from J. Cannon *Parliamentary Reform 1640–1832*, Cambridge University Press, 1973.

The higher number of contests before 1747 was a reflection of the more contentious nature of politics. The 1722 election illustrated the vigour of the contest for political power between Whigs and Tories while that in 1734 was the result of an invigorated opposition to Walpole's policies, especially his failed excise scheme of the previous year. These two elections can be contrasted with that of 1784 where, it has usually been maintained, public opinion rejected Charles James Fox in favour of William Pitt.

The case for the independence of the electorate in the first half of the eighteenth century has been buttressed by a numerical argument. In the early 1710s there were an estimated 250,000 electors which, using figures produced by the statistician Gregory King in the late seventeenth century as a base for national population,[14] gives an electorate of 4.7 per cent of the total population, whereas after the 1832 Reform Act the figure was 4.2 per cent. After 1715, it is argued, the electorate was deliberately shackled by more efficient management of elections and by the Septennial Act. But having the vote and actually being able to exercise it were two different things. Turnout seems to have been low: Geoffrey Holmes found that gentry turnout in the Suffolk and Hampshire elections of 1710 was 39 and 30 per cent respectively and only 18 per cent in the West Riding election of 1708.[15] Added to this is the evidence that regular voters far outnumbered casual voters who turned out for one election. If this evidence applies nationally – and there is every reason to think it might – then there is little to support the argument for a large body of politically articulate and electorally active men defending their interests via the hustings.

Electoral contests during the eighteenth and early nineteenth centuries were not the preserve of an independent and politically conscious electorate but of local political elites. In this more deferential model of political activity the voters were susceptible to the influence of their acknowledged superiors. By focusing on events at the centre of government historians have placed an emphasis on electoral politics which gives them an unjustified modernity and assumes that no contest meant that there was no political dimension to that election. As Clark argues:

> A falling number of contests after the Hanoverian accession is more remarkable in that the traditional occasions for conflict did not disappear. Normally, the old social divisions were still there. . . . The politics were of a different sort, and contests were not a necessary part of the system . . . the cry was not generally raised that electors were deprived of a right to participation by the absence of a contest. It is a modern assumption that there is, and ought to be, a contest in each constituency at each election in order that the system may function properly as a system of representative government.[16]

How was the Commons managed? – The MPs

The decline of an independent electorate was paralleled, some historians maintain, by the emergence of 'oligarchic' government. The individual was excluded from politics, and power monopolized by self-interested political managers. This views politics in terms of a centrist oligarchy containing a democratic populace struggling to be 'free'. What this convenient polarization neglects is that eighteenth-century government was always government by a few, that the notion of 'the political nation' was a similarly narrow one, that politics was determined by the responses of different elements of the dominant elite at both local and national levels and that 'popular' politics, where it made any impact at all, was generally local rather than national. The perspective of politics looked at from the centre was different from that of the county, borough or region.

People became MPs for different reasons, of which power is but one. In the eighteenth century perhaps the most important reason was for the 'advantages' it brought. The ways in which these advantages were perceived could, to a certain extent, determine the direction in which an MP faced. Though it is fashionable to criticize the notions of 'Court' and 'country' in seventeenth- and eighteenth-century politics, they do provide ways of looking at how contemporaries perceived advantage. Those who looked to the Court sought advantage from the patronage and offices at the Crown's disposal. Since royal favour could be fickle, this predisposed those MPs to support the current governing ministry. The Brudenell family were courtiers and special favourites of George III. George Brudenell, 4th Earl of Cardigan, was created Duke of Montagu in 1766 and his younger brother, Thomas, was made Earl of Ailesbury ten years later. Ailesbury controlled the boroughs of Great Bedwyn and Marlesborough and always ensured the return of MPs who were absolutely faithful to government. Another brother, Robert, an MP between 1756 and 1768, was in the army and, despite not seeing active service, died in 1768 as colonel of the 16th Foot and Lieutenant-Governor of Windsor Castle.

By contrast, those who took a stance based on the 'country' looked back to their localities and sought advantage there in terms of enhanced standing and influence. Sir Gregory Page Turner, MP for Thirsk at the end of the century, claimed that 'whatever his abilities were . . . his property rendered him independent and he always delivered his sincere sentiments according to his conscientious opinions'.

Benjamin Hammett, MP for Taunton 1782–1800, became a banker in London and Somerset, acquired considerable urban property and was largely responsible for the rebuilding of Taunton. His election put a final seal on the classic story of the local boy made good. Support for a particular ministry was determined, to a certain extent, by the consequences of its actions and policies in that locality. This was not, however, an introverted form of provincialism but an articulate stance based on identifiable local needs within a somewhat vaguer notion of national issues. It would, however, be an overstatement to see such MPs as 'independent' members who voted as their consciences dictated. Though their voting behaviour in the Commons could be volatile most showed a general tendency either to support or oppose an administration. These broad groupings were not mutually exclusive but they can be distinguished from those MPs who sought advantage in being professional politicians.

This hard core of professional politicians, whose primary interest was power, who occupied the front benches in the Commons and engrossed the attention of contemporaries and historians, grouped themselves together to gain the main advantage. Whether these groupings can be termed 'parties' is a difficult and controversial subject. In addition to these were various pressure groups or lobbies of City interests hoping for lucrative contracts which could be obtained from supporting an administration. The East India Company is a good example of a lobby and its representatives grew from about 10 MPs in the 1750s to some 45 MPs by the 1790s. Growth in the number of its representatives was a reflection of the increasing power the Company had in India. The West Indian interest also had parliamentary representation, though never as large as contemporaries believed. On average there were never more than a dozen 'West Indians' in the Commons. William Beckford, for example, was elected in 1754 and remained one of London's MPs until his death in 1770. He owned large estates in Jamaica as well as an estate in Wiltshire. This gave him the opportunity to develop an interest in Salisbury, where his brother Julines was returned in 1754. A second brother, Richard, was elected for Bristol at the same time. These lobbies were not the same as those MPs who supported the Court position and their support, particularly if their interest was affected by foreign policy, was significantly more volatile.

How was the Commons managed? – Patronage and 'party'

How did successive ministers manage the House of Commons in the eighteenth century?[17] It is important to consider the role of patronage and party in this process. Namier placed patronage centre stage, though his view has recently been revised. Patronage alone was rarely either a sufficient or rigid determinant of political behaviour. But though its significance should not be overestimated neither should it be ignored. Kinship and patronage networks were based on reciprocal and balanced relationships which imposed obligations on both sides, though deferential attitudes were not the same as political subservience. To view the eighteenth century as a 'political desert' where issues played no role and where politics was simply about manoeuvring for power completely misses the important point about the potentially volatile nature of patron–client relationships. Certainly by the 1810s and 1820s there was increasing conflict between peers' voting in the House of Lords and their clients' voting in the House of Commons especially over religious issues like Catholic emancipation and the repeal of the Test and Corporation Act and constitutional issues like the Reform Act.

'Parties'

Because MPs grouped themselves together in the eighteenth century as a way of obtaining power it is possible to identify 'parties'.[18] Some historians, Namier among them, argued that party could be banished from the eighteenth-century political landscape entirely. But Namier employed modified party labels in all his writings. This blanket denial would, however, not have been accepted by contemporaries, though they would have recognized that no single attitude to party existed. Lord Dupplin classified MPs elected in 1734 as either 'Whigs' or 'Tories', and it can be assumed that he would not have used the terms if they had no contemporary meaning.[20] Closer examination of the 410 MPs classed as 'Whigs' shows them to be followers of the Duke of Newcastle, the Duke of Bedford, the Prince of Wales and half a dozen smaller party leaders, but their voting behaviour could never be guaranteed even by their own leaders. The 106 'Tories' acknowledged no leader but saw themselves as 'independent' members. Historians have often assumed that it is possible to treat all forms of eighteenth-century political organization in the same way. In reality contemporaries held different attitudes according to the type of political organization being discussed. Eighteenth-century definitions of party varied and, as John Brewer stated,

> to talk of Hanoverian party or parties is to talk of widely differing phenomena which should be distinguished not simply by locating or tabulating their different individual members . . . nor by the modern

criterion of the two-party model or party government, but by ascertaining their different political purposes and means of legitimation.[19]

The Whigs were better able than the Tories to exploit the political advantages gained at the accession of George I. Though the number of Tory MPs in the Commons declined after 1714 – in the last parliament of Queen Anne there were 358 Tories and 200 Whigs but after the 1715 election the numbers were 217 and 341 respectively, by 1742 there were only 136 Tories in the Commons, and only 117 after 1747. Whig hegemony was supreme during the 1720–50 period but it was shattered in the 1750s, leading to the factionalism of the 1760s which Namier described. Namier's decade was marked by an absence of party polarity. The crucial issue for historians is precisely when the party system re-emerged after 1770.

Before the 1680s the basic political pattern within the localities had been that of an Anglican gentry majority, often with significant corporate identity, challenged at its flanks by the alternative minority ideologies of Protestant Dissenters and Roman Catholics. The Glorious Revolution of 1688–9 clarified this situation. The country gentry was unanimous in rejecting James II's policies and the position of the two minorities was marginalized by a formula combining toleration of worship with substantial, though flexible, exclusion from political participation. 1688 marked the triumph of Anglicanism, locally and nationally. But it was a triumph which from the 1690s was to leave the Anglican majority split down the middle into Whig and Tory. This split was at its root religious and dynastic: did Anglican theology allow the succession to be altered? If it did, was the Church merely a department of the state? Who was the rightful king? The 'High' and 'Low' church positions offered fundamentally different interpretations of the common Anglican inheritance, the first grounded in notions of Divine Right and the second on a more pragmatic and ambiguous notion of 'resistance' to tyranny. In this scenario the breakdown of the party system in the 1750s can be seen as the result of the removal of Jacobitism as a viable alternative political ideology and the need for a reappraisal of party alignments. The Whigs may have held ministerial power until the 1750s but Britain was hardly a 'one-party state'. Both Tories and the various groupings of 'opposition Whigs' posed viable threats to Whig hegemony.

WALPOLE

The parliamentary supremacy of Walpole in the 1720s and 1730s provides an excellent example of how politics could be managed in the early and mid-eighteenth century.[21] George I and George II wanted ministers who supported policies of which they approved and whom they could trust. This put the Tories, suspect for their believed if not actual Jacobitism, out of the running. After 1720 it was evident that Walpole was willing to accommodate monarchical wishes. The early relationship between George I and the Whigs was, however, far from cordial, and came to a head in 1717 with the Baltic crisis. Swedish involvement in a Jacobite plot because of Hanover's interest in territorial gains from Sweden in North Germany led George I to ask Parliament to support hostile moves in early April. The Whig ministry was split over support for Hanover's interests and opposition to the Northern War and several leading Whigs, including Walpole and Townshend, resigned or were dismissed. Walpole allied himself with the Tories in opposing the Stanhope–Sunderland Whig ministry. Despite serious challenges, however, it survived and in 1720 Walpole and Townshend were brought back into the ministry. The aftermath of the South Sea 'Bubble' demonstrated Walpole's fiscal acumen and political skills to great advantage. By April 1721 he was again Chancellor of the Exchequer, in addition, First Lord of the Treasury and clearly 'Prime Minister'.

Walpole consolidated his position in the early years of the 1720s. Opposition Whigs, like Cowper and Wharton, co-operated with the Tories, but with only limited success. The 1722 general election increased Whig control of a large number of constituencies, capitalizing on the supposed threat of the Atterbury Plot, a conspiracy to combine an Irish Jacobite invasion from France with a rising in London as soon as George I left for his summer vacation in Hanover. Some of Walpole's success was due to chance factors: the continuation of Anglo-French co-operation and the deaths of his principal Whig opponents and much of the episcopacy. The former allowed him to complete his control over the Whigs, a potential source of conflict not resolved in 1720. The latter permitted him to strengthen the Whig position in the Lords. Though an alliance emerged in the mid-1720s of Tories and Opposition Whigs, led by William Pulteney, their differences over church and foreign policy made co-operation difficult and this plus the support of both Georges, explains ministerial success in surviving attacks. George II genuinely valued Walpole's abilities and consistently supported him during the ministerial disputes of 1729–30, during the excise crisis of early 1733 when Walpole sought to extend customs duties to wine and tobacco and after the death of Queen Caroline in 1737.

The Opposition was in a difficult position. Tory opposition to Hanoverian commitments and subsidies to the Landgrave of Hesse-Cassel for troops to protect Hanover between 1726 and 1732 helped to consolidate royal support for Walpole. There was also the question of how far the Opposition could safely oppose policies in which the king had an interest and on how best to persuade the king to change his ministers. Walpole's attitude to opposition did not help them either. He correctly saw that Whig hegemony could easily be compromised if his policies created tension. Tories were not proscribed in the localities, retaining their control of church livings and their place on the Commissions of the Peace. As Jeremy Black says:

This ensured political control of the localities, and the desired operation of the local governmental and legal system. There was no need to extend it to a wholesale purging. The local political elites were to be disciplined, not destroyed . . . there was no attempt to introduce a new level of local government directly under the control of the national government.[22]

Walpole avoided intervention whenever possible because he believed that it was neither essential nor politically expedient. The use the Opposition made of the revival of the salt duty in 1732 and the excise crisis of the following year demonstrated the potential tensions of directed reforms.

The Commons lay at the heart of Walpole's system. He realized that control of the Commons could not be left to second-rate managers while he sat in the Lords. The Lords, with its Whig character reinforced by changes on the episcopal benches, was managed by Townshend and, after 1730, by the Duke of Newcastle. Walpole could let popular bills pass the Commons, often unopposed, knowing they could always be stopped in the Lords. He managed the Commons by a combination of oratory, approachability and experience. He ruthlessly controlled patronage, using offices, small or large, to the best political advantage. A significant number of Walpole's meetings with George I and George II concerned this. Placemen who voted against the ministry were dismissed. He was not only expected to manage Parliament but also win elections. Control of the means of corruption enabled him to do this, increasing the ministerial Whig majority in 1722 and 1727, though not in 1734 or 1741.

Walpole's fall from office in 1742 showed that to be successful a minister needed the support of both king and Commons. Though his majority had been reduced in 1734 Walpole was still able to govern successfully. The general election of 1741 saw defeats in two areas of the country where the ministry was usually strong: Cornwall and Scotland. Even so, the ministry survived with a slight majority but it was increasingly disunited. Dissatisfaction with the Spanish war was used to advantage by the opposition among independent MPs. Leading supporters like Newcastle and Wilmington were jockeying for position in a leadership contest. These developments lost Walpole control of the Commons. In December 1741 a division for the chairmanship of the Committee of Privileges and Elections was carried against the government by four votes and in January 1742 an election petition from Chippenham was also lost. Opposition control of this crucial judicial, but also political, mechanism meant, as Walpole realized, the inexorable erosion of government support in the Commons. Walpole simply could not go on and, despite the continued support of the king, resigned and went to the Lords as the Earl of Orford.

THE ROLE OF IDEOLOGY

Recently historians have been at pains to place ideology at the centre of the political stage.[23] The view that 1688 marked the end of 'Divine Right' and its replacement with a Lockian 'liberal' and secular political ideology is now seen as oversimplistic. John Locke's writings, especially his *Two Treatises of Government* written in the late seventeenth century, have been seen by historians as the basis for post-revolutionary government and were used to underpin the much-celebrated notion of political stability. This was developed by historians in the 1960s and rested on an unchallenged acceptance of an ideological consensus grounded in the preservation of property which predicted non-party or one-party tranquillity. In this perspective conflict was over the workings of an agreed constitution not about principle. The idea that English life and thought dramatically changed after 1688, was quickly secularized and 'modernized' and accepted Locke's views on government has come under increasing fire in the last decade.

Clark argues that this modernist perspective omits both the continued centrality of the religious dimension and traditional, hierarchical and deferential forms which dominated thought and behaviour and determined relations between the aristocracy and the rest of society. It also overestimated the extent of bourgeois influence upon those relations. The emergent middle and professional classes worked within the existing social framework throughout most of the eighteenth century, only asserting their ideological difference clearly after 1780. Eighteenth-century politics and ideology cannot be explained on the assumptions about political conduct prevalent after 1832 or 1867. Part of the problem of analysing ideology in the eighteenth century comes from an overestimate of the importance of John Locke. Clark cites three main objections to historians looking at Locke from a nineteenth-century perspective. First, Locke's political ideals did not correspond to even the most advanced governments of the eighteenth century. Secondly, Locke never advocated a vision of a more libertarian and egalitarian political or social structure. Finally, whatever the logical implications of his work, his theory did not function as a practical justification for representative government in the eighteenth century. It was not until the late eighteenth century that the radical potential of Locke's political ideology was appreciated and extended by radicals such as James Burgh, Richard Price, Joseph Priestley and Thomas Paine. Locke's theories can be portrayed as being 'first ignored, then misunderstood (Englishmen failing to perceive their profoundly subversive implications), then relegated to the harmless role of platitudinous defences of the existing order'.[24] Locke's influence on eighteenth-century Britain was as an advocate of theological heterodoxy, attacking the established nature of the Church, rather than of political democracy. Anglicans could answer abstract theories of contract or natural rights with a view of man which was ultimately religious. It was Lockian heterodoxy which turned contract theory into a virulently revolutionary creed.

If Locke's ideas cannot properly describe the mental world of the early and mid-eighteenth century what ideology can? Clark has suggested that the dogma of Divine Right did not disappear in either 1688 or 1714. Britain remained an hereditary monarchy and this gave Divine Right continued relevance to the practice of government. But it was precisely the hereditary nature of monarchy which caused the problem. Both the Jacobites and Hanoverians claimed to be Britain's rightful rulers. Both claimed that position by Divine Right. The debate was between different proponents of Divine Right. The Jacobites subscribed to four linked doctrines: the divine institution and status of monarchy; the descent of the title to the Crown by indefeasible hereditary right; the accountability of kings to God alone, not to subjects possessing the right of deposition; and scriptural injunction of non-resistance and passive obedience, even towards monarchs of whom the subjects might disapprove. The Whigs stressed the providential nature of Divine Right, rejecting the second and third elements of the Jacobite position, but sought to salvage the rest. Divine Right posed problems particularly for the Tories. There was a tension between their Anglican theological position and its practical implications, a Catholic dynasty. For Whigs it became a political strategy, a means for defending the Hanoverian claims to the throne and the threat from the Jacobites.

The 1745–6 Jacobite rising marked a major crisis for the Hanoverian state. It demonstrated how deeply rooted indefeasible Divine Right was in British society and how easily the Hanoverian dynasty could have been overthrown. Culloden ended Jacobitism as a credible military threat to the Hanoverian throne and without the possibility of the use of force the full doctrine of indefeasible Divine Right was placed beyond hope of retrieval. It led to changes in Whig and Tory political ideologies which had focused on the dynastic element. In the next fifteen years it is possible to identify a transformation of the Divine Right ideology, a process paralleled by the disintegration of the existing political parties in the 1750s. Clark argues that

> The uniting of the old Whig and old Tory allowed the monarchy to be progressively hedged with a certain divinity, but as a diffused sense of reverence which also embraced the whole social order, not as the sharply-focussed spotlight which early eighteenth-century dynastic conflict had made it. . . . In respect of the nature of allegiance, therefore, a choice between dynasties translated itself after 1760 into a choice between parties. . . . [25]

It was the issues of allegiance and sovereignty rather than representation and reform that were raised, according to Clark, by both the American crisis in the 1770s and 1780s and the threat from France from the 1790s.

These issues helped to sustain a conservative ideological consensus of great unity and strength, not merely the reactionary and unthinking one of the radical critique.

ISSUES – STABILITY AND CONFLICT

It is difficult to focus on the issues that dominated early and mid-eighteenth-century politics. It is not that issues were absent but that they tend to be leitmotifs underlying political activity, emerging at various times as 'crises'. Government tended to be concerned with administration rather than any overall legislative plan for reform. The poet Alexander Pope's dictum that 'whate'er is least administered is best' sums up early and mid-eighteenth-century attitudes to policy-making. Historians who categorize Walpole's policies in terms of 'let sleeping dogs lie' are making the same point. Policy-making, as a consequence, tended to take the form of 'crisis management'. Norman Gash has identified as 'the great paradox of the eighteenth-century'

> a centralized legislature and a decentralized administration, a parliament legislating for the whole country but not always or often for the country as a whole . . . the greater part of the legislation of this period was not law but regulation, involving not legal principles but administrative details. . . . [26]

Who actually made policy in the eighteenth century was left, conveniently, undefined. In general terms it was made as a result of agreement, tacit or overt, between monarch and minister and, with a few exceptions, it worked. The royal veto on legislation was never employed after 1708; the government never lost a general election; there were no major disputes between Commons and Lords, and nearly every parliament lasted its full term. The crises which punctuated eighteenth-century politics have been seen as 'the limits of mutual tolerance',[27] demonstrating that ministers could not survive without the support of both the Commons and the king. George II could not save Walpole in 1742. But George III could dismiss the Fox–North coalition in 1783 and replace it with the minority Pitt administration which survived until it gained electoral supremacy the following year. Pitt was, however, to resign in 1801 over royal opposition to Catholic emancipation.

'Opposition' and 'party'

It is important to note that the phrase 'His Majesty's Opposition' was coined, and then in jest, only in 1826. The suspicion, if not the flavour, of immorality that clung to the notion of a 'formed opposition' can be seen as a central facet of eighteenth-century government. Opposing on a specific issue was perfectly legitimate; opposing the system was factious.

Discussion of the formulation of the notion of 'Opposition', especially by the Rockingham Whigs, has been made difficult since historians have previously imposed the logic of the mid-nineteenth-century two-party system – government and opposition – upon a political system alien to it.[28] To most politicians in the eighteenth century both party and opposition were suspect. Party was condemned as partial, for the advantage of the few rather than the many and, despite containing honest (but deluded) people was often intended to overthrow the government and undermine the constitution. Opposition, attempting to remove the king's ministers by 'storming the king's closet', was to constrain the constitutional powers of the Crown to appoint and dismiss ministers. The balance of the constitution would be subverted by those who created political disorder to satisfy personal ends.

By the 1760s there were three arguments designed to legitimate opposition and, by extension, party: the country-party position; the conception of 'measures not men'; and the notion of 'honourable connections'. The country-party argument was based on the premiss that while other parties were illegitimate because they pursued particular ends and corrupted the constitution this was not the case with the country party. Its political affiliation was loyalty or disloyalty to the constitution for the common good. Opposition to 'wicked ministers' was, consequently, justified only in defence of the balanced constitution. The country party sought a 'broad-bottomed' administration, replacing self-interest politics by the politics of virtue. The 'measures not men' argument based itself upon the notion of solely attacking a minister's measures rather than the minister himself, thus avoiding calling the king's prerogative of appointment into question. The distinction between measures and men was, however, difficult to maintain in practice and it was viewed not as an argument for organized opposition but as a way in which MPs could follow their individual consciences on specific issues. These justifications for opposition had developed during the early eighteenth century and 'measures not men' was even regarded as an intrinsic part of the post-1688 settlement.

The difficulty of maintaining the distinction between measures and men led, in the 1760s to the notion that 'honourable connections' were politically and constitutionally legitimate. Edmund Burke, at this time a Whig, was the leading theorist of this position. His *Thoughts on the Cause of the Present Discontents*, first published in 1770, gave the clearest exposition of this view. He drew a distinction, similar to that of the country party, between partisan groups and 'a body of men united for promoting by their joint endeavours the national interest upon some particular principle in which they are all agreed'. Burke's argument was in certain important respects different from previous arguments. He sought not merely to legitimize opposition but party as well, though he did not go so far as to suggest that party and government should be coterminous. He argued, unlike the country party and 'measures not men' exponents, that party and opposition were not constitutionally subversive but, in an unperverted form, beneficial to the body politic. To Burke opposition acted as a 'responsible' check on existing administrations. Political disagreement was an inherent part of free government and helped to preserve the freedom and liberties intrinsic to the British Constitution.

Stability?

Throughout the eighteenth century notions of opposition were distrusted from whatever quarter and, despite Burke's *Thoughts*, politics as primarily the interplay of government and opposition was very much a thing of the future. But just how politically stable was Britain in the first half of the eighteenth century? In 1967 J. H. Plumb published *The Growth of Political Stability in England 1675–1725*. He asked why political stability, which deserted England for most of the seventeenth century and which eluded successive monarchs and ministers in the forty years after 1680, had been restored under a Whig ascendancy by Walpole. Few historians have challenged the three essentials of Plumb's thesis:

> that some of the raw materials of stability, for example the great resources of patronage at the Crown's disposal, had already become available under the later Stuarts; that until Anne's death there were crucial vitiating factors – major political and religious problems still unresolved – which made it exceptionally difficult in an age of party strife to put these materials to good use; and that the Whig achievement after 1714 was and remains a notable one, whether or not we are content to personalise it as much as Plumb does.[29]

In support of this historians have pointed to the management of bitter political feuds after 1688 within strictly constitutional channels, parliamentary elections and frequent meetings of Parliament. Geoffrey Holmes writes

> It was symbolic that the one successful revolutionary coup of the whole period, that of 1688 itself, was so profoundly respectable that it made the election of a 'free parliament' – in which political divisions could be legitimized – its main agreed objective.[30]

This view of a Whig stability established after 1720 is far less certain than Plumb maintained. 1688 inaugurated a period of serious dynastic insecurity lasting until the slaughter of Culloden in 1746. The Jacobites and emerging Anglo-French rivalry posed a major challenge to the stability of the British state. Plumb emphasized England and, to a lesser extent, lowland Scotland in his thesis. William III may have been easily able to secure England and Wales, but Ireland and much of Scotland had to be conquered and held down. Walpole's achievement in the 1720s and 1730s of good relations, or at least neutrality, with France was the cornerstone of his emasculation of the Jacobite position. The breakdown of that under-standing in the 1740s precipitated the '45 rebellion. External pressures were combined with internal problems. The Tory party, as Linda Colley shows,[31] did not simply disintegrate after 1714.

There was little sense of stability in religion. The Anglican Church was split into 'high' and 'low'. Toleration had been extended to Dissenters in 1689, but only to trinitarians. Catholics were even more suspect and both were denied full civil liberties. Walpole preserved this status quo. Relations between Anglicans, Dissenters and Catholics were generally good in the localities and after the widespread riots of the 1710s there were few religious disturbances until the anti-Methodist riots of the 1740s. This seeming stability was far from obvious in Scotland and Ireland where religious belief was probably more of a political statement than in England. Historians are increasingly aware of the continued importance of religious disputes. Though it is important to emphasize the social and political continuities of the early eighteenth century there were still major political and religious differences which could, and did, produce conflict. As Jeremy Black says,

> it is too easy to underrate the political challenges of the period. The Jacobite rising of 1745–6 is an important commentary on the Walpole period, and was seen as such by many contemporaries. The nature of the military crisis in 1745 should not be underrated. Though very few were willing to fight for the Jacobites, few were prepared to fight for the Hanoverian succession, which was shown to rest on a very narrow base. . . . The political fragility revealed in 1745 vindicates the import-ance Walpole attached to not rocking the boat. . . .[32]

MONARCHS AND MINISTERS

How George III was perceived by his contemporaries

The final section of this chapter examines the relationship between mon-arch and ministers and focuses on the period between the accession of George III in 1760 and the appointment of William Pitt as Prime Minister in late 1783.[33] The first issue historians have to face is the way in which George III was perceived by contemporaries and how this influenced subsequent writers.[34] Butterfield wrote that

> The most important, perhaps, of all the issues presented to us, and all the topics of controversy ever provoked by the reign of George III, is the question of the framework of ideas and purposes which shaped the attitudes and conditioned the conduct of that king at the beginning of his reign.[35]

The problem is not simply one of unravelling the psychology of a very complex person but of determining, in a period when older political traditions were in flux, who was progressive and who conservative. What actually happened is not in real dispute but why certainly is. Contemporary accounts tend to be sympathetic to George's problems, though not to the solutions he put forward. These have supplied the main elements of the 'Tory' and 'Whig' interpretations round which discussion ranged until recently. The 'Tory' interpretation can be illustrated by the work of Nathanial Wraxall and John Adolphus. The latter wrote:

> I can without hesitation declare my opinion, that, in the period on which I have written, the throne has been filled by a monarch who has sought the love of his subjects through the means of public spirit and private virtue; and who has tempered a noble desire to preserve from degradation the authority he inherits, with a firm and just regard to the constitution and liberties which conducts him to the throne, and which will ever form its best support.[36]

In this view the king was the preserver of the Constitution against the self-interested ambitions of Whig politicians who had usurped many of the royal powers. George was seen as 'the Patriot King' acting not out of self-interest but out of love for his country and the need to replace corruption in the political system by the actions of virtuous men. George III was not content to play as passive a role as his predecessors and was determined to regain those powers left him under the Revolutionary Settlement. The alternative 'Whig' position can be found in Horace Walpole, Robert Walpole's youngest son:

> No British monarch has ascended the throne with so many advantages as George the Third. . . . A passionate, domineering woman, and a Favourite without talents, soon drew a cloud over this shining prospect. . . . The views of the Court were so fully manifested afterwards, that no doubt can be entertained but a plan had been early formed of carrying the prerogative to very unusual heights. . . .

and, in 1770, Edmund Burke

> These singular advantages inspired His Majesty only with a more ardent desire to preserve unimpaired the spirit of that national freedom to which he owed a situation so full of glory. But to others it suggested sentiments of a very different nature. They thought they beheld an opportunity . . . of drawing to themselves by the aggrandisement of a court faction, a degree of power which they could never hope to derive from natural influence or from honourable service. . . . The discretionary power of the crown in the formation of ministry, abused by bad or weak men, has given rise to a system, which without directly violating the letter of any law, operated against the spirit of the whole constitution.

The Whigs maintained that there was a deliberate and consistent effort to increase the power of the Crown which was against the 'spirit' of constitutional arrangements that had operated since 1688. George III, under the influence of his tutor, Bute, and of the Jacobite Bolingbroke's *The Idea of the Patriot King*, published in 1738, a book which Walpole saw as 'inculcating the worst maxims of government and defending the most avowed tyrannies', sought to destroy politicians who did not owe their position to the Court. Pitt owed his political strength to his popularity, especially in the City. Newcastle's influence came from ability to influence and manipulate elections. Both had to go. The king then established his own minister, Bute, who relied totally on Court power. The failure of this scheme led to a system where ministers ostensibly governed but in which important decisions were taken backstage. The constant shuffling of ministries in the 1760s meant that no independence of government could be established, political parties were destroyed and ministers were completely subordinated to the king and his cabal. The independence of Parliament was then curbed by the skilful use of the 'influence' at the Crown's disposal.

This less favourable view of George III, a view in which his supposed 'madness' was taken as a partial explanation, became the orthodox view during the nineteenth century. To historians like Erskine May and William Lecky, George tried to stop progress towards the nineteenth-century system of government, a view reinforced by the injection of the assumption that party-political responsible government had come into existence between 1714 and 1760 and functioned on lines familiar to politicians of late Victorian England. May wrote that George attempted 'to revert to a polity under which kings had governed, and ministers had executed their orders, [this] was a dangerous regression in the principles of constitutional government'.[37]

Did George III increase royal power?

The assumption was made, by both George III and subsequent historians, that royal power had been lost before 1760 and that after his accession he set out to recover it. As Ian Christie says:

> We have here a classic form of a common problem in history: Given A, which of two answers follow from it, X or Y? The normal expectation is that closer investigation will establish either X or Y as the correct conclusion to the exclusion of the other. In 1957 Butterfield still considered the problem as posed in this form. The question he did not ask was, are we correct in postulating A? And yet if we are not correct in doing so, the whole shape of the problem changes and so does the answer. Substitute B for A, and the answer simply turns out to be Z.[38]

Both Tory and Whig interpretations drew conclusions about the impact of 1688 on royal power, the roles of George I and George II and of the nature of British politics after 1714 which, as we have already seen, does not stand up to close scrutiny. Kingship continued to function in the hands of George III very much as it had under his grandfather: there had been no diminution of monarchical power before 1760 and therefore no restoration after it. George III had been grounded in both the theory and the history of the British Constitution and his reverence for it was informed and genuine and, by the standards of his generation, completely orthodox. There is no evidence in his thinking that George wished to subvert the Constitution or adopt designs for arbitrary government. Liberty was not waning but broadening in the years after 1760 as treatment of John Wilkes and the press showed. As for his 'madness' this was shown, as some contemporaries believed, not to be a consequence of mental instability but physical illness (porphyria caused by genetic defects). But the new view of George III still maintains that he suffered from delusions. His perceptions of the situation of the Crown in 1760 were as deluded as those of Burke and the Rockingham Whigs that the constitution was under threat from a secret cabal. 1760 saw a change of monarch but very little else.

Monarchs and ministers – a dialogue

Eighteenth-century writers saw relations between king and minister in terms of a dialogue between the two concepts of ministerial responsibility and the royal prerogative.[39] Ministers were responsible for the conduct of government, including the exercise of many powers legally vested in the monarch and were accountable to Parliament and more specifically to the elected MPs for their actions. This did not negate the responsibility of ministers to the king, who could appoint and dismiss them. The advantages of ministerial responsibility are seen by John Brewer as twofold. First, it preserved the notion that the king was above politics and that it was ministers rather than monarchs who were culpable for errors. Secondly, the distinction between monarch and minister provided the opportunity of redress for the subject if government policy was unfair, and this acted as a constraint on the executive. Legitimate opposition to the measures of the king's ministers was seen as one of the pillars of a free constitution. Ministerial responsibility and the exercise of the royal prerogative were seen as complementary.

The operation of these abstract conventions was, however, more complex and it was the absence of any adequate definition of the relations between king, ministers and Parliament that left scope for argument in the 1760s. The Court position was that ministerial appointments were a matter of the personal choice of the king. Ministers were, in George's words, his 'instruments' or 'tools'. Opposition was characterized as attempts to curb the power of the Crown as head of the executive. Attacks on the measures of a ministry, which had received royal support, were a direct attack on the king's authority. The 'independence' of the Crown was an implicit rejection of the idea of responsible government. The opposition argued that a completely independent king constituted unlimited monarchy since there were no constraints on executive power. Their argument was that the king ought to appoint a popular man, one of weight and credit in the nation, to be his minister and that failure to do so could lead to removal on the grounds of ministerial unpopularity.

The 1760s

This opposition view was fully articulated in the 1760s largely because of the political conspicuousness and unpopularity of Bute. As the king's tutor in the 1750s he was able virtually to monopolize royal favour in the early years of the reign and seemed to personify all the worst facets of personal royal rule. On his accession George III inherited the coalition led by Pitt 'the Elder' and the Duke of Newcastle. The former was the 'minister of measures', directing the war against France and making policy. Newcastle was the 'minister of numbers', responsible for manipulating the political system and crucial for his role in financial matters. Both epitomized all that George detested: Pitt with his popular support and Newcastle the self-interested corruption of power. Bute was added to the government in March 1761 as a Secretary of State but, despite the resignation of Pitt in late 1761 and Newcastle in May 1762 it has traditionally been argued that he was unable to establish himself successfully and resigned the following April. Recent work has, however, suggested that Bute did establish himself successfully and that he resigned because he had always intended to do so out of distaste for office.

Bute was seen by contemporaries as upsetting the balance of the Constitution and was opposed by politicians who could not agree on anything else. It was argued that, as the king's favourite, Bute monopolized the affection of the Crown and isolated the king from his subjects. Unpopular ministers, especially favourites, brought the king into disrepute and created political instability. The attacks on Bute's personal and public character, the expressions of hostility in the localities all helped to affirm the existence of a system based on favouritism. As Brewer says: 'Bute became a political scapegoat, forced to suffer because of the conflict between the king and the nation's political leaders.'[40]

Once Bute resigned it should have been possible for an accommodation to have been reached between the king and the politicians. But this failed to materialize until 1770. Politicians believed that Bute was still a major influence on the king's thinking. George III's fumbling political interventions in August 1763, March–April 1765, February 1766 and June 1767 and the emergence of a party composed chiefly of Bute's former associates, the King's Friends, helped confirm this.

The result was a series of unstable and unsatisfactory ministries headed by George Grenville (1763–5), the Rockingham Whigs (1765–6), William Pitt, now Earl of Chatham (1766–7) and finally the Duke of Grafton (1767–70). This instability was a matter of confidence: the confidence of the king in his ministers and vice versa. This can be seen in the stipulations made by the leaders of the various political groupings about who should be excluded from power. In 1765 the exclusion of Bute was agreed to by all parties and in 1766 Pitt insisted that Newcastle be kept out of any ministry he might form. This ministerial control of the powers of the Crown was a statement that ministers should not simply enjoy the semblance of royal power but have the full and complete confidence of the king. For example, Grenville appeared not to have had the confidence of the king from mid-1763. In August the king, perhaps on the advice of Bute and certainly with his help, began negotiations with Pitt behind his ministers' backs. Grenville was able to exploit his discovery of these negotiations, regularly asking the king to confirm his faith in his ministers. This outward expression of confidence did not alter George's increasing distaste for Grenville and he was dismissed as soon as the king could make alternative arrangements.

Lord North

The experience of Bute and Grenville illustrates the consequence to successful government of not having the confidence of both the House of Commons and the king. Lord North was able to gain the confidence of both from the early 1770s and retained them until government entered a period of crisis from 1778.[41] North was a 'manager', of both king and Commons, in a way which the ministers of the 1760s were not. He was a sure administrator, good political manager as his success in the 1774 and 1780 general elections showed, and he restored financial stability in the early 1770s, reducing taxation for the first time since 1756. What opposition there was had fallen apart and, until the war in the American colonies began to go badly in 1777–8, North was careful not to provoke issues on which there was marked disagreement.

The outbreak of the American war led to an increase in taxation and lack of military success invigorated the opposition. By the late 1770s the battle lines were drawn between the opposition Rockingham Whigs and the king. George III believed totally in his right to choose his own ministers and in his personal responsibility for retaining his sovereignty over the colonies. The Whigs were more pragmatic. Some, like Charles James Fox, never recognized the colonists as rebels but as British subjects defending their liberties. Most stood for the recognition of America and the salvaging of as much commercial well-being as possible. By late 1779 the combination of American problems, opposition from Europe, problems in Ireland and demands for political and institutional reform in England posed a major threat to North's ability to govern.

The crisis of 1782–3

North retained the confidence of the king but the 1780 general election reduced his majority in the Commons. The surrender of Yorktown in late 1781 convinced North of the need for peace. His resignation in March 1782 inaugurated a period of political instability which ended only with the appointment of William Pitt 'the Younger' in late 1783. Between March and his death in July 1782 Rockingham was first minister leading a disunited party. Shelburne succeeded but resigned the following February. The king found himself in the position of having to accept a coalition led by Lord North and Charles James Fox in April. The period between April and December 1783 was one of determination of the coalition to remain in power and the king to get rid of them. Throughout 1782 and 1783 George III actively intrigued to bring down ministries and was not above intervening in the legislative process to do so. This can be clearly seen in his intervention in the House of Lords to ensure the defeat of the coalition's India Bill in December 1783, an action which has been widely interpreted as unconstitutional. George III argued that in dismissing the coalition he acted to conserve not violate the constitution. His unorthodox action had a sense of propriety to contemporaries because it was needed to counter the unorthodox actions of the coalition in its India Bill. Confidence was only restored with the success of Pitt in the 1784 general election. The display of public opinion in favour of the king's action before and during the election may be seen as sufficient justification for his action. There is no evidence of a settled design pursued since 1760 of enlarging the prerogative powers of the Crown and the role of monarchy. The 1760s and 1782–3 demonstrated that mutual confidence of king and minister was the essential ingredient for successful government.

CONCLUSIONS

There is an important sense of continuity in government between 1714 and the 1780s. The successful application of power was based on confidence between monarch, minister and Parliament. Corruption, 'influence' and the advantage of office for oneself and one's friends provided the necessary political cement. Policy was based on the acceptance of a dialogue between monarch and minister. This form of government worked well when there was agreement and understanding between its various parts but its stability could be threatened by sudden or prolonged 'crises' or by antipathy between king and minister. Government was reactive, coping with situations and problems as they emerged, rather than proactive and determining its own political agenda.

NOTES

1 The most useful general surveys of the eighteenth century are W. A. Speck *Stability and Strife: England 1714–1760*, Edward Arnold, 1977 and I. R. Christie *Wars and Revolutions: England 1760–1815*, Edward Arnold, 1982. D. Marshall *Eighteenth Century England*, 2nd edn, Longman, 1974 covers the whole period to the 1780s in one volume. P. Lanford *A Polite and Commercial People, England 1727–1785*, Oxford University Press, 1989 is a detailed study. The background before 1714 is best examined in J. R. Jones *Country and Court: England 1658–1714*, Edward Arnold, 1978 and the collection of essays edited by G. Holmes *Britain After the Glorious Revolution 1689–1714*, Macmillan, 1969. C. Jones (ed.) *Britain in the First Age of Party 1680–1750*, Hambledon, 1987 is a seminal collection of essays.
2 On Namier see the essay by John Cannon in the book he edited entitled *The Historian At Work*, Allen & Unwin, 1980, pp. 136–53 and L. Colley *Namier*, Weidenfeld, 1989.
3 What follows draws on two recent review articles by J. Black in *Teaching History* 47, February 1987 and W. A. Speck in *The Historian*, Autumn, 1986. See also Black's critique of Clark 'England's Ancien Regime?' *History Today* March 1980 pp. 43–51. See also R. Porter 'English Society in the Eighteenth Century Revisited' in J. Black (ed.) *British Politics and Society from Walpole to Pitt 1742–1789*, Macmillan, 1990.
4 On the Constitution see W. A. Speck *Stability and Strife* op. cit. pp. 11–30 and J. Carter 'The Revolution and the Constitution', in G. Holmes (ed.) op. cit. N. Gash 'The English Constitution in the Age of the American Revolution', in his *Pillars of Government*, Edward Arnold, 1986, pp. 3–15 is a stylish essay.
5 Voltaire, *Letters on England*, 1st edn 1733, Penguin, 1980 pp. 47, 45.
6 Montesquieu *De l'esprit des lois*, Gallimard edn, 1970, book xi, ch. v, p. 168.
7 N. Gash op. cit. p. 4.
8 N. Gash ibid. p. 7.
9 See S. Baxter *William III*, London 1966 and R. Hatton *George I Elector and King*, Thames & Hudson, 1978 for studies which do use foreign archives.
10 Further details on Dunning and the context in which he made his speech can be found in J. Brooke *The House of Commons 1754–1790*, Oxford University Press, 1964, pp. 116–18.
11 Clarke explores this issue in *English Society 1688–1832*, Cambridge University Press, 1985, pp. 15–41.
12 See Chapter 2.
13 D. Marshall op. cit. p. 54.
14 For King's population figure see the table in H. Perkin *The Origins of Modern English Society 1780–1880*, Routledge, 1969, pp. 20–21.
15 G. Holmes *British Politics in the Age of Anne*, Macmillan, 1967, rev. edn Hambledon Press, 1987 and his *The Electorate and the National Will in the First Age of Party*, Lancaster, 1976 provide detailed analysis of contemporary poll-books.
16 J. C. D. Clark *English Society 1688–1832*, Cambridge University Press, 1985 p. 21.
17 The discussion on how the Commons was managed draws heavily on the general works cited above and the revisionist work of J. C. D. Clark. In addition see J. Black (ed.) *Britain in the Age of Walpole*, Macmillan, 1984, J. Brewer *Party Ideology and Popular Politics at the Accession of George III*, Cambridge University Press, 1986, L. Colley *In Defiance of Oligarchy: The Tory Party 1714–1760*, Cambridge University Press, 1982 and B. W. Hill *The Growth of British Parliamentary Parties 1689–1742*, Allen & Unwin, 1976 and *British Parliamentary Parties 1742–1832*, Allen & Unwin, 1985.

18 I will examine 'party' in more detail in later chapters.
19 J. Brewer op. cit. pp. 40–1.
20 J. Brooke op. cit., pp. 271–2.
21 For Walpole in addition to J. Black (ed.) op. cit. especially pp. 23–44 and the general works cited above, see J. H. Plumb *Sir Robert Walpole, The Making of a Statesman*, Cape 1956 and *Sir Robert Walpole, The King's Minister*, Cape, 1960 which take the story down to the 1734 election, H. T. Dickinson *Walpole and the Whig Supremacy*, University of London Press, 1973 and B. Hill *Sir Robert Walpole*, Hamish Hamilton, 1989. P. Langford *The Excise Crisis: Society and Politics in the Age of Walpole*, Oxford University Press, 1975 is a good study of opposition to a specific policy and more generally. J. Black *Robert Walpole and the Nature of Politics in Early Eighteenth Century Britain*, Macmillan, 1990 is an essential synthesis.
22 J. Black (ed.) op. cit. p. 10.
23 On party ideology Clark's work provides an important revisionist slant. Recent work includes J. P. Kenyon *Revolution Principles: The Politics of Party 1689–1720*, Cambridge University Press, 1977, H. T. Dickinson 'The Eighteenth Century Debate on the "Glorious Revolution" ', *History*, 61, (1976) pp. 28–45, *Liberty and Property: Political Ideology in Eighteenth Century Britain*, Weidenfeld, 1977 and the collection of sources he edited *Politics and Literature in the Eighteenth Century*, Dent, 1974. On Locke see the work of John Dunn, especially his brief study, *Locke*, Oxford University Press, 1984.
24 J. C. D. Clark *Revolution and Rebellion*, Cambridge University Press, 1986, p. 112.
25 J. C. D. Clark *English Society 1688–1832*, Cambridge University Press, 1985, pp. 194–5.
26 N. Gash op. cit. p. 13.
27 ibid. p. 7.
28 See the useful discussion in J. Brewer op. cit., chapter 4.
29 G. Holmes 'The Achievement of Stability: the Social Context of Politics from the 1680s to the Age of Walpole', in J. Cannon (ed.) *The Whig Ascendancy: Colloquies on Hanoverian England*, Edward Arnold, 1981, p. 2.
30 ibid. p. 3.
31 L. Colley op. cit.
32 J. Black (ed.) op. cit. p. 20.
33 For a detailed narrative of events see I. Christie op. cit. and D. Marshall op. cit.
34 J. Brooke *King George III*, Panther, 1974 is a sympathetic biography and I. R. Christie 'George III and the Historians – Thirty Years On', *History*, 71 (1986), pp. 205–21 is an excellent summary of the historiographical issues.
35 H. Butterfield *George III and the Historians*, Collins, 1957.
36 Extracts from the works of Wraxall, Adolphus, Walpole and Burke can be found in E. A. Reitan *George III: Tyrant or Constitutional Monarch?* D. C. Heath, 1964, pp. 1–27.
37 E. A. Reitan op. cit., p. 31, quoting from Erskine May *The Constitutional History of England since the Accession of George III, 1760–1860*, 11th edn, London, 1896, Vol. I, pp. 1–17.
38 I. R. Christie op. cit., p. 212.
39 For the discussion of ministerial responsibility and the power of the Crown see J. Brewer op. cit., pp. 112–36.
40 ibid. p. 122.
41 See P. Thomas *Lord North*, Penguin, 1976 for a useful biography. K. Perry *British Politics and the American Revolution*, Macmillan, 1990 considers politics from 1754 to 1783.

4 Politics in the eighteenth century II

The previous chapter showed that politics in the period between 1714 and the appointment of William Pitt as Prime Minister in late 1783 was grounded in the relationship between monarchs, whose powers and scope of political manoeuvre had not been reduced as much as historians previously thought by the 1688 Revolution, and ministers, whose authority rested on monarchical support and the effectiveness of their management of the House of Commons. The closeness of the relationship between king and minister played a major role in determining the stability of the political system. This chapter is concerned with four major areas of political action: first, the issue of Jacobitism which, arguably, dominated political discourse and decision-making until the late 1740s; secondly, the question of popular politics; thirdly, the major political developments in Wales, Scotland and Ireland; and finally, foreign and colonial policies focusing on relations with France and Europe generally, India and the problem of the American colonies.[1]

JACOBITISM

J. C. D. Clark has recently asked 'Why does Jacobitism matter?' This may seem a rather strange question except that until recently Jacobitism did not matter to most historians.[2] The image many people had of Jacobites was of wearing the white cockade, drinking loyal toasts, raising the clans, the débâcle of Culloden and the heroic-tragic fate of the 'Bonnie Prince'. The Jacobites did not pose a real threat to either the later Stuarts or the early Hanoverians. Underpinning this view of the past lay the ideological bankruptcy of claims to Divine Right and a secularizing view of political ideology. A Lockian consensus had quickly been established after 1688 and fundamental ideological conflicts were consequently absent from England. This 'neat' view of the eighteenth century owed much to looking at history through the eyes of the successful rather than the failures, albeit romantic ones. The continued importance of Divine Right ideologies has already been stressed and questions raised about the impact which Locke's ideas had on eighteenth-century political thinking. Dynastic questions continued to dominate British politics until 1760. The Stuarts posed a real threat to the Hanoverian state which was neither as stable nor as secure as historians have believed. Jacobitism is firmly back on the agenda for historians of the Walpole era.

Jacobitism and the Tories – a debate

The relationship between Jacobitism and internal English politics is a matter of some disagreement, particularly the question of whether the Tories were Jacobite or not. Two main views have been advanced. Eveline Cruickshanks maintains that Jacobitism was the distinguishing feature of the Tory party. She first stated this thesis in the early 1970s when many historians still doubted whether the Tory party survived after 1715 let alone that it survived because of its adherence to a dynastic ideology. In 1979 she restated her position in *Political Untouchables: The Tories and the '45'*, claiming that the disintegration of the Jacobite option was at the heart of the confused nature of party politics in the 1750s. By contrast, Linda Colley maintains, especially in her study of the Tory party between 1714 and 1760, that the Tories were a well-organized party, whose loyalty to the Hanoverian succession was clear because they had serious prospects of office. The Tories had not been driven to Jacobitism by their proscription from the spoils of power. Dr Colley shows that the Tory party was well led both in Westminster and in the constituencies and enjoyed considerable public support. However, her thesis that their loyalty was determined by the prospect of office is more difficult to substantiate and the evidence she cites is weak. She claims that in 1717, 1721, 1725 and 1727 monarchs went some way towards examining the practicality of a mixed Tory–Whig ministry. Given the fundamental incompatibility between the Hanoverian and Tory notions of Divine Right, Tory opposition to Hanoverian influence on British foreign policy and support for a 'High Church' ecclesiastical policy, it seems unlikely that a mixed ministry was more than an attempt, in a time of potential crisis, to pacify the opposition.

Jacobitism and the Tories – some conclusions

Jeremy Black suggests that 'three facts' are 'clear' as a result of this debate.[3] First, there is a lack of evidence on the attitudes of the Tory rank and file members to Jacobitism. Secondly, the degree of Tory support for Jacobite conspiracies was highly ambiguous, again because of lack of concrete evidence. The Jacobites always claimed widespread support as part of their strategy for obtaining foreign assistance but it is difficult to assess just how widespread it actually was. Finally, and in the context of the politics of the first two Georges, there were advantages for Walpole and his supporters in maintaining that the Tories were Jacobites. Walpole may genuinely have feared a successful restoration of the Pretender and believed that Tories were crypto-Jacobites but others were able to exploit people's fears for their religion and liberties.

However widely Jacobite views were held after 1714, it was dangerous to express them publicly. One consequence of this was the development of an underground culture of loyalty to the Stuarts expressed through secret societies with elaborate rituals and much drinking, especially on Stuart anniversaries like the execution of Charles I. Jacobite assertions remained possible through these societies but also in anonymous publications, secretly printed and distributed. It was possible for Walpole to suppress a popular culture of printed ballads and broadsheets in the 1720s but he was less successful in muzzling the Jacobite press or silencing the indefeasible Divine Right ideology. Some attempt was made to control the universities and schools, whose teachers were often suspected of Jacobitism. In 1724, for example, a purge of senior posts took place at Winchester and into the 1740s and 1750s the leaders of the parliamentary Tory party emerged from legitimist, High Church Oxford University. Pitt the Elder complained that prints of the Young Pretender were openly on sale in Oxford in the 1720s. Though it is important not to overstate support for Jacobitism there is little doubting its popular appeal until the 1720s and perhaps even later. Irrespective of whether Jacobitism posed an actual threat to the Hanoverian regime it did provide an alternative ideology to the Whig notion of 'Liberty and Property'.

POPULAR POLITICS

What part did popular politics play between 1714 and the 1780s?[4] Historians have had some difficulty in defining what 'popular politics' was during this period. It is important to distinguish between popular politics and radicalism, though even here there was considerable overlap.[5] There was an important division between those who, through extra-parliamentary means, attempted to influence the decision-making process or reform it and those who held ideological views which were incompatible with existing social and constitutional conventions. Between 1714 and the 1790s the former is much easier to identify than the latter.

Popular pressure under Walpole

The degree to which British politics under Walpole was dominated by a narrow Whig oligarchy and was increasingly stable provides only a limited perspective and, as Dickinson states,

> can only appear convincing if we concentrate exclusively on the narrow confines of court, Parliament and a loose federation of country houses . . . politics was not simply the preserve of the narrow landed oligarchy that dominated court and Parliament.[6]

The Septennial Act reduced the frequency of elections and, it has been argued, this diminished the independence of the voters. This view over-estimates the extent to which the system of patronage and corruption led to a submissive electorate. Even small constituencies needed careful management by those who wanted to maintain their electoral influence and the loss of seats in the larger constituencies in the 1734 and 1741 elections marked a major reversal in Walpole's popular appeal. MPs in these constituencies could not afford to take the electorate for granted. John Scrope, for example, was defeated at Bristol in 1734 because he supported Walpole's Excise scheme contrary to instructions sent him by the city corporation.

Pressure groups, organized by powerful mercantile interests and by the leaders of religious opinion, formed a second strand in popular politics. Lobbying of MPs and the use of printed propaganda by these groups could sometimes persuade the government to take action to promote or defend their sectional interests. On several occasions Walpole responded to politi-cal demands from the Bank of England and the chartered trading compan-ies. The West India interest was able, through carefully orchestrated petitioning and propaganda campaigns, to obtain a series of measures in their favour including the 1733 Molasses Act and 1739 Sugar Act which promoted the interests of both merchants and planters. Effective lobbying by the Quakers encouraged the major dissenting sects to establish a joint committee of London Dissenting Ministers in 1727 which co-ordinated pressure in favour of Indemnity Acts to allow Dissenters to hold office without taking the Anglican sacrament and the Committee of Dissenting Deputies which, in 1736 and 1739, lobbied vigorously but unsuccessfully for the repeal of the Test and Corporation Acts.

Pressure group activity could, in periods of political crisis, take on a nationwide character. In 1733 there was considerable national protest against the Excise Bill while between 1738 and 1742 there was concerted pressure against Walpole's political conduct in general and his handling of the crisis with Spain in particular. Though Walpole claimed that both campaigns were instigated by leaders of the parliamentary opposition, they also demonstrated the degree of genuine popular hostility to Walpolean policies. In 1738 the London merchants took the lead in their attack on Walpole demanding tougher action against Spanish attacks on English commerce. Petitions from Bristol, Liverpool and Glasgow and an organ-ized press campaign forced the government on to the defensive. Increas-ingly Walpole's conciliatory policy towards Spain became less tenable and in 1739 he yielded to the clamour for war. His inability to pursue the war successfully led to renewed opposition and in the 1741 general election most of the open constituencies and a majority of the electorate voted against his supporters. His resignation in 1742 was a direct consequence of this.

A third way in which central government was pressurized was through the political activities of the emergent urban bourgeoisie and, to a lesser extent, the lower orders. Each had its own reasons for resisting the authority of local ruling oligarchies, especially the importance of the patronage and deference aspects of local political and economic systems. The degree to which urban centres were 'open' played a major role in the extent to which bourgeois and plebeian political culture and action had a real effect. Political struggles tended to be over local issues but sometimes they became emmeshed in national issues. This was certainly the case in the City of London with its special privilege of petition and address to Parliament and its city corporation divided into a Court of Aldermen and a Common Council. Though Walpole could generally count on the support of the rich merchants and financiers who dominated the Court of Aldermen, he increasingly alienated the smaller, independent merchants and the urban bourgeoisie, who dominated election to the Common Council, and the city's four MPs. Attacks on the independence of the corporation electorate and the limitations on the powers of the Common Council contained in the 1725 City Elections Act acted as a focus for criticism. It led to a broadly based anti-ministerial coalition in London which, by 1741, had reduced Court interests on the Common Council and the Court of Aldermen and secured the election of all the city's MPs. The Court lost political control over London for the first time since 1688. The experience of London spread to other large boroughs. There was conflict between the corporation party, representing the interests of the richer inhabitants, and an independent opposition hostile to the claims of oligarchy in Exeter, Bristol, Tiverton, Colchester, Norwich, Worcester, Nottingham, Leicester, Liverpool and Coventry. This conflict often had a religious character: Anglican corporation versus Dissenting opposition.

Pressure from the labouring population

Electoral contests, pressure groups and petition campaigns were largely confined to bourgeois urban politics, rarely involving the poorer sections of society. Crowd demonstrations could, however, influence the political decisions of those in power. Though there were isolated occasions when crowd activity took a markedly Jacobite flavour, as for example during the riots on the Pretender's birthday at Bridgwater in 1721 and at the Coventry election in 1722, they were symbolic not of widespread Jacobite support but of a traditional popular defiance to the ruling Whig oligarchy. As Dickinson says:

> The poor did not expect to decide who should rule them, but they did seek to circumscribe how the ruling oligarchy should exercise its authority. Far from rising in armed resistance to overthrow established authority, most rioters were concerned to enlist the support of that authority in defence of their customary rights.[7]

Popular protest sometimes forced government to think again, recognize the limits of its authority and retreat from or rethink contentious policies. In 1720, for example, serious persistent rioting and over ninety petitions resulted in government action to stem the flow of imported printed calicoes which had created unemployment among weavers in London and elsewhere. Rioting among weavers in south-west England in 1726 led to action on wages in 1727. The dropping of the Excise Bill in 1733 and the embargo on grain exports in 1740 followed widespread rioting.[8]

The press

The expansion of the press from the early eighteenth century, with its constant emphasis on the liberty of the subject, helped to bring politics out of the restricted arena of Court and Parliament and into the literate and increasingly politically conscious urban environment. Political items from London's newspapers and periodicals were reprinted in the provincial press. Walpole attempted to control the press by the 1725 Stamp Act, the prosecution of hostile printers and journalists and by subsidizing a proministerial press but his government frequently lost out in the propaganda war. The press was not simply critical of specific policies but of the whole, Walpolean system. It increasingly upheld the liberties of the subject and attacked the corruption and abuse of power by the executive. Demands for the return of triennial Parliaments, attacks on the size of the national debt and the standing army and the injustice of the existing distribution of parliamentary seats demonstrated that the oligarchic nature of government did not go unchallenged. In general terms the political system created by Walpole was sufficiently flexible to contain the views of different interests and to make concessions or abandon policies if opposition became too vocal or violent. Stability and strife were opposite sides of the same coin.

John Wilkes

The importance of the relationship between Parliament and extra-parliamentary groups increased after 1760 as the cases of John Wilkes and the Association Movement illustrate.[9] From the 1750s there was an evolution of London opinion from being part of the parliamentary opposition into an expression of independent extra-parliamentary opposition. William Beckford, as one of the City's MPs between 1754 and his death in 1770 and as Lord Mayor in 1762-3 and 1769-70, was the architect of this change. He not only led London opposition to the 1763 Peace of Paris which successfully ended the Seven Years War but had, as early as 1761, criticized rotten boroughs and supported parliamentary control over pensions and places and in 1770 he declared himself in favour of extending the franchise. With James Townsend and John Sawbridge, Lord Mayors in 1772–3 and 1775–6 respectively, he built up the City as a powerful force for political change, willing to work with opposition politicians like the Rockinghamites and Chathamites as well as with John Wilkes.

The Wilkes affair dragged on for over a decade with major crises between 1763 and 1765 over 'general warrants' and 1768 to 1774 over his election as MP for Middlesex. Wilkes had conducted a campaign in the *North Briton* defending Pitt against the press attacks made in Bute's newspapers. Though not a great orator in the House of Commons Wilkes excelled as a satirical journalist, attacking the supposed, though unfounded, liaison between Bute and the king's mother and comprehensively denouncing the 1763 peace treaty in no. 45 of the *North Briton*. In April 1763 Wilkes and a number of printers and publishers were arrested on a general warrant as suspected publicists of a putative libel of the government. Wilkes, imprisoned in the Tower, secured his release by suing for a writ of habeas corpus. He promptly commenced his, eventually successful, attack on the supposed legality of general warrants which failed to name the accused but merely specified the crime. This entitled those executing the warrant to seize indiscriminately the papers and personal effects of any suspect. Despite success, Wilkes was unable to avoid expulsion from the House of Commons, was wounded in a duel with a government supporter and, with legal proceedings pending against him, thought it prudent to go abroad.

He remained in exile until 1768, condemned by the English courts for blasphemy and seditious libel and with outlawry and threat of criminal sentence hanging over him if he returned. The 1768 general election saw his successful election as MP for the county of Middlesex. Having won parliamentary victory, he waived it, surrendered to the authorities and was sentenced to twenty-two months in the King's Bench Prison for his authorship of the *North Briton*. Wilkes' election had prompted riots and demonstrations in Westminister, in the City and at Southwark. These came to a head on 10 May 1768 at St George's Fields where crowds had gathered to cheer the imprisoned Wilkes. Troops attempting to keep order opened fire, killing six people and wounding a further fifteen. Wilkes mounted a further attack on the government from his prison cell and in early 1769 was once again ejected from his parliamentary seat. Between February and April 1769 Wilkes was again elected as MP for Middlesex and again expelled by the House of Commons. Though the House had the right to expel MPs, eligibility for election was a matter of common and statute law and the unseating of Wilkes raised issues which critics of the government and more radical thinkers could focus upon. In late 1769 a small group of radical lawyers and merchants banded together in the Society of Supporters of the Bill of Rights, initially to support Wilkes and pay his debts but soon as advocates of extensive reform programmes embracing the form and administration of the law and the nature of the representative system. They successfully infiltrated the government of the

City of London and in 1771 used their power to prevent the arrest of the printers of parliamentary debates. As Ian Christie says:

> Like the challenges to general warrants after 1763 this success marked an important step towards greater freedom of the press, more open government, and the exercise of greater popular influence over the actions of politicians. . . . Contrary to their claims that they were fighting off the onset of a Tory authoritarian reaction, Wilkes and his friends in various minor ways were extending the range of civil liberties, liberalising the constitution, and opening the way for developments that would only mature in the years after Waterloo.[10]

Popular pressure in the 1770s and 1780s

Wilkes had received a great deal of support from the American colonies which identified with his professed oppression by an intolerant, insensitive and unreasonable government and by the raising of the issue of representation. The Assembly of South Carolina, for example, sent £1,500 for Wilkes' cause and reformers in Boston asserted that 'the fate of Wilkes and America must stand or fall together'. Support for the American cause and opposition to the confrontational policies of Lord North intensified in the early 1770s as war drifted closer. Though public opinion at large was generally behind North's policies, London radicals suggested that the fault lay with the monarch and his advisers and Wilkes, now Lord Mayor, petitioned the king for conciliation with the colonies. Royle and Walvin comment that

> many Englishmen (often friends of the colonists) [sought] to find in the turmoil of the years 1776–1783 some theoretical and political solutions to the confusion which had descended on British politics.[11]

Wilkes unsuccessfully proposed the reform of parliamentary representation in March 1776, but the drive for reform came from outside in the form of political pamphleteering. Major John Cartwright called for annual Parliaments and equal representation in his tract *Take Your Choice*, which was clearly influenced by American ideas. Their influence can also be seen in the work of John Jebb, Richard Price, Joseph Priestley, John Horne Tooke and Thomas Brand Hollis but what was needed was an organizational structure to turn their ideas into reality. James Burgh suggested in his *Political Disquisitions*, published in 1774–5, that a national association of men of property was needed to test opinion and which could then petition and press for reform.

The outbreak of hostilities with the colonies in 1775 and the conduct of the war had a profound impact upon British domestic policies, and the evolution of British radical politics in these years cannot be considered independently of these events. British politicians gradually realized that the American conflict was one which they could neither afford, control or win, a situation exacerbated by the entry of France on the American side in 1778. Objectors to the war in principle found common cause with those concerned by the conduct of the conflict. The costly use by ministers of patronage and pensions to maintain their positions was thrown into high relief and raised again the question of the domination of the legislature by the executive. Whig politicians led by Rockingham and his secretary Edmund Burke renewed their demands for 'economical reform', the purging of placemen and pensioners which would reduce the cost of government. This soon broadened into a vigorous nationwide campaign led by county associations.

The roots of the Association Movement lay among the discontented country gentlemen of Yorkshire led by Christopher Wyvill. Inspired by Yorkshire's example other counties took up the demand for economical reform and, following a meeting of county delegates in London in early 1780, more radical proposals for parliamentary reform emerged. The usefulness of these Associations to political reformers was limited because Wyvill was among a minority of Associations' members favouring moderate changes in representation. The result was the establishment in April 1780 of the Society for Constitutional Information (SCI), a body influential in disseminating arguments for parliamentary reform and in laying the foundations for subsequent radical activities. The SCI was moderate, reformist and respectable but, unlike the early Wilkes movement, was prepared to aim its propaganda at the lower sections of society though its proposals involved little more than tinkering with representation.

Parliament was willing to accommodate demands for economical reform but was not prepared to concede parliamentary reform. William Pitt showed himself to be a friend to the reformers in the early 1780s and those reformers following Wyvill supported Pitt, working hard to secure his electoral victory in 1784. The following year Wyvill's county supporters in Yorkshire petitioned Pitt for reform, but found that support had declined in other areas of the country. Pitt, however, did propose a limited measure for abolishing a number of rotten boroughs, despite opposition from the king and a majority of his own cabinet. It was rejected by the House of Commons and its defeat reduced even further nationwide support for reform. The Association Movement collapsed and the SCI became inactive. As Royle and Walvin say:

But it is interesting to remember that Pitt, the young parliamentary torch bearer of the reforming cause in the years 1784–5, was the man who, a decade later, was to be responsible for the vigorous and punitive repression of men and organisations seeking a radical reform of Parliament. . . . The cause of parliamentary reform languished, paradoxically, under the government of the one chief minister who above all others had seemed to herald the brightest prospects in living memory for government-backed reform.[12]

WALES, SCOTLAND AND IRELAND

Wales and Scotland had been integrated into the English state by 1714, the former since the 1540s, though the latter only since 1707. Ireland retained its own legislative identity until 1801. This section is concerned with examining the major developments in these three countries. The following questions will be borne in mind. How far did their political systems operate in similar ways to that in England? How far were their political agendas controlled by English politicians? How far were political actions a reaction to these agendas? What role did nationalism fulfil in these countries? What impact did English popular and radical politics have? How far did these three countries develop differently from England and why?

Wales

Wales[13] was more closely integrated into English social and political life than either Scotland or Ireland. Few Welshmen held government office and the great majority had no particular devotion to national, as opposed to local, politics. It is difficult to identify a specifically 'Welsh interest', MPs had no separate parliamentary identity nor did they have the same political force as the Scottish members. Political contests were fought not over matters of national policy but between the great landowning families and their clients. The smaller squires fell out of the race for power leaving the field clear for the great landed gentry who were, unlike their English counterparts, not squeezed between the aristocracy and the emergent and vigorous commercial and professional sections of society. Wales was represented in Parliament by an increasingly restricted circle of county families – the Bulkeleys in Anglesey, the Williams-Wynn in Denbighshire, the Morgans in Monmouth and Brecon and the Mansels in Glamorgan – who represented county and borough virtually unchallenged for most of the century.

Parliamentary politics

A seat in Parliament was seen as a mark of social distinction, giving the member's family priority in their own district, a say in the nomination of the Lord Lieutenant and control of a considerable amount of patronage. As in England, county members tended to be more independent than borough members. Most of the Welsh MPs saw politics as a leisurely activity rather than as a career. However, attachment to party labels was real and lip service was at least paid to party principles, though there was little difference between Whig and Tory in terms of social background and interests. In Cardiganshire the Vaughans of Crosswood upheld the Whig banner against the Pryses of Gogerddan, in Pembrokeshire it was the Owens of Orielton against the Phillipses of Picton Castle, in Monmouthshire the Tory dukes of Beaufort against the Whig Morgans of Tredegar. Party was a matter of family tradition, not of policy and bore little relation to divisions on national policy. Rival candidates were often both supporters or both opponents of the minister then in power. Boroughs and counties increasingly came under the sway of particular families. By 1700 the Bulkeley family controlled Anglesey and Beaumaris and possessed great influence in the shire and borough of Caernarfon. But in 1715 Viscount Bulkeley declined to stand for Beaumaris because, as a Jacobite, he disliked the Hanoverian succession. Instead he arranged for Meyrick of Bodorgan to replace him on the understanding that his seat would be returned when he wished. However, Meyrick refused to stand down in the 1722 election and it cost Bulkeley £10,000 to regain the seat. A few other families – the Vaughans of Corsygedol in Merioneth and the Mostyns in Flintshire – also had secure possession of county seats but in most shires several families disputed the representation. This sometimes led to a compromise where seats were held in turn but occasionally elections were contested. In 1741 there was a contest in Denbighshire between the Myddeltons of Chirk Castle and Sir Watkin William Wynn of Wynnstay. The latter had taken the seat in two hard-fought elections in 1716 and 1722 and, in a last attempt to recover the seat for the family, John Myddelton had in 1739 obtained Walpole's support. The campaign lasted two years, cost Wynn £20,000 and led to each side creating over 400 additional leasehold voters. In the May 1741 poll Wynn defeated John Myddelton by 1,352 votes to 933. The Walpole-appointed sheriff, William Myddelton, then disqualified nearly 600 of Wynn's voters and duly declared his relative elected. Following Walpole's resignation in 1742 the result was reversed, Wynn was awarded the seat and William Myddelton sent to Newgate prison and heavily fined. Wynn hegemony in the seat was not threatened for over a hundred years.

Wales and Monmouthshire returned twenty-three Tories but only four Whigs in the 1713 general election and Jacobite feelings remained strong after 1714 though, as the Young Pretender's assessment indicates, this rarely led to decisive action: 'I will do as much for my Welsh friends as they have done for me; I will drink their healths.'

There were constant reports of seditious gatherings and public disturbances. In 1715 Pembrokeshire squires used truncheons to break up loyalist meetings, while a Jacobite mob rioted in Wrexham. In 1717 a proposed landing at Milford Haven failed to materialize. The area between Machynlleth and Aberystwyth was, according to local Whigs, in a parlous state by 1720. Squires openly drank treasonable toasts; their agents interfered with the mail; they ran an escape network for fugitives and corresponded with the exiled Jacobite court. A number of secret Jacobite organizations came into existence, like the Society of Sea Serjeants and the Cycle of the White Rose, but they were of social as much as political importance. There is no evidence of any attempt to link the Jacobite societies or co-ordinate action between them and they increasingly degenerated into drinking clubs. The 1745 rebellion was also a non-event in Wales.

Welsh Jacobitism

Welsh Jacobitism was an affair of the country gentry with a few leading families in each county affected: the Pryses in Cardiganshire, the Kemeys, Lewises and Raglan associates in Glamorgan; the Wynnstay, Brogyntyn and Baron Hill families in North Wales; the Picton Castle and Slebech families in Pembrokeshire and the Beaufort family in Monmouthshire; and they drew lesser families into their orbit. The Jacobite movement suffered from the over-optimism and dalliance of the Welsh gentry. The 1721 survey by Jacobite agents and that of a French envoy in 1743 betrayed poor intelligence of the actual situation and an unrealistic assessment of individuals leading to an assumption of Jacobite control in Wales that was grossly inflated. Whatever hold the Jacobites had on Wales was slackening by the 1740s as even committed Jacobites were becoming tired of political sterility and being debarred from local as well as national office. The mellowing of Welsh attitudes and Welsh Jacobite inactivity during 1745 resulted in the readmission of Tories into local government offices and by 1748 Tory JPs were appointed in Cardiganshire. Jacobitism was recognized in Wales, as elsewhere, as a romantic sentiment rather than a practical political alternative after 1745 and the accession of George III enabled Tories once more to associate with the throne and Jacobites like Sir John Philipps made their way to Court.

Welsh Whigs

From the 1720s one significant development was the organization of political activity in the constituencies. After 1720 Sir Watkin William Wynn built up a territorial political base in North Wales. Sir John Philipps attempted something similar in the south-west and after 1761 a bloc emerged in Radnorshire led by the Marquis of Carnarvon. What political conflict there was occurred when Whigs, often supported by the English patronage machine long dominated by the Duke of Newcastle, attempted to dislodge Tories from their long-entrenched positions. The 1727 election was the first to return more Welsh Whig than Tory MPs. The 1733 Excise Bill excited political passions in Wales because of traditional prejudice against excisemen and their influence at elections. The Commons vote was more or less on party lines though some Welsh Whigs voted with the opposition. Walpole deprived the Duke of Bolton of his Lieutenancy of Carmarthenshire as a result. The 1734 general election was fought before the dust settled not without interference from England. Newcastle's election agent, Jessop, prepared the way in the Welsh border counties and troops were quartered at Knighton after Walpole's effigy was burnt.

The Whigs spent more time preparing for the 1741 election, laying plans especially to counter the Wynn influence in North Wales. A Whig sheriff had been chosen for Denbighshire in 1740 but this did not prevent the victory of the Wynn family who held Denbighshire (Sir Watkin William Wynn after a petition), Montgomeryshire (his brother Robert) and the borough of Flint (his other brother Richard). Only in the Denbigh boroughs did the Whigs have some success. In anticipation of the 1747 election the Tories joined with Frederick, Prince of Wales and, although the election confirmed the Pelhams in office, this move signified the political reorientation of the Tories now willing to exploit the reversionary interest to bring them to power. Newcastle's influence, through the Earl of Powis as his election agent, was evident in the Welsh elections of 1754 and 1761, when there were disagreements between Whig families over seats in Caernarfonshire and Cardiganshire.

Newcastle's fall in 1761 was followed by the distintegration of the Welsh Whigs some of whom attached themselves to Bute, others to George Grenville, though most of them supported the Peace of Paris which ended the Seven Years War, conduct of which they had approved under Pitt but which had since become a matter of economic hardship. Protest centred round the Cider Tax. Though it was not simply a matter of mob violence there were riots and fears that public order would break down in southern and south-east Wales. Lord Egmont noted:

> the Welsh counties adjacent, Monmouth and Hereford, are made of stuff to kindle with a very little fire, and Somerset, Devon and Cornwall are divided from Glamorgan by the Severn alone.

The issue of taxation merged with that of John Wilkes, which evoked some sympathy in Wales. When he was released from prison in 1770 balls were held in his honour at Denbigh and Ruthin and a coffee-house in Denbigh named after him, though there is no evidence of a petition from Wales during the petitioning campaign of 1769–70. In the 1770s and 1780s new political alignments emerged. The new reformers represented a striking coalition of gentry and industrialists (often former Tories and Jacobites) together with liberal Dissenters. Not a party in the modern sense, they tended to call for a common body of reforms which can broadly be described as populist rather than revolutionary. In terms of parliamentary politics they provided a focus for the series of elections in the 1780s.

Scotland

Scotland enjoyed a state of 'semi-independence' in the eighteenth century.[14] It did not participate in British politics because such a concept did not exist. Scottish affairs and issues were largely separate and distinct and, according to Alexander Murdoch, for much of the eighteenth century revolved round the basic problem of national development:

> The union had destroyed a Parliament, but it allowed many different Scottish institutions to survive. These institutions and the society which supported them . . . [sought] not . . . assimilation, but parity with English society. Government mirrored this situation. . . . Semi-independence (a quasi-Union?) allowed the Union settlement to work by providing a buffer between English government and assumptions and Scottish institutions and society in general.[15]

So how was Scotland governed after 1707? The negotiated union was as much a result of social and economic as political crisis. English attempts to suppress the commercial power of the Dutch Republic had forced Scottish merchants to readjust their pattern of trade towards large-scale commerce with England. The abortive Company of Scotland, founded in 1695, was obstructed by England and was prevented from access to the money markets of London, Amsterdam and Hamburg, leading to great Scottish bitterness. Harvest failures between 1695 and 1699 led to widespread famine and by 1700 the Scottish commonwealth teetered on the edge of bankruptcy. The surrender of its legislative independence was the price Scotland paid for the gamble by its political elite that the solution to their domestic problems lay in economic union with England.

1707 and after

The 1707 settlement stopped at legislative union and Bruce Lenman argues that

> Provided the Protestant Succession went through, and Scottish political life was abolished at a national level, Westminster was not fanatical about details. The upshot was that the Union was almost as interesting for what it kept apart as for what it joined together.[16]

The Church of Scotland was kept independent because had it opposed Union it might have mobilized opinion hostile to the surrender of national identity. The legal system was also left untouched largely because the Scottish legal profession was closely linked to landed society. The constitutional settlement of 1707 made Scotland and England one state but could not resolve the social, economic and cultural differences between the two countries. There remained

the flourishing national institutions of the law, the church and the universities. . . . Scottish local government, the Scottish electoral system, the Scottish banking system and the metropolitan society of Edinburgh . . . [17]

but there were also negative features:

the national animosities which came to be represented by the Jacobite pretenders, the Duke of Cumberland, Lord Bute and John Wilkes. National distinction was not only present, it was pronounced.

After the abolition in 1708 of the Scottish Privy Council, the chief executive organ of government in Scotland, constitutional authority lay with the British Privy Council. In reality policy was formed not in the Privy Council but in the cabinet and real decision-making was usually restricted to an inner cabinet dominated by the chief minister reporting directly to the king 'in the closet' (that is, in private conversation). Except during the 1715 and 1745 rebellions Scottish business was rarely considered sufficiently important to warrant cabinet discussion, which resulted in individual government departments having most influence on the normal administration of Scottish affairs. Between 1708 and 1725 and again briefly from 1742 to January 1746 there was a separate Scottish Secretary of State. From 1725 to 1742 and again from 1746 to 1754 Scottish business was under the Duke of Newcastle who was Secretary of State for the Southern Department 1724–48 and for the Northern Department 1748–54. Scottish affairs were the responsibility of the Northern Secretary until 1782, when they were transferred to the new Home Department. Judicial appointments, presentations to parishes in the gift of the Crown, the disposal of Crown offices in Scotland and correspondence with Crown officers all went through this department but, because it had no control over the revenue offices, the army or navy in Scotland, its influence over government patronage was limited. The Treasury, by contrast, was responsible for Scottish revenues, salaries of Scottish officers, administration of Crown property in Scotland, bounties for Scottish manufactures and the appointment of customs officers. It had greater scope for patronage and increasingly became more important in British government from both a political and an administrative standpoint.

A Scottish 'minister': the Earl of Ilay

The necessity of advice on Scottish conditions and custom led to the emergence of the unofficial office of Scottish 'manager' or 'minister' representing Scottish interests and mobilizing the Scottish MPs and representative peers behind the government. From 1725 to 1761 Archibald Campbell, Earl of Ilay (and after 1743, third Duke of Argyll) managed Scottish affairs. His family represented the largest and most influential aristocratic interest in Scotland in the early eighteenth century and this encouraged Walpole to seek an alliance with Ilay and his brother John, second Duke of Argyll in 1725. In return for control over most government patronage in Scotland, Ilay kept the bulk of Scottish MPs behind the government, submitted recommendations for offices, advised government on its election plans and, through his own independent power base exerted influence over government policy. Ilay both managed Scottish affairs for England and represented and guarded Scottish national interests in Westminster.

The pressures of the Seven Years War led to Ilay's power being at its greatest in the last four years of his life. It also provided a common crisis and common enemy which united English and Scottish ruling elites under a new British and imperial patriotism. Ilay's death was followed by a vacuum not filled until after the appointment of Henry Dundas as Lord Advocate in 1775 and the consolidation of his position in the early 1780s. Dundas went on to become a British politician in a way that was never possible for Ilay:

> At the heart of this distinction . . . lies the growth of an imperial consciousness amongst the ruling elite of Britain. The nature of the British state was changing from a national basis to an imperial one, and this development had to affect the political conduct of the elite which maintained the state. Like Argyll, Dundas saw to the management of the Scots for the government, but whereas Argyll had protected the Scots from English interference, Dundas won them a piece of the imperial pie.[18]

It is difficult not to conclude that Scotland was under-represented in the British Parliament. Her 45 MPs only just exceeded the 44 returned by the grossly over-represented county of Cornwall. There were only about 2,300 voters in the 33 Scottish counties and most of them were subject to a few hundred landowners. In the burghs only the town councils had the franchise. Scottish MPs rarely wanted to offend by representing grievances and most served government for profit. The 16 so-called 'representative' peers were similarly tools of government. The decision of the House of Lords in the Brandon case of 1711, when the House refused to admit the Duke of Hamilton on the strength of his rank as Duke of Brandon in the British peerage, shut important routes to social and political position for the higher Scottish aristocracy. Court support was now the only means of access to the legislature for nearly all Scottish peers.

It is important to distinguish between the role of the Lord Advocate who spoke for the government in the House of Commons, produced Scottish legislation and acted as a sort of government whip for Scottish MPs and the Scottish 'manager' who represented Scottish interests within the executive bureaucracy and who managed the Scottish electoral system for the government. In the 1720s and 1730s Ilay wished to maximize ministerial influence while in his later years he merely wanted to buttress or at least recognize the dominant interest in a locality through control over the distribution of patronage.

Full participation in Scottish politics involved a public acknowledgement of the Hanoverian Succession. Convinced Scottish Jacobites were non-players in this game and all the other participants were, after 1715, Whig. Until 1725 the Whigs polarized into two party structures. The 'Squadrone' were a small group of country Whigs distinguished by family traditions of opposition to the Stuart monarchy and a close network of matrimonial alliances. Their identity of interest made up for their lack of numerical strength; they numbered about a quarter of the Scottish MPs and representative peers in the first British Parliament and rapidly declined as a political force in the early 1720s when they unsuccessfully supported Stanhope and Sunderland against Walpole. The second grouping were followers of the duke of Argyll or Argathelians and dominated Scottish affairs from the 1720s until the 1760s. Not every member of the Scottish political establishment was firmly committed to either party, but they had to live with them.

Scottish Jacobitism

Jacobitism seemed to be dying as a cause after 1715, shaken by the mismanagement of the rising that year by the Earl of Mar. It increasingly became a conservative backlash led by discontented lairds and nobles, especially in the Highlands, and it seems that the Scottish nobility in general was convinced that it had little future. The easy crushing of the 1719 rising in north-western Scotland confirmed this view. Apart from significant Mackensie support it was very much the work of Scottish exiles, themselves pawns in a quarrel between Spain and England which had no bearing on Scotland at all. By 1745 in many respects Jacobitism was a social and political anachronism in Scotland as elsewhere. Its ultimate aim was to turn the clock back before 1688, end the Protestant Succession and link Britain in alliance with France. In this it underestimated the extent that Scotland had benefited from the rivalry in trade and colonial power between England and France. Jacobitism could not compete with the upturn in Scottish trade and manufacture in the 1740s. Scotland's advantage lay, particularly in the Lowlands, with the economic benefits of British imperialism not in dynastic politics.

Conclusions

Alexander Murdoch maintains that there are three views of Scottish politics after 1707.[19] First, the Scottish allies of a given ministry simply carried out instructions from their English masters. Secondly, Ilay and others bowed to the inevitable when faced by English pressure but otherwise carried out their own policies to cope with the needs of the Scottish political nation. Finally, an interpretation can be adopted that Scottish ministers were responsible to English ones but that the relationship was not one-sided and based on the successful or unsuccessful representation of Scottish interests by the Scottish manager. Emphasis on the submissive aspects of Scottish government can result in underestimating the extent to which a separate Scottish political identity was maintained by negotiation. Scotland may not have had high priority in government policy-making, may even have been ignored, but it still had to be managed and controlled.

Ireland

The government and politics of eighteenth-century Ireland[20] was different from that of Wales and Scotland in two important respects. First, Ireland retained its own legislative integrity, if not independence, throughout the century. Secondly, Ireland was religiously a Catholic country even if the focus of authority lay with the Protestant minority. The relationship between Catholic and Protestant mattered far more in Ireland than on the mainland and could not be ignored. Was the Catholic majority a potential threat to Protestant political hegemony? How far could Ireland be left to govern itself? How important was Irish politics and policy in Westminster?

Governing Ireland

How did Walpole govern Ireland? His policy has been interpreted from two different perspectives. English historians have argued that Walpole sought to exclude Irishmen from government, used English party hacks and as a result alienated the 'natural rulers' of Ireland, paving the way for the 'nationalism' of Flood and Grattan. Irish historians, by contrast maintain that Walpole introduced a system of 'undertakers', contracting out Irish parliamentary management to Irish politicians who carried through English policy in return for a say in that policy and control over a large amount of patronage. Each interpretation contains some truth.

Irish politics throughout the eighteenth century was a 'dialogue' between four main elements: internally, the Anglo-Irish, the Presbyterian Scots of Ulster and the Irish Catholics and externally, the British government through the Irish administration based at Dublin Castle. The Anglo-Irish, Protestant and dominant landowners, saw themselves as a beleaguered minority, threatened on two sides by the Catholic peasantry and emergent middle class and the Presbyterian Scots who had settled in Ulster in considerable numbers from the mid-seventeenth century, both of whom were denied full participation in the political system because of their beliefs. The Anglo-Irish felt dependent on English support, particularly military aid, to defend them against the Catholic threat. The successful campaign of 1690 and the defeat of James II at the Boyne effectively ended any real prospect of a successful Catholic uprising in Ireland. The

Catholics were deprived of their natural leaders as a result of the exile of the so-called 'wild geese' and the continued decline of a coherent Catholic gentry. Only with aid from France and the exiled Jacobites did the Catholics have a real chance of regaining power. Ireland was a divided and antagonistic society with potential for conflict not just between Catholic and Protestant but between Protestants. There was no sub-structure of small owner-occupiers and gentry between the Catholic peasantry and the Protestant landowners. Irish society was dependent upon support either from Protestant England or from Catholic Europe.

In theory the executive in Dublin Castle (the Lord Lieutenant and in his absence a commission of Lords Justices) was appointed from England and was responsible to English ministers. The Crown enjoyed considerable 'hereditary revenues' in Ireland. The Irish Parliament – elected until 1768 for the life of the monarch – had no right to prepare legislation. This was produced by the Irish Privy Council, itself accountable to the English Privy Council, and the Irish Parliament could only accept or reject it without amendment. The Westminster Parliament could legislate for Ireland if necessary. In practice the situation was far less clear-cut. By 1714 the Irish Parliament had developed a power of the purse. Secondly, there was an important development in the legislative process. Legislation began its life in the Irish Parliament as 'heads' of bills not in the Irish Privy Council, which risked difficulties if it tampered with them. Money bills over which the Irish Commons claimed a monopoly, were seldom altered. Generally Irish issues made little impact on Westminster. There was an Irish lobby, as in 1731 under Lord Perceval, but it concentrated on specific issues especially in trade and industry. What an English ministry wanted from its Irish policy was a peaceful and quiet island.

Ireland under Walpole

Changes in the pattern of Irish politics after 1714 made it easier in some respects for English ministers to get what they wanted. The two-party system, much in evidence under Queen Anne, broke up quickly. Irish politics swung decisively towards the Whigs, a situation confirmed in the 1715 general election. Some discontented Whigs later joined the remaining opposition Tories who were themselves split. By the mid-1720s the significant unit of parliamentary organization was the family or territorially-based 'connection'. The result of this was the re-emergence of matters of 'patriotic' concern as a popular focus for the hybrid opposition. Irish political concerns were refocused in the 1710s and 1720s, culminating in the campaign against Wood's Halfpence between 1722 and 1725.

The rivalry between the two most prominent Irish politicians, Alan Brodrick and William Conolly, dominated the period from 1714 to 1727. In 1714 Brodrick became Lord Chancellor while Conolly assumed the more overtly political office of Speaker of the Commons. Conolly's strategy was to make himself indispensable at all times. Brodrick became increasingly isolated and expected dismissal following his breaking with Sunderland in 1719. Walpole's return to power shifted the balance and he was willing to protect the Brodricks, whom he saw as potential allies, from Sunderland. Parallel to the conflict between Conolly and the Brodricks was the constitutional problem of the Irish House of Lords. In 1714 the Whigs inherited a Tory-dominated Upper House. A batch of new Whig bishops and the creation of peers was not sufficient to turn the Lords into an automatic rubber stamp. Many of the new creations were Irishmen, who outnumbered Englishmen in the House, and when any 'national' issue arose a patriot coalition, led by Archbishop King of Dublin and the Tory Irish primate Lindsay, could often defeat the court. The Lords became embroiled in a constitutional conflict over their appellate jurisdiction, brought into question by an appeal from Ireland to the British House of Lords. In the 1720 Declaratory Act the Westminster Parliament reaffirmed its rights both to hear Irish appeals and to make laws for Ireland.

In July 1722 William Wood was given the patent to mint copper coins for Ireland. The campaign against the Halfpence between 1722 and 1725 can be compared to the Excise struggle of 1733 in England. The Halfpence was seen as a symbol of English oppression and as a real threat to the Irish economy. By September 1723 when the Irish Parliament met opposition was mounting and both Houses addressed the king against the Halfpence. Swift's *Drapier's Letters* of 1723–4 ridiculed Wood, attacked Walpole and raised the wider theme of Ireland's constitution and the rights of the Anglo-Irish as 'free people'. But the issue was not simply support for or opposition to the Halfpence but between Brodrick and Conolly to see who should 'govern', a conflict eventually resolved in favour of the latter. The whole Wood affair demonstrated the ineptitude of Walpole's understanding of Ireland. He mishandled Irish public opinion by underestimating opposition and the depth of feeling against the Halfpence. He obstinately continued to support it and, when compelled to back down, saw more in the patriotism of the Anglo-Irish than actually existed.

Management of both Houses of the Irish Parliament necessitated that the chosen undertaker(s) be afforded clear support. But Walpole took a different view and concentrated on the jurisdictional dispute, the stridency of opposition to the Halfpence, and he was obsessed by the notion of Anglo-Irish 'independency'. The importance of having a capable Commons 'undertaker' was amply demonstrated after Conolly's death in 1729. But Walpole was now at the stage where he distrusted all Irish politicians and was determined that the fruits of patronage should be given to Englishmen. This underlined Ireland's dependence, reinforced the 'English' interest especially in the Lords and created a political counter-balance to the power of the Commons 'undertaker'. If Irish politics was unstable under Walpole then, as David Hayton says, 'Such troubles as Walpole endured were for the most part of his and his colleagues' own making'.[21]

In the 1720s and 1730s the Protestant Ascendancy had neither the confidence nor the resources to challenge English constitutional and economic paternalism. Walpole's interventions, guided by a faulty evaluation of Irish politics, were rarely helpful, frequently damaging and motivated by English considerations.

Demands for reform

The 1760s and 1770s saw the emergence of growing dissatisfaction with the government of Ireland. Pressure by Irish Catholics for repeal of the penal laws gathered momentum after 1760 with stress being placed on the economic and political advantages of enabling Catholics to invest freely in land hence giving them a stake in the established order. Protestants showed a growing desire to reaffirm Irish constitutional rights which challenged the control of the British executive over Irish legislation. The balance between the British government and the Irish 'undertakers' increasingly came under strain. British government found itself in the position of first encouraging and then restraining the development of an Irish national movement.

From the early 1760s the Irish Commons, led by Henry Flood and Henry Grattan, began to express resentment at the denial of basic constitutional rights and liberties. Demands for a Habeas Corpus Act and for a Bill to limit the duration of the Irish Parliament emerged in 1763 and in 1765 this was extended to include a bill giving judges security of tenure during good behaviour. In return for Irish agreement to finance an extra 3,000 troops, the British government was prepared in 1767–8 to carry constitutional reform. Lord Townshend, the Lord Lieutenant, managed to pass the Irish Octennial Act in 1768 but British obstruction proved fatal to carrying out the rest of the bargain. Security of tenure for judges was blocked by a British insistence that petitions for their removal might come from the Westminster as well as the Dublin Parliament. There were second thoughts about Habeas Corpus and Irish interest in having their own Mutiny Act was not even discussed. Townshend's problems increased since the disappointed 'undertakers' of Irish politics had been suspended and now joined the patriot parliamentary opposition. Parliamentary management became increasingly difficult and expensive.

The outbreak of the American war provided a further stimulus for both commercial and constitutional questions in Ireland and during the late 1770s and early 1780s Lord North encountered growing difficulties in governing from Dublin. There were conflicting responses to the American revolution in Ireland. Politically aware Catholics supported imperial authority and gave assistance with military recruiting, a development treated with extreme suspicion by many Protestants. The Irish Establishment's support for British policy in America was cool and ambiguous. Loyal Irishmen had no desire to see the colonists secede but they also recognized that Ireland had a common interest with America over the defence of constitutional principles against the claims of the British Parliament. The attitude of Ulster Presbyterians was distinctly hostile.

Grievances against the British government were exacerbated by the end of economic prosperity as Ireland lost overseas markets, first for linen in the American colonies and then in Europe with the dislocation of trade following the entry of France and Spain into the conflict. Demands for commercial reform began in the Irish Commons from 1776, gaining momentum in 1778. The logic of Lord North's case in refusing to endorse change was destroyed by the sweeping offers made to the Americans in the terms of the Carlisle Peace Commission of 1778, and the small concessions made to Ireland in 1779 were insufficient to reduce popular agitation. The defenceless state of Ireland and the threat of invasion in 1778–9 led to the emergence of the Volunteer Movement. Though largely a Protestant militia, the Volunteers proved a highly responsive sounding board for Irish discontent and its connection with an influential part of the Irish electorate had a marked effect on the Irish House of Commons. By the autumn of 1779 the Volunteers were said to number 40,000 men and on 4 November 1779 the Dublin Volunteers paraded on College Green with field guns labelled 'Free Trade or this'. Lord North capitulated to threats to the Irish economy and public order and in early 1780 substantial commercial concessions were made. Restraints on the export of Irish wool, woollens and glassware were removed and acts prohibiting the carrying of bullion into Ireland repealed. The Irish were conceded freedom to trade with the British colonies on the same terms that the British enjoyed.

Economic concession was followed by Grattan and his followers turning to the constitutional question of Ireland's legislative independence. Westminster believed that Protestant politicians, aware of their vulnerability as a minority in Irish society, would not push this issue too far. Lord North had already taken action to defuse one element of Irish discontent, that of the underprivilege caused by religion and had taken toleration rather further than the Protestant Ascendancy wanted. In 1778 penal laws were lifted from English Catholics and the statutes prohibiting Catholics from buying forfeited Irish estates were repealed. The Irish Parliament followed suit with a limited Catholic Relief Act though the Catholic purchase of freeholds was delayed until 1782. Discrimination against Irish Presbyterians was removed by an Irish enactment of 1780 repealing that part of the 1704 Irish Test Act which had imposed a sacramental test for those holding local appointments or offices under the Crown. Despite the alarm caused to the gentry and larger landowners by this and middle-class agitation in Dublin for political participation and radical attacks on Irish pocket boroughs, the effects of these developments and attempts to fan anti-Catholic feelings were limited throughout 1781–2. Mass meetings of the Volunteers in 1781 and 1782, especially that at

Dungannon, passed resolutions demanding the establishment of an independent Irish legislature.

Fears that Ireland might go the way of America led to Rockingham and his Whig administration conceding full and equal constitutional rights to Ireland in May 1782. Protestant prejudice had been overcome by a sense of solidarity with Catholics as Irishmen and Ireland had, unlike America, gained its legislative independence as well as maintaining its connection with Great Britain. But it is important not push this notion of 'independence' too far. The mainland still possessed considerable influence over Irish politics particularly at the level of administration. The Lord Lieutenant was appointed under the British great seal and Royal Warrants countersigned by three British Lords of the Treasury were used to notify the Crown's decision on Irish administrative matters (issue of public money, appointments, pensions and the regulation of government departments). The Crown retained a theoretical veto in the case of colonial legislation, though this was only used eighteen times before the Union of 1800–1. Demands for reform of the Irish Parliament and the franchise began to be heard in the summer and autumn of 1782 but within a year the Volunteer movement was in decline and the Irish political nation again split along broadly sectarian lines. The defeat of Pitt's reform bill in Westminster in April 1785 effectively killed any government action for Irish reform. As John Cannon says: 'It is sufficient comment on the limits of that legislative independence Ireland had achieved in 1782 to note that the effective decision was still made in England.'[22]

FOREIGN POLICY

The final section of this chapter is concerned with British foreign policy. I do not intend to give a detailed narrative of this subject but will confine myself to the objectives, machinery and patterns of foreign policy between 1714 and the mid-1780s. More detailed studies can be found in the notes.[23]

A 'Whiggish' propensity?

It is possible to identify a 'Whiggish' approach to Britain's foreign policy and international relations similar to the Whig interpretation of domestic history as a natural progression towards parliamentary democracy.[24] Because all the European great powers – Britain, France, Russia, Austria-Hungary, Prussia, the Ottoman Empire – had already been involved on the international stage since 1648 it was understandable that the diplomatic relations of the period from 1648 to the 1790s should be treated in terms of the analysis of the nineteenth century. Stress was therefore placed by historians on informed policy-making and long-term rational planning. In this analysis war tended to be regarded as a device of deliberate policy based on a rational consideration of perceived national advantage. Ideology and domestic pressures were generally ignored except for Britain and other states, whose system of government was different from those described as 'absolutist'. Recently, however, historians have begun to argue that international relations were not fundamentally different after the Treaty of Westphalia of 1648 than before.

Two issues need to be considered if the continuity of pre- and post-1640 is to be maintained. First, how far was there what Michael Howard has called 'a cultural predisposition to war' in this period?[25] The belief that war appears to be a natural and inevitable part of human conduct and a proper way of adjudicating disputes would have been readily accepted in the seventeenth century but did attitudes change during the eighteenth century? Certainly there were more critics of war after 1700 than before, but whether there was the shift in sensibility towards rationally organized warfare as a major instrument of state policy which Howard identifies is more questionable. The extent to which Frederick the Great was more 'modern' in his notions of foreign policy and the role of warfare than Louis XIV is a matter of degree and style rather than of fundamental difference.

Secondly, two major elements of international relations – the role of dynastic concerns and the continued habit of discussing relations in religious terms – suggest continuity between the eighteenth century and the two centuries preceding it. The role of religion has received relatively little attention from historians but there is sufficient evidence for diplomatic intervention and tension because of the treatment of coreligionists in other countries. For example, the Hanoverian decision in 1730 to support the Protestant town of Hildesheim against its Catholic Wittelsbach Prince Bishop led to tension and military action. The 1725 Austro-Spanish treaty of Vienna was seen by Protestant Europe as a Catholic plot, visible evidence of a conspiracy in support of the Jacobite claim to the British throne. The Seven Years War (1756–63) was portrayed in propaganda as a religious conflict. Alliances in the eighteenth century, however, rarely conformed exactly to confessional lines. In 1725 the Alliance of Hanover, formed to confront the Austro-Spanish pact, linked Britain and Prussia with France and in 1726 Prussia changed alliances. Sweden fought Prussia in the Seven Years War. The continued importance of religion as a major factor in foreign policy can best be seen in the religious symbolism surrounding military and naval victory and defeat. In 1756 Edward Weston, a senior official who had dealt with foreign policy, wrote an anonymous pamphlet entitled *The Fast* calling for a national fast day to win divine support for an immoral and irreligious country. National fast days were held in Britain in all but one year of the War of American Independence. Newspapers, like *The Monitor* often saw the hand of Providence at work during the Seven Years War. By placing their emphasis on the 'modern' aspects of the eighteenth century, especially the emergence of rationalist philosophy, historians have neglected the extent to which Europe was a religious society and how far issues were expressed in religious rather than rational terms.

Dynastic considerations

The central role of monarchy and the importance of dynastic considerations also ensured a basic continuity in the conduct of foreign policy between the sixteenth and eighteenth centuries. George Frederick Handel's 1743 Dettingen *Te Deum* was an expression of both religious ideology and a celebration of the power of royal majesty. Making war was one of the most impressive functions of monarchy, displaying both its coercive power and legitimate authority and was the most extreme expression of dynastic purpose. George I was willing to fight in 1714 had a pro-Stuart coup attempted to prevent him inheriting the British throne and he had to fight the Jacobites the following year. Between 1714 and 1760 dynastic considerations lay at the heart of British foreign policy. Successful diplomacy or war conferred greater acceptability on monarchs and brought political popularity and success to ministers. This took place in the context of a Court culture, predisposed to war as a heroic endeavour, and of an emergent imperialist culture which saw war in terms of commercial advantage.

British monarchs had far more control and room for manoeuvre in the making of foreign policy than any other matter of state. This was not simply the result of an entrenched royal prerogative but of the need for secrecy of deliberation and immediacy of response which Parliament could not provide. George I and George II both had continental commitments in Hanover which they often placed above the interests of Britain. Both spent long periods away from England, which necessitated the repeal of the clause in the 1701 Act of Succession preventing royal travel abroad without parliamentary approval. The diplomatic implications of continental involvement were generally accepted in England. The restoration of the Stuart line and what was perceived as an alien Catholic absolutism was seen as a potential consequence of failure to do so. This did not mean that continental involvement was accepted uncritically and between the 1720s and 1750s the cry of Hanover was exploited to great effect by politicians. George III ostentatiously renounced Hanoverian policies at the beginning of his reign in his attempt to appear a patriotic British monarch, a decision which he later regretted. His attachment to an Austrian rather than Prussian alliance was a consequence of opposition to his policies in the 1760s and he played a crucial role in the diplomacy of the American War of Independence. Eighteenth-century British monarchs were not mere ciphers in foreign policy.

How was foreign policy conducted?

The conduct of the king's foreign policy was the responsibility of the two Secretaries of State for North and South, who divided foreign policy between them, until 1782 when the modern division between Home and Foreign Offices was established. They were supported by a small bureaucracy of under-secretaries and clerks in Whitehall. Overseas relations were conducted, in key areas of Western Europe, by ambassadors and elsewhere by envoys and lesser officials. There were certain problems with this system. The division of duties between two Secretaries of State could make the development of consistent and coherent policy difficult though, in practice, one or other Secretary was recognized as superior and key decisions tended to be the result of discussions between the monarch and other ministers. For example, the Duke of Newcastle first had to defer to his colleague Townshend and, when he achieved primacy, expected his colleague as Secretary of State to be subordinate. In the late 1740s and early 1750s this led to a succession of ministers – Harrington, Chesterfield and Bedford – before he obtained a compliant colleague in the person of Holderness. The creation of a single Foreign Secretary in 1782 therefore did not have a dramatic effect on the practice of foreign policy. More problematic was the question of the appointment of individuals with the necessary expertise and technical ability when appointment was the result of patronage rather than merit. Lord Chesterfield summed up the problem in the 1750s as follows:

> Most of our ministers abroad have taken up that department occasionally, without ever having thought of foreign affairs before; many of them without speaking any one foreign language; and all of them without manners which are absolutely necessary towards being well received, and making a figure at foreign courts.[26]

Parliament had little or no constitutional standing in foreign policy. Negotiations took place, treaties were made and war declared by the monarch as head of state. Financial expediency, however, gave the legislature considerable influence over the direction of policy and no government could afford to provoke parliamentary displeasure at its foreign policy. Monarchs could not afford to wage war or develop ambitious military or foreign policies after the establishment of the Civil List in 1697 and ministers knew that credibility abroad depended on the ability to obtain financial assistance at home. Parliamentary approval of policy was therefore essential and throughout the eighteenth century the executive normally presented treaties for parliamentary approval. Foreign allies viewed this parliamentary influence with considerable disquiet. The notion of 'Perfidious Albion', that Britain could not be trusted to carry out its commitments because of its powerful Parliament, became a useful

propaganda weapon among continental rulers and was not without a modi-
cum of truth.

The role of Parliament in foreign policy reflected and reinforced the ill-
defined and ambiguous power of 'public opinion'. In this the burgeoning
press played a central role.[27] By mid-century some politicians felt that
freedom of the press represented a significant threat to the conduct of
foreign policy. Foreign news took up the majority of space in eighteenth-
century newspapers even when there were significant domestic issues. But
foreign coverage in the press was often sensational, inaccurate, partisan
and, at times, stridently xenophobic and militantly patriotic. Ill-informed
and propagandist as the press might be, ministers were unwise to ignore
its influence. The reduction of the electorate's influence over foreign policy
was one of the justifications used in 1716 in the debates on the Septennial
Act. However, the deep concern of propertied opinion was also expressed
in addresses and petitions to Parliament and the Crown. In 1739 there
was a national campaign in support of war against Spain and in 1756
addresses on the loss of Minorca. Lobbies, for example monopoly companies like the East India and Levant Companies, formal committees like
those of the West India and North American merchants, financial interests
in the City and looser groups all had vested interests and expected their
views to be taken into account when foreign policy was made. As Paul
Langford says,

> During the eighteenth century foreign policy was almost always the
> most important matter before the political nation . . . the pride of place
> given to foreign affairs in the press was an authentic tribute to the
> interest attached by the public to them.[28]

Objectives of foreign policy

What were the objectives of eighteenth-century British foreign policy?
The use of 'objectives' may, as has already been stated imply a long-term
rationality to policy which was in reality lacking. Poor communications
often meant that the Secretaries of State were making decisions or advising
the monarch on foreign intelligence that had been superseded by events,
and ambassadors and envoys adopting attitudes based upon ministerial
policies which had since changed. To a significant extent, therefore, the
day-to-day operation of foreign policy was pragmatic, haphazard and often
uninformed. However, with this proviso, it is possible to identify certain
issues lying behind policy and decision-making during this period. From
1688 through to the 1750s preservation of the Protestant Succession against
the Jacobites played a major role in the conduct of foreign affairs. France,
Spain, Austria, Sweden, Russia and Prussia all meddled at one time or
another in Jacobite intrigues, with important results for Whitehall. How-

ever, what was happening in Europe would have been of concern to English ministers without the German interests of the first two Georges.

The threat of invasion made war at sea and the state of the navy matters of central concern to successive British governments. During the eighteenth century the idea of the two-power naval standard developed, with Britain having sufficient ships to deal with the fleets of France and Spain simultaneously and also capable of using its navy as a weapon of the blockade against continental Europe. This policy was expensive and was unpopular as a result. Those who paid taxes tempered the bellicosity of William Pitt in 1761–2 and George III to fight the American colonists to the death and forced a sense of realism upon those responsible for making policy decisions.

In Europe Britain's interests lay in three main areas. First, it was concerned in keeping the Low Countries either neutral or in friendly hands. Divided into the Austrian Netherlands (basically present-day Belgium) and Holland, the Low Countries were strategically placed opposite Britain's North Sea and Channel coast. No British minister could afford to have a potentially hostile power controlling this area. Secondly, the connection with Hanover necessitated what contemporaries saw as expensive involvement in continental Europe. Thirdly, there was an increasingly strategic focus in the Mediterranean on protection of British interests in the Middle East. The growth of British trade in the eighteenth century saw a shift from European to non-European markets. Tension and conflict with Spain over South American trade and with the French in America, the West Indies, Africa and India led to a colonial and maritime contest which exploded in the Seven Years War. Economic advantage was central to diplomatic and military action. Lord Holderness in the mid-eighteenth century said:

> I am convinced you will agree with me in one principle, that we must be merchants while we are soldiers, that our trade depends upon a proper exertion of our maritime strength; that trade and maritime force depend upon each other, and that the riches which are the true resources of this country depend upon its commerce.[29]

A chronological division

Paul Langford has divided Britain's foreign policy between 1688 and 1783 into three phases: the defence of the succession 1688–1721; the influence of Hanover 1721–54 and the lure of empire 1754–83. While any chronological division is, to a certain degree, arbitrary and there is considerable overlap between these themes, Langford has successfully identified the basic pattern and themes of foreign policy in this period. In 1714 Britain had just successfully ratified the Treaty of Utrecht ending twenty years of hostility against France. Though it may be an exaggeration to see Utrecht as creating Britain as a major power, it did mark a major change in the balance of power in Europe and an important stage in the gradual erosion of French dominance. Marlborough's wars prevented the Low Countries and Italy falling under French control and the capture of Gibraltar and Minorca gave Britain an important say in Mediterranean affairs. The Protestant Succession had been successfully defended but the neutralization of a perceived, if not always actual, Jacobite threat was to play a major role in foreign policies of Stanhope, Townshend and Walpole. The wars between 1689 and 1714 had been both an economic and financial strain and the need for stability was both fiscally expedient and politically popular.

The rising in 1715 was defeated and Spanish and Swedish support for Jacobites neutralized. The Anglo-French alliance of 1716 brought about a startling diplomatic revolution and was used to great effect in the Mediterranean, where Spain and Austria still refused to accept the partition of the Spanish empire as final. Pressure from the alliance brought Austria into line but it required British naval action at Cape Passaro in 1718 before eventually Spain brought its grievances to an international conference at Cambrai in 1724. In northern Europe Hanover was a far greater consideration and the British navy was used first against Sweden and then Russia in support of electoral interests. This northern policy split the Whig party in 1717, a rift healed in the early 1720s, but it did raise the question of the malign influence of the Hanoverian connection.

Throughout the 1720s the French alliance remained central to London's strategy. Austrian and Spanish rivalry in Italy posed the major threat to European peace between 1720 and 1725. But Townshend's policy in defence of a balance of power and Anglo-French hegemony had the effect of driving Austria and Spain into alliance in 1725. Townshend's response was rapid and confrontational and the formation of the Alliance of Hanover resulted in a state of 'cold' war between 1726 and 1729 and open naval confrontation between Spain and Britain before Spain and Austria climbed down. Townshend's policy was adventurous and positive but carried with it the risk of full-scale war and in 1730 Walpole took full control of foreign policy.

Walpole sought peace, which brought domestic popularity because of lower taxation, permitted further consolidation of the Hanoverian Succession and deprived the Jacobites of active support. He kept Britain out of the confrontation between Austria and France which erupted in 1733 in the War of the Polish Succession despite pressure from George II and Austria. Though peace reduced the possibility of a Jacobite invasion, it did lead to the loss of the French alliance in 1731. By the late 1730s Walpole was being pressurized by the parliamentary opposition, commercial interests and patriotic opinion into responding to Spanish attacks on British trade and, though he strove to arrest the spiral into war, in 1739 the War of Jenkin's Ear began. Walpole's failure to manage the war effectively and repeated failure in the West Indies campaign played a major role in his fall from power in 1742.

The Anglo-Spanish war was quickly absorbed in the War of the Austrian Succession (1740–8). Britain gained little from the war and the Treaty of Aix-la-Chapelle returned her to the pre-war position with both Spain and France. Between 1742 and 1744 Carteret adopted policies oriented exclusively towards Europe in an attempt to remodel the balance of power. His loss of credibility at home and abroad discredited his Hanoverian or continental policy. Britain no longer saw herself as a continental power in the same way that France operated. The focus of attention and Anglo-French rivalry moved away from Europe to colonial and commercial confrontation.

Between the 1740s and 1763 conflict between British and French interests became more marked in North America, the West Indies and in India. When the Seven Years War broke out in 1756 Britain's involvement in the European aspects of the conflict and the security of Hanover, ensured by subsidy treaties with both Prussia and Russia, were of second-ary rather than primary concern to Pitt though not to George II. Control of Canada and India was wrested from the French and the supremacy of Pitt's maritime policy established. The humiliation of both France and Spain in 1763 by the Peace of Paris was almost bound to lead to a war of revenge at a later date and resulted in their support for the American colonies in the late 1770s and early 1780s. Direct British continental intervention was costly but European alliance or subsidies did provide a diversion essential if a global strategy was to be successfully pursued. The failure of the American war demonstrated the fallacy of the argument employed by the parliamentary opposition that European alliances weak-ened domestic interests. The Treaty of Versailles of 1783 was remarkable for what Britain saved from the wreck of the American war and for the rethinking of foreign policy that followed. Paul Langford sums up Britain's foreign policy as follows:

The eighteenth century finally witnessed that realisation of Britain's natural capacity for aggressive commercial and industrial expansion overseas, which Tudor and Stuart monarchs had only intermittently favoured and frequently obstructed, and was to provide the basis for Victorian hegemony . . . one thing that cannot be said of the British in the eighteenth century is that they under-valued maritime and overseas objectives, or overrated the lure of the Continent. And Victorians were to owe much to their predecessors' understanding at least of this fundamental fact of political and economic life.[30]

NOTES

1 References to the major general works on eighteenth century politics can be found in note 1 of chapter 3. J. Black (ed.) *British Politics and Society from Walpole to Pitt 1742–1789*, Macmillan, 1990 is a valuable collection of papers covering different aspects of this chapter.
2 A useful bibliography of the recent debate on Jacobitism can be found in J. C. D. Clark *Revolution and Rebellion*, Cambridge University Press, 1986, pp. 174–7. Of the works cited see B. Lenman *The Jacobite Risings in Britain 1689–1746*, Methuen, 1986, E. Cruickshanks (ed.) *Ideology and Conspiracy: Aspects of Jacobitism 1689–1759*, John Donald, 1982 and J. Black (ed.) *Britain in the Age of Walpole*, Macmillan, 1984. F. McLynn *The Jacobites*, Routledge, 1987 is a excellent study as is his biography *Charles Edward Stuart*, Routledge, 1988. P. Monod *Jacobitism and the English People*, Cambridge University Press, 1989 and E. Cruikshanks and J. Black (eds) *The Jacobite Challenge*, John Donald, 1988 summarizes recent work.
3 J. Black (ed.) op. cit. pp. 4–5.
4 On popular politics and radicalism see the methodological discussion in J. C. D. Clark op. cit. pp. 97–103. G. Rudé *Paris and London in the Eighteenth Century*, Collins, 1970 and J. Stevenson *Popular Disturbances in England 1700–1870*, Longman, 1979 are essential on the subject. For the first part of the eighteenth century see H. T. Dickinson 'Popular Politics in the Age of Walpole', in J. Black (ed.) op. cit. pp. 45–67. J. Black *The English Press in the Eighteenth Century*, Croom Helm, 1987 is the most recent introduction to the 'fourth estate'.
5 I shall consider the nature of popular protest and radicalism in more detail in Chapter 11.
6 H. T. Dickinson op. cit. p. 46.
7 ibid. p. 62.
8 Popular protest is considered in Chapter 11.
9 E. Royle and J. Walvin *English Radicals and Reformers 1760–1848*, Harvester, 1982 is a useful introductory work. J. Cannon *Parliamentary Reform 1640–1832*, Cambridge University Press, 1972 covers both Wilkes and Wyvil. For the Wilkite movement see G. Rudé *Wilkes and Liberty: a Social History of 1763 to 1774*, Oxford University Press, 1962 and John Brewer's reassessment 'The Wilkites and the Law 1763–1774', in J. Brewer and J. Styles (eds) *An Ungovernable People*, Hutchinson, 1980. The Association Movement is fully discussed in I. R. Christie *Wilkes, Wyvil and Reform*, Macmillan, 1962.
10 I. R. Christie *Wars and Revolutions: Britain 1760–1815*, Edward Arnold, 1982, p. 79.
11 Royle and Walvin op. cit. p. 26.
12 ibid. pp. 30–1.
13 G. H. Jenkins *The Foundations of Modern Wales 1642–1780*, Oxford University Press, 1987 is essential but also see the following general works: E. D. Evans *A History of Wales 1660–1815*, University of Wales Press, 1976, D. Fraser *The Adventurers: Wales in History 1485–1760*, University of Wales Press, 1976, G. E. Jones *Modern Wales: A Concise History c. 1485–1979*, Cambridge University Press, 1984, A. J. Roderick (ed.) *Wales Through the Ages*, Vol. II, Christopher Davies, 1960 and D. Williams *A History of Modern Wales*, 2nd edn John Murray, 1977. T. Herbert and G. E. Jones (eds) *The Remaking of Wales in the Eighteenth Century*, University of Wales Press, 1988 contains valuable sources.
14 The major general works on Scotland in the eighteenth century are: W. Ferguson *Scotland 1689 to the Present*, John Donald, 1969, R. Mitchinson *Lordship*

to Patronage: Scotland 1603–1745, Edward Arnold, 1983 and B. Lenman *Integration, Enlightenment and Industrialisation Scotland 1747–1832*, Edward Arnold, 1981. T. C. Smout *A History of the Scottish People 1530–1830*, Fontana, 1972 gives essential background. A more detailed picture can be found in B. Lenman 'A Client Society: Scotland between the '15 and the '45' in J. Black (ed.) op. cit., pp. 69–93 and in the contrasting yet complementary works of A. Murdoch *The People Above: Politics and Administration in Mid-Eighteenth Century Scotland*, John Donald, 1980 and R. M. Sunter *Patronage and Politics in Eighteenth and Early Nineteenth Century Scotland*, John Donald, 1985.

15 A. Murdoch op. cit. p. 27.
16 B. Lenman op. cit. p. 70.
17 A. Murdoch op. cit. p. 3.
18 ibid. p. 133.
19 ibid. pp. 32–3.
20 On Ireland T. W. Moody, F. X. Martin and F. J. Byrne (eds) *A New History of Ireland*, Vol. IV, Oxford University Press, 1986 is the most recent survey. E. M. Johnston *Ireland in the Eighteenth Century*, Gill, 1974, D. Dickson *New Foundations: Ireland 1660–1800*, Helicon, 1987 and R. Foster *Modern Ireland 1600–1972*, Allen Lane, 1988 are shorter and more usable. For the Walpole era see D. Hayton 'Walpole and Ireland', in J. Black (ed.) op. cit. pp. 95–119. R. B. McDowell *Ireland in the Age of Imperialism and Revolution 1760–1801*, Oxford University Press, 1979 is basic for the later period.
21 D. Hayton op. cit. p. 119.
22 J. Cannon op. cit. p. 102.
23 On foreign policy P. Langford *The Eighteenth Century 1688–1815*, A & C Black, 1976 and J. R. Jones *Britain and the World 1649–1815*, Fontana, 1980 are the best general surveys. On Walpole see J. Black *British Foreign Policy in the Age of Walpole*, John Donald, 1985 and his essay in J. Black (ed.) op. cit. pp. 145–70 and on relations with France J. Black *Natural and Necessary Enemies: Anglo-French Relations in the Eighteenth Century*, Unwin-Hyman, 1986. On the imperial issue P. J. Marshall *Problems of Empire: Britain and India 1757–1813*, Allen & Unwin, 1968 and I. R. Christie *Crisis of Empire: Great Britain and the American Colonies 1754–1783*, Edward Arnold, 1966 are still essential reading. On the American question the literature is voluminous as the bibliography in E. Countryman *The American Revolution*, Penguin, 1987 shows but see, R. C. Birch *1776: The American Challenge*, Longman, 1976 for a study with documents and M. J. Heale *The American Revolution*, Methuen, 1987 is concise and readable. H. M. Scott *British Foreign Policy in the Age of the American Revolution*, Oxford University Press, 1990 appeared too late to be considered.
24 The discussion of Whiggish notions of foreign policy draws on J. Black (ed.) *The Origins of War in Early Modern Europe*, John Donald, 1987, especially the editor's introduction.
25 M. Howard *The Causes of War and Other Essays*, Oxford University Press, 1983, p. 13.
26 Quoted in P. Langford op. cit. pp. 6–7.
27 See the useful discussion in J. Black *The English Press in the Eighteenth Century*, Croom Helm, 1987, pp. 197–243.
28 P. Langford op. cit. pp. 12–13.
29 Quoted ibid. p. 24.
30 ibid. p. 244.

5 The changing nature of religion 1700–1800

> If God were not a necessary Being of Himself, He might almost seem to be made for the use and benefit of men.[1]

> Many a long dispute among divines may thus be abridged: It is so. It is not so. It is so. It is not so.[2]

Christian belief was a vital and pervasive feature of British society in the eighteenth and nineteenth centuries. It determined people's attitudes, aspirations and their social and political relationships. It symbolized, through its rituals, its churches and chapels, its art, music and architecture, a continuity of individual and social experience, tradition and control. It legitimized actions, particularly by the state and was an expression of the cultural hegemony of those in authority. John Tillotson was not alone in recognizing its instrumental nature, 'made for the use and benefit of men'. But people worshipped and perceived their belief in different ways and this was tolerated to lesser or greater extents. The Christian belief system was riddled with so many contradictions and exceptions that by 1700 the identification of the Christian Church with the whole of organized society had ceased to be plausible even as an ideal,[3] though it still had rhetorical value for pro- and anti-ecclesiastical propagandists. This chapter is concerned with religion in the eighteenth century. A detailed consideration of developments from the late eighteenth century through to the Religious Census of 1851 can be found in Chapter 14.

THE NATURE OF 'RELIGION'

What do historians understand by 'religion' and how has its social role been interpreted?[4] To begin with, religion is an internal and external phenomenon and has generated ceremonies, religious buildings, officials and art. These can be seen and, in that sense, are 'external'. But their significance needs to be approached through the inner life of those who use these externals. Consider communion where wine is drunk and bread eaten. How can historians understand this, except by knowing what communion meant to Christians and by knowing the hopes and feelings of those who participated in the occasion? Why have people viewed communion differently? Does the bread and wine actually 'become' the Body and Blood of Christ or does it 'represent' them? The external and inner meanings of religion are fused together. To understand developments in eighteenth-century religion in Britain it is not enough to chronicle events. Historians must try to enter into the meanings of those events.

Dimensions of Christian religion

The problem is compounded by the different dimensions of Christian religion. First, the ritual dimension. Religion tends, in part, to express itself through worship, prayers and offerings. Even the simplest form of religious service involves rituals, some form of outer behaviour (kneeling during prayers, for example) linked to an inward intention to make contact with, or participate in, the world of the spirit. But ritual may degenerate into a mechanistic or conventional process. Secondly, Christian religion has a theology or formal system of doctrines which attempt to give system, clarity and intellectual focus to what is revealed through the language of religious faith and ritual. Thirdly, Christian religion incorporates a code of ethics which lays down standards of behaviour for the community. Fourthly, religions are not just systems of belief but also organizations or parts of organizations. They have a communal or social dimension. It is important to distinguish between the ethical and social dimensions of religion. The latter is the process by which a specific religion is institutionalized and through its institutions and teachings affects people in the community. The doctrinal and ethical dimensions express a religion's claim about the nature of the invisible world and about how people's lives ought to be shaped. Finally, and some would say centrally, is the experiential dimension, the ways in which through personal religion individuals 'experience' or hope to experience the invisible world of the spirit. People may be familiar with Christian rituals and with the Christian theology but these lack 'real' meaning without some sort of deeper understanding of the Christian faith, something achieved through a particular personal experience or through revelation. Belief necessitates conforming to the ideas, attitudes, values and actions of a church or chapel but this is not a sufficient definition of 'belief'. It is only through the merging of the external and inner meanings of religion that people can get closer to knowing what belief is.

A functionalist view

The experience of belief is intensely personal, a conviction born of revelation that defies historians' logic. So how can the need for religion in society been explained? Some sociologists argue that its contribution to society should be seen in terms of satisfying basic human needs. They maintain that society requires a certain degree of social solidarity, value consensus, harmony and integration between its parts. Durkheim argued in his *Rules of Sociological Method*, first published in 1895, that social life would be impossible without a 'collective conscience' of shared values and moral beliefs and that these are strengthened by religious worship. Defining religion as 'sacred' provides legitimation for directing human actions. Collective worship strengthens the unity of the group and promotes social solidarity through an expression of faith in common values and beliefs. Religion is part of a cultural system and provides guidelines for human actions and standards against which individual conduct can be evaluated. It makes sense of all experiences in terms of an integrated and consistent pattern of meaning. Suffering and poverty can thus be meaningful; inequalities explained.

This functionalist view of religion emphasizes its positive contributions to society but neglects the many instances when religion has been a disruptive and divisive force. It ignores internal divisions within communities over religious ritual and dogma leading to intolerance or open conflict. It gives little consideration to hostility between different religious groups in society where belief is a direct threat to social order.

A Marxist view

In a Marxist perspective religion is seen as an illusion, a series of myths which justify and legitimate the domination and privilege of those who rule and something which eases the pain caused by exploitation and oppression. It does not solve society's problems but is simply a misguided attempt to make them more bearable. Religion does this in four main ways. First, it promises a paradise of eternal bliss after death, salvation from bondage and misery in the afterlife. Secondly, some religions make a virtue of the sufferings caused by oppression and poverty, particularly if borne with dignity. The reward for suffering is the promised redress of injustice after death. Thirdly, it offers the hope of supernatural intervention to solve problems on earth: the millenarian belief in 'heaven on earth'. Finally, religion often justifies the social structure and an individual's place in it. Society was divinely ordained, social arrangements immutable, inequalities inevitable. In this perspective religion becomes an instrument of social oppression. It tends to keep people in their place, makes unsatisfactory lives bearable, diverting attention from the real source of their oppression and as a result helping to maintain the power of the ruling class.

Religion and capitalism

For both functionalists and Marxists religion is a means for individuals to understand their places and roles in society. The ways in which individuals gave meaning to their lives and the motives and purposes for actions derived, to a certain degree, from attitudes both to and by religion. That religious belief can direct economic action was argued by Max Weber. He examined the relationship between the emergence of certain forms of Protestantism and the development of Western capitalism. Underpinning the practice of capitalism was the 'spirit' of capitalism, a set of ideas, ethics and values. Making money and working effectively became both a religious and a business ethic.[5]

'Church'

It is important to distinguish between different types of religious organizations.[6] The term 'church' refers to a large, formal organization with a hierarchy of officials (with bishops, or episcopalian, as in the Church of England or without, as with Presbyterianism in Scotland). It claims social exclusiveness in a given territorial area in relation to a given ethnic group (as in the case of the Church of England) or universally (as with the Roman Catholic Church). A church which identifies with the state becomes part of the 'Establishment' and is integrated into the socio-economic structure of society. It frequently regards itself or is seen as the guardian of the norms and values of society and jealously guards its monopoly on religious truth. Those who do not accept its doctrines are often seen as being outside society, not citizens in the fullest sense of the word and consequently suspect.

'Denomination'

A 'denomination', by contrast, hardly ever has a social majority and is formed of individuals who have either been converted to its beliefs or are members as the result of family tradition. It approves of the separation of church and state but does not reject the wider society *per se*. Denominations draw their members from all levels of society. They accept the norms and values of society though they may impose additional restrictions upon their members – for example, moderation in the consumption of alcohol. Denominations have a hierarchy of officials and a bureaucratic structure, though there is greater stress on the role of the laity than in churches.

'Sect'

A 'sect' is a relatively small, exclusive religious group, but one which if successful may develop into a larger denomination. They are often closed against the larger society, rejecting its norms and values and are most likely to arise within groups which are socially marginal. They offer their frequently unprivileged members a sense of honour either in the afterlife or in a future 'new world' on earth after the Second Coming. They institute a strict pattern of behaviour for members to follow and make strong claims on their loyalty; belonging to a sect is often the dominant factor in an individual's life. As small face-to-face groups they do not need either a hierarchy of paid officials or a bureaucratic structure. Worship in sects is usually characterized by an intensity and commitment often not present in either churches or denominations. Both sects and millenarian movements reveal a close relationship between tensions in traditional social relationships and religious activity. Millenarian movements promise that the world will be transformed suddenly and soon, prophesying the merger of the visible and invisible worlds. Both sects and millenarian movements tend to arise during periods of rapid social change when traditional norms are disrupted, social relationships are inconsistent and the traditional social ethos is undermined. To those in authority both are suspect because, through their emphasis on a revolutionary Second Coming, they challenge existing socio-political order.

RELIGION IN 1700

In 1700 the Christian religion can be seen in terms of systems which expressed hierarchical or more egalitarian structures; of emphases on local autonomy or national and international centralism; of bureaucratic control or small group interaction; of whether it coexisted or colluded with the state or rejected it, and of membership based upon mutual personal consent, birthright or personal choice. These can be examined with ease. However, once historians move from these categories into areas of fantasy, revelation, myth and fear – the domain of the psyche and psychic – matters become far less safe.[7] It reaches beyond to subjectivity and individual experience, something which has only recently become an area of serious historical study.

Voltaire wrote in the 1730s that

If one religion only were allowed in England, the government would very possibly become arbitrary; if there were but two, the people would cut one another's throats; but as there are such a multitude, they all live happily and in peace.[8]

Though he overstated the case – certainly if it had been extended to Wales, Scotland and Ireland – Voltaire was correct in identifying a 'multitude' of religions in mid-eighteenth-century Britain. Though membership of the Anglican or the Scottish Presbyterian Churches was a prerequisite for full membership of civil society, other forms of Protestantism and Roman Catholicism were tolerated, depending on the prevailing political climate, while being discriminated against overtly through legislation and covertly through prejudice, fear and distrust. In 1700 it is possible to identify three major religious groupings in the United Kingdom: the Church of England or the Anglican Church; Dissent which was largely made up of Presbyterians, Independents, Baptists and Quakers plus smaller, often exotic sects like the Muggletonians; and the Roman Catholics. By 1800 the major changes in religious observances had been an evangelical revival in the Established Church which led to Methodism as an expression of 'new' Dissent and to an evangelical party within Anglicanism, the revival of 'old' Dissent and to splits within the Scottish Presbyterian church.

THE ANGLICAN CHURCH

There is little doubting the pervasive influence of the Anglican Church throughout politics, law and society during the eighteenth century.[9] Established by legislation during the sixteenth and particularly seventeenth centuries, its links with the state were symbolized by the presence of its twenty-six bishops and two archbishops in the House of Lords. The Test and Corporation Acts confined the reality of political power to its communicant members. The elaborate machinery of the law was partly operated through church courts (bishops' courts and archdeacons' courts) which controlled matters relating to wills as well as regulating church matters. Though the supremacy of statute and lay courts had long been acknowledged, the ecclesiastical courts continued to play an intrusive role in people's lives. The suspension of Convocation, the official representative body of the Church, for over a century after 1717 symbolized to contemporaries and to later historians the inhibiting effect which the alliance between Church and state had upon the former, sapping its energies and impairing its effectiveness.

'Church and State'

The intimate relationship between Church and state was clearly demonstrated by the control which lay patrons had over half of the clerical appointments to livings. The right to present an individual to a living or 'advowson' was as much a piece of property as a landed estate and resulted in an alliance, sometimes a turbulent one, between squire and parson. The parson's income came from several sources: from the 'glebe', land attached to the living which the clergyman might farm himself or rent out; income from 'tithes' and fees from the clergyman's services. This income either went directly to the clergyman, who was then styled a 'rector', or it could be 'appropriated' by the bishop or dean and chapter of the cathedral or 'impropriated' by the lord of the manor or a body of local gentry who then paid their 'vicar' a fee or 'stipend' from the proceeds. Glebe, tithes and fees brought in variable income and good management was essential if clergymen were to maintain their standards of living. They needed to be as competent in their legal rights as in theology. This led to criticism of 'worldliness' and interference in the economic and social life of the community, a claim reinforced by the widespread incidence of clerical magistrates.

Anglicanism under threat?

In what ways had these close links weakened the potential of the Anglican Church to realize its universalistic goals? Were these weaknesses? Weakness is a relative concept and it is important to emphasize that the Anglican Church was an immensely powerful social and religious institution in the early eighteenth century. But its real vulnerability lay in the unpreparedness of its parochial organization for demographic, locational and social change. Its powers for adaptation were initially limited.

During the sixteenth and seventeenth centuries the Anglican parochial system was severely damaged economically while at the same time it was being defended politically as a bulwark against subversive Dissent and Popery. Parishes were exploited by impropriating gentry who farmed the profits of the Church. For example, an Essex benefice worth £800 was provided with a clergyman who received a stipend of only £55 per annum. The result of such practice was a direct increase in pluralism, clerical absenteeism and ignorance and decay in the fabric of many churches materially and spiritually. By 1700 derelict churches were not an uncommon sight. The impact of this 'plunder of the Church' had been recognized by the mid-seventeenth century and sporadic attempts were made to augment poor livings, particularly by Queen Anne's Bounty after 1704. But these provided minimum compensation for previous impropriations and in 1806 William Wilberforce cited the case of a curate-weaver at Lastingham in Yorkshire. The Rev. Mr Carter with thirteen children and a stipend of £20 per annum supplemented his living by angling and his wife kept a public house. Little had changed during the eighteenth century and in 1812 a parliamentary inquiry found that there were 4,813 incumbents who were non-resident but there were only 3,694 curates serving their parishes. Over a thousand parishes in England and Wales were simply unattended by ministers of the Established Church. This created a vacuum of indifference into which more evangelical religion could impinge.

'Dependency'

In retrospect the precarious position of the Anglican Church is clearly evident. To contemporaries it was far less obvious. Close links between a resident clergyman and the local landowners and magistracy could result in high rates of religious practice and make religious Dissent untenable. The main problem for the Anglican parson within a 'dependency' system of paternalism and deference was that the system was not over-responsive to changing conditions and inhibited easy adjustment to the religious needs of an emerging industrial society. This and the weakening of its monopoly

of religious practice presented the Anglican Church with a dilemma. Tolerance of religious deviance and apathy had increased considerably in the
half-century after the Act of Toleration of 1689. Anglican monopolistic
pretensions required a religious prescription and conformity which no
longer existed. Its choices were limited to either resisting the social tendencies towards voluntary adherence to a plurality of churches or undergo-
ing radical structural and religious-cultural changes. To accept the latter
would have meant recognizing religious practice as a voluntary associational commitment, not a legally or socially prescribed one. To traditional
Establishment theory this was not just novel but subversive, threatening
all traditional authority structures.

The ability to impose religious uniformity ultimately lay with the lay
elements in society not with the clerical leaders of dioceses and parishes.
This and the identification of High Churchmen with Toryism and the
Jacobites meant that the Church of England was ill-prepared for the more
tolerant religious climate of the early eighteenth century. The existence
of the Nonjurors, a group of at most 20,000 adherents who had seceded
when they refused, on the grounds of conscience, to take the oath of
allegiance to William III after 1688, did not help the Anglican case.
Between 1690 and 1740

> The abnegation of authority which had occurred had been essentially
> political and social rather than ecclesiastical. Abandoning the tra-
> ditional policy of endorsing clerical authority in the interests of social
> cohesion, the early Hanoverian State under the Whigs had come into
> conflict with precisely those sections of Anglicanism which would have
> been likely, under different circumstances, to have shared a strong
> alliance with the State.[10]

Attacks on theology

Parallel to the weakening of the position of the Anglican Church economically and politically were attacks on its doctrinal position. Its formal creed
was embodied in the Thirty-Nine Articles but providing this belief was
affirmed at ordination or induction into a parish by clergymen, no detailed
interpretation was insisted upon. Questions of theology were hardly
thought to be involved. General assent to the system was what was needed:
conformity for conformity's sake. The prevailing spirit was 'latitudinarian',
the prevailing tone was that of reason. The Anglican Church was, politically and socially, a 'broad' church. It was suspicious of zeal and 'enthusiasm', concerned to retain the status quo rather than adapt. The most
important distinction within Anglicanism was between those who took
Calvinist and Arminian positions. Calvinists believed that an individual's
salvation was predestined while Arminians maintained that salvation was
achievable by all through 'justification by faith'. Anglicanism placed its

emphasis on 'practical Christianity', for example, the giving of alms, setting up charity schools, running musical festivals in aid of the county hospital. It was firmly placed within the external world of social relationships and control and, though it did not ignore the invisible world of the spirit, it could easily be criticised by contemporaries for doing so. The theology of the Anglican Church paralleled its organizational and personnel structures in being focused on a world-view that was predictable, unchanging or only changing gradually, and politically and socially traditional. It too was not easily adaptable to the threat posed by the revival of the Spirit by the Wesleys or by demographic changes from the 1740s.

National decline, local diversity

This national picture of decline in the Anglican Church is far less clearly mirrored when specific localities are examined.[11] In Devon, for example, the Church was not only highly organized but closely and actively interwoven with the society it served. Through its courts, the Church acted as moral policeman, settling disputes and protecting people's rights; through the Charity Schools and later the Sunday Schools, it shouldered almost alone the burden of providing education for the poor; and even pioneered schemes of social insurance as well as administering endowed charities.

The impact of the Church in Devon can be seen, in particular, in the area of education. The Charity School movement made a serious attempt during the late seventeenth century to offer entirely free education to the poor. Its aim was to make its pupils into good people, but also good citizens, so sustaining monarchy, the Protestant Succession and established order. In 1699 it was taken over by the Society for the Promotion of Christian Knowledge (SPCK) and by 1704 fifty schools had been established in London. The SPCK had no coercive powers, depended on local patronage for financial support and encouraged managers of existing schools to join their movement. In 1700 Devon already had several grammar schools, but these offered only limited free education and in 1707–8, following a sermon by the Bishop of Exeter, Offspring Blackhall, to Exeter's mayor and corporation on the need for Charity Schools in the city, a decision was made to set up three schools each for fifty pupils (two for boys, one for girls) funded by public subscription. By the end of 1709 all three schools were functional. Sermons continued and within two years a second girls' school for fifty pupils was opened with other schools at Crediton and Topsham. By 1724 schools had been set up in twenty-five towns and villages and in a further fifteen places by 1800. The Sunday School movement had its origins in the early eighteenth century but was not fully popularized by Robert Raikes until the 1780s. The zeal of the Devon clergy for this movement was considerable and in 1831, of the 103 Devon parishes, 41 mention no other provision for the education of the poor. The Church in Devon provided an education, albeit one directed towards obedience to political and religious authority, for a substantial proportion of children, both girls and boys. The inertia which was evident in the national picture needs to be modified by local and regional experience.

An 'era of disaster'?

From 1740 to the beginning of the nineteenth century was 'an era of disaster' for the Church of England, according to Alan Gilbert.[12] There may have even have been an absolute decline of conformist practice during these years, despite demographic growth. A sample of thirty Oxfordshire parishes showed a progressive decline in the number of communicants: 911 in 1738, 896 in 1759, 868 in 1771 and 682 in 1802 – a decline of 25 per cent. How representative this experience was is conjectural but Oxfordshire may have fared better than some areas. Even if the incidence of conformist practice did not decline absolutely, Anglicanism did experience massive decline both in relation to the size of the wider society and in relation to the strength of rapidly growing extra-Establishment religious movements. Historians may disagree about the effectiveness of its pastoral and administrative structure but 'by virtual consensus they have recognized the eighteenth-century Church as a static institution, characterised by inertia if not always complacency'.[13]

The crisis that faced Anglicanism after 1740 came from two main directions: first, the impact of Methodism and secondly, the speed and direction of social and political change. Both challenged the 'influence' of the established order, calling into question the conformist affirmation of the basic moral values, social conventions and cultural and integrative mores of the community. In this situation the Church was identified with the 'old order' and with the traditional ruling classes striving to maintain control in a society where traditional authority structures were breaking down and where the integration of the stable community was giving way to the anomie of new and relatively unstructured communities.

The claim that Anglican uniformity had an important cohesive social function which was made at the beginning of the eighteenth century became increasingly difficult to sustain after 1740. Anglicanism became blatantly partisan and patently reactionary. This can be seen in the definite hardening of Anglican attitudes towards Methodism and Dissent. But people in increasing numbers

> turned from the Church to the voluntary associations of Nonconformity not merely because the Church was inefficient, not only because it continued to behave like a monopoly in a competitive 'market situation', but also simply because it was the 'Establishment'. It became an axiom of English radicalism that, while religion itself was intrinsically 'kind and benign', an established religion was a pernicious thing.[14]

EVANGELICALISM WITHIN ANGLICANISM

Evangelicalism was not confined to Methodism and some clergymen, converted by contact with Wesley and Whitefield, chose to stay within the Church and operated within their own parishes.[15] This was initially a 'quiet' movement of individuals awakened by the vision of Christ as the believer's Saviour. They did not possess a uniformity of view except in holding the doctrine of justification by faith. Most were Calvinist in theology. John Berridge (1716–93), a Cambridge don who accepted the living of Everton in Bedfordshire in 1755, is a good example of an early evangelical.[16] His own conversion came within a year of settling in his parish

> as I was sitting in my house one morning and musing upon a text of Scripture, the following words darted into my mind with a wonderful power and seemed indeed like a voice from heaven. Cease from thine own works. . . . The tears flowed from my eyes like a torrent. The scales fell from my eyes immediately . . .

This conversion is reflected on his tombstone

> Was called up to wait on Him above. Reader, Art thou born again? No Salvation without a New Birth! I was born in sin, February 1716. Remained ignorant of my fallen state till 1730. Lived proudly on Faith and Works for Salvation till 1754. Admitted to Everton Vicarage, 1755. Fled to Jesus alone for Refuge, 1756 . . .

The effect of his preaching was electric. A neighbour wrote in 1761 that

> B preached with his usual vehemence, and was full of agitation. His audience, according to their different affections, felt and showed the effects in the strangest manner. Some wept, some screamed, some laughed, some sang, some fell into fits, and almost all into surprising attitudes, noise and confusion . . .

His evangelism was successful in the country districts round Everton, though socially limited. A sympathetic observer said of his followers

> Upon the whole I remark, that few ancient people experience anything of this work of God; and scarce any of the rich. These generally show either an utter contempt of or an emnity to it . . .

Country parishes

The evangelical revival first showed its power in quiet country parishes. It was led by clergymen who made their own discoveries and preached to their own parishioners. Conversion provided the essential dynamic and, as in the case of Methodism, preaching, hymn singing and the circulation of devotional literature were fundamental. The early evangelicals were conscious of their isolation and it took time for the movement to spread from its rural roots into the universities, bishops' palaces, the homes of the rich and London. No evangelical was entrusted with a diocese until 1815 when Henry Ryder was made Bishop of Gloucester. This seriously weakened the impact which evangelicalism had before 1800. In addition, there was no guarantee that the message of an evangelical incumbent would be carried on by his successor. Evangelical parishioners might then drift toward Dissent. The evangelicals' attitude towards the Anglican Church was in certain senses ambivalent and the itinerant nature of many of the early evangelical clergymen often led to tension in parishes where they preached between parishioners and their vicars.

The penetration of evangelicalism into the Church was achieved gradually and was not directed at merely securing major appointments. William Pitt, despite his friendship with William Wilberforce, was unaffected by 'vital Christianity'. In a society where appointments in the Church were decided more on political and social than on religious criteria, it is not surprising that evangelicals, suspect for their 'enthusiasm' as well as for their orthodoxy, were not promoted. The problems encountered by William Romaine, for many years the only evangelical spokesman in London, were indicative. His message was so little appreciated by the gentry that his own churchwardens refused to provide lights for his evening services – he preached holding a candle.

Charles Simeon

Central to changing attitudes was the work of Charles Simeon (1759–1836) who, through his base at Holy Trinity Church, Cambridge, motivated generations of undergraduates. Converted in 1779, Simeon's major contributions to evangelicalism were twofold. He recognized first, the need for a professionally trained clergy and secondly, the necessity of ensuring that there was continuity of ministers in a living. To achieve the latter he bought up the advowson in a considerable number of key parishes – biblically indefensible but a pragmatic necessity, he maintained. Simeon supported the emergence of the great national societies designed to stimulate the parishes. His work was to have a profound impact on nineteenth-century religion.[17]

By 1800 the two elements which characterized evangelicalism had taken shape. The personal belief in conversion, the notion of justification by faith alone, the importance of preaching, the centrality of religion to the family through reading the Bible and conducting family prayers at home, its missionary zeal which characterized the early evangelicals was combined with the more practical need for a committed and trained evangelical clerical profession championed by Simeon. Evangelicalism became more outward looking, concerned not merely with conversion at home but also, through its support for foreign missions, with conversion of the heathen abroad.

The 'Saints'

William Wilberforce (1759–1833) links the evangelicalism of the eighteenth and nineteenth centuries.[18] Converted in 1785, Wilberforce personified the second-generation evangelicals: he was wealthy, the son of a Hull merchant; he was close to those with political power as MP for Yorkshire from 1784 to 1812 and through his friendship with William Pitt; he was well-informed on subjects and understood the techniques of political persuasion. Building on the work of the early evangelicals, Wilberforce and the 'Clapham Sect' demonstrated the need for machinery to make their work more effective and built on the work which John Wesley had done to create a national organization. Henry Thornton's house at Battersea Rise became the Sect's strategic headquarters. Charles Grant, Zachary Macaulay, James Stephen, Thomas Clarkson, William Smith, John Venn, the Vicar of Clapham and others brought different strengths to the Clapham Sect and this diversity accounts in part for its considerable influence. Wilberforce, though author of the influential *A Practical View of the Prevailing Religious System of Professed Christians in the Higher and Middle Classes in this Country Contrasted with Real Christianity* in 1797, wrote only with great difficulty and was extremely disorganized in keeping his papers. These defects were made up by the organizational and clerical skills of Zachary Macaulay and Thomas Clarkson. By contrast Wilberforce was an impressive orator and his social position gave him an entrée into the best houses. The aims which Wilberforce expressed in 1787 – 'God Almighty has set before me two great objects – the abolition of the slave trade and the reformation of manners' – were those of the Clapham Sect but the interests of the various members of the Sect added other things to their platform: the conversion of the heathen, especially in India; the spreading of 'gospel Christianity' among the lower orders, pioneered by Hannah More through the Cheap Repository Tracts launched in 1795; a measure of church reform especially against non-residence and pluralism; schemes for education and philanthrophy and an aggressive programme to strengthen the evangelical party within the Church of England.

Wilberforce's religious radicalism was linked to a political conservatism, though to brand him a mere conservative moralizer neglects important aspects of the social programme of the Clapham Sect. It pressed for some control over working conditions, the rescue of chimney boys, the abolition of naval press gangs, civil rights for Roman Catholics, prison reform, some measure of parliamentary reform and church schools for the poor. Neither is it possible to maintain, as Ford K. Brown did in his *Fathers of the Victorians* (Cambridge University Press, 1961) that the work of the Clapham Sect was conspiratorial as its members timed their campaigns and, in their overt propaganda of their moral objectives, sought to undermine the legislative supremacy of Parliament. Planning and organization can be seen as sinister only because the Clapham Sect was the first pressure group to use them effectively.

The focus of Wilberforce's crusade was twofold: the abolition of the slave trade and the reformation of manners. In 1787 he secured a Royal Proclamation against Vice and Immorality and formed a Proclamation Society to put it into effect by attempting to check indecent literature and enforcing Sunday observance. But in the public mind the vigorous anti-slavery agitation was the principal achievement of the Clapham Sect.[19] The campaign was launched in 1787, the slave trade was abolished in the British Empire in 1807 and slavery itself in 1833. Success was achieved by a combination of effective propaganda (petitions, lobbying, speeches, pamphlets) and changes in the economic importance of the slave-based sugar colonies after 1790.

The position of the evangelicals in politics was contradictory. They contracted the concerns of politics to a moral imperative but widened the whole sphere of politics through their techniques of mass agitation. Anthony Armstrong sums up their achievement:

> The Evangelicals saw a way of harnessing the new moral and religious sentiment in Britain; they formulated new colonial and philanthropic attitudes, and thus they became a striking feature of the nineteenth-century scene.[20]

By 1800 the Church of England was in a defensive position. Pressure came from the dissenting sects, especially Methodism, which were detaching parts of its actual or potential congregation in the process. The work of the evangelicals was regarded by many churchmen as exhibiting many of the most objectionable characteristics of Methodism. To orthodox clergymen both Dissent and evangelical Anglicanism seemed to deny the significance of a central Anglican rite, that of baptism. Rivalry with evangelicalism did little to remove the essential administrative, parochial and manpower weaknesses which contributed most to the Church's slackening hold on its constituency. The Church had become complacent and was unable to counter the enthusiasm of the evangelical revival. It stood for a uniform national church in a period when religious pluralism became more acceptable.

ANGLICANISM OUTSIDE ENGLAND

Wales

If the national position of the Anglican Church in England was static or in decline, its status in Wales, Scotland and Ireland was far more precarious. The organizational problems that existed in England were magnified in Wales. The diocese of St Davids, for example, embraced the greater part of South Wales and was the second-largest diocese in England and

Wales. Administrative machinery at the level of the archdeaconary and rural deanary was weak and often non-existent, removing any effective link between bishops and clergy. Parishes were over-large and churches badly sited. Parochial revenues were always inadequate and patronage of livings was largely in lay hands: for example, the Bishop of Llandaff did not have a single living under his control in the Glamorgan half of his diocese. The power of the bishops to reform the system, even if they had the disposition, was thus far more limited than in England. The ministry was inadequate because of a shortage of clergy, which encouraged pluralism. The poverty of the Welsh Church was reflected in the calibre of the clergy whose ignorance stemmed from their lack of education because there was no provision for clerical education. The number of graduates in the Welsh ministry was small because many Welshmen sought more remunerative livings in England – this is illustrated by the number of Welshmen who served as prison chaplains in London during the eighteenth century. Queen Anne's Bounty, a means of supporting poor benefices out of the royal proceeds from first fruits and tenths (two taxes on ecclesiastical offices) from 1704, had a considerable impact on the Welsh Church because of its large number of livings worth less than £50 per annum.

There was some revival of Church life in the early eighteenth century but the Hanoverian succession brought a crop of fresh problems as well as exacerbating old ones. The High Church Party, dominant under Queen Anne, was succeeded by Latitudinarians, which led to the nomination of people with 'broad views' to episcopal and other high offices. In Wales this led to a cleavage between the High Church lesser clergy and the 'broader' episcopacy. In addition the Hanoverian bishops were English. When John Evans was translated from Bangor to Meath in Ireland in 1716, Wales was deprived of its last Welsh-speaking bishop until 1870. Being a Welsh bishop was a step on the road to higher office and as a result translations were frequent: for example, of the nine bishops of Bangor between 1714 and 1760, eight were translated. Absenteeism became much more accentuated after 1714 and, when appointments were made, they were often non-Welsh-speakers. Some bishops like Shute Barrington (Bishop of Llandaff 1770–82) were very careful about appointing Welsh-speakers to Welsh-speaking parishes, unlike Drummond (Bishop of St Asaph 1748–61) who thought it desirable to eradicate the Welsh language as soon as possible. Matters came to a head in 1766 with the appointment of an Englishman, Dr Bowles, to two parishes in Anglesey where only five of the five hundred parishioners understood English. In the Trefdraeth test case the Court of Arches ruled that ignorance of Welsh was sufficient to bar a person's appointment to a Welsh-speaking parish though added that, as Dr Bowles had been properly instituted, he should continue to enjoy the living. Despite this ruling the practice of English appointments continued and even liberally-minded bishops showed little appreciation of the language problems.

The parish clergy have frequently been unfairly castigated by historians. Though forming the most numerous professional class in Wales their status was low and there was no close affinity between squire and parson as in England. Comments about the irregularity of services and infrequent communions were widespread but the number of communicants was small and, despite the religious ferment of the eighteenth century, as in England there does not appear to have been a significant increase in numbers. The parish clergy did, however, play an important part in the education of the poor, especially their central role in the work of the SPCK in Wales. Between 1699 and 1736 96 schools were established throughout Wales contributing much to the printing of books in Welsh. This was continued through the Circulating Schools set up by Griffith Jones and Thomas Charles and the Sunday Schools.[21]

The general picture which emerges of the Welsh Church in the eighteenth century is of a church with inadequate resources, both human and material. As in England there were many abuses which were in need of reform. The Welsh Church was, however, probably more institutionalized than its English counterpart. Its bishops lacked initiative and enterprise. They saw the Welsh language as a threat to English cultural values rather than as a medium through which religious experience and commitment could be achieved.

Scotland

The development of Protestantism in Scotland until the settlement of 1690 was one of conflict and compromise between Presbyterians and Episcopalians. The settlement of 1690 abolished episcopal rule, though 500 clergy refused to accept this and formed the Episcopal Church. It suffered from its association with Jacobitism and its clergy were Nonjurors, penalized by the Abjuration Oath of 1719 and victims after '1745' of further legal proscription under the Acts of 1746 and 1748 which prevented them holding services anywhere other than in their own homes. The Church did not make its peace with government in London and Edinburgh until after the death of the Young Pretender in 1788. Penal laws against the clergy were repealed in 1792 and during the next few years the Scottish bishops directed their attention to recovering control over the independent Episcopal congregations which had come into existence served by clergy ordained in England or in Ireland. At the Synod of Lawrencekirk in 1804 a formula was devised under which a number of these agreed to reabsorption. Episcopalians accounted for a small minority of Scottish worshippers, perhaps 80,000 people by the 1790s. Their appeal was limited, especially by the taint of Jacobitism, and the landed classes tended to be attracted more by Anglican than by Scottish Episcopal tradition. The Union of 1707 had confirmed Presbyterianism as the established religion in Scotland and by the end of the eighteenth century it occupied a very similar social position to the Church of England.[22]

Ireland

Protestant traditions had long been established in England, Wales and Scotland. In Ireland, however, this was not the case. The vast majority of the Irish remained Roman Catholic and Protestantism was the imposed, alien and repressive religion of the governing minority. During the eighteenth century with four archbishops, eighteen bishops, 2,000 clergymen and a gross annual income of nearly £1 million, the Church of Ireland was both over-staffed and over-endowed for an establishment ministering to the needs of less than a seventh of the population. Pluralism and sinecures were widespread and many clergy were stationed in parishes with congregations of less than ten people. Oppressed by penal laws and by the Anglican tithe (until 1825 levied exclusively in tillage land as pasture had been exempted by an Act of 1735) friction between the mostly arable-farming Catholics and the largely pastoral-farming Protestant was widespread. The Church of Ireland was on the defensive after the relaxation of the penal laws in the second half of the eighteenth century, a process of decline that was marked by the reorganization of the 1830s and the final disestablishment of 1869.[23]

Conclusions

The Established Church was a powerful force for conservatism and tradition during the eighteenth century. It symbolized the stability of the established order and was supported, tacitly or otherwise, by the vast majority of people in England despite its inefficiencies, obvious abuses and failure to provide a uniform spiritual support. Its ability to adapt to changing circumstances was limited. But it could still claim to be the Church of England in 1800. In Wales, Scotland and Ireland different traditions brought different responses to the Established Church. In Wales Anglican traditions were less strong and the problems of organization worse. In Scotland Presbyterianism was the established church, and the Church of Ireland ministered to only a small minority of the Protestant population. Established by Parliament the Church was susceptible to the whims of political pressure and to the need to make compromises. It was here, as much as in its organisational structure, that the real weakness of the Established Church lay.

ANGLICANISM 'IN DANGER'?

Was the Anglican Church 'in danger' during the eighteenth century? Certainly in the 1700s many clergymen and a few bishops believed that its exclusive privileges, guaranteed by the 1662 Act of Uniformity, the Test and Corporation Acts and the Licensing Act, had been removed and that Dissent and irreligion were increasing. After the 1688 Revolution exclusive Anglican worship had been undermined by the 1689 Toleration Act which allowed Dissenters to hold services in their own conventicles provided they were Trinitarian Protestants. Occasional conformity, whereby Dissenters took communion in the Church of England to abide by the letter of the Test and Corporation Acts and the rest of the time worshipped in their own conventicles, broke the Anglican monopoly of political power. The Licensing Act lapsed in 1695, resulting in a deluge of anti-Anglican and anticlerical literature which would never have passed the former ecclesiastical censors. The meeting of Convocation in 1701 made the divisions within the Church more obvious. Most of the bishops favoured the revolutionary settlement while the inferior clergymen opposed it, forming respectively the Low and High Church parties. The Whig party regarded the High Church party as more dangerous than the Dissenters but was unable to prevent an Occasional Conformity bill becoming law in 1711 or the 1714 Schism Act which made the separate education of Dissenters illegal.

The succession of George I in 1714 brought further power to the Whigs, the ascendancy of the Low Church party and the ending of High Church influence. Under Walpole a close alliance was formed between Church and state with Bishop Gibson of London ensuring that only Walpole supporters sat on the bishops' benches in the House of Lords. The suppression of Convocation in 1717 removed a national sounding board from the High Church party. Ecclesiastical patronage was controlled by the Duke of Newcastle after Walpole quarrelled with Gibson in 1736. The votes of bishops became crucial for the government in the House of Lords and they were consequently obliged to spend the parliamentary sessions in London rather than in their dioceses. Political rather than spiritual imperatives took priority.

If there was a danger to the Anglican Church in the early eighteenth century then, High-Churchmen believed, it would come from an alliance between a Whig ascendancy and a resurgence of Dissent. This danger never materialized and, far from making inroads into Anglicanism, until the 1740s Dissent was in decline.[24] It was not until the emergence of evangelical Methodism or 'new' Dissent that real inroads were made into the Anglican constituency. I will discuss 'old' Dissent throughout the eighteenth century before moving on to examine the growth of Methodism.

'OLD' DISSENT

In 1715 the total number of Dissenters in England and Wales was probably about 300,000 out of a total population of about 5.5 million. The principal sects were the Presbyterians, who made up two-thirds of the whole, the Independents or Congregationalists, the Baptists and the Quakers. Numbers of Dissenters remained static, or may even have declined, until the mid-eighteenth century and Dissent ceased to be, as it had been before 1688, the vibrant alternative to Anglicanism. Why was Old Dissent an increasingly demoralized, introverted movement? Why had it lost much of its original social and cultural impetus? There was an important shift in its social composition. Support among the aristocracy had already declined by 1715, though Dissent still drew quite substantially on the support of the gentry. By 1740 this too had declined. As E. R. Bebb pointed out: 'first the socially distinguished, then the economically powerful sections of early Nonconformity almost disappeared, having been for the most part re-absorbed into the Anglican Communion.'[25] The loss of gentry support led to some contraction of Dissent in the countryside, and concentration in towns made the erosion of the dissenting interest seem even more spectacular at the time than in retrospect. Significantly Dissent failed to appeal effectively to that section of society – the working population – from which it might have replenished its numbers. This was something that Methodism was to do very successfully.

The campaign against the penal legislation imposed after 1660 gave Dissent a common ideology of protest. 'Persecution' kept Dissent together under Charles II and Queen Anne. Although denied full civil rights, generally Dissenters were not persecuted after 1714. In 1719 the Occasional Conformity and Schism Acts were repealed and, though the Test and Corporation Acts remained in force, annual Indemnity Acts secured Dissenters against malicious prosecution after 1728. In 1722 the Quaker objections to the terms of earlier legislation were overcome by enabling them to affirm rather than swear oaths. Paradoxically Dissent declined when it was tolerated, something which Low-Churchmen had predicted. Dissenters were being won over to the Established Church by conciliation.

Dissent also suffered from disputes over dogma in the 1710s and 1720s which left it much weakened. The theology of the three major sects had strong similarities. It was officially Calvinist and accepted the doctrine of the Trinity. The crucial difference between the Baptists and the others was the practice of adult baptism by immersion. The difference between Presbyterians and Independents was one of church government: the former had a hierarchical system while the latter gave decisive authority to individual congregations. The rift between Trinitarian and Unitarian Presbyterians came to a head in 1719. An attempt to resolve it at Salter's Hall in London was indecisive, giving congregations control of whether they expelled ministers whose views on the Trinity they disliked. Authority from the centre simply did not exist and many Dissenters troubled by the breach with orthodoxy, were ripe for conversion by the Methodists.

In terms of motivation, social composition and doctrinal certitude Dissent had ceased to have a broad appeal. It was fragmented, highly argumentative and individualistic and its adherence to Calvinist principles stultified conversionist zeal. The potential appeal of Dissent was thus diluted, leaving a vacuum which Methodism exploited.

An evangelical revival

The evangelical revival from the 1740s not only produced 'new' Dissent, but also had a revitalizing effect on some sections of old Dissent. There was an influx into the ranks of Dissent of evangelicals who could not reconcile their conversion with continued membership of the Established Church. The Baptist churches which numbered 283 congregations in 1716 were reduced to about 200 by 1751 but an accelerated expansion in the second half of the century brought the number to 532 by 1808. Similar expansion was experienced by Independent congregations of which 95 traced their origins to the period 1700–49 compared with 269 from 1750–99. While these sections of Dissent recovered rapidly after 1750, Presbyterianism continued to decline and by 1808 its congregations were vastly outnumbered by both Independents and Baptists. The Quakers were not, like the Presbyterians, facing virtual extinction in 1800, but they too played no part in the massive expansion of Dissent which had taken place among Congregational and Baptist communities.

The revival of 'Old' Dissent led to a renewed collision with the Anglican Church and once again Dissenters began to press for legal concessions. In 1779 Parliament conceded their case by an Act substituting a declaration of acceptance of the Bible as the basis of Christian faith for the obligation of subscribing to the Thirty-Nine Articles. The late 1780s saw an unsuccessful campaign for the repeal of the Test and Corporation Acts led by Presbyterians whose Unitarian views received no legal protection under the Toleration Act. Concessions were blocked by the counter-revolutionary atmosphere of the 1790s and harassment of Dissenters, as for example the chemist James Priestley in the Birmingham riots of 1791, increased. Magistrates, often Anglican clergymen, began to refuse leave to preachers to take the declaration of 1779, did not give preaching licences and prosecuted those who preached without licence. Not until 1811 and 1812 did the influence of the evangelicals in Parliament end this campaign of harassment and secure the repeal of the Conventicle and Five Mile Acts while in 1813 the provisions of the Toleration Act were extended to cover Unitarians.

Welsh Dissent

Welsh Dissent, which emerged in the half-century after 1660, acquired a very distinct Welsh character, particularly with regard to language. The social composition of congregations in Wales was more socially diffuse than in England: membership was a statement not just of religious conviction but also of incipient Welsh nationalism. An analysis of ten Dissenting congregations in Monmouthshire at the end of the seventeenth century showed that their 1,300 members included 1 squire, 37 'gentlemen', 115 yeomen, 137 merchants, 85 farmers and 167 labourers. Welsh Dissent in the late seventeenth century was characterized by 'gathered' churches, organized on a county or even wider basis, which gathered together periodically for the celebration of communion and were subject to a common discipline. Exclusiveness was a characteristic of the 'gathered' church since membership was only offered when a person had shown proof of conviction and then only after a long period of preparation. Presbyterians, Baptists and Independents were also found in 'gathered' churches and Baptists and Independents were often yoked together, a consequence of their congregational system of organization.

The Independents and Presbyterians responded to the Toleration Act by setting up a Common Fund in London two years later, in 1691, to support their churches and particularly to make provision for ministerial education. Resentment against the interference of the Fund men was often expressed, and some churches insisted on keeping their independence by refusing Fund support. The Common Fund led to doctrinal differences between sects being accentuated and in 1694 the Congregational Board set up its own separate fund. By 1700 'gathered' churches were declining in importance and there was a growing tendency for the different sects to sort themselves out on the basis of doctrinal belief.

Welsh Dissent had rejected the Anglican faith, the 'religion of the magistrate', and was equally opposed to any authoritarianism in matters of belief. Belief was a matter of individual personal conviction. This intellectual rather than emotional approach led Dissent, particularly the Presbyterians towards an increasingly rationalist position. There was a gradual move away from Calvinism even among sections of the Baptists and Independents. Welsh Dissent became increasingly select in its appeal, moral and anti-ritualistic in attitude and schismatic in character. To join Dissent was to distance oneself. The doctrinal debate between Calvinism and Arminianism tore many congregations apart after 1700. The Independents were particularly affected but the Baptists did not go unscathed. The 'first schism' began in Wrexham in 1707 and spread to Cardiganshire when the Calvinists were forced out of the Church. Dissenting sects were far from monolithic, the situation remained fluid until after 1800 and schisms were almost endemic.

As in England, an effect of Methodism was to transform the character of Welsh Dissent from a narrow, intellectual exclusive group into a more popular evangelical movement. The Baptists and Independents grew just as quickly as Methodism especially in Glamorgan and Monmouthshire while in North Wales their position was largely unchallenged. Even Presbyterians, although never very numerous, increased in numbers in Cardiganshire, a Methodist stronghold.

Presbyterianism in Scotland

Only in Scotland did Presbyterianism retain its central place. This did not mean that the majority of Scottish people belonged to one church since from 1700 onwards the established Presbyterian church was rent by schism especially over the issue of lay patronage. Popular Presbyterianism insisted on the right of the congregation, or at least the elders, to choose their own minister. The Patronage Act of 1712, however, reasserted the right of lay patrons to appoint ministers. This marked an important change since landowners increasingly looked to England for their cultural models and wanted a minister in the manse as friendly and polite to the laird as the average Anglican parson was to the squire.

The result was a growing number of splits between 1700 and 1800. The Sandemanians seceded in the 1720s, condemning the Church–state link. New and Auld Licht Burghers and Anti-Burghers faced each other as four hostile factions of the Secession Church formed after 1740, professing a rigid, puritanical Calvinism increasingly out of touch with the mid-eighteenth-century Scottish Enlightenment. The two New Licht groups, which represented less ossified Calvinist views, did unite in 1820 to form the United Secession Church. The secession of 1752 produced the Relief Presbytery, led by Thomas Gillespie of Dunfermline, a moderate and evangelical church. None of these churches made any attempt to join the Cameronians of 1690, who in the eighteenth century were reorganized to form the Reformed Presbyterian Church. By 1800 the total of dissenting Presbyterians was substantial. The churches tended to have geographical bases, for example, the United Secession Church was centred on the western side of the Central Lowlands of Scotland especially in Glasgow. They tended to be more earnest and puritanical than the Established Church and appealed in particular to the lower middle classes, the artisan and the peasant. This related back, not to the theological implications of lay patronage, but to the resulting appointment of ministers with little in common with their congregations.

More importantly secession weakened the position of 'evangelicals' or the 'high flyers' in the General Assembly. They were a popular party which adhered to dogmatic Calvinism but were not willing to secede and were opposed by the 'Moderates' led until 1780 by the historian William Robertson. The Moderates fostered a latitudinarian outlook similar to that which had earlier overtaken the Church of England. While not challenging the central tenets of the Church's system, they tended to gloss over many of its implications in practice. Under Robertson's successor, Principal George Hill of St Andrews University, the close links between the political establishment and the Moderates led to an increase in the prestige of the evangelicals, though they did not achieve a majority in the General Assembly until 1833.

The outcome of secession and the dominance of the Moderates was a

Presbyterian church in some respects ill-fitted to cope with the strains contained in social change after 1780. Like the Church of England it lacked evangelical zeal and was similarly hampered by the unadaptiveness of its traditional parish organization. It faced competition from independent churches similar to that encountered by the Church of England from Dissent and Methodism. Non-Presbyterian churches failed to gain wide popular support until the 1790s when Charles Simeon and Rowland Hill and later the brothers James and Robert Haldane adopted an evangelical mission. The response of the General Assembly initially was entirely negative and in 1799 it passed an Act restricting preaching to ministers. The result was to foster the forces of Dissent and the work of the Haldanes led to the creation of both the Scottish Baptist and Scottish Congregational Churches and the Congregational Union of Scotland in 1813. Both north and south of the Border by 1800 the Established Churches were increasingly challenged by the vigorous expansion of evangelical activity and their responses were similar.

Dissent in Ireland

During the second half of the seventeenth century a rift emerged between the increasingly Presbyterian north of Ireland and the Anglican Establishment in Dublin. The decisive defeat of the French and Jacobite forces in 1689–91 made the prospect of invasion remote to the Protestant Establishment and led to penal restrictions against Presbyterians as well as Catholics. This was motivated by the scale of the Scottish influx of the 1690s and until the repeal of the Irish Tests Acts in 1780 Dissenters were not eligible for office. A contrast emerged between areas which retained support for the Church of Ireland among Protestants and areas where Presbyterians became predominant. Scottish immigrants and their descendants had more resources than the Church of Ireland members. The result was that the Church of Ireland remained immobile, retaining its predominance in relatively backward west Donegal, in Fermanagh and Monaghan but gained no new areas to compensate for its loss of dominance in the more fertile Ulster. The tensions created by the division between Anglicans and Presbyterians and between Protestants and Catholics were more stark in Ireland than elsewhere in the British Isles.

METHODISM

For many people in the early eighteenth century the religion espoused by both the Anglican Church and 'old' Dissent had become too rational in character. It had lost its zeal, had ceased to be an expression of 'experimental' religion. The 'Methodist Revival' was the major eighteenth-century response to this. Emphasizing an initial sense of sin followed by experience of conversion and realization of 'justification by faith', an impetus was given towards evangelical missionary activities. As a result new and more flexible forms of organization than the Church of England provided developed.[26] The critical questions which need to be considered are: How did Methodism first develop? How can the evangelical revival be explained? What was the chronology of Methodist growth until 1800? What opposition was there to Methodism? What was its relationship to the Church of England? What was its impact on eighteenth-century society? Did it prevent revolution in the 1790s?

Evangelicalism – an international movement

The eighteenth-century evangelical revival was an international and inter-continental movement. In Germany, America and in England and Wales it was an attempt to return to the religious fervour of an earlier age – to the Reformation belief in justification by faith and the Puritan insistence on personal conversion. Three independent revivals occurred in the early eighteenth century. The earliest was in the English colonies in America. A second focus was the religious community which grew up in Berthelsdorf in Saxony on the estates of Count Nicholas von Zinzendorf, was reinforced by persecuted remnants of the Protestant church of Bohemia and Moravia who were given sanctuary on his estates – hence 'Moravian' – and sought to revitalize existing churches rather than develop an independent one. A third revival began in Wales in 1735. These three independent movements were brought into contact with each other through the medium of a group of Oxford graduates and students who, from 1729, had met for prayer, study and good works in a methodical manner, which resulted in them being scornfully branded by their contemporaries as 'Methodists'.

Calvinist Methodism

George Whitefield provided the link between the English, American and Welsh revivals, crossing the Atlantic thirteen times. He joined the Methodists' 'Holy Club' soon after entering Pembroke College as an under-graduate, experiencing conversion around Easter 1735. Whitefield shared the Calvinist theology of both American and Welsh evangelicals and was the greatest popular preacher of the evangelical revival until his death in 1770. However, he did not have either Wesley's or the Welsh evangelical Howell Harris' organizational inclinations – this is exemplified by the 433 Welsh Calvinist societies in existence by 1750 compared to only 29 English Calvinistic Methodist societies and a further 23 preaching stations. Selina, Countess of Huntingdon, after her conversion in the 1730s did attempt to give English Calvinistic Methodism a degree of permanence, appointing evangelical clergymen, providing opportunities for them to preach to members of the aristocracy, building chapels in fashionable resorts like Bath, Brighton and Tunbridge Wells and opening an evangelical training college at Trevecca in 1768. But her authority over her connexion was moral rather than legal. Calvinist Methodism began to decline after her death in 1791. As Michael Watts says:

> In any case Lady Huntingdon's mission to the upper classes was no substitute for Whitefield's failure to organise his converts among the lower classes. Whitefield's unconcern with organisation guaranteed that English Methodism would become almost Arminian in its theology.[27]

The Wesleys

The Wesley brothers, Charles and John, came from the High Church wing of the Established Church. John Wesley was sent by his Tory father to Christ Church, Oxford in the early 1720s when Oxford was regarded as the home of High Church Toryism and suspected of Jacobitism. John took his degree in 1724, became a fellow of Lincoln College in 1726 and acted as tutor there from 1729 to 1735. It was his dissatisfaction with the worldliness of Oxford which prompted him to join the 'Holy Club'. Influenced by the Nonjuror William Law's *A Serious Call to a Devout and Holy Life*, published in 1729, which urged Christians in their private lives to demonstrate the piety that would set them apart from non-believers, he was persuaded to go to the new colony of Georgia in 1735 by its Tory founder General Oglethorpe. This mission failed largely because he tried to treat the colonists as members of the Holy Club in Oxford. He was, in W. A. Speck's words, 'still too much the high-church Oxonian'.

Other influences affected Wesley on his return to England in 1737. He had been impressed by the Moravians when on board the ship bound for Georgia, particularly by their indifference to the threat of death during storms they encountered. The Moravians emphasized the importance of the individual 'knowing' Christ:

> Salvation came from a new birth in Christ, which was a sudden, miraculous regeneration: 'one moment is sufficient to make us free to receive grace, to be transformed by the image of the little lamb.'[28]

Wesley's conversion came at a religious society meeting in Aldersgate Street, London, on 24 May 1738. Early Methodism owed much to the Moravians, especially their stress on the new birth which converted people from nominal to real Christianity. The intercession of Christ led early Methodists to dwell more on the New Testament than the Old, on the love of Christ rather than on the wrath of Jehovah. The Moravians emphasized hymn singing, which also played a central part in Methodist services – it was in this area that Charles Wesley made his greatest contribution. The Wesleys broke with the Moravians in 1740 because of their passive attitude towards religion, waiting for inspiration from the Holy Spirit. This 'stillness' was unacceptable to the Wesleys, who were men of action as well as men of God.

Wesley's evangelicalism owed much to the example of George White-field although he followed a different theological tradition. Whitefield was a Calvinist, believing that only the elect were predestined for salvation. The Wesleys, however, were Arminians, believing that Christ died for all men. Whitefield's views were more in line with early Puritanism while the Arminianism of the Wesleys owed much to High Church traditions.

Whitefield and the Moravians provided Wesley with a model for evangelical action. William Law and the Arminian tradition provided a theological basis for 'real' and 'practical' Christianity which was not exclusive but could appeal to all people who wished to be saved. Wesley's real contribution was his co-ordination of Methodists into a coherent organizational structure. Even here Wesley borrowed the pattern from the semi-formal and more elaborately organized religious societies which had sprung up in the late seventeenth century. Some were small groups where people met for prayer or Bible readings but others had broader aims like the reformation of manners and the SPCK. Methodists were organized on similar lines to the Oxford Holy Club. Wesley divided devout followers into 'bands' of between five and ten people, composed of either men or women further divided into married and single Methodists. He drew up rules for the bands in late 1738. Select societies for more pious members and united societies for the less zealous were first established in Bristol and London in 1739. These early societies were large and argumentative with a fluid membership and resulted in the unique Methodist institution, the class. The first class was formed in Bristol in 1742, as a money-raising device. It consisted of twelve members under a class leader who collected one penny a week from those in his charge which was then given to the steward of the local society. Wesley recognized the potential of the class as a spiritual dynamic and as a means for exercising control over the membership. Classes began to meet regularly for prayer, for argument and for the consideration of the scriptures. Class leaders were appointed, not elected, reinforcing Wesley's personal control. As a Tory Wesley's attitude to government was authoritarian:

> the greater the share the people have in government, the less liberty, civil or religious, does a nation enjoy.

> As long as I live, the people shall have no share in choosing either stewards or leaders among the Methodists. We have not, and never had, any such custom. We are no republicans and never intend to be.[29]

The Wesleys kept in touch with their supporters by travelling and preaching. At first they concentrated on an axis bounded by Bristol and London but in 1742 John visited Newcastle. London, Bristol and Newcastle became the points of a triangle marking the main area of the Wesleys' activities. England and Wales was divided into seven 'circuits' in 1746, growing to 114 in the British Isles by 1791. Inside these large units Wesley's preachers moved and select ones – his 'assistants' – were given charge of circuits. The Conference was first called in 1744 though Wesley saw it as an advisory rather than a governing organ. It met annually and was made the governing body of Methodism by the Deed of Declaration of 1784 which vested control of the Connexion, after Wesley's death, in one hundred preachers chosen by Wesley himself. This did little to modify Wesley's autocratic direction but his successors, though they may have had constitutional authority, lacked the same degree of moral authority. Protests at the excessively clerical and autocratic nature of the government of the Connexion led to the secession of Alexander Kilham in 1797 and the formation of the New Connexion in which ministers and laymen were included in equal numbers. Secessions, motivated by criticisms either of intolerable autocracy or declining evangelical zeal increased after 1800. Methodist organization did not suffer from the ossification which threatened the Church of England. If the latter wanted to set up a new parish or build a new church it required an Act of Parliament. All Wesley had to do was to redraw boundaries between societies and circuits.

It is important for historians to consider W. H. Speck's statement that 'Too often methodism is described as a crusade by the Wesley brothers and Whitefield when they were but the most conspicuous among a large number of like-minded men'[30] seriously. Wesley proceeded in certain areas by a series of takeover bids taking over existing small, more loosely organized connexions. In the West Riding William Grimshaw and John Nelson developed societies on similar lines to the Methodists which were later simply absorbed into Wesley's system. Wales retained its distinctly Calvinist character and Wesleyan Methodism made little impact until after 1800.

Explaining an evangelical revival

How can the success of the Methodist Revival be explained? Methodists attributed it to the awakening to the workings of the Holy Spirit but this explanation does not explain why people were more open to the influence of evangelical zeal in the 1730s and 1740s than in the earlier decades of the eighteenth century. Field preaching and the use of itinerant preachers enabled the Methodists to reach those sections of society who were simply not catered for by the Anglican Church. The Established Church, even if it had the inclination, did not have the same flexibility as Methodist organization and could only proceed piecemeal. The focus of Anglican church building was social rather than spiritual, catering for the wealthy rather than the poor. The gap between demand and provision was growing, especially in areas of demographic expansion. Manchester, for example, had only one parish church in 1750 to cater for about 20,000 people.

Methodism deliberately set out to fill this vacuum and preaching in the open air enabled contact to be made with thousands. When chapels were built Wesley insisted they should be plain with seating on a first come, first served, basis. Methodism made a particular appeal in industrial areas, making less impact in agricultural areas. The tin-mining and fishing areas of Cornwall, the industrial areas of Lancashire, Yorkshire, Durham, Northumberland and Staffordshire became Methodist strongholds while the agrarian counties of Wiltshire, Hampshire and Surrey were 'Methodist waste-lands'.

The contemporary denigration of the movement for associating its members with the 'rabble' failed to acknowledge that Methodism struck roots at various levels of society. Whitefield's Calvinist evangelicalism had its supporters among the aristocracy though Wesleyan Methodism did not attract many from the governing elite. The difference between Whitefield and Wesley was not simply one of theology. Whitefield maintained that aristocratic vice and corruption percolated from the top of society to the bottom and that reform must follow the same route. By contrast Wesley saw that successful religious reform must begin with the poor and move upwards. This distinction is between a closed and open conception of evangelical revival.

Methodism appealed to craftsmen and tradesmen for economic as well as spiritual reasons. Drunkenness, immorality and swearing, at whatever level of industry, was bad for business. Methodism took over the reforming attitudes of the religious societies but adopted a more positive attitude to business, an extension of the work ethic which had played such an important role in seventeenth-century Dissent. Wesley urged a scrupulous standard of fair trading upon his members and bankrupts were sometimes expelled from the society. The approach had appeal to artisans because economic change threatened their status in society. Wesley encouraged Methodists to buy from and help each other. He did not condemn competition or the role of the market as long as they operated fairly, did not exploit people and led to some profits being used to support the poor.

The impact of Methodism was most profound among the labouring poor, other than farm workers. Methodism appealed especially to miners, such as those in the Kingswood colliery near Bristol, Cornish tin miners and those on Tyneside in particular. The previous religious affiliation of, for example, the Kingswood miners, was High Church rather than Dissenting, they had supported Sacheverell in 1710 and were suspected of Jacobitism under George I hence the appeal of Arminian Methodism.

The response from the poor was not always favourable and Methodist leaders frequently faced hostile crowds particularly in the 1740s and 1750s. Wesley had to cope with demonstrations in Staffordshire in 1743, Cornwall in 1745 and Lancashire in 1748. In Staffordshire rival mobs of Darlaston and Walsall fought a pitched battle for the privilege of tormenting Wesley. Methodists denounced popular pastimes like cock-fighting, dancing and drinking, which led to spontaneous objections when preachers were in a locality. Other demonstrations were encouraged, usually not openly, by landlords, Anglican clergymen and discontented sections of the aristocratic elite who, despite Wesley's support for the social hierarchy, believed that Methodism threatened social dislocation. Why did the poor support Methodism which condemned their pastimes and supported the existing social system? Unlike Anglicanism it offered more than a reward after death and its revivalist preaching appealed to the emotions of the poor. Wesley believed that Methodism could alleviate the lot of the poor on earth and that a fairer distribution of goods could reduced hardship. He also opposed the notion that the reason for poverty was idleness. Charity went further than just relieving poverty and in 1746 a fund was established to provide capital for Methodists to set themselves up in trade. Methodists also looked after the sick, educated the poor, so they could improve their life-style, and distributed vast amounts of cheap and sometimes free literature. Wesleyan Methodism provided both the prospect of improvement for the poor and a means of achieving it.

Other explanations have been put forward for the success of Methodism. Eighteenth-century revivalists found their most appreciative audiences among unsophisticated communities, where emotional beliefs in witches and ghosts, and the stark contrast between good and evil were widespread. Powerful preaching may have weakened the power of inhibition in individuals giving free rein to affective responses. This led, especially in the 1740s and 1750s, to wild enthusiasm and demonic frenzy. At a Methodist service at Llangeitho in 1746, for example, a sermon by Daniel Rowland flung

> almost the whole society into the greatest agitation and confusion possible – some cried, others laughed, the women pulled one another by the caps, embraced each other, capered like, where there was any room. I never saw greater instances of madness even in Bedlam itself.

Wesley and his preachers may have regarded these outbreaks as God's will but they seem to have been caused by the sermons which brought home to the listeners their fears of death, judgement and damnation. People in eighteenth-century Britain were highly susceptible to appeals to escape from the wrath to come. Death was an ever-present threat – from disease, from the effects of starvation, from war and from natural disasters like the Lisbon earthquake of 1755 – and this inclined people to take religion more seriously. The reasonable nature of Anglicanism provided less of an answer than the enthusiasm of Methodism.

Methodist growth

Methodism may have made significant advances after 1750 but it was still only the religion of a small number of people. In 1811 there were about 150,000 Methodists in all the sects set against a national population of 10 million, and in 1851 worshipping Methodists made up only 4 per cent of the total population. Methodism was also geographically concentrated and in areas like Kingswood, Cornwall and Newcastle it had become virtually the established religion. It is important not to overestimate the scale of the Methodist Revival. However, statistics do not add up to influence or effects. There is little doubt that organizationally Wesley was able to operate very effectively in areas where the influence of the Church of England had been diluted, either demographically or spiritually. Wesley's real achievement was to establish an organizational structure which could capitalize upon an evangelical attitude to religion – the minimal impact of Calvinist Methodism in England shows the effect of failing to establish good organization. But many problems were still unsolved on Wesley's death in 1791.

The 1790s – a crisis for Methodism

The 1790s was a decade of crisis for Methodism. One problem concerned the relationship between Methodism and the Church of England. John and Charles Wesley remained members of the Church of England all their lives, though there was friction between them and their fellow Anglicans from the start. Wesley saw Methodism as a means of reforming the Anglican Church from within and some bishops found aspects of Methodism appealing. In many aspects of theology it was orthodox. It encouraged more frequent taking of Holy Communion. But it upset the Anglican way of doing things and, some believed, threatened the Anglican basis of society. Wesley, however, refused to face the realities of the situation by not recognizing the logic of separation. Yet from 1739 Wesley was compelled to appoint lay preachers since insufficient Anglican clergymen joined him and from the 1750s he was under increasing pressure to ordain ministers. A number of lay preachers began to administer to sacraments in the early 1750s and, although John seemed prepared to fudge the issue, his more resolutely Anglican brother was alarmed and sought support against his brother's indecision. The 1755 Leeds Conference resolved that separation 'was no ways expedient' though it was not until the 1760 Bristol Conference that Wesley categorically refused to ordain a separate ministry.

The separation of American from English Methodism in 1784, following the American War of Independence, brought the issue of breakaway into focus again. In appointing a 'superintendent' and two 'elders' for service with his societies in America, Wesley had been compelled to act since the Bishop of London could no longer ordain clergymen for the now independent colonies. This did not alter his practice in England, though he did appoint preachers to administer the sacraments in Scotland and in the colonies. Following Wesley's death, separation occurred. 'Church Methodists' objected to the sacraments being administered by preachers in their chapels and wished to continue attendance at parish churches for this purpose. The ban imposed on the sacrament in chapel in 1792 was overturned at the Manchester Conference in 1795. The Plan of Pacification permitted the administration of the sacrament in chapels where the trustees at one meeting and the stewards and leaders at another, agreed to it. Conference had also to approve. This was a highly successful compromise:

> [there are] numerous examples of Methodists societies which continued to take the sacrament in the local parish church until well into the nineteenth century, especially if the incumbent was an evangelical. . . . The Methodists could no longer claim with conviction that they were merely the Church of England at prayer.[31]

Parallel to the issue of ordination was the question of the building and licensing of chapels. This created problems under the Toleration Act which only allowed conventicles for dissenters from the Anglican Church. Wesley's opponents argued that he should apply for licences for them as a Dissenter. Wesley fought a long legal battle for the right of his followers, as Anglicans, to worship in their own chapels without the need for a licence under the Act. In 1803 the Methodists formed a Committee of Privileges to defend their interests in both Parliament and the courts and in 1811–12 faced a challenge from both. The result of successful agitation was the so-called 'New Toleration Act' which repealed the Five Mile and Conventicle Acts and which gave itinerant preachers the same legal rights as clergymen.

Despite the debates over ordination and licensing and the Kilhamite secession in 1797 over the question of clerical autocracy, Methodism sustained rapid growth during much of the 1790s. One explanation, associated particularly with E. P. Thompson, suggests that Methodist revivalism occurred during periods of political repression; it is portrayed as 'The chiliasm of the defeated and the hopeless'. An alternative solution, provided by W. R. Ward, identifies a crisis in religion as well as politics in the 1790s and views Methodism as a challenge to the paternalistic Anglican Establishment. Popular evangelicalism, in this perspective, is a religious expression of radicalism and not a substitute for it. To Thompson religion was a conservative force while for Ward popular religion was diverse and radical. This difference was reflected in contemporary perceptions: radical leaders thought of Methodism as a conservative deflection from temporal objectives while Anglican bishops denounced it as a form of ecclesiastical Jacobinism.

Methodism outside England

What impact did Methodism have outside England during the eighteenth century? In Scotland its impact was minimal. The importance of the Irish branch of Methodism was established by Wesley's twenty-one visits. In 1789 Methodist membership exceeded 14,000, insubstantial compared to the total Irish population, but representing a 500 per cent increase since

1770. Much of this growth was in Ulster; Methodism was relatively strong in areas of long-standing English Protestant influence, including market towns, but had only limited success among the Catholic peasantry, despite the efforts of Irish-speaking evangelists. There was a sprinkling of support from merchants, professionals and minor gentry but Methodism made little impact on those at the top and bottom of society. The real impact of Methodism in Ireland was to occur after 1800.

The Calvinistic Methodist movement in Wales[32] had its origins in the 1730s and, though part of the broader evangelical revivals, was largely independent of those in England. Dominated in the 1730s and 1740s by Howell Harris, an outstanding preacher and organizer, Daniel Rowlands, who earned the nickname 'Holy Rollers' because of the effects of his sermons and William Williams, a lyric poet and hymn writer, the movement's growth was slow, though always highly organized. Scattered local societies sent representatives to a monthly meeting, over these were set a quarterly meeting, and after 1740 power of decision-making and policy lay with the Association. Individual congregations were left with more independence than in England and from the 1740s there were several secessions. Like Wesleyan Methodism the Welsh movement was firmly within the Church of England despite the hostility it encountered, especially in the north and west, where the gentry organized mobs against them. The decision to separate was deferred until 1811. Their Calvinism stemmed from Harris' service as Whitefield's deputy when he was in America and, although Wesley made forty-six sorties into Wales, he and Harris reached an agreement in 1746, probably at Neath, to channel their energies separately. The first Wesleyan chapel in Wales was not built until 1802.

As in England, Welsh Methodism drew its support from across society, extending from minor gentry and farmers to labourers though rural artisans were most prominent. Geographically Methodism was firmly established in west Wales – Harris' influence was, for example, paramount in the counties of Brecknock, Radnor and Mongomery – but it lost out to the Independents and Baptists after 1750 in industrializing Glamorgan and Monmouthshire. Little real progress was made in North Wales following the failure of missionary work after 1738 and it was not until after 1785, as a result of the spread of Sunday Schools, that real advances were made. The expansion of Welsh literacy was a major consequence of the resurgence of evangelicalism:

> the Welsh learned to read in an almost totally religious context. They learned to express themselves, indeed define themselves, in the language, imagery and concepts of the Bible and of Protestant sectarianism.[33]

The impact of Methodism

What impact did Methodism have upon eighteenth-century society? It appealed to the people's aspirations in a way that Anglicanism did not, hence the number of contemporary references to Methodists as 'respectable'. The debate over whether Methodism prevented revolution in the 1790s, a debate that tends to present conservative and radical arguments which are not mutually exclusive but interdependent, has been largely inconclusive. Wesley's control and clericalism led to autocratic government, a trend continued after his death, but this is hardly a sufficient explanation for Methodist support for the status quo or the prevention of revolution.[34] Religion had a far greater appeal than secular radicalism to the thinking active minority in Britain. For some its satisfaction was spiritual. To others it provided a degree of social self-fulfilment, lack of which might have led to political discontent. It legitimated self-improvement and economic endeavour, what Ian Christie calls 'a guide for successfully meeting the challenge of the Industrial Revolution . . .'.[35] Also Methodism was limited numerically and geographically. In 1811 there were about 150,000 Methodists in England. They were geographically concentrated, but even in Yorkshire made up only a small part of the total population. But this does not reflect the extent of Methodism's influence. What Methodism may have done was to divert potential radical leaders away from political to spiritual concerns. In the 1790s political radicalism suffered from the same lack of broad appeal and penetration as Methodism as far as the bulk of British society was concerned.

Harold Perkin has argued that 'religion was the midwife of class',[36] in the sense that it enabled people to escape from dependence on the gentry and gave them a 'model of class organisation'. This, combined with the methodist emphasis on respectability, eased the process of social change. Methodists were educated, disciplined and, through running the Methodist machine, trained in organization. This, combined with Methodist attitudes to 'industry', stimulated the rise of newly respectable and increasingly wealthy Methodists: for example, ironmasters like the Guest family in South Wales, the Walker family of Masborough and the partners of the Thorncliffe ironworks and the Ridgways, the Hanley potters. An incentive now as well as in the future was provided for prospective Methodists.

How far did Wesley's attitudes to contemporary issues affect the impact of Methodism on eighteenth-century society? Though both Wesleys supported all the characteristic forms of philanthropy – charity schools, hospitals, dispensaries etc. – no distinctly Methodist form of philanthropy was devised. Paradoxically, given the structure of Methodism, its philanthropic activities were individual, local and lacking organization. His attitude to slavery was certainly ambivalent before the 1770s and not until the publication of his *Thoughts on Slavery* in 1774 did Wesley attack the entire system of slavery, returning to the issue just before his death. His admiration for Wilberforce's 'glorious enterprise' was taken up by Methodists generally and they provided an important source of support for the abolition movement.

Wesley also admired John Howard, the prison reformer, and the 1776 Conference encouraged preachers to visit prisons. There is, however, no evidence that he urged prison reform though he did recognize the threat of execution as a major aid in the work of conversion. Wesley's attitude to education was significant, though some contemporaries and later historians regarded it as retrograde. He recognized the importance of literacy as much for its part in effective organization as in education but believed that content should be carefully controlled. Education, Wesley saw clearly, could lead to radicalism and perdition as easily as to salvation. His control over what the Methodist Connexion published was absolute and he was a compulsive writer and editor of Christian texts. The criterion used by Methodists to decide whether to publish a book or pamphlet was one of 'improvement' or moral uplift. This has been seen as a form of religious censorship and may have led to a stifling of creative energies among some writers.

Wesley was at pains to paint himself as a social conformist and this was reflected in the way his views on philanthropy, prison reform and education mirrored contemporary attitudes. This was also evident in his views on Catholicism. While sympathetic to Catholic mysticism, his political attitude to Papists was openly conventional. He objected to the Saville Act of 1778 which lifted some of the penal laws and was sympathetic to the views of Lord George Gordon and the Protestant Association, visiting Gordon in the Tower after the 1780 riots. Methodist opinion generally followed Wesley. His anti-Catholic prejudice was strongly influenced by his experience of Ireland and it had several strands. First, his hostility was directed at the theological system rather than its adherents. Secondly, he believed that the religious, political and economic problems of Ireland were caused by Catholicism, pointing to the contrast between the living conditions of Protestant Ulster and the Catholic south. Third, as a result of a selective reading of seventeenth-century Irish history, he concluded that given the opportunity Irish Catholics would be disloyal to the British Crown. This needs to be balanced by the favourable comments on Catholic congregations and individuals found in his *Journal*. Wesley was undeniably anti-Catholic but he was not a bigot. He was prepared to grant freedom in religion to anyone who knew what 'freedom' meant. The Roman Catholic Church did not deserve freedom, Wesley maintained, because it was not prepared to grant it. As David Hempton says:

The irony is that Wesley, who pioneered the formation of a non-sectarian religious association, should have been instrumental in heightening sectarian rivalries at the end of the eighteenth century. Indeed, Wesley's anti-Catholicism was one of his profound and enduring legacies to the Wesleyan connexion and the connexion's vigorous anti-

Catholicism . . . was a most important determinant of Wesleyan political attitudes during the nineteenth century.[37]

ROMAN CATHOLICISM

Being Roman Catholic in the early eighteenth century involved severe social and legal disabilities, having rights of religious practice restricted and being subject to official surveillance.[38] Catholics faced general suspicion in a society deeply imbued with anti-Papist prejudices dating back to the Reformation. The association of Catholicism with Jacobitism meant that insinuations of disloyalty had some foundation, though it appears that apart from periods of acute anxiety, such as in 1715, 1722 and 1745, penal laws were laxly enforced and English Catholics were allowed to live in peace.

Until the second half of the eighteenth century English Catholicism may have been in decline; certainly some contemporary Catholics believed this to be the case. Growing numbers of wealthy Catholic families, faced with their seemingly permanent marginality in society, turned to Anglicanism. The survival of Catholicism among the rest of society was heavily dependent on the patronage of this elite who funded Catholic chapels and priests. In 1770 there were perhaps 200 Catholic heads of landowning families whose households were focal points for congregations. The estimated Catholic population of 115,000 in 1720 declined to some 70,000 by 1770. This was heavily concentrated in certain largely rural areas, chiefly the north, lowland Lancashire, Staffordshire, Worcestershire and Monmouthshire, but made up at most only 20 per thousand of the population. Elsewhere Catholics were thinly scattered and in Wales and the south-western counties their numbers were negligible. The most significant shift in Catholic orientation was to urban areas and this eventually led to the collapse of gentry control over Catholicism. By 1800 76 per cent of Catholic clergy served in missions independent of landed families while in 1700 two-thirds of the clergy had been employed by Catholic nobility or gentry. Both English Catholic and Irish Catholic immigrants were attracted to the opportunities offered by growing industrial centres and the bulk of the increase was among artisans and the poor. Catholicism was able to benefit in the same way as Dissent from the vacuum left by the Church of England.

By 1755 the Catholic church in Scotland numbered only 16,000 adherents. Tarred by the brand of Jacobitism it had almost been pressured out of existence. The largest concentration of 10,000 people, depending on the protection of the Huntleys, was around Aberdeen with the remainder scattered about parts of the Western Highlands and the Islands. Popular hostility survived longer in Scotland than England but by 1800 the Catholic community showed signs of recovery especially in the Clyde valley, the focus of Irish immigration into Scotland. By 1800 there were an estimated 30,000 Catholics in Scotland.

Anti-Catholicism may have had popular appeal after 1750 but the political will to maintain the penal laws was in decline. The 1778 Act allowed Catholics who subscribed to a new oath to purchase, or legally to inherit land in England and abolished the prosecution of priests. An attempt to legislate on similar lines for Scotland in 1779 led to serious rioting in several Scottish cities. A Protestant Association was formed early in 1780 to campaign for the repeal of the 1778 Act and, when its leader Lord George Gordon presented a petition to Parliament, riots broke out with widespread attacks on Catholics, their property and Catholic sympathizers in London. A movement for Catholic emancipation in England in the 1780s, led by Charles Butler, resulted in the 1791 Act which gave legal existence to registered Catholic places of worship and admitted Catholics to the professions.

The situation in Ireland was different largely because of the scale of Catholicism and its clear identification with Roman Catholic orthodoxy. English Catholicism took a more independent stance and the Cisalpine Club, founded in 1792, stated that it would resist any outside ecclesiastical interference which might obstruct its freedom. Catholic Ireland was seen as a standing threat to the unity and security of the British Isles, a view reinforced by the 1798 Rebellion. But religious exclusion was only one of a whole range of grievances: social, economic and ultimately nationalist. The Franchise Act of 1793 gave parliamentary suffrage to Irish Catholic 40-shilling freeholders but this was insufficient for those who hoped it would lead to the final repeal of all disabilities. Irish Catholics did not oppose the Irish Union Act of 1800, thinking that the new united Parliament was more likely to grant them emancipation than the old Irish one. Indeed Pitt had given the impression he would do so but George III would not countenance such a measure. Pitt resigned. The Catholic question, in Ireland if not elsewhere, remained a political rather than a religious question into the nineteenth century.

CONCLUSIONS

Support for established religion, whether Anglican, Dissenting or Catholic, is difficult to estimate with any degree of certainty. There are statistics which give figures for congregations in the eighteenth century but, although it is possible to identify broad trends from these, they cannot be called absolute numbers. Contemporaries expressed concern about the growing indifference of large sections of the population: 'Tis plain and indisputable that Christianity in this kingdom is very much declining', and 'religion hath lost its hold on the minds of the people.'

This may be true in terms of attendance at services but there was an important underlying religiosity based on a tacit if not overt acceptance of Christianity as a guide for life. Historians should not underestimate the impact which religion had on the life of British society in the eighteenth century.

NOTES

1 John Tillotson *Sermons*, London, 1694.
2 Benjamin Franklin *Poor Richard's Almanack*, London, 1743.
3 R. W. Southern *Western Society and the Church in the Middle Ages*, Penguin, 1970, especially pp. 15–23, provides an elegant analysis of the medieval social environment which still haunted eighteenth-century society.
4 For the discussion of 'religion' see N. Smart *The Religious Experience of Mankind*, Fontana, 1971, especially pp. 11–44 and D. Martin *A Sociology of English Religion*, Heinemann, 1967. J. D. Gay *The Geography of Religion in England*, Duckworth, 1971, though more useful for the period after 1800, is worth study.
5 M. Weber *The Protestant Ethic and the Spirit of Capitalism*, Allen & Unwin, 1930.
6 A useful typology of church, denomination and sect can be found in D. Martin op. cit. pp. 79–80.
7 This approach is exemplified throughout J. Obelkevich, L. Roper and R. Samuel (eds) *Disciplines of Faith: Studies in Religion, Politics and Patriarchy*, Routledge, 1987.
8 Voltaire *Letters concerning the English Nation*, London, 1733, p. 45.
9 For the Church of England in the eighteenth century see A. Armstrong *The Church of England, the Methodists and Society 1700–1850*, University of London Press, 1973 especially chapter 1, A. Smith *The Established Church and Popular Religion 1750–1850*, Longman, 1971 and D. L. Edwards *Christian England*, Vol. III, Collins, 1984, especially part one. More detailed consideration can be found in A. D. Gilbert *Religion and Society in Industrial England*, Longman, 1976, E. R. Norman *Church and Society in England 1770–1970*, Oxford University Press, 1976 and E. G. Rupp *Religion in England 1688–1791*, Oxford University Press, 1986. P. Virgin *The Church in an Age of Negligence: Ecclesiastical Structure and Problems of Church Reform 1700–1840*, Cambridge University Press, 1989 is an essential study of the Georgean church.
10 A. D. Gilbert op. cit. p. 11.
11 For what follows I have used A. D. Warne *Church and Society in Eighteenth Century Devon*, David & Charles, 1969 for examples.
12 A. D. Warne op. cit. p. 27.
13 ibid. p. 28.
14 ibid. p. 81.
15 On Anglican Evangelicalism, see D. L. Edwards op. cit. pp. 754–80 and A. Armstrong op. cit. pp. 121–30. See also M. Jaeger *Before Victoria: Changing Standards of Behaviour 1787–1837*, London, 1956, F. K. Brown *Fathers of the Victorians: The Age of Wilberforce*, Cambridge University Press, 1961 and I. Bradley *The Call to Seriousness: The Evangelical Impact on the Victorians*, London, 1976. Boyd Hilton *The Age of Atonement: The Influence of Evangelicalism on Social and Economic Thought 1785–1865*, Oxford University Press, 1988 is essential. As is D. W. Bebbington *Evangelicalism in Modern Britain*, Unwin Hyman, 1989.
16 On John Berridge see P. L. Bell *Belief in Bedfordshire*, Belfry Press, 1986, pp. 93–7.
17 On Simeon see H. E. Hopkins *Charles Simeon of Cambridge*, London, 1977 for a convenient analysis of his life and impact.
18 Useful biographies of Wilberforce are by R. Coupland, Oxford University Press, 1923, R. Furneaux, London, 1974 and J. Pollock, London, 1977.
19 Detailed discussions of the slave trade and its abolition can be found in B.

Davidson *Black Mother*, Penguin, revised edn, 1980 and R. Anstey *The Atlantic Slave Trade and British Abolition 1760–1810*, Macmillan, 1975.

20 A. Armstrong op. cit. p. 155.
21 On Welsh developments in addition to general works cited earlier see M. Clement *The SPCK and Wales*, SPCK, 1954 and M. G. Jones *The Charity School Movement*, Cambridge University Press, 1938.
22 On Scotland see A. L. Drummond and J. Bulloch *The Scottish Church 1688–1843*, St Andrews Press, 1973.
23 On Ireland see the earlier chapters of D. H. Akenson *The Church of Ireland: Ecclesiastical Reform and Revolution 1800–1885*, Yale, 1971. J. E. Bradley *Religion, Revolution and English Radicalism*, Cambridge University Press, 1990 considers Dissent and politics.
24 For the discussion of 'Old' Dissent see A. Armstrong op. cit. pp. 35–43, 173–5 and A. D. Gilbert op. cit. pp. 14–17, 32–41. M. Watts *The Dissenters*, Oxford University Press, 1978 especially chapters 4 and 5 is more detailed.
25 E. R. Bebb *Nonconformity and Social and Economic Life 1600–1800*, Epworth Press, 1935, p. 57.
26 Literature on Methodism is large. In addition to the general works cited above see S. Andrews *Methodism and Society*, Longman, 1970, E. G. Rupp and R. E. Davies (eds) *A History of the Methodist Church in Great Britain*, Vol. I, Epworth Press, 1965, B. Semmel *The Methodist Revolution*, Heinemann, 1974, *J. Wesley and the Church of England*, Epworth Press, 1970, R. F. Wearmouth *Methodism and the Common People of the Eighteenth Century*, Epworth Press, 1945. D. Hempton *Methodism and Politics in British Society 1750–1850*, Hutchinson, 1984 examines the political and social consequences of Methodism.
27 M. Watts op. cit. p. 401.
28 Quoted in W. A. Speck *Stability and Strife: England 1714–1760*, Edward Arnold, 1977, p. 108.
29 Quoted in A. Armstrong, op. cit., p. 66. For a fuller discussion of Wesley's Tory attitudes see B. Semmel op. cit., pp. 56–80.
30 ibid. p. 111.
31 D. Hempton op. cit. p. 66.
32 On Methodism in Wales see A. H. Williams *Welsh Wesleyan Methodism 1800–1858*, Bangor University Press, 1935 especially pp. 15–84 for a discussion of why Wesleyan Methodism did not strike roots until after 1800 and E. T. Davies *Religion in the Industrial Revolution in South Wales*, University of Wales Press, 1965, especially pp. 44–96. T. Herbert and G. G. Jones (eds) *The Remaking of Wales in the Eighteenth Century*, University of Wales Press, 1988 contains sources.
33 G. A. Williams *When Was Wales?* Penguin, 1985, p. 155.
34 See the Ford Lectures of I. R. Christie *Stress and Stability in late Eighteenth-Century Britain*, Oxford University Press, 1985 for the most recent discussion of the subject and pp. 183–214 for the churches and 'good order'. R. Mole *Pulpits, Politics and Public Order in England 1760–1832*, Cambridge University Press, 1989 examines the relationship between religion and politics.
35 ibid. p. 213.
36 H. Perkin *The Origins of Modern English Society 1780–1880*, Routledge, 1969, pp. 176–216.
37 D. Hempton op. cit. pp. 42–3.
38 For Roman Catholicism two books will be found useful: J. Bossy *The English Catholic Community 1570–1850*, 1975 and E. R. Norman *Roman Catholicism in England*, Oxford University Press, 1986.

6 William Pitt and his legacy 1783–1812

One of the most pervasive platitudes of eighteenth-century constitutional theory was that governments ought to be patriotic in character;
that administrations should be broadly based seeking to embrace the
widest possible range of political support; and that loyalty to the Crown
and to the establishment in Church and State should be an assumed
pre-requisite for office. Governments were supposed to be coalitions
of men of good will, motivated by a desire to serve the State rather
than the agents of faction or party.[1]

Between 1760 and 1783 British politics was marked, first, by a ten-year
period of ministerial instability as George III sought a minister acceptable
both to himself and Parliament, and then by thirteen years of administration largely by Lord North. Plagued by the American crisis, which
turned into war after 1775, and by the perennial problem of Irish government North survived until early 1782. Short-lived Whig administrations
led first by Rockingham, Shelburne and by Fox and North initiated a
period of political instability which ended with the peremptory dismissal
of the Fox–North coalition in December 1783. This chapter will examine
political developments between William Pitt's appointment as Prime Minister in 1783 and the assassination of Spencer Perceval in May 1812.[2] It
will examine the nature, extent and limitations of Pitt's achievement as
Prime Minister between 1783 and 1801 and the nature of his legacy in the
period of less stable government both before and after his death in early
1806.

A POLITICAL 'CRISIS'

Between 1782 and late 1783 there was a succession of administrations
which did not have the support of the king and found it difficult to weld
together a reliable majority in the House of Commons. Lord North's
resignation in late March 1783 led to a period of political and constitutional
crisis not finally resolved until the general election a year later. Whig
administrations, led by Rockingham and, after his death in July 1783, by

Shelburne, found themselves working with a monarch resentful at losing Lord North. Effective government proved difficult though 'economical reform' was pushed forward and a peace was negotiated with America at Versailles. George III's resentment turned to blind anger when, in early 1783, his former trusted minister formed a coalition with the Rockingham Whigs now effectively controlled by Charles James Fox. With no alternative administration possible George III was compelled to accept one which he regarded as an affront to the royal prerogative and which he schemed to remove through royal influence in the House of Lords. Faced with an East India Bill, which attacked both the chartered rights of the East India Company and royal patronage, the king and William Pitt used their influence to ensure its defeat in the House of Lords. Under sustained royal prompting the coalition was twice defeated there in two days and in mid-December 1783 was dismissed. Pitt in accordance with his pledges formed a new administration.[3]

The king's blatant interference was controversial and, given the convention governing the independence of parliamentary proceedings, unconstitutional. George III argued that his action was justifiable because of the actual or intended incursions of the coalition politicians on the powers of the Crown. The king had considerable popular support and the unprecedented scale of the addresses to the Crown in early 1784 revealed that many people believed that a threat to the balance of the constitution had been averted. It was also possible that even without monarchical interference the House of Lords would have rejected the India Bill for which there was growing revulsion and that the king making his feelings known merely acted as a catalyst.

PITT IN POWER

Initially Pitt did not have a Commons majority and was opposed by a coherent grouping of ex-ministers and their supporters led by North, Fox and the Duke of Portland. A Whig hostess said that 'it will be a mincepie administration' just before the Christmas recess, while the historian Edward Gibbon observed that 'Billy's painted galley will soon sink under Charles' black collier.' John Robinson's estimate of the strength of groups in the Commons in late 1783 gave the supporters of the Fox–North coalition 231 votes while Pitt could only muster 149. With independent support of 74 for Fox and 104 for Pitt, the opposition could rally 305 MPs while Pitt could only count on 253. Fox and North underestimated Pitt's political acumen and, as he became increasingly competent, Pitt won the admiration and votes of many independent members and the majorities against him began to fall. They also underestimated the degree of support which Pitt had outside Parliament. He had a reputation as a reformer and as an individual 'above party'. Pitt could stand for purity, virtue and youth unlike his opponents. In March 1784, once the opposition's majority had

dwindled to one and it was clear that Pitt could rely on support other than
the use of Crown electoral influence, George III used his constitutional
prerogative and dissolved Parliament, three years earlier than the septennial convention required. The appeal was highly successful and coalition
supporters were routed both in the larger constituencies, where Pittite
popular support was in evidence and in many of the smaller ones where
royal influence was expertly manipulated by John Robinson, George's
election agent.

The 1784 election

It is difficult to give precise election figures. One estimate gave the Pittites
315 MPs, the Foxites and Northites 213 and Independents and doubtfuls
30 but these figures contain large numbers of independent members who
declared themselves for either Fox or Pitt on the hustings but who did
not see themselves as 'party' men. The *Annual Register* commented that
'So complete a rout . . . is scarcely to be credited.' Pitt himself wrote that
'We are more successful everywhere . . . than can be imagined.' Two
things are, however, quite clear. First, that Pitt now had the majority
necessary for effective government and that he had restored the principle
of a minister governing with the support of both king and Commons.
Secondly, despite the loss of both party members and sympathetic independent MPs – the so-called 'Fox's Martyrs' – the Rockingham Whigs had
weathered the storm more successfully than many people believed. They
had not been destroyed as a potent political force. By the end of the 1780s
the term 'leader of the opposition' was coming into use and was applied
to Charles James Fox in the Commons rather than Portland, the nominal
leader of the Whigs, who sat in the Lords. Public perceptions of notions of
'government' versus 'opposition' were heightened by the personal rivalry
between Pitt and Fox and throughout the 1780s the opposition Whigs
more or less maintained their voting strength.

By 1788 Pitt was firmly in control of both Commons and Lords. One
estimate of government support gave Pitt 280 MPs, 185 of whom owed
their primary loyalty to the king, 50 or so who attached themselves to Pitt
and just over 40 who owed their allegiance through family or patronage
to other ministers, principally those Scottish MPs controlled by Henry
Dundas. The opposition of the Portland–Fox and North groups had about
155 MPs while independent members made up the remaining 122 MPs.
Pitt extended his control over the House of Lords through George III's
willingness to create peers, something he had not been willing to do for
other ministers. Almost half of the peers created when Pitt was Prime
Minister were ennobled between 1784 and 1790.

Early attempts at reform

Pitt may have won a substantial victory in the 1784 election but it is important not to overestimate the extent to which the following decade was without political strains. He was able to embark upon a programme of national recovery but within a political framework in which a conservative consensus dominated. Between 1784 and 1786 Pitt was defeated on four substantial issues, including defence, parliamentary reform and economic union with the United States and Ireland. Pitt's support came from those who believed in strong, stable government, and it was consequently looser and more heterogeneous. He wrote to the Duke of Rutland in mid-1785 during the debates on Ireland that

> We have an indefatigable enemy, sharpened by disappointment, watching and improving every opportunity. . . . Our majority, though a large one, is composed of men who think, or at least act, so much for themselves, that we are hardly sure from day to day what impression they may receive. . . . Any new circumstance of embarrassment might have the effect, sooner than can almost be imagined, of reversing our apparent situation of strength and security.

To these supporters nationalizing administrative structures was more acceptable than legislative programmes particularly if it produced more efficient and especially cheaper government. Pitt was content to work within this system and never attempted to fashion a popularity in any way independent to that of the king. His achievement was to reduce the temperature of political debate in the Commons, just as the opposition was able to preserve the essentials of party identity under adverse conditions. As Asa Briggs says, Pitt

> was always willing to serve, just as Fox was always willing to oppose, and this, rather than any desire to be popular, was the key to his political career. Freedom for him lay in the recognition of what he regarded as necessity, the supremacy of the royal will. . . . Above all he was anxious to apply both his will and his ability to the urgent tasks of recovery and reconstruction which he believed were far more important than prolonged discussion of general principles.[4]

The Regency crisis 1788–9

The most serious threat to Pitt's tenure of office was the Regency crisis of 1788–9.[5] When George III was stricken by an attack of apparent madness in late 1788 the Whigs were in a state of disarray. The Fox–Portland group had been associated with the reversionary interest round George, Prince of Wales, for six years. To some extent it was a relationship of convenience. The Whigs saw the succession of the Prince as their route to office while he was willing to use the Whigs both as an embarrassment to and lever against his father. This support was a two-edged sword for the Whigs. The application to Parliament for additional money to clear the Prince's unpopular debts was necessary while the admission that he had contracted an unlawful marriage with the Catholic Maria Fitzherbert in 1785 alienated Portland and other aristocratic leaders. These stresses within the Whigs surfaced in 1788 shortly before the king's illness, highlighting the dependence of the Whigs on the Prince if they were to achieve power. Fox found himself in the position of relying on the future king for power which brought home the illogicality of his denunciation of Pitt who owed his advancement to the existing king.

Pitt and his supporters, recognizing their dependence on royal support, framed a Regency Bill closely limiting the power of the Regent. The Whigs, by contrast, demanded an 'unrestricted' regency. This played straight into Pitt's hands, and he was able to point to Fox's reversal as the champion of parliamentary authority; unlike Fox, he showed himself very able at dealing with the historical and constitutional precedents. Despite a few desertions and the intrigues of Thurlow, the Lord Chancellor, the one cabinet minister who had no real loyalty towards the government, Pitt's majority held and he was able to push his bill through Parliament. By mid-February the bill was reaching its final stage in the Lords but the process was ended with the rapid recovery of the king. Pitt, however, did not have control over the Irish Parliament which declined to model its proceedings on those in London and passed addresses inviting the Prince of Wales to assume royal functions without limitations. The close relationship between monarch and minister is made clear in a letter George III wrote to Pitt during the evening of 23 February 1789, which ended 'I am anxious to see Mr Pitt any hour that may suit him tomorrow morning, as his constant attachment to my interest and that of the people, which are inseparable, must ever place him in the most advantageous light.'

Fox and the Whigs

During the Regency crisis the Whigs had made some important tactical blunders, and disagreements between Fox and Portland threatened the cohesion of the party. Fox had come across as opportunistic rather than principled and reluctant to impose discipline on younger Whigs like Richard Sheridan and Charles Grey. Few had taken seriously Edmund Burke's theoretical defence of the hereditary succession as justification for an unlimited Regency Bill and this led Burke to question the party's seriousness of purpose. Despite the débâcle of 1788–9 the Whigs entered the 1790 general election in reasonable shape. For this William Adams was largely responsible through his central organization of the party[6]

The achievement of the party managers of the 1780s therefore, was to consolidate the [Whig] Coalition into a party, to absorb smaller opposition factions and, between the elections of 1784 and 1790, to stabilise the size of the parliamentary opposition around 130–40 MPs.

THE FRENCH REVOLUTION

The French Revolution transformed British political life. Between 1790 and 1794 tensions within the opposition Whigs, personal as well as ideological, led to division. The first public split was provoked by the publication in November 1790 of Edmund Burke's *Reflections on the Revolution in France*.[7] His polemic against the Revolution was grounded in attacks on the principle that people were born with inalienable natural rights and that their most basic expression lay in the right of citizens to choose their rulers by democratic processes. He challenged the notion of equal natural rights, maintaining that government did not derive its authority from the explicit consent of the governed but from custom, practice and experience. Without the traditions of the past Burke believed that the social order, preservation of which was the prime duty of government, would break down. Speculative ideas, even if based in reason, were no basis for stable government. But Burke was no reactionary, arguing that any state which did not permit change had lost the means of conserving itself. As Eric Evans says: 'In attacking [the] revolution's philosophical basis, he also laid down principles subsequently identified as central to the ideology not of Whiggery, but of modern Conservatism.'[8]

Fox under pressure

In April 1791 Fox disowned Burke, asserting that the French were imitating the principles of Glorious Revolution to which defence the Whigs were dedicated. Burke only took a few supporters with him but the rift within the party widened during the following year. Fox's argument that the Revolution was a 'Whiggish' event could only be maintained so long as he could control reformist Whigs. In April 1792 a group of radical Whigs led by Grey, Sheridan and Samuel Whitbread formed the Association of the Friends of the People, in an attempt to commit the party to parliamentary reform. The Whig tradition, this group argued, was as committed to parliamentary reform as it was to removing religious disabilities and that this meant putting themselves at the head of reforming movements which attracted support down the social hierarchy and so would neutralize any 'democratic' excesses. The Whigs were placed in the position of having to make an uncomfortable choice. Burke had emphasized the dangers of well-meaning reforms leading to revolution and chaos and increasingly the debate within the Whig party polarized over whether it should emphasize reform and liberty or order and public security.

Fox did not join the Association though he sympathized with its aims.

He became increasingly convinced that Pitt intended to subvert English liberties after the militia was summoned to help defend the country against an alleged insurrection, and in December 1792 he was driven to a defence of both the French Revolution and parliamentary reform. As a result William Windham, MP for Norwich, and thirty conservative Whigs distanced themselves from Fox and Portland and declared their support for the government. Windham acknowledged that however desirable reform actually was it was being used by those who sought to overthrow the constitution. The execution of Louis XVI in January 1793 and the outbreak of war with France the following month exacerbated Whig problems. Fox opposed the outbreak of the war. Portland regarded it as a regrettable necessity. Fox supported Grey's motion for parliamentary reform in the Commons in May 1793; Portland opposed it. Neither Burke nor Portland saw themselves as ceasing to be Whigs, they still wished to conserve the Whig constitution, but what separated them from Fox was their view of how this could best be done. By mid-1793 what opposition unity remained was severely stretched and, after nearly a year, Portland and the conservative Whigs formed a coalition with Pitt. The formation of the coalition in July 1794, when Portland became Home Secretary and four other conservative Whigs, Fitzwilliam, Mansfield, Spencer and Windham, entered the cabinet, marked a realignment of political forces and, according to Frank O'Gorman, a reaffirmation of the strength of party in politics.

A 'new' Tory party?

Some historians have seen the rebirth of the Tory party in the formation of the coalition in 1794. This may be a misrepresentation of the nature of the coalition government. Pitt certainly did not see himself as a Tory, always referring to himself as an independent Whig. Portland and the conservative Whigs did not abandon the Whig creed nor did they lose their long-standing distrust of Pitt. John Derry argues that the crisis caused by revolution and war necessitated the formation of a government of national unity but that it was not a party ministry.[9] Derry's argument holds up far more where Pitt is concerned than with the conservative Whigs. Pitt's approach to the French threat was pragmatic and insular in 1790 and remained so until his death. Pitt needed peace if his fiscal and commercial reforms were to bring economic benefits and he saw the preservation of a free constitution as the basis for this economic prosperity. Defence of the constitution was a defence of the economic welfare of the nation. Derry argues that

> This helps to explain why the government tended to follow opinion rather than to anticipate it, and why under both Pitt and Liverpool there was a general reluctance to make innovations in constitutional

law and practice. Men who were obsessed by a reverence for the constitution and who were convinced of its unique nature, were as reluctant to make innovations of reactionary character as they were to yield to radical demands.[10]

Social, political and religious attitudes in the early 1790s symbolized by the creation of loyalist associations and Church and king riots, veered towards a conservative preservation of the constitution, defence of property and an enhanced sense of patriotism. This repressive opinion both reinforced and was reinforced by Pitt's ministry. Pitt maintained that the repression initiated by the State Trials of 1793–4, the suspension of Habeas Corpus in May 1794 and the Treasonable Practices and Seditious Meetings Acts of 1795 was a temporary and regrettable expedient. The extension of state power and its assumption of an apparently permanent vigilance can be explained by prevailing public opinion as much as by Pitt's desire to repress opposition. It was difficult for government to assess objectively the threat which revolutionary radicals posed to public order and contemporaries were quick to point to irrational hysteria in repressive legislation. Public order may well have been as threatened by loyalist actions as it was by any real or apparent revolutionary activity. The conservative Whigs did more than the Pittites to emphasize the anti-reformist nature of Toryism after 1794. But Pitt was not opposed to all change. His response to the attempt by Samuel Whitbread in February 1796 to fix minimum wages was neither reactionary nor unsympathetic, though his bill to improve poor relief was ferociously attacked in the Commons and withdrawn.

Between 1794 and 1797 Pitt could count on the support of over 500 MPs, consisting of 426 Pittites plus independent MPs who generally supported the government on important issues and 77 Portland Whigs. The Foxite opposition numbered about 55. This unequal division was between those men of solid property who perceived a threat to their economic well-being in revolutionary attacks on the constitution and the Foxites who represented the government as the major threat to British liberties, and supported Fox's calls for a negotiated peace and Grey's parliamentary reform motions. From 1797 to 1800 the Foxites renounced regular parliamentary attendance though secession was never complete and Pitt's resignation over Catholic emancipation in 1801 brought them flooding back to Parliament.

POLITICAL INSTABILITY 1801–12

Between 1801 and 1812 seven administrations ruled Britain, none lasting more than three and a quarter years.[11] These years were marked by the metamorphosis of the Pittites into Tories and the re-emergence of the Foxite Whigs as a credible opposition. The large governing coalition which Pitt had formed in 1794 was split by his resignation over Catholic emancipation into groupings of Pittites (60), Addingtonians (30–40), Grenvilles (20–30) and Canningites (10–15). Supporters of Court and Treasury numbered between 200 and 230 and, in a House of Commons increased to 658 MPs with the addition of 100 Irish members. This led to unstable and unpredictable ministerial support. Any stable administration needed the alliance of at least two elements of the old Pittite coalition to lead the Court and Treasury grouping. It took eleven years before three of these groups reunited under Lord Liverpool – Grenville delayed joining the ministry until 1821.

The period of political instability between 1801 and 1812 was, to some degree, a result of Pitt's refusal to transform his supporters into a party. There had always been potential for division before 1801 but Pitt had skilfully held this in check. After 1801 personal differences sharpened and divisive issues emerged. The factions were divided on abolition of the Slave Trade – Addingtonians were against, Grenvilles for and the Canningites divided – and on Catholic emancipation – Addington's and later Perceval's group against, Canningites and Grenvilles in favour. However, there was an underlying unity on issues like parliamentary reform and on law and order. Pitt had based his political dominance and large-scale support in Parliament on administrative ability and political success. His was a government of administrators and patriots not of party. Resignation and defeat ended this personal hegemony. Between 1801 and 1812 politicians sought an alternative to the political cohesion provided by Pitt's genius.

Addington 1801–4

When Henry Addington formed his administration in 1801, most Pittites stayed on with the approval of their leader. Pitt had readily agreed not to oppose the ministry as Addington's condition for accepting office. Canning refused to serve and, although Portland remained in office, Windham and Spencer left. In 1802 Lord Grenville went into open opposition against Addington's Peace of Amiens and, with Windham, formed a separate war party of about thirty MPs. Despite Pitt's benevolent neutrality, Addington's incompetence and the renewal of war in 1803 could not long delay the inevitable. In April 1804 Addington eventually resigned and Pitt returned for a second administration.

Pitt returns 1804–6

Between 1801 and 1806 the Foxite Whigs was the main group to benefit from instability. The June 1802 election demonstrated the degree of popular support for the Peace of Amiens and the Foxites slightly improved their position adding public vindication to parliamentary approval for their peace policy. Within a year, because of Napoleon's imperialism, they reversed their long-standing peace policy and in May 1803 Fox supported a declaration of war. Addington would not consider coalition with Fox to strengthen his Commons majority and, in what can only be seen as calculated opportunism, a coalition between Fox and Grenville was negotiated in 1804. As Frank O'Gorman says: 'Now that Pitt had acquiesced to a cowardly peace and Fox had come to terms with the war, the coalition was a natural stepping stone on the road to office.'[12]

Pitt was unable to reunite his old supporters between 1804 and his death in January 1806. The Fox–Grenville group deprived him of support from one quarter and he did not enjoy assistance from Addington. Support for his ministry was unstable and narrow. But initially the opposition was disunited. The Grenvilles did not fully understand the personal animosity between Pitt and Fox and the two opposition groups took time to work together effectively. By late 1805, however, the opposition coalition was performing both effectively and actively and there was little doubt that a substantial and revitalized opposition existed for the first time since 1791.

'All the Talents' 1806–7

George III had no alternative after Pitt's death but to turn to Grenville and, with reluctance, Fox. The 'Ministry of All the Talents', as it was widely dubbed, was led by Grenville, with Fox as Foreign Secretary and, though Whig-dominated, was a coalition of politicians including the group round Addington, since 1805 ennobled as Viscount Sidmouth. No action was taken on either religious concessions to Ireland or parliamentary reform, both of which were unacceptable to the Addingtonians. The death of Fox in September removed the ministry's most talented member and the 1806 general election added little to its popular support. The ministry was seen as politically inconsistent. It refused to entertain discussions on parliamentary reform. Ministers fell over each other to woo the king, despite the criticism of secret royal influence frequently expressed while they were in opposition. The Lord Chief Justice was brought into the Cabinet to please Sidmouth and the king in direct contravention to the independence of the judiciary. Faced with a war that was going badly, the king was lukewarm in his support and there were increasing attacks from a revitalized Pittite opposition. The ministry lingered until dismissed in March 1807.

Portland 1807–9

Sidmouth's resignation over the removal of disability against Catholics becoming officers in the navy and army throughout Great Britain and Grenville's refusal to give the king a written promise that he would not raise the question again was the cause of the dismissal of the Talents.

Many people believed that the king had acted in an unconstitutional way but, as in 1783–4, the immediate reaction to his actions in the form of petitions and the result of the 1807 general election showed that his intervention was generally approved. Public opinion was vehemently anti-Catholic. The electorate were given a clear choice between Whigs and Tories, denoting opposition or support for the king's position and alignment on religion. The 1807 election was a clear victory for the Tories. Portland could count on the support of about 370 MPs while the opposition could only muster about 290. The Whigs were not to hold office again until late 1830.

Between Pitt's death and the formation of the Portland ministry in March 1807 the Pittites began to make themselves the basis of a Tory party. On 20 January 1806 they decided as a group to support the Talents only if the basis of Pitt's policies was left untouched. In February they voted as a group against the inclusion of Lord Justice Ellenborough in the cabinet. They negotiated as a group when Grenville tried to include them in the coalition in June. In July they decided to oppose systematically a ministry they believed did not enjoy royal confidence and by December were determined to drive the Whigs from office. Portland, though old and ill, was widely respected and acted as party leader.

Perceval 1809–12

The development of Toryism between 1807 and 1812 was far from smooth. Personal rivalries, which went so far as a dual between Castlereagh and Canning in 1809, and the final mental collapse of the king with the establishment of the regency in 1810–11, were obstacles to stable government. So too was the erratic progress of the war, which resulted in increased taxation and commercial dislocation and the revival of extra-parliamentary radicalism. Portland retired in 1809 and his successor, Spencer Perceval, could not hold the Pittites together. Canning refused to serve and Perceval was unable to gain the support of the Whig opposition which believed that the advent of the regency would enable them to take office independently. It was only divisions within the Whigs in September 1809, early in 1811 and February 1812 that enabled Perceval to remain in power. Not until March 1812 did his government look secure with the return to Sidmouth and Castlereagh to strengthen its anti-reformist base. After Perceval's assassination in May 1812 the appointment of Lord Liverpool, despite the eventual length of his administration, was neither immediate nor inevitable.

PITT AND POLICY

1783 to the early 1790s

It is possible to divide Pitt's ministry between 1783 and 1801 into two: from 1783 through to the early 1790s when he was responsible for what successive historians have seen as a 'national revival', and from the early 1790s to his resignation in 1801 when he was largely concerned with the impact and implications of the French Revolution.[13] Given Pitt's reputation as a defender of the constitution and social order in the 1790s it is important to recognize that he was known as a cautious reformer in the early 1780s though he never allowed this to interfere with the needs of administrative expediency. In 1785 he unsuccessfully attempted to abolish thirty-six rotten boroughs and transfer their seats to London and the counties, failed to achieve economic union with Ireland and had already dropped the notion of economic union with America which he had considered when Shelburne was Chancellor of the Exchequer. These failures confirmed Pitt's inability to lead the country in his own reforming terms because of the extent of opposition. Parliamentary reform was lost in the Commons by 248 votes to 174 and he abandoned economic union following opposition from British manufacturing and commercial interests. The framework of government within which Pitt operated was overwhelmingly 'administrative', reacting to problems when they arose rather than initiating programmes of a fundamental reforming nature. Pitt can best be seen in the first part of his ministry as an individual concentrating on streamlining and improving the machinery of government. He was primarily a pragmatic administrative reformer.

Restoring national finances

The first area where administrative reform occurred was in the restoration of national finances. In 1783 government expenditure exceeded income by £10.8 million, largely a result of the cost of the American War and inefficiency in collecting excise duties. Government had difficulty in raising loans and confidence in a recovery of national finances was at a low ebb. Between 1783 and 1791 annual governmental revenue was increased by almost £4 million of which half came from new taxes and reducing smuggling and fraud and the remainder from increasing the efficiency of collection.

Pitt's initial priority was to raise revenue and his first target was the smugglers. It is difficult to estimate the extent of smuggling and the effect this had on national finances but perhaps a fifth of all imports was contraband. The finances of the East India Company had been undermined by smuggled tea which in the early 1780s amounted to between 3 and 4.5 million tons per year. Pitt adopted a two-pronged strategy. He introduced restrictive legislation to reduce the attractiveness of smuggling and extended the rights of search over suspect cargoes. An extended 'Hovering Act', for example, authorized the confiscation of certain types of vessel carrying contraband goods found at anchor or 'hovering' within four miles of the coast. Parallel to this he embarked on a massive reduction of duties. The 1784 Commutation Act reduced the duty on tea from 119 to a uniform 25 per cent and this was followed by reductions on wines, spirits and tobacco. The tightening up on revenue agencies and the transfer of more business to the excise department led to increased yields: 29 per cent on spirits, 63 per cent on wines and 39 per cent on tobacco by 1790. Pitt did not destroy smuggling but he made it a far less profitable and far more risky business.

The loss of revenue occasioned by reductions of duties was recouped by the increased efficiency with which taxes were collected. Pitt has the not unjustified reputation for being one of the most efficient tax-gatherers ever to govern England. His taxation policy was based on the prevailing orthodoxy that all should bear a share but that the poor should not be overburdened. Luxury goods were consequently the major taxable items: pleasure horses, hackney carriages, gloves, hats, ribbons, candles, servants and hair powder plus a graduated increase in the tax on windows. Eric Evans rightly sees this as representing little more than a 'shuffling of the Hanoverian pack'. Taken as a whole Pitt's taxation policy was sensible but could be both unpopular and misguided. The window tax may have held back the development of the glass industry. A projected tax on coal was withdrawn because of opposition and taxes on linen and cotton in 1784 had serious economic implications and were also withdrawn. Pitt's only real innovation was a tax on shops, introduced in 1785, but withdrawn in 1789 after widespread opposition and public disturbances in London.

In 1783 the national debt stood at £238 million with interest charges amounting to about a quarter of government expenditure. Pitt wanted to reduce this through the extension of a 'sinking fund', a device whereby annual sums were set aside for buying government stock to pay off the debts. A sinking fund had existed since 1716 but its potential value was reduced by ministers raiding it for other purposes. Richard Price had in 1772 argued for a regularly supported and inviolate fund and, as in many other areas of policy, Pitt was willing to use other people's ideas. The reform of the sinking fund in 1786 was perhaps more important in restoring national confidence than producing financial improvement. The sinking fund was placed under the control of a board of six commissioners and was made inviolate. Given peace, prosperity and continued parliamentary approval for taxation, there was little wrong with the scheme and by the outbreak of war in 1793 some £10.25 million of stock had been acquired and the debt was beginning to run down. After 1793, however, it proved a liability and was ended in the 1820s.

Administrative efficiency

In 1780 Lord North persuaded Parliament to appoint an independent commission to examine public finance and by December 1783 it was about half-way through its deliberations. Its fifteen exhaustive reports with their detailed description of existing practice and recommendations for improvements provided the basis for reform which Pitt was willing to implement. The existing system of government had developed to satisfy political rather than administrative criteria. Offices, whether sinecures or not, were rewards for political support, a consequence of the needs of patronage. Creating financial stability meant rationalizing this system. Radical reform would have encountered widespread opposition from the entrenched power of patronage-mongers and consequently Pitt operated in a more circumspect manner. Sinecures were simply allowed to lapse on the death of their occupants. Most of the 180 posts the public accounts commissioners recommended should be abolished in 1786 disappeared in the next twenty years. Lord Liverpool said that Pitt had all but destroyed the patronage network. In reality, as John Bourne has shown,[14] administrative patronage increased with the enlarged role of government. What had gone were 'offices of profit'. Efficient departmental management was gradually built up piecemeal but with a greater degree of Treasury control with a Treasury Commission of Audit, created in 1785, overseeing public expenditure. The Board of Taxes was reinforced by transfers from the Treasury and the Excise Board. People with talent, like Richard Frewin at Customs, were promoted and encouraged to develop administrative policies on their own initiative. The creation of a central Stationery Office in 1787 secured economies in the supply of stationery to the departments. The practice of the Treasurers of the Navy having their funds under their own management was brought under control by requiring that any moneys issued should be kept in an account at the Bank of England and withdrawn only when required. This was part of Pitt's tightening of naval expenditure where he relied heavily on its Comptroller Sir Charles Middleton, later Lord Barham, who was largely responsible for the creation of a navy capable of responding to the French challenge between 1793 and 1815. More radical naval reform with the introduction of promotion by merit and seniority, salaries rather than fees and a strengthened Naval Board, was only prevented by the Regency crisis of 1788–9.

Prior to 1787 there were 103 separate exchequer revenue accounts and revenue collectors forwarded funds under 68 different accounts. Under the Consolidated Fund Act of 1787 most revenues collected were paid into a single consolidated fund account at the Treasury. The exceptions were the Civil List annuity and the land and malt taxes on which specific blocks of funded Exchequer bills were secured. This marked a major step forward in efficient administration and led to economy of labour and the reduction of confusion. Initially new taxes were accounted for separately but this was removed in 1797.

Commercial policies

Financial solvency and administrative efficiency at home were paralleled by an enlightened commercial policy which encouraged buoyant and growing trade. The value of imports doubled to £20 million between 1783 and 1790 and exports rose from £12.5 million in 1782 to over £20 by 1790. Given the problems of empire in the early 1780s this was a major achievement. Economic recovery, it was maintained, necessitated the continuance of the old monopolistic system in the West Indies. The United States was seen as a threat to British commercial and naval supremacy in the New World. Shelburne's notion of economic union with America, when he was prime minister in 1782 and 1783, was jettisoned and Pitt's new Committee of Trade, under the influence of Charles Jenkinson, rejected the reduction of trade barriers. Trade with America was not to be reciprocal. The Navigation Acts were maintained with vigour; in 1783 American shipping was excluded from the West Indian islands; trade with America for cheaper meat and fish via the French and Spanish islands was made illegal by order in council in 1787 and by statute the following year. Jenkinson's protectionist policy towards American trade was indicated in the passage of the last Navigation Act in 1786. The Americans saw it as a vindictive action aimed at disadvantaging the shipping of the northern states but Jenkinson's calculations were strictly commercial. If America could be prevented from developing a challenge to Britain's merchant shipping then, although there had been loss of political control, Britain could still retain economic and commercial hegemony. Jenkinson's policy was contrary to prevailing trends which tended to emphasize trade with the Americas rather than with Europe. By 1785 British exports to America had returned to the levels achieved in the early 1770s and by the 1790s the tariffs acted only as a minor irritant. The outbreak of the French war and the more sympathetic views of Grenville and Dundas, now overshadowing those of Jenkinson (ennobled as Lord Hawkesbury) led to the Jay Treaty of 1794 which opened certain markets to American shipping. The effects were dramatic: Britain's exports to America more than doubled between 1793 and 1799 and by 1800 America was taking more than 25 per cent of British exports. This more liberal policy was a recognition of the growing economic importance of the American market for exports and the dependence of Britain's textile industry on imported cotton.

The immediate economic advantages of Canada were limited in the 1780s. Its furs, fish and timber were important but its scattered population did not offer a large market for British goods. Yet relations with Canada were handled with care. An arena of Anglo-French conflict, it was only brought under the British Crown by conquest in 1760. In Quebec there was still potential for tension between English- and French-speakers. Canada's population had been substantially increased by the migration of many American loyalists north: some 25,000 settled in Nova Scotia and a further 20,000 in upper Quebec. The costs of administering the Canadian provinces of Quebec, Nova Scotia and New Brunswick were largely borne by the British government. Canada assumed greater importance after 1783 as a barrier to possible American expansion. The 1791 Canada Act, which radically recast the government of the province of Quebec, reflected an imprecise desire to give some self-determination to colonial development and to prevent any penetration of American republican influence.

The loss of the American colonies focused the attention of government on India and the East, with their underdeveloped but potentially large markets. Pitt had come to power as a result of the abortive Fox–North India Bill and the issue was quickly dealt with in his East India Act of 1784. The East India Company kept its patronage but effective political and strategic control passed from it to a Board of Control made up of ministers of the Crown. Responsibility for Indian affairs passed to Henry Dundas in London and in India to Earl Cornwallis, Governor-General from 1786 to 1793. Sinecures were suppressed and able recruits enlisted. Effective British administration, based on colonial control and native assistance, dated from the Cornwallis period, though he was unable to secure government control of company troops. Trade in the East improved under Pitt, though this was as much a result of his ending of tea-smuggling as administrative rationalization.

There was an important commercial thread in Britain's rehabilitation in Europe after 1783, when she was starkly isolated. Pitt's policies were novel only in the scale on which they worked. Negotiations were opened with all the leading courts of Europe for reciprocally lowered tarriff duties. The Eden trade treaty with France, signed in September 1786, was the only real, though temporary, achievement of this policy. French wines entered Britain at the same preferential rates as the Portuguese and, although opposition from manufacturers kept the silk market protected, France was opened to British goods in a general tariff reduction of 10–15 per cent. Within three years French manufacturers were complaining that the treaty was unfairly weighted in favour of British manufacturers. In reality their complaint was a reflection of competitiveness of the early stages of British industrialization. As Eric Evans says:

> The liberalisation of trade was bound to favour the most efficient producers; Britain's later commitment to free trade by no means represented an intellectual conversion to a persuasive doctrine. Her manufacturers were backing a horse which could not lose.[15]

Commercial considerations played a part in challenging French expansion into the Low Countries though Britain also wished to stop France using

Dutch overseas bases like Cape Town. Britain's isolation in Europe was emphasized by the French alliance with the Dutch in 1785 which involved a reduction in the powers of the pro-English House of Orange. A successful Prussian invasion in 1787 revived Orange fortunes and was followed by a Triple Alliance between Prussia, the United Provinces and Britain. This ended Britain's diplomatic isolation and its unity enabled Britain success-fully to exert her authority in the North Pacific in 1790 when Spain seized ships from a British trading base for furs and fish at Nootka Sound, off western Canada. Pitt was less successful in his support of Anglo-Prussian policy over Russian gains round Ochakov on the Black Sea. Demands that Russia return the area to the Ottoman Empire were resisted and Pitt abandoned his policy following large-scale opposition to his warlike stance in the House of Commons.

Conclusions

Pitt was an efficient rather than a innovative minister. He rationalized the existing systems of government and taxation rather than embark on a radical programme of reform. His approach was cautious, following rather than leading opinion, and responsive to the influence of opposition. This can be shown in his attitude to the ideas of Adam Smith. Historians frequently argue that Pitt has a reputation as an individual committed to free trade. This may be true but it did not divert him from the practicalities of politics. Diplomatic and commercial realities meant that Pitt's commit-ment to free trade was always limited. 1786 saw both a Navigation Act and the Anglo-French treaty. Britain's commercial success had been built on protection, and the move to freer trade was a result of British industries no longer needing protection as much as the intellectual attraction of the new system. The outbreak of war in 1793 drove the British government back to protection. Improving the efficiency of free government contrib-uted decisively to growing wealth and economic power. Pitt said in 1792 that:

> It is this union of liberty with law which, by raising a barrier equally firm against the encroachments of power and the violence of popular commotion, affords to property its just security, produces the exertion of genius and labour, the extent and solidarity of credit, the circulation and increase of capital; which forms and upholds the national character, and sets in motion all the springs which actuate the great mass of the community through all its various descriptions. . . .[16]

PITT AT WAR

In his 1792 budget speech Pitt reduced defence expenditure and asserted that Europe could expect at least fifteen more years of peace. A year later the French National Convention declared war on Britain. Was Pitt complacent to the threat from France, as some historians have argued? Did he fail to appreciate that the French Revolution created the atmosphere for a crusade? Pitt had first spoken on events in France in February 1790, striking a balance between hope and caution:

> The present convulsions in France must, sooner or later, terminate in harmony and regular order . . . [but] he trusted that . . . gentlemen [ought] not to relax their exertions for the strength of the country.

Burke found in 1791 that 'there was no moving ministers from their neutrality'.

It is important to see Pitt's actions not with hindsight but in the context of traditions of non-interference in the affairs of European powers unless there was a direct threat to British interests. Pitt initially saw his responses to radical movements in Britain and military and naval action against France as temporary and regrettable expedients. They were a means of restoring the stability necessary for economic prosperity.

Pitt made this clear in his response to Fox during the debate on the suspension of Habeas Corpus in May 1794: 'the Bill was limited in its duration; that it was but a temporary measure, adapted to a present existing evil, and was to continue in force for little more than six months . . .'.[17]

Pitt did not participate in the war for general considerations. No action was taken when first Prussia and then Austria declared war on revolutionary France in 1792. The September Massacres, the declaration of the French Republic and the trial and execution of Louis XVI were insufficient to push him into war though he shared contemporary horror at these events. It was the French victory over Austrian forces at Jemeppes in November 1792 followed by the fall of Antwerp and the opening of the Scheldt estuary in defiance of treaty to all shipping which upset the balance of Britain's diplomacy. In addition the French showed themselves willing to export their revolutionary ideas by offering assistance to all people seeking to break the yoke of monarchy and tyranny.

Why France posed a threat

In two important respects France now posed a potent threat to what Pitt perceived as Britain's 'security' and once France declared war in February 1793 he could justify his actions as self-defence. From November 1792 Pitt and his Foreign Secretary, William Lord Grenville showed themselves willing to let France resolve her own internal problems if she withdrew her forces from Belgium and renounced interference with the internal government of other countries. Pitt's objective was to restore the balance of power in the Low Countries and remove the French threat from the United Provinces. French domination of the entire coastline of north-west

Europe was a threat both to Britain's domestic security and trade and it was to contest the ambitions of France in an area sensitive to British interests that Pitt went to war.

Secondly, France posed a threat to the stability of Britain's constitution through its revolutionary ideology. Reaction against reforming ideas pre-dated the outbreak of war. Edmund Burke split from the mainstream Foxite Whigs in 1791 over the revolution and took his place on the Treasury benches in 1792. Portland allowed his friends to support Pitt from late 1792, though he did not formally join Pitt's ministry as Home Secretary until 1794. 'Church and King' societies and later the Reeves Associations provided popular incentives for the government's attack on the reforming societies and from late 1792 Pitt began a campaign of repression. A Royal Proclamation condemned 'divers wicked and seditious writings' in 1792 and there was isolated prosecution of reformers between 1793 and 1795. Habeas Corpus was suspended in 1794 and in 1795 the Seditious Meetings Act banned public meetings. In 1796 stamp duties were raised on newspapers and a system of registration of printing presses was introduced. Corresponding Societies were banned as 'unlawful Combi-nations and Confederacies' in 1797 and two further acts in 1799 and 1800 banned workers' combinations. The more repressive nature of anti-reform activity was the result in part of the perceived threat from revolutionary France but also needs to be seen in the context of rising prices and inflation caused by the war and a series of poor harvests from 1794. Reform agitation outside Parliament was checked by both legislation and the strength of the anti-reform movement in the localities. Reform activity inside Parliament declined and the decisive defeat of Charles Grey's parlia-mentary reform bill by a substantial margin in 1797 reflected the strength of the conservative reaction. Patriotism and conservatism successfully countered radicalism and reform.

War policies

Pitt and Henry Dundas, his Secretary of War, thought of war in a tra-ditional eighteenth-century way.[18] This entailed a two-pronged approach. First, a 'blue-water' maritime strategy was employed where the Royal Navy was used to blockade the French coast and to pick up enemy colonies which could later be used as bargaining counters in subsequent peace negotiations. Secondly, a continental war was fought using small units of British forces, paid mercenaries and subsidized allies. Broadly the first part of this strategy was successful, the second part less so. The major problem facing Pitt in the summer of 1793 was which of the various conflicting war aims to pursue. Should he concentrate his energies in securing the Low Countries against French aggression? Should he aid counter-revolutionary forces within France to destabilize the revolutionary regime, as urged by Burke and Windham? Should the main thrust of the campaign be against French colonies? The first and third options reflected the approach used throughout the century. It was the second option which was different and brought to the war an ideological element. Both sides could see their actions in crusading terms, for and against revolutionary and republican dogmas. The conflict between these two options – peace either through military and naval victory or through the restoration of the Bourbon monarchy – was reflected within the coalition ministry: Pitt and Dundas supported the former while Burke and Windham saw the war as the means of eliminating the Jacobin heresy.

Britain could not defeat revolutionary France, with its new armies, a 'nation in arms' led by generals using unorthodox and mobile tactics, alone. The British army was too deficient in numbers and training to provide an effective continental force. Of the 50,000-strong army, half were needed for police and garrison work in Britain and most of the rest were scattered abroad. The government therefore turned to German allies for mercenaries: 14,000 Havoverians and 8,000 Hessians were taken into pay. Britain could only raise 7,000 men under the Duke of York for the Flanders campaign which began in April. Expeditions in support of French royalists in the Vendée and in Toulon were both inadequate and too late. The campaign in Flanders continued into 1794 but it was increasingly clear that Prussia and Austria were more concerned with the affairs of Poland than with the west. Austrian defeat at Fleurus compelled York to retreat across Holland, though he evacuated most of his force from Bremen in April 1795. Between 1795 and 1797 the first coalition collapsed. Prussia made peace at Basle in April 1795. The government of the United Provinces entered an alliance with France in May 1795. Spain withdrew and made a defensive–offensive alliance with France and the utter defeat of Austria in 1796 and 1797 led to peace at Campo Formio.

What gains Britain made between 1793 and 1797 were either colonial conquests or naval victories. Sea power cut the French off from their overseas empire and French and later Spanish and Dutch colonies were occupied. French settlements at Pondichery and Chandernagore in India were secured in 1793 though French influence still remained, especially in Mysore. In the West Indies Britain took Tobago in 1793 and supported a rebellion in Santo Domingo. Control was extended over the French islands of Martinique, St Lucia and Guadeloupe in 1794, though it had abandoned the last two by the end of the year. Haiti, rich in coffee, sugar and cotton, seemed to have been wrested from France and Spain when the coastal towns were captured in 1794 but it was never secured. With 40,000 men killed and a similar number incapacitated by disease, Britain lost more men in the West Indies than Wellington was to lose in the Peninsular campaigns after 1808. The Franco-Dutch alliance of 1795 led to Britain's seizure of Dutch colonies at the Cape of Good Hope, in Ceylon and in the West Indies. From the British point of view, even before the Austrians made peace, the war was reaching a stalemate. British trade and empire had been achieved through military operations backed by naval supremacy. But French mastery of Western Europe seemed complete. Two attempts were made to make peace in 1796–7: in October 1796 Lord Malmesbury was sent to Paris and this was followed by a second series of negotiations the following July at Lille. French resolve was hardened by the *coup d'état* of 18 Fructidor which marked the reassertion of Jacobin influence in the Directory government of France and negotiations foundered on demands that Britain should surrender all her conquests while France should keep all hers.

Events became increasingly unfavourable to Britain from late 1796 and Pitt found himself totally isolated and facing what has been seen as the greatest threat to national security between 1588 and 1940. The external threat of invasion was exacerbated by problems in Ireland which France was willing to exploit, naval mutinies, high prices and inflation. Naval victories over the Spanish at Cape St Vincent and the Dutch at Camperdown in February and October 1797 respectively ended French hopes of invasion. Napoleon Bonaparte persuaded the Directory of the merits of an attack on British power in India and in early 1798 French agents began to intrigue with the East India Company's greatest enemy in southern India, Tipu of Mysore. Napoleon invaded Rome and extinguished the freedom of Switzerland and, using his naval control of the Mediterranean, took Malta and defeated the rulers of Egypt. The military advantage which he had gained was eliminated by the destruction of the French fleet by Nelson at Aboukir Bay in August 1798. The implications of Nelson's victory were far-reaching. The French lost their naval supremacy in the Mediterranean and their army was stranded, though not actually defeated until 1801. In India Tipu was defeated and killed at Seringapatam in 1799 and the territorial power of the East India Company extended. In Europe the failure of the French Egyptian expedition encouraged those states with grievances to show their hand. The Ottoman Empire declared war on the invaders of their Egyptian province. With difficulty Lord Grenville reassembled a second coalition against France of Britain, Russia and Austria. As with the first coalition, early limited success was followed by disunity and defeat. Austria was defeated at Marengo and Hohenlinden in 1800 and made peace at Lunéville in 1801. Russia withdrew her support and during 1800 France cultivated good relations with Russia, Prussia and Denmark with a view to closing northern Europe to British trade. These moves threatened Britain's domestic stability since poor harvests necessitated imports of Baltic grain. Retribution for the formation of the 'Armed Neutrality of the North' and the invasion of Hanover by Danish and Prussian troops was swift. In March 1801 the Danish fleet was destroyed at anchor at Copenhagen, the invading troops were withdrawn from Hanover and relations between Britain and Russia thawed.

The consequences of the formation of the first and second coalitions were similar. In both 1797 and 1801 Britain was left isolated after France had successfully defeated the coalition armies and countries which lacked trust in each other. France's grip on Europe had been gradually tightened. The British Navy had saved Britain from invasion in 1797 and had successfully defeated the navies of France, Spain, Holland and Denmark. It had secured Britain's colonial possessions and enabled the conquest of enemy colonies in the West Indies, Africa, India and Ceylon. But it could not defeat Napoleon in Europe and its success encouraged France to concentrate more on its armies, thus increasing pressure on Britain's allies. Sea power and land power had fought each other to a standstill, each dominant in its own sphere. A compromise peace was a logical option in 1801–2 to give both sides breathing space.

Pitt fought the French War between 1793 and 1801 much as his father would have done – using Britain's naval supremacy to blockade Europe and pick off enemy colonies while subsidizing allies to fight the land war. His failure, if it can be called that, was that he had a 'limited' rather than a 'total' conception of the conflict. Pitt fought the war for commercial rather than ideological reasons and, within those limits, it was fought successfully. The logic of the effort expended to control the West Indies and India demonstrated a keen awareness of the tilt of Britain's trade away from Europe and towards American and Asian markets. This commercial bias represented nothing new. It had been a major objective of every war since the mid-seventeenth century. Pitt has been unjustly criticized for an indiscriminate and poor use of subsidies. Of the £66 million paid in subsidies between 1793 and 1815, only £9.2 million was provided before 1802. The lack of military success which these bought was a consequence of several things. Pitt's concern to keep the Low Countries out of French control was not shared by members of the two coalitions, both of which were loose federations of distrusting states. Prussia was more interested in the Baltic than the North Sea and looked to the partition of Poland to pick up more territory. Austria wished to sever her connections with Belgium and consolidate her position in central Europe. In addition the French had superior armies, generals and tactics and the British army was in no position to sustain a long continental campaign. In Europe reliance on others was unavoidable.

The expenses of war

The war was expensive for Britain and ended Pitt's economic reforms. He was hesitant about pushing up taxes and relied heavily on borrowing to finance the war which increased from £4.5 million in 1793 to £44 million by 1797. The effect was inflationary and in 1797, following a run on the banks occasioned by the French landing at Fishguard, the government authorized the Bank of England to suspend cash payments and to issue notes for small denominations (£1 and £2). Inadvertently Pitt had stumbled upon one aspect of successful wartime fiscal policy. It was not until he announced his proposals for an income tax in 1798 and its collection in 1799 that Pitt pursued other aspects of wartime fiscal policy. This graduated tax was a logical, if unpopular solution and was only accepted on the understanding that it was a temporary wartime expedient. It raised about half the £10 million Pitt had hoped to raise annually and one explanation of the support for the negotiations leading to the Peace of Amiens between 1801 and 1802 was the belief that income tax would be abolished.

Wartime ministers, especially if they do not provide outright victory, have rarely been seen as successful either by contemporaries or later historians. Pitt may well fall into this category. But to condemn him outright as inadequate fails to acknowledge his appreciation of the commercial implications of the war, the advantages which colonial conquests were to bring and the naval supremacy for which his reforms in the 1780s and early 1790s had laid the foundations. War was a necessity forced upon Pitt, who needed to make commerce and constitution secure.

AMIENS TO WATERLOO

The Peace of Amiens, negotiated by Hawkesbury (later Lord Liverpool) and Cornwallis and ratified by Parliament in May 1802, received a poor press from contemporaries and subsequently from historians.[19] The surrender of Austria deprived Britain of any leverage in Europe and Addington accepted terms which recognized French predominance on the continent and agreed to the abandonment of all overseas conquests. Grenville and Windham regarded these concessions as a disgrace and refused to give the ministry further support. This opened a split between them and Pitt, who was still prepared to give Addington assistance. Viewed simply in territorial terms Amiens was disastrous but Addington and his ministers saw it as a truce, not a final solution. Britain had been at war for nine years and Addington, previously Speaker of the House of Commons, was fully aware of growing pressures from MPs and from the nation at large for peace. Canning, one of the most vehement critics of the Peace, willingly admitted that MPs were in no mood to subject its terms to detailed scrutiny and that they would have ratified almost any terms.

Amiens to Trafalgar

In the twelve months between Amiens and the inevitable renewal of the war Addington made military and fiscal preparations which placed Britain in a far stronger position than it had been in 1793. British naval and military strength was not run down. The remobilization of the fleet proceeded well in 1803. Addington retained a regular army of over 130,000 men of which 50,000 were left in the West Indies to facilitate the prompt occupation of the islands given back in 1802 when the need arose. 81,000 men were left in Britain which, with a militia of about 50,000, provided a garrison far larger than anything Napoleon could mount for invasion in 1803. The 1803 Army of Reserve Act produced an additional 30,000 men of whom more than half later accepted transfer to the regular forces. He revived the Volunteers, backed by legislation giving him powers to raise a levy *en masse*. This raised 380,000 men in Britain and 70,000 in Ireland and by 1804 they were an effective auxiliary force. Reforms by the Duke of York improved the quality of officers and in 1802 the Royal Military College was set up. Addington improved Pitt's fiscal management of the war in his budgets of 1803 and 1804 by deducting income tax at source. This was initially set at a shilling and raised by Pitt in 1805 at 1/3d. in the pound on all income over £150. Fox, who bitterly denounced Pitt's 25 per cent increase in 1805, had now to defend a further 60 per cent increase the following year. Once war was renewed in 1803 Addington adopted a simple strategy: blockade French ports, sweep French commerce from the seas, re-occupy colonies recently returned to France and her allies and seek allies on the continent who were willing to resist French expansion.

Continuity of strategy

From 1803 until about 1810 there was little difference in Britain's strategy to that employed in the 1790s or its level of success. Addington gave way to Pitt in April 1804. Napoleon recognized that final victory depended on the conquest of Britain and during early 1805 preparations were made for an invasion. To succeed he needed to control the Channel and to prevent the formation of a European coalition against France. He failed on both counts. The destruction of a combined Franco-Spanish fleet at Trafalgar in October 1805 denied Napoleon naval supremacy and the hesitant moves of Russia and Austria against him meant that troops intended for invasion had to be diverted. Between late 1805 and 1807 France confirmed its military control of mainland Europe. Austria was defeated at Ulm and Austerlitz in October and December 1805 respectively and in January 1806 Austria made peace at Pressburg. Prussia, which had remained neutral in 1805, attempted to take on France single-handed and was defeated at Jena in October 1806; Russia, after its defeat at Friedland, made peace at Tilsit in 1807. Britain once again stood alone.

'Economic warfare'

With the prospect of successful invasion receding as a means of defeating Britain, Napoleon turned to economic warfare. This was not new. Both Pitt and the Directory had issued decrees aimed at dislocating enemy trade and food imports. The difference between Napoleon's continental system and the attempts in the 1790s was one of scale. Between 1807 and 1812 France's unprecedented control of mainland Europe meant that British shipping could, at least in theory, be excluded from the continent.

In practice, however, there were major flaws in Napoleon's policy. First, it was impossible to seal off Europe completely from British shipping: parts of the Baltic remained open as did Portugal and in 1810 Russian ports were reopened to British commerce. Secondly, in the face of French agricultural interests, Napoleon did not ban the export of wines and brandies to Britain and during the harvest shortages of 1808–10 he allowed the export of French and German wheat under licence. Thirdly and most importantly, he had no control over Britain's trade with the rest of the world and it was to this that Britain increasingly looked. Though the continental system and particularly Britain's Orders in Council were blamed for economic crisis in 1811–12 by both manufacturers and the Whigs, it has been suggested that a better explanation can be found in industrial overproduction and speculation in untried world markets. Napoleon failed to achieve an economic stranglehold because he did not have naval supremacy and because Britain's economic expansion was directed at non-European markets. The British blockade inflicted far more harm on France, whose customs receipts fell by 80 per cent between 1807 and 1809 than exclusion from Europe ever did to Britain.

The British response to the creation of the Continental System came in the form of Orders in Council. In January 1807 the Talents ministry prohibited any seaborne trade between ports under French control from which British shipping was excluded. To avoid unduly antagonizing the United States, trade by neutral shipping from the New World to French-controlled ports was unaffected. The Portland ministry took a harder line and, under pressure from the Chancellor of the Exchequer Spencer Perceval, far more draconian Orders were issued in November and December 1807. These extended exclusion to all shipping from French-controlled ports and compelled neutral traffic to pass through specific British ports, paying transit duties in the process. The major purpose of the Orders was to dislocate European commerce and as a result create discontent with the Napoleonic regime. Success in this area was achieved at the cost of further deterioration in relations with the United States. Demand for British goods meant that trade continued largely uninterrupted until America passed a Non-Importation Act in 1811. British exports to her largest single market plummeted from £7.8 million in 1810 to £1.4 million in 1811. There was a corresponding reduction in imports of raw cotton which were 45 per cent lower in 1812–14 than in 1809–11. The Anglo-American war of 1812–14 was fought largely about the Great Lakes, since the primary objective of the American 'hawks' was the conquest of Upper Canada. The New England states opposed the war vigorously and had the Orders in Council been withdrawn a few weeks earlier it would probably not have been approved by Congress. Little was achieved militarily and the most famous incident of the war, the repulse of a British attack on New Orleans, was fought a month after the war ended but before news of the Peace of Ghent reached America. The peace settled nothing and not one of the original causes of the war – for example, the boundaries between the United States and Canada or maritime rights – received any mention.

Total victory

The final phase of the war began in 1808 when Napoleon attempted to exchange influence for domination in the Iberian Peninsula. Nationalist risings in Spain against the installation of Napoleon's brother Joseph as king and anti-French hostility in Portugal, which had been annexed the previous autumn, prompted Castlereagh, Secretary of War and the Colonies, to send 15,000 troops in support. This approach conformed to the strategy used since 1793 of offering limited armed support to the opponents of France. In the next five years British troops, at no time more than 60,000 strong, led by Arthur Wellesley (created Viscount Wellington in 1809) and his Portuguese and Spanish allies fought a tenacious war with limited resources. Wellington's victory at Vimeiro in August 1808 was followed by the Convention of Cintra, negotiated by his superior, which repatriated the French troops and set Portugal free. By the time Wellington returned to the Peninsula in April 1809 it seemed that this campaign was to be no more successful than the Walcheren expedition to the Low Countries was to prove later that year. The Peninsula campaign drained Napoleon's supply of troops which he had to divert from central Europe. Calling the war the 'Spanish ulcer' was no understatement. Wellington gradually wore down French resolve and military might and it was from the Peninsula that France was first invaded when Wellington crossed the Pyrenees after his decisive victory at Vitoria in August 1813.

Napoleon's position in Europe was weakened by the unsuccessful and costly Russian campaign of 1812 and by the spring of 1813 the British government was absorbed in creating a further anti-French coalition. The Treaty of Reichenbach provided subsidies for Prussia and Russia. Separately negotiated treaties, usually under French military duress, had been a major problem of the three previous attempts at concerted allied action. Castlereagh, now Foreign Secretary, saw keeping the allies together long enough to achieve the total defeat of France as one of his primary objectives. Austria was at first unwilling to enter the coalition, fearing the aggressive aspirations of Russia as much as those of France. Castlereagh knew that a general European settlement was impossible without total victory. When he arrived in Basle in February 1814 French troops were everywhere in retreat – Napoleon had been defeated in the three-day 'Battle of the Nations' at Leipzig the previous October and Wellington had invaded south-west France – but the allies were no more trusting of each other's motives. Castlereagh demonstrated his skills as a negotiator and achieved the Treaty of Chaumont in March by which the allies pledged to keep 150,000 men each under arms and not to make a separate peace with France. Napoleon's abdication and exile to Elba in 1814 allowed Castlereagh to implement his second objective: the redrawing of the map of Europe to satisfy the territorial integrity of all nations, including France. The Congress of Vienna of 1814–15, within limits, achieved this. Napoleon's final flourish in 1815 which ended at Waterloo made no real difference.

DOMESTIC POLICIES 1806–12

Between Pitt's death in January 1806 and the formation of Liverpool's administration in 1812 domestic politics was broadly in a state of flux as the various political groupings sought formulas which would allow them to govern effectively. Fragile ministries survived from 1807 to 1812 largely because of the impotence of the Whig opposition, especially their inability to exploit popular feeling against the ministries. Attitudes towards parliamentary reform and Catholic emancipation provided the two most important constraints on achieving ministerial stability. Addington and his supporters, for example, were prepared to support the Talents ministry as long as Catholic relief was not pushed and withdrew their support when it was. Personality and ambition also played a major role. Wellington's elder brother harboured ambitions to be prime minister when Perceval's foreign secretary and antagonism between Canning and Castlereagh went so far as a duel in 1809. The parameters within which positive change could be achieved were therefore limited.

'Moral' politics

The numerical importance of the 'moral wing' in the House of Commons, personified by William Wilberforce, led to the abolition of the slave trade in 1807 and to significant attacks on corruption. Henry Dundas, Lord Melville, was unsuccessfully impeached by the Talents ministry. The Portland ministry was dogged by charges of corruption and the Duke of York was forced to resign as Commander-in-Chief following an army promotion scandal involving sale of commissions by his actress-mistress Mary Clark. Perceval took the initiative and steered a Sale of Offices Prevention Act which made soliciting money for procuring offices a penal offence. The principle was carried forward in Curwen's Act which stopped the sale of parliamentary seats, preventing the Treasury from giving financial support to the proprietors of parliamentary boroughs. There were allegations of East India Company corruption which touched Castlereagh and charges of electoral malpractice in Ireland. From 1810 to 1811 George III's final illness led to the introduction of the Regency. The assassination of Spencer Perceval in May 1812 only altered this situation in retrospect.

MANAGING WALES AND SCOTLAND

English political control and management of Wales and Scotland in the late eighteenth and early nineteenth centuries continued to mirror the methods used before 1780. Two circumstances were different. First, both Wales and Scotland began to industrialize and urbanize though both remained predominantly agrarian economies until after 1815. Secondly, reforming and revolutionary ideas reflected a revived nationalist spirit which challenged the existing anglicized social, economic and political hegemony. It is on the reaction of the governors that this section of the chapter concentrates. Ireland, by contrast, proved a far more intractable problem to the English government and, for various reasons, the late 1780s and 1790s saw a breakdown in the ability of the Protestant Ascendency to govern Ireland effectively, which led to the loss of its separate legislature in the 1800 Act of Union.

Wales

Self-interest activated the political conduct of many Welsh MPs during the American War of Independence. Some, like Edward Lewis, Capel Hanbury, Herbert Mackworth and the ironmaster Anthony Bacon held lucrative government contracts and initially backed North's policy of coercion when others doubted the wisdom of continuing the war. After 1778 there was a fall-off of Welsh support, partly as a result of lack of military success but also because North instituted an inquiry into encroachments on Crown land in Wales. Lord Bulkeley, the young Sir Watkin Williams Wynn and the members for Anglesey and Caernarfon formed 'a little parliamentary phalanx' of patriots and in five crucial divisions in 1782 more Welsh MPs voted against than for the government. North's fall brought Lord Shelburne into office and in carrying through the peace negotiations in late 1782 and early 1783 he had the support of most of the Welsh members; when Pitt came to power in late 1783 they transferred their allegiance to him.

The outbreak of the French Revolution had a far greater impact than the American Revolution, contributing much to the political education of the Welsh people. But it also bred divisions in society which were to rend the nation in the nineteenth century. The reaction to the Revolution was led by the gentry and particularly the Anglican clergy, emphasizing that the Church of England was the *only* bulwark against atheism and republicanism. Bishop Horsley of St David's wanted churchmen to extend hospitality to French Catholic clergy, arguing that he had more in common with them than with Dissenters. Prejudice stirred up by Anglicans, which led to the Birmingham riots in 1791, was exhibited at Wrexham where the ironmaster John Wilkinson was accused of French sympathies because he held interests in the French iron industry and paid his men in tokens which could only be exchanged by local Presbyterians. Loyalist associations developed in many Welsh towns in 1792: Paine was burnt in effigy in Cardiff, Carmarthen and Llandovery and loyalist workers in Merthyr execrated his name by setting their hob-nails in the pattern of his initials which they then trod under foot. Loyalist pamphlets were translated into Welsh.

The outbreak of war in 1793 greatly altered the situation since it was contrary to what all those favourable to the Revolution had expected. Religious prejudice was exploited at elections, especially by candidates who favoured Catholic emancipation, and Dissenters had to be on their guard. In 1793 the three denominations in the south-west held a meeting at Newcastle Emlyn and asserted their loyalty and respect for the constitution; the Independents' meeting at Bala hoped that reasonableness would soon return. Recruitment to the Volunteer Movement, launched in 1794, was widespread in Wales, especially after the abortive French landing at Fishguard in 1797. The Welsh gentry saw the Volunteers as a means of maintaining public order as much as security against invasion. This was reinforced by widespread rioting in 1794–5 occasioned by high food prices, extensive protests against rack-renting by landlords and the activities of the press-gang.

The gentry and clergy believed that behind the 1797 landing was the French assumption that the Welsh would rise spontaneously, though there is no evidence of widespread links with Wales as there is with Ireland. Suspicion in Pembrokeshire led to the trial of two local Dissenters who were acquitted after six months in prison. Whether this was a plot laid by the gentry and clergy against Dissenters as William Richards asserted in his *Complaint of the Afflicted*, published in Welsh in 1798, hostility against Dissenters was stepped up and the Methodists suffered by association. A Methodist 'plot' was alleged, even though the Methodists did everything possible to show their loyalty and had little sympathy with the Dissenters. Anglicans, however, were not convinced and resorted to unsuccessful harassment to try and stem the proliferating tide of societies and Sunday schools. In Merioneth, Edward Corbet, a JP, indicted local Methodists for worshipping in an unlicensed meeting-house at Corris and on his own authority had it demolished. Unlicensed preachers were brought before quarter sessions and the Bala magistrates imprisoned one for preaching at Llanrwst.

Demands for reform had been submerged by the conservative reaction of the 1790s. The first decade of the nineteenth century, however, saw increasing criticism by Welsh MPs of the workings of government and they supported moves to remove corruption and inefficiency. In the debates on the Scheldt expedition of 1809, for example, they were divided equally for and against the government. Between 1790 and 1815 certain trends in Welsh political life were becoming more obvious. First, there was a growing divergence between MPs and the people they represented. Secondly, the exploitation of the crisis caused by revolution and war by Anglican clergy had estranged them from the outlook of large sections of the population. Politically and religiously there was a growing gulf between rulers and ruled in Wales.

Scotland

For twenty-five years after 1780 the political management of Scotland was dominated by Henry Dundas of Arniston.[20] Lord Advocate in 1775, Dundas tried to expand his electoral influence in Scotland in the late 1770s to increase his bargaining power at Westminster. Of the 45 MPs elected in the 1780 election 41 reliable supporters of the government were returned and of these Dundas personally controlled twelve. The characteristic pro-government nature of the Scottish MPs is well illustrated by their voting on the Dunning proposal of the 'influence of the Crown' in 1780: 23 against, 15 absent, 7 in favour. On North's fall in 1782 Dundas transferred his allegiance to Rockingham, Shelburne and, during the Fox–North coalition, to William Pitt. In the 1784 general election he had some sort of grip over 22 Scottish seats.

Dundas as 'manager'

The 'Disannexing Act' of 1784 returned estates forfeited by the descendants of the Jacobites who had forfeited them after 1745. Dundas had agitated for this since 1775. The return of the estates, and any accumulated debts, was far more significant as political symbolism than as a transfer of property. Lenman argues:

> It set the final seal on the total reconciliation between the Scottish aristocrat, and a British government which as late as 1746 had harboured doubts as to whether there was such an animal as a reliable Scotsman. . . .[21]

Dundas, was, however, less favourably disposed to mercantile demands for reform of burghal government, the most indefensible and corrupt part of the Scottish political power structure, because his political power rested on existing social structures.

Unlike Ilay, Dundas did not expand his empire of electoral influence through collateral branches of his own family, most of whom loathed him, but by tactical alliance with regional magnates. In 1784 his influence was still centred on the Lothians in alliance with Henry, third Duke of Buccleuch. The extension of his influence in north-east Scotland in alliance with Alexander, fourth Duke of Gordon is a good example of his techniques. Late in 1783 Gordon embraced Dundas as both political guide and friend, mentioning only an English peerage as an appropriate object of his ambition. He achieved a hereditary seat in the Lords in 1784 when he was made Baron Gordon of Huntly and Earl of Norwich. Yet the Dundas–Gordon axis faced opposition from the rival electoral interests of the Earl of Fife and by 1787 Dundas was trying to force through a compromise with the earl, which was eventually successful. The Wemyss interest in Fife was bought out with British and West India appointments in 1788, and the enlarged alliance swept the north-east in the 1790 elections. A similar pact finalized in 1789 with the Earl of Eglinton gave Dundas control of Ayrshire. The overall success of Dundas' strategy can be seen in the 1790 election where only nine counties and seven burghs were contested and up to 34 of the 45 MPs were of the Dundas interest. The Scottish ruling class had moved, partly out of conviction, partly through systematic pressure and corruption and partly for gain, into becoming supporters of William Pitt.

Dundas represented both the internal and external expansion of the British state. The patronage he obtained through his interest in India was used to bind together his domestic political empire. Dundas was one of the leading members of the Board of Control set up by the India Act from its inception in 1784 until 1801 and in 1793 the salaried office of President of the Board of Trade was created for him. In his Indian appointments Dundas favoured his fellow Scotsmen and looked after his relatives: for example, Sir Archibald Campbell was appointed Governor of Madras in 1787, Colonel Colin Mackensie rose to be the first Surveyor-General of India from 1815 to his death in 1822. Scots, like the soldier Sir David Blair and the administrator Mountstuart Elphinstone, were prominent in the conquest and organization of the successful Mysore and Maratha wars between 1798 and 1805.

Bruce Lenman argues that the greatest achievement of the Pitt–Dundas axis was the general overhauling and professionalization of government in the aftermath of the American war. Scotsmen played a major part in the redefinition of the appropriate place of the state in society. Scottish intellectuals like Sir James Steuart and especially Adam Smith made a fundamental contribution to economic and fiscal policies. They were to the fore in most areas where state power was being consolidated, rationalized or made more morally defensible. Patrick Colquhoun, a former Glasgow merchant who became a London magistrate, was a leading figure in the debate on law and order in the 1790s. Scottish intellectuals also played an important role in the single most successful gesture of moral validation undertaken before 1832, the campaign against negro slavery. The degree of influence which the Scottish educational system, and especially its medical schools, had on England was a reflection of its higher quality and of the fact that opportunities for advancement were greater in England than they were in Scotland.

The outbreak of the French war consolidated Dundas' grip on Scottish political life. He crushed disaffection by the Marquis of Tweeddale in Haddingtonshire in 1795 and wrested control of Kircudbrightshire from the Earl of Galloway by a flood of patronage the same year. He was made Home Secretary and, in 1794, Secretary of State for War and these offices, as well as his Indian interest, enhanced the patronage at his disposal. Detailed management of Scotland was transferred to his nephew, the Lord Advocate Robert Dundas of Arniston. His task was eased since virtually the entire membership of Scotland's ruling class rallied to the regime under the pressures of patriotism and social panic. The 1796 election confirmed his hegemony. He supported Pitt's union of Ireland and resigned with Pitt over Catholic emancipation in 1801.

From Dundas to Dundas

From 1801 Dundas' power was less secure though still strong. He supported Addington's administration in the 1802 election, securing the return of a squad of 31 MPs. This marked a marginal but nonetheless significant erosion of his interest, especially as he lost control in Fife and Stirling. Elevated to the peerage as Viscount Melville by Addington, he returned to office as First Lord of the Admiralty in Pitt's new administration, but charges of corruption led to his resignation and impeachment in 1805. Pitt's death in early 1806 finished Dundas as an active politician. The restoration of the Dundas regime was led by his only son, Robert Saunders Dundas, which occurred in the next two years. The 1807 election saw a Dundas phalanx of only 24 MPs but its control over the peers' election was impressive and by 1811 Robert, second Viscount Melville had already smoothly succeeded to his father's regional political empire.

Henry Dundas' control of the Scottish political system must not be overestimated. Comprehensive as it was, he was unable to crush all opposition. The party manager of the Foxite Whigs after 1789 was William Adam, a Scottish laird from Fife but in general Scottish Whigs, initially led by James Maitland, eighth Earl of Lauderdale and then by an Irish earl, Lord Moira, were rarely effective. Dundas was able, for example, to exclude Lauderdale from the Lords in 1796 and 1802. The conservative reaction in Scotland had been very successful but at a cost that became evident after 1815. English Tories became more pragmatic and within limits, reformist but at the cost of internal conflict and division. Scottish Tories, locked into a system in which politics had been reduced to the manipulation of patronage, had no such flexibility.

IRELAND

Ireland generally proved more difficult to manage and govern than Wales or Scotland during the eighteenth century.[22] Jacobitism never achieved the same numerical significance as Irish Catholicism and, although it created rifts within Welsh and Scottish societies they were largely within the ruling elites. Religious belief in Ireland created a chasm within society between minority Protestants who had authority, wealth and civil liberties and majority Catholics who were generally poor and subject to political, social, religious and educational discrimination. Irish society was inherently more unstable than the societies in mainland Britain and it was this instability which accounted for the impact which external factors had, particularly in the 1790s.

Problems of governing

The problem of governing Ireland was not simply one of Protestant versus Catholic. The debate on the proper relationship between England and Ireland was between Protestants as well as between Catholics and Protestants. Though the eighteenth century saw the emergence of an intelligentsia, particularly in Dublin, the bulk of the Catholic population was uneducated, with stunted political aspirations and highly conservative views. Their aims were primarily economic, though they can also be seen as attacks on an alien agrarian and religious system; the reduction of rents and the end of the tithe. Their tactics and the responses of landlords were fairly basic. The Whiteboys, the collective term for the various agrarian terrorist organizations, burnt ricks, maimed animals, destroyed crops and attacked those fellow Irishmen who buttressed the system. The landlords used their powers of eviction to exert economic and social intimidation. The political dimension was in embryonic form and it was the Protestant minority, Anglican and Presbyterian, who took up the broader question of political rights. Between 1778 and 1782 concessions were granted by Westminster. The American War of Independence was unpopular since it closed one of the few substantial markets permitted by Britain but there was also considerable sympathy with American struggles to free themselves from English control. The threat of French invasion after 1778 and the growing strength of the 'Patriots' in the Irish Parliament led to concessions: in 1779–80 Ireland was given the right to export wool and glass and to trade with all Britain's overseas possessions except those administered by the East India Company and in 1782 the Dublin Parliament was given legislative autonomy, though this was far from meaning independence for Irish Protestants or the Irish nation as a whole.

Pitt's early policies

The potential dangers of this constitutional situation became clear in the early part of Pitt's ministry. The emancipation of the Irish Parliament made the British ministry's control over Irish tariff policy difficult despite the assumption that the co-ordination of policies was an explicit part of the commercial concessions of 1779–80. In 1783 popular demands in Dublin for protection of the nascent sugar-refining industry cut across that settlement and threatened the interest of mainland sugar refiners. The prospect of a tariff war between Ireland and Britain was made more likely by widespread rioting in Dublin in early 1784 and, as a result, Irish politicians approached Westminster with a request for additional concessions. Parallel to this were demands for further political reform including a limited emancipation of Catholics. It was this issue, as well as the radical nature of many of the reform proposals, which led to the rejection of reform bills introduced in November 1783 and March 1784 by the Dublin Parliament.

Pitt took on board both the economic and political issues in 1785. He was prepared to give substantial commercial concessions and strengthen the power of the Irish Commons, though only as an instrument of the Protestant Ascendancy, provided Dublin would bind itself to making a contribution to imperial defence which would increase in proportion to the country's wealth and revenue. His proposals were vehemently opposed in both Britain and Ireland. British manufacturing and commercial interests, led by Josiah Wedgewood, thought Pitt had gone too far in his trading concessions. The Irish Parliament wanted acceptance of their demands for local tariff protection against British goods, not free trade. There were also good political reasons for rejecting Pitt's scheme. Irish parliamentary leaders were on the defensive against the radical, largely middle-class, movement for political reform which they believed aimed at reducing aristocratic government and increasing the prospects of Catholic emancipation. Though Pitt amended the proposals they were dropped when it became obvious that they would not pass the Irish Commons. Anglo-Irish commercial co-operation remained dependent on the 1779–80 concessions and in fact proved quite successful. In 1786 the Dublin legislature adjusted tariffs in line with the Anglo-French treaty and in 1787 passed a Navigation Act which conformed to the British 1786 Act.

Pitt fails

Pitt's failure to achieve substantial economic reform revealed that the Irish Parliament might at any time run out of control and could not be relied upon to conform to policies put before it by Westminster. The major difficulty was over what the political concessions of 1782 actually meant in practice. Parliamentary independence did not mean that Ireland had been freed from British executive control through the Crown-appointed Lord Lieutenant and Chief Secretary. After 1782 great care was taken to ensure that Irish administration was controlled by men loyal to the British interest. By contrast Dublin parliamentary reformers and the extra-parliamentary radicals of the 1790s believed that 1782 had given them independence of action and that without substantial political reform that independence could not be fully expressed. The Irish House of Commons was far more 'managed' than the British and this did not change after 1782.

The economic prosperity of the 1780s had different effects on Irish society. For those with property, Ireland shared in Pitt's national revival. The 1784 Corn Law encouraged the production of grain for British markets. The linen trade expanded and exports tripled between 1781 and 1792. But the bulk of Irish society did not benefit from these improvements. Demographic growth – Ireland's population rose by 29 per cent between 1781 and 1801 compared to a rise of only 13 per cent in England – created a major agrarian crisis. Land was subdivided to such an extent that by 1800 more than half the population tilled soil which could not support their needs. The move to grain cultivation did little to alleviate the situation since grain was grown for the British market and was too expensive for the bulk of the Irish population. Rural terrorism and incendiarism increased as a result. There was little difference between the approaches to exploiting land hunger of Protestant landowners and the small minority of Catholics who, since 1778, held equal rights in the purchase and disposal of estates. Both pushed up rents and held down wages.

France and Ireland

The French Revolution led to renewed demands for political reform and to the final breakdown of the government of the Protestant Ascendancy. The reform agitation of the 1780s in both Britain and Ireland had been largely among the land-owning interest but in the 1790s it was concentrated among shopkeepers and skilled urban workers. The Belfast Society of United Irishmen, formed under the initial leadership of a Protestant lawyer Wolfe Tone, sought full reform of the Dublin Parliament and the establishment of a legislature free of religious discrimination. The United Irishmen alarmed reformers like Henry Grattan because they attempted to forge a new alliance between the politically literate Presbyterian minority in Dublin and Belfast and the rural Catholic majority. The problem they faced was one of different levels of political consciousness: an enlightened, urban ideology in which sectarian supremacy and bitterness had no place and a crude, bitter and sectarian Catholic ideology. Outside the major urban centres the original United Irishmen's intentions broke down into violent, sectarian feuding between the Protestant 'Peep O'Day Boys', which developed into the Orange Society after 1795, and Catholic 'Defenders'.

Pitt did not accept the majority view of the Dublin Parliament that Anglo-Irish interdependence could be guaranteed only by continued Catholic oppression and he attempted to win over the Catholic gentry. In 1792 an Irish Catholic Relief Act freed Catholics from remaining disabilities relating to mixed marriages, education and the profession of the law. In 1793 they were given the same municipal and parliamentary franchise as Protestants and most civil and military offices were opened to them. However, they remained debarred from membership of the Irish Parliament or from holding military rank above colonel and in practice they remained excluded from borough guilds and corporations. Attempts to make the dominance of the Protestant Ascendancy less unpalatable resulted in the reduction of the number of pensions, the disfranchisement of revenue officers and the disqualification of certain place-holders from membership of the legislature.

Rebellion

Pitt's reforms satisfied nobody. Protestant fears of eventual Catholic domination were heightened and there was a further hardening of sectarian divisions. Radicals like Tone condemned them as sham reforms, pinning their hopes on a French invasion to coincide with the rebellion they were striving for. Sectarian divisions were increased by measures designed to protect Ireland from invasion: between 1793 and 1796 a Militia Act was passed, a new Protestant Yeomanry formed, an Insurrection Act, which made oath-taking a capital offence, became law and Habeas Corpus was suspended. The appointment of Earl Fitzwilliam, a leading Portland Whig, as Chief Secretary in early 1795 focused attention on the issue of how far Pitt could uphold the interests of the Protestant Ascendancy. Fitzwilliam believed that the stability and loyalty of Ireland necessitated both the purging of the dominant party of John Beresford, Commissioner of Revenues since 1780, and conceding Catholic claims for equal political rights. Fitzwilliam was replaced by Pitt's friend, the second Earl Camden in March 1795, falling victim to Portland's conviction that the newly formed coalition must be held together. Beresford and other officials were reinstated and emancipation dropped. Ian Christie maintains:

> Probably whichever way events in Ireland had gone in 1795 the results would have been divisive. As it was, bitterness was kindled between the Catholics and the Protestant Ascendancy and grievances remained to provide a pretext for extremists.[23]

The appeal of the United Irishmen was to Irish nationalism. They exploited every grievance, commercial or otherwise, which could be attributed to the British connection and fostered a sense of Irish identity based on geographical separation. Officially suppressed in 1794, the United Irishmen went underground and Wolfe Tone and his immediate circle were prepared to accept French assistance to achieve revolution in Ireland. Bad weather prevented the French landing troops at Bantry Bay in December 1796 and British repression in 1797 in Antrim and Down significantly weakened the northern United Irishmen. The 1798 rising was, in many respects, a prolonged and flabby failure. Most of the Dublin leadership of the United Irishmen were arrested in March 1798. Repression in 1797 kept the Ulster rising within manageable proportions. The Catholic rising in the south-east was, after some initial success, shattered at Vinegar Hill in June and the French landed too late to be of any real value.

Union

Sectarian violence finally convinced Pitt that the Protestant Ascendancy could not keep Ireland loyal. Constitutional union of the two kingdoms became increasingly attractive in ministerial circles and by June 1798 it emerged as the only safe solution. Camden was replaced by Earl Cornwallis as Lord Lieutenant and Commander-in-Chief with Lord Castlereagh as Chief Secretary. Between late 1798 and the successful passage of the Union Act in 1800 they worked together to obtain safe majorities in both Houses of the Irish Parliament. This proved far from easy. Pitt, Grenville and other liberal-minded politicians believed that removal of the remaining disabilities against Catholics was essential to ensure their support for union. In this they faced opposition not only from the Protestant Ascendancy and politicians in Westminster, but from George III. An initial rejection of a bill of Union in Dublin in January 1799 was followed by a year of negotiation and bribery which ensured the passage of the bill a year later. At Westminster the Act of Union was approved without any difficulty. Critics denounced Castlereagh's activities as pure corruption but recent investigation has shown that the swing of Irish parliamentary opinion between 1799 and 1800 cannot be explained simply in these terms. Only twelve MPs who opposed the bill in 1799 voted for it in 1800. Some potentially dangerous opposition was bought off by giving financial compensation to those who were to lose the benefits of pocket boroughs: Lord Downside, who opposed union, pocketed £50,000 while Lord Ely, who supported it, got £15,000. The bulk of support for the 1800 Act came from MPs elected to the sixty seats which changed hands between the two votes on union. In Ulster Presbyterians supported union on the grounds that the Westminster Parliament would be less hostile to them than that in Dublin and accepted Castlereagh's argument that the linen trade in Londonderry and Belfast could only gain from the closer economic association with the British empire of trade which union would bring.

Each of the 32 Irish counties retained their two representatives. Two were given to Dublin and Cork and one to Dublin University and the 31 single-member Irish borough constituencies. This eliminated the mass of rotten- and pocket-borough representation that characterized the old Irish electoral system. Ireland was given a representation of 29 in the Westminster House of Lords, election being for life. One archbishop and three bishops, chosen on the principle of rotation, spoke for the Established Church. Irish peers, who did not become representative peers, could sit in the Commons for mainland constituencies. The Anglican Churches of England and Ireland were united and Ireland was to contribute almost 12 per cent of the UK budget, though the two Exchequers remained separate until 1817. The Act conferred full equality of commercial rights and privileges though Castelreagh did secure twenty years' modest protection for Irish textile manufacturers.

The Act of Union did nothing to resolve the major issues of alienation and tension within Irish society: land tenure and religion. Demographic growth intensified land hunger after 1801 and the identification in the popular mind of landlord interests with Union was a guarantee of continued disaffection. Economic discrimination buttressed religious cleavage with Presbyterian and prosperous Ulster set apart from the Catholic agrarian south. The response of the UK Parliament was to increase landlord powers of eviction and each addition to the statute books reinforced Catholic beliefs that rights could only be gained by direct action.

Committed as Pitt and some of his colleagues were to Catholic emancipation, in 1800 they were unable to win over the king and in February 1801 Pitt resigned over the policy which he saw as necessary. Far from eliminating the Catholic question, Union merely pushed it more directly on to the British political scene. By 1805 Catholic demands for political emancipation were under the leadership of the young wealthy Catholic, James Ryan, and as a result of his efforts, the first of many petitions on the subject was presented to Parliament. Rebuffed by the Talents ministry in 1806, Ryan formed the more broadly based Catholic Association in Ireland to co-ordinate and intensify the campaign. By the beginning of 1807 the ministry suggested that concessions should be made but, as in 1801, the king refused to accept them and dismissed the ministry. The 1807 general election showed the overwhelmingly anti-Catholic nature of popular sentiment in Britain. A Relief Act in 1813 did little more than remove inconsistencies in Acts passed in Dublin and London before Union and made no concession to Irish claims to full emancipation. Up to 1815 Irish Catholicism was, according to Ian Christie, 'an unsatisfied and potentially revolutionary force'.[23]

NOTES

1 J. W. Derry 'Governing Temperament under Pitt and Liverpool', in J. Cannon (ed.) *The Whig Ascendancy: Colloquies on Hanoverian England*, Edward Arnold, 1981, p. 125. J. W. Derry *Politics in the Age of Fox, Pitt and Liverpool*, Macmillan, 1990 provides the most recent general survey.

2 The most convenient general works on this period are A. Briggs *The Age of Improvement 1783–1867*, Longman, 1959, I. R. Christie *Wars and Revolutions: Britain 1760–1815*, Edward Arnold, 1982 and E. J. Evans *The Forging of the Modern State: Early Industrial Britain 1783–1870*, Longman, 1983. H. T. Dickinson (ed.) *Britain and the French Revolution 1789–1815*, Macmillan, 1989 contains excellent essays.

3 I. R. Christie *The End of the North Ministry 1780–1782*, Macmillan, 1958 and J. Cannon *The Fox–North Coalition: Crisis of the Constitution 1782–4*, Cambridge University Press, 1969 provide the detailed narrative.

4 A. Briggs, op. cit. pp. 84–5.

5 J. W. Derry *The Regency Crisis and the Whigs 1788–9*, Cambridge University Press, 1963 deals with the crisis facing Pitt. The position of and problems facing the Whigs can best be approached briefly in E. J. Evans *Political Parties in Britain 1783–1867*, Methuen, 1985, B. W. Hill *British Parliamentary Parties*

1742–1832, Allen & Unwin, 1985 and F. O'Gorman *The Emergence of the Two Party System 1760–1832*, Edward Arnold, 1982 and in more detail in L. G. Mitchell *Charles James Fox and the Disintegration of the Whig Party 1782–94*, Cambridge University Press, 1971, D. E. Ginter *Whig Organisation in the General Election of 1790*, University of California Press, 1967 and F. O'Gorman *The Whig Party and the French Revolution*, Macmillan, 1967. J. Derry 'The Opposition Whigs and the French Revolution 1789–1815', in H. T. Dickinson (ed.) op. cit. pp. 39–60 is an excellent summary.

6 F. O'Gorman *The Emergence*, op. cit., p. 20.

7 On Edmund Burke there is a convenient collection of his major writings selected and edited by B. W. Hill entitled *Edmund Burke on Government, Politics and Society*, Fontana, 1975 and Conor Cruise O'Brien had edited *Reflections of the Revolution in France*, Penguin, 1973. C. B. Macpherson *Burke*, Oxford University Press, 1980 is a convenient and short, if contentious, study of his life.

8 E. J. Evans op. cit., p.13.

9 J. W. Derry 'Governing temperament' op. cit.

10 ibid. p. 128.

11 H. D. Harvey *Britain in the Early Nineteenth Centry*, Batsford, 1978 provides the most detailed, recent account of this period. J. J. Sack *The Grenvillites 1801–1829: Party Politics and Factionalism in the Age of Pitt and Liverpool*, University of Illinois Press, 1979 and J. P. Jupp's biography of Grenville, Oxford University Press, 1985 are substantial contributions to party political history. M. Roberts *The Whig Party 1807–1812*, Macmillan, 1939 is still essential for the Whig dilemma.

12 F. O'Gorman op. cit. p. 34.

13 Two of the three proposed volumes of Pitt's biography by J. Ehrman have appeared so far: *The Younger Pitt: The Years of Acclaim*, Constable, 1969 and *The Younger Pitt: The Reluctant Transition*, Constable, 1983. J. Holland Rose *William Pitt and the Great War*, 1911 is still of value for the later period. C. Emsley *British Society and the French Wars 1793–1815*, Macmillan, 1979, is excellent on the impact of the war as is his paper in H. T. Dickinson (ed.) op. cit., pp. 211–28.

14 J. M. Bourne *Patronage and Society in Nineteenth-Century England*, Edward Arnold, 1986.

15 E. J. Evans *The Forging of the Modern State*, op. cit. p. 31.

16 *Speeches of William Pitt*, London, 1806 Vol. II, p. 46.

17 In addition to the discussion of the war in the textbooks cited above see the readable general accounts of A. Bryant *The Years of Endurance 1793–1802*, 1942 and *Years of Victory 1802–1812*, 1944. On the naval war see G. J. Marcus *A Naval History of England*, Vol. II, *The Age of Nelson*, 1971. Diplomacy can be approached in P. Langford *The Eighteenth Century 1688–1815*, A & C Black, 1976 and M. Duffy 'British Diplomacy and the French Wars 1789–1815', in H. T. Dickinson (ed.) op. cit. pp. 127–46.

18 Developments in the period between 1801 and 1812 can be approached in A. D. Harvey op. cit. and through biographies. P. Ziegler *Addington: A Life of Henry Addington, first Viscount Sidmouth*, Collins, 1965 is a sympathetic account of an individual castigated throughout his career. D. Grey *Spencer Perceval 1762–1812, the Evangelical Prime Minister*, Manchester University Press, 1965, N. Gash *Lord Liverpool*, Weidenfeld, 1984, W. Hinde *George Canning*, 1973, J. W. Derry *Charles James Fox*, 1972 and *Castlereagh*, Allen Lane, 1976 and E. Longford *Wellington: The Years of the Sword*, Weidenfeld, 1969 cover the major protagonists.

19 B. Lenman *Integration, Enlightenment and Industrialisation: Scotland*

1746–1832, Edward Arnold, 1981 is the most accessible study. H. Furber *Henry Dundas, First Viscount Melville 1742–1811*, Oxford University Press, 1931 is still the standard biography.

20 B. Lenman op. cit. p. 75.
21 In addition to the general works of Ireland cited in earlier chapters see E. T. Johnston *Great Britain and Ireland*, Edinburgh, 1963, A. P. F. Malcolmson *John Foster: The Politics of the Anglo-Irish Ascendancy*, Oxford University Press, 1978, G. Bolton *The Passing of the Irish Act of Union*, Oxford University Press, 1966 and the early sections of J. W. Derry's biography of Castlereagh, op. cit. T. Pakenham *The Year of Liberty*, Panther, 1972 provides a useful narrative of 1798.
22 I. R. Christie *Wars and Revolutions* op. cit. pp. 221–2.
23 ibid., p. 300.

7 The aristocratic elite and the political process – the Liverpool Administration 1812–27

... little in Liverpool's career suggests a Prime Minister of other than modest capabilities. His strength was his capacity for survival, a capacity buttressed by the willingness of innately more able men to serve under him rather than under an abler rival to themselves.[1]

In December 1828 the most underrated prime minister of the century died almost unnoticed. Liverpool's government, in structure and appearance the last of the long eighteenth-century administrations, in outlook and achievement was the first of the nineteenth-century conservative ministries. . . . The essence of the Liverpool system was opposition to constitutional changes combined with innovation in administrative and social policy.[2]

Benjamin Disraeli called Liverpool 'an arch mediocrity' and, until recently, this view of him has been largely accepted by historians.[3] Was he a politician of limited ability who only retained power because more capable colleagues were more prepared to serve under him than under each other? Or was he a skilful politician combining reactionary and forward-looking policies using the collective talents of his ministers? When he became Prime Minister in 1812 Liverpool already had considerable experience in both the Commons and the Lords. Born in 1770, Robert Banks Jenkinson sat as MP for Appelby from 1790 to 1796 and for Rye from 1796 to 1803 when he became Baron Hawkesbury. He became second Earl of Liverpool in 1808. He was Master of the Mint from 1799 to 1801, Addington's Foreign Secretary between 1801 and 1804, Home Secretary 1804–6 and 1807–9 and, under Spencer Perceval, Secretary for War and the Colonies. One thing, however, is certain: Liverpool's ministry is most easily remembered for its longevity. Unlike most ministries it was not one of growing strength and gradual decline. It was at its weakest between 1815 and 1822 when its popularity in the country was at a low ebb. In contrast between 1822 and 1827 it had a strength which was impaired only by conflicts within the cabinet. Its end came suddenly with Liverpool's physical collapse in February 1827. This chapter will examine the ways in which the Tory and Whig parties developed between 1812 and

1827, focusing on the three different phases of Liverpool's rule and the inability of the Whigs to mount a consistently successful opposition. It will consider the major problems which government faced at home and the ministry's responses to these challenges. Foreign policy will be examined in Chapter 17. Finally it will consider developments in Wales, Scotland and Ireland.[4]

EIGHTEENTH-CENTURY ASSUMPTIONS UNDER THREAT

Political and constitutional assumptions

Just how far had the processes which characterized eighteenth-century politics changed by 1812 and how did this affect Liverpool? What impact did the wars between 1793 and 1815 have on British society? These questions need to be approached first because they, to a certain extent, set the parameters within which Liverpool thought and worked and the challenges which faced him and his ministers. British government in 1812 was, as it had been in 1714, based upon a Protestant Ascendancy. The fundamental feature of the constitution remained the identification of Church and state, meshed together under aristocratic supervision. At local and national levels the basic assumption was that only men with property, preferably landed property, were fit to be given power and authority and that they should be in communion with the Anglican Church or, in Scotland, the Presbyterian Church. The justification for this situation was threefold. First, only men of property could be trusted to act responsibly since they alone had a stake in the community. Secondly, Dissenters and Catholics had shown themselves, especially in the seventeenth century, to be unreliable and subversive and thirdly, the three sources of power in Parliament – Monarch, Lords and Commons – balanced each other, preventing a drift into distorted and repressive constitutional forms.[5]

By 1812 the assumptions behind this interlocking constitution were seen by many as increasingly dubious. The gradual decline of the power of the Crown, not evident until after 1780, called the notion of constitutional balance into question and raised the prospect of a struggle for power between the aristocratic and popular elements; any fundamental reform of Church or state threatened the dismantling of the entire system. By 1812 demands for concessions by those excluded from power – Dissenters and, especially in Ireland Catholics, the expanding 'middling classes' and the 'lower orders' – were growing. Pitt's claims that economic, social and political security depended on the constitution was echoed by Huskisson in his opposition to the Repeal of the Test and Corporation Acts in 1828 when he insisted that religion could not be treated in isolation. The Acts were part 'of the system as a whole, one portion of which could not be properly dealt with. . . . The strength, and security, and prosperity, of the empire mainly depended on the present system.'[6] In the 1780s and especially under the threat from France in the 1790s Pitt could justify this view. It had popular support and could be sustained against a radical attack. By the late 1820s despite the continued importance of anti-Catholicism, it could not.

The impact of revolution and war

Liverpool and his colleagues turned to images of the 1780s and 1790s – national revival and revolutionary threat – in the aftermath of the French war for their models of government and administration. Clive Emsley writes that

> The men who governed Britain in 1815, and for the next fourteen years, had inherited the watchwords 'Church and State' together with great fear of popular disorder and revolution. . . . Their desire for government efficiency to win the war led them to support, and often initiate administrative reforms; such reform was rarely apparent to the public at large. Their fear of organic change in the Constitution, to which they were indebted for their position and their power, led them to set their face against all popular demands for major reform.[7]

For many who played major roles in British politics in the 1810s and 1820s Pitt was, in Michael Bentley's words, 'a mental reference-point of luminous importance'. This looking backwards for a definition of statesmanship and successful government – a recurrent feature in British politics – helped to determine how politicians perceived change since 1793.

The suggestion that the French wars were generally beneficial to both British society and economy tends to be based on the fact that, unlike in earlier or later conflicts, Britain fought a major war and actually got richer.[8] Historians, however, differ in their estimation of their impact. E. P. Thompson suggests that the wars were crucial in reducing the pre-war socio-economic status of the labouring population and that this led directly to the emergence of a working-class consciousness. Asa Briggs maintains that cotton and pottery industries would have expanded more without the war and that the iron industry and agriculture would have been spared post-war recession.

In 1793 Britain was already the most powerful trading nation in the world and her internal economy was geared to overseas commerce to a greater extent than any of her rivals. This commercial lead was, in part, due to superior technology, though it is important not to exaggerate the extent of this advantage. Britain's economy expanded more rapidly than her rivals not because of labour-saving devices but because commercial and industrial sectors had more capital investment and entrepreneurial enterprise. From 1793 until the introduction of the Continental System and Britain's retaliatory Orders in Council in 1806–7 industries, especially those with a direct interest in war, showed continued growth. Progress in cotton and woollen textiles was interrupted only by the financial crises of 1797, 1799 and 1803. American imports of raw cotton grew from £0.5 million in 1793 to over £10 million by 1801. Demand for ordnance was the main cause of growth in the iron industry, though unreliable imports from Sweden and Russia and growing domestic demand played an important part. There was a marked increase in capital investment in agriculture. Enclosure continued rapidly and wasteland, in peacetime an unprofitable asset, was brought into cultivation. Output increased by half between 1795 and 1815. Landlords benefited from higher rents and tenants from wartime prices. Prices fell between 1801 and 1804 but generally during the war years they were consistently and significantly higher than prices since 1714. Britain's naval supremacy enabled her to eliminate foreign trading competition and the 'Atlantic sector' of the European economy more or less collapsed. Neutral countries benefited from the war, as long as they remained neutral. The United States, for example, made net profits of $42 million in 1807 but this declined with deteriorating relations with Britain and by 1814 had slumped to $2.6 million. American trade did not return to its 1807 level for twenty years after 1814.

Despite the expansion of both trade and industry it is important not to paint too optimistic a picture of the British economy during the wars. There were domestic difficulties leading to a decline in the real (and sometimes the nominal) earnings of the working population, precipitating food riots and industrial unrest. Luddism, for example, was caused less by recession than by the ready availability of industrial capital which made the introduction of mechanized processes economically advantageous.

First, there was wartime inflation. Between 1793 and 1815 domestic prices rose at about 3.3 per cent per annum. This was caused by a combination of bad harvests and trade fluctuations periodically forcing up prices while the increased money in circulation prevented them from returning subsequently to their former levels. The suspension of cash payments in 1797 and the introduction of paper money was not accompanied by any control over the amount of paper in circulation. The face value of notes in circulation may have more than doubled by 1815. That inflation was no more than 3.3 per cent per annum was an indication that economic expansion absorbed most of the increase in the money supply and easy money was probably the crucial factor enabling wartime expansion. A. D. Harvey maintains that industrial entrepreneurs and farmers were more able to exploit ready money than employees, landlords and rentiers and that these years saw a 'substantial accumulation of economic power in the hands of entrepreneurs, at the expense both of bourgeois rentiers and workers'.[9] Harvey also argues that taxation favoured entrepreneurs. Taxable income from industrial and commercial profits hardly increased between 1803 and 1813 while income under agricultural profits went up by a half in the same period. It was much easier for entrepreneurs than farmers to evade taxation.

That government contributed little to this economic expansion is not surprising.[10] Its creation of easy money after 1797 was the result of political expediency rather than any rational calculation of economic advantage. The scope of central government was small and the size of its executive departments and the revenues at their disposal correspondingly limited. Inflation, rising levels of personal taxation and the expansion of the national debt increased popular prejudice against enlarging the cost of state administration. Calls for 'cheap and efficient government' were characteristic not simply of radical and reformers but of opposition politicians, independent MPs and cabinet ministers. Liverpool did not express a minority opinion when he said: 'government or Parliament never meddle with these matters [industrial relations] at all but they do harm, more or less'.[11]

State intervention, as well as costing money, was seen by contemporaries as an attack on vested interests and the rights of property and as an unwarranted enlargement of executive powers. This is not to say that government never intervened. For example, the 1817 Poor Employment Act authorized loans for providing public works and the 1819 Factory Act protected children in cotton mills. But these measures tended to be responses to specific circumstances and piecemeal solutions rather than part of any coherent programme for social and economic protection. Such was prevailing opinion that what Thomas Carlyle saw as 'an abdication on the part of the governors' occurred with the repeal of obsolete and unwanted statutes, like the Statute of Artificers, which had provided a structure of legislative control and protection for society at large. But problems do not simply disappear and gradually, beginning under Pitt and continued under Liverpool, government administration became more efficient and complex and less pragmatic. The notion of planned change, grasped in embryonic form by Pitt's decision to base his fiscal changes on recommendations from the Public Accounts Commissioners, became an accepted part of government under Liverpool. Government had ceased merely to react, it had begun to initiate in a positive manner.[12]

Michael Bentley is critical of historians who discuss Britain's political arrangements in terms of 'the unreformed system'. What existed was hardly systematic nor part of a conscious design but a consequence of tradition and long-term historical development – Walter Bagehot later called it the 'cake of custom' – but it informed equally the perspectives of politicians and those outside the political nation. Paradoxically these seemingly ossified arrangements were capable of shifts of emphasis and Liverpool had fewer resources at his disposal to maintain his position than William Pitt.

A decline in the 'power of the Crown'

There had been a significant decline in the power of monarchy since 1780. George III may have been able to dismiss the 'Talents' ministry in 1807 and influence the outcome of the general election later that year but the slide towards monarchical impotence was to be an absolute one. The final breakdown of the king in 1811 and the establishment of the Regency continued the process. George IV, as regent and king, had neither the personal respect or political authority of his father. The power of the monarch to control cabinets and manipulate electors had receded before the attack on sinecures and all forms of patronage. Parallel to this were changes in the House of Lords which, according to Bentley, 'had begun its transition from power to rank, from the pinnacle of the political structure to the apex of social hierarchy'.[13] This was a gradual process and peerage control over cabinet places only declined slowly after 1812. In 1810 there were only two ministers who were commoners. This had become six by 1818 and remained at that level for much of the rest of the century.

Parliament

The decline in the power of the Crown and the, as yet indeterminate, alteration in the House of Lords resulted in the House of Commons being the centre of political ambition and executive preoccupation. The composition of the Commons remained in 1815 little different from that of 1780. There was no noticeable influx of army officers or merchants. Lawyers had been powerful throughout the eighteenth century but did not reach their greatest influence until after 1832. Family connection retained its importance as a bonding agent. Two important developments were, however, evident by the 1810s. First, the basic weakness of the constitution can be shown by the looseness of control of the executive over the legislature. This was far more apparent to ministers than to the public. Radicals assumed that the Commons was under the domination of ministers through their concentration on the defects and abuses of electoral arrangements. The existence of bribery and nomination and the less tangible factors of influence and connection pointed to a corrupt system of government in which county elections were often settled by agreement between the dominant interests and borough seats could easily be bought. This belief has to be seen in the context of the degree of independence inside and the power of public opinion outside the House of Commons and the impact of 'economical reform' upon the physical ability of the executive to 'manage' the legislature.

Secondly, the House of Commons, though it still bore the characteristics of a body whose historic function was to criticize government and obtain redress of grievances, 'reverted to the doing of business rather than presenting an arena for oratorical display or the consideration of local and individual complaint'.[14]

The amount of executive business accelerated and from 1811 the government took priority on Monday and Friday, the Order Days. There was an increased use of select committees, membership of which significantly reflected the balance of forces in the Commons. A Private Bill Office was established in 1810 and a working library in 1818. Parliament only sat between late January and July and business did not usually begin until four in the afternoon. Government had limited room for manoeuvre and this meant that controversial legislation could easily be obstructed and called for considerable effort by ministers to get it on to the statute book. Liverpool frequently found himself in a weak position in the Commons, as he could not longer rely on patronage and a disciplined party system had yet to develop. His ministers did not yet possess sufficient bureaucracy to leave them free from administrative detail in order to take their places as 'political' leaders in the House. He could not even guarantee that the government would get its way on major matters of policy.

'Party'

'Party' was, in Michael Bentley's words, 'a floating presence, sometimes central to political action, sometimes by-passed by it'.[15] 'Tory' and 'Whig' were not without meaning but that meaning was not finite. Since 1809 Toryism had developed as a language of Pittite resistance against the enemy within and was based on the land, its deferential tenantry and Anglicanism. Whiggery developed its ideology round the belief that the Pittite reaction made the 1689 settlement more attractive. Both sought power through an appeal to history: the Tories to past tradition, the Whigs to past events. Both placed emphasis on family, land and money. But political decisions in 1815 were not only, if they ever were, made in London. Changes in the nature of the economy and their impact on society meant that demands for political reform could be resisted less easily. Concession to radical demands could be achieved either from within the existing political structure or by force from outside. Radical change from within this structure proved more difficult to launch and sustain than pressure from outside but, in the long term, it was to be more successful. The problem facing the Whigs was how to convert a belief in the necessity for parliamentary reform into practice without establishing democracy. For the Tories the problem was how to cope with change in the social and economic structure without fundamental political change. Between 1812 and 1827 the inadequacy of eighteenth-century responses was clearly demonstrated and an appraisal and reconstruction of political attitudes gradually began to emerge. Liverpool's strength lay in his ability to sponsor administrative while resisting fundamental change and the débâcle of 1827–30 demonstrates how difficult this balancing act was.

LIVERPOOL IN POWER 1812–27

Appointment

Spencer Perceval's assassination on 12 May 1812 was followed by almost a month of negotiations before Liverpool finally became Prime Minister on 8 June. Initial plans for Liverpool to assume the premiership with the Sidmouthite Nicholas Vansittart as Chancellor of the Exchequer failed and the Cabinet resigned when a back-bench supporter of Canning carried the Commons against ministers in a request for a strong administration. Between 21 May and early June negotiations took place for a broad-based administration first by Wellesley and then by the Prince Regent's friend, Lord Moira. By setting reasonable, but unacceptable, conditions, the Regent manoeuvred to ensure that Grey and Grenville excluded themselves from any new arrangement. Wellesley's unacceptability to the old ministers made it impossible to recruit a ministry from either side and in June Liverpool reconstituted the government, keeping Sidmouth and Castlereagh by allowing freedom of conscience in the Cabinet on Catholic emancipation and establishing a ministry which Canning, the leading dissident, had no grounds to oppose. Wellesley was out-manoeuvred and lacking a strong personal following, went into virtual retirement, though he made his peace with Liverpool in 1821 and became Lord Lieutenant of Ireland. The disbanding of the Canning faction in 1813 and its absorption into the government in 1814 signalled the virtual reunification of the old Pittite coalition. Only the aristocratic Grenvilles remained outside but finally gave their support to the government as the result of a patronage compact in 1821.

Elections

The September 1812 election, called following victories in Spain, did not dramatically strengthen Liverpool's position.[16] Between 1812 and 1818 firm government supporters numbered 253 plus 78 waverers while the opposition could muster 149 and 83 respectively. This left only 102 'independent' MPs. Liverpool's administration was not proof against attack from a combination of opposition and independents as in 1816 when the proposal to extend the lucrative income tax into peacetime was rejected. The 1818 election, when 38 per cent of constituencies were contested, increased the strength of both government and opposition, seemingly at the expense of independent MPs: 261 plus 80 waverers for the government, 171 and 16 for the opposition. Independent MPs seem to have fallen to 49. The 1820 election, called after the death of George III, saw a revival of independent MPs to 114 with government supporters plus waverers at 349 and opposition plus waverers at 220. F. O'Gorman concludes from his analysis of voting behaviour that 'party' outnumbered 'non-party' divisions. Just over half the MPs in the parliaments elected in 1812, 1818 and 1826 never deviated in that behaviour and between 1812 and 1827 there was a remarkable consistency of support for government and opposition.

A Pittite Cabinet

The Tory Cabinet established in 1812 showed that Liverpool was the heir of the Pittite tradition. Bathurst, Harrowby, Mulgrave and the second Lord Melville had all worked directly with Pitt. Sidmouth, as Henry Addington, had been his Speaker in the House of Commons and it was to him that both Castlereagh and Nicholas Vansittart owed their initial advancement in British politics. Most ministers had been born in the early years of George III's reign, owned estates, though not as grand as those of the Whig leaders, and were connected to the world of administration through their fathers' involvements in the Commons, the army, the law, the diplomatic service or the East India Company. Though Castlereagh and Melville provided Irish and Scottish dimensions respectively, the ministers had limited geographical vision, southern English and agrarian, lacking any real understanding either of the plight of the agricultural worker or of the urban and industrial unrest and radicalism of northern England and lowland Scotland.

1815–21

The economic dislocation at the end of the French wars and the revival of extra-parliamentary radicalism perhaps, paradoxically, helped in the long term to strengthen Liverpool's parliamentary position. The threat of social and economic instability between 1815 and 1821 resulted in a growth of partisanship between government and opposition. But there were areas of common ground between them, especially over attacks on the social hierarchy, the preservation of property and the need for public order. This common ground weakened the extent to which the opposition posed a real threat to Liverpool. The major problem facing Liverpool in 1815 was restructuring the government finances. Falling wheat prices led to an attack from an increasingly desperate farming lobby resulting in the protective 1815 Corn Law. Liverpool did not face major problems in Parliament, since the opposition, like the government, consisted of landowners. The problem lay outside Parliament with widespread disturbances in London which had the effect, not of preventing the government pressing ahead with legislation, but of making it more difficult for it to change course without appearing to have backed down in the face of popular pressure. The sessions in 1816 and 1817 found Liverpool in a weak position. He lost divisions on the politically unpopular property, malt and income taxes when uncommitted Tories sided with the opposition in 1816 and his only success seemed to be bringing George Canning back into the cabinet as President of the Board of Control. The transition from a war-time to a peacetime economy severely strained social and economic relationships. There was a sharp reduction in demand leading to unem-ployment which was aggravated by high prices for essential commodities. Sidmouth as Home Secretary and Eldon as Lord Chancellor were obsessed with potential insurrection which the launching of William Cobbett's unstamped *Political Register* in November and the disorder at the Spa Field meetings in London supporting demands for political reform in November and December seemed to confirm. Liverpool was faced by a perceived threat to public order but lacked the revenue essential to govern-ing effectively. It was revenue, not revolution, which the Whigs identified as their cause and significantly during 1817 they did not plan to exploit the supposed revolutionary threat but sought to manufacture a parliamentary majority to oust Liverpool, based on the relative virtue of retrenchment and parliamentary reform. The Whig Brougham wrote to his friend Thomas Creevey in early 1816:

As to home politics here we should make our main stand; and the ground is clearly retrenchment, in all ways, with ramifications into the Royal Family, property tax, jobs of all sorts, distresses of the landed interest, etc. . . . In short, it is the richest mine in the world.

Two years later Lord Holland wrote to Francis Horner, a leading Whig in the Commons: 'It is through the unpopularity of the expenditure that we must get at the foreign system of politics, which in my conscience, I think the cause of it.'

Liverpool's fortunes began to revive in 1817. The attack on the Prince Regent's coach on 28 January resulted in a shift of opinion behind a government which declared the preservation of public order and the defence of property its major priorities. Liverpool did not believe that the mass of the population were disaffected but that politically motivated agitators could instigate panic and disorder which his government did not have the policing resources to control. Habeas Corpus was suspended and a Seditious Meetings Act was quickly passed. The march of the Blanke-teers, the Pentrich and Huddersfield risings proved abortive. Parliamen-tary reform was not an issue around which the Whigs could yet confidently rally: the Grenville faction seceded at the end of the parliamentary session and splits were revealed between radical Whigs and more cautious figures who, by 1819, included Grey himself. Grey had said in Newcastle in September 1817 that

I am still a reformer but with some modifications of my former opinions: with more fear of the sudden and inconsiderate changes, with a most complete conviction that to be successful reform must be gradual and must be carefully limited. . . .

Adroit exploitations of events only partly explains Liverpool's improved position by the end of 1817 and consideration needs to be given to an easing of economic conditions which probably took the sting out of the recession and quietened radical agitation more effectively than legislation.

The general election of 1818 was hotly contested. It had little to do with insurrection, all to do with retrenchment and cheap government which may account for an estimated fifteen overall gains for the opposition. Agitation seemed to have been wiped out, Habeas Corpus was revived early in the year and the Seditious Meetings Act was allowed to lapse in July. 1819 and 1820 were years of major crisis for the government and wasted opportunities for the opposition. Radicalism revived in 1819 and repression was reimposed in the 'Six Acts' which gave the government powers to bear down hard on the merest symptom of discontent. There is little doubt that the ruling establishment were panicked by events like Peterloo but what Liverpool legislated against was no imminent revolution but the spread of agitation and the willingness of the opposition to sponsor and champion its advance. J. E. Cookson is not overstating the case when he writes: 'The Whigs were as much the intended victims of the Six Acts as the Radicals.'[17]

The death of George III in early 1820 precipitated a general election and the mishandled affair of the Queen's Trial. Canning resigned over the latter in late 1820. The Cato Street conspiracy when a group led by Arthur Thistlewood planned to assassinate the Cabinet and establish a republic revived fears of a national insurrection. The government was the object of widespread vilification throughout 1820. It was demoralized and only the reconstruction of the ministry in the early 1820s restored its composure.

A reconstituted ministry

Historians have been accustomed to divide Liverpool's administration into two phases: a 'reactionary' one from 1812 to 1822 when anti-reforming ministers like Sidmouth and Eldon introduced legislation to suppress liberties and defend public order; and a 'liberal' one from 1822 to 1827 when 'Liberal Tories' like Huskisson, Robinson and Peel introduced reforms in fiscal policy, trade and the legal system. Liverpool's administration was neither reactionary nor suddenly reformist in 1822. Cookson argues that an awareness of the importance of 'respectable' opinion, not formally represented in the institutions of government, characterized every notable transaction of the government. This may overstate the case. Liverpool certainly did not depart from an aristocratic view of government and was not insensitive to demands issuing from outside the narrow political establishment but he took a Pittite 'national' view rather than one based on interest or class. Maintaining 'harmony' and 'improvement' were central moral as well as pragmatic imperatives consequent on this view.

Change, Liverpool argued, had to be carefully regulated and the deliberate action of those who were in the best position to calculate its effects, not the consequence of extra-parliamentary radical agitation. Liverpool's general economic strategy had been agreed during 1819 and 1820 in the form of a decidedly Pittite notion of national revival through a policy of sound money and stimulus to trade. His close relationship with Huskisson suggests a long-term commitment to reducing tariffs and a recognition of the need to reconcile the potentially divergent interests of land and industry in the national interest. Frederick Robinson's 1824 budget which reduced excise duties had been approved in outline by his predecessor. Some of Peel's penal reforms had been proposed under Sidmouth. Canning's foreign policies were a direct continuation of Castlereagh's. The difference between the 1820s and the 1810s lay, not in policies, but the revival of the economy and the not unrelated decline in threats to public order. Huskisson, Peel and Robinson were operating in calmer and more expansionist times than Sidmouth and Vansittart.

It is, however, important not to underestimate the reconstruction of Liverpool's ministry in 1821–2. The general election of 1820 favoured the opposition more than the government and it faced a series of attacks from currency reformers, protectionists and retrenchment radicals as well as from the Whigs. In the 1821 session a group of dissatisfied agriculturalists sided with the opposition to repeal the tax on farm horses and Liverpool was defeated on a proposal to establish a Committee of Enquiry into the State of Agriculture. Over 250 MPs professed support for the government: while they would oppose Liverpool on specific issues, they were also prepared consistently to support him on issues of confidence. Reverses on sectional issues did not prevent the ministry from proceeding with its policies to promote Britain's economy.

Canning's resignation in December 1820 confirmed the supremacy of Castlereagh as both Foreign Secretary and leader of the House of Commons. He had good reason to believe that the king would never give him high office and that the opposition would be unable to help him in the immediate future. He felt both excluded and humiliated. The Whigs had problems of their own. Their image among the electorate was clearly sharper in 1821 than in 1812 but the Grenville faction split from the Whigs in the autumn of 1821 and their policies still had to harden into a recognizable form. Castlereagh's suicide in August 1822 threw Liverpool and his ministry into crisis. Castlereagh had to be replaced in two posts. To make Canning leader of the House had obvious attractions if only for his oratorical skills. But Peel, who had replaced Sidmouth as Home Secretary earlier in the year, hoped for the position. He needed to move Vansittart from the Exchequer and Huskisson, who since 1814 had masterminded economic policy from the secretaryship of woods and forests, demanded improved status. Liverpool eventually gave Canning both Castlereagh's posts and in a reshuffle in early 1823 brought in Huskisson at the Board of Trade and Robinson at the Exchequer. Robinson did not have a better claim than Huskisson but Liverpool recognized that making the latter Chancellor of the Exchequer would offend Vansittart and create dissension with the ministry. Huskisson's annoyance was partly salved by the Presidency of the Board of Trade, which carried cabinet rank. The significance of cabinet changes in 1822–3, according to Michael Bentley, lay in the emergence of a new style of politics.

A changed style of politics?

Contemporaries identified this change of style in ministerial responses to events on the continent and in Ireland. Wellington, a minister since 1819, viewed foreign policy in the 1820s from a legitimist and pro-French stance and increasingly saw Canning's views as revolutionary and pro-Spanish. Through 1823, and especially in August when Canning refused to send troops to Portugal to defend its king against revolution, Wellington's estimation of Canning declined and a growing split became evidence within the ministry. Liverpool, Canning and Wellington all threatened resignation in 1824 over whether certain South American colonies should be given official recognition by the British government. Wellington saw opposition to this policy as discouraging revolutionary barbarians while Canning based his support on economic considerations: principle versus expediency. The same polarities appeared in the Irish context and the reshuffle of 1822–3 did have important consequences for religious policy. Canning, Huskisson and the Grenvilles all favoured increased political liberties for Roman Catholics throughout Great Britain, Wellington and Peel opposed any concessions to the Catholics.

Liverpool's solution to the revival of demands for Catholic emancipation in 1823, with the formation of the Catholic Association by Daniel O'Connell, was to declare it an 'open' question on which ministers might legitimately disagree. Whig support in the Commons ensured majorities for Canning's bill in 1822 to admit Catholic peers to Parliament and for the 1825 Relief Bill of Sir Francis Burdett but 'Protestant' support in the House of Lords ensured ultimate defeat. The Catholic question was prominent in the 1826 general election and, as in the 1807 election there is evidence that although 'Protestants' made a limited number of gains it did not remove the question. The events of 1827–9 showed that the Catholic question had to be faced by government and that only a Protestant government would have sufficient strength to do this. By early 1827 when Liverpool was incapacitated by a stroke, the constitutional, religious and landed bases of Toryism were under attack. The repeal of the Test and Corporation Acts, Catholic Relief and parliamentary reform began the process of change from Toryism to Conservatism, a process completed by the split occasioned by Peel's fiscal policies of the early 1840s and his repeal of the Corn Laws in 1846.

Whig ineffectiveness

Why were the Whigs unable to dislodge Liverpool from power? Part of the problem was lack of leadership. Fox was not succeeded by one leader after his death in 1806 but by two, Grey and Grenville but both were, after Grey's elevation in 1807, in the House of Lords. Leadership in the Commons proved an intractable problem. Lord Henry Petty, the only figure of distinction, also moved to the Lords on the death of his father, Lansdowne, in late 1809 and Grenville would not accept the radical Samuel Whitebread. In the end George Ponsonby, an affable, honest individual who did his best for the party, was chosen and remained leader of the opposition in the Commons until his death in 1817. The suicides of Whitebread and Samuel Romilly in 1815 and 1818 respectively removed two of the most promising Whig leaders. Between 1818 and 1821 George Tierney led the party but his selection was largely the result of the need not to antagonize moderate elements in the party which the more radical contenders, Samuel Romilly and Henry Brougham would have done. Tierney's failure to topple the government in 1818–19 weakened his authority and health and between 1821 and 1830 the party drifted leaderless. Royal hostility to the Whigs, particularly Brougham following an intemperate attack on the Regent in 1816 and, less rationally, to Grey, strengthened Liverpool's position. The attitudes of George IV in the 1820s were not the same as those of the Prince of Wales in the 1780s. It is not coincidental that the Whigs stayed in opposition while he lived. In the Lords neither Grey nor Lansdowne provided much evidence of leadership and the Grenville faction seceded after 1818. Whig weaknesses and uncertainties in the Commons counterbalanced the government's relative lack of debating talent there before 1822.

The problem was, however, not simply one of leadership. There was a significant difference between opposing government measures and having an alternative programme of policies on which to campaign. The cardinal element of early nineteenth-century Whiggism was its insistence on political liberty upon which all other liberties were based. Commitments to repeal the Combination Acts, to reform parliament, to repeal the Test and Corporation Acts and to pursue Catholic emancipation were grounded in long-established demands for civil liberties. Whig resistance to the Six Acts and their defence of Habeas Corpus, press freedom and Queen Caroline is evidence of the persistence of this tradition. The limitations of this ideology were twofold. First, its focus was political and it neglected the newer social and economic problems caused by industrial and demographic change. This helps to explain the confusion and indifference that some Whigs showed to many of Liverpool's economic and financial policies and the problems they faced with these issues after 1832. Secondly, attitudes to these political policies within the party were equivocal and divisive. Grey, the radical agitator of the 1790s was resistant to younger

Whigs by the 1810s and had become pessimistic about the successful achievements of reform. Yet it was parliamentary reform which Grey perceived by the early 1820s as the issue which could bring power. He had never abandoned the Whig belief in its historic role of moderating between the forces of ministerial despotism and radical anarchy by providing leadership for the propertied men of the middling orders. Increasingly Grey and other younger aristocrats – Russell, Althorp, Milton, Tavistock and Ebrington – saw a return to power as the result not of a royal manoeuvre but of a vote in the House of Commons. There was a fundamental shift in perceptions in the 1820s from seeing themselves merely as an opposition to offering a credible alternative government.

DOMESTIC POLICIES

It is possible to examine the domestic policies of the Liverpool administration in terms of its responses to the problems of the economy, to demands for political reform, to the need for administrative reform particularly in the legal system, and finally its reaction to religious questions. Its record of success was greater on economic and social questions, issues which could be resolved using administrative solutions, than on questions of political and religious reform which attacked the fundamentals of the constitution.

ECONOMIC POLICIES: 'CORN' AND 'CASH' AND 'COMMERCE'

It is debatable whether Liverpool's ministry was the first to develop coherent economic policies or whether it was the last to regard industrial developments as a malignant aberration.[18] It is, however, clear that Liverpool's economic policies emerged from the increasingly complex nature of the British economy. 'Cash and Corn' dominated the debate in the 1810s and 'Commerce' was added in the 1820s. They raised a series of fundamental questions which dominated debates until the 1840s: what should the place of agriculture be in an industrialized society? What should the relationship between consumers and producers be? How could the competing claims of agriculturalists and industrialists be resolved? What should the proper role of government be in the economy?

The French wars had stimulated certain sectors of the economy, especially agriculture. Rents, prices and costs had risen sharply since the 1790s and the future of the British corn trade was discussed in Parliament as early as 1813. Concern was expressed about the effects of the end of the war upon inflated prices. The bumper harvest of 1813 sent prices crashing down and peace in 1814 brought foreign grain imports and the promise of more to come. Irish landlords, like Sir Henry Parnell, were first to point to the 'malady of peace'. A Select Committee in 1813 recommmended the imposition of high import duties, the abolition of preferential tariffs on Canadian grain and free exportation, and a second committee the following year concluded that a fair figure for wheat was 80 shillings a quarter, an approximate wartime average. By 1814 the protectionist movement was dominated not by Irish but by Scottish landlords. Initially in Scotland, as in England from 1815, the corn question divided town and countryside, producers and consumers. For some, protection was an issue of principle but for most it was a matter of survival. But protection was much less an issue in Scotland than in England after 1815. Good harvests in 1814 and 1815 brought prices down to half their 1812 levels. Farmers and tenants who had improved marginal land found themselves particularly at risk. Lower prices and continuing high levels of taxation meant that they had considerable difficulty in repaying bank loans on which high interest was acceptable in inflationary conditions but disastrous in deflationary ones. This led to a large number of bankruptcies, to rent and wage reduction and to agrarian distress. The farming interest was not united in its demands, with farmers on good land often indifferent to demands for higher protection because they stood to gain more from the decultivation of poorer soils.

Protection: 1815

Liverpool was faced with demands for protection from parts of the landed interest and opposition from manufacturers and the urban working population. The cabinet could not be indifferent to the fate of the country's largest single economic interest, whose votes they needed in the Commons. But the fact remained that the 1814 and 1815 Corn Laws were designed to maintain farming in its wartime state and to keep prices, profits and rents at wartime levels and this could be portrayed by opponents as beneficial to one section of society at the expense of the rest. Public disorder in London hardened rather than weakened the resolve of Parliament and the 1815 Corn Law, a compromise solution reached at meetings between leading members of the cabinet and protectionists, prohibited the import of grain until the price fell below 80 shillings a quarter for wheat. Liverpool could defend protection as likely to provide the country with a more stable supply of food than would result from reliance on intermittent and costly imports and could argue that rural prosperity could only be achieved on the basis of high arable prices. Opponents pointed to the inequity of this particular law. Previous corn laws had tried to maintain a judicious balance between the interests of producers and consumers by maintaining prices at levels satisfactory to both. The 1815 Act clearly favoured the interests of producers. Liverpool and Vansittart may have seen the 1815 Act as transitional, to help agriculture return to normality after the artificiality of the wars. However, the excellent harvest of 1815 and the distress of 1816 confirmed the view, expressed by William Cobbett, that it would bring no real economic benefits and would exacerbate social conflict. Distress spread from the poorer soils on to the better-quality land whose occupiers, lukewarm protectionists in 1814 and 1815, began to join the campaign.

Protection: further demands from farmers

Demands for protection from early 1816 were orchestrated by a Gloucestershire solicitor and farmer, George Webb Hall. Though he did not initially obtain a great deal of support, by late 1818 a movement for general protection began to take shape and in January 1819 he formed a Central Agricultural Association designed to weld agriculturalists into a force to counter what were seen as the pernicious free-trading influences of the Board of Trade. By the end of 1819 twenty English counties had sent representatives to the Central Association but its leadership consisted of small squires and large tenant farmers rather than members of important landed families. A semi-political movement, the Central Association was not altogether to the liking of the landowning gentry and Webb Hall's economic theories proved to be rather naive when exposed to cross-questioning by experts on the 1821 select committee. Its influence waned after 1821.

Protection: the 1821 Committee

Agriculturalists managed to carry a motion against the government in May 1820 for the appointment of a Select Committee but it was effectively emasculated by severely limiting its terms of reference. Continued distress – caused by four consecutive good harvests from 1819 – led to a second Select Committee being set up the following year. The 1821 Committee has often been regarded as a protectionist body which was forced by Huskisson and Ricardo into producing a free trade report. In fact the committee was much more finely balanced but its final report, drafted by Huskisson did little to satisfy protectionists. Economically ministers felt that the agricultural industry should learn to adjust to peacetime conditions. Politically, it was drawn between the benefits of cheap food for the whole country and the need for political support from agriculturalists in the Commons for other policies. The 1821 Report suggested that a duty on imported grain, counterbalanced by a lowering of the level at which imports were permitted might help ease the sudden transition from total prohibition to free importation at 80 shillings under the existing law. A flood of petitions led to the revival of the committee in 1822 but it merely repeated its earlier recommendations. On this basis the government introduced the 1822 Corn Law which imposed graduated scales of duties on foreign corn between 70 and 85 shillings. Since the 1815 prohibition at 80 shillings was never repealed and prices never reached that level during the lifetime of the Act, it remained a dead letter.

Protection: the 1822 Corn Law

Liverpool was at his weakest in the House of Commons during 1821 and 1822 in the aftermath of the 'Queen's Affair', the abortive attempt by George IV to divorce his estranged wife, the 1820 general election and during the reconstruction of his ministry. The 1822 Corn Law is only explicable as an interim action while he considered a more permanent solution. The debate on agricultural distress had stirred up a whole range of other issues. Attacks were made on government expenditure. County gentry hoped for reduced taxation to offset reduced rent. Farmers thought tithes and poor rates were a more pressing problem. Radicals sought solutions in renewed demands for parliamentary reform and currency reformers called for an end to 'cheap money'. In addition to these different economic arguments, independent county MPs became increasingly restive and tried to take control of policy. Liverpool, however, made his position very clear in a debate in February 1822: 'The agricultural is not the only interest in Great Britain. It is not even the most numerous.' Boyd Hilton is correct in his identification of a new agricultural policy from 1821.

Protection: 1823–7

Rising wheat prices from 1823, the 1825 financial crisis and the manufacturing depression of 1826 brought fresh demands for the abolition or reduction of duties on foreign corn. A revival of industrial unemployment and social unrest led Liverpool to reduce prices to alleviate the food situation and he made it clear that he intended to revise the 1815 Act the following year. Norman Cash argues that the 1826 session

> marked the point, at which the landed interest went permanently over to the defensive against the claims of the rest of the community. . . . 'The charm of the power of the Landed Interest', pronounced the whig Creevy in May 1826, 'Is gone.'[19]

But the ground-rules had been laid in the 1821 Report and 1822 Act. The 1827 and 1828 Corn Laws, introduced by Canning and Huskisson respectively, completed that process, providing a sliding scale of duties to operate around the pivot point of 60 shillings, ceasing entirely at 70 shillings a quarter. In his attitude to agriculturalists since 1821 Liverpool had demonstrated that the national interest had priority over narrow sectional ones. It was the same attitude which Sir Robert Peel demonstrated in 1846. Gladstone suggested in the 1870s that Whig victory in 1830 delayed the passage of repeal by a decade and he is possibly correct. Liverpool, Canning, Huskisson, Peel and even Wellington were more liberal economically than their Whig counterparts though this was not for humanitarian reasons but to allay the potential of revolutionary discontent.

'Cash'

The second strand in Liverpool's economic policies was 'cash'. The wars with France had been expensive, taxation had been high, and 'cheap' paper money had been circulating since the late 1790s. In 1814–15 government expenditure exceeded income by 45 per cent and servicing the national debt cost £30 million. Reducing public expenditure and paying off old debts – a process of retrenchment – became a primary concern of Liverpool's ministry from 1815. Outside Parliament there were also demands for retrenchment and widespread petitioning stated that the large army and the property tax were one and the same evil. A petition from Farringdon in the City of London opposed Liverpool's desire to retain income tax:

> . . . this obnoxious and inquisitorial Tax can only be proposed with a view to maintaining an enormous Military Establishment in a time of profound peace, a measure hostile to the spirit of the British Constitution, and highly injurious to the best interests of society.

Henry Hunt used more colourful language at the first open-air meeting at Spa Fields on 15 November 1816:

> Everything that concerned their subsistence or comfort was taxed. Was not their loaf taxed, was not beer taxed, were not their coats taxed . . . was not everything that they ate, drank, wore or even said taxed?

Retrenchment

Liverpool accepted that heavy government expenditure would continue for several years after 1815 and that it would never return to its pre-war levels. Britain already had commitments to finance the army of occupation in France and to pay already contracted allied subsidies. Britain had acquired a further seventeen colonies and their defence needs had to be taken into account. The value of the pound had fallen. But the period of transition Liverpool needed was denied him by the campaign against income tax, which realized 20 per cent of government income in 1815. Income tax had always been unpopular, but was tolerated because of the needs of the war. In the general opposition to income tax which continued in peacetime, the Whigs saw an issue on which to defeat the government and organized a national campaign of agitation. The government's weakness lay, not in their proposal, but in their inability to publicize their case through the press. No prominent newspaper was prepared to support them. Despite important concessions on the scope of the tax, Liverpool was defeated in the Commons by 238 to 201 votes. He had hoped to carry the proposal by 40 votes but his Irish supporters abstained and some 80 MPs who usually supported the government voted against him.

This defeat, which left the government with revenue of only £12 million to cover expenditure of £30 million, had both social and economic consequences. Unlike the Corn Laws it did not worsen relations between industry and agriculture but it did deepen the gap between rich and poor. Abolition was popular but, in this contest, shortsighted. Liverpool was obliged to fall back on indirect taxation to cover his costs and these weighed more heavily upon the poor. Abolition and the introduction of the Corn Laws can both be seen as sectional decisions. Economically Vansittart was forced to fudge finances by continuing to borrow from the money markets at higher rates of interest to pay off older debts, thus increasing the national debt.

Calls for 'sound money'

The defeat on income tax strengthened calls for 'cheap government' and the need for 'sound money'. Liverpool pursued a determined policy of cutting government costs from 1816. The armed services were further reduced, the Civil List was pared down, government departments were repeatedly pruned and a 10 per cent cut was made in official salaries. Between £50 and £55 million revenue was raised annually after 1815 compared to about £16 million before the wars. To opponents like Cobbett this difference was a striking one. Liverpool, however, could do little to reduce it further. In 1818 he controlled only about 9 per cent of this revenue, the rest was swallowed up servicing the interest on the national debt, war pensions and interest on loans necessary to meet a deficit of £13 million. The continued existence of the 'sinking fund', where money was borrowed at a higher rate than the fund designed to pay it off, was an economic absurdity and its retention can only be explained as an irrational reverence to the memory of Pitt. Radicals could easily attack this system of finance, condemning the 'tax eaters' and 'fundholders' who seemed to sap the country's strength. The landed interest, Liverpool's natural supports, were disadvantaged by the combination of high interest rates and lower agricultural prices as they too struggled with loan repayments. Economically and politically, the case for a revision of the financial system was overwhelming.

Resumption of 'cash payments'

Liverpool believed that only the re-establishment of 'sound money' could ensure a sustained growth in the economy. In 1819 the government embarked on a more constructive policy and two select committees were established in the Commons, one on currency, the other on public finance. Peel chaired the currency committee, but it included all the leading cabinet ministers, and in May it recommended gradual resumption of cash payments by 1823. Most financial experts, including David Ricardo, favoured the end to wartime paper currency on the grounds that a return to a fixed gold standard was essential to a sound money policy. The transition was accomplished ahead of time and from 1821 Britain was effectively on the gold standard. The recommendations of the finance committee led to Vansittart's 1819 budget, characterized rather extravagantly in a government pamphlet as a 'new system of finance'. It imposed £3 million of new taxes and took £12 million out of the sinking fund as a means of balancing the budget; the remainder was made up by Exchequer bills and loans in the usual way.

The importance of this budget lay in its acceptance of a principle Huskisson had been attempting to instil: that what should be aimed for was a surplus of revenue over expenditure and that this would restore public confidence in the government. The problem with this view was that the major sources of revenue, customs and excise, fluctuated with the levels of economic activity. Liverpool, in true Pittite fashion, looked back to the 1780s and saw a recovery of trade and manufacture as the next stage of the process: 'commerce' was the third strand of his policies.

Commerce

For Liverpool and Grenville it was essential to stimulate the sluggish British economy, and removing tariffs and loosening the commercial regulations which controlled the flow of British trade was the way to do this. But theirs was a belief grounded in political expediency not dogma. Tariffs, especially on wool, were actually increased between 1815 and 1822 and the commitment of the mercantile and manufacturing interests to freer trade has been exaggerated. Many merchants saw things pragmatically, supporting monopoly in areas which they dominated and free trade in areas where they had the competitive advantage. London merchants were sceptical and their free-trade petition presented to Parliament in early 1820 owed more to the economist Thomas Tooke than to widespread conviction. But on 26 May 1820 Liverpool gave a firm statement of the advantages of an unrestricted freedom of trade in a speech to the House of Lords. But it was not unequivocal: he reassured his audience that he did not envisage abandoning agricultural protection and believed that absolute free trade was out of the question. Two committees were established, one in each House, to examine the question of foreign trade and lay down strategies for the new approach. The Commons report, introduced by Thomas Wallace, Vice-President of the Board of Trade, was outspoken in favour of freer trade, arguing that it would ease manufactures out of depression, stimulate entrepreneurial searches for new markets and create employment. It is important not to undervalue the roles of Vansittart and Wallace. They drew up blueprints for the reforms which Robinson and Huskisson initiated after 1823. Between 1819 and 1820 Liverpool had captured the initiative in both financial and commercial policy.

Reforms 1822–7

Implementing the planning of 1819–20 was delayed until 1823–6. The Queen's Affair reduced support for Liverpool's ministry inside and outside Parliament to its lowest ebb. The ministerial changes of 1822–3 gave the ministry the firm leadership it lacked. Vansittart's 1822 budget was in surplus and his successor started off with nearly £5 million excess revenue. In 1823 Robinson was able to budget for a surplus of £7 million of which £5 million was used to repay debts leaving £2 million for tax cuts. In 1824 and 1825 clear surpluses enabled him to reduce excise duties on a wide range of consumer goods and raw materials, including coal, iron, wool, silk, hemp, coffee, wine and rum. Despite lowering duties, rising consumption and growing trade kept excise revenue buoyant. The financial crisis of 1825 and the recession the following year did not lead to alterations in policy and Robinson was still able to reckon on a small revenue surplus in 1827. The general trade recession which lasted from 1827 to 1831 had inevitable results on revenue and, though there were budget surpluses up to 1830, they were insufficient to justify further tariff reductions. Important as Vansittart's and Robinson's budgets were, as early as 1824 Liverpool had realized that the limits of tax reduction had been reached and that the only way out of this financial stalemate was to reduce indirect taxation and reintroduce direct taxes. John Herries, Chancellor of the Exchequer under Goderich, was preparing to reintroduce income tax when the ministry collapsed and Henry Goulburn, Wellington's Chancellor, was only prevented from incorporating a proposal for a modified income tax in the 1830 budget by the Prime Minister's opposition.

Both the financial and commercial policies were in all essentials the same as Pitt's in the 1780s. In 1821 Wallace reduced the duties on timber imported from northern Europe and the following year he simplified and liberalized the complicated structure of the Navigation Acts. In 1823 Wallace resigned in protest at Huskisson's promotion over his head and has not received the credit for laying down the programme which Huskisson then implemented. In 1823 the Reciprocity of Duties Act reduced tariffs if other countries would follow suit and by 1827 most European states and America had negotiated agreements for mutual abolition of adjustment of discriminatory duties. The success of this policy can be seen in the 64 per cent increase in tariff revenue between 1821 and 1827 compared to only 36 per cent for Pitt between 1784 and 1792.

Huskisson and reform

Huskisson's contribution to the economic reforms of the 1810s and 1820s was twofold. First, he believed that the inflexibility of the mercantile system was responsible for the loss of the American colonies and consequently argued for a more liberal and preferential policy towards colonial possessions. Colonies had as much right to prosperity under the imperial flag as Britain so that a solid and mutually beneficial imperial union could be created. Secondly, he foreshadowed Richard Cobden in seeing free trade as a moral force for international harmony and co-operation. But he was not a doctrinaire free-trader and his notion of preferential colonial tariffs cut across strict free-trade theory. His policies were based on a hard-nosed assessment of the potential advantage to Britain of exploiting her economic superiority.

A 'freeing' of the economy?

It is important to see the 'freeing' of the economy implicit in fiscal and commercial policies in the context of social policy which in certain circumstances ignored prevailing economic theories. Most of it was remedial in character, limited in scope and largely ineffective in practice. Liverpool supported the campaign to regulate the employment of children in textile mills which resulted in the 1819 Factory Act. In 1816 demobilized soldiers were allowed to set up in trade in any part of the kingdom and the Poor Employment Act of 1817 offered government loans for public works schemes to alleviate unemployment. In 1819 an Act was passed to encourage Friendly Societies by giving them special safeguards and privileges, beginning a process of self-help for the working population. Liverpool and Huskisson supported the abolition of all legal restrictions on the export of machinery, emigration of artisans and trade combinations. The 1828 Passenger Transport Act imposed regulation on north Atlantic emigration traffic and restrictions were reimposed on trade unions in 1825. In each case the government argued that its action would benefit the individual and stimulate economic expansion.

The 'liberalization' of the economy underwent a severe test in 1825. The loosely unified and private nature of the banking system, with the exception of the Bank of England, made it inherently unstable. Many country banks had limited resources and bank failures were not uncommon. The return to 'sound money' in 1821 and the prosperous conditions of the early 1820s led to a speculative boom in South America and the floating of enterprises of a questionable nature. The Bank was slow to raise its interest rates to dampen the boom, though it is only fair to say that the Usury Law prevented this beyond 5 per cent. The collapse of about a hundred London and provincial banks hastened the emergence of a more modern system of financial administration. The ban on joint-stock companies, theoretically illegal under the Bubble Act of 1720, was lifted in 1825. The Bank Act of the following year introduced joint-stock banks which helped stabilize the system and prohibited banks, in England and Wales, printing paper money under the value of £5.

Liverpool's economic policies were designed to spread economic prosperity and as a result remove discontent. Norman Gash sees this as being 'at bottom . . . a social policy'. Like Pitt, Liverpool sought to create social harmony, constitutional security and national revival through economic expansion. The government-inspired pamphlet *The State of the Nation*, published in 1822, explained this policy in an important exercise in public relations.[20] Pitt had had to take account of public opinion when initiating his reforms in the 1780s and on occasions had bowed to its pressure. Liverpool was faced with a more vocal and organized public opinion that Pitt. The economic and social environment within which he worked had shifted since the 1780s away from agriculture and towards manufacturing. Pitt was not faced with a farming lobby demanding protection for its interest. Liverpool was. Unwilling to reform a broadly landed Parliament, Liverpool had to rely more on persuasion than legislation to achieve his objectives. His economic policies sought to reconcile the contradictions within both the economic and political systems. He sought to govern an increasing industrial and urban society through an agrarian-based legislature. Economic conditions and his pragmatic, though increasingly free-trading, economic policies enabled him to do this. But parliamentary concessions on economic and administrative matters were to lead to demands for concessions of a more fundamental nature between 1827 and 1832. Liverpool and the Tories were able to resist these pressures between 1812 and 1827. His successors were not.

A THREAT TO PUBLIC ORDER

The second major problem which faced Liverpool and his government, particularly between 1815 and 1821, was the threat to public order posed by demands for parliamentary reform.[21] Surges of radical agitation in the nineteenth century tended to correspond to periods of 'distress' and this is clearly demonstrated between 1815 and 1821. The end of the wars brought considerable social and economic dislocation. Jeremy Bentham wrote in 1817 that 'The plains, or heights, or whatsoever they are, of Waterloo will one day be pointed to by historians as the grave not only of French but of English liberties.' Agricultural prices, which had begun to fall before 1815, continued to fall after. The 1815 Corn Laws did little to prevent this slide, provoking violence in London and widespread discontent in urban and industrial centres where people felt that prices were being kept artificially inflated for the benefits of the landed interest. Declining conditions for the bulk of the rural population led to 'bread and blood' riots in East Anglia in 1816. There was a widespread belief among governing circles in the existence of a widespread revolutionary situation which public disorder in 1816 and 1817 did little to allay. The Spa Field riots in late 1816, the 'Blanketeers' march and Pentrich rising in 1817 resulted in the tightening of anti-radical laws and to the suspension of Habeas Corpus.

Tension relaxed following the good harvest in 1817 and, though in 1818 the state of trade provoked some serious strikes, political agitation and mass meetings declined. The 1818 harvest was again poor and, for Liverpool's government, 1819 proved to be a climactic year with the Peterloo Massacre in August and the passage of the Six Acts. The Cato Street Conspiracy of 1820, though largely irrelevant to popular politics, raised the political temperature in London but Liverpool was soon embroiled in the potentially far more damaging trial of Queen Caroline. The popular momentum of 1819–20 declined with the revival of the economy from 1821. Energy was diverted into religion, with Methodist revivals in Lancashire and Cumberland, and into trade unionism. Successful parliamentary pressure led to the repeal of the Combination Acts in 1824, though, following widespread strike action, some restrictions were reimposed in 1825.

Unrest and agitation, though it may appear to have a nationwide character, is best seen in terms of responses to particular social and economic conditions. In this situation it was the local magistracy rather than central government which was at the cutting edge of reaction. The coercive resources available to Liverpool were limited and the small peacetime establishment army was already stretched to its limits. The Home Office was, however, prepared to advise magistrates and manufacturers to make use of the law to deal with conspiracy and agitation. Home Office officials were convinced, like local gentry and magistrates, that not only was there widespread activity by demagogues but that there was also a general wish to start a national revolution. Liverpool and his ministers reached this conclusion on the basis of evidence from magistrates, army officers and their own spies who often exaggerated the nature of economic disputes and sometimes initiated the illegal activities on which it was their business to report. Liverpool's response to the potential threat to public order was frequently based upon defective and, on occasions, deceptive information.

Was Liverpool's response dictatorial?

Was the attitude of Liverpool's ministry to demands for reform dictatorial? His policy was a largely preventive one. His emphasis on law and order aimed to reassure the weak and propertied and prevent the slide into arbitrary rule. If he over-reacted to events it was because of inadequate information on the extent of popular activity and a desire not to run risks. Peel thought there was over-reaction to the December 1816 riots. He wrote:

> It will be thought by sensible and moderate men that the Government really wishes to magnify a mob into a rebellion in order that . . . the public attention [is] diverted from economy and a pretext made for maintaining the military.

Like William Pitt, Liverpool sought to distinguish between genuine social grievances and deliberate radical action. Radicals and Whigs argued that in his defence of the constitution he subverted both laws and liberties and they point to the 1819 Acts as evidence of this. In fact these Acts were relatively moderate in character and largely ineffective in practice. Parliament generally supported Liverpool and Whig attacks on Tory subversion of the constitution were unsuccessful. The exception to this was the Queen's Trial where Liverpool found himself under attack from Whigs and popular opinion. Liverpool took the brunt of the antipathy which people felt for a king whose actions were seen as hypocritical and unjust. The government's case was doomed from the start and it was saved from censure and defeat by the queen's opportune death in 1821.

Attempts at reform

Liverpool showed himself willing to deal with particular cases of electoral corruption. In 1821 the borough of Grampound was disfranchized. The country gentlemen overruled the ministry and voted to transfer the seats to Leeds but this was rejected in the House of Lords and they went to the West Riding. The decision of the Commons gave the first real demonstration that normally conservative MPs were willing to concede piecemeal parliamentary reform. In 1822 Lord John Russell's reform motion attracted 164 votes, the highest since Pitt's 1785 proposals, and the following year Lord Archibald Hamilton's proposal to reform the representation of Scottish counties was only defeated by thirty-five votes. For those, like Liverpool, who were opposed to a systematic reconstruction of the electoral system, these events were worrying in two respects. First, they raised the likelihood of conflict between Commons and Lords over the nature of the constitution: how long could the Lords resist demands for change and act as the watchdog of the old constitution? Secondly, the Whigs realized that it was politically advantageous for them to pursue the reform question. J. C. Hobhouse wrote in his diary in January 1821 that 'Lord Milton owned to me that Reform was gaining ground in his mind. Indeed I never saw so great a chance as to Reform in my life.' Government support derived largely from the Irish and Scottish seats and from English closed boroughs while the Whigs gained their votes from English counties and the more popular urban constituencies. Parliamentary reform posed a far greater electoral threat to the Tories than the Whigs. Economic prosperity and the government's efficient and 'liberal' policies of the mid-1820s saw this threat recede.

LEGAL REFORM

The third area of concern for Liverpool's administration centred on reforming the legal system. In the late eighteenth and early nineteenth centuries people had become increasingly concerned about the effectiveness of the legal system. In civil courts cases were often subject to long delays, procedure was obsolete and there was a backlog of undecided cases. This situation was exacerbated by the existence of two competing and sometimes contradictory systems: common law was administered by the Courts of King's Bench, Common Pleas and the Exchequer and the system of Equity through the Court of Chancery and by the Lord Chancellor. Criminal law, though harsh on paper, was in practice much more lenient. There were over 200 capital offences and a further 400 resulting in transportation. Juries often refused to convict for petty capital crimes. There was no regular police force in England, save for a totally insufficient body in London and, after 1792, in Middlesex. Radicals in and out of Parliament had been campaigning for reform on humanitarian and utilitarian grounds for years. The growth of legal chaos and the state of prisons led to harsh criticism of the system by John Howard, Sir Frederick Eden and Elizabeth Fry, and continental influence favouring penal reform influenced thinking.

Sir Robert Peel's promotion to the Home Office resulted in a widespread reform of the system.[22] As with fiscal and commercial policies Peel was able to build on initiatives in the earlier part of Liverpool's administration particularly the recommendations of Sir James Mackintosh's 1819 Committee. Peel's reforms fell into two distinct types, reform of the legal system and the prevention of crime, and ran respectively behind and ahead of public opinion. Between 1822 and 1827 Peel consolidated and amended the administration of civil and criminal law. The prison system was reformed and central control tightened in 1823, but a central prison inspectorate was delayed until 1835. Many capital offences were swept away, though in practice most of these had ceased to be punished by hanging. The law on theft was clarified in 1827, when Peel was briefly out of office, and the Game Laws reviewed in 1828. Some inroads were made into the administration of civil law in the 1825 statute.

These reforms did not go as far as many Whig reformers would have liked but Peel was anxious that legal reform should not be viewed in isolation and thought that there needed to be an improvement in the detection and prevention of crime. He had already set up an efficient police system in Ireland during the 1810s and he wished to extend this to the mainland. A parliamentary committee in 1822 rejected this notion, evidence of the prejudice of both politicians and the general public against infringement of traditional British liberties. Like parliamentary reform and Catholic emancipation, the introduction of policing was seen as a constitutional question, an attack on long-established rights. Peel was finally successful in establishing a Metropolitan Police Force in 1829 but the spread into borough and rural areas was resisted and it was not until the County and Borough Police Act of 1856 that raising a police force became obligatory.

RELIGION: THE CATHOLIC QUESTION

The final area of concern for Liverpool's administration was religion.[23] Discrimination in favour of the Anglican Church continued until after 1827 but increasingly it encountered difficulties in maintaining its numerical position, particularly in the burgeoning urban centres. Evangelicals within the Anglican Church provided considerable inspiration for regenerating the Church but their enthusiasm was criticized by the High Church Party which pressed the government to take action over the lack of church accommodation. In 1818 the Church Building Act secured a £1 million fund for the building of new churches and a further £0.5 million was added in 1824. The limited attempts to reform abuses in the structure of church organization in 1796 and 1803 had done only a little to meet the problems of non-residence and curates' stipends. In 1813 Lord Harrowby's Act laid down minimum stipends varying with the size of parish and in 1817 a general Act consolidated the previous legislation. The reforms, which came to fruition in the 1830s and 1840s, had already begun.

The Catholic question was a permanent irritant throughout Liverpool's premiership. The government was squeezed between the 'Catholic' Whigs and the 'Protestant' bulk of the Commons without any unity or coherent policy. Between 1812 and 1822 an agreement existed that the cabinet would remain neutral on the subject and would not raise it as a matter of government business. If it was raised independently ministers would be able to vote as their consciences dictated. The ministeral reconstruction of 1822–3 and renewed Catholic agitation in Ireland led by Daniel O'Connell revived interest in the issue. Bills giving varying concessions to Catholics passed the Commons in 1821, 1822 and 1825 but were all rejected in the Lords. The 1825 bill precipitated a major political crisis for Liverpool with the 'Protestant' Peel and then the 'Catholic' Canning threatening resignation. Canning argued that the government could no longer remain neutral on the issue. His 'Catholic' colleagues persuaded him otherwise and the 'agreeing to disagree' formula was re-established. The crisis had been postponed because of the need to preserve the government. Liverpool's stroke in February 1827 led to a revival of division. Fundamental reforms could no longer be resisted.

POLITICS OUTSIDE ENGLAND

Wales

Wales, Scotland and Ireland were more 'Tory' than England throughout Liverpool's administration. A writer in the *North Wales Chronicle* declared in 1809: 'Depend upon it gentlemen, the system is so complete and so perfect within itself that you cannot strip it of any of its parts without endangering the whole.'[24] And in his election address in 1812 John Jones talked of 'the spirit of our constitution by which religious and civil liberty ought to be secured to every Briton'.[25]

Welsh MPs showed considerable weakness in distinguishing reactions to social distress from legitimate expressions of political unrest as did many of their English counterparts. The suspension of Habeas Corpus was widely approved of and the editor of the journal *Seren Gomer* argued that it would have been unnecessary if the effectiveness of the appeals of Welsh sheriffs and others in authority had been paralleled in England. Cries of loyalty and choruses of satisfaction with the existing constitution followed Peterloo and the Six Acts. Only four Welsh MPs supported Russell in 1822. The Tory nature of Wales in this period can be explained by the growing religious gulf between the rulers, who were overwhelmingly Anglican, and the ruled, who were Nonconformists. The changing economic structure, especially of the south, was beginning to challenge the hold of the landlords but, until the late 1820s, the advantage lay with Toryism. It had the financial resources, the influence and patronage, the fear of revolution and, unlike England, the press. But it was a Toryism on the defensive.

Scotland

Scotland was effectively managed by the Melville interest, a political machine grounded in the scale of the patronage at its disposal and in the gross venality of the Scottish ruling class. Scottish Tories, so their opponents argued, were more reactionary than those in England and 'liberalization' after 1822 had no Scottish equivalent. Neither the Scottish Whigs nor Scottish radicals made any real impression on this ascendancy and when it finally broke up after 1827 it was from within. Catholic emancipation made tensions within Scottish Toryism explicit. The 1832 Reform Act completed the process of destruction.

Ireland

The Act of Union meant the removal of the forum of debate on Irish politics from Dublin to London. The Irish administration remained in Dublin but the initiative on the issues of land and religion lay very definitely with Westminster and British reformers. Power in Dublin lay with the Lord Lieutenant and the Chief Secretary: the former was usually an aristocrat who had already gained distinction in politics or diplomacy, the latter a young politician with ambitions to satisfy and a reputation to make.[26] The permanent officials centred round an Under-Secretary who had effective day-to-day running of the administration. The relationship between Lord Lieutenant, Chief and Under-Secretaries varied during this period and focused on the willingness of Lord Lieutenant and Chief Secretary to surrender their initiative to the Under-Secretary. The allocation

of patronage was significant and, although in more important appointments the wider political consideration involved sanction from London,
the Castle administration controlled appointments to the Bench, bishop-
rics, certain military ranks, corporation offices and a large number of
sinecures and clerkships. Unaffected by the 'economical reform' movement before Union, Irish administration was rationalized and made more
efficient after 1800. Irish government was made cheaper by the consolidation of various institutions, for example the two Exchequers in 1816
which gave the Treasury firmer control over Irish expenditure.

In county government the administrative authority lay with the Grand
Jury. It was a non-elective body, selected by the Sheriff. Until 1816
appointment as sheriff, was virtually in the gift of the local MP, and even
the adoption of the English method of selecting sheriffs from lists supplied
by Assize judges altered little. Grand Juries would sanction certain
schemes of public works, have a surveyor estimate the costs and then
make claims for the sums involved at the next assize. Expenses for public
works were levied as county cess on all occupiers of land, an unpopular
system as the actual payers of cess were not consulted when plans for
expenditure were being drawn up. This inefficient system was reformed
in 1817, when procedures for claiming expenses were tightened up and
specially qualified county surveyors appointed and in 1836 when payers
of cess were given some control over proposals for public work projects.
Urban government was probably more corrupt and inefficient than that
operating in the counties and corporations were generally non-elective
and exclusively Protestant bodies.

Maintaining law and order was the principal responsibility of the Dublin
administration. Catholics were excluded before 1829 but there were significant reforms during Liverpool's ministry. In 1814 the Lord Lieutenant
was given powers to appoint special stipendiary (paid) magistrates in
disturbed areas and this was extended in 1822 to include any area where
the local magistrates requested a stipendiary magistrate. The list of magistrates was revised in 1822 and alterations were made in the selection of
sheriffs from 1816. Sir Robert Peel took steps to improve the Irish police
system and in 1814 the Lord Lieutenant was given the power to appoint
a chief police magistrate with a specially appointed Peace Preservation
Force to disturbed areas. Its creation signified a tendency of central
government to assume powers which had previously been left to local
interests. In 1822 the Constabulary Act resulted in the appointment of a
chief constable to each barony and called on local magistrates, or the
Lord Lieutenant if they refused, to provide a certain number of constables
for each district. This created two forces, the Police Preservation Force
and an Irish Constabulary, and they were not placed under unified control
until 1836.

The Irish economy, like that on the mainland, suffered from depression
after 1815. The process of change from an arable wheat economy to a

pastoral one had its origins in farmers' responses to the post-war market situation where grassland farming was more profitable than tillage. Fundamental to British policy towards Ireland throughout the nineteenth century was a belief that economic prosperity would remove Irish social and political unrest. The Ejection Act of 1816 and the Subletting Act of 1826 made the consolidation of holdings easier but growing population led to the continued reclamation of marginal land in small plots, especially for potatoes. Rents for these plots were determined by land hunger rather than the productivity of the soil. In 1817 and 1821 there were serious potato failures and, on both occasions, private charity and government-funded public works schemes attempted to alleviate the distress. Rural exploitation, land hunger and distress led to a serious escalation of rural disorder. The government passed a succession of insurrection and White-boy acts to deal with the situation. Ireland lacked the capital to create sufficient alternative employment and the famines of the 1840s provided a massive impetus to a process of emigration that had its origins in the 1810s.

Irish Catholics demand emancipation

The Catholic question was left unresolved by Union and until 1823 the issue stagnated. The reason for this stagnation lay largely in divisions among the Catholic leaders over the series of 'safeguards' which the government deemed necessary accompaniments to emancipation. These safeguards centred on two issues: that the state should have some control over the appointment of Catholic bishops and priests and that some state provision should be made for the payment of Catholic clergy. Until the early 1820s these safeguards frustrated every effort to resolve the problem. This was particularly evident in the differences between Catholic bishops, who favoured the state provision for payment, and the parish priests who preferred a voluntary support system. The Catholic laity were equally divided over safeguards with some, like Daniel O'Connell, rejecting the notion altogether. By the early 1820s the Catholic cause in Ireland was divided and bankrupt. O'Connell recognized that even with a pro-emancipationist majority in the Commons, the House of Lords and the king could easily block change. The result was a fresh political initiative with the formation of the Catholic Association in the spring of 1823. O'Connell realized that, working through the Church, he could mobilize the mass of the Catholic population, which the Establishment viewed with some alarm. The votes of the tenantry had, for the most part, been an integral aspect of the landlord's property but in 1826 in many places the 40-shilling freeholders disobeyed their landlords and voted for the candidates favoured by local Catholic agitators. The Clare election of 1828 provided Wellington's government with a choice: emancipation or rebellion.

CONCLUSIONS

Lord Liverpool was the last of the non-party leaders of Parliament who sought to improve the detail, though not the fundamentals, of the economic, social, political and constitutional structure. Faced with growing problems – the dislocations of returning to a peacetime economy, tensions between the industrial and agricultural sectors and between town and countryside, mounting pressures for political and religious reform – he was generally able to put together a programme which received support from Parliament. He held together, particularly after 1822, a divided and contentious cabinet of ambitious individuals. It is true that many of his problems were solved, not by legislative action, but by trends in the economy and the ineffectiveness of the Whig opposition. But his approach was firm if not always sure, improving if not innovative. Disraeli's condemnation of Liverpool as 'an arch mediocrity' is an exaggeration and misunderstands the nature of the man and the problems he faced.

NOTES

1 E. J. Evans, *The Forging of the Modern State: Early Industrial England*, Longman, 1983 p. 187.

2 N. Gash, *Aristocracy and People: Britain 1815–1865*, Edward Arnold, 1979, p. 128.

3 Norman Gash's view of Liverpool can be examined in *Lord Liverpool*, Weidenfeld, 1984 and in articles in *History Today* 'Lord Liverpool: A Private View', May 1980 and 'The Tortoise and the Hare: Liverpool and Canning', March 1982.

4 In addition to E. J. Evans op. cit. and N. Gash *Aristocracy and People*, op. cit., good accounts can be found in A. Briggs *The Age of Improvement*, Longman, 1959, D. Beales *From Castlereagh to Gladstone 1815–1885*, Nelson, 1969 and M. Bentley, *Politics Without Democracy 1815–1914: Perception and Preoccupation in British Government*, Fontana, 1984. E. Halévy *The Liberal Awakening 1815–1830*, most recent paperback version Ark, 1987, is still of value. More detailed accounts can be found in J. E. Cookson *Lord Liverpool's Administration: the Crucial Years 1815–1822*, Scottish Academic Press, 1975 and A. J. B. Hilton *Cash, Corn, Commerce: the Economic Policies of Tory Governments 1815–1830*, Oxford University Press, 1977. E. J. Evans *Britain before the Reform Act: Politics and Society 1815–1832*, Longman, 1989 combines text and sources.

5 See the discussion by J. Cannon 'New Lamps for Old: the End of Hanoverian England', in J. Cannon (ed.) *The Whig Ascendancy: Colloquies on Hanoverian England*, Edward Arnold, 1981, pp. 100–24 and J. C. D. Clark *English Society 1688–1832*, Cambridge University Press, 1985 chapter 6, pp. 349–93.

6 Quoted in J. Cannon (ed.) op. cit. pp. 103–4.

7 C. Emsley *British Society and the French Wars 1793–1815*, Macmillan, 1979, p. 181.

8 On the impact of the French wars see C. Emsley op. cit. and A. D. Harvey *Britain in the Early Nineteenth Century*, Batsford, 1978, pp. 323–39.

9 A. D. Harvey op. cit. p. 336.

10 For changing conceptions of the proper role of government see chapter 15.

11 Quoted in N. Gash op. cit. p. 45.
12 For conditions in 1815, E. Halévy *England in 1815*, London, 1924 reprinted several times but most recently with an introduction by A. Briggs, Ark, 1987 is a goldmine of stimulating ideas and information.
13 M. Bentley op. cit. p. 23.
14 ibid. p. 24.
15 ibid. p. 26.
16 On Tory and Whig positions generally during Liverpool's administration see F. O'Gorman *The Emergence of the British Two-Party System*, Edward Arnold, 1982, B. W. Hill *British Parliamentary Parties 1742–1832*, Allen & Unwin, 1985, D. Beales *Political Parties in Nineteenth Century Britain*, The Historical Association, 1971 and E. J. Evans *Political Parties in Britain 1783–1867*, Methuen, 1985. For the Tories, R. Stewart, *The Foundation of the Conservative Party 1832–1867*, Longman, 1978 has a useful section on pre-1832; A. Mitchell *The Whigs in Opposition 1815–30*, Oxford University Press, 1967 is the standard work on the Whigs. N. Thompson *Wellington after Waterloo*, Routledge, 1986 is essential on a major political player.
17 J. E. Cookson op. cit. p. 186.
18 On economic policies see A. J. B. Hilton op. cit. and J. E. Cookson op. cit. T. L. Crosby, *English Farmers and the Politics of Protection 1815–52*, Harvester, 1977, is excellent on the controversies over the Corn Law. B. Gordon, *Political Economy in Parliament 1819–23*, Macmillan, 1976 and *Economic Doctrine and Tory Liberalism 1824–30*, Macmillan, 1979 are useful on the impact of economic ideas on policy.
19 N. Gash op. cit. pp. 122–3.
20 See the detailed discussion of 'The State of the Nation' in N. Gash (ed.), *Pillars of Government*, Edward Arnold, 1986, pp. 26–42.
21 Radicalism between 1815 and 1822 is examined in chapter 12.
22 On Peel see N. Gash *Mr Secretary Peel: The Life of Sir Robert Peel to 1830*, first published 1960, new edn Longman, 1985.
23 A more detailed consideration of the crisis of Anglicanism can be found in chapter 14.
24 *North Wales Chronicle* 25 February 1809.
25 *Carmarthen Journal* 15 June 1812.
26 For Peel's period as Chief Secretary of Ireland (1812–18) see N. Gash op. cit., chapters 4–6 especially the useful discussion of the administration of Ireland in chapter 4. See also D. McCartney *The Dawning of Democracy: Ireland 1800–1870*, Helicon, 1987.

8 The constitutional revolution 1827–32

The power of prerogative was succeeded by the influence of patronage. The efficiency of the latter has passed away. What talent can now attain itself in this country is so much beyond anything in the gift of a Minister to bestow, that those despise the gift who are most capable of rendering him service. He must now look to the sound opinion of the thinking part of the community. . . . It will equally avail him against the writings of the old Whigs; the defections and bickerings of the ultra Tories; the arts of demagogues; the ravings of dinner and other meetings; the combinations and the violence of portions of the people.[1]

Between February 1827 and late 1832 the British political system underwent major changes which, at least for one historian,[2] marked the end of the *ancien régime*. The stark chronology is straightforward. In 1828 the Test and Corporation Acts were repealed. The following year Catholics were emancipated, ending the spiritual monopoly of Anglicanism. In 1832 there was a measure of parliamentary reform which, though conservative in both intention and effect, did extend the franchise to the 'respectable' sections of society, especially those in towns. This chapter is concerned with examining these events and their impact not simply on England but on Wales, Scotland and Ireland, and with their impact on the political groupings at Westminster.[3]

MINISTERS, MINISTRIES AND ISSUES

Canning in power

Lord Liverpool's stroke in February 1827 and his resignation the following month released tensions over religion and reform which had previously been held in check.[4] Michael Bentley may be correct in maintaining that Liverpool's Toryism was 'dead and buried' before February 1827 but this neglects the role which he had had in reducing the political temperature on the controversial issues of corn, Catholics and the franchise during the 1820s. Between 1827 and 1832 there was a 'confusion' or 'flux' of party as both Whigs and Tories underwent major divisions and realignments. Frank O'Gorman contentiously argues that:

> By the end of it, both had repaired their damaged cohesion and were preparing to adjust themselves to the new electoral world in which they now had to live. The ability of the parties to ride out the political upheavals of these years says much for their strength as parties and for the extent to which politics was hardening into a two-party mould before 1832.[5]

Lord Liverpool was one of the few Tory ministers to work successfully with George Canning whose appointment as Prime Minister was bound to be controversial. George IV accepted Canning, an individual for whom he had the deepest personal antagonism, for good reasons. Canning commanded the House of Commons, most Tory MPs wanted him, he was popular in the country and ambition meant he would accept nothing less. His appointment combined royal convenience, parliamentary assent and popular approval. But leading Tories refused to serve under him. Wellington, Peel, Eldon and four others resigned from the cabinet and this prompted thirty-five resignations from minor office-holders.

The revolt against Canning was, however, far more than an expression of dislike for an individual but the result of fears among sections of the Tory party which had been gathering momentum since 1821. Canning's political identity was defined by his belief in the desirability of Catholic emancipation, the need to restructure the Corn Laws and the pursuit of a foreign policy designed to enhance Britain's global trading position. Each of these positions was suspect and exposed fundamental divisions between Tories. Through the 1820s Tory 'Protestants' and agriculturalists had been unable to persuade the Commons to reflate the economy, arrest the tendency towards free trade, reinforce agricultural protection and repeal the malt tax. Robinson's corn bill had been forced on the landed interest in 1826 to quieten agitation in northern manufacturing towns and the success of O'Connell in Ireland meant that the Catholic question could no longer be ducked. The most common reason given by those who resigned was that Canning was an advocate of Catholic emancipation, but this neglects the fact that he had no intention of promoting it as a government measure. Catholic emancipation remained an 'open' question in his cabinet.

Suspicion of his motives and ambitions was sufficient reason for some leading Tories to remain outside Canning's government. The political vacuum created on the ministerialist side was filled by a small group from within the Whig party. Lansdowne, Devonshire, Tierney and Lamb accepted office and others offered support from outside. Grey disowned them publicly. Ellenborough pressed for firm opposition and the radical Whigs around Althorp wanted no part. This alliance between liberal Tories and some Whigs promised to realign politics during the ministries of Canning and Goderich on the basis of liberals prepared to contemplate constitutional reform and Ultra Tories and diehard reactionaries for whom reform was unthinkable but within a year it had collapsed.

There were no great parliamentary trials of strength during Canning's short ministry. The 1826 election had reinforced the 'Protestant' representation in the Commons and Burdett's second parliamentary attempt to Catholic relief failed there, the first motion to do so since 1819. Canning would obviously do everything possible to avoid 'Ireland' when Parliament sat. Parliamentary reform was also to be avoided. Canning had consistently opposed it and it was unacceptable to his Tory supporters. The Whigs liked Canning's Greek liberalism and the St Petersburg protocol of 1826 was hardened into the Treaty of London the following spring. Canning's attempt to reform the Corn Laws was diluted in the Commons to make it tolerable to his supporters but destroyed in the Lords by Wellington, who emerged as a public statesman for the first time.

Goderich: an inadequate leader

Canning's health had begun to fail early in 1827 and in August he died. George IV was unwilling to have a Whig Prime Minister nor would he have Peel, whom he disliked, or Wellington, of whom he was afraid. He turned to Robinson, ennobled by Canning as Viscount Goderich. An efficient Chancellor of the Exchequer, Goderich was painfully aware of his inadequacies as Prime Minister and the six months he held 'power' were marked by a revival of royal power. The king bullied Goderich into accepting Herries as Chancellor of the Exchequer and kept his Whig supporters out of office. Herries' resignation following a trivial argument with Huskisson persuaded Goderich to resign in January 1828 without meeting Parliament. The king's only alternative was a remodelled Tory government with Wellington as Prime Minister and Peel leading the Commons. The Whigs returned to the opposition benches in obvious embarrassment while the more liberal Tories headed by Huskisson stayed in office. Wellington appeared to have restored the normal pattern of two-party politics, continuing the characteristic economic and fiscal policies of the early 1820s. But the attempt to rebuild the Tory party as it had been under Liverpool stood little chance of success. Wellington and Peel had difficulty in keeping the ministry together and Huskisson and his allies left office in May 1828. Wellington lacked Canning's popular appeal and when events compelled the ministry to give way over repeal and emancipation his coalition was shattered. Increasingly the ministry became incapable of governing.

Wellington: general as Prime Minister

Wellington had been in the cabinet since 1819 but as Master of the Ordnance, hardly a position on which to build a political reputation. His battles with Canning over foreign policy had not been in public and he had even acted as Canning's plenipotentiary at St Petersburg during Anglo-Russian mediation between Greece and Turkey in 1826. What was not in question, however, was his commitment to Protestantism and his defensiveness on agriculture. During 1827 he assumed the role of Protestant pillar and defender of protectionism. In the first he was aided by the death of the Duke of York, the king's brother and heir to the throne, in early 1827. York had consistently opposed emancipation and his death advanced the Catholic cause in two important respects. First, it silenced a fanatical opponent who, as heir to the throne, had commanded great resources of propaganda. Secondly, it meant that William, Duke of Clarence would succeed on the king's death and he seemed to contemporaries to be potentially 'a very decent king'. Wellington attracted to himself much of the charisma that York had acquired and his actions following Liverpool's resignation in leaving government and destroying Robinson's corn bill in the Lords further enhanced his reputation as the Protestant champion. Some Tories were, however, uneasy about his becoming commander-in-chief in the Goderich ministry – was this the beginning of his capitulation to the Canningites?

From the beginning Wellington's government was narrowly based. Until May 1828 it included the Canningites led by Huskisson, but it lacked the strength to command events or to control Parliament. As economic depression and dislocation returned at the end of the 1820s, agitation for fundamental reforms reached new heights. Wellington's dilemma was a stark one. Concessions which threatened the absolute supremacy of the Anglican Church, particularly emancipation, threatened a backlash from the backbench ultra Tories. Failing to act in line with what Peel recognized in 1828 as increasingly liberal public opinion could unite Canningites and Whigs within Parliament and raised the spectre of revolutionary activity outside. O'Gorman argues that during 1828 and 1829 Wellington's government went through a process of 'reluctant self-liquidation' as first repeal and then emancipation was conceded.

Religious emancipation

Repeal of the Test and Corporation Acts was championed by a strong alliance of extra-parliamentary Dissenters with a strong national organization. Lord John Russell's motion for repeal was, however, prompted as much by the new party configurations as by external pressures. The statutes were hardly ever enforced and the government bowed to the will of the majority and to the mood of the moment, reversed its earlier opposition and allowed Peel to pilot the legislation through the Commons. In the Lords there was an even more emphatic collapse of the will to resist and the bench of bishops overwhelmingly supported the proposal. The Ultras tolerated repeal but Catholic emancipation was a different matter.

The real obstacle to emancipation, however, lay in the Court and in the House of Lords and the events of 1828–9 showed that resistance was even crumbling there. The resignation of Huskisson and his supporters precipitated a by-election in County Clare with the appointment of Vesey Fitzgerald to head the Board of Trade, bringing the matter into focus. O'Connell's victory in July 1828 and his inability as a Catholic to take his seat in the Commons faced Wellington and Peel with two alternatives. They could either use force, which they did not have, to put down the threat from the Catholic Association or concede emancipation. Calling a general election would resolve nothing since, as the 1826 election had shown, anti-Catholic feelings were strong on the mainland and it was probable that British rule of Ireland would be thrown into question by the election of ineligible Catholic MPs. Wellington came to the conclusion that emancipation must be conceded and as a result undermined the 'Protestant' basis of his ministry.

Wellington was faced with opposition from the king and sections of the Tory party, the growth of the Protestant Brunswick movement inspired by the Duke of Cumberland and Lord Eldon – by mid 1829 over 200 Brunswick Clubs existed in England and Ireland to defend the existing constitution – and the increased activities of the Catholic Association. By early 1829 the Ultras were a party within a party. Wellington and Peel achieved emancipation but at the cost of splitting the Tories and creating an atmosphere of personal distrust, particularly of Peel, which returned in the 1840s. A fundamental tenet of Tory belief had been abandoned by their own.

Wellington's ministry limped on for over a year after emancipation, supported with little relish by some Tories and opposed with little real vigour by the Whigs. Economic depression in late 1829 brought widespread distress to manufacturing and agricultural areas and denied Wellington the calm conditions necessary to allow the political situation to settle. Reform was still on the agenda and there were demands for parliamentary reform as well as calls for currency reform and the repeal of the Corn Laws. The Whigs, though still unable to defeat the ministry, showed signs of revival in early 1830 and Russell's unsuccessful attempt to enfranchise Manchester, Leeds and Birmingham in February brought Whig and radical sentiments together. Grey perceived the strength of reform feeling at this time. Lord Althorp provided long-needed leadership for the Whigs in the Commons and there were even suggestions that Huskisson and his supporters might be brought into a Whig government.

The 1830 election

Wellington did not fully appreciate the weakness of his position in January 1830 when Parliament reconvened and his room for manoeuvre was further reduced by the death of George IV on 26 June. This had two important consequences. First, it removed the royal veto on Grey and the Whigs, significantly weakening Wellington's ministry. Secondly, a general election had to be held within six months which opened up the political and parliamentary system to popular influence. Although the July revolution in France did not affect the outcome of the general election – Halévy believed it had and historians supported this until Norman Gash provided evidence that only a minority of seats were undeclared when news of the revolution reached England – it did provide an important reference point for the rest of 1830 especially as there were widespread 'Swing' disturbances across much of southern and eastern England.

The election ran against the government, though it is difficult to estimate gains and losses. There were some outstanding Whig victories – Brougham's virtually unopposed victory in Yorkshire was the most spectacular – but less than a third of constituencies were contested. It seems that the government lost between ten and fifteen seats and the opposition gained between twenty-five and thirty. Wellington could count on the support of about 250 MPs, and opposition supporters (Whigs and Canningites) about 200, with 212 doubtful or uncommitted. Was the 1830 election a victory for reformers? Certainly there was evidence of widespread reformist sentiments in the country but general elections before the late nineteenth century were rarely fought on specific issues – those of 1784 and 1807 were exceptions. There was, however, no doubting the lack of enthusiasm for the government and the permanent shift of opinion, perceived most clearly by the Whigs, among the emerging middle classes against the existing system of representation.

Wellington's primary concern was to keep his government in existence and to this end he attempted to bring the Canningites back into the Tory fold. Huskisson's death in September, following an accident at the opening of the Liverpool–Manchester railway, opened the possibility of a Whig arrangement with the Canningites now led by William Lamb, Viscount Melbourne and Henry Temple, Viscount Palmerston. They had been impressed by the strength of reforming opinion in the country and were willing to contemplate the reform of Parliament, something Canning would never have accepted. Their refusal to take office without the Whigs threw Wellington back on the Ultras but they were equally unwilling to reinforce his ministry. The bitterness created by emancipation made reconciliation difficult even over opposition to reform. Wellington's statement on 2 November that the constitution was perfect and possessed the confidence of the people may be seen as a last-ditch attempt to get ultra support but it had disastrous effects. It united the Whig, Radical, Ultra and Canningite opposition and Wellington resigned on 16 November 1830 following defeat on the Civil List the previous day by 233 to 204.

The Whigs in power

Wellington was defeated by a broad coalition of groups, Whig and Tory. The reform issue created a temporary confusion of parties but the Tories and Ultras returned to their natural home before 1832. On the Whig side there was a more significant realignment of party groupings with the absorption of the Canningites. The government which Grey formed in late 1830 was, however, far from an exclusively party ministry. It contained 'old' Whigs like Lansdowne, Carlisle and Lord Holland; the Canningites Goderich, Grant, Melbourne, at the Home Office, and Palmerston at the Foreign Office; a few ultra Tories including the Duke of Richmond in the cabinet while Durham and Brougham represented radical Whiggism. It was not until reform was achieved that the non-Whig office-holders were shed and that Grey's ministry became a party one.

Crisis and reform

The Reform crisis of 1831–2 heightened party activity and deepened public involvement in the political conflict at Westminster. The government initially performed badly, its revenue proposals were torn apart in the Commons and reform was the one issue on which it showed any real flair. To achieve substantial reform Grey had to gain sufficient support in the Commons and Lords and from the king. The first reform bill passed the Commons by one vote and when an adverse amendment was carried in committee Grey persuaded a reluctant king to dissolve Parliament. The general election of April and May 1831 brought victory for the reformers, who won almost all of the 'open' boroughs while only six of the thirty-four county MPs who had voted against reform on the second reading or on the critical amendment got back into Westminster. The MPs split into 370 pro-reformers, 235 anti-reformers and 53 doubtful. Grey could now get his bill through the Commons. A second reform bill passed in September 1831 only to be defeated by 41 votes in the Lords on 8 October. Grey was faced with three options. First, he could abandon reform altogether. This was ruled out by his ministry's public commitment to the issue and the momentum of public opinion outside. Secondly, he could try to persuade a significant number of peers to change their minds. Grey attempted unsuccessfully to negotiate with a group of 'waverers' led by Wharncliffe and Harrowby who saw greater disaster in rejecting the next bill than accepting an amended form of it. Thirdly, he could threaten to swamp the Lords with new Whig creations and compel acceptance of reform. Durham, Brougham and Russell enthusiastically supported this option but Grey, Richmond, Althorp and the king were nervous.

A third bill passed the Commons before Christmas 1831 and it seemed certain that, with the agreement extracted from the king to create Whig peers, it would pass the Lords. But Grey was defeated in a division and the king accepted the resignation of the government rather than countenance the creation of peers. Ten days were wasted while the king tried to create an administration led by Wellington. With nowhere to turn, Grey was recalled and, with the guarantee of creations, the bill passed the Lords in June.[6]

A 'constitutional revolution'

Between 1828 and 1835 the *ancien régime* was transformed and this was recognized by contemporaries – a contributor to the *Quarterly Review* spoke of a new political era with a new constitution. The five pieces of legislation which led to this transformation – repeal of the Test and Corporation Acts, Catholic Emancipation, parliamentary reform in 1832, the Poor Law Amendment Act of 1834 and the Municipal Corporations Act of 1835 – were connected chronologically and by internal political logic. Repeal in 1828 pointed directly to Catholic emancipation which led to the reform of Parliament. Municipal reform was linked to both civil and ecclesiastical reform, giving Dissenters urban power by reforming Anglican corporations. The Poor Law Amendment Act, it was argued, went some way to depriving the landed interest of one of their major functions in the counties.[7] Just how big a transformation was this 'constitutional revolution'? Was it a compromise to prevent revolution? Did it really alter the balance of power within the British political system?

CHANGE AND CONTINUITY

Tensions and crises

There had always been tensions and crises of confidence in the traditional institutions. Radical attitudes before the French Revolution have recently been focused upon by several historians: John Brewer sees the 1760s as the 'crucial decade', Colin Bonwick has pointed to the great strides taken by radicalism in the 1760s and 1770s and Walter Shelton has highlighted the 'shock waves' which the food riots of the 1760s sent through English society. The 1790s saw an enthusiastic revival for the traditional constitution caused by revulsion at the excesses of the French Revolution and the patriotism of a country at war. John Cannon and J. C. D. Clark are not alone in believing in the strength of the Protestant constitution into the 1820s. So why did the situation change? One explanation is that those excluded from power grew stronger while the conviction of the governing classes that they should be excluded grew weaker. This is, however, not in itself sufficient explanation for the 'constitutional revolution'. As long as those excluded from power did not join forces – a major difficulty given hostility between Dissenters and Catholics and the unlikelihood of co-operation between the emergent middle classes and those without property – concessions on fundamental issues could easily be resisted. In addition the Whigs, the only political grouping committed (more or less) to funda-mental reform were themselves excluded from office. For reform to be successful it was necessary for certain conditions to exist. First, those excluded from power should have lost confidence in the existing system to such an extent that they were willing to take concerted and, within limits, united action to achieve their objectives. Secondly, those with power needed to believe that the alternative to conceding reform was potentially worse than the reform itself, and so would be willing to act accordingly. This created problems because, given the interconnected nature of the constitution, once reform had begun it gained a momentum of its own which was difficult either to control or stop.

Religious reform

Between 1780 and 1820 there was no massive conversion by the population of Britain to either religious toleration or political reform. What was clear, however, was the gradual erosion of the numerical position of Anglicanism and the related growth of Protestant Dissent and unbelief,[8] and by 1828 the continued exclusion of thousands of loyal Protestants from full partici-pation in the political life of the country could no longer be justified. Dissenters profited from the success of Catholic claims and to Anglicans could even seem allies in defence of the Protestant constitution. Lord John Russell introduced a motion for repeal of the Test and Corporation Acts which passed the Commons on 26 February by 237 to 193 votes with remarkable ease. Peel made a token opposition but the government had no automatic majority and the dissenting interest was strong in many constituencies. Between February and May 1828 Peel piloted a repeal bill through the Commons and Wellington made no attempt to mobilize the Lords in opposition. No bishop opposed the bill and, as it passed the Lords, no division was forced on the principle of the measure, though some amendments were accepted. The *Annual Register* noted that it was: 'the first successful blow that had been aimed at the supremacy of the Established Church since the Revolution',[9] and that it demonstrated a marked change in the nature of English society.

Catholic emancipation

For those who opposed the repeal of the Test and Corporation Acts, the debates took place in the shadow of Catholic emancipation.[10] Repeal established the principle that the constitution *could* be changed. The question of Catholic emancipation was bound up with Ireland but, as

J. C. D. Clark says 'Religion, nationalism and allegiance were as inseparable in the Irish case as in the English.'[11]

The 1826 general election had shown the depth of anti-Catholic sentiment among the British electorate, attitudes exacerbated by the influx of Irish immigrants after 1800 and especially after the 1821 famine. Lancashire was particularly badly hit and the resources at the disposal of poor law officials were badly strained. Bristol overseers of the poor petitioned for assistance and select committees investigated the problem of the Irish poor in 1823 and 1828. The Catholic Irish, concentrated in London and other cities, were perceived as a political threat to the Protestant Establishment and, for much of the nineteenth century, government was haunted by the spectre of union between Irish nationalism and radical agitation. But there had been major changes in Ireland which made resistance by Wellington's government increasingly untenable. There had been a marked alteration in the demographic balance between Ireland and England and Wales. By 1821 there were some 6.8 million Irish to 12 million people in England and Wales – the Irish had increased to over half its population. From the 1780s concessions for Catholics and Protestants had been prised from successive British governments but, as the 1798 rebellion showed, these had been insufficient to eliminate religious tensions. The Act of Union pushed Irish problems directly on to Westminster but, contrary to Pitt's original intention, brought in the Irish without Catholic emancipation and denied the possibility of establishing a more stable and sympathetic relationship between the two countries.

The County Clare election in July 1828, caused by the promotion of Vesey Fitzgerald to the Board of Trade, brought the issue of emancipation to a head, though opponents like Lord Eldon expected the ministry to capitulate on the issue even before the election. Resistance to Catholic emancipation inside Westminster had been crumbling since 1812 – in 1813 a motion had passed the Commons only to fail by one vote in the Lords; in 1823 Nugent's bill, supported by Peel, passed the Commons by 59 votes only to be wrecked in the Lords; and in May 1828 there was a majority of six for emancipation in the Commons – though it is ironic that it was finally carried by perhaps the most 'Protestant' Commons elected since 1800.

Wellington and Peel were faced by two contradictory pressures in late 1828 and early 1829. O'Connell's victory at County Clare brought the prospect of civil war in Ireland much closer. But English public opinion was overwhelmingly opposed to any further concessions. In the event County Clare was a fortunate accident for it allowed Wellington and Peel to represent their introduction of emancipation as a prudent act of political necessity to forestall widespread disturbances in Ireland. The king's speech on 5 February 1829 in effect announced the government's intention to introduce emancipation. It was followed by a widespread petitioning campaign and by March, when the first reading of the bill took place, there had been 957 petitions in opposition compared to 357, mostly from Ireland, in favour. Despite opposition in the Commons and the campaign led by Winchelsea and Eldon in the Lords emancipation was easily achieved.

The cost for Wellington and Peel was high. They were both castigated as betrayers of the ancient constitution and Church. Peel felt obliged to offer himself for re-election to his constituents at Oxford University and was defeated. Wellington fought a duel with the Ultra Lord Winchelsea, though Peel declined to vindicate his honour against his equally savage critic, Sir Charles Wetherell. More important was the legacy of bitterness within the Tory party. A group of Ultras announced their conversion to parliamentary reform as the only way of defending what was left of the existing constitution. For the Ultras Parliament had been corruptly influenced and the executive had acted against the wishes of public opinion.

PARLIAMENTARY REFORM: ISSUES AND TENSIONS

The issue of parliamentary reform can be seen as a dialogue between three groups within British society: the 'lower orders', the middle classes and the ruling aristocratic elite.[12] Catholicism and Dissent were reasonably defined units during the campaigns for repeal and emancipation. By contrast the 'lower orders' and the middle classes were vague terms and masked ambiguities of response to demands for reform, and the ruling classes were themselves far from unanimous in their attitudes.

Peel denied that the lower orders were excluded from power under the existing system of representation and there certainly were examples of unreformed boroughs where very humble people had the vote. But they were isolated, few in number and possessed little real political clout and it is hardly surprising that they came to see their vote as a marketable commodity. William Cobbett, who stood as a non-bribery candidate for Honiton in 1806, was accused of taking bread out of the mouths of the poor. The lower orders were therefore not unanimous in their support for reform. There was massive involvement of the working population in the reform agitation but it centred on traditional pre-industrial groups rather than those spawned by factory and machine. The Reform riots of 1831 took place in Derby and Nottingham, manufacturing centres but not factory towns; Bristol, a commercial centre, and Bath and Worcester, both some distance from industrial centres. However, there were certain developments evident by the late 1820s compared with the 1810s. The lower orders were generally more politically aware, less deferential towards their social superiors, increasingly organized and with better prospects of finding allies. This growing political consciousness can be seen in two important ways. First, there was an increase in the scale of petitioning: in 1784 Bristol and Glasgow submitted petitions of 5,000 and 4,000 names apiece but by 1829 this had risen to 39,000 and 37,000 respectively. Not everyone who signed was from the lower orders but the sheer size of some petitions

– 81,000 in an anti-Catholic petition from Kent – means that many poor people must have signed. Other petitions stated that they came from less prosperous groups. Secondly, there was an increase in the circulation and numbers of newspapers, which indicates that a large proportion of the lower orders must have had some knowledge of contemporary events. Newspapers like the *Gorgon* and the *Poor Man's Guardian* were specifically aimed at the lower orders. Increased political consciousness did not necessarily mean that it either could or would be translated into actual political power.

It was, however, not the numerical strength of the lower orders which was of real importance in the late 1820s but the conversion of many of the middle classes to the cause of reform. The middle classes did not form a homogeneous group in the early nineteenth century. Many of them qualified as voters in both counties and boroughs and played a role in local government as councillors and aldermen, as JPs and in public offices. There was little indication that this situation was resented in either rural or urban settings. By the 1820s the middle classes had taken a more prominent position in demands for reform than the lower orders. They challenged the philosophical justifications behind a Parliament dominated by the landed interest. This represented a growing awareness of their numbers and of their role as producers of wealth. It also marked a growing suspicion of the willingness of Parliament to legislate on behalf of the community at large rather than just for a particular section of society. A Wolverhampton manufacturer said that:

> Fifty years ago we were not in that need of Representatives which we are at present. . . . We now manufacture for the whole world and if we have not members to promote and extend our commerce, the era of our commercial greatness is at an end.

The introduction of the Corn Laws increased middle-class suspicion that government was prepared to introduce *laissez-faire* measures only when they served its purpose while protecting the farmer. The feeling of difference and separation from the aristocratic elite was exacerbated by the Nonconformity of the middle classes and led to a religious challenge to the spiritual monopoly of Anglicanism. In general terms they did not as yet seek universal suffrage or a position outside the existing aristocratic system. But the lack of middle-class representation in most industrial towns was increasingly unacceptable given their developing industrial and manufacturing power. For the Whig ministers in 1830–2 the vital thing was to break the radical alliance between the middle classes and the working population and, in Grey's words, 'to associate the middle with the higher orders of society in the love and support of the institutions and government of the country'.

This emphasis on extra-parliamentary pressure is open to the serious objection that the aristocratic elite never lost their parliamentary domination. John Cannon argues that there was a marked lack of unity within the governors and that three basic attitudes among politicians were present.[13] First, an important section of the aristocracy, primarily Whig, sympathized with the claims of the middle classes and were prepared to reconstruct the political system on more 'liberal' lines. Secondly, there were many politicians who, while unenthusiastic about reform, were prepared to make concessions rather than risk direct and potentially revolutionary confrontation between rich and poor. Thirdly, there was a vociferous group, especially strong in the House of Lords, opposed to all change in the social and political system. Opposed to repeal and emancipation, initially in favour of reform, the Ultras were vocal, quotable and losers. They fought each major issue from 1828 to 1835 tooth and nail and on every occasion they lost.

Why did the Whigs favour reform?

Why did the Whigs, a predominantly aristocratic party, take up the banner of reform? It would seem that in doing so they were acting against their own interests. In fact reform was both advantageous and necessary for the Whigs. By the 1820s they had established a powerful claim to be considered the least successful of modern political parties, doomed to a permanent political wilderness. It is not surprising that some should begin to question the merits of a system under which they did so conspicuously badly. The increased attacks on the inadequacies of the electoral system and their belief in the need to give expression to middle-class opinion were undoubtedly important but at the heart of their commitment to reform was the political advantage it would bring. By disfranchizing the smaller boroughs dominated by the Tory interest and removing industrial from county interests the Whigs could strengthen their position in the Commons and their prospects of office (see Table 8.1).

Table 8.1 The potential impact of reform

	Tory	Whig
Boroughs over 10,000	25	34
5–10,000	24	25
under 1,000	55	16

Source: From a lecture given by E. A. Smith, Reading University, 1969 and based on an 1825 memorandum in the Fitzwilliam Papers.

Political advantages, belief in the necessity of attaching the 'respectable' to a modified but still overwhelmingly aristocratic parliamentary system and the effective mobilization of public opinion in a situation of political excitement and flux lay at the heart of the Whig strategies in the debates on and passage of reform between 1830 and 1832.

Reform as a focus for discontent

Derek Fraser sees the reform movement as an amalgam of 'discontents, policies, motivations, activities and personalities of fluctuating and regional intensity'.[14] Crucial to the reform issue were six interrelated strands. First, the reform demands of the Ultra Tories were a direct legacy of 1829. They argued that if Parliament could pass Catholic emancipation against what they saw public opinion to be it was in need of reforming since it did not reflect the nation's wishes. Ultra Tory attacks – like the radical one – were directed against pocket boroughs through which, they believed, the executive dominated Parliament. The significance of their demands for reform lay in making the cry for reform more general.

Secondly, the political excitement, particularly in urban areas, consequent on the 1830 general election and the July Revolution in France helped to maintain the political momentum already created. Thirdly, the existence of discontent, even before the 1830 election, can be explained by the economic distress which affected rural and urban areas between 1829 and 1832 and which, with the cholera outbreak of 1831–2, maintained the intensity of protest. Poor harvests in 1829–30 ushered in a period of depression and throughout the agitation there were high poor rates, widespread unemployment, slack trade and low wages. There was considerable fear among the governing classes that this would result in some sort of union between middle-class radicals and the protests of the lower orders where, as in Birmingham, the structure of society and industry was conducive to such a development. Fourth, this led to the formation of the Birmingham Political Union (BPU) by Thomas Attwood in December 1829 and the subsequent creation of political unions elsewhere based on the Birmingham model. Political unions were the typical local lobbying unit during the reform agitation, organizing local opinion through the dual channels of public meetings and petitions. Reform was not necessarily always the primary concern of these unions and the Tory Croker claimed that in the vast majority of petitions the most prominent demand was not for parliamentary reform but the reduction of taxes and the abolition of tithes. The political unions were characterized by their emphasis on constitutional legality – the BPU motto was 'Peace, Law and Order' – and on co-operation between the middle classes and the lower orders. Attwood later claimed that the unions had achieved three things during the agitation: they had created a public opinion which favoured reform; showed that they were not law-breaking bodies and had kept enthusiasm at boiling point. This exaggerated the degree of success which the unions had over industrial Britain. Birmingham artisans may have been able to identify with the emerging middle-class ideology of 'respectability' but opinion elsewhere was less restrained. Manchester weavers, Leeds croppers and Leicester framework knitters did not identify as closely with the middle classes and were consequently more radical and less law-abiding in their approaches to the issue.

Fifthly, a more menacing aspect of the reform agitation was attacks on property. Fraser argues that England was 'standing on the edge of a precipice of disorder throughout the years of agitation'.[15] Nobody in authority was happy about civil disorder *but* neither were the leaders of the reform movement, who judged correctly that the threat of public disorder was a powerful lever but that actual disorder was political suicide. Threats to property, feared by the aristocratic elite and embarrassing to reformers, were an integral aspect of these years. The decision of the Anglican Church to oppose reform in 1831 led to widespread attacks on the clergy. Popular organizations began to break free from more moderate leaders. Bishops were in physical danger: the bishop's palace in Bristol was burned down during three days of rioting and that in Exeter was only saved by armed force. The non-payment of tithes and church rates was threatened and Disestablishment became a widespread cry. In 1832 the disorders known as the 'Days of May', when the king and the Lords again resisted reform, seemed to many to be a preliminary to civil war.

Finally, it is important not to underestimate the enormous influence wielded by the press on behalf of reform. By 1830 many of the London papers – *The Times*, the *Examiner*, the *Globe* and the *Westminster Review* – had all cited parliamentary reform as one of the great issues of the times. But it was in the provinces that the real power of the reform press lay since the fulcrum of reform was there rather than in London.[16] The *Leeds Mercury*, edited by the Baines father and son, had already adopted a liberal stance in 1815, supported repeal and emancipation and opposed the privileges of the Church of England, campaigned for Brougham's election for Yorkshire in 1830 and actively promoted moderate reform. Archibald Prentice adopted a radical Benthamite tone in the *Manchester Guardian*, founded in 1828. He was a staunch advocate of universal suffrage and vote by ballot and contended optimistically that middle and working classes were now united in support of thorough but rational reform. Prentice played a leading role in establishing the Manchester political union which aspired to bring together men and masters, spoke at all the chief meetings in Manchester in support of the three reform bills, accepted the need to create peers to overcome opposition in the Lords and rejoiced, when the Reform Act finally passed, that 'the people and the press are, thank God! triumphant'.

1830–2: a revolution thwarted?

The emotional atmosphere created outside Parliament and the tensions between opponents and supporters of reform did not make reform a foregone conclusion in the summer of 1830. The alliance of the Whigs with the Ultras made Grey's ministry, to a striking degree, one of blue blood and great landowners. The Reform Act, ironically, was framed and passed by those who had most to lose and who believed they were acting wisely and liberally to preserve the existing social order. The Act eventually passed in 1832 was moderate, at least in principle if not in its effects. The ballot, universal suffrage, annual Parliaments, equal electoral districts and the payment of MPs – the more extreme radical demands – had no place in the perspective of Grey and many of his colleagues and would certainly not have received parliamentary approval. The Whig reform focused on the form of the franchise and the redistribution of seats and this left almost endless scope for negotiation, debate and resistance.

Grey appointed a committee consisting of Durham, his son-in-law, J. W. Ponsonby (who became Viscount Duncannon in 1834), Lord John Russell and Sir James Graham in late 1830 to consider some reform measure. Its brief was, however, limited since Grey added the proviso that it must retain 'the essential character of the Constitution'. By the end of January 1831 when it reported Grey was already advocating a 'conservative' measure. There had been riots in rural England in late 1830, which had already frightened the Ultras, and news of revolution in Belgium and Poland and unrest in Italy. He squashed the idea of the secret ballot and only accepted the £10 household franchise when the Office of Taxes showed that £20 householders were too thinly spread to make the higher threshold worthwhile. On 1 March 1831 Russell introduced the first reform bill into a stunned House of Commons. He proposed to disfranchise boroughs of less than 2,000 inhabitants while boroughs with under 4,000 people lost one member. This created 168 vacancies of which 34 were to be given to unrepresented boroughs, 55 to the counties and 9 to Scotland. The remaining vacancies were not to be filled, with a resulting reduction in the overall size of the Commons. The existing 40-shilling freehold franchise was to remain in the counties and a uniform borough franchise was proposed for the occupation of buildings, as owner or tenant, with an annual value of £10. Grey had identified three cardinal principles behind reform – disfranchising rotten boroughs, enfranchising new towns and the uniform £10 household franchise – and these aimed to amend the existing system to make it acceptable rather than create a new one.

These proposals were hardly 'revolutionary' but the Tories stressed five major objections in their opposition to the measures. First, they argued that the bill was an uncompensated confiscation of private property and of corporate and customary rights. Secondly, it was as full of anomalies as the old system. Thirdly, there would be an inevitable transfer of 'influence' from the landed to the industrial areas of the country. Fourthly, the new system would make it impossible for government to be carried out because there would be insufficient patronage to back up the executive. Finally, it would 'open the floodgates' and eventually result in the destruction of the existing constitution. The Whigs countered these charges by claiming that ordered change was necessary and that their proposals were the result of a sensible assessment of the situation. They emphasized that the extension of the franchise was both limited and moderate, that landed property would still be represented – the county representation was to be extended – but so would commercial and industrial areas and that by not introducing reform the floodgates of uncontrollable popular demands would be opened and the existing constitution destroyed.

Most of these arguments were used in the debates during March 1831 but it was soon painfully clear that Whig control over the House of Commons was tenuous and that the bill would certainly be defeated in the Lords. The division on the second reading, on 23 March, the famous victory of 302 to 301, was decisive. Most of the Ultras divided with the opposition; of the 140 identifiable Ultras only 28 voted for the bill. The victory was achieved by a combination of the Irish members, who backed the bill by 51 to 36, and English county members, who similarly backed reform by 51 to 25. The English borough members were opposed by 205 to 174. This was an insufficient majority to carry the bill, but sufficient to persuade William IV to agree to a general election when the ministry was defeated in committee in April.

The 1831 general election followed only a week after the snap dissolution and, according to J. C. D. Clark, 'voting took place in a semi-revolutionary mood of excitement and resentment against the Bill's opponents'.[17] The result was a landslide against the Ultras. Public opinion made itself felt in the large 'open' boroughs and in the English counties, and the extent of public commitment to reform became evident. Of the 82 English county members, 76 were returned in favour of reform. The pro-reform victory gave Grey a majority of between 130 and 140 and the Tory opposition to reform, especially that led by Peel, was increasingly 'measured', if not 'indifferent'. He refused to align himself with the Ultras and was instinctively drawn to compromise and concession, but to 'rat' again would have been political suicide. For opponents of reform the Whig majority meant that it was no longer an issue of principle but one of the degree of that reform.

On 24 June Russell introduced a second bill, which passed its second reading by 136 votes (367 to 231) and though the committee stage dragged on through the summer it finally passed the Commons on 22 September (345 to 236). One important concession which was made to the landed interest was government acceptance of the so-called 'Chandos clause' which proposed enfranchising tenants-at-will paying annual rentals of £50. Attention now shifted to the Lords where, following five weeks of debate, the bill was defeated by 41 votes (199 to 158). Popular violence, especially riots in Nottingham, Bristol and Derby left ministers undecided about their next move. Melbourne at the Home Office thought the crisis not merely dangerous but quite new in its intensity. Peel dashed to Drayton Manor to protect his family from the Birmingham Political Union and the Derby rioters. The decision to prorogue Parliament, ban any military organization among the Political Unions, and then return just before Christmas to introduce the bill again, along with the intensity of the cholera epidemic may have helped to quieten the situation.

Grey found three alternatives open to him in the autumn of 1831. First and quite unacceptably, he could abandon or defer reform. Secondly, he could attempt to persuade members of the House of Lords of the untenable nature of their opposition. Finally, he could threaten to swamp the Lords with new Whig peers and steamroller the bill through. Grey briefly flirted with the second option in negotiation with a group of peers known as the 'waverers' but soon realized that success could only be achieved through either the threat or the reality of a massive creation of Whig peers. A third, revised, bill was introduced on 12 December 1831, was passed by the Commons before Christmas by 162 votes (324 votes to 162) and was then passed to the Lords. On 13 April 1832 it passed its second reading by nine votes (184 to 175) but, despite consultations between Grey and opposition leaders, it encountered difficulties at the committee stage. A wrecking amendment was carried in the first week of May and, when the king refused to create sufficient Whig peers, Grey resigned. This led to the crisis known as the 'Days of May' when the king investigated the possibility of Wellington forming a government which would then pass a more modest reform measure.

This Tory interlude was accompanied by widespread extra-parliamentary activity. Property owners threatened to withhold taxes. Westminster was flooded with anti-Tory petitions. Francis Place suggested that investors should withdraw their assets from banks immediately, precipitating a financial as well as a political crisis – 'To stop the Duke, Go for Gold' – and armed insurrection was threatened. Peel's refusal to join any government committed to reform meant that Wellington could not form an alternative government. Grey returned with the king's assurance that he would create Whig peers and this was sufficient to get the bill through its committee stage. On 6 June it finally passed the Lords by 106 votes to 22, receiving the Royal Assent the following day.

THE REFORM ACTS

The 1832 Acts: England and Wales

The major changes which the Reform Act brought about in England and Wales were as follows. In English and Welsh counties the franchise was given to adult males owning freehold property worth at least 40 shillings per annum, those in possession of a copyhold worth at least £10 per annum or those leasing or renting land worth at least £50 per annum (the result of the 'Chandos clause'). In the boroughs there was a uniform franchise for those occupying property worth at least £10 per annum as well as those who exercised a borough vote before 1832. There was a major redistribution of seats following the disfranchising of 56 English boroughs which lost their representation entirely; Weymouth lost two of its four MPs and 30 boroughs lost one of their two members. In England 22 new parliamentary boroughs were created with two members and 19 with one member. English county representation was also increased. Yorkshire elected six rather than four MPs. Twenty-six counties were split into two divisions each with two MPs, and seven counties received a third member. Six counties retained two members and the Isle of Wight became a separate single-member constituency. In Wales the old system of grouping boroughs was retained but two new single-member constituencies were established for Merthyr Tydfil and Swansea. In Wales three counties now returned two members while the remaining nine retained their one member. The most important and far-reaching of the other clauses of the Reform Act related to the registration of voters for each constituency.

The 1832 Acts: Scotland

In Scotland the constitutional revolution between 1827 and 1832 coincided with the end of Melville management of its political system.[18] The Whig approach to reform in Scotland was through belief in the need for complete assimilation of the Scottish and English political systems as the best way of preventing a resurgence of political management. Their strategy combined a liberal approach to the destruction of Melville-style management with a conservative approach to the franchise. This conservatism consisted in wanting property to prevail against numbers rather than in wanting to preserve institutions. At this stage the Whigs wanted to bring Scottish affairs firmly under the control of the Home Office, limit the role of Lord Advocate to purely legal questions and as far as possible abolish all other Scottish offices.

As in England, arguments for reform hinged on where to set the franchise qualification. If too low, then the Whigs would encourage dangerous popular pressure on the government; if too high, it might push previously 'safe' opinion into the arms of the radicals. The 1830 general election increased support for reform among MPs from 13 to 17 but, with the exception of four MPs, the burghs remained largely impervious to popular opinion. In the counties the Whig representation had doubled in ten years and the election brought them to power. The Whig Lord Advocate, Francis Jeffrey, piloted the Scottish parliamentary reforms through Commons and Lords and they received the Royal Assent on 17 July 1832.

Fear of too great a movement towards democracy determined that the Scottish Reform Act contained not just compromises but deliberately conservative elements. In addition, its passage through Parliament in the wake of the English bill meant that little attention was given to its details and as a result numerous anomalies in its working emerged. The franchise increased the electorate sixteen-fold to about 65,000. In the counties the purpose of the Act was to consolidate the power of the landed gentry. There were few changes in the distribution of the 30 county seats: 27 counties returned one member each and Elgin and Nairn, Ross and Cromarty and Clackmannan and Kinross were joined with each group electing one member. Some of the smallest counties – Bute, Peebles, Sutherland and Selkirk – were separately represented and their MPs continued to be appointees of local magnates. Owners of land with a yearly value of £10 were enfranchised but the rules for leaseholders and tenants were stricter than in England. In the burghs the Whigs intended to destroy the power of local cliques and the vote was given to every owner of property worth £10 a year. Eight extra seats were created with Edinburgh being given an extra member, while Glasgow with two seats and Aberdeen, Dundee, Greenock, Paisley and Perth with one seat were represented separately for the first time. But many of the smaller, more easily corruptible, burghs were allowed to retain their status.

The 1832 Acts: Ireland

Ireland had already undergone recent parliamentary reform before the 1832 Irish Reform Act.[19] The 1800 Union Act eliminated all the smaller boroughs and only slight changes were necessary to the representative system in 1832. The real issue was over franchise. The franchise for boroughs was the same as in England but some cities were legally considered as 'counties of cities' and the right to vote was extended to £10 freeholders and leaseholders. This broke the corporation monopoly and loose nomination system in over half the Irish boroughs. The Catholic emancipation legislation, by replacing the 40-shilling freehold franchise with a uniform £10 freehold qualification, had drastically reduced the electorate. This was augmented in 1832 by leaseholders to the value of £10 with leases of at least twenty years, which increased the number of those entitled to vote to a respectable, though not pre-1829, level. There was no redistribution of county seats, with the 32 counties retaining their two members. 31 boroughs retained their members but an extra member was added to Belfast, Galway, Limerick and Waterford. A second seat was given to the University of Dublin with a franchise extended to all holders of M.A. and higher degrees. As on the mainland, registration of voters was introduced, though until the reforms of the 1850s this was far from accurate.

The right to vote

In broad terms the three Reform Acts redefined who was eligible to vote in both counties and boroughs while permitting those with 'ancient rights' to retain their franchise (many were still doing so when the 1867 Reform Act was passed). Redistributed seats increased the representation, especially in England, of areas of marked demographic growth and introduced a system of registration of voters. What did this mean in practice and what was the significance of reform?

Tables 8.2–8.4 show the effects the Reform Acts had on the electorate and on the composition of the House of Commons.

Table 8.2 Comparison of voters

	Counties	*Boroughs*
England and Wales	1 in every 24 inhabitants	1 in every 17
Scotland	1 in every 45 inhabitants	1 in every 27
Ireland	1 in every 116 inhabitants	1 in every 26

Source: K. T. Hoppen *Elections, Politics and Society in Ireland 1832–1885*, Oxford University Press, 1984 p. 2.

Table 8.3 Approximate size of electorate, 1831 and 1833

England and Wales	*1831*	*1833*	*% increase*
Counties	201,859	370,379	83
Boroughs	164,391	282,398	71
Combined	366,250	652,777	78

Source: E. J. Evans *The Great Reform Act of 1832*, Methuen, London, 1983, p. 50.

Table 8.4 Changed composition of the House of Commons, 1820 and 1832

	County seats		*Borough seats*		*University*		*Total*	
	*1820**	*1832*	*1820*	*1832*	*1820*	*1832*	*1820*	*1832*
England	80	144	405	323	4	4	489	471
Wales	12	15	12	14	–	–	24	29
Scotland	30	30	15	23	–	–	45	53
Ireland	64	64	35	39	1	2	100	105
Total	186	253	467	399	5	6	658	658

* 1820 was taken as a convenient pre-reform starting point since the borough of Grampound was disfranchised in 1821 and its seats transferred to Yorkshire.
Source: As Table 8.3, p. 51.

Comment

Like contemporaries, historians have found it difficult to reach agreement over the Reform Acts. Were they, as Grey observed, essentially 'aristocratic measures' aimed at preserving the landed interest? Were they dangerously democratic in conception as Wellington asserted? Or did they, by eliminating working-class representation, leave the path open to the middle-class oligarchy feared by Peel? There was a range of motives and opinion on the measures among the cabinet, among MPs generally and in the country at large. It is far easier to say what the Acts did not do than what they did.

It is necessary to examine what the Acts actually did and the impact which this had on the operations of the political system. Norman Gash argues that:

> emotional reaction against the scenes which accompanied the bill inevitably coloured many men's views of the bill itself. . . . Divorced from its contemporary context and analysed dispassionately, the Reform Act represented no more than a clumsy but vigorous hacking at the old structure to make it a roughly more acceptable shape. . . . A complete recasting of the electoral system would have been impossible in 1832. It was not only beyond the intention but outside the power of the Whig cabinet. They lacked the necessary statistical information and experience; and they were working in haste to carry out a political pledge. They did not profess to be logical; they were neither doctrinaires nor democrats.[20]

Reform was therefore necessary to the Whigs strategically and tactically, reflecting Grey's anxiety to prevent further radical advance. As in 1793, Grey believed that moderate reform was the only secure route to political stability and away from the slide into revolutionary chaos. It was unnecessary to abandon aristocratic government to achieve this objective. It was, Grey paradoxically maintained, possible to frustrate demands for democracy, not by reactionary strategies, but by a liberal extension of the franchise and by concessions to expansive areas by a redistribution of seats. The existing constitution could be strengthened by attaching to it the new forms of propertied interests. The Acts removed only the most glaring defects of the unreformed system, perpetuated many anomalies and inequalities of representation and were never intended to supply an accurate political mirror of the distribution of economic and social consequence in the country.

In many senses the Reform Acts were a hotchpotch solution, though as has already been noted they were the only solution which the Whigs could really have been expected to achieve given the circumstances. A lack of balance remained between southern and northern England and between county and borough. The south continued to be overrepresented in terms of population and interests at the expense of the north and, even more, of London. Southern counties had about a quarter of the English population but had a third of the MPs. However, there were major changes. Cornwall's representation dropped from 44 to 13 seats and of the 22 new two-member boroughs 14 were in the growing industrial areas of the Midlands and the North and 5 in London. The replacement of Old Sarum and Dungeness by Huddersfield and Rochdale was a belated recognition of the political consequences of industrialization and demographic growth. There was enormous difference in the size of constituencies. Middlesex, for example, was still significantly under-represented with 14 MPs compared to Lancashire's 26. It is possible that, with increased party activity after 1832 and the resulting increase in the number of contested elections, bribery and corruption actually increased.

The Act's treatment of the countryside was strongly influenced by political calculations, in particular the importance to political managers of revitalizing and strengthening the powers of the landed interest. The pre-reform Parliament failed to represent the opinions and interests of the country landowners, many of whom sat not in the open county constituencies but for rotten or pocket boroughs. The Whigs responded by increasing county representation and by purifying it of urban and non-agricultural voters. County MPs were increased from 188 to 253 and the distinction between county and borough made to correspond more closely than before to the economic and social distinction between country and town. The agricultural character of county electorates was boosted by giving 40-shilling freeholders who previously voted in counties but who owned urban property borough votes *and* by enfranchising the middling and large tenant farmers through the Chandos clause. In the counties the most contentious aspect of the English Reform Act was the Chandos clause, an amendment which enfranchised £50 tenants-at-will and increased the county electorate by about 30 per cent more than the Whigs intended and which was superficially feared as a means of increasing the influence of the aristocracy. The importance of the Chandos clause was, according to Norman Gash, exaggerated both at the time and afterwards. Landlord influence continued much as before and most of the new county voters were of the same Tory persuasion as their landlords. But to argue that this was a consequence of the Chandos clause is unjustifiable. Proprietors could, and on occasions did, evict tenants who were politically hostile but this never occurred on a large scale and would have been to the disadvantage of landlords especially if the tenants were good farmers. It was poor farming and low profits by tenants which determined eviction rather than non-deferential electoral behaviour. The Chandos clause cannot be seen as a trade-off by the Whigs, a sophisticated device to strengthen the landed interest while making only minor concessions to the urban middle classes. There was no complete separation between borough and county in the 1832 Act. Urban 40-shilling freeholders voted in the county and many small boroughs were enlarged by taking in the surrounding rural areas. In Wallingford, for example, the electorate voted 2:1 against Blackstone, a local landowner, before 1832 but with the extension of the borough into the surrounding countryside that situation was reversed after 1832. Some dilution of county electorates with urban blood remained and was of political importance in the industrial counties. The Whigs had calculated correctly that an increase in landlord influence would benefit the Tories and therefore retained the urban counterweight in counties which they or their liberal allies might later turn to advantage. Giving a major position in the political nation in the 1830s to the landed and rural elements was not simply a matter of privilege, tradition and property but reflected contemporary economic and political reality. Industrial change, though dynamic and in high focus, was far from complete.

The Whigs initially considered a £20 borough household qualification but this was changed to £10 when it was discovered that this would actually reduce the electorate in some constituencies. The purpose of the uniform franchise was twofold. First, it aimed to keep out non-property owners, though in some areas like London many of the householders were artisans. Secondly, it reformed the chaotic pre-1832 borough franchises. The effects of the change were markedly different across the country since rental values varied. It is clear that the £10 householders did not constitute a single social class. Though this property qualification covered virtually all middle-class family men, in some areas it also brought artisans and skilled workers into the franchisal net. In bringing the urban middle classes within the political nation – Grey had spoken of them as 'the real and efficient mass of public opinion . . . without whom the power of the gentry is nothing' – the new franchise brought in something more varied *and* more traditional than simply an industrially based middle class. This was more a consequence of the existing social structure than of Whig political calculation. The proportion of £10 houses was anything between 15 and 50 per cent. For example, the percentage of £10 houses in Wigan was half that in Reading. In London there were many skilled workers with permanent residences and rental values were high. In Cornwall and parts of Wales they were low and shopkeepers did not find themselves on the electoral register. The older established towns tended to have a higher proportion of £10 households than those of more recent origin. In general terms the borough franchise can be viewed as more 'democratic' in the south than in the industrial north and Midlands.

The 1832 Act removed the worst abuses of the old borough system and the number of borough members was reduced from 465 to 399. Rotten boroughs were abolished and the franchise in corporation boroughs substantially increased: Bury St Edmunds increased from 35 to 620 electors and Portsmouth from 49 to 1,295. But proprietary boroughs remained and in some cases were created. Gash estimates that between 60 and 70 MPs continued to fill parliamentary seats because of patronage. A minority of

English boroughs after 1832 had over 1,000 voters; 123 boroughs had under 1,000 voters and of these 92 had between 300 and 1,000 electors and 31 fewer than 300. The 1832 Act still allowed considerable scope in the boroughs for the expression of private interests, many of which derived from aristocratic and landed sources.

The 1832 Acts innovated but they also preserved and it is the continuity between the pre- and post-1832 situation that Norman Gash emphasizes. The December 1832 general election saw little real change in the types of people elected as MPs. Between 70 and 80 per cent of MPs were still from the landed interest. No more than a hundred were from the professional and industrial middle classes, a number comparable with elections before 1832. It was not until the 1840s that a significantly higher number of middle-class MPs were elected and not until the 1870s that overall aristo-cratic control of the House of Commons was lost. The middle-class urban electorate seemed happy to continue to elect MPs from within the landed interest and it is interesting to compare their conservative attitude to national elections with the ferocity with which they fought local elections and paid attention to issues such as local education, public health and civic amenities. There is little evidence in the 1830s and 1840s that the middle classes wished to seize national political power. They had extracted recognition from Parliament but did not wish to challenge the aristocratic hegemony *per se*. Grey's calculation that they would act as a conservative force was brought home clearly in the late 1830s and 1840s in their general opposition to the Chartists. Extending the franchise had, as Grey calcu-lated, strengthened the status quo.

The Crown emerged rather unhappily from the reform agitation. This continued the reduction in the political patronage at its disposal. The disfranchising of many nomination boroughs should, however, not be exaggerated for the ability of the Crown to 'make a House' had already disappeared. The clauses on registration contributed to the growth of local party organizations. The electoral system after 1832 may have retained too much private and personal influence for party to be all-pervasive but the direction in which the dynamics of political organization would develop was already clear.

The Reform Acts had a profound effect on the politics of the United Kingdom as a whole. The conservatism of the English Act must be set alongside the more far-reaching Acts for Scotland and Ireland. Before 1832 successive governments relied on the more easily managed Irish and Scottish seats to counterbalance the independence of English county members and the representatives of the larger boroughs. After 1832 the essential conservatism of the English seats was faced with the essential liberal radicalism of Scotland and Ireland. 1832, for all its imperfections, initiated the process of gradual, non-violent change. Whatever many con-temporaries felt, Sir Robert Peel was correct in his belief that reform could not be final.

NOTES

1 *The Result of the Pamphlets or What the Duke of Wellington has to look to*, London, 1830.
2 J. C. D. Clark *English Society 1688–1832*, Cambridge University Press, 1985, chapter 6, pp. 349–420, especially pp. 393–420.
3 For standard textbook discussion of this period see A. Briggs *The Age of Improvement*, Longman, 1959, N. Gash *Aristocracy and People: Britain 1815–1865*, Edward Arnold, 1979, pp. 129–55, E. J. Evans *The Forging of the Modern State: Early Industrial Britain 1783–1870*, Longman, 1983, pp. 204–11 and M. Bentley *Politics Without Democracy 1815–1914*, Fontana, London, 1984, pp. 59–95. Two detailed studies of the 1830s contain useful discussions of reform: G. B. A. M. Finlayson *England in the Eighteen Thirties: Decade of Reform*, Edward Arnold, 1969 and A. Llewellyn *The Decade of Reform: The 1830s*, David & Charles, 1982. R. Stewart *Party & Politics 1830–52*, Macmillan, London, 1989, is a good brief study. An approach through the biographies of central figures of the period is useful: see N. Gash on Peel, Longman, Elizabeth Longford on Wellington, Weidenfeld, Vol. II, 1972, Philip Ziegler on William IV, Collins, 1971 and on Melbourne, Collins, 1976, Muriel Chamberlain on Lord Aberdeen, Longman, 1983, Kenneth Bourne's first volume on Palmerston, Allen Lane, 1982, E. A. Smith on Lord Grey, Oxford University Press, 1989 and John Prest on Lord John Russell, Collins, 1972.
4 On the 'flux of party' see E. J. Evans *Political Parties in Britain 1783–1867*, Methuen, 1985, F. O'Gorman *The Emergence of the British Two-Party System 1760–1832*, Edward Arnold, 1982 and B. W. Hill *British Parliamentary Parties 1742–1832*, Allen & Unwin, London, 1985. On the emergent Conservative party see R. Stewart *The Foundation of the Conservative Party 1830–1867*, Longman, 1978, B. Coleman *Conservatism and the Conservative Party in Nineteenth Century Britain*, Edward Arnold, 1988, and R. Blake *The Conservative Party from Peel to Thatcher*, Fontana, 1986. For the Whigs see A. Mitchell *The Whigs in Opposition 1815–1830*, Oxford University Press, 1967. N. Thompson *Wellington after Waterloo*, Routledge, 1986 is essential for the Tory position.
5 F. O'Gorman op. cit., p. 116.
6 Discussion of the Poor Law Amendment Act and the Municipal Corporations Act can be found in Chapter 9.
7 U. Henriques *Religious Toleration in England 1787–1833*, Routledge, 1961 discusses the repeal of the Test and Corporation Acts and Catholic Emancipation.
8 Quoted in N. Gash *Aristocracy and People*, op. cit., p. 137.
9 On the Catholic question see G. I. T. Machin *The Catholic Question in English Politics 1820–1830*, Oxford University Press, 1964. On Ireland see D. McCartney *The Dawning of Democracy: Ireland 1800–1870*, Helicon, 1987, pp. 63–109 and R. B. McDowell *Public Opinion and Government Policy in Ireland 1801–46*, Oxford University Press, 1952. O. MacDonagh *The Hereditary Bondsman: Daniel O'Connell 1775–1829*, Weidenfeld, 1987 is the first volume of what may well be a definitive biography.
10 J. C. D. Clark op. cit., p. 354.
12 The discussion of reform by D. Fraser in J. T. Ward (ed.) *Popular Movements 1830–1850*, Macmillan, 1970 and J. Cannon 'New Lamps for Old: the End of Hanovarian England', in J. Cannon (ed.) *The Whig Ascendancy: Colloquies on Hanovarian England*, Edward Arnold, 1981, pp. 100–24 are both extremely useful. M. Brock *The Great Reform Act*, Hutchinson, 1973 is the standard work and E. J. Evans *The Great Reform Act of 1832*, Methuen, 1983 provides a shorter starting point. J. Cannon *Parliamentary Reform 1640–1832*, Cambridge

University Press, 2nd edn, 1980 looks at the issue from a longer perspective. N. Gash *Politics in the Age of Peel*, Harvester, 2nd edn, 1978 and *Reaction and Reconstruction in English Politics 1832–1852*, Oxford University Press, 1965 provide the best analysis of the electoral system after 1832 but should be read in relation to D. C. Moore *The Politics of Deference*, Harvester, 1976, a difficult but rewarding alternative view. C. Flick *The Birmingham Political Union and the Movements for Reform in Britain 1830–1839*, Archer Books, 1978, is an excellent study of the archetypal political union. D. J. Moss *Thomas Attwood*, McGill Queen's University Press, 1990 is a definitive biography.

13 J. Cannon 'New Lamps for Old' op. cit., pp. 114–17.
14 D. Fraser op. cit.
15 ibid., p. 38.
16 On the role of the press in the provinces see D. Read *Press and People 1790–1850: Opinions in Three English Cities*, Edward Arnold, 1961.
17 J. C. D. Clark op. cit., p. 404.
18 For Scotland before 1832 and after see I. G. Hutchinson *A Political History of Scotland 1832–1924*, John Donald, 1986 and N. Fry *Patronage and Principle: A Political History of Modern Scotland*, Aberdeen University Press, 1987.
19 The best approach to the impact of reform on Ireland is K. T. Hoppen *Elections, Politics and Society in Ireland 1832–1885*, Oxford University Press, 1984, pp. 1–32.
20 N. Gash *Aristocracy and People* op. cit., p. 152.

Addendum: two recent books should be noted, I. Newbould *Whiggery and Reform 1830–1841: the Politics of Government*, Macmillan, 1990 and P. Mandler *Aristocratic Government in the Age of Reform*, Oxford University Press, 1990.

9 The Whig reforms 1832–41

The tone and language of our Ministry is not quite in common with that of those parties of men to whom we owed our Elevation and continuance in office. Lord Grey naturally and laudably looks to closing his career and leaving the country in tranquillity and prosperity. He is consequently averse to the agitation of any great questions that are not actually forced upon him . . . [but] the language of such among our party as are by nature more Tory than Whig and more conservative than reforming . . . produces an appearance of unpopularity and encourages Hume, Cobbett, O'Connell, Attwood and Whittel Harvey to ferment discontent and turbulence.[1]

WHIG GOVERNMENT – INTRODUCTION

In mid-1833 Henry Richard Vassall Fox, third Lord Holland, noted three aspects of Whig government in his diary which were to have a great bearing on government and policy-making for Grey and Melbourne, his successor as Prime Minister. First he pointed to the growing difference between the nature of Whig rule and the aspirations of those who elected it to power in 1830 and whose support in the 1831 election was largely responsible for parliamentary reform the following year. Secondly, he noted Whig reticence to take action on any of the 'great questions' which were still in need of solution. Thirdly, he identified divisions within the Whigs, held in check by the necessities of reforming Parliament, between 'conservatives' and 'liberals'. These issues need to be examined in relation to the breakdown of 'tranquillity and prosperity' in the mid-1830s through a combination of economic crisis and extra-parliamentary agitation.[2] This chapter focuses on the following questions: in what ways did party politics develop during the 1830s and why did the Whigs lose the 1841 general election? what further reforms did the Whigs undertake during the 1830s and what pressures were they responding to?

THE WHIGS – A COALITION OR A PARTY?

The government Grey formed in late 1830 was a coalition of groups which favoured reform but it can also, with some justice, be seen as 'Whig'. It is important to assess the political characters of those ministers who, though prepared to support reform in 1832, found themselves having to govern a society after 1832 which had not only been politically reformed but which during the 1830s encountered major economic and social upheaval. The Canningites, leaderless after the death of Huskisson in September, were courted and won. Melbourne became Home Secretary. It had been his appointment as Chief Secretary for Ireland in 1827 which had persuaded the Whig Lord Lansdowne to throw in his lot with Canning. Melbourne retained his position in the Wellington ministry, remaining an advocate of Catholic emancipation, and followed Huskisson in resigning over the failure to allocate seats from the disfranchised borough of East Retford to Manchester. Melbourne, Palmerston and the other Canningites declined to join Wellington in late 1830 when he refused to consider a moderate reform of Parliament. Melbourne was not a reformer by choice and was among the most conservative of Grey's ministers, maintaining that 'change is of itself a great danger and a great evil'.

People

Other Canningites entered government. Lord Palmerston became Foreign Secretary only after the office had been refused by Lord Holland and Lord Lansdowne. He nearly broke up the ministry by his reluctance to insist on the Reform Bill without modifications, but was soon immersed in foreign affairs and extricated himself from Grey's domination. Charles Grant became President of the Board of Trade and Viscount Goderich Secretary for War and Colonies: the latter was to continue as an inept administrator, the former became one.

Viscount Althorp became leader of the government in the House of Commons. At forty-eight, he had been a Whig most of his life but lacked experience of high office and was neither a financial expert nor an accomplished orator. But he had earned the respect of Whigs in the Commons and, despite his relatively advanced political views, as the eldest son of Earl Spencer he had impeccable aristocratic breeding. Melbourne and Palmerston, though far from enthusiastic, had accepted him as leader of the Commons, since the alternative was Henry Brougham. A powerful orator and energetic advocate of legal and administrative reform, Brougham was considered a little too radical but had sufficient standing both in the Commons and in the country to ensure that he could not, safely, be ignored. Brougham's reputation was surpassed only by his ambition and Grey had little difficulty in persuading him to become Lord

Chancellor. This seemed to temper his more outlandish ideas but he held no office after 1834.

Sir James Graham was one of the most competent of the moderate Whigs. His appointment as First Lord of the Treasury led to an impressive departmental reorganization. Lansdowne, Carlisle and Holland with Grey were the core of the old Whig party in the Lords. Lansdowne became Lord President of the Council, Carlisle minister without portfolio and Holland Chancellor of the Duchy of Lancaster. Lord Durham, Grey's son-in-law, was appointed Lord Privy Seal, a post which gave status without great demands being made on one's energies. The Duke of Richmond, an ultra Tory and recent convert to reform, was appointed Postmaster-General.

Grey's original cabinet consisted of thirteen men, nine of whom were in the Lords and one, Palmerston, an Irish peer in the Commons. On the periphery of the cabinet were Lord John Russell, son of the Duke of Bedford and an enthusiastic reformer, Viscount Duncannon, an Irish peer and another relative of Grey and Melbourne, and Edward Stanley, heir to the dukedom of Derby. The cabinet may have accommodated Canningites and even an ultra Tory but its motive force was undoubtedly Whig. Contemporaries agreed that both the Grey and Melbourne ministries were Whig.

Perceptions of 1830–2

Events between 1830 and 1832 were dominated, in Grey's perception of the situation, by the need to reconcile hierarchical assumptions with the compelling need to embrace the middle orders within the political nation. He maintained that the Reform Act was a concession which averted revolution and as a result preserved the existing institutions and aristocratic ascendancy. During and after the reform agitation Grey contended that government must direct and control currents of improvement and reform and 'endeavour to adapt its institutions and policy to publick opinion and gain the affection and confidence of the governed'.[3]

In responding to the ambiguous notion of 'public opinion' the major effect of the Reform Act was to elevate the House of Commons into a position where it overshadowed both the Lords and the Crown. This ill-defined supremacy was ratified by Melbourne's pledge in 1836 that his government would resign only if it lost the Commons' confidence and his resignation following electoral defeat in 1841 put this into practice. The problem the Whigs faced was how the 'community' should now be defined: did it remain an association of corporate interests or was it now an aggregation of individuals? The Reform Act in its vague distinction between interests and recognition of numbers, however qualified by property or wealth, implied a reluctant acknowledgement of the representation of numbers. But it was to remain a problem which was not finally resolved until the reform legislation of the 1870s and especially the 1880s.

1832 and Whig reforms after 1832

Historians have been slow to examine the relationship between parliamentary reform and the other significant legislation of the 1830s: factory reform, the Poor Law Amendment Act, abolition of slavery in the empire (excluding St Helena, Ceylon and India: it was not abolished in the latter until 1843), the Municipal Corporations Act, concessions to Dissenters in the form of the marriage and registration Acts. But the degree of Whig responsibility for them has hardly been evaluated. While municipal reform can be considered a Whig measure the same cannot be said of the others. Factory and poor law reforms owed their main support to paternalistic Tories and radicals. In general legislation to improve the conditions of the 'lower orders' was not 'Whig' legislation though individual ministers may at times have sympathized and even promoted specific measures. Abolition of slavery and the continued relief of Dissenters, reforms involving liberty and the institutions of Church and state, were more congenial to the earlier Whig traditions. It is accurate to say that the Whigs presided over rather than initiated much legislation in this 'decade of reform'. Concession for the sake of stability, clearly evident in the implementation of parliamentary reform, was a major dimension of government policy throughout the 1830s. The preservation of institutions remained the Whigs' prime consideration. 'Reform on a truly conservative principle', as expressed by Grey, could be applied to every established institution and became both a virtual Whig maxim and a cause of major dissension within the party.

Ireland

The problems of reconciling 'popular' with aristocratic interests and difference within the party was particularly evident over Ireland. Demand for the abolition of tithes, the consequence of the fusion of traditional grievances about land tenure and religion was the most immediate Irish problem to face Grey's ministry. Many Whigs doubted whether Ireland was 'fit for Free Government' and, without a substantial middle class, the cleavage between property and poverty was more obvious than in England. Attacks on established institutions could, in this situation, be seen as a threat to public order. Resistance to the tithe was identified as a prelude to resistance on the payment of rent, a far greater threat to institutional stability.

The reform of civil and religious liberties evident in the limited Irish legislative programme announced in 1831 showed that the Whigs were persisting with their traditional emphases on civil, constitutional and religious issues. The proposed legislation included reform of Grand Jury presentments, education, reform of corporation monopolies, some reform of the Vestry Act, repeal or alteration of the Subletting Act and some provision for the poor but was not intended to deal with the problems of land tenure. By the autumn of 1831 Anglesey and the Irish Secretary Stanley agreed that delay in reforming the tithe system was potentially dangerous. It was in the context of the need for tithe reform that the issue of the appropriation of surplus revenues of the Irish Church for secular purposes arose. This policy brought two Whig principles into conflict: the inviolability of property and the necessity for concessions to ensure stability. Althorp maintained that the government must remain popular and, with measures like the regulation of church rates in England and the abolition of slavery in the empire, he emphasized the need for Irish Church reform. Grey and Stanley were not convinced of the need to make this concession and the cabinet reluctantly agreed not to consider the matter in the 1833 session.

Towards the 'Derby Dilly'

Melbourne and Stanley were, by mid-1832, impressed with the need for additional powers if Irish government was to maintain order. Anglesey, the Lord Lieutenant, argued successfully for harsh coercive legislation. Even 'liberal' Whigs like Russell supported a measure which attempted to reconcile the needs of liberty and the preservation of property. The Coercion Act and an Irish Church Temporalities Act passed in 1833 failed either to resolve the problems within Ireland or to face the issue of appropriation. The disunity in the cabinet, evident over policy towards Portugal as well as Ireland, dogged the ministry throughout 1833 and early 1834. Russell failed to convince his colleagues and the tithe bill which Stanley introduced contained no appropriation clause. Russell, in Stanley's words, 'upset the coach' in May 1834 by revealing in the Commons the divisions within the cabinet over the issue. Stanley, Graham, Richmond and Goderich (since promoted to the earldom of Ripon) resigned before the end of May. The question of the renewal of the Coercion Act, which the Prime Minister supported, and over which Brougham and Althorp entered unauthorized dealings with O'Connell to prevent renewal, gave Grey the excuse to resign. The inability to find a solution to the Irish problem revealed the contradictions and limitations of Whiggery.

Grey has been considered a weak prime minister but this fails to do him any real justice. In many ways Grey was a prime minister in the eighteenth-century mould. The personal loyalty he commanded, perhaps more than any other single factor, sustained a ministry increasingly divided on fundamental issues. He smoothed over the growing animosity between Durham and Stanley which threatened the Whigs in late 1832, and moderated the distraught Russell in 1833–4. He could occasionally impose his own views on reluctant colleagues. The best examples of this were his delay in creating peers in 1831–2 and, less fortunate, the renewal of the Irish Coercion Act in 1834. Like Lord Liverpool, Grey guided rather than dominated his cabinet and was careful to submit tactical decisions to his colleagues.

Melbourne and Peel 1834–5

Melbourne's government, formed in August 1834, ran into difficulties almost immediately. The Irish problem remained unresolved. Radical Whigs, especially Brougham who was not given office, were insubordinate. On the right, Althorp was lukewarm in his support. The king had wanted Melbourne to form a moderate coalition government with Wellington and Peel to ensure stable government, an offer which had been refused. In September Brougham and Durham tried publicly to outbid each other as the originator of reform. In November Althorp became Lord Spencer on the death of his father, and moved to the Lords. Melbourne had formerly stressed to the king the importance of Althorp to the feasibility of the ministry in the Commons and compounded this by suggesting Russell as a replacement. The king dismissed him in November 1834 and invited Peel to form a minority Tory administration. Norman Gash comments that

> William IV in a real sense made Melbourne and Peel the first leaders of the Victorian Liberal and Conservative parties by the simple process of asking them to form a ministry. In November 1834, like his father in 1784, he hoped to secure himself against policies to which he objected by bringing in a minister of his choice who might win public approval.[4]

Stanley and Graham refused to join the Conservative ministry and the general election in early 1835 failed to give Peel a parliamentary majority. His government finally came to an end in April 1835 but his 'hundred days' had given the Conservatives a unity and direction they had lacked since 1829. But it did much the same for the Whigs. The general election, where the Whigs had significant losses in the English boroughs, trimmed the size of the difficult Whig 'reform' majority and brought the quarrelsome forces of the left to their senses. Peel was vulnerable to concerted attacks from the Whig, Irish and radical MPs. The problem was forging that alliance. The Lichfield House compact of February 1835 achieved at least short-term agreement to evict Peel.

The 'divided' Whigs

The central issue dividing political opinion remained the use of surplus revenues of the Irish Church: should the revenues be appropriated for secular purposes or should they be reserved for strictly ecclesiastical ends?

Richard Brent argues that the Whigs were divided on this issue into three groups.[5] 'High Churchmen', led by Stanley, wished to make no concessions to Catholics in Ireland or Dissenters in England and left the Whig party in 1834. 'Old Foxites', like Grey, inheriting a certain religious scepticism from the eighteenth century, were often indifferent to church reform. The third group, the 'Liberal Anglicans' (Althorp, Morpeth, Ebrington and Duncannon with Russell at their head), was deeply impressed by the religious revival of the period and believed it right to stress the common ground between Catholics, Dissenters and Anglicans. By 1835, Brent maintains, this group guided Whiggery in policies which sought to gather Protestant and Catholic Dissenters into the political nation. In practice it sponsored educational and ecclesiastical reform aimed at completing the transformation of the constitution from an Anglican notion into one which was almost entirely non-sectarian, yet Christian.

Other parliamentary groupings

Apart from the Whigs and Conservatives three further groupings can be identified in the Commons after 1835. First, the 'Philosophic Radicals', once believed to be the motive force behind reforming policy in the 1830s, but who are largely discounted in Brent's view.[6] They and other radical MPs had never developed into a coherent group and failed to act as an organized left-wing to pressurize the Whigs even when, as in 1837, they held the balance between Whigs and Conservatives. The radicals were faced after 1835 with the dilemma of either supporting the Whigs or opposing them and letting in the Conservatives. They were individuals rather than party men and concerned more with specific issues like the ballot or financial retrenchment than with general policy. As a more 'liberal' Whig party took shape after 1835 the genuinely independent radical MPs were gradually absorbed and by 1841 fewer than ten remained.

The Irish party,[7] led by O'Connell, formed the second group. After 1835 he proved a loyal ally of the Whigs, suspending his campaign for repeal of the Union until the advent of a Conservative government. This resulted in a process of consolidation in the Irish party and O'Connell's electoral influence was perceptibly weakened. The Whigs began to eat into the Irish constituencies and in the 1841 election they were the largest party, closely followed by the Conservatives, with O'Connell's Repealers holding only eighteen seats.

The final grouping was the 'Derby Dilly' named after Stanley, heir to the Derby earldom, and its vacillating position in the political system, which stood between the two main parties and enjoyed a brief period of influence as the larger parties vied for its support. Formed by the resignations over appropriations in 1834, Stanley and Graham gradually moved towards the Conservatives and were to be important ministers in Peel's 1841–6 ministry and, in the case of Stanley, a future leader of the party.

Melbourne in power 1835–41

Melbourne returned to power in April 1835 and the history of his party until defeat in 1841 has been seen as one of steady electoral decline. But to view Whiggery as alternately crass, lazy, over-confident and hyperactive neglects the extent to which the period was one of parliamentary growth for the emergent Liberal party. Russell had made Melbourne's acceptance of appropriation a condition of his accepting office. It was an issue that divided the cabinet and failed to obtain permanent ministerial support. The Lichfield Compact seemed to make O'Connell respectable. This made appropriation more difficult though by late 1835 Lansdowne openly and Melbourne tacitly were ready to drop it. Not until 1838 did Russell signify the government's willingness to abandon the issue and it was not until 1840 that Irish municipal reform finally wound up the Whig programme of Irish legislation. Tory propagandists made much of O'Connell's support for the Whigs and there is little doubt that they had opened themselves to the charge of conceding much to retain his support.

The association with O'Connell was clearly an insufficient cause of Whig electoral decline after 1835. More important were the limitations on their power and the character of the Whig leadership. The House of Lords proved a formidable obstacle. The reform agitation and the threat of creating new peers may have frightened the Lords but it had not intimidated them. It may even have stiffened their resistance to change. The Whigs, however, were undoubtedly intimidated by the Lords and were prepared to accept almost any provocation rather than face another crisis like that of 1831–2. Whig legislation was as a result mutilated or delayed by a body clearly acting as a political party opposed to the elected ministry and using its legislative power in a co-ordinated way to overrule both the executive and the majority in the Commons. Liverpool and Pitt had been able to rely on the unconditional support of the Lords. Melbourne could not. The upper house was no longer an adjunct of government but had become an independent and partisan legislative counterbalance to the Commons. The diarist Charles Greville, clerk to the Privy Council, wrote that in the Lords 'All are either Whigs or Tories arrayed against each other and battling for power.' This change from many of the Lords being 'the party of the Crown' supporting the king's ministers simply because they *were* his ministers was not as dramatic as this implies. The fifty years of Tory rule from Pitt to Wellington had masked the inherent Toryism of the upper house. The advent of Whig government led to its 'Toryism' being explicitly seen. The obstruction of the Lords reached its climax over municipal reform in 1835. Peel and Wellington had already accepted the principle of reform and had hoped to pass a limited measure themselves but their fall in April had pushed the matter back to Melbourne. But it was Peel who 'threw over the Lords' and co-operated with Melbourne in a compromise over municipal corporations which the Tory peers in the end accepted. The Whigs may have taken the initiative in legislating after 1835 but, as the 1835 Act demonstrates, the hallmark of this period was co-operation between the two major parties in producing compromise solutions.

Melbourne did not always welcome compromise but he was usually prepared to accept it. He was a practical politician sometimes lacking in energy, concerned less with the larger and more principled political issues than with holding his cabinet together. His can be contrasted with the more populist approach of Russell who was at the height of his influence in the 1830s, Gash argues that:

> Russell's defects were a certain littleness of mind and a temperamental infirmity of purpose. . . . His misfortune was that in the decade when he was at the height of his powers, he was not in command of the party.[8]

Growing problems

The apparent dynamism of the 1835 Act was followed, in 1836, by a parliamentary session of such inactivity and boredom that commentators were talking of it in terms reminiscent of 1824. The Whigs were given an easy year's government with victories in the first municipal elections, economic prosperity and the still irregular co-operation between Peel and the Stanleyites. Apart from Irish appropriations, an issue increasingly seen as Russell's fetish, they appear to have had little to talk about. Surprise by-election defeats, like that in Renfrewshire in early 1837, counselled against dissolution. The Whigs appeared, and felt, insecure and the death of William IV on 20 June 1837 added to that insecurity.

Superficially the Whigs were successful in the 1837 general election. The Conservatives gained only thirteen seats and this was partly offset by losses in Scotland and Ireland. But Peel's failure to dislodge Melbourne must be seen in the context of the general movement towards the Conservatives in by-elections since 1835, a process which continued after 1837. More important, the Whigs lost seats in both English boroughs and counties. Melbourne was left with a majority of thirty, barely sufficient to underpin a ministry in which there were major disagreements. Russell diagnosed the problem precisely in a letter to Melbourne in August 1837: 'If we attempt little their friends grow slack and if they attempt much their enemies grow strong.'[9]

Between 1837 and 1841 the parliamentary strength of the Whigs declined and its sense of purpose waned. Melbourne had hardly been an active prime minister since 1834 and after 1837 he attempted even less.

He spent an increasing amount of his time playing father figure to the young Victoria and her court and less time in the day-to-day administration of government and the cabinet. By default Russell, as Home Secretary and Leader of the Commons, became the major strategist of an emergent Liberal party.

The major problem which Russell faced was how to give the government a sense of purpose. Russell had swung away from his radical stance over Ireland and in his speech on 20 November he announced his belief that the 1832 settlement was 'final'. This checked those in the party with ambitions to confront the House of Lords and convinced the radicals that they faced a threat. In retrospect it is arguable that the reorientation of Whig into more 'liberal' policies between 1838 and 1841 marked Russell's major contribution to the emergence of the Liberal party. Brent argues that he succeeded in altering the concerns of Whiggery from an interest in the mechanics of the constitution to a consideration of its moral foundations. Under Russell the Whigs began their transformation into a party of conscience.

Melbourne gave way reluctantly in 1838 and 1839 to changes in both men and measures, part of the Whig search for a new electoral identity. Economic dislocation since 1837 combined with a revival of widespread political unrest and popular agitation in urban Britain. The Anti-Corn Law League focused attention on the morality of some sections of the economy being protected to the disadvantage of the consumer. The rebellion in Canada, which began in December 1838, provided a vital test of the liberal credentials of the government at precisely the time that Russell called them into question. Melbourne's response was to send Durham, the most powerful spokesman of radicalism now with an earldom, to check on the unrest there. This diverted attention from Charles Grant (now Lord Glenelg), the incompetent Colonial Secretary, who was not dismissed and replaced by Lord Normanby until February 1839. Melbourne's handling of this problem was shrewd and, though the Durham Report marked a milestone in Canadian constitutional developments, the domestic impact of Durham's removal showed the fundamental weakness of parliamentary radicalism after 1837.

The resilience and, to some extent, toughness which Melbourne showed over the Canadian crisis was not paralleled by his response to the problem of Jamaica. The government's position over Jamaica was contradictory. It needed to maintain executive authority over the colonies as well as ameliorating the position of the blacks. The cabinet decision to suspend the Jamaican constitution was taken because of resistance by planters to British intervention and the acceleration of the abolition of negro apprenticeship which began with the abolition of slavery in 1833 and negro apprenticeship was due to expire in 1840. The government's dilemma was that if it betrayed the negro then it offended the 'Saints' while if it attacked the ethics of representative government it offended the radicals. In May

1839, with some radicals abstaining and some voting with the opposition, the government's majority fell to five and Melbourne resigned.

The 'Bedchamber crisis', 1839

Melbourne's decision was hasty and ill-conceived and was made worse when he was recalled to office a few days later. Peel had refused office when he quarrelled with the Queen over the appointment of new ladies of the Bedchamber. Melbourne had acquired a personal influence over the young queen in appointing himself her private secretary and Peel saw the replacement of Whig ladies of the Bedchamber by Tories as a matter of confidence in his administration. Cabinet changes followed. Spring-Rice, the Chancellor of the Exchequer, retired in August and moved to the House of Lords. Poulett Thomson, the government's best economist, would not succeed him in the Treasury because of his lack of confidence in his colleagues and went to Canada as Governor-General. The timid and conventional Francis Baring took the post. Grey's son Lord Howick resigned in a huff over Melbourne's 'stationary' system. Three 'liberal' Whigs – Clarendon, Labouchere and Macaulay – were brought into the cabinet.

The one issue which might perhaps have revived the Whigs and renewed their sense of purpose was a fresh burst of parliamentary reform. Russell had suggested that the ballot should be made an 'open' question in the cabinet in 1837 but Melbourne had refused. Russell's consequent attempt to assert a firm cabinet policy in his 'finality' speech had diminished his own popularity and the hopes of his 'liberal' supporters. In 1838 Grote's ballot motion was defeated by 315 to 198 with Melbourne and some 60 Whigs voting with Peel and the opposition. Changes in policies as well as persons marked the return of Melbourne to power in 1839. Making the ballot an 'open' question in 1839 was a painful necessity in order to reconcile the radical Whigs who had been alarmed by the narrow escape from a Conservative government. Despite this, in June 1839 the ballot failed to pass the Commons. The Whigs were still caught in the dilemma that faced them in 1830 – how could they reconcile being a party of government with pressures for popular reform from extra-parliamentary sources?

The concessions in 1839 exacerbated the weaknesses within the government. The economic and social problems of the late 1830s threw the inadequacies of Whig fiscal policies into high relief. Between Althorp's mangled budget of 1831 and 1837 the government relied increasingly on indirect taxation which was vulnerable to economic slump. By 1838 there was a budget deficit and by 1840 Baring, faced with a projected deficit of £2 million, reversed the trend towards 'cheap government' with increases of 5 per cent in Customs and Excise and 10 per cent in Assessed Taxes. Faced with a bankrupt fiscal policy the Whigs suddenly became converts to free trade and tariff reform. Constitutional reform had been exhausted and fiscal policy marked a fertile area for fresh impetus to rouse flagging enthusiasm. Poulett Thomson wrote to Baring from Canada in May 1841 that

> It does not meddle with religious prejudice; it does not relate to Ireland; it does not touch on any of the theoretical questions of government on which parties have so long been involved. It is a new flag to fight under.[10]

It was also a 'radical' flag, but it came too late to prevent electoral defeat.

The 1841 election – why did the Whigs lose?

It is important to understand why the Whigs lost the 1841 election. J. P. Parry argues that:

> It is no coincidence that the only two elections between 1832 and 1886 which the Conservatives conclusively won – indeed the only two at which they collected over 250 English seats while the Liberals held under 200 – followed the two periods of most intense speculation that nonconformist and Catholic pressure might force the incumbent Liberal government into radical religious reform.[11]

Given that parties won support by appealing to the emotions and prejudices of the electorate it is not surprising that religious issues remained of central importance in determining electoral behaviour. The major difficulty faced by the Whigs, and especially the 'liberal Anglicans', was that the political and religious behaviour of both Nonconformists and Catholics in the 1830s was frequently based on emotionalism and enthusiasm and this was worrying to those whose view of Protestantism was profoundly rational.

Following 1832 the Whigs had been inspired to tackle a series of religious grievances. In 1833 they gave the first state grants to both the Anglican National Society and the Nonconformist British and Foreign Schools Society which promoted education in England. Six years later Russell increased the grants but made them conditional on satisfactory state inspection. The most radical religious initiatives were reserved for Ireland, with the reform of the Church of Ireland in the Irish church Temporalities Act of 1833, though the Whigs failed to achieve any success on the appropriation issue. Two years earlier a national system of Irish elementary education had been established which aimed both at improving educational provision and diminishing the power of Catholic priests. It was designed to reduce sectarian hostility by educating Catholics and Protestants together, at least for secular subjects. The Whig objective of improving the prospects of stability, in a non-coercive way, and of Protestantism was initially thwarted by the Catholics gaining effective control of the system and by Protestants continuing with their voluntary schools.

Whigs and Nonconformists

It was, however, the Whig relationship with provincial British Nonconformity which proved crucial in the 1841 election. After 1832 the Whigs satisfied some Nonconformist grievances: in 1835 the Municipal Corporations Act broke Anglican control of corporations far more effectively than the repeal of 1828 and established 'liberal' majorities in most large towns for the next fifty years; in 1836 the Civil Registration and Marriages Acts instituted civil registration for births, marriages and deaths and allowed Nonconformist chapels to be licensed for weddings; and, also in 1836 a charter was granted allowing the non-sectarian University of London to confer degrees and Russell introduced a measure which provided for the commutation of tithes to a money payment.

Questions concerning the Church of England were, however, more difficult to resolve. The Whigs recognized its role as an agent of social stability and that it had an immensely useful spiritual purpose. The 'liberal Anglicans' did wish to see it reformed, partly as a result of their attack on the corruption of unreformed institutions. Peel was also prepared to accept internal reform and took the matter up in his short-lived Conservative ministry in 1834–5. His proposals were broadly implemented by the Whigs when they returned to power, in the 1836 Established Church Act which set up the Ecclesiastical Commission to administer changes. By emphasizing the spiritual dimension of the Church, as opposed to its doctrinal and organizational exclusiveness, however, the 'liberal' Whigs hoped to persuade Nonconformists to rejoin the Establishment or at least identify with its function in a brotherly spirit. This 'rationalist' approach, however, satisfied neither Anglicans nor Nonconformists. It led to the claim by the high Anglican Tractarians, based in Oxford, that the Church was 'in danger' and to increasing radicalism among those Nonconformists who saw disestablishment as a potential solution.[12]

Whigs and Nonconformists first came into conflict after 1832 particularly on the question of church rates. While the Whigs recognized that there was a pressing need to remove this grievance they also felt that, since the Church was a national institution for the preservation of order and sound religion, some payment from government funds for the upkeep of its fabric was legitimate. There was a widespread assumption that attack on the church rates was a preliminary to an all-out onslaught on the Church Establishment itself. In 1837 the government's compromise proposal, which would have made the Church financially responsible for the upkeep of fabric, was withdrawn after extensive opposition from defenders and opponents of the rate. A private member's bill proposing abolition two years later did not even receive government support.

Divisions within Nonconformity between moderate and more radical strands created problems for the Whigs in the 1830s. The leadership of political Nonconformity between 1780 and the mid-1830s was dominated by Unitarians who broadly shared the moral vision of the Whigs, working for civil liberties and moral reform and against corruption but not for disestablishment. Congregationalists and Baptists, however, took the lead after 1832 and became a powerful force in rousing radical, provincial political Nonconformity. This radicalization was first seen in their attitude towards church rates in the late 1830s and led to the establishment of the Anti-State Church Association in 1844. Radical Nonconformity had many weaknesses. Many evangelical Nonconformists felt that they had nobler aims outside politics; the Wesleyans, the largest single denomination, were happy to receive education grants and its leader Jabez Bunting had distinctly Tory views. Moderate Nonconformity was generally pleased by Whig commitment to ending the slave trade and by Church policy. But in their mobilization of feeling the Nonconformists, moderate as well as radical, affected the political situation. The spectre of disestablishment was a powerful weapon of political propaganda and organization. The revival of Anglicanism was in some respects synonymous with the revival of Conservatism: 'The revolutionary temper of the times had thrown all Churchmen on the Conservative side . . .'.[13]

FROM TORY TO CONSERVATIVE PARTY

The revival of the Conservative party between 1832, when it was without an acknowledged leader, with no agreed policies and with little organization save the recently founded Carlton Club, and 1841 cannot, however, be explained simply in terms of the religious dimension.[14] Events between 1828 and 1832 had shattered the Tory party and its membership in the House of Commons slumped to around 175 MPs in the election to the reformed Parliament. Three options, which broadly corresponded to three groups within the party, were open to the Tories after 1832: they could remain a reactionary, aristocratic, landed interest group, enter into a Tory–Radical alliance or continue the liberal Tory traditions of the 1820s.

A reactionary interest group?

Remaining a reactionary interest group appeared to be a viable option in the two years after 1832. As Ultras they had opposed Catholic emancipation in 1829, helped to bring down Wellington's ministry in 1830 and now found themselves associating with radicals like Attwood and Cobbett in attacks on Whig financial policy especially over the malt tax in 1833. They claimed, with some justice, that their belief in 'protection, protestantism and no popery' reflected the conservative attitudes of possibly a majority of the electorate. But, as Peel and other moderate Conservatives realized, the landed interest by itself constituted too narrow a base on which to build either a viable opposition or a national party. Between 1835 and 1841 no distinctly recognizable ultra wing operated within the Conservative party but the landed interest remained.

The concentration of agricultural strength in one party was one of the most significant developments of the 1830s. That community regarded the Conservative party as its natural political champion and, unlike in the 1820s, Whigs and radicals as its natural enemies. For Peel the movement of the landed interest *en bloc* into Conservative ranks posed a potential danger to party unity and policy. Their relationship with Peel was an uneasy one. They regarded his actions over Catholic emancipation as a betrayal and blamed many of their economic problems on the return to gold, which Peel had managed. Lord Chandos refused to enter the cabinet in the 1834–5 ministry without a pledge of some concessions on the malt tax and in March 1835 made an independent attempt to secure its abolition. In the crisis over Maynooth and the Corn Laws in 1845 and 1846 the agricultural interest overwhelmingly voted against Peel.

The extent of Tory penetration into rural areas during the 1830s can be demonstrated by comparing election results. In 1831 reformers had won all but 6 of the 82 English county seats. In 1841 the Conservatives took all but 23 of the 159 English and Welsh county seats. The growing importance of the landed interest to the revival of Conservatism was reflected in the increase in Tory county MPs at the expense of the Whigs in the 1835 and 1837 general elections but it coincided with the revival of the campaign against the Corn Laws. Peel defended agricultural protection between 1838 and 1841 on specific, practical grounds. Though he did not regard the landed interest as a privileged class he did stress the special burdens on the land – tithe, poor rate, county rate and land tax – and the fact that not only agriculture but industry as well still enjoyed significant tariff protection. Like Liverpool, Peel recognized the interdependence of land, industry and commerce but argued that protection for farming was justified for the benefits it brought to the whole community. However, Peel had said on several occasions that, if it could be demonstrated that the laws adversely affected national prosperity or were opposed to his views of national needs, he would be ready to amend or repeal them. Protection was a negotiable issue for Peel but, as he discovered in 1846, it was not for the agricultural interest.

A Tory–Radical alliance

The second grouping within the Conservative party during the 1830s looked towards the attractive option of forging a Tory–Radical alliance to combat the emergent politicization of the middle classes. This strategy may seem somewhat odd when it is remembered that reform in 1832 was, in many Tory eyes, forced through by combined middle- and working-class pressures. However, the alliance between these two social groupings was short-lived and the gulf between them widened especially with the growth of Chartism. The negotiations between some of the Chartists, led by William Lovett, and the Complete Suffrage League of Joseph Sturge in 1842 showed the extent of this gulf and that there was potential mileage in the Tory strategy.

Tories could appeal to the socially dispossessed for support against their common enemy, the middle classes. This appealed to individuals – Robert Blake calls them 'idealists, romantics, escapists' – who looked back to a supposedly 'golden age' and feared or despised the harsher realities of economic change. Their call was for a return to the reciprocal values of paternalism, a sense of responsibility for the lower orders, and had its roots deep in the traditions of landed society.[15] This motivated the actions of individuals like Richard Oastler and John Wood in their opposition to the new poor law in the 1830s. High Tory paternalism was associated not only with protectionism but with a strong attachment to the Anglican Establishment. The Conservative press in London and in the north was overwhelmingly against the new poor law and leadership of the 'Ten Hour' movement and the anti-poor law agitation drew heavily on the passionate oratory of Tory evangelicals.

Tory Radicalism was never a coherently organized section of the parliamentary party and by 1841, as a distinct movement, it was a spent force. This should not mask its importance as an expression by defenders of the values of a rural society under siege. Tory Chartism, campaigns against the poor law and in favour of factory reform, the writings of Thomas Carlyle were all manifestations of popular Toryism. 'Young England' marked its most romantic expression. The name was given to the small group of youthful aristocratic Tories elected to the 1841 Parliament: George Smythe, later seventh Viscount Strangford, Lord John Manners, later sixth Duke of Rutland, Alexander Baillie-Cochrane and, within limits, Benjamin Disraeli.[16] Young England was essentially escapist and nostalgic and was dead by the beginning of 1846, killed by the Maynooth debate in which its members voted on different sides. Like other strands of Tory Radicalism, Young Englanders maintained that property had its duties as well as its privileges and showed some consciousness of the gulf between the 'Two Nations'.

Tory Radicalism had serious defects which explain why it evoked so tepid a response in the party. Its focus was in most respects opposed to the economic orthodoxies of the day, involved Conservatives in co-operation with unpalatable allies and promised no electoral return. On the issue of the poor law it was against the economic interests of Conservative agriculturalist supporters. For Peel, Tory Radicalism threatened to turn back the progress that had been made in transforming the old Tory party, based on hierarchical and agrarian principles, into a modern Conservative party alive to the needs of industry. It only made sense if Peel contemplated enfranchising large sections of the working population and, as Blake says: 'Rightly or wrongly, [he] had no intention of risking it, and that fact alone ruled Tory-Radicalism out of the realm of practical politics.'[17]

Both the Ultra and Tory Radical groups within the emergent Conservative party had, to some extent, been neutralized by the late 1830s. This is not to say that their ideas ceased to be important but that a moderate form of Conservatism personified by Peel had gained a dominance confirmed by the electoral victory in 1841. This dominance was, however, based on fragile foundations, as Peel found to his cost in 1845 and 1846.

'Liberal' Toryism and Peel

The Conservative weakness, as Peel correctly saw, lay in the weight of their history, their root-and-branch opposition to the Reform Act and the popular perception of them as the party of reaction. Peel's achievement in the 1830s was to alter this perception, to make the party attractive and politically acceptable and to attract Whigs who were not prepared to stay in a party of radicalism but who were still in favour of reform. This led Peel broadly to accept the realities of the industrial revolution, to compromise with the forces of change and adapt traditional institutions to new social demands and to a libertarian fiscal policy which would bring increased affluence to every class in society, relaxing revolutionary potential. This was not a new policy, rather a reversion to the 'liberal Toryism' of the 1820s, a policy perverted by the events of 1830 to 1832.

A genuinely Conservative party saw protecting executive authority and restraining the Whigs from making unreasonable popular concessions as central to their principles. Peel made this very clear in a speech to the House of Commons in February 1833 in which he unequivocally accepted the Reform Act and declared his readiness to consider gradual and deliberate reform of 'every institution that really required reform'. The defence of the constitution against unwarranted attack had its fullest expression in the Tamworth Manifesto of December 1834 and it remained the basis of the party's parliamentary behaviour for the rest of the decade. It was seen as a 'reasonable' policy by the electorate and resulted in a shift of electoral advantage to the Conservatives and away from the Whigs. The roots of the Conservative victory in 1841 can be identified in 1835 and 1837.

Electoral growth

The events of 1834–5 were crucial to the development of the Conservative party. Appropriation led to secession from the Whigs, the dismissal of Melbourne's ministry and to the appointment of Peel as prime minister of a minority Conservative administration. Some historians have seen Peel's acceptance of office as 'premature' but this neglects the extent to which the political crisis benefited the Conservatives. Robert Blake identifies three reasons why office was important.[18] First, it established Peel's leadership of the party unequivocally so that when he gave his Tamworth Manifesto he did so as prime minister and leader of the Conservative party. Secondly, it caused a general election and this compelled the Conservatives to organize themselves both nationally and in the constituencies. Thirdly, the general election, though it did not result in victory, increased Conservative representation by a hundred seats. Office transformed the formerly disjointed opposition into a coherent party and alternative government. In the 1837 election they made additional gains, some thirty-five seats, giving them a majority in the English and Welsh seats. Ireland and Scotland and the queen kept the Whigs in power. The attitude of the monarch, which had been so helpful to Peel in 1834, frustrated him in 1839 with Melbourne's resignation and the ensuing 'Bedchamber crisis'. Victory had to wait until 1841 when the Conservatives achieved a majority of 76.

The Conservative recovery after 1834 and its cohesiveness in opposition can be compared with the problems which beset the Whigs. Belief in principles and policies, as the Whigs discovered, were, without effective organization, insufficient to either retain or gain political power. The transformation of the Conservatives was largely, though not exclusively, the result of better organization. Inside Parliament there were regular party meetings and an improved system of whipping. After 1837 the Chief Whip was Sir Thomas Freemantle, an inspired choice since, as a country gentleman from Buckinghamshire, he could appeal to the 'independence' of the agricultural county MPs and he was straightforward, discreet and popular. This helped to raise levels of 'party' consciousness and reduced the occasions when substantial numbers of MPs voted against the wishes of the leadership.

Party organization

Increased party solidarity in the House of Commons was paralleled by the emergence of Conservative party organizations in the constituencies. The registration clauses of the Reform Act acted as an important stimulus to this development. The institutionalizing of party was already taking place in Ireland by the time of the 1832 election, where the Protestant Conservative Association provided the Tories with a capable central headquarters raising weekly subscriptions of nearly £600. Newark Conservatives were the first to form an association in 1831 and between 1832 and 1836 this was reproduced throughout the country. By the beginning of 1837 there were several hundred such associations attesting that the Conservative revival had a popular base and was something more than just the reassertion of influence by Conservative landowners and borough patrons.

Some central direction was supplied by the Carlton Club, professionally run by Francis Bonham, though the autonomy of the local associations limited his room for manoeuvre. It had four chief departments of electoral management – registration, selection of candidates, payment of expenses and canvassing – but rarely did the Carlton act as the prime mover. Power, in the first instance, remained the preserve of the local associations. The Carlton collected information and distributed it to both the localities and the party leadership. It could, as a result of its up-to-date intelligence, prod constituencies into action but it had no power to compel. Patronage remained the principal link between Westminster and the constituencies.

The geography of the Conservative victory in 1841 was important as it was the only victory until 1874. Peel drew his strength from England, not Scotland and Wales, and from the agricultural counties and small boroughs not the densely populated, manufacturing centres. Though the Whig parliamentary party was, like the Conservatives, composed almost entirely of Anglicans and to a lesser extent members of the landed interest, by 1841 it was the Conservatives who were the party of the Church and the land. This was both Peel's greatest strength and his Achilles' heel as Norman Gash recognized:

> In 1841 Peel claimed and won for himself a free hand; but this necessarily had its limitations. It entitled him to decide what he wished; but what decided whether he could carry it out was the available material in Parliament. He held office as leader of a party: the brute votes in the lobby which had put him into power. . . . Whatever the proportions of Conservative strength in the country, in the parliamentary party the intellectual Peelite wing was in a minority.[19]

THE WHIG REFORMS 1832–41

Between 1832 and 1841 various reforms were passed by the Whig-dominated Parliament. The extent to which they can be considered 'Whig' in intention has already been considered and they may best be seen as having broad parliamentary backing rather than as the result of doctrinaire party policies. Asa Briggs called this period one of 'reform by instalments', though this may overestimate reform as a rational development of the 1832 Reform Act.

Reforms of the 1820s continued

Reform after 1832 took three main directions. First, the Whigs continued with some of the reforms already undertaken by the Tories before 1830. There was a continued rationalization of the criminal law code and of legal procedures with Brougham as Lord Chancellor presiding over the establishment of the central criminal court and the Judicial Committee of the Privy Council. The Whigs abolished slavery in the British Empire in 1833 and in 1838 removed the last monopoly of the East India Company with the ending of the China trade. Secondly, the constitutional reforms of 1828 to 1832 were continued with the Municipal Corporations Act of 1835 and the establishment of the Ecclesiastical Commissioners. Finally, there was a restructuring of the administrative apparatus of the state, including a somewhat reluctant acceptance of increasing centralized administrative obligations which owed something to Benthamite energies but also to ad hoc responses to the imperatives of a rapidly industrializing and urbanized society. It is with the constitutional and 'social' reforms that the rest of this chapter is concerned.

CONSTITUTIONAL REFORMS

English local government in the early nineteenth century was a patchwork of infinite variety, an inconsistent consequence of historical, religious and administrative traditions. The Whigs undertook some reform at the lowest level of government in the parish and major reform in the towns. In the counties the justices of the peace remained supreme and the county bench possessed both judicial and administrative functions. These unpaid officials were viewed by some as the bulwark of English liberties but as a tyrannical oligarchy imposing class rule on people immune to its opinions by many radicals. They remained in control of county government until the late nineteenth century, the symbol of landed authority and power.

The vestry

The vestry was the major political institution at parish level.[20] Its authority came from its power of taxation. The consent of ratepayers was required for most parochial expenditure associated with the church fabric and relief of the poor and nominal consent was necessary for spending involving highways, improvement, scavenging and watering. Population growth had swelled the size of vestries to unmanageable proportions and the main aim of the Sturges Bourne Acts of 1818 and 1819 was to restore the exercise of power to property. The introduction of multiple voting, where the number of votes an individual had depended on the size of his property, was intended to redress the balance in favour of wealth as against mere numbers and this principle was later enshrined in the Poor Law Amendment Act.

The emasculation of the vestry was widely resented, was seen as an attack on the liberties of the people and as a restoration of oligarchic control. In 1831 the Whigs passed the Vestries Act which ensured that the vestry could be elected by all ratepayers, male and female, where desired. Secret ballots were provided for under the Act as were annual elections for the third of the vestry who retired each year. This could have introduced household suffrage into parishes but the reality was different since the Act was permissive and was not widely adopted.

The result of the Sturges Bourne Acts and the 1831 Act was a politicization of parish government. People deprived of political opportunities elsewhere sought success and achievement in parochial and township administration. Liberal vestries counterbalanced Tory oligarchies and, from the 1850s, artisan and working-class vestries had the same effect on bourgeois-dominated councils. Parochial affairs may have been unimportant in a national context – for example, whether the bells should be rung at the ratepayers' expense or not – but they did have a local political significance. Reform in the nineteenth century, at whatever level of government, was followed by politicization of the institution.

Municipal reform, 1835

The municipal reform of 1835 is often discussed as a codicil to the 1832 Reform Act and its importance consequently underestimated. The greater part of the industrial and commercial middle class lived outside London in or near the rapidly growing urban centres and, following the demonstration of their political strength and cohesion in 1831–2, they were in a position to insist on self-government in their own cities. For many Tories therefore municipal reform had far more sinister political implications than the 1832 Act.[21]

Nineteenth-century towns fell into two main categories. Unincorporated towns, which had no charter, were under control of the county bench and liable to pay the county rate. Though some achieved a degree of independence from county control and others gained corporate status, most were unaffected by reform in 1835 and were outside the mainstream of urban local government until the late nineteenth century. Corporate towns had charters but were private rather than public institutions, responsible to their members, the freemen, rather than to the citizens as a whole. Whether a town was incorporated or not was an accident of history not a function of size. As a result many rapidly growing towns, like Manchester, Birmingham and Sheffield, were without corporations. Reform of urban local government was a pressing need.

It is possible to identify four major pressures for reform. First, both national and local government were concerned with the growing problem of law and order in towns. Lord Liverpool feared that the large cities were becoming ungovernable because of the volatility of their undisciplined crowds. The lack of an effective civil police force was seen as crucial to the creation of an ordered, stable society. The 'reform riots' of 1831 provided convincing proof that municipal reform was necessary if only to maintain order. Secondly, the political and religious exclusiveness of the unreformed corporations was increasingly unacceptable to the emerging commercial and industrial urban elite. Reform, it was argued, would lead to a balance between the economic interests in the towns.

The third element concerned the method of appointment to corporations. The unreformed corporations were generally self-elected and self-perpetuated. To radicals and to the middle classes self-election was the source of corporate evil and the means by which an illegitimate oligarchy maintained itself. Finally, municipal reform was a necessary part of parliamentary reform bringing the representative system more closely into line with a developing urban industrial society. Joseph Parkes in 1835 described reform as 'our Postscript to the Reform Bills; in fact, Municipal Reform is the steam engine for the Mill built by Parliamentary Reform' and *The Times* explained two years earlier that 'the fact is that Parliamentary Reform, if it were not to include Corporation reform likewise, would have been literally a dead letter'.[22]

Althorp announced his intention of introducing legislation but this was deferred until after the report of a Select Committee established in February 1833. The scale of the problem led it to recommend the creation of a Royal Commission which was appointed the following July. The advantages of Royal Commissions – the Whigs had already established one to look into the poor laws – over the previously popular Select Committee were numerous. Membership was not restricted to members of the two Houses of Parliament. They could call on expert advice rather than simply have them as witnesses. They were sufficiently independent of Parliament to offer objective and authoritative reports on which to base legislation.

Unbiased and objective in theory, both the Poor Law and Municipal Corporations Reports were ammunition for already conceived courses of action. This was clear from the brief of the Municipal Corporations Royal Commission to 'collect information respecting the defects in their constitution'. Lord Brougham selected individuals for membership on the basis of their sharing Whig desires for a more representative form of local government. Both the chairman John Blackburne, radical MP for Huddersfield, and the secretary, Joseph Parkes, ensured that the Whigs got the kind of report they wanted. Local Whig accusations about the corruption of corporations were accepted at face value and Tory defences summarily dismissed. The resulting report, produced after widespread local study, was a massive and detailed indictment of the injustice, inefficiency and corruption of the existing corporations. Few contemporaries could quibble with this.

In June 1835 Lord John Russell introduced a bill, drafted by one of the commissioners, J. R. Drinkwater, with frequent comment from Parkes. It proposed to sweep away the old corporations and replace them with councils elected by household suffrage and a three-year residence and ratepaying franchise. Freemen and aldermen were to be abolished; borough magistrates were to be elected by the council and one third of the council was to retire each year. Licensing was to be in the hands of the

council, which would be headed by an elected mayor. This radical proposal
– Melbourne had had to be persuaded of the case for household suffrage
– quickly passed the Commons and in July 1835 was sent to the Lords.
Peel admitted the need for reform – he had not wound up the Royal
Commission during his minority administration in 1834–5 – and was content to make minor amendments. The Tory peers led by Lord Lyndhurst
were not so compliant and the bill promised a major split in the Tory
party and the prospect of constitutional confrontation between Commons
and Lords. Peel refused to support the Lords' amendments, the Whigs
proved willing to compromise on some issues and dropped others. Aldermen were to remain and make up a quarter of a council. Councillors were
to have substantial property qualifications and in boroughs of over 6,000
inhabitants the town was to be divided into wards. Magistrates were to
be appointed by the Crown and retain their licensing authority. Freemen
retained their parliamentary, though not their municipal, franchise. As
amended, the bill received the Royal Assent in September 1835.

Under the Municipal Corporations Act 178 corporations were abolished
and replaced by elected councils. A uniform franchise was established by
which all occupiers with a three-year residence qualification could vote
for the first council and after that annually for one third of the council.
Each council elected its own mayor and aldermen, all debates would be
open and accounts publicly audited. The Act also laid down the procedure
by which a town could petition for incorporation.

Municipal reform was possibly more important in a political than a
constitutional context. Contemporary attitudes were conditioned by perceptions of the political implications of reform. Whig concerns centred on
the reform of judicial administration and the need for effective public
order and the distinct possibility of party advantage. The County Police
Act of 1839 attempted to introduce effective policing into rural areas and
municipal reform was geared to the same task in the boroughs. The only
compulsory duty imposed on the new town councils was the formation of
a watch committee and the establishment of a borough police force. Parkes
maintained that the Act 'will be poison to Toryism . . . we may defy Peel
and any union of Tories or Coalition he may effect'.

The reasoning behind this was very sound. Most of the unreformed
corporations were dominated by a Tory monopoly of electoral patronage,
and abolition would remove much Tory influence. This was recognized by
Lord Lyndhurst who concluded that 'It was a Whig measure – Whig in
its principle, Whig in its character and Whig in its object.' One of the
achievements of the 1832 Reform Act was to create an alliance between
a liberal middle class and a Whig landed aristocracy. The 1835 Act formalized the legal context in which the urban elite could exercise hegemony
over their own communities and may be seen as a further stage in the
same process.

Tory opposition to the Act was based on what they saw as its political bias. But behind the rhetoric lay a Tory concern to defend the rights of property and, throughout the debates, the Tories argued that government by nomination was more likely to produce respectable government than government based on elections. But it was fear of household suffrage that underlay all Tory protests. The corporations were, Lyndhurst argued, a barrier between the throne and raw democracy. Opponents maintained that municipal government would be thrown into the hands of radicals and Nonconformists, confirming the trend towards republicanism begun in the 1832 Act. In reality the municipal franchise did not prove as democratic as the Tories maintained.

The radicals hoped that municipal reform would lead to democracy in local government and form part of their attack on the aristocratic system of government. It offered to radicals the reassuring prospect of administering a *coup de grâce* to the Tory party. But by 1841 the radicals had lost much of their parliamentary representation and Peel had won a major electoral victory.

Did the 1835 Act inaugurate a 'municipal revolution'? The most profound changes were the reform of the 178 boroughs and an ability, through the incorporation clauses, to maintain a reforming momentum. Twenty-two new boroughs were incorporated within twenty years, including Manchester and Birmingham in 1838. The municipal revolution occurred in the half-century after 1835 when simple representative institutions were transformed into powerful agencies with wide social purposes. The system did not change in 1835; that had to wait until after the County Councils Act of 1888. The personnel of urban government did, however, alter. 1835 saw a change of representatives, 1888 a change of system.

SOCIAL POLICIES

The 1830s saw the beginnings of policies which aimed to deal with the specific needs, abuses and problems of an industrializing and urbanized society. It has been said that 'Social policy in industrialising Britain did not really begin until the Reform Parliament elected in 1832.'[23] Though passed by a Whig Parliament these policies can only be called 'Whig' to a limited extent. In fact most of the measures cannot be seen, except perhaps in retrospect, as grounded in any particular ideology but rather as

the product of the interplay between general ideology (the presence of evangelicalism, humanitarianism, philanthropy and Benthamite utilitarianism) and the apparently semi-fortuitous appearance of dedicated individuals.[24]

The enhanced role of the state was largely the result of actions by the middle classes.[25] This is not to deny the existence of pressure from the labouring population and the emerging trade unions, but is merely a recognition that the focus of sustained initiatives came from the bourgeoisie. The labouring population was generally suspicious of state regulation of working conditions and in their agitations for reform their emphasis, with the notable exception of the debate on the implementation of the poor laws, lay on the struggle to extend the franchise.

The labouring population and the middle classes had different sets of expectations from the Whig government as a result of parliamentary reform. If there was an underlying strand in the social reforms it can be seen in the need politically to detach the middle classes from the labouring population. Whether it was social reform which led to this division or whether it was the result of the disaffection of the labouring population is open to question but the legislative floodgates were opened: 1833, first effective Factory Act, first government grants for education and the ending of slavery in the British empire; 1834, the Poor Law Amendment Act; 1835, the Municipal Corporations Act and the setting up of a prisons commission; in 1840 a Royal Commission investigated child labour. As a social policy it was, from the government's point of view, very cost effective. Charges were borne by either local property owners in the case of the poor law or by businesses affected by the Factory Act.

Poor law reform

The reform of the poor laws extended the growing chasm between the middle classes and the working population.[26] The poor law, as it existed in the early 1830s, was not a system but, in Sydney Checkland's words, 'an accretion', determined by statutes passed two centuries earlier in a different economic and social world, without central organization and left to the discretion and vagaries of local parishes. Economic distress in the mid-1790s led to the introduction of 'allowances in aid of wages', generally though not accurately known as the 'Speenhamland system' after its first application in Berkshire in 1795. What was initially perceived as a temporary expedient became a necessity for the labouring population in the depressed agrarian south after 1815. Escalating costs, changing ideological perceptions and the 'Swing' riots of 1830 led to an increasingly focused challenge to the existing system which was seen as corrupting and lenient and for demands that more rigour should be imposed on the poor.

The ideological debate was between a humanitarian evangelical approach to the poor in which there was a strong imperative of humane social responsibility and the arguments of the political economists and the 'common sense' of businessmen and many landowners that labourers must operate within the framework of the free market economy and 'social discipline'. The latter had the better of the argument and by the early 1830s it had become a commonplace wisdom among the middle classes and many of the aristocratic elite, especially the Whigs, that the poor laws encouraged indolence and vice. The Royal Commission set up in 1832 to investigate the workings of the poor law quickly confirmed what the Commissioners had set out to prove. There may have been exaggeration of the abuses of the old poor law in the 1834 Poor Law Report, and Mark Blaug has shown that its economic consequences were not understood by contemporaries or by later historians, but there was no misunderstanding of purpose by those who framed the Poor Law Amendment Act, especially Edwin Chadwick, its guiding force.

The 1834 Act did not aim to deal with the nature or lack of provision, but only with excess. It had not been politically practical to abolish public relief completely but the relief for those unwilling or unable to make provision for themselves was to be on terms less favourable than those obtained by the lowest paid worker in employment (the principle of 'less eligibility'). This would eliminate abuse and fraud. Pauperism was a defect of character as there was always work available at the prevailing market price if it was sought strenuously enough. Hard work and thrift would always ensure a level of competence, however modest the level at which individuals were working. These values, reflecting emergent middle-class ideology, made a lasting impression on society for the rest of the century. The sense of shame at the acceptance of public relief, the stigma of the workhouse (the Act did not, however, require local authorities to build them) and the dread of the pauper's funeral were central facets of the attitudes of the working population and played a major role in the definition of 'respectability' that emerged among both middle classes and labourers. The 1834 Act embodied the ideology of the political economists but it could be presented by its opponents as an abuse of the poor: the poor law agitation before 1834 was aimed at amelioration but after 1834 the rigour of the system generated a counter-pressure in favour of easement. Maurice Harcourt wrote of the Act that

> Oh! glorious was that mortal's skill
> Who first devised the Poor Law Bill,
> To teach in this enlightened time,
> That poverty's the vilest crime.

The 1834 Act was important in three respects. First, unlike factory or mine reform, the thinking behind the Act was rural rather than urban in basis. This led to the adoption of a programme entirely unsuitable and unworkable in the industrial urban setting of northern England and accounted for the widespread opposition to its introduction after 1836. A simple reversal from relaxation to rigour could succeed in the agrarian south to a considerable extent but matters were different in the industrial north. There the new poor law was politicized, first by the anti-poor law agitation and then by the effect of the introduction of the electoral principle into poor law affairs.[26] Secondly, 1834 was the result of a generalized view of a whole range of problems and contained a moral rather than an environmental view of the poor; within this framework it aimed at comprehensiveness and internal consistency. Finally, it created the first effective element of centralized British bureaucracy, intended to preside over a general social policy with central control and supervision and local administration.

The standardizing intentions of national legislators almost immediately came into conflict with the responses of local people who dealt with the realities of immediate situations. Localities could and did ignore or evade the instructions of the Commissioners. Outdoor relief could not be withheld in seasonal employment like agriculture or during trade depressions in industrial centres. Checkland has argued that this 'generated a kind of schizophrenia when placed alongside the concepts embodied in the governing Act of 1834 . . . [producing] concessions to common sense and common humanity'.[27] Despite this there is no doubt that imposing 'rigour' resulted in much hardship under the Act. There are accounts of deficient diet, penal workhouses, families torn apart and the denial of dignity to the old. The poor were abused because of a combination of indifference to their plight and social zealotry because of the dogma enshrined in the enabling legislation.

The 1834 Act was intended as an attack on a structural problem: the conditions and behaviour of the labouring poor, especially in agrarian regions. Its intention was to reduce abuse, and to stop confusion between wages and relief. Can this be seen as an expression of middle-class values grounded in the ideology of political economy? In simplistic terms it probably can but the relationship between political economy and poor law policy was in practice far more complex. The uniformity of support by the middle classes for political economy can easily be exaggerated and the nature of the trade cycle resulted in their refusal to implement the full rigour of the 1834 Act in their industrial centres. Middle-class ratepayers joined opposition to the Act which would entail considerable expense in reorganizing the administration of poor relief without bringing the benefits intended for agricultural districts.

The Poor Law Report may have been over-optimistic in believing that uniformity of practice was possible but its principles established attitudes to poverty which still have significance. U. Henriques maintains that

> In 1834 the new development was given a scope, a momentum and a character which made it irreversible. The change was more immediate and more complete in the south than in the north, but it was lasting. . . . The Victorian workhouse and all it stood for . . . was perhaps the most permanent and binding institution of Victorian England. Not until the working class had obtained the vote and entirely different attitudes to poverty in general and unemployment in particular began to creep in at the turn of the century did the principles of 1834 start to lose their grip.[28]

Factory reform

The second area of social policy in which the Whigs undertook reform was factory conditions.[29] Technological change and the development of new work conditions had gained sufficient strength by the 1830s to necessitate a serious and sustained effort by the state to regulate their application. Both employers and workers believed themselves to be locked into a system of attitudes, actions and responses. Employers regarded their position as defined by the laws of a competitive market over which they had no control. Insensitive, repressive and largely indifferent to the conditions of their workers, many were motivated by a belief in profit, a belief buttressed by their subversion of religious piety. Endemic drunkenness among the workforce, as escape from these pressures, seemed to confirm employer belief that the workforce could and would not respond to better treatment. These attitudes percolated down into the workforce itself and there is ample evidence of the exploitation of and cruelty towards workers, especially children, by fellow workers. Masters and workers had been related to each other by simple contract and face-to-face contact but industrialization had created a new set of relationship patterns. Workers had become 'operatives', human extensions of new technology, 'dehumanized' and 'dehumanizing'.

The Health and Morals of Apprentices Act of 1802 was extended in 1819 from parish apprentices to cover all textile factory children. But the 1833 Factory Act was the first really effective attempt to control workers' conditions. The origins of the Act lay in extra-parliamentary pressure from the Ten Hour Movement which resulted in the Whigs establishing a Select Committee in 1831 to examine factory conditions. The publication of its report in January 1833 highlighted the stark realities of conditions and led Anthony Ashley Cooper, parliamentary spokesman of the Ten Hour Movement, to introduce a factory bill. Criticisms, largely justified, that the 1833 report was somewhat one-sided as it had only heard the workers' views resulted, in April 1833, in the government setting up a Royal Commission to investigate the employment of children in factories. The Whigs had effectively taken reform out of the hands of the Ten Hour Movement, and it became a government-sponsored issue.

Why did the Whigs take control of factory reform? Extra-parliamentary agitation occurred in the context not only of conflict between capital and labour but of other economic and social rivalries. Social, ideological, religious and political rivalry between industrialists and neighbouring agriculturalists was exploited by operatives, who turned for protection from mill-owners to county JPs. The result was an Anglican Tory–Radical alliance on the factory question, grounded in notions of paternalism rather than the tenets of political economy and less inhibited than Whig Radicals in support of the industrial poor. This alliance was weakened by the reform agitation of 1831–2 but remained important through the anti-poor law agitation until the late 1830s and the onset of Chartism. Parallel to this Tory paternalist approach was one supported by some Whig radicals and a group of philanthropic mill-owners in which Nonconformist belief was a unifying force. The agitation in Yorkshire had already convinced the Whigs that a Factory Act was inevitable. Determining the composition of the Royal Commission ensured that the range of options available to them would be wider and less unpalatable to manufacturers than a Ten Hours bill.

The Royal Commission Report was placed in the hands of Edwin Chadwick. The report, produced in forty-five days, looked at factory conditions far less emotionally than the Select Committee. Its conclusions were not based on humanitarian grounds, the position adopted by the Ten Hour Movement, but on the question of efficiency. Chadwick argued that human suffering and degradation led to less efficient production and that a good working environment would lead to health, happiness and an efficient workforce. Its recommendations were firmly placed on the question of children's employment and consequently it was criticized for failing to deal with the issue of adult labour. The 1833 Factory Act which implemented its recommendations was confined to children's work and applied only to textile mills but it did establish a small inspectorate to enforce the legislation.

Inspection was the prime condition of effectiveness, making enforcement possible and, perhaps in the early stages more importantly, providing a continuous stream of information about the conditions of workers in a range of industries. The prevailing view among historians that the early factory acts were never adequately enforced was effectively challenged by A. J. Peacock in an article published in 1984. He showed that in nineteen of the years between 1833 and 1855 the conviction rate was above 80 per cent and in twelve of those years it was over 90 per cent. Despite the intense criticism of the 1833 Act and the problems encountered in enforcement, it is unfair to underestimate the Whig achievement. The debates in 1832 and 1833 led to the issue being publicly aired as never before. The extra-parliamentary movement may have been frustrated and the 1833 Act may not have been based on any real principles, but it did mark an important stage in the emergence of effective factory legislation and underpinned the developments of the 1840s.

Education

The religious dimension which emerged in factory reform was a more explicit feature in the educational debates of the 1830s. Both Tory and Whig politicians acknowledged the need to provide elementary education for the poor. They differed, however, over the kinds of religious education this entailed. The Whigs found themselves in the invidious position of having to choose between different conceptions of the role religion should play in children's development.[30]

Anglican determination to dominate educational provision was a pervasive theme throughout this decade, a result of Nonconformist growth and radical attacks on Anglican wealth, privilege and tithes. Preserving control over education was seen as essential to preserving its establishment status. There was a traditional rivalry between the primarily Dissenting British and Foreign School Society (BFSS) founded in 1808 and the Anglican National Society founded three years later. The educational techniques adopted by both were virtually identical, variations of the monitorial system or learning by rote. The foundation of the Central Society for Education in 1836 marked a new departure in both the means of educating and the religious education to be provided. Its opposition to the monitorial system resulted in responses from both the National Society and the BFSS, resulting in its abolition by the latter in 1847. Neither society, however, responded to the Central Society's call for united but secular education.

Richard Brent is critical of those historians who see developments in early nineteenth century education exclusively in terms of 'social control', because they neglect the extent to which there were differences in party view about the society which it sought to control. Liberal Whig politicians saw education as the agent for establishing a liberal Anglican state. But their notion of a 'common Christianity' was criticized by those religious groups for whom doctrine and faith were inseparable, and as a consequence a truly national system of education was an impossibility.

The constitutional revolution of 1828–32 had made it politically impossible to ensure that the religious education offered by the state would be exclusively Anglican. Anglican Tories therefore wanted the existing system of sectarian societies to continue, supplemented by financial aid from the state while resisting all government interference in the kind of education to be provided. Grants had been made as early as 1813 to the Dublin Society, royal letters instructing the clergy to preach charity sermons on behalf of the National Society had been issued since 1823, in 1833 building grants to both religious societies had commenced and in 1835 a grant of £10,000 was approved for the construction of normal schools to train teachers. The need to improve both the quantity and quality of education had already been acknowledged by the Whigs.

Russell's plans in 1839 were, however, far more controversial. A Select Committee report on the education of the poorer classes urged greater state expenditure and the Whigs reacted by proposing to increase the state grant to £30,000 to appoint school inspectors and to establish a state 'normal school' for non-sectarian teacher-training. The Whigs were, however, painfully aware of the narrowness of their parliamentary majority and the limits of their national support and, faced with strident Anglican and Tory opposition, diluted their principles. The 'normal school' idea was dropped and the money earmarked for the project diverted to the religious societies. In the spring of 1840 the government conceded the Anglican Church's control of appointments to the inspectorate of state-aided schools. Brent comments that this marked the political limit of liberal Anglicanism.

Limitations of Whig reforms

How far did the Whigs succeed through their reforms in fostering differences between the middle classes and the working population? The working population felt deeply betrayed by the 1832 Reform Act, which failed to give them either the vote or the secret ballot. Municipal reform in 1835 did not redeem the Whigs in their eyes. Representation remained firmly rooted in the possession of property, whether middle class or aristocratic mattered little. Neither factory nor poor law reform satisfied the labouring population: one deprived them of their children's wages, the other deprived them of their dignity and outdoor relief. For the middle classes parliamentary and especially municipal reform brought political respectability if not immediate power. Social and ecclesiastical reforms had been achieved but with differing degrees of middle-class approval. But the Whigs made little effort, except in the final years of their government, to deal with twin issues of the economy and free trade. The limitation of the Whig achievement in the 1830s has, perhaps harshly, been criticized as follows:

> The immediate legacy of the 1830s lay in what reform failed to achieve rather than what it had achieved. Chartism and the Anti-Corn Law League were both manifestations of this failure. . . . Peel and the Conservatives coming into office in 1841 were, then, the heirs to this legacy: a legacy of political frustration, social grievance, class bitterness, economic dislocation, radical protest.[31]

ECONOMIC PROBLEMS

Between 1830 and 1841 the Whigs were faced by economic problems of unprecedented proportions, what has been called the first crisis of industrial capitalism or the 'condition of England' question. Gramsci maintained that there was a 'crisis of hegemony' as the moral legitimacy of government was challenged by extra-parliamentary forces. How did the Whigs respond to these challenges? They inherited widespread agricultural disturbances in southern England when they came to power in late 1830. Motivated by distress and poverty rather than radical sentiments the 'Swing' rioters hoped for alleviation of their conditions, attacking tithes, the poor law and any form of farm machinery that replaced manual labour, and demanding higher wages. Magistrates and gentry showed some sympathy for the plight of the labourers and had to be reminded by the Home

Office of their duty to defend property. Despite this, retribution was light compared to the 1816 East Anglian riots and only three men were hanged, though 450 were transported to Australia. Public opinion was uneasy about exacting too harsh punishment.

Local magistrates, however, reacted in a more alarmist manner in 1834 to the spread of agricultural unions in Dorset. The Tolpuddle Martyrs were transported not for forming a trade union, itself a legal act, but for in ignorance administering an illegal oath. Melbourne supported the local magistracy in making an example of six labourers who were sentenced to seven years transportation. The unjust nature of the sentence provoked widespread public disquiet and agitation and Russell revoked the sentences in 1836.

Neither 'Swing' nor the Tolpuddle Martyrs did much to change the conditions of agricultural labourers in southern England. The new poor law, though much resented and hated, was introduced despite widespread opposition. Landed authority was maintained, though rural incendiarism reflected continued resentment that little was being done to alleviate conditions. Unity of interest between Whigs and Tories ensured that landed hegemony was maintained during this decade.

The Whigs faced more difficulty in urban and industrial centres in maintaining their authority. The main reason for this, other than the intensity of the urban and industrial crises, was that alternative ideological solutions were being put forward.[32] This was not the case in rural areas, where protest was almost entirely concerned with restoring past conditions. Detaching the middle classes in general from the radicalism of the labouring population was an important aspect of the Whig strategy. This is not to deny the crucial importance of middle-class sympathy and leadership in areas that affected the labouring population – factory reform, anti-poor law agitation and the anti-corn law agitation – but a recognition of the common interests which the aristocratic elite and middle classes had in denying economic and political power to the rest of society.

The Whigs faced their greatest challenge with the emergence of the diverse Chartist movement and to a lesser extent the Anti-Corn Law League.[33] Chartism began as a broad-based movement drawing support from skilled artisans and some members of the middle classes as well as from the labouring population. The Whigs, firm in their historic tradition of civil liberty, were anxious not to appear too repressive, as they believed this could exacerbate the situation. At the Home Office Russell and, after August 1839, Normanby were criticized for underestimating the potential danger but this was based on assumptions that Chartism was simply the product of political agitation, which it was not. The army shadowed the Chartists and the new police forces were created, but major confrontations were avoided. Whig authority was maintained through a judicious combination of defusing situations, coercion when property and order were threatened and tact and judgement in the use of the courts.

A CRISIS OF HEGEMONY?

Was there a major hegemonic crisis in the 1830s? How did the Whigs react to it? Gramsci argued that during the 1830s the ruling political groupings underwent a process of restructuring which ensured their survival and which led to the creation of a new balance of political forces, the reshaping of state institutions and the formation of new ideologies.[34] John Saville and others see this as the process which established the 'bourgeois state'. The Whigs suppressed Swing and attacked attempts at general unionism, the Poor Law Commission set out to discipline the poor, the Board of Trade resisted demands from the handloom weavers and factory workers for controls on production and the new police forces provided coercive backing. Paul Richards argues that there was a policy break by the Whigs after the 1837 general election with alarm at the anti-poor law agitation in the north and the emergence of Chartism.[35] Both the liberal Whigs and Peelite Conservatives agreed that the basic solution to national crisis lay in the revival and expansion of industrial capitalism but that renewed industrial and urban expansion had to be subject to greater 'physical and moral' regulation. Concessions to the working population can be seen as part of a wider strategy to contain popular radicalism and to give cohesion to the strained social and economic system. The defeat of Russell's original education proposals in 1839 and the foundation of the Education Department marked a cultural closing of ranks by Whigs and Tories against threats to their hegemony. Peel's victory in 1841 was not simply a defeat of the Whigs but a shift in liberal opinion to the right.

Between 1828 and 1841 England underwent a revolution of sorts in its constitutional, ecclesiastical, social and economic systems. A combination of concession, reform and coercion ensured that the existing political elite was able to absorb the 'respectable' and keep out the masses. The 1830s have long been known as the 'decade of reform' and, even if the achievements of the decade no longer seem to eclipse those of the 1820s, the title is apt. It was not expected that every government, whatever its party label, would be a reforming one. But the possession of property rather than 'numbers' remained the basis for political authority and power. Hegemony was challenged but successfully maintained through a realignment of dominant economic and social forces.

NOTES

1 A. D. Kriegel (ed.) *The Holland House Diaries 1831–1840*, Routledge, 1977, p. 209.
2 Standard textbook discussions can be found in A. Briggs *The Age of Improvement*, Longman, 1959, pp. 236–85, N. Gash *Aristocracy and People: Britain 1815–1865*, Edward Arnold, 1979, pp. 156–219, E. J. Evans *The Forging of the Modern State: Early Industrial Britain 1783–1870*, Longman, 1983, pp. 219–45 and M. Bentley *Politics Without Democracy 1815–1914*, Fontana, 1984,

pp. 86–111. G. B. A. M. Finlayson *England in the Eighteen Thirties: Decade of Reform*, Edward Arnold, 1969 and A. Llewellyn *The Decade of Reform: The 1830s*, David & Charles, 1972 provide a more detailed consideration of the decade. R. Stewart *Party & Politics 1830–1852*, Macmillan, 1989 is an excellent study.

3 A. D. Kriegel (ed.) op. cit., 17–19 July 1833, p. 232.

4 N. Gash op. cit., pp. 159–60.

5 R. Brent *Liberal Anglican Politics: Whiggery, Religion and Reform 1830–1841*, Oxford University Press, 1987 provides a cogent analysis.

6 W. Thomas *The Philosophic Radicals*, Oxford University Press, 1979 is a full-length study but also see his shorter paper in P. Hollis (ed.) *Pressure from Without in Early Victorian England*, Edward Arnold, 1974.

7 A. Macintyre *The Liberator: Daniel O'Connell and the Irish Party 1830–1847*, Oxford University Press, 1965 is the best study of the subject. O. MacDonagh, *The Emancipist: Daniel O'Connell 1830–1847*, Weidenfeld, 1989 should be used to supplement Macintyre.

8 N. Gash op. cit., p. 173.

9 Russell to Melbourne, quoted in M. Bentley op. cit., p. 102.

10 Quoted in N. Gash *Reaction and Reconstruction in English Politics 1832–1852*, Oxford University Press, 1965, p. 180.

11 J. P. Parry *Democracy & Religion: Gladstone and the Liberal Party 1867–1875*, Cambridge University Press, 1986, p. 13.

12 On these issues see Chapter 14.

13 Dean Church quoted in N. Gash *Aristocracy and People*, op. cit., p. 176.

14 On Conservatism in the 1830s see R. Stewart *The Foundation of the Conservative Party 1830–1867*, Longman, 1978, B. Coleman *Conservatism and the Conservative Party in Nineteenth Century Britain*, Edward Arnold, 1988 and R. Blake *The Conservative Party from Peel to Thatcher*, Fontana, 1985. On Peel see N. Gash *Sir Robert Peel*, Longman, 1985 edition and D. Read *Peel and the Victorians*, Basil Blackwell, 1987.

15 See D. Roberts *Paternalism in Early Victorian England*, Croom Helm, 1979.

16 On 'Young England' three works are of particular value: R. Blake *Disraeli*, Methuen, 1966, chapter 8, M. Girouard *The Return to Camelot: Chivalry and the English Gentleman*, Yale, 1981, especially pp. 67–110 and R. Faber *Young England*, Faber, 1987.

17 R. Blake *The Conservative Party from Peel to Thatcher*, Fontana, 1985, p. 25.

18 ibid., pp. 38–9.

19 N. Gash *Reaction and Reconstruction in English Politics 1832–1852*, Oxford University Press, 1965, pp. 147–8.

20 On the vestries see D. Fraser *Urban Politics in Victorian England*, Leicester University Press, 1976, pp. 25–54.

21 On municipal reform see D. Fraser op. cit., D. Fraser *Power and Authority in the Victorian City*, Basil Blackwell, 1979, pp. 1–21, 149–73 and the brief discussion in J. Saville *1848: The British State and the Chartist Movement*, Cambridge University Press, 1987, pp. 9–10. G. B. A. M. Finlayson has contributed two important articles: 'The Municipal Corporation Commission and Report 1833–35', *Bulletin of the Institute of Historical Research*, 36 (1963), pp. 36–52 and 'The Politics of Municipal Reform, 1835', *English Historical Review*, 81 (1966), pp. 673–92.

22 Parkes and Lyndhurst quoted in D. Fraser *Power and Authority in the Victorian City*, Basil Blackwell, 1979, pp. 13, 14.

23 ibid., p. 85.

24 A detailed discussion of the broad issues contained in the emergence of a 'bourgeois state' can be found in Chapter 15.

25 The debate on the poor laws can best be examined in J. D. Marshall *The Old Poor Law 1795–1834*, Macmillan, 2nd edn, 1985 and M. E. Rose *The Relief of Poverty 1834–1914*, Macmillan, 2nd edn, 1985. G. R. Boyer *An Economic History of the English Poor Laws 1750–1850*, Cambridge University Press, 1990, defends much contemporary criticism. A. Digby *The Poor Law in Nineteenth Century England and Wales*, The Historical Association, 1982 is a short introduction to the operation of the 'new' system. A. Brundage *The Making of the New Poor Law 1833–39*, Hutchinson, 1979, and S. and E. Checkland (eds) *The Poor Law Report of 1834*, Penguin, 1974 are essential on the introduction of the new system; see N. Edsall *The Anti-Poor Law Movement 1833–1844*, Manchester University Press, 1971 and J. Knott *Popular Opposition to the 1834 Poor Law*, Croom Helm, 1985 on the scale of opposition. G. Himmelfarb *The Idea of Poverty: England in the Early Industrial Age*, Faber, 1984 is simply the best book on the subject. L. Rose *'Rogues and Vagabonds' Vagrant Underworld in Britain 1815–1985*, Routledge, 1988 adds a valuable dimension. On Chadwick, see the biographies by J. E. Finer, Methuen, 1952 and A. Brundage, Pennsylvania University Press, 1988.

26 On the politicization of poor law elections see D. Fraser *Urban Politics in Victorian England*, Leicester University Press, 1976.

27 S. Checkland op. cit., pp. 91–2.

28 U. Henriques *Before the Welfare State*, Longman, 1979, p. 59.

29 The shortest introduction to factory reform is U. Henriques *The Early Factory Acts and their Enforcement*, The Historical Association, 1971 and J. T. Ward *The Factory Movement 1830–1855*, Macmillan, 1962 is the most detailed.

30 See the useful discussion in R. Brent op. cit., pp. 218–51.

31 G. B. A. M. Finlayson *England in the Eighteen Thirties*, Edward Arnold, 1969, p. 104.

32 P. Richards 'State Formation and Class Struggle 1832–1848', in P. Corrigan (ed.) *Capitalism, State Formation and Marxist Theory*, Quartet Books, 1980, pp. 49–78 is a useful examination of alternative ideologies.

33 See Chapters 12 and 13 for a full discussion of these issues.

34 See J. V. Femia *Gramsci's Political Thought: Hegemony, Consciousness and the Revolutionary Process*, Oxford University Press, 1981.

35 P. Richards op. cit., pp. 73–8.

Addendum: See note at end of Chapter 8.

10 The Peel Administration 1841–6

A constitutional statesman is in general a man of common opinions and uncommon abilities. . . . No man has come so near to our definition of a constitutional statesman [as Sir Robert Peel] – the powers of a first-rate man and the creed of a second-class man. . . . He was a great administrator. . . . A great administrator is not a man likely to desire to have fixed opinions. . . . [1]

Sir Robert Peel aroused great emotions of admiration and antipathy during his lifetime and was used as the model of a constitutional statesman after his tragic death in 1850. He had a long and distinguished parliamentary life. Born in 1788 near Bury, Lancashire, the son of an enlightened cotton manufacturer, Peel was consciously prepared for politics by his father and had a brilliant academic record at Harrow and Christ Church, Oxford. He entered Parliament in 1809 as a colleague of Castlereagh and had a varied ministerial career – Under-Secretary for War and the Colonies between 1810 and 1812, Irish Secretary 1812–18, Chairman of the Financial Committee on Cash Payments 1819–21 and Home Secretary 1822–7 and 1828–30 – before he became Prime Minister, first in 1834 and then in 1841. This chapter is concerned with his administration between 1841 and 1846 and with his influence in politics between his resignation and his death in July 1850.[2] Politics in Wales, Scotland and Ireland between 1832 and 1846 will also be considered.

THE 1841 ELECTION

The general election of 1841 produced a comfortable overall Conservative majority of between 75 and 78. This result did not mark a sudden surge of opinion towards Peel but one built on the two previous general elections, trends evident in by-election results and on superior party organization. The obvious strength of the Conservatives in some constituencies meant that 113 seats went to them without a contest compared to only 55 in 1837.

The Whigs recognized the need for fiscal reform in the late 1830s and had come out in favour of a fixed duty on corn in place of the existing sliding scale. The Conservatives preferred to continue with the existing structure. Published election addresses show that this was the major issue of the campaign, mentioned by 60 per cent of the candidates. For the Conservatives the second issue, mentioned by 40 per cent of their candidates, was defence of the Church and resistance to both O'Connell's Irish Catholics and English Dissenters. Twenty per cent of Conservative addresses were critical of the 'new' poor law, criticisms supported by *The Times* but not by Peel. Neither party advocated free trade in corn, though many Tory agriculturalists thought the Whigs were heading in that direction.

Conservative gains were made mainly in the English counties – they held 137 out of 159 seats – and these contributed significantly to Peel's victory. This reinforced the assumption that the Conservatives were above all the party of the land. The number of Peelite Conservatives, found to be about a hundred in the crisis of 1845–6, was not markedly increased in 1841 and it can be argued that this reflected Peel's failure to convince many of his party and much of the electorate of the validity of his version of Conservatism. Peel was obviously more popular in 1846 than he had been in 1841 and achieved this largely by increasingly acting apart from his party and eventually by standing above party. He issued no new 'Tamworth Manifesto' in 1841, for he was still acting in the spirit of 1834, and many of the Conservative candidates he asked the electorate to vote for were patently much less liberal than he was himself. Michael Bentley argues that

> The electorates in [the] constituencies did not comprise the broad base at which Peel's rhetoric since Tamworth had been directed; and the election overall had not reflected, in any simple way, the urban domination established by the Conservative party in the second half of the 1830s. Office, indeed, had come from the very direction which had then seemed so unpromising, that of county-based resistance politics.[3]

The potential for tension within the Conservative party was evident from the outset of Peel's administration. The Earl of Ripon, strategically placed as President of the Board of Trade, said to Sir James Graham in 1841 that the administration must take 'an enlarged view of what the actual condition of society demands'. This prognosis was fraught with dangers for the Conservatives.

MINISTERS AND MINISTRIES

Melbourne did not resign immediately but waited for the inevitable defeat in the Commons and on 30 August Peel took office. There were no constitutional problems as there had been in 1839 and, largely because of the influence of Prince Albert, the Queen quickly developed a deep admiration for Peel. His cabinet drew on surviving ministerial talent from the 1820s as well as on rising new men. Two former Prime Ministers, Goderich (now Earl Ripon) and Wellington, received cabinet office. The first was uncomfortable between 1841 and 1843 at the Board of Trade and then from 1843 to 1846 as President of the Board of Control responsible for Indian policy. Wellington had suffered two strokes in 1840 which put the Foreign Office beyond him and he came in as minister without portfolio. By default Lord Aberdeen returned as Foreign Secretary, a post he had previously held under Wellington in the late 1820s. Lord Wharncliffe, a waverer in 1832, was Lord President of the Council until 1845, and the Duke of Buckingham – the Chandos of 1832 – was Lord Privy Seal until 1842. They symbolized respectively the voice of moderation and a defence of the land. Lord Lyndhurst was again Lord Chancellor. These individuals brought broad experience of government to the cabinet.

Sir James Graham took a great step forward by accepting the Home Office and he quickly established himself as second-in-command to Peel. Henry Goulburn undoubtedly suffered from Graham's advancement and though he became Chancellor of the Exchequer his influence was limited by the overwhelming degree to which Peel dictated fiscal policies. Lord Stanley, with Graham one of the Whig defectors of 1834, took the Colonial Office, an area which he later recognized was of less importance in the politics of the 1840s than it had been in the years of Canada and Jamaica. He also began to move away from Peel, which eventually led him to the Toryism of Bentinck and Disraeli in 1846. The only minister capable of confronting Peel on questions of trade and economy was the Vice-President, and from 1843 President, of the Board of Trade William Ewart Gladstone. Benjamin Disraeli was not given office, despite his pleas, which nurtured a sense of denial that played an important influence on his attitude in 1845–6. Robert Blake says that

> The Tory ministry of 1841–6 was one of the ablest of the whole century. It contained five past or future prime ministers [Goderich, Wellington, Aberdeen, Stanley and Gladstone], and the adhesion of the 'dilly' [the group which seceded from the Whigs in 1834–5] gave a notable boost to its talent.[4]

PEEL'S ATTITUDES

Peel made it clear from the outset to both his party and to the country that it was his duty to govern. He inherited the eighteenth-century political tradition that the executive must provide direction for the House of Commons and should not be subservient to it. He accepted that the Commons had the right to veto ministerial actions but maintained that the cabinet should hold the initiative in the conduct of government and administration; entirely when it came to executive action and largely so in terms of legislation. He placed the responsibility firmly on backbench MPs to support his ministers in policies the government chose to undertake in the national interest. Within a fortnight of forming his administration Peel said in the Commons that he would not by 'considerations of mere political support' hold office 'by a service tenure which would compel me to be the instrument of carrying other men's opinions into effect'. From 1841 to 1846 the parliamentary battle that mattered was within the Conservative ranks.

Peel's attitude to ordinary MPs was based on his belief that the Conservative party existed to provide majorities not to make difficulties. This 'disciplined' approach to party looked forward to the later nineteenth and twentieth centuries but it created tensions within the ranks of the backbenchers among whom the eighteenth-century tradition of 'independence' was still strong. The quantity of patronage available to reward MPs and their constituents was by 1841 considerably reduced and Peel frequently complained that he spent too much time absorbed in patronage business without any tangible results because it caused disaffection. Peel did not pay sufficient attention to his backbenchers' views and in 1845 and 1846 he was to ask them to accept too much.

By contrast, Peel over-supervised his colleagues. It was clear from the outset that it was *his* government with his dominance of the cabinet and awareness of the major concerns of all his departments. Peel's was a highly organized and businesslike administration and he was impatient with MPs who wanted quick results and who failed to understand how slowly the machinery of the state moved. By placing his sense of duty as Prime Minister above his perception of his commitment as leader of the Conservative party he was endangering his position as both while ensuring his position as one of the few great statesmen of the century.

There is a neat logic in examining Peel's ministry solely in the light of 1845–6 but free trade in corn no more entered his mind in 1841 than it entered Russell's, and this neglects the extent to which repeal was a surprise as much to the Anti-Corn Law League as it was to Peel. There were more pressing problems.

The constitutional and religious issues of the 1830s had either been solved or shelved. They had been succeeded by a major economic and social crisis which originated in the mid-1830s and this reached its peak as Peel took office. His concern for the conditions of the people was not mere show and he accepted that ministers had a major role to play in encouraging the welfare of the nation and in finding the best course of action to ease social and economic distress.[5]

FINANCE

The most pressing problem which faced Peel in 1841 was finance. No failure had so dogged the Whigs in the late 1830s as their inability to balance the budget and Conservatives had seized upon that failure as *the* mark of Whig incompetence. There had been budgetary deficiencies for the previous three years and the Whigs had been defeated when the House of Commons expressed its lack of confidence in their ability to regain fiscal solvency. Peel's approach to the question was dominated by the difficulties of raising revenue, but he had already decided that, when he returned to power, he would reintroduce income tax though he was careful to present this as a temporary expedient to overcome deficiencies. A natural consequence of this decision was a review of the tariff system which had hardly been touched since Huskisson's tenure at the Board of Trade in the 1820s. Peel accepted that reimposing income tax would be politically unpopular and that reviewing tariffs could hardly fail to bring up the corn question.

The 1842 budget

The cabinet discussed the problem throughout the winter of 1841–2. The corn question and tariffs were approached first on the basis that the promise of cheaper living conditions and encouragement of trade would make income tax more acceptable. This was a sensible tactical move. The new corn bill, introduced in February 1842, made drastic reductions in the duties imposed in the 1828 Act. A scale was drawn up which imposed a duty of 20 shillings on foreign wheat when the price of home wheat was 51 shillings a quarter, dropping to a nominal 1 shilling when domestic prices rose to 73 shillings. Tariffs on other cereals were reduced pro-portionately. Buckingham, 'the farmer's friend', resigned on the issue though he was prepared to support Peel on any other issue. Conservative backbench opinion was, however, far more amenable and, though a higher level of protection was called for, the representatives of the English coun-ties were prepared to support their leader. The impotence of free traders, despite an extensive petitioning campaign, was demonstrated by the crush-ing defeat of Villier's repeal motion by 395 to 92.

Peel then outlined the rest of his government's plans. In March he announced, much to the surprise of the Whig opposition, the reintroduc-tion of income tax (7 pence in the pound on incomes over £150 for the next three years). Its yield was estimated at £3.7 million with the rest of the £4.3 million that was needed made up of miscellaneous taxes. The unpopularity of income tax was tempered by the new tariff proposals. Duties were reduced on 600 imports, including timber, involving a loss of revenue of £1.2 million. Peel emphasized that the aim of tariff reduction was the reduction of the cost of living for every class in society. Whig opposition, given their own budget the previous year, was muted and attempts to amend the proposals came largely from within Conservative ranks. 'The danger,' Peel said, 'is not low prices from the tariff, but low prices from the inability to consume.' He therefore shifted the burden of taxation away from the less well off by moving to direct taxes so, he argued, increasing the purchasing power of the consumer. Peel refused to make any modifications, precipitating the first split in Conservative ranks when an amendment to the clause admitting foreign meat and cattle was defeated by 380 to 113 with 85 of Peel's own party among the minority.

Widespread disorder and agitation in the summer of 1842 added to the grumbling of the agriculturalists. They distrusted the free-trade tendencies of the government and accused Peel of giving in to extra-parliamentary pressures. His responses to their complaints were blunt and clear: Britain was fast becoming an industrial, urbanized nation whose population increasingly depended on trade and manufacture and nostalgia for a rural past could not alter that development. Falling domestic wheat prices in late 1842 focused the attention of English farmers and their reaction to the Canada corn bill in 1843 showed just how sensitive they were.

In 1842 the Colonial Secretary had virtually guaranteed free entry of Canadian corn into Britain so long as safeguards against the inclusion of illicit American wheat could be provided. Agriculturalists saw this as an attempt to weaken the modified protection offered in the 1842 Corn Act. Stanley argued that the decision was justified on the grounds of imperial preference, a principle which went beyond Huskisson to the 1815 Corn Act and he, with Peel, was able to convince government supporters. Resistance to the proposal was, as a result, limited to some amendments, most of which came from the Whig opposition, and the bill passed both Houses with minimum embarrassment to the government. Around twenty Conservatives voted against the government, some of whom did so to appease their local constituencies.

More serious for Peel was a further loss of confidence by the county electorate in the ministry. Party sensitivity had been offended, again. The Duke of Richmond's son expressed a widely held view: 'Are we to agree to every motion which we think most prejudicial to agriculture because they threaten us with retiring?' Suspicion of Peel's manner and increasingly his motives was compounded by the formation, after the Smithfield Show in December 1842, of an 'Anti-League' to resist further attacks on the agricultural interest. In June 1843 a speaker at a Kent county meeting had asked whether, given the experience of Catholic emancipation, agriculturalists could trust Peel. He had defended the revised Corn Law in the Commons in 1843 but he refused to be bound to it in principle. The practical working of the Act was now his sole criterion for the continuance of protection.

Finance and party tensions 1843–5

The economy had not recovered as quickly as Peel had hoped in 1843 and the success of the 1842 budget still hung in the balance. 1843 saw a budget deficit of £2 million instead of the modest £0.5 million Peel had envisaged.

The continued depression in manufacturing industry and the lateness in setting up the machinery for collecting income tax were largely responsible. Peel did not regard this as a setback since it was clear that the worst of the depression was over and that, in a full year, income tax would yield considerably more than had been estimated. The government reaped the benefits of their fiscal policies in 1844 with the April budget in which Goulburn announced that both customs and income tax had yielded more than expected and that expenditure had been reduced. The massive surplus of £4 million allowed Peel to absorb the deficit of the previous year and still leave a small credit balance.

The strain on party loyalties evident in 1843 continued in 1844 when Peel decided that cotton, wool and sugar duties must be removed. Sugar was the most valuable dutiable commodity to enter Britain, a major item on the cost of living and a significant source of revenue. Proposals to reduce sugar tariffs were regarded as a challenge to the whole notion of colonial preference and led to an alliance of liberal free traders who wanted to admit all foreign sugar irrespective of origin and conservative protectionists. Led by Philip Miles, MP for Bristol, the protectionists were not to be converted by Peel's appeal to a party meeting and on 14 June a wrecking amendment was carried by 20 votes with 62 Conservatives voting against the ministry. Peel's immediate response was to consider resignation but he was persuaded otherwise. Three days later the Commons reversed the decision but, according to Michael Bentley, Peel recognized that

> he must soon fall. If he knew this, moreover, historians cannot be allowed to pretend that they do not: Peel's last months were acted out in the foreknowledge of doom and must be analysed accordingly.[6]

while Norman Gash argues that

> the relationship called for tact and management; and in 1844 Peel mismanaged the situation as badly as any in his long career. Overwork, disillusionment, the strains of office stiffened the autocratic tendencies in his nature, making him increasingly indifferent to party claims and the party's future.[7]

The Bank Charter Act

1844 did, however, mark the passage of the Bank Charter Act which Peel regarded as one of the chief legislative achievements of his career. Peel had previously shown himself willing to intervene decisively and in detail to promote a sound basis for economic enterprise. The 1844 Act reinforced the work which he had begun as chairman of the Currency Committee of 1819. It strictly separated the 'issue' and 'banking' departments of the Bank of England and laid down that the specie reserves of the former, which covered the note issue, should not be used to sustain the latter. Any note issue over £14 million was to be backed by bullion. This concentrated the issue of banknotes in the Bank of England and, as a result, country and joint-stock banknotes slowly began to drop out of circulation. Though the Act was very successful in psychological terms, encouraging business confidence, the strict division between the two departments proved a problem during commercial crises. In the 1847 crisis the banking department reserves were almost exhausted while the issue department was left with ample reserves and the Treasury agreed to a transfer of funds. This did not prove necessary but in the 1857 crisis a transfer in contravention to Peel's rules proved unavoidable.

The 1844 Act was the basis of Britain's currency policy for the next eighty years and the ease with which it passed through Parliament reflected Peel's impressive reputation for financial skill. But the gold standard was not under serious threat in the 1840s and many contemporaries and some later historians pointed out that as a defence of bullionism Peel was fighting battles won in the 1810s and early 1820s. One of the reasons why the Act worked so effectively up to 1914 was that Peel failed to take into account the increasing volume of banking deposits. The Bank of England quickly learned to manipulate these deposits and consequently influenced the level of money supply. In this light the Bank Charter Act was perhaps a less fundamental measure than Peel believed.

The 1845 budget

In 1845 general economic prosperity and the healthy state of national finance enabled Peel to plan further advance. The 1842 budget had been a large-scale experiment with its risks covered by the reimposition of income tax. The 1845 budget was a far safer measure introduced in a more tranquil economic climate. Peel introduced the budget himself in February, renewing income tax for a further three years and, as a result, enabling sweeping reductions in tariffs. The available surplus was calculated at £3.4 million of which £3.3 million were to be returned to the public in the shape of lower sugar duties, the abolition of all export duties on British goods and free entry for more than half of imports still carrying duties, including cotton and industrial raw materials.

Sugar again provoked much open dispute but generally the budget was generally approved. *The Times* saw it as 'popular in tendency', emancipating commerce at the expense of property and favouring the poor. Agriculturalists complained that land was not mentioned but Peel retorted by arguing that any increase in commerce increased demand for agricultural products and so benefited farmers and labourers. The *Derby Mercury*, a protectionist newspaper, argued that 'the Cabinet is essentially a commercial Cabinet' while the *Morning Post*, which had supported the 1842 budget, now openly attacked Peel as the individual who had destroyed the Tory party in 1829 and who had since 1841 been busily destroying the Conservative party.[8]

Finances: successful policies?

Peel's financial policies proved a resounding success. The estimates presented to Parliament in 1846 showed that the surplus was over £2.5 million rather than the estimated £700,000. The financial solidarity of the government in 1845 enabled Peel in 1846 to produce a third free-trade budget in which duties amounting to over £1 million were removed. Between 1842 and 1846 Peel had largely accomplished the work of transforming Britain into a free-trade country, only leaving Gladstone some tidying up to do in 1853 and 1860.

Peel pointed out in May 1845 that

> They cannot deny that Trade is prosperous. That the people are contented, That the Labourer has a greater Command than he ever had over the Necessities and Comforts of Life. . . . That the Revenue is so prosperous that our calculations of deficiency are certainly baffled. That our monetary system is sounder than it has ever been, and yet there has been boundless activity in commerce and in all speculation of gain. That even Land is increasing in value in consequence of the prosperity of Commerce. . . .[9]

However, Peel's achievement in creating firm foundations for both government finances and the banking system neglects his failure to control the railway mania of 1845. The problem was whether and how he should intervene to control speculative private railway ventures. The 1844 Railway Act had already been weakened by pressure from the railway interest and the Railway Board created in August 1844 to vet proposals for new lines was dissolved the following June. As the mania intensified in the second half of 1845 Peel recognized that the detached attitude of the government could not be maintained but he remained slow to act. In April 1846 the *Illustrated London News* criticized the slowness of government action and remarked that it had missed the opportunity of creating the best railway network rather than one determined by speculative advantage. Peel's enthusiasm for railways was not paralleled by any sense of the advantages of a major directing role for the state.

SOCIAL POLICIES

Tension within Conservative ranks over economic policies was duplicated, on occasions with equal passion, in social policies. Conservative policies were either a gloss or an extension on measures introduced in the 1830s and, as in economic matters, reflected Peel's conviction rather than attempts to seek party unity. On both the poor law and factory reform

Peel held views contrary to those of many of his backbenchers: 53 primarily northern Conservative MPs opposed the former and supported the latter. He would have won their warm approval had he opposed the 1834 Act but he had reminded the Conservatives in 1840 that the leaders of the party had helped the Whigs introduce the new system and promised continued support. In 1842 Peel's government secured an extension of the poor law until 1847 with minor modifications.

Factory reform

Peel remained steady in his opposition to the Ten Hour Movement right up to the passage of the 1847 Factory Act. He had adopted the argument of political economists that wages would fall under a ten-hour day and the cost of production would increase with consequences for rising prices. He also did not like interfering in the free operation of the market or in the contractual relationship between masters and men. This was not a doctrinaire approach but one grounded in a genuine concern for the welfare of workers. In 1841, however, this concern was mistaken by a West Riding short-time deputation as an acceptance of the ten-hour principle. This led to widespread and misleading publicity, raising then shattering workers' hopes and intensifying their hostility to the government during 1842.

Peel was, however, prepared to accept intervention to control working conditions when convinced that the moral case was overwhelming. He opposed Ashley over ten-hour legislation because he believed that the moral case was weaker than the economic one. But he was prepared to accept the moral arguments implicit in the 1842 Mines Act which excluded women from underground work.

Peel's good intentions were insufficient to dampen class and sectarian antagonisms, which intensified during the industrial distress and disturbances of 1841 and 1842. Fear and prejudice came together in the opposition to Graham's Factory Bill in 1843. The Whig educational initiative of 1839 foundered on the unwillingness of most people to accept secular education and the unacceptability of any system in which the Established Church did not have a leading role. Peel and Graham agreed on the importance of improving educational provision for the working population and making the educational clauses of the 1833 Factory Act effective. Graham's proposal for state assistance in the education of factory children – motivated by the need to raise the 'moral feeling' of the people as a counter to radical agitation – was thought by Nonconformists and Roman Catholics to favour the Church of England unfairly. Parliamentary and extra-parliamentary opposition resulted in the whole bill being abandoned.

A revised factory bill, shorn of its contentious educational clauses, was reintroduced in early 1844. It proposed to limit children in textile mills to no more than six hours work per day, but did not reduce the permitted twelve hours of women and young persons. Ashley moved a ten-hour amendment which carried with 95 Conservatives supporting it. Nearly a third of the Conservative party had taken Lord Ashley's side against the cabinet. Their motives for doing so were mixed but, as Peel informed the queen:

> A great body of the agricultural members partly out of hostility to the Anti-Corn Law League, partly from the influence of humane feelings, not foreseeing the certain consequences to the Corn Laws of new restrictions upon labour, voted against the government.

Peel refused to accept ten hours or compromise with eleven hours and the bill was only passed when he threatened resignation unless his wayward supporters rescinded their earlier vote. The crisis revealed different attitudes towards party and its relationship to the executive held by backbenchers and by the cabinet. Yet if party was to replace the Crown as the means of ministerial stability then the executive needed to know it could rely on the support of its party members.

TOWARDS SCHISM

In both economic and social policies an estrangement built up between Peel and his party and this deepened in 1845 into outright rebellion. Peel was a firm supporter of the Anglican Church but the debates over education in 1843 confirmed him in his belief that the power of non-Anglican and non-Protestant opinion was so great that government could no longer discriminate in favour of the Established Church. He recognized the need for more churches in manufacturing areas but was not prepared to face the inevitable non-Anglican protest that he used taxpayers' money to provide these. One in five electors were Nonconformist by the 1840s and, though a significant minority of Wesleyans supported Peel in 1841, most favoured 'liberal' or Whig policies. Peel realized that adopting an aggressively Anglican policy would antagonize non-Anglicans and damage further the position of the Anglican Church.

Peel's difficulties over religion, corn and his insensitivity towards his own backbenchers came together in problems associated with Ireland: successively, O'Connell's agitation for repeal of the union, the Maynooth grant crisis of 1844–5 and finally the failure of the Irish potato crop in 1845 with its profound social and political consequences throughout the British Isles.

The Irish dimension

Ireland's problems had been obscured by England's during 1841 and 1842 but a mass movement dedicated to the repeal of the Union with Britain had gathered considerable momentum under the leadership of O'Connell.

During 1843 a surge of support, especially from among Ireland's Roman Catholic priests, made it formidable and Peel was compelled to act. A mass meeting at Clontarf in October was banned and O'Connell was arrested, tried, imprisoned and then released. Peel and Graham felt that Ireland teetered on the edge of rebellion and that coercion was insufficient as a solution. Peel had considerable first-hand experience of the Irish situation and he recognized that there were two main obstacles to good government there: poor relations between tenant and landlord, and bad relations between the British government and the Catholic middle class and moderate clergy.

The exploration of the first problem was delegated to a Royal Commission headed by the Earl of Devon set up in 1843 and his solutions for the other half of his programme were put forward in a series of cabinet memoranda in the spring of 1844.[10] Only if, Peel argued, the moderate Catholic clergy could be detached from the repeal movement would the Church of Ireland be able to retain its privileges. But a policy of religious appeasement was fraught with difficulties. Irish Conservatives were unwilling to give offices to Roman Catholics despite Peel's entreaties since 1841. The less moderate members of his cabinet, not least Stanley and Gladstone, were implacably hostile to concessions and there was widespread alarm at the spread of the doctrinally suspect Tractarian movement within the Church of England. The changed state of British public opinion towards Catholicism was equally important. Anti-Catholic feeling had hardened since 1829 because of disillusion at the failure of emancipation, the violence of O'Connell's movement and increasing numbers of Irish Catholics on mainland Britain. Opposition was, however, grounded in more than native prejudice. There was a deeply held conviction about the proper relationship between Church and state which did *not* include giving aid to a church whose members owed their first loyalty to Rome and were therefore tainted with at least the suspicion of disloyalty to the Crown.

Peel identified charitable endowments as an area of reform which would benefit Irish Catholics and the 1844 Charitable Bequests Act aimed to remove obstacles to endowments to the Catholic Church. Without directly recognizing the Roman Catholic hierarchy, a supervisory Charitable Trusts Board was created with Catholic members to facilitate endowment of chapels and benefices. The Act was not immediately welcomed by many Catholic bishops and clergy but it was soon recognized as a beneficial working solution and as the first gesture of conciliation.

In 1845 Peel turned to Irish education, both to the better training of Catholic priests at Maynooth College, near Dublin, and to the creation of improved higher educational facilities. Each proposal ran into strong, prejudiced opposition. The principle of state support for Maynooth went back to 1795 but the grant of less than £9,000 was seriously inadequate. Peel wanted it increased to £26,000 plus a special building grant of £30,000 and aimed to raise the social and intellectual level of the priesthood, hoping this would make priests more moderate. In late 1844 he had pulled back from this proposal in the face of opposition from Stanley (now promoted to the House of Lords) and from Gladstone, who left the cabinet in January 1845.[11]

Peel introduced his Maynooth Bill in April 1845 without fully appreciating the nationwide hostility to the proposal. The timing was unfortunate – it corresponded to the Tractarian crisis in Oxford – and this simply increased the alarm and indignation of evangelical Protestantism. The double principle of religious endowment by the state and encouragement of Roman Catholicism struck deep into the prejudices and fears of contemporary Protestants. Anglican Ultras saw the commitment to Maynooth as implicit official recognition of the Roman Catholic church and as a challenge to the established position of the Church of Ireland. Nonconformists opposed the payments because they disliked any link between Church and state. From different directions Anglicans and Nonconformists briefly came together, a joint central Anti-Maynooth Committee was set up to organize the agitation and over 10,000 petitions poured into Parliament between February and May.

Peel pressed ahead with his plan in the face of vehement opposition by many of his own party and much of the country. For opponents Maynooth was yet another example of Peel's 'flexibility' and they pointed to 1829 when he had argued that Maynooth's charter should be revoked and Irish priests brought under government control. Despite widespread extra-parliamentary opposition from the Central Anti-Maynooth Committee the bill went through, as emancipation had in 1829, with large cross-bench majorities. The combination of office-holders, liberal conservatives, erastian Whigs and Irish Catholic MPs was too strong for the ultra-Protestant and doctrinaire radicals.

The debate on Maynooth is important less for the discussion of the principles of the bill than for the vehemence of attacks on Peel's 'betrayal'. Ashley wrote that Peel was 'the most unpopular head of a party that ever existed' and Sir James Graham knew that the government had 'lost the slight hold which we ever possessed over the hearts and kind feelings of our fellows'. Peel maintained that his government had the right to do what it felt necessary without reference to what had happened in the past. The Conservative party, egged on perhaps by Disraeli's scathing attacks, split 159 to 147 in favour of the bill on the second reading but 149 to 148 against it on the third.[12] At issue was far more than the bill itself it was the place of party and its proper use in a parliamentary constitution.

Peel's third proposal, the Academic Institutions (Ireland) Act, was intended to improve the education of the Irish middle class in the hope that this would make it more resistant to political extremism or clerical influence. Ultra-Anglicans were damning in their criticism of the idea of the non-denominational 'Godless colleges' proposed for Cork, Galway and Belfast. Irish Catholic attitudes were split and in July 1846 the Vatican decided that such institutions would be harmful to the Catholic faith.

Of Peel's three reforms, two proved successful and one a failure. To a limited extent the Charitable Bequests and Maynooth Acts broke up the combination of Irish Catholics but the collapse of the Irish Repeal movement cannot be directly attributed to Peel's actions. The price of concessions to Ireland was the breakup of Peel's own party which never recovered from the shock administered to it by the Maynooth grant. The Irish famine administered the *coup de grâce*.

Corn Laws

By the summer of 1845 the press and many politicians were predicting the ending of the Corn Laws. The news of the potato blight and the imminence of widespread famine merely brought the matter to a head since it was likely that Peel would have anyway attempted further revision of the Corn Law in the 1846 session. His appeal, particularly to the middle classes, became increasingly irresistible. He ceased to be a party leader who had sought support irrespective of party and became a charismatic statesman who put himself above party. There is an evident change in the press's attitude to him: the opportunist politician who, even though he introduced reforms, was not entirely trustworthy, the great political survivor not a statesman became, largely as a result of the 1845 December crisis, popular, trusted and respected.

Peel had no illusions about the effects the potato blight would have. As Irish Secretary, he had lived through the famine of 1817. A scheme of national relief at the taxpayers' expense would have to be organized before the full effects of famine were felt the following spring. Could the taxpayer be asked to contribute to the feeding of Ireland and still tolerate the existence of the Corn Laws? Peel had three alternatives open to him: leave the law intact, suspend it until the Irish problem was resolved or abolish it. Leaving the law intact was a non-starter. Suspension posed certain problems: the length of suspension was unpredictable but was likely to be for more than a year which meant that an unpopular resumption of the law would occur in 1847 when a general election was due. He had already intimated to Prince Albert in December 1845 that he intended to prepare the country gradually for a change of policy and fight the elections due in 1847–8 on a platform of free trade, so depriving the Whigs of the electoral advantage to be gained from cries of 'cheap bread'. He also believed that the aristocracy, which he was intent on upholding as central to national affairs, would bring about its own downfall by tying its fortunes to the maintenance of the Corn Laws. Peel wrote in January 1846 that: 'The worst grounds on which we can now fight the battle for institutions – for the just privileges of Monarchy and Landed Aristocracy is on the question of food.' The problem with abolition was that Peel could not count on the support of either his own party or the majority of his cabinet.

Between the end of October and early December Peel tried unsuccessfully to convince his cabinet colleagues that drastic modification of the Corn Laws was inevitable. They were prepared to support the measures Peel and Graham had already taken: instructions to lord lieutenants to set up relief organizations, the secret purchase of American maize costing £100,000 and a search for possible European sources of food. But they held back from making the crucial decision. Some ministers opposed the question of modification or abolition in principle, while others did not consider the situation warranted a reversal of party policy. On 6 November only Aberdeen, Graham and Herbert supported Peel in cabinet and his delay in making a final decision was motivated largely by giving waverers time to make up their minds. Delay worsened the position of the government and failed to bring about the agreement Peel wanted. On 4 December Lord Stanley and the Duke of Buccleugh indicated that they would resign rather than support a complete change in policy. The following day the cabinet concluded that with the loss of Stanley and Buccleugh it would be unable to carry Peel's bill suspending the Corn Laws and Peel announced that in such circumstances he felt duty bound to resign.

Peel returned to power after eleven days. Lord John Russell, though he had already announced his conversion to total repeal in his 'Edinburgh Letter' of 22 November, and the Whigs were in a minority in both Commons and Lords. His party was not united or enthusiastic over corn. Peel's promise of general support, while accepted by Russell and most of his senior colleagues, was suspected by others. Russell's decision was to hand power back to Peel who was convinced that the corn issue had to be resolved in the national interest and that he was the only politician who could achieve this.

All the members of Peel's old cabinet, except Stanley, rejoined him. He proposed to make a last round of tariff changes in which corn would be treated as an ordinary commodity and at the end of January he announced his plans to the Commons. They included abolishing or reducing duties on a large range of goods and a progressive reduction of corn duties leading to their abolition in 1849 with compensation for farmers in the form of government loans for improvement and various forms of relief for county rates. If Peel intended through these proposals to placate the protectionists or blunt their resistance he failed completely. The political battle broke out immediately. The Central Protection Society held meetings all over England promoting petitions to Parliament and exacting pledges from constituency MPs against repeal. Within Parliament Lord George Bentinck, for whom Peel was a 'dishonest jockey', and Benjamin Disraeli emerged as protectionist leaders and their personal attacks on the Prime Minister widened the emotional gap between Peelites and Protectionists. Protectionists argued that if the famine was the cause of Peel's

action then suspension *not* abolition was called for. To them his decision
was part of a long-matured 'secret design' and as a result Peel was accused
of 'deception' in attributing his decision to conditions in Ireland. The
depth of the division within Conservative ranks can be shown in the second
reading when 231 MPs voted against the proposal and only 112 with, and
on the third reading 241 against and 106 for. Repeal was achieved by a
combination of Peelite, Whig and Irish MPs.

It was simply a matter of time before Peel resigned. Bentinck was set
on revenge at the passage of repeal through the Commons and Peel had
only just over a hundred supporters he could count on. On 25 June repeal
passed the Lords and later that evening the Protection of Life (Ireland)
bill was defeated by 73 votes in the Commons. Less than a third of the
protectionist MPs voted with the Whigs and nearly half supported Peel
but this was insufficient to ensure victory. On 29 June Peel announced his
resignation.

In his resignation speech Peel commended a free-trade commercial
policy to the next government and maintained that he would have built
on the restoration of law and order in Ireland by further concessions to
Catholics and an attempt to resolve the problems of tenure between
landlords and tenants. His speech was, however, remembered for two
things: his wish to be remembered favourably by the working population
and his tribute to Richard Cobden as the real architect of repeal. On the
first he was criticized for 'pathos' by many protectionist newspapers though
Peel believed that repeal would remove a feeling of injustice and showed
that a landed legislature could be responsive to the unfranchised masses.
For the second time he was accused of 'claptrap'. Contemporaries recognized that it was only Peel who could have secured the abolition of the
Corn Laws at that time and that the Anti-Corn Law League was surprised
by events.

PEEL'S DECADE

In or out of government Peel dominated the politics of the 1840s.[13]
Between 1846 and 1850 he had a unique position in public life. He provided advice for Prince Albert on foreign and domestic policy. Charles
Wood, the Whig Chancellor of the Exchequer sought his opinion. In 1849
the Whig Irish Lord Lieutenant, Clarendon, persuaded Russell to include
some of Peel's proposals after hearing a speech on Ireland. He was called
upon to lend his support to the government over the repeal of the Navigation Acts in 1849 and was asked to use his authority with the Peelite
peers. Praised though Peel's stance was in the country, his reluctance to
give positive leadership to his parliamentary supporters resulted in an
unsteadiness in politics. He may have been determined not to take office
again but the Peelites, alienated from the protectionists and suspicious of
the Whigs, looked for a coalition of moderates in which Peel would

inevitably be forced to play a major role. Gladstone was particularly critical of Peel's self-indulgent attitude after 1846 both at the time and later. Whether Peel was 'in a thoroughly false position', as Gladstone maintained, between 1846 and 1850 and whether he could have maintained this 'heroic' mantle into the 1850s, there is no doubting his popularity to the mass of the middle class and a large section of the working population. He had sought to justify the flexibility of aristocratic government and its ability to adapt to the needs of society as a whole rather than sectional interests. The Protectionists may have overemphasized the significance of repeal but as a moral symbol of Peelite pragmatism it cannot be cheapened.

Peel was an outsider by traditional Tory standards. He was of humble birth: Wellington complained on one occasion that 'Peel has no manners'. He was academically brilliant at both Harrow and Christ Church, Oxford. He possessed a comprehensive and detailed grasp of machinery of government, saw himself as Pitt's natural successor and was a professional politician when most saw politics as an amateur occupation for 'gentlemen'. He was a conservative by nature and instinct, passionately attached like Pitt to the constitution and to traditional ways of doing things. Yet he was aware that preserving a fundamentally sound system from violent overthrow meant that it had to be made more acceptable and efficient. Conservatism demanded well-judged and carefully timed but none the less fundamental reforms to achieve this. A sensible rationalization of commercial policies lay at Peel's heart and could, he believed, be used to popularize government.

His commercial and professional attitudes proved too radical for some of the Tory country gentlemen. But the irrational dislike by many Tories of one of their most powerful and successful leaders cannot be explained on policy grounds alone. His birth, his haughty personality and authoritarian approach to government and to his own backbenchers offended Tory sensibilities and the events of 1845–6 turned offence into schism. But Peel had created his own political culture and those, like Gladstone, who practised it dominated politics in the quarter-century after 1850.

WALES, SCOTLAND AND IRELAND

Wales

The difference in status between Wales on the one hand, and Scotland and Ireland on the other, became more acute during the nineteenth century.[14] Wales had no accepted capital and its boundary with England was artificial. The Act of Union with England had been followed by a systematic creation of administrative uniformity culminating in the abolition of the Court of Great Sessions in 1830. There was from the perspective of Westminster no distinction between English and Welsh problems.

Despite this administrative effort, the separate existence of a Welsh community was maintained in two important respects. First, the Welsh language survived, serving as the normal medium of communication in most parts of Wales until the 1870s. Secondly, Welsh society was quite different from English society, with a different network of class relationships. Land was farmed in less commercial ways and a growing divergence emerged between Anglican, Tory, English-speaking landowners and increasingly Nonconformist, Welsh-speaking tenants. There were scattered elements of a middle class but these did not form a large group, were located largely in the more anglicized southern and eastern counties and consisted of professional rather than mercantile classes.

Demographic and industrial growth lent a new complexity to the economy and society of the country, dividing Wales further into distinct cultures and creating new connections with England. More fundamental was the rise of Nonconformity which proceeded side by side with industrialization from 1800. By 1850 it had created important lines of division within Welsh society, polarizing opinion in different areas in ways that class affiliations were not able to do.

The power of Nonconformity was demonstrated in the protest against the repeal of the Test and Corporation Acts in 1828–9 and Nonconformists' cautious support for parliamentary reform in 1831–2. The 1832 Reform Act, however, had only limited effect. In the county seats, the hold of the gentry remained unimpaired and the balance between county and borough representation was unchanged. Five new seats were given to Wales: Glamorgan, Monmouthshire and Denbighshire received a second MP and the Glamorgan borough seat was divided in two with Merthyr obtaining a seat. At a parliamentary level, the political life of Wales maintained its quiet and undistinguished course until the 1860s. Despite population change the stranglehold of the landed interest was as firm as ever and, for the bulk of the population, the only politics possible was the politics of protest.

Between 1832 and 1850 there was a gradual change in the outlook of Nonconformity as it rediscovered its links with English Dissent and copied its political activity. On the surface Nonconformists retained their political conformity and Methodists, in particular, warned their flock of the dangers of subverting worldly authority. In practice Welsh Dissenters campaigned against the Church Rate and Tithe Commutation Act of 1836, had close links with Chartism and the Rebecca rioters. The campaign of Lewis Edwards against the Corn Laws was slowly transformed into a challenge to the hegemony of squire and parson and into a wider struggle for national equality.

Scotland

In 1832 many in Scotland saw the passage of parliamentary reform as creating a 'Scotch millenium', the beginning of a new era.[15] The Whig party won a huge majority both of parliamentary seats and of the popular vote in the 1832 election: it won all but ten of the 53 Scottish seats. It prided itself in having achieved major constitutional change without alteration to the country's underlying social or political structure. As in England the next nine years showed increasing Whig complacency and the assumption that further reform could be achieved not by frenetic political activity but through moral enlightenment, social reconstruction and economic advance.

Whig principles, as in England, were of little help in dealing with the major problems posed by the working population. The Whigs did not want to provoke trade unions by imposing new restrictions. They thought repeal of the Corn Laws would reduce the cost of living. They recognized the need to improve relief of the poor, but were determined that this should not mean higher taxes. Some Whig MPs believed that urban problems and the changes in the Highlands could be resolved by widespread emigration.

Reform of the burghs required immediate attention. The Tory regime before 1832 had recognized burghal government as a problem and since 1800 there had been a number of private Acts to maintain administration in a reasonably efficient state. The Whigs had various changes in mind: a popular franchise in municipal elections was considered essential and they also contemplated depriving decayed burghs of their charters and abolishing the distinction between royal and non-royal burghs. In 1833, two years before equivalent legislation in England, reform was achieved. Three statutes were passed: the first allowed more burghs to set up police authorities limiting the persistent influence of vested interests on the councils; the others, one for royal burghs and the other for the rest, extended the franchise to all £10 householders and provided for triennial elections.

The Whigs experienced considerable difficulty in running the reformed system between 1832 and 1835. Dominated by Jeffrey, Cockburn, Abercromby and Kennedy who had achieved political revolution in 1832, the Whigs now found themselves plagued by raised expectation. The Whig party managers were harassed by Whig MPs who expected all the patronage which had previously been reserved by the Tories to come to them. The problem was that there was no Scottish Minister as such: Kennedy was a junior Lord of the Treasury advising on patronage and elections in Scotland and whipping Scottish MPs, Jeffrey was Lord Advocate but lacked the phalanx of subservient MPs to use as a bargaining counter for Scottish affairs while Cockburn hoped to take over general political duties from Jeffrey, though this never occurred. None was a member of the cabinet and the Prime Minister entrusted business to either Brougham, who thought himself familiar with Scottish affairs but did nothing about them, or to Melbourne, who was at best indifferent. Frustration and disillusion resulted in Jeffrey, Cockburn and Kennedy retiring from active politics during 1834.

Indifference by Westminster towards Scotland continued after the brief Conservative interlude of 1834–5. John Murray became Lord Advocate in 1835 but he was not taken seriously in London. Robert Steuart, Scottish Lord of the Treasury, similarly had little influence. It was easier for those concerned with patronage to communicate directly with William Gibson-Craig, boss of the Edinburgh Whigs or with the Clique, the circle of dominant merchants in Glasgow. Murray was alarmed by the revival of agitation among the working population and by crisis in the Kirk which was to lead to the Disruption in 1843. In the first case he was hostile and himself led the prosecution of trade unionists in 1838. On the second he was indecisive, unwilling to offend the interests involved. Murray was an ineffective, indecisive minister – only 22 of his 51 bills were passed – and in 1839 he took the opportunity of opting for the Bench. His successor, Andrew Rutherford, was harsh, overbearing and partisan and took little opportunity to lead Scottish politics.

Why was Whig rule of Scotland so ineffective during this period? All of the leading politicians were advocates and the Bench creamed them off before they were able to establish themselves politically. None achieved the status or reputation in Scotland or in England that Dundas or Melville had done and, as a consequence, there was no coherent Scottish interest in Parliament and the Whigs were less independent of London than their Tory predecessors. But Whig failings went deeper than this. Between 1830 and 1832 they had pursued positive policies but whether their spectacular success exhausted their ideas, especially in Scotland, is an open question. As in England, they became increasingly cautious and conservative, tinkering with issues rather than proposing radical solutions. Scotland was regarded as peripheral by Westminster and Scottish Whigs steadily lost electoral credibility and confidence in their ability to find solutions to labour problems and religious strife.

Popular dissatisfaction with the feeble performance of Whig governments in the 1830s was exacerbated by the attitude of Radicals who sought more substantial reforms and a more rapid pace of change. From 1832 to 1835 the Radicals drifted away from collaboration with the Whigs to confrontation, while moderate Whigs were increasingly alarmed by the steepening Radical platform. The Radical challenge, as in England, was not sustained in 1836–7 and, as the church issue emerged, the challenge for mainstream Whigs was to resist the intrusion of religious zeal into party politics without alienating political support among Dissenters and elements within the Presbyterian Church.

Political passivity was compounded by an inferiority of electoral organization which helps to explain why the Whigs were unable to press their advantage in the 1841 election. There was little central co-ordination from either London or Edinburgh and organizational impetus was left to local initiative. There were few able local leaders, little cash for organization and fewer patronage resources in the counties than in the burghs which remained overwhelmingly Whig in 1841.

Scottish Tories were faced with a daunting task after 1832. They retained only one burgh seat and nine counties in the election to the reformed Parliament. They were widely hated both for ruthlessly manipulating unreformed Scottish politics since the 1780s and for using their power to sustain a Toryism more reactionary than in England. This had particularly been the case in the 1820s when no equivalent of 'liberal Toryism' developed in Scotland and when a monolithic resistance to any change emerged. In the face of such widespread hostility, it was unlikely that a Conservative recovery, which led to a decisive majority in England in 1841, would be repeated in Scotland. But significant advances were made, especially in the counties, in 1835 and 1837 at almost the same rate of increase as in England, though this was not maintained in 1841. Conservative share of the 53 Scottish seats increased from 10 in 1832 to 15 in 1835, 19 in 1837 and 22 in 1841.

This advance cannot be explained simply by organization. There were many other issues which the Conservatives could exploit. Many people thought that enough had been conceded in 1832 and that further reform should be resisted. Progressive voters saw the Conservatives rather than the Whigs as firmer supporters of social reform. But, just as in England, they gained significant support from being supporters of the Established Church while the Whigs, suspicious of religious zeal and mindful of electoral support they received from Dissent, talked much about disestablishment. Scottish Conservatives were not prepared to compromise on religious issues and only two Scottish MPs supported Peel in 1845 over Maynooth.

Scottish politics was riddled with religious antagonism. The Presbyterian Church was regarded as the spiritual leader of Scottish society and had far more independence from the state than the Church of England. In the absence of direct control from Westminster the Kirk had control over education from school to university, supervised poor relief and still exerted significant moral guidance. But its position was under considerable strain and it needed to modernize rapidly. It had not responded to the twin pressures of population change and urbanization. Schools were too few and there were claims that moral standards were falling. The working population was turning to alternative ideologies – dissent and radicalism – and Irish immigrants, who made up much of the industrial workforce of western Scotland, retained their loyalty to Catholicism.

Between 1832 and 1843 the Church of Scotland was broadly divided between moderates, who held to traditional values, and evangelicals, who sought a new social position for the Church.[16] This difference of emphasis showed itself in challenge to the notion of state patronage which had been established in 1712. Moderates wanted to retain the existing system while evangelicals supported the right of congregations to elect their own ministers. Evangelical control of the General Assembly of the Church of Scotland in 1834 led to demands for change. It asked Westminster for a grant of £10,000 to build new churches, money which was not ultimately forthcoming. It passed the Chapels Act which strengthened the role of towns and cities in the Kirk and finally it passed the Veto Act which gave congregations the right to veto ministerial appointments. These measures calmed the situation and for a few years there was both Conservative and Whig support for the Veto Act and 200 churches were built by voluntary contribution.

Conflict emerged over the operation of the Veto Act and in 1838 a legal decision effectively restored the operation of the Patronage Act, denying the people generally any control over the appointment of ministers. This intrusion by the state in the affairs of the Kirk was deeply resented but neither Melbourne nor the Conservatives were prepared to intervene to remedy the situation. Both Whigs and Tories were suspicious of what they saw as an unwelcome democratization within the Church. Whig attempts at finding a compromise contained in Aberdeen's bill foundered on opposition from those evangelicals opposed to state intrusion and this was compounded by the Conservative victory in 1841. The outcome of the dispute over patronage came to a head when the Kirk split in May 1843 into the Established Church and the Free Church of Scotland. The political importance of the Disruption was felt for the remainder of the century. The Church of Scotland remained the voice of Conservatism while the Free Church adopted a liberalism devoted to moral principles and antagonism towards privilege in any form which was markedly different from the complacent pragmatism of Whiggery.

The split within the Established Church, the only Scottish institution which could justifiably claim to speak for the whole nation, reinforced London's position as the centre for Scottish affairs. Westminster legislated on issues like education, poor relief, public health and factories, which would previously have been within the scope of the Kirk. This can be seen in the reform of the poor laws in 1843. There was no doubting the inefficiency of the existing system and in early 1843 a Royal Commission was established to investigate it. Disruption meant that the Kirk could no longer alone administer relief and the Conservative Lord Advocate, Duncan McNeill, introduced legislation. A central board, nominated by the government, was established in Edinburgh with overall responsibility for Scottish poor relief, effectively superseding the Kirk's role. The central board still had to work through local agencies – each parish established its own board and an inspector – which required the consent of electors before levying a poor rate. The central board had a liberal attitude to relief but its attempts to set minimum standards, though they led to a doubling of poor law expenditure by 1850, fell far short of the effort needed to counter the extent of pauperism and destitution.

Scottish independence was also surrendered in banking. It had not been subject to any English legislation and had successfully resisted attempts to extend the 1826 English legislation. In 1845, however, Scottish banking was remodelled on the English system, bringing its vigorous expansion to an end.

How did Whig and Conservative governments respond to radicalism in Scotland during this period?[17] The Corn Laws were unpopular in Scotland not only because they inflated food prices but because the efficiency of farming made them unnecessary. There were few supporters of the laws among the landed interest and there was little of the clear conflict between city and country that existed in England. The Whigs favoured the replacement of the sliding scale with a small fixed tariff and the Scottish members of Melbourne's cabinet, Macaulay and the Earl of Minto, were already arguing for changes in the law by 1840. Decisive influence could not be exerted by Scotland alone and there was increasing support for the activities of the Anti-Corn Law League. After 1842, when its campaign slackened in England, it took on new intensity in Scotland. By 1845 the Whigs were prepared to support repeal and it was no coincidence that Russell published the letter committing his party to ending the Corn Laws in Edinburgh in late 1845. It was the Irish crisis which eventually precipitated repeal in 1846 but Scotland's part in the victory was to have remained so firmly behind repeal. Peel could rely on the solid support of Scottish MPs.

The Corn Law agitation was largely a middle-class affair. The working population took little part in a campaign led by employers who fought trade unions and opposed factory reform. This reflected a growing divergence within radicalism between those who could and those who could not vote. For workers it was parliamentary reform not repeal that was the focus of agitation. This began as militant trade unionism in 1837–8, when there were violent disturbances, particularly in Glasgow, over reductions in wages and the use of blackleg labour. Revulsion at the nature of trade union activities was not confined to the middle classes and helps to account for the moralistic, rather apolitical character of Scottish Chartism.

Between 1832 and 1846 the position of Scottish politics was effectively marginalized. The Whigs began the process which the Conservatives completed in the early 1840s. Peel's administration, so beneficial for Britain as a whole, had the opposite effect on Scotland. It was indecisive in coping with problems, a situation not helped by its ignorance of them. Conservative failure to prevent the Disruption left Peel without a vehicle in Scotland to carry through his social programme. The old patriarchal society rested on the twin pillars of the Church and the Tory gentry and after 1843 both were cut off from the mainstream of national life. Conservatism, already far more exposed than in England, went into a terminal decline.

Whig hopes for a 'Scotch millenium' also proved illusory. The Whigs sought in 1832 to legitimize the existing social order in a proper political constitution. Their attempts to pursue, in a disinterested spirit, policies for the public good were perceived as conscious anglicizing. By 1846 this vision was in tatters. The Kirk had been shattered by the Disruption, the landed gentry had turned to conservatism and the political system was in confusion. The Whigs had failed to maintain the existing system and the Conservatives were unable, through ignorance of Scottish politics and electoral weakness, to put forward a real alternative. The one-party Tory state of the early nineteenth century was replaced by a one-party Whig state after 1832: stagnant oligarchic government based on patronage remained the norm.

Ireland

The Act of Union abolished many of the rotten boroughs that existed in the old Irish Parliament and reduced the number of Irish MPs in Westminster to 100.[18] Until 1832 these seats remained largely under the control of individual patrons, continuing the tradition established in the seventeenth century that they should provide support for the administration and a useful patronage resource. The influence of the large landowner over the electorate was the result of various factors. There is evidence of electoral apathy and loyalty to the landlord's wishes. Eviction was more often a threat than reality for anyone who went against the landlord's electoral preference but more subtle economic and social pressures appear to have been used. Bribery and patronage were essential elements of the electoral system well into the nineteenth century and up to the Waterford election in 1826 the Tory Protestant ascendancy retained control over the political system.

The 1832 Irish Reform Act was conservative and, compared to the English Act, its outcome was disappointing. Although there was an increase in the number of voters the possibilities of bribery, corruption and impersonation remained high. The effect of the Act can be demonstrated by examining the constituencies of County Carlow and the borough of Carlow. There was an increase in contested elections: of the eleven parliamentary elections between 1800 and 1832 only three were contested compared with eight out of the ten elections between 1832 and 1852. In the borough thirteen burgesses, often related to each other and controlled by the borough patron the Lord Charleville, elected the MP before 1832 and electoral contests were unknown. After reform there were 278 electors for the borough and all but one of the seven borough elections between 1832 and 1852 were contested.

Before 1832 the overwhelming majority of Irish MPs were Tory. After 1832 liberal-Whigs and Repealers were able to challenge Tory dominance. The new electoral system introduced by emancipation and reform opened up greater possibilities than had been envisaged. The liberals, who had sponsored emancipation in the 1820s, became the natural allies of Irish Catholics in the 1830s and 1840s. This broke the Tory-Protestant ascendancy that had dominated Irish politics before 1832.

Daniel O'Connell launched his attack on Protestant control of Irish parliamentary seats from the outset and in the 1832 election his repeal party won 39 seats compared to 36 liberal-Whig and 29 Conservative seats. This was the largest grouping he led: it dropped to 32 in 1835, 31 in 1837 and by 1841 it had fallen to 18 though it did recover to 35 by 1847. This numerical decline reflected the nature of his supporters as a loose bloc rather than as a disciplined party. Throughout the 1830s O'Connell adopted a pragmatic but highly visible approach to politics in order to break the control of local landowners opposed to repeal. He used local liberal Protestants, promoted repealers from outside the area and even imported English Whigs. Two opposing views of politics were at stake: the older view that parliamentary seats were an extension of personal property and a more novel, reforming and radical notion that representation should be based on democratic ideals of liberty and equality.

The Whigs in London were fully aware of the problems of Ireland and of the need to find solutions to make rule from Westminster more acceptable. The police, magistracy, jury system and the courts needed reform, a poor law for Ireland had to be devised, something had to be done about tithes and the unreformed municipal corporations. The informal compact between O'Connell and Melbourne at Lichfield House in 1835 in which the Whigs were kept in power by O'Connell's MPs in return for good government, reform and better administration in Ireland was assisted by the appointment of Thomas Drummond as Under-Secretary at Dublin Castle.

Drummond vigorously pursued a campaign of reform. He was a bureaucrat rather than a politician and so was less intimidated by vested interests. He was determined that the police, military and legal system should not be used as an arm of the Protestant ascendancy. He kept the Whig side of the Lichfield House Compact by effectively opening large areas of official employment and patronage to Catholics. The yeomanry, which had long been under the control of local landlords, had already been abolished in 1834. He refused to allow the police or military to collect tithe arrears and in 1836 brought the entire police force under the control of an inspector-general, began recruitment on non-sectarian lines, initiated training procedures and provided Dublin with its own metropolitan police. He increased the number and functions of stipendiary magistrates, reformed the jury system and for the first time Catholics were appointed to the Bench. Drummond's administration aimed to make the legal system and the machinery of enforcement more acceptable to Ireland.

The Whig government attempted to improve conditions in the country by reform acts dealing with tithes, the poor law and municipal corporations. In 1838 a Tithe Act wrote off all arrears and converted tithes into a rent charge payable by the head landlord who passed the charge down to sub-tenants, exempting only the lowest class of cottiers and tenants. Tithes had previously led to widespread disturbances especially between Catholic and Protestant clergy and the Act, despite its limitations, ended the endemic tithe war. However, the rent charge merely transformed the confrontation into one between tenants and landlords.

The Irish Poor Law Act, passed in 1838, which set up workhouses, was opposed by O'Connell on moral and economic grounds. The Whigs ignored their own Royal Commission set up years earlier which concluded that importing the English post-1834 system would be unsuitable. By 1841 Ireland had been divided into 130 poor law unions with elected boards of guardians, and Catholic ratepayers gained their first experience of local government and administration. The Irish Municipal Corporations Act of 1840 broke the control of the Protestant and Tory Orange organizations over the administration of Irish cities and towns. As in England the unrepresentative and inefficient nature of urban government was attacked. The Act provided elective town councils for ten of the largest cities and towns and handed over the administration of the smaller and poorer towns to the poor law guardians. Though considerably less liberal than O'Connell wanted, the 1840 Act did free municipal government from the absolute control of borough patrons and enabled Catholics to have a role in local administration.

O'Connell was disillusioned with the Whigs and with their reforms by the end of the 1830s. He also recognized that a Conservative victory was likely in the next general election. He increasingly argued that the only way of solving Ireland's problems was the restoration of an independent Irish Parliament and the ending of Union. The creation of the Repeal Association in 1840 and the reduction of his MPs to 18 in the 1841 election led O'Connell to concentrate on extra-parliamentary agitation. The 'monster meetings' and O'Connell's claim that 1843 would be the 'Year of Repeal' worried Peel's administration but, instead of waiting for the campaign to run out of steam, he decided to act. O'Connell was arrested in October 1843, charged with conspiracy to incite disaffection, and imprisoned. Though he was released after four months the enthusiasm of the 'Year of Repeal' could not be replicated. Peel's policies for Ireland in 1844 and 1845, outlined earlier, attempted to kill repeal with kindness and detach the moderate Catholic clergy and middle class from repeal. Famine with its deep social, economic and psychological effects changed Ireland's political agenda. Under O'Connell Ireland had been generally loyal and pacifist. That loyalty and pacifism perished in the Famine and O'Connell himself died in May 1847. Whether English rule was in fact to blame for the Famine mattered less than the belief that it was. John Mitchel was not alone in believing that 'the Almighty indeed sent the potato blight, but the English created the famine'.

NOTES

1 W. Bagehot 'The Character of Sir Robert Peel', 1856, reprinted in N. St John-Stevas (ed.) *Bagehot's Historical Essays*, Dennis Dobson, 1971, pp. 185, 194.

2 General textbook discussion of Peel's ministry can be found in A. Briggs *The Age of Improvement*, Longman, 1959, pp. 325–43, N. Gash *Aristocracy and People: Britain 1815–1865*, Edward Arnold, 1979, pp. 220–49, E. J. Evans *The Forging of the Modern State: Early Industrial Britain 1793–1870*, Longman, 1983, chapters 23–7 and M. Bentley *Politics Without Democracy 1815–1914*, Fontana, 1984, pp. 111–42. N. Gash *Sir Robert Peel*, Longman, revised edn 1986, is essential but can be usefully supplemented with D. Read *Peel and the Victorians*, Blackwell, 1987. P. Adelman *Peel and the Conservative Party 1830–1850*, 1989, combines text and sources.

3 M. Bentley op. cit. p. 112.

4 R. Blake *The Conservative Party from Peel to Thatcher*, Fontana, 1985, p. 50.

5 On the policies pursued see, in addition to the works cited above, T. L. Crosby *Sir Robert Peel's Administration 1841–46*, David & Charles, 1970. R. Stewart *The Foundation of the Conservative Party 1830–1867*, Longman, 1978 is a valuable study and N. Gash 'Peel and Wellington', in D. Southgate (ed.) *The Conservative Leadership 1832–1932*, Macmillan, 1974 looks at personality and policies. R. Stewart *The Politics of Protection*, Cambridge University Press, 1971 looks at Stanley and the protectionists from 1841 through to 1852 and can be used alongside T. L. Crosby *English Farmers and the Politics of Protection 1815–52*, Harvester, 1977. N. Gash *Reaction and Reconstruction in English Politics 1832–1852*, Oxford University Press, 1965 is essential reading.

6 M. Bentley op. cit., p. 120.

7 N. Gash *Aristocracy and People*, op. cit., p. 231.

8 See D. Read op. cit., pp. 147–8 for further reactions to the 1845 budget.

9 ibid., pp. 148–9.

10 D. A. Kerr *Peel, Priests and Politics*, Oxford University Press, 1982 provides the best account of Peel's attempts to resolve the Irish problem.

11 On Gladstone's position during this period see R. Shannon *Gladstone, vol. I, 1809–1865*, Hamilton, 1982, especially chapters 3–4, H. C. G. Matthew *Gladstone 1809–1874*, Oxford University Press, 1986, pp. 59–87 and P. Stansky *Gladstone: A Progress in Politics*, Norton, 1979, pp. 34–47.

12 See R. Blake *Disraeli*, Methuen, 1966 for the definitive biography.

13 For Peel's position after 1846 see D. Read op. cit., J. B. Conacher *The Peelites and the Party System 1846–1852*, David & Charles, 1972 for leaders and issues and W. D. Jones and A. B. Erickson *The Peelites 1846–57*, Ohio State University Press, 1972 for organization and membership.

14 On Wales during the 1830s and 1840s G. Jones *Modern Wales: A Concise History c. 1485–1979*, Cambridge University Press, 1984 is a good outline. The opening chapter of K. O. Morgan *Wales in British Politics 1868–1922*, University of Wales Press, 1970 places Wales in British politics before 1868.

15 On Scottish politics in this period D. and S. G. Checkland *Industry and Ethos: Scotland 1832–1914*, Edward Arnold, 1984, provides a good introduction and can be supplemented by the more detailed studies of M. Fry *Patronage and Principle: A Political History of Modern Scotland*, Aberdeen University Press, 1987 and I. G. C. Hutchinson *A Political History of Scotland 1832–1924: Parties, Elections and Issues*, John Donald, 1986.

16 For a fuller discussion of the problems of established religion in Scotland see Chapter 14.

17 Chapter 13 looks at radicalism in the 1830s and 1840s more fully.

18 For Ireland F. S. L. Lyons *Ireland Since the Famine*, Fontana, 1973, especially

chapters 1–3, provides a readable summary of the situation and the issues in the mid-nineteenth century. D. McCartney *The Dawning of Democracy: Ireland 1800–1870*, Helicon, 1987 is a good recent study. K. T. Hoppen *Elections, Politics and Society in Ireland 1832–1885*, Oxford University Press, 1984 is essential for electoral politics, while his *Ireland since 1800: Conflict and Conformity*, Longman, 1989 provides a more general sweep.

11 'Bread and blood' – the nature of popular protest

Here I am, between Earth and Sky – so help me God. I would sooner lose my life than go home as I am. Bread I want and Bread I will have.[1]

Good bye, good bye and God bless you all – I hope my fate will be a warning to you all, and I hope you gentlemen farmers will give the young men work; it was the want of work that brought me to this.[2]

The first statement was made by an agricultural labourer William Dawson after the 1816 Littleport and Ely riots and the second by George Pulham, a twenty-two-year-old agricultural labourer, on the scaffold in 1835. Without the vote, lacking political cohesion and organization, how could individuals like William Dawson and George Pulham influence those who governed society, nationally and locally? What circumstances led to the mass of the population reacting in some form of popular protest to the actions of their governors? What form did this reaction take and how successful was it in influencing those in authority? This chapter examines the changing character of popular protest during the eighteenth and first half of the nineteenth century. The succeeding two chapters examine the nature of political protest from the 1790s through to the demise of Chartism and the Anti-Corn Law League.

LOOKING AT CROWDS

Issues

The last thirty years have seen an upsurge in the theoretical[3] and historical[4] examination of popular protest and of the parallel study of public order. The wave of riots and disturbances that swept Europe and America in the 1960s over civil and student rights, the emergence of football hooliganism, race riots and 'issue' protest may have contributed to this yet it cannot be seen simply as a passing academic fashion cashing in on social concerns.

There has been a gradual but fundamental revision of contemporary assumptions and accounts of the development of modern Britain. These had emphasized a peaceful and logical evolution of national institutions, a characteristic that made Britain unique among developed nations. This view, perhaps best exemplified in the 'Whig' school of historiography, regarded the seventeenth-century conflict between Crown and Parliament as the critical period of Britain's development. The eighteenth century was merely a period of political stability and national expansion in which radical traditions played little or no part. 'Whig' historians had little incentive to search for symptoms of disorder or protest in these develop-ments. This emphasis can perhaps best be explained in terms of national insularity and chauvinism with an implied distaste for the political insta-bility and revolutionary excesses of continental Europe, especially after 1789. Popular protest was either viewed as an aberration or ignored alto-gether. Politics was viewed from the top down.

There were notable exceptions to this. R. F. Wearmouth had analysed aspects of eighteenth-century popular protest, the Hammonds had dealt with the social effects of industrial and agrarian change, Max Beloff had examined popular disturbances between 1660 and 1714 and F. O. Darvell had looked at the Luddites but it was not until the pioneering work of George Rudé that a new dimension was given to the study of popular protest. His examination of the Parisian crowd and the London 'mob' in the eighteenth century opened new lines of enquiry.[5] First, he showed that crowd action had an important influence on the course of political events. Secondly, his work on crowd composition and motivation demon-strated that the stereotypes commonly applied to the 'mob' by both con-temporaries and later historians were very misleading. Thirdly, this led him to use the less pejorative term 'crowd' rather than 'mob' which had overtones of irrationality and violence that were not borne out by a close study of crowd actions. Rudé's constructive achievement has been to bring popular politics within the orbit of traditional politics, especially in the eighteenth and early nineteenth centuries.

The awareness of collective behaviour and its relationship to political disturbances and action led historians to examine the diverse nature of popular protest. Charles Tilly argued for the 'political' nature of all forms of popular protest, especially in its violent form. Eric Hobsbawm wrote of 'collective bargaining by riot' to explain the influence of popular protest on the status quo. Both are concerned with the emergent role of 'public opinion' and recognized that popular protest in Britain was usually con-ducted in a full and conscious awareness that public opinion could be lost or won by the behaviour of the participants, both those in authority and those protesting.

Popular protest can reveal the stage of political development and the nature of political feelings among otherwise inarticulate sections of society. Rudé, for example, has shown the importance of 'rights' and 'liberties' which, mingled with a strong strain of anti-Catholicism and xenophobia, formed an early justification for popular intervention in politics. E. P.

Thompson has suggested that a coherent set of assumptions about the world in which people lived formed a basis for the emergence of popular radicalism. Rudé and Hobsbawm have shown that in the 1830 Swing riots rising economic and social factors were the prime motives for action rather than specifically political ones. This view echoes earlier work by W. W. Rostow whose 'social tension' chart, constructed from the movement of wheat prices and fluctuations in the trade cycle, saw the presence of popular protest as a barometer of socio-economic 'distress'. Most recent studies have been rightly sceptical of Rostow's rather simplistic approach, while others have rejected his 'gross economic reductionism' entirely. Though it has become increasingly obvious that economic causes were simply part of a much more complex process, it is important not to neglect contemporary attitudes that popular protest was a 'bread and butter issue' and 'a rebellion of the belly'.

Whether there was a direct relationship between economic deprivation and popular protest is a matter of some disagreement. Marx equated periods of socio-economic distress and popular, especially violent, protest and saw distress both as a symptom of discontent and an instrument of change. According to him violence was

> the midwife of every old society which is pregnant with a new one; it is the instrument with the aid of which social movement forces its way through and shatters the dead, fossilised political forms.[6]

Social unrest, in this scenario, is the result of lack of harmony between the political and social systems. De Tocqueville, by contrast argued that

> Revolutions are not always made by the gradual decline from bad to worse. Nations that have endured patiently and almost unconsciously the most overwhelming oppression often burst into rebellion against the yoke the moment it begins to grow lighter.[7]

It is not necessarily actual conditions but how people perceive those conditions which accounts for popular protest. J. C. Davies has taken de Tocqueville's thesis further and suggests that

> It is a dissatisfied state of mind rather than the tangible provision of 'adequate' or 'inadequate' supplies of food, equality or liberty which produces revolution. . . .[8]

If people perceive themselves to be underprivileged and if there is a threat to what they perceive as their basic needs – physical in terms of food for example, or mental in terms of popular notions of what is 'just' or 'fair' – then they are more likely to turn to popular forms of collective action.

The remainder of this chapter will concentrate on four major areas. First, it will examine the nature of crowds and ask why the character of traditional forms of protest changed during this period. Secondly, it will consider the social and cultural milieu in which protest occurred and especially the views of E. P. Thompson. Thirdly, a typology of different forms of popular protest for mainland Britain will be considered and finally the character of protest in Ireland will be examined.

Canetti and Rudé

In 1962 Elias Canetti produced his *Crowds and Power*, an extremely broad examination of crowds and the psychology of crowds. The following discussion attempts to draw together Canetti's views with those of George Rudé on the 'pre-industrial' crowd. First Canetti distinguishes between the 'open' and 'closed' crowds. An 'open' crowd has

> no limits whatever to its growth; it does not recognise houses, doors or locks and those who shut themselves in are suspect. 'Open' is to be understood in the fullest sense of the word; it means open everywhere and in any direction. The open crowd exists so long as it grows; it disintegrates as soon as it stops growing.[9]

Its breadth of purpose is its initial strength and ultimate weakness and by absorbing everyone it falls to pieces. There are parallels between the 'open' crowd and Rudé's characteristic of the pre-industrial crowd as having 'spontaneity' and lack of coherent organization. A common feature of pre-industrial crowds was their transformation from a small beginning – for example, a meeting of housewives outside a baker's shop or a discussion in a public house – into a widespread attack on property and a full-scale disturbance. A 'closed' crowd has renounced growth in favour of permanence or semi-permanence. It has and accepts defined boundaries and objectives, sacrificing its capacity for growth by remaining a social and political force. Trade unions and political parties, Rudé recognizes, have their 'spontaneity' limited but make up for this with coherent organizational patterns.[10]

So how does a 'crowd' develop and decline? Canetti argues that the crowd is created through 'discharge': 'it is the moment when all who belong to the crowd get rid of their differences and feel equal'.[11]

Distinctions of rank, status and property are imposed from outside and only within the relative anonymity of the crowd can they be thrown off. Rudé reinforces this with his view of crowds as 'mixed' in social composition.[12] This did not mean that all social groups were either represented or represented in more or less equal proportions. Those 'in authority', especially among the aristocratic elite or the emergent middle classes, played little part in riots or street disturbances for most of this period. It was the emergence of a radical and active middle-class agitation from the 1820s that was one of the important changes in the nature of popular protest in this period. Crowds were 'mixed' only in relation to the lower orders of society, both male and female: cottagers, small freeholders, agricultural labourers, rural workers in textile industries, crafts-men and miners in rural areas; skilled and unskilled workers, small shop-keepers, artisans and master craftsmen in the towns.

The 'destructiveness' of the crowd is also important. This destructive-ness was sometimes symbolic – the burning of the villain of the day in effigy (sometimes actual); the pulling down of property, the burning or smashing of labour-saving machinery, arson – and sometimes egalitarian – the handing out of illegally obtained grain or flour to all in the crowd. Both pulling down property, whether it was houses or fences, and arson had a symbolic importance to crowds by removing and purifying the perceived threat to the existing social system. In early nineteenth-century Ireland, for example, turnip crops were frequently destroyed because they seemed to symbolize the new capitalist system of agriculture which threatened more traditional forms of farming. Parallel to the destructive-ness of the largely 'open' crowd was the emergence of more 'modern' forms of protest: petitions to Parliament, marches and modern-type indus-trial disputes of a more or less peaceful character.

'Eruption' is an important stage in the development of the crowd, marking the point when it changes from 'closed' to 'open' and attempts, with an evangelical determination, to reach everybody.[13] Parallel to this is the emergence of a sense of 'persecution'. This sense of fear and uncertainty is something which those in authority can play on by con-cession or repression or a combination of the two. For example, the acceptability of parliamentary reform to the middle classes in 1832 came as much from their perceived fear of the forces of democracy, something played on by the Whigs, as from their support for fundamentally conserva-tive changes. Ultimately a crowd can give way to 'panic'. This often occurred when authority asserted or reasserted itself, anonymity and equa-lity ceased and the boundaries of people's individuality became clear to them again. Persecution becomes individual not collective and the crowd disintegrates into its individual parts.

Canetti summarizes the main attributes of the crowd in relation to four things: crowds always want to grow and in that dynamic lies their destruction; within the crowd there is equality and anonymity and once that is lost the crowd disintegrates; crowds love density; and finally crowds need direction if they are to continue as a crowd.[14] So where does that direction come from? Canetti argues that 'crowd crystals', small rigid groups of people, usually men, precipitate crowd action. Rudé takes the notion of leadership further. He argues that the typical leader of the pre-industrial crowd comes from 'without' rather than from 'within' the crowd, especially in more sophisticated forms of protest.[15] He identifies three levels of leadership. First, there was the 'leader-in-chief,' who may have acquired that position either voluntarily or involuntarily, in whose name the crowd protests. Secondly, the 'intermediate leader' – whom Rudé calls 'a sort of NCO' – who passes on slogans and directs destruction. Thirdly, the most articulate or militant among the rioters themselves may acquire a leadership that is local and purely temporary. These leaders alone emerge from 'within' the crowd and may be anonymous figures, may adopt pseudonyms like 'Rebecca', 'Ludd' or 'Swing' or may be known by their real names. After 1800 temporary leaders gave way to more permanent and articulate individuals who formed the core of Canetti's 'crowd crystals'.

All forms of collective behaviour are grounded in ideas and perceptions about what is right or wrong, fair or unfair, just or unjust. 'Invisible' crowds are based upon fear of the invisible dead and/or their ideas.[16] This can be seen in the concern expressed about burying Tom Paine's bones in England in 1817. The fear, real to those who feel it, of the unknown and of radical change is far from rational, though it may appear perfectly logical to those concerned. From the 1790s through to 1850 fear of the ideas of revolution played a major role in the thinking of the aristocratic governing elite. 'Baiting' crowds were 'open' and characterized by a specific aim.[17] The crowd is out to kill – symbolically or actually – and everyone wants to get involved and emotions run high. The Gordon riots in 1780 and the 'Church and King' riots in the 1790s fall into this category. 'Flight' crowds were created by a threat like the new machinery which motivated some Luddites in the 1810s and agricultural labourers in the Swing riots in 1830.[18] 'Prohibition' crowds were created by a refusal by people to continue with what they had previous been doing and obey a prohibition that was sudden and self-imposed.[19] Finally, Canetti identifies 'reversal' crowds which are concerned with delivering themselves from the stings of command in a rigidly stratified society.[20] 'Invisible', 'baiting', 'flight' and 'prohibition' crowds all, in various ways and to varying degrees, demand a return to the status quo while 'reversal' crowds want the structure of society and political power to be radically altered.

Canetti and Rudé provide a useful model for examining the crowd and popular protest in this period. What needs to be stressed is the extremely diverse and changing nature of popular protest in the period between 1700 and 1850. Movements, if that is what they can be called, varied enormously in terms of objectives, social composition, tactics and geographical location. A broad, though not mutually exclusive, distinction may be drawn between traditional protest which has the restoration of the status quo as one of its prime objectives and radical protest which was concerned with changing the nature and composition of the existing political system. This chapter focuses on the former and the succeeding two chapters on the latter.

A polarized society?

Throughout the period between 1700 and 1850 British society was highly conscious of an individual's position in the social hierarchy. Birth, wealth, occupation, gender, race and life style all played a major part in the ways individuals perceived other individuals in a community and the ways in which they were perceived. By 1700 British society was already polarized and that process continued throughout the eighteenth and early nineteenth centuries. This polarization was in part cultural, detaching the gentry and some of the middling ranks from artisans, labourers and the poor. Whether it is possible to talk accurately of a 'national culture' as such in eighteenth-century Britain, a whole range of artistic and intellectual interests marked the aristocracy and gentry off from the rest of the population. They contributed to, and benefited from, the development of a 'consumer' society after 1700, a standardized 'national' cultural tone set by the shops which lined the expanding urban streets, the development of the provincial press, the multiplication of spa towns, the emergence of 'refined' theatre, novels, circulating libraries, assemblies, balls, landscape gardening, follies, the obsession with fox-hunting and horse racing and the Game Laws.

'Refinement' and the sense of certainty it symbolized was contrasted with a 'brutal' popular culture rooted in a view of life that was uncertain, largely unplanned and, according to E. P. Thompson, based on the lack of a 'predictive notion of time'. It was largely spontaneous and this spontaneity was transferred to popular protest. Popular identity was rooted in a sense of belonging to particular local environments in which there were different local dialects, diet and special festivals and customs, leisure, the ale-house and fiction distributed by itinerant pedlars and music which remained fundamentally oral.

During the eighteenth and early nineteenth centuries a growing series of polarities in speech, dress, manners, living conditions, leisure pursuits and literary interests emerged which eroded the common heritage of assumptions about social integration and interaction. The gulf between a 'patrician' and 'plebeian' culture was never simply a gulf between the literate and illiterate but did mark a distancing of one part of society from the other.

That British society did not fragment further in the eighteenth and early nineteenth centuries owed much to the acceptance that 'the rule of law' was the birthright of every male citizen, unlike on the continent where the operation of the law was often at the whim of individuals and where social groups had exclusive legal privileges. Everybody was subject to the same laws and there was an expectation that their exercise would be seen to be 'just'. Disorder and popular protest was one face of the belief that it was right to participate in seeking justice; order was its obverse. The operation of the law was marked by both technical rigidity and sensitivity and flexibility in practice. There was acceptance and understanding of the frailties of men and women.

During the eighteenth century the system of criminal justice, based on close social relationships, came under strain. Douglas Hay argues that the law was increasingly used as an instrument of 'gross coercion' and that this was masked by a rhetoric of 'majesty, justice and mercy' and the theatre of public execution.[21] His theory has been questioned by other historians, who have pointed to labourers and middling men playing a central role within the judicial system and to the difficulty of seeing the law as the tool of a particular class. In both cases the crux of social relationships lay in the hegemony of the landed classes, who were quite prepared to subject themselves to the system of law because they were supremely well placed to use it to protect their own interests. After 1700 popular notions of 'justice' and hegemony notions of 'order' came into conflict.

A 'moral economy'

The ideas of E. P. Thompson and their critique provide a valuable way of further amplifying the motivational aspects of collective mentality.[22] Thompson is primarily concerned with explaining the motives behind food riots. He does not accept that they can be explained by 'spasmodic' elements like harvests and food prices but that there was 'some legitimizing notion . . . they were defending traditional rights or customs, and, in general this popular consensus was endorsed by some measure of licence afforded by the authorities'.[23] He moves on to argue that, although riots were often triggered by rising prices,

> these grievances operated within a popular consensus as to what was legitimate and what were illegitimate practices in marketing, milling, baking etc . . . they were grounded on a consistent traditional view of social norms and obligations, of the proper economic functions of several parties in the community, which, taken together, can be said to constitute the moral economy of the crowd. An outrage to these moral assumptions, quite as much as actual deprivation, was the usual occasion for direct action.[24]

Thompson believes that it is possible to talk about a 'bread-nexus' in the eighteenth century and, in an economy where bread formed the main foodstuff for the labouring population, a highly sensitive form of consumer consciousness developed where 'the friction of the market-place takes us into a central area of the nation's life'.[25]

In his paternalist model Thompson saw marketing as being, as far as possible, direct from producer to consumer. Many restrictions were placed on selling corn and on millers and bakers, paternalist forms of market supervision and consumer protection respectively:

> the paternalist model had an ideal existence and also a fragmentary real existence. In years of good harvests and moderate prices, the authorities lapsed into forgetfulness. But if prices rose and the poor became turbulent, it was revived, at least for symbolic effect.[26]

The repeal of legislation regulating the internal corn trade between 1767 and 1772 resulted in the development of 'an anti-model – a direct negative to the disintegrating Tudor policies of provision'.[27]

The new political economy, exemplified by Adam Smith, accepted the natural operation of supply and demand in a free market which would maximize the satisfaction of all parties and establish the common good. The market mechanism was best regulated when left to regulate itself without legislative or moral sanction.

Confrontations with the market in the pre-industrial society were more universal than any other form of protest and had applications outside Thompson's specific food riots. Protests over enclosure, custumal rights, attacks on deer parks, anti-poor law riots, arson and poaching can all be seen as expressions of collective mentality based on recognition of moral if not legal 'justice'. By the end of the eighteenth century, Thompson maintains, the 'bread-nexus' was gradually being replaced by the 'cash-nexus'. The belief in the importance of wages led to a more vigorously organized and potentially seditious form of protest: the 'open' crowd gave way to the 'closed' one.

A. W. Coats and E. Fox Genovese both provide valuable critiques of the 'moral economy'.[28] Coats disputes the contention that the free-market model invariably worked against the poor. He does, however, accept that this does not dispel the reality of the food riot and that Thompson's traditional model better assured the provisioning of the labouring population. But this did not remove the very real existence of misery.

Elizabeth Genovese and John Stevenson criticize his depiction of the eighteenth century. Thompson implies that industrial society emerged from traditional society directly, presumably without a 'proto-industrial' stage, and fails to identify the outstanding characteristic of eighteenth-century England: that it was, if not an industrial society, definitely a capitalist one. By 1700 England already possessed a highly sophisticated trade in foodstuffs and the corn trade was undoubtedly most important. During the eighteenth century this trade continued to expand, stimulated by growing population and urbanization but there was considerable strain upon the total food supply of the country. The London market played a major role in the development of a national trade in foodstuffs and by 1720 up to 80 per cent of England's internal corn trade was devoted to supplying the capital. It was the dominance of London which stimulated the development of a transport network, gradually creating a more unified national market for foodstuffs, especially grain. The loosely related regional economies with their own price levels which made up the English economy in 1700 were gradually eroded during the rest of the century and price differentials were reduced. Arthur Young was, in 1772, impressed by the degree of uniformity and prices in England. However, differences in prices between regions were not incompatible with the existence of a national market.

The eighteenth-century consumer lived in a far more sophisticated economy in which the links between consumer and producers were becoming more complex than Thompson envisaged. The food trade was becoming more specialized.[29] In 1750 a covered Corn Exchange was set up in London where sale of grain was by sample to a small group of dominant factors. Marketing became more complex: mealmen and flourmen entered the processing side of the trade, becoming mill-owners and millers; farmers moved into milling and malting; home baking began to decline with the emergence of professional bakers. The move to a self-regulating market economy predated the decline of the 'moral economy'.

Government had begun to abdicate its responsibility for regulating the corn trade from the mid-seventeenth century. Tudor policy had accepted market mechanisms but regulated the corn trade in line with clear priorities: supplying London, the armed forces and the poor in periods of scarcity. In 1663 the medieval statutes against monopolistic offences were practically abolished, though only finally repealed in 1772. Good harvests in the first half of the eighteenth century encouraged a lenient attitude by government to the activities of middlemen but retained the right to reimpose sanctions during periods of scarcity. The old paternalistic framework of price control, through the use of the Assize of Bread in many towns, became increasingly irrelevant to the operation of the food market. The Assize was unable to keep up with developments in the corn trade and the specialization of the milling and baking industries, and even when it set a price was unable to enforce it.

Between 1660 and 1814 there was important regulation by government of the external corn trade. After 1660, and especially 1689, the corn export trade was stimulated by the use of bounties to producers of wheat, barley, oats and rye. The bounty on grain was 5 shillings per quarter on wheat, as long as home prices did not rise above 48 shillings. This system helped producers dispose of surpluses when prices were low and keep out foreign imports until prices rose; it remained the basis of state regulation until the Corn Laws of 1814 and 1815. These laws abolished the export bounty and made exports free at all times. Between 1700 and 1814 government had only a minimal role to play in relation to foreign trade: it could temporarily suspend or lower duties on imports or ban exports, usually in periods of scarcity. Otherwise the import–export trade was left free to operate under existing regulations with little interference.

When examining Thompson's thesis it is important to recognize the limited nature of state regulation of the corn trade after 1700. The existence of a complex and 'de-regulated' corn trade, whether regional or national, predated, often substantially, the disturbances which Thompson says arose from its operation. Stevenson says that

This means that we are not dealing with a straightforward reaction to the onset of market capitalism in the food trade. If that had been the case, there should have been many more food riots, much earlier.[30]

Stevenson may be right but the lack of food riots before 1750 can be accounted for by low food prices, while the increased incidence in the succeeding half-century was the result of rising prices and growing population. The reaction was not against the introduction of a capitalist system but against the failure of that system, literally, to supply the goods.

TYPOLOGY OF CROWD ACTION

Food riots

Food riots were the most common form of popular protest in the eighteenth and early nineteenth centuries.[31] It is, however, a mistake to see this period as punctuated by an almost unbroken succession of riots. They generally occurred in the wake of bad harvests and shortages which sent food prices rocketing and were often the direct outcome of the fear of shortages rather than of shortages themselves. The second half of the eighteenth century saw more lean years than the first half, with peak years in 1766, 1795 and 1799–1800. In the nineteenth century there was a progressive decline in food riots and, except for the East Anglian riots in 1816 and 1822 and parts of the Swing riots in 1830, these were confined to the fringes of Britain. The chronology of food riots in the next section will be followed by a general discussion in which comparisons and contrasts will be drawn out.

The 1690s saw widespread food rioting but the next decade saw a lull, the result of lower prices, which was broken between 1708 and 1710 when prices rose again. There were seven major protests in 1709. Riots in the Wrexham–Chester area marked the first appearance of food protest in North Wales. Localized protest occurred in 1727–9 and 1737 in Cornwall and North Wales. This sequence of riots, though unrelated, did have certain characteristic features. First, they were protests at the movement of grain outside the areas concerned: for example, in 1700 a Truro corn-dealer's store was attacked and in 1709 corn dealers who had been buying up grain for export to France in North Wales went in fear of their lives. Secondly, there is evidence that direct pressure, like the march of the Kingswood colliers into Bristol in 1709 or of the Cornish tin miners to Falmouth and Truro in 1727 and 1729, led to a lowering of prices.

There were major disturbances in 1740–1 following the harsh winter of 1739. Most of these occurred in the major grain-growing regions and shipping ports of eastern England, north of the Thames, and in North Wales. Riots in western and southern counties were less numerous and taken less seriously by the authorities. Riots spread, for the first time, to the West Riding of Yorkshire, Teeside and Tyneside (though its keelmen had rioted in 1709–10), north of the border to the Edinburgh region and west into Pembrokeshire. A recurrent theme in reports of these riots was popular hostility to the export of grain from regions where shortages were anticipated or already felt. Within a 'moral economy', it was maintained, local markets should always be adequately supplied before merchants should be allowed to profit from exports. The 1740 riots were exacerbated by the failure of the authorities to restrain exports and properly regulate the corn trade.

Food riots in 1756–7 were, both in scale and intensity, among the most severe of the century. From an initial outbreak in the Midlands in August 1756 they spread rapidly to the north, south, south-west and to Wales. By December 1757, when they stopped, thirty counties in England and Wales had been affected and over 140 incidents reported. As well as the dramatic increase in the quantity of riots there was a marked extension of the variety of protest. Crowd action to prevent the export of grain, which had marked riots earlier in the century, remained important but other forms of riot, price-setting protest, attacks on mills, retailers and grain dealers, became more important. The severe outbreak of riot in the Midlands occurred because of difficulties in feeding growing urban populations when food prices rose.

In 1766 England was in the middle of a major economic slump. Manufacturing industries, buoyant during the Seven Years War, experienced a painful return to peacetime conditions. This, combined with cattle murrain, crop failure, exceptional foreign demand and government inactivity, ensured that food prices were high. In August 1765 the government allowed the parliamentary provision which admitted corn duty-free to lapse and the bounty of 5 shillings per quarter on exported wheat automatically came into effect. As a result corn merchants, who had previously imported corn without paying duties, were allowed to export the same corn for a profit. Corn dealers took advantage of this situation to ship out as much corn as possible. Riots in early 1766 in Hampshire and Dorset led to the government temporarily re-establishing the export embargo until August.

The corn harvest in Scotland and northern England in 1766 was exceptionally good but was poor in southern England. Had Chatham's government acted to prevent export after the temporary embargo lapsed on 26 August it is likely that further riot would have been avoided. It did act but, if anything, its actions made things worse. A confused proclamation on 10 September made it clear that, without parliamentary sanction, the government could not prohibit grain export and that, as Parliament would not meet for seven weeks, no sanction would be available until November. Much of the rioting in September and October came in response to this situation which inadvertently directed attention towards corn dealers and determined the main areas of protest. Farmers sought either to export their grain as soon as possible or to store it until prices rose.

Crowds were remarkably successful in forcing concessions by indirect means – through physical intimidation, threatening letters, non-violent visits – thought the degree to which this removed hunger was probably limited. More important was the local magistrates' and townsmen's vigorous programmes of relief. Government repression was used only when the scale of disturbances exceeded the abilities of the magistracy to contain them through concessions. The twelve peacetime regiments were concentrated by Barrington, Secretary at War, at the centre of the rioting in Wiltshire and, to a lesser extent, in the Midlands and order was quickly restored. Seven men were executed and 57 others, who were convicted of felonies, suffered lesser penalties. Government action in reimposing the corn embargo on 26 September and the stabilizing of the economy brought protest quickly to an end.

Good harvests in 1768 and 1769 were followed by a succession of five poor harvests between 1770 and 1774. There were disturbances in five areas of Britain. In the winter of 1772–3 industrial depression in Scotland caused unemployment and wage cutting in the local linen industry which coincided with a sharp rise in grain prices. The result was crowd action in Tayside and central Scotland to prevent the shipment of grain to England. There was collective action by cloth workers in Essex and Suffolk associated with the general decline of the industry in the area and higher prices. Attacks on mills and millers led to farmers, shopkeepers and dealers being forced to reduce prices. There were protests in Devon and Somerset in 1772, in Bedfordshire and Buckinghamshire and Cornwall in 1773.

The twenty years between 1773 and 1793 were relatively quiet compared to the preceding and succeeding years. Harvests were generally good and protests were distinctly regional. In southern and eastern England there were only three food riots, one of which was linked to labourers' demands for higher wages. There were protests on the east coast of Scotland in 1784, 1792 and 1793. Secondly, there was a series of riots down the west coast of Britain: in 1783 at two ports in south-west Scotland; in 1789 in North Wales; in 1793 in Liverpool and Swansea and in 1789 and 1793 in Cornwall. Finally disturbances occurred in the industrial centres of the west Midlands and the West Riding of Yorkshire. Rioters used a variety of strategies to reduce prices or obtain grain: waggons were stopped on the road and grain seized, warehouses and mills were attacked, farmers and corn-dealers were threatened.

There were four major outbreaks of food disturbances in the period between 1794 and 1820, all of which corresponded to periods of harvest failure and high prices. E. P. Thompson calls 1795 the 'climactic' year for food riots in England, with no region free from protest. John Stevenson estimates that there were 74 major disturbances. The poor harvest of 1794, which was about 25 per cent below that of 1793 and led to deficiencies in the pre-harvest period in 1795, provides only part of the reason for the upsurge of protest. Many industrial workers were laid off or took wage cuts in 1795 because of the sensitivity of trade to grain prices. The French war disrupted grain imports and the authorities seemed unaware of the scale of the problem. These circumstances combined to produce a major subsistence crisis.

There was a scattering of riots in 1794 and early 1795 but major protests did not begin in earnest until March. In Cornwall and North Wales crowd action prevented the export of grain. In other areas the main aim was 'price regulation'. By the autumn of 1796 it was clear that, because of the poor harvest, the authorities must take measures to alleviate food shortages. Action was taken to increase the supply of food and to regulate prices by both local authorities and private individuals. This was sufficient to prevent major disturbances in England and Wales in 1796. The only area where there was widespread protest was in Scotland which, because its staple oat crop had not failed in 1794 or 1795, had previously been untroubled. What caused protest was the impact of England's food shortages, and rioters attempted to prevent the movement of Scottish barley and potatoes south.

The three harvests between 1796 and 1798 were good but in 1799 there was a shortfall of between 25 and 40 per cent. This pushed British grain prices up sharply between December 1799 and May 1800. This, combined with the beginnings of a trade depression, led to the earliest disturbances being located in the industrial centres of Lancashire (October–November 1799 and January–February 1800), Yorkshire (April 1800, though there had been an earlier riot at Huddersfield over potato prices), the Midlands (February, April, May 1800), the urban centres of the Central Lowlands of Scotland (from February 1800) and South Wales. In many rural areas – west Wales, the Lake District, south-west and north-east Scotland – there were sporadic protests mainly connected with the movement of foodstuffs. The first crisis of 1799–1801 was ended by the government actively encouraging imports: it did not want a repeat of the mid-year crisis of 1795.

Good weather helped to relieve tensions and prices fell in anticipation of a good harvest. Widespread rain in August left grain too wet to be threshed and prices began to move upwards. This had a marked effect on consumers, who believed that the harvest was good and that price increases were due to speculation in the grain market by farmers, dealers, shopkeepers and merchants. These individuals became the focus for crowd action. Major incidents occurred in London. This was very unusual because government always tried to maintain the food supply of the capital. There were also incidents along the coasts of north Kent, Hampshire, Dorset and the south-west, in the south Midlands and the Black Country, Nottinghamshire, Derbyshire, South Yorkshire and Lancashire. Scotland, by contrast, was generally quiet. In England high prices persisted through the winter of 1800–1 and industrial recession was now at its height. Prompt government action in instructing magistrates to deal quickly with any protests resulted in the levels of rioting not matching the continuing inflated prices.

Food riots between 1810 and 1813 and 1816 and 1818 were clearly related to food shortage and high prices. There were disturbances in Cornwall and Devon and round Carlisle but the major problem lay in the industrial centres of Lancashire, north-east Cheshire and the West Riding of Yorkshire which were suffering from acute commercial distress, industrial Luddism and radical agitation. Protest in Scotland was on a smaller scale than in England and there were no disturbances in Wales. The pattern of food riots that had begun to emerge in 1799–1801, with their increasing concentration in urban and industrial centres completely separate from the countryside, continued between 1810 and 1818. The exception to this changing emphasis was the Fenland protests of 1816.

Between 1795 and 1818 there is little evidence for a major subsistence crisis apart from a small increase in burials. The disturbances that occurred must be placed in the context of shortage and hardship rather than real famine and starvation. As in the earlier riots of the century the issue was one of transporting food from area to area to relieve shortages. Urban growth exacerbated this problem and helps to explain why the focus of food riots altered from rural to industrial settings. Food riots declined in number after 1815 and were replaced by other protests aimed at defending living standards which were more suited to the industrial environment. After the 1810s food riots were confined to two main areas: the remoter areas of Britain and some of the poorer urban slums. There were riots in Cornwall in 1830–1, in the south-west, in north-east Scotland round Aberdeen and in Jersey in 1847 and in Devon in 1867. In urban areas there were attacks on food shops in Manchester in 1826, in other parts of Lancashire in 1829 and in the Potteries in 1842.

Two features stand out in the location of food riots in Britain: the influence of the communication system and the growing importance of the distribution of the manufacturing population. Many disturbances took place in ports, market towns or trans-shipment points, irrespective of whether they were in prosperous or marginal areas. The sight of grain moving from one area to another or being shipped from small ports could inflame popular sensibilities. This was particularly important in East Anglia and in the southern counties which served the food needs of London. Equally important was the presence of a large non-agricultural population, dependent on local markets for food supplies and vulnerable to rapid fluctuations in prices. During the eighteenth century colliers were the most important such group: tin miners in Cornwall, the Kingswood colliers round Bristol, Black Country colliers, colliers in Lancashire and Cheshire and the pitmen of Tyneside. Cloth workers formed another group with a long tradition of defending their rights by collective action. Itinerant workers, like canal navvies, were frequently blamed, though not always justly, for disturbances. Their involvement illustrated the difficult position of labourers in semi-rural conditions where provisioning was often difficult and dependent on the unreliability of local markets. The widespread incidence of riots in Cornwall and the relatively undisturbed situation in the north-east can be explained by poor and good communication networks, the location of industrial centres inland or on the coast and a willingness to use alternative food grains to wheat and more extensive use of potatoes.

Participants in food riots were usually a cross-section of local inhabitants. The coincidence of riots with market towns and manufacturing centres meant that participants reflected urban populations rather than rural ones. Country areas were rarely short of grain. The major exception to this was the Fenland riots of 1816. Women frequently played a dominant role in riots and initially felt the frustrations and anxieties of price fluctuations more acutely than men. In 1800 the *Leicester Journal* remarked that 'all public disturbances generally commence with the clamour of women and the folly of boys'.

The relationship between price movements and food riots is far from simple. The pre-harvest months saw real discontent about prices but the post-harvest period was one of rumour and resentment with complaints that farmers and middlemen were regulating the supply of grain to maximize their profits. Riots, like those in 1766 and 1795–6, did not occur when prices were at their highest but simply because of the rate and direction of price movements. Collective action was rarely motivated simply by prices, though frequently they acted as a stimulus to protest. Feelings of fear, injustice, a perceived attack on traditional values, the complex psychology of individuals and crowds as well as prices led to growing resentment which could spill over into protest.

Land protests

Protests over individual, especially tenants', land rights can be divided between those in Wales, Scotland and upland England and those in lowland England during this period. During the eighteenth century the focus of land protest moved first to southern Scotland and then to northern Scotland and Wales. The reason for this is twofold. First, the development of large-scale pastoral farming required the 'clearance' of tenants in some areas. Secondly, landowners asserted their property rights over commons and upland wastes against customary rights of tenants and labourers.

In the lowlands of Galloway on the western borders of Scotland, the Levellers' Revolt of 1724 was a movement against enclosure and eviction.[32] By contrast on the eastern borders there was little protest against enclosure. Explanation for these contrasting responses lies in different types of farming. Galloway was remote from any sizeable demand for corn, had an economically underdeveloped tenantry lacking the capital to develop large-scale cattle farming and who were cleared from the land to enable landowners to farm it directly. The 1724 Revolt was shortlived and was unsuccessful in stopping further enclosure. The landowners had troops, the legal system and the Church of Scotland broadly on their side, though there was unease at the disruption to an ordered society that enclosure caused. Some tenants were incorporated into the new economy and prospered but the vast majority was left defeated and demoralized. In the east, landowners found it more profitable to be involved in the grain trade than pastoral farming. They co-operated with their tenants, allowing the latter to prosper and getting increased rents in return. There was a gradual reaction of tenant numbers and wholesale evictions proved unnecessary.

The link between agrarian and industrial change may explain the relative absence of protest from the southern Scottish Highlands and the eastern parts of South Wales. The expansion of industry adjacent to these areas and its need for supplies of labour led many tenants to 'vote with their feet'. In the southern Highlands the gradual change in tenurial arrangements was related to the gradual transformation of clan chiefs into private landowners. These changes were blunted not only by their gradualness but by their undermining of the solidarity of communities. Widespread and permanent migration to more lucrative industrial centres was an accepted part of the community's life. There were complaints about hardship but there was no overt collective action.

In contrast the dramatic ending of ways of life in the northern Scottish Highlands and in western Wales led to widespread resistance.[33] In the Highlands protests were related solely to the development of capitalist sheep farming on such a large scale that it made the clansmen redundant. The traditional view was that clearances were passively accepted because there was little antagonism between clansmen and chief. Though this may well have reduced the level of opposition, the clearances were accompanied by widespread resistance which marked the transformation of clan chiefs into private landowners and a move away from communal to capitalist sheep farming.

The clearance disturbances, after two protests in the 1780s, occurred in 1792, 1813 and 1820–1. The 1792 rising was the result of a clash between traditional black cattle rearing and the new sheep farms rather than over the direct threat of eviction. A peaceful plan was conceived largely by the men of Strathrusdale and Ardross to round up all the sheep and drive them out of the northern Highlands. They hoped that others would take up their cause and push the sheep further south. The authorities responded quickly and three companies of the Black Watch were mobilized but, on their arrival at Boath, they found 6,000 sheep unattended.

The Kildonian protests of 1813 were a response to the wholesale clearance of the strath as part of the economic development of the Sutherland estates. There was again the call to drive out the sheep and a rudimentary attempt to co-ordinate the actions of different areas. The disturbances of 1820–1 seem at first sight to be unconnected apart from occurring during another phase of major clearances. In 1819 Thomas Dudgeon's Sutherland Transatlantic Emigration Society was established. It focused attention on the clearances but certain leading members were reported to have called for resistance to eviction and, under pressure from the authorities, its leadership disbanded. Rank-and-file Dudgeonites, however, were present in communities throughout the Highlands. Evictions in the early summer of 1819 were carried out peacefully but disturbances broke out in response to similar clearances the following year.

The islands and the west coast of Scotland had been insulated from the effects of clearances because large numbers of men were still needed for the lucrative kelp industry. By the late 1820s an irreversible contraction of the industry had set in and sheep farming became increasingly important. The centre of gravity for protests consequently shifted from the east to the west coast and the islands. With the exception of the protest in Caithness in 1835, all the riots in the east were concentrated in the Strathcarron area, a region that had already seen protests in 1792 and 1820. Evictions in the 1850s were, however, carried out more easily in the west than those in the east earlier in the century. The major reason for this was the smaller scale of eviction and the inaccessibility and isolation of many of the communities which made concerted resistance more difficult to organize.

The clearances ended whatever remained of the economic basis of the clan system – its political and military significance did not survive Culloden – and demolished whatever remained of the old communities based on kinship. Those who remained in the Highlands – many chose emigration – reverted to a barely subsistence economy and lived in a vast rural slum. The potato became a staple diet and the effects of the famine of the 1840s were as severe, though less recognized, in Scotland as in Ireland. The clearances were the result of demographic and economic forces, operating on a dependent and insecure society, which were beyond the control of local landowners who had little alternative but to respond to market forces.

In Wales there were regional differences in responses to enclosure. In the Welsh uplands enclosure was needed to establish proprietary rights to allow the commons to be used for large-scale pastoral farming. In North Wales land was enclosed largely to meet the needs of the developing slate industry; it was not primarily a question of agricultural improvement. Landowners needed to exert their rights over waste and common land before slate development could occur. Most of the protests occurred during the French wars. The opposition of squatters and small farmers in south and mid Wales to enclosure between 1815 and 1820 followed on from the general disaffection in the west and south-west of Wales which lasted from the 1790s through to 1813. After the 1820s Wales was remarkably free from direct collective action over land rights.

In contrast to Scotland and Wales there was a marked absence of protest over land in lowland England, especially after 1800. The main reasons for this lay in the nature of agrarian change and the power of the enclosers. Drainage and enclosure had already taken place in many areas before 1700, though not without resistance in some places, and a more ordered agrarian society had begun to be established, based on wages and rent. By 1750, when enclosure was resumed in earnest, many communities that had previously resisted were so changed that no protests, comparable to those in Scotland and Wales, developed.

In the first half of the eighteenth century protests were primarily linked to the use of land for social prestige rather than for monetary gain. In the Northamptonshire forests and in the Forest of Dean there was opposition to enclosure and on Cannock Chase the struggle continued to prevent the creation of rabbit warrens. The most serious protests were concerned with 'blacking', systematic and organized attacks on deer parks in royal forests and on private estates.[34] Blacking was a response to the attempts of George I and II to revitalize the forest authorities and to the enlargements of private deer parks as visible evidence of the power and prestige of the new Whig elite. Deer poaching represented a symbolic attack on what was threatening people's livelihoods: enclosing wasteland, a capitalist exploitation of the timber resources, the grazing of deer on crops standing in the fields. Fish ponds were attacked because when they were enlarged they flooded gravel and peat pits. Landscaped parks brought an end to common rights. The Black Act of 1723 did not end foresters' resistance to change but diverted it from overt to covert forms: arson, maiming animals, breaking gates and fences.

With the increase of agricultural prices from 1750 and the greater possibilities of higher rents and returns, landlords turned to widespread enclosure and drainage. There was opposition to schemes in the Somerset Levels and in the Lincolnshire fens (1768–73). The defence of wastes under the threat of enclosure by industrial workers was widespread in the Midlands. The town fields of Leicester were the scene of protests in 1754 and in 1771–2 the Earl of Uxbridge was faced with widespread protest to his proposal to enclose the parishes round Burton-on-Trent. There were protests at Reddich in 1772 and Malvern in 1778.

After 1780, despite the scale of the enclosure movement, few communities took direct collective action and most of these took place before 1800. In Oxfordshire from 1786 to 1831 the men of Otmoor opposed all attempts to enclose and drain the moor. Protest was, on occasions, successful in holding up enclosure and drainage but generally only for a short time.

Turnpike protests

There were fragmented and localized disturbances over turnpikes and over the militia during the eighteenth and early nineteenth centuries. Despite the widespread development of turnpikes protests occurred in only four areas where the high concentration of toll-gates meant that even short journeys were liable to be expensive: round Bristol, 1727–35, 1749 and 1793; in the Gloucester and Ledbury area, 1734–8; in the West Riding, 1752–3 and in southern Scotland, 1792. Similar complaints over the number of turnpike trusts arose in south-west Wales in the period before 'Rebecca'. The location of these riots, and the customary destruction of the toll-gates, coincided with areas where communities of small farmers, independent colliers, artisans and clothiers existed rather than in areas where industrial and agrarian capitalism were well advanced.

The Rebecca riots,[35] which occurred in west Wales in 1839 and again between 1842 and 1844, have usually been represented as protest by an oppressed peasantry particularly against the burdens of the toll-gates. In reality the problems which led to protest were far more deep-seated, the consequence of a fractured society. The gulf between the small west Wales communities, which had become largely Nonconformist, and the anglicized landowners and magistrates had visibly widened. These were communities under increasing pressure from social and economic change and in which there was widespread unrest.

Toll-gates were but one grievance among many. People complained of tithes, high rents, the poor law, church rates and the insensitivity of clerical magistrates and land agents. Bad harvests between 1839 and 1841, the collapse in prices in 1842–3 and the extension of toll-gates on country roads transformed unrest into collective action. Attacks on gates along the Carmarthen–Pembrokeshire border occurred in 1839 but the main phase of action was from the winter of 1842 until 1844. The intervening years saw attacks on workhouses, burning of hayricks, threatening letters and the destruction of salmon weirs, all countersigned by Rebecca.

Farmers were widely involved in the 1839 attacks but there is evidence for a significant shift in the social composition of later riots. Unemployed workmen and iron-workers became more active in west Wales and many farmers, frightened for their own property and by the breakdown of law and order, shifted their support to those in authority, co-operating with the commission of enquiry set up by the government in 1843. There was also a shift in the way in which the protesters tried to influence events. There was a gradual decline in the number of riots and more widespread use of mass meetings to discuss grievances and to petition government. The turnpike system in west Wales was reorganized by Lord Cawdor's Act of 1844 – rationalized but not removed – and the toll-gate problem was largely resolved. David Williams argues that the coming of railways helped to remove remaining tensions within the isolated communities by facilitating migration to the industrial centres. Other legislation helped alleviate the conditions of the small farmer: the General Enclosure Act of 1845, the repeal of the Corn Laws in 1846 and the poor law of 1847 which humanized the administration of poor relief. By the 1850s the pressures of population were slackening – the population of rural Wales reached its peak in 1851, farm labourers were able to take advantage of the higher wages and better conditions of life in the towns – and there was a revival in economic prosperity. The fundamental cause of the riots had been removed.

Militia riots

There were militia riots in 1757 and 1795–8. Following the new Militia Act of 1757 disturbances were confined to the eastern part of the country, especially Yorkshire, Lincolnshire and Bedfordshire. The new Act provided for a ballot to which every man in England between 18 and 50 years was subject, with certain exceptions. The labouring population saw the Act as an attempt by the wealthy landowners to use the poor to defend their property. This, added to rumours that militia service meant service overseas, exacerbated the situation. In most areas rioting was only ended by a determined defence of landowners or the use of military force.

There were sporadic disturbances over the militia after 1757 but the next major outbreak occurred between 1795 and 1798. The 1786 Militia Act required each county to draw up an annual list of men eligible for service which was then returned to central government. The threat from France meant that it was first implemented in 1795, at a time of high prices, increasing taxation and resentment over military and naval recruitment. Protest took similar forms to those in 1757 – attacks on officials and destruction of militia lists – though there is evidence in Lincolnshire that there was more planning and organization than in 1757. Pressure in Scotland had meant that no militia had been set up in the 1750s. The 1797 Act was the first to be implemented there and was met with massive reaction. As in England, much of the problem seems to have emerged from lack of explanation by the authorities of the meaning of the Act, which was consequently easily misrepresented.

Militia recruitment opened up the divisions within rural society. The rich could easily buy themselves out of the militia leaving the poor to protect their property. In both 1757 and 1795–8 implementation corresponded to periods of high prices and widespread disturbances over food. The riots, especially in England, occurred in areas free from food protest and they can be regarded in these areas as equivalent to the food riots of industrial workers.

Agricultural labourers in protest 1790–1850

Agricultural labourers were rarely at the centre of protest in the eighteenth century but this situation changed after 1790. It is necessary to consider why this change happened and why the protests of farm workers were largely confined to southern and eastern England. Enclosure, initially at least, required an increased supply of, particularly unskilled, labour. This and the decline in the number of long-hired farm servants led to the emergence of waged agricultural labourers who gradually became a group separate from the patriarchal control of their employers.

The agricultural boom during the French wars and the post-war depression did much to shape the consciousness of agricultural labourers of their new position in rural society. Wage differentials emerged between farm workers in southern and northern England and between areas which had alternative sources of employment to agriculture and those that did not. In 1795 Berkshire magistrates meeting at Speen introduced a system of relief to supplement the wages of labourers. Similar schemes were introduced across southern England. Though historians frequently call this the 'Speenhamland system' the name gives the schemes a uniformity which in practice they did not possess. Allowances in aid of wages did not fully make up the difference between high prices and wages and many labourers viewed wage supplements as an attempt to revive paternalistic bonds between masters and men. The insistence on wage increases and, in the case of Norfolk labourers the rejection of wage supplements, may indicate that the gulf between employers and workers was growing.

Wartime farming decisions had transformed much of southern and eastern England into a region dominated by wheat production. Boom conditions ended abruptly in 1815, grain prices slumped while rents, fixed during wartime inflation, did not. Farmers were faced with falling profits and sought to cut costs by cutting wages, quite possible in a labour market saturated by the demobilization of the armed forces, or by introducing economies of scale which technological innovations like the threshing machine offered. The East Anglian disturbances of 1816 can be seen as the first concerted series of collective protests largely by agricultural labourers.[36]

Industrial workes, townsmen, cottagers, fenmen and agricultural labourers were linked together in 1816 in a way that they were not in 1822 or 1830. There were three main types of protest, depending on location. There were incidents in some market towns which were a continuation of the long tradition of food riots and collective action by textile workers. Agricultural labourers took little part in these. On the loam and clay lands of Essex, Suffolk and Norfolk labourers were at the centre of protest over the use of mole ploughs and threshing machines and over demands for a subsistence wage. These followed on from similar protests between 1793 and 1805.

The third series of disturbances was in the Fens, centred on Downham Market, Littleport and Ely. The diversity of rioters – one in three arrested was not an agricultural labourer and one in seven had some land – reflected the heterogeneity of the fenland society, the impact of enclosure and drainage and the particular effect of depression. Riot was a response to the threat from enclosure and drainage to the independence of the way of life in the Fens but it was also a response to specific economic circumstances. The authorities at local level had limited resources at their disposal to stop riots spreading and, especially in the Fens, there were too few gentry to act collectively. Magistrates could make concessions to stop protest but the dramatic breakdown of law and order in Littleport and Ely could not be tolerated by central government. Sidmouth ordered the military to be deployed in force throughout Norfolk and Suffolk, not just in the Fens. Magistrates who had made concessions were overruled and draconian sentences were passed on the fen rioters. Five were executed and this, as much as anything, ensured that rioting spread no further.

Agricultural labourers may have been tentative in 1816 but during the protests six years later they were more assertive. There were three areas in Norfolk where collective protest occurred in late February and early March 1822. All three involved the destruction of threshing machines and in contrast to 1816 these attacks were not simply symbolic, drawing attention to the plight of the labourer, but were a campaign to sweep the machines away. Local magistrates acted quickly to prevent any widespread disturbances and the use of the military and yeomanry drove the main rising underground.

The Swing riots in 1830 lasted from August until well into December and took several forms.[37] In some areas there were demands for higher wages; in others tithes were the issue; poor law officials and workhouses were attacked but most widespread was the destruction of threshing machines. The major difference between the protests of 1816 and 1822 and those in 1830 was one of scale. The Swing riots were not confined to a single area but spread across most of southern and eastern England. Why was there such a widespread mobilization of agricultural labourers in 1830?

The 1830 riots began slowly and, initially, machine breakers were given lenient sentences. These were interpreted by many labourers as tacit approval of their actions and of the justice of their grievances and led to protests gathering momentum. Revolution in France in July, the growing agitation for parliamentary reform and the alienation of the middle classes from the Tory administration gave rural protest a more threatening dimension than in either 1816 or 1822. The newly established Whig government made the suppression of the disturbances its first priority on achieving power in mid-November. Concerted local action, especially by the gentry of Wiltshire and Hampshire, the use of troops and unwillingness of Lord

Melbourne, the Home Secretary, to countenance weakness or compromise on the part of local magistrates gradually restored order.

Swing did not destroy the willingness of agricultural labourers to protest, as some historians have maintained. There was widespread, though largely unsuccessful, action against the imposition of the Poor Law Amendment Act in 1835, rural trade unionism in the south-east and at Tolpuddle and covert protests in the form of arson. Agricultural protest may have had less of an impact nationally after 1830 but close examination of the local press gives a different story. Labourers were experts in slacking in highly effective and almost undetectable ways. More seriously they could steal their employers' corn, fruit and game despite the severity of sentence if caught. Sheep and horse stealing were capital offences until 1831 and arson remained so until 1837. Poaching was endemic in rural areas. Stacks could be fired, farm buildings lit, fences pulled down, animals maimed and drainage channels breached.

Rural protest in the early and mid-nineteenth century can be explained by the lack of understanding of the nature of change by both labourers and their employers. Change imperfectly understood aroused fear which could easily be fanned by rumour. This was made worse by 'want' and 'distress', under- or unemployment and consequent loss of status in the community.

It is evident from the discussion above that there was no clear division between rural and urban protest. It is, however, necessary to examine industrial and urban disturbances because they occurred as much as food riots and because they were often better reported.

Labour protests

Labour disputes were among the most frequent causes of collective action in the eighteenth and early nineteenth centuries. Eric Hobsbawm's phrase 'collective bargaining by riot' is not without validity. In the period before legal trade unions workmen and women often resorted to violence as a means of putting pressure on employers and local authorities as well as developing a sense of social and economic solidarity. Labour disputes were attended in their most typical forms by attacks on machinery, destruction of materials and tools, intimidation of strike-breakers, parades, lobbying of employers as well as peaceful negotiation.[38]

Labour disputes involved workers from many areas of the country and from many occupations: for example, Kingswood colliers, silk weavers from Spitalfields, woollen weavers of Norwich, Yorkshire and the western counties. The textile industries had a long history of disturbances, going back to the seventeenth century. In some cases disputes were over technical change. In 1768–9 there were riots in Blackburn when spinners attacked the house of James Hargreaves and destroyed his spinning machines. There was a systematic campaign against machines for carding and roving invented by Richard Arkwright in 1779 and the Grimshaw factory in Manchester, the first to use Cartwright's powerloom, was burnt down in 1792. There were disturbances over loss of status and the decline in the effectiveness of protective legislation. Gloucestershire weavers took action in 1755–6 because, they maintained, their employers were ignoring the legislation of 1726 and 1728 to regulate their wages. Cloth workers and other textile workers were concerned about the dilution of trade caused by abuse of apprenticeship laws. There were disturbances over the use of Irish wool and against weavers working on East Indian fabrics.

All these forms of collective action appear to have been motivated by a desire to maintain the status of workers, and defend their customary practices. They were overwhelmingly defensive in character, resisting 'unfairness' and change. 'Combination' and the use of the strike as a means of industrial pressure to preserve or improve living standards became a growing practice and the Combination Acts of 1799 and 1800 were as much a reaction against the growing and proved strength of trades unions in the 1790s as an extension of the Pittite 'reign of terror.'

The city 'mob'

The city 'mob' has been characterized by Eric Hobsbawm as 'a pre-political phenomenon . . . [but this] does not mean that it had no implicit or explicit ideas about politics'.[39] There is evidence that mobs often rioted 'without ideas', reacting spontaneously against unemployment, higher living standards and taxation but mobs also demonstrated some of the characteristics of pressure groups. Mobs expected that the authorities would be sensitive to their demands and frequently directed their attentions against the rich and powerful. They were often hostile to 'foreigners', that is to non-townspeople. Rudé sums up the complexity of the problem:

> Anomic and associational movements, social protest and political demands, well organised and clear-sighted interest groups and 'direct action' crowds, leaders and followers came together in a chorus of united opposition in which, however, the individual parts can still be distinguished and identified.[40]

The nature of urban popular protest is best exemplified by the experience of London during this period.[41] With a population of over half a million in 1700 London was by far the largest urban community in Britain. It had played a central role in the religious and constitutional struggles of the seventeenth century and the city 'mob' had a reputation for opposition to government and its policies. There were riots in 1710 in support of Sacheverell, gin riots in 1736, riots over the Jewish Nationalization Act in 1753 and in support of John Wilkes between 1763 and 1771. Urban protest was at its most successful when there was a broad alliance between different social groups in the city and least successful when the mob rioted alone. Popular protest in this situation was a means of putting pressure on government to change policy and was overtly 'political' in character, though there were as yet no 'recognized channels' to translate collective action into effective political pressure. Success or failure to influence policy owed much to the sensitivity of government to the particular pressure within Parliament.

The Gordon riots in 1780 marked an important stage in the dissociation of the propertied from popular clamour. The origins of the riots lay in the Catholic Relief Act of 1778 which had aimed to clarify the position of Roman Catholics. Attempts to pass similar legislation for Scotland led to a violent Presbyterian reaction. There was a powerful and emotive anti-Catholicism in Britain and in 1779 a Protestant Association was formed to resist any further attempts to ameliorate the position of Catholics in Scotland. Widespread rioting in Edinburgh and Glasgow and in smaller towns led to the withdrawal of the Scottish bill.

In February 1779 a similar association was formed in London and in November Lord George Gordon, who had been prominent in Scotland, was asked to become its president. In May 1780 it was determined to present a monster petition against the 1778 Act to Parliament. The Association had widespread support among the lower orders in London, illustrating the continuance of the bigotry and superstition. In early June Gordon and a large crowd of petitioners went to Westminster amid widespread disorder. For over a week London seemed to be at the mercy of the mob – the Fleet prison was attacked and many houses were destroyed. By 9 June, however, troops had regained control and Gordon was on his way to the Tower.

Gordon had tapped the anti-Catholicism of London to an extent which he was himself unable to control. Rudé has suggested that behind the 'No Popery' slogans there was a considerable amount of social bitterness. Destruction and violence was not concentrated solely in areas where the poorer Irish Catholics lived. The major difference between the 1780 riots and earlier orchestrated pressure during the Excise crisis or the Wilkes affair was one of scale. The spectre of mob violence which the events of 1780 presaged meant that London politicians became more cautious about mobilizing popular clamour in the future. There were limits beyond which popular campaigns could not be carried without severe risks to the Establishment, whether in London or at Westminster.

London remained the focus for many of the major political agitations for the next forty years. The radical societies of the 1790s took their lead from the London Corresponding Society. After 1815 it was the scene of several popular agitations: opposition to the passing of the Corn Laws, the reform agitation of 1816–18, and support for Queen Caroline in 1820. But London's pre-eminent position was being eclipsed by the emergent provincial and industrial centres in the north and Midlands. Lobbying and petitioning Parliament, a process aided by the emergence of the railway system, were 'managed', not spontaneous. London remained the centre of government and commerce and consequently central to political agitation, but increasingly it was a 'stage' for demonstrations which derived most of their support from outside the capital.

'Church and King' riots

'Church and King' riots, of which the Gordon disturbances were an extreme example, were something of a two-edged movement because their popular social basis resulted in ambivalent situations embarrassing to those whose interests were being overtly promoted. Rudé argues that they were more typical of agrarian than industrial countries yet during the eighteenth century they were more common in urban than rural settings. The London crowd was clearly motivated by 'Church and King' rather than radical-political issues in its frequent appearances on the streets in the 1710s. Methodists, their houses and chapels were frequent targets for attack in the middle of the century, for example in Exeter in 1745 and Norwich between 1751-2. Crowds were often stirred up by the antagonism of local clergy who branded Methodists as political subversives, crypto-papists and Jacobites. Quakers were attacked in both 1776 and 1800, though the motivation for this seems to have been their success in commerce and industry, especially the grain trade.

The 'Church and King' tradition was at its height during periods of political tension like the 1710s and 1740s and the pace of persecution slackened until the 1790s. Revolution in France and the beginnings of the campaign to repeal the Test and Corporation Acts after 1787 led many Anglicans to believe that their religion and their monarchy were threatened, providing the most important ingredients in the tensions which erupted after 1790. The position of Dissenters was exacerbated by their wide support for parliamentary reform, especially in the major provincial centres. 'Church and King' clubs sprang up and these acquired support from the 'lower orders' motivated as much by economic resentment as religious zeal: there were food riots in Birmingham in 1782 and 1792 and wage movements in Nottingham in 1783, 1790 and 1793. It is perhaps not surprising that Manchester, Birmingham and Nottingham had a history of difficult relations between the economically powerful dissenting minority and the Anglican Establishment, and that the latter was prepared to 'use' popular forces to defend its position.

The most serious disturbances took place in Birmingham in July 1791. The focus for protest was the scientist and theologian Joseph Priestley and other Unitarians. During four days of rioting his house and some twenty others were destroyed or damaged. Magistrates did not over-exert themselves, giving the impression that Dissenters were fair game. Though the Priestley riots were the most celebrated 'loyalist' disturbances of the early 1790s, attacks on reformers and French sympathizers intensified as the revolution in France became more radical. There were widespread 'patriotic' protests in Nottingham in 1792 and 1793 and in Manchester in late 1792, directed against popular radicalism.

Crowd action: possible explanations

There is no all-embracing explanation for popular protest in mainland Britain during this period. Economic conditions certainly affected levels of social tension and William Cobbett's statement that 'I defy you to agitate a man on a full stomach' reflected the experience of many reformers that periods of economic depression provided fertile conditions for popular agitation. However, protests like those associated with Sacheverell, the Militia Acts and Lord Gordon had little or no connection with adverse economic conditions.

Protesters were rarely motivated by a single issue. Turnpikes may have been the 'trigger' for action in South Wales and the spread of new technology for Luddites and 'Swing' rioters but their protests were symptomatic of a deeper malaise. Absolute deterioration in conditions was perhaps less important than 'relative deprivation', popular perceptions and experiences that status, living standards or accepted practice was changing. Whether low wages, high prices, feelings of injustice or perceptions of change beyond individuals' control, the most striking feature of much popular protest was its essentially defensive nature with the preservation of the community and its values and the restoration of the vaguely perceived but vigorously defended 'moral economy' as its fundamental objective.

The gap between protest by 'riot' to the growth of articulate and nonviolent means of expressing demands, which historians once saw as characterizing this period, has been significantly narrowed by the recognition that riots were much more restrained and rational procedures and less 'primitive' than previously believed. Riots did not operate outside the existing economic, social and political systems; in fact many rioters could claim that they were defending that establishment. But their lifespan was short, limited by the nature of the crowd which created them. The more 'modern' forms of protest had greater permanence, rational organization, long-term aims and were eventually recognized, though sometimes reluctantly, as valid institutions through which pressure might legitimately be exerted on employers and government.

PROTEST IN IRELAND

The nature of popular protest in Ireland was different in two important respects from that on mainland Britain and this justifies dealing with it separately. Protest had a sectarian intensity and high levels of violence to an extent generally unknown in Britain and this underlay much of the tensions within Ireland[42]. This brief survey will do no more than sketch the main protest movements between the 1760s and 1840s.

Growing tensions

The 1760s saw signs of tension within rural society with a sharpening of sectarian antagonism. The southern margins of Tipperary saw an agitation by small tenants against the enclosure of common pasture and this was exploited by Protestant politicians as evidence of a Catholic conspiracy. High prices for pastoral land after 1760 were reflected in rising land values, especially in Munster cattle country, which put marginal mixed farmers and smallholders under pressure. The result was the 'Whiteboy' disturbances, the first widespread popular action since the Connacht disturbances of 1710–11.

The agitation spread out from south Tipperary into west Waterford, north Cork and Limerick and the catalogue of grievances expanded. Ex-tenants resented not having their leases renewed. The poor resented the collection of tithes through intermediaries, and especially resented the level of tithe on potatoes. The participants were largely Catholic and of low social rank but they did receive some support from above, some of it for reasons of private revenge, some on the grounds of compassion. The nerve of the local magistracy was strengthened by the reinforcement of local garrisons by several Ulster-recruited regiments and the agitation subsided. The local magistracy and the army general subscribed to a Catholic conspiracy theory but a special commission set up to investigate the protests discounted this dimension and took economic grievances at face value. Retribution was swift but, by eighteenth-century Irish standards, mild: only twelve people were sentenced to death.

Later in 1762 protest welled up again in Tipperary and in parts of Kilkenny and survived sporadically for three years. Enclosure ceased to be an issue but tithes remained a common denominator. Tithes were not objected to on simple sectarian grounds – they were a grievance for all denominations – nor was it that tithes were the greatest financial burden on tenants – land rents were several times higher – but because they were collected in an arbitrary and uneven manner. The aim of the agitation was not the elimination of tithes but their regulation and reduction. Attempts by the Whiteboys to enforce a schedule of 'fair' tithe charges formed an important precedent for later redressing movements.

The Whiteboy disturbances were closely connected to the intra-gentry religious tensions in Tipperary, and Protestant families sought to use the conspiracy theory to attack both the Catholic gentry and clergy in the county. The local gentry's view of what caused the agitation conflicted with the basically economic views of government in Dublin. But many Protestants, especially in rural Munster, supported harsh treatment for those suspected of fomenting rebellion. Contemporary perceptions were clearly illustrated by the 700 people who subscribed to a new Cork edition of Sir John Temple's *History of the General Rebellion of 1641*.

The summer of 1763 saw the first signs of large-scale social protest in the six Ulster counties. The 'Oakboy' movement was a much more public movement than the nocturnal Whiteboys. It gathered its supporters together in larger numbers, did little physical damage and was more successful in its objectives. It was essentially a tax revolt by all denominations against the Anglican clergy for indiscriminately levying fees and against the gentry whose enthusiasm for road-building had pushed up the county rate or 'cess'. Repression was swifter and sharper than in the south but the criminal prosecutions which followed nearly all failed either because witnesses did not materialize or because the juries, dominated by Presbyterian and Anglican 'middle orders', sympathized with the actions of the protesters.

Sectarian rivalry

In the late 1780s religion was a major element in two waves of local communal disturbances. In County Armagh protest involving Catholic and Protestant weaver-farmers began in 1784. The status of many Catholics in this prosperous and religiously mixed county caused much resentment, and the involvement of a small number of Catholics in local volunteering in 1783–4 raised the temperature. The volatility of this area has been explained by the breakdown of traditional family discipline because of the large number of independent young weavers of all denominations. Groups of Protestants, soon known as 'Peep-o'-day boys' began raiding large Catholic houses, ostensibly in search of weapons. Initially there was considerable disquiet among all the gentry at these activities but sympathies weakened when Catholic counter-groups, known as Defenders, appeared. By the late 1780s there were occasional shows of strength by both parties. Some gentry openly recruited Peep-o'-day boys into Volunteer corps and defenderism spread south and east into Down and Louth.

In the south agitation against the tithe system re-emerged in 1785–7. The 'Rightboy' movement was far more sophisticated and peaceful than the movements of the 1760s and had coherent demands for tithe reduction. The attack on tithes was not in essence sectarian as the extension of the agitation to certain Catholic clergy who were accused of levying excessive tithes demonstrated. But Richard Woodward, Anglican bishop of Cloyne, adopted strident sectarian tones towards the campaign, presenting it as the beginnings of a general attack on the Established Church. This attracted criticism from both Presbyterians and Catholics but was an understandable response by a church which perceived itself as being under siege.

By the mid-1790s Defender networks had spread through predominantly Catholic districts in fourteen counties. In response to this Protestants began to establish local oath-bound 'Orange' lodges. Linked to this was a campaign of arson and intimidation against Catholic smallholders in north Armagh and in the Lagan valley; the victims were paying the price of the actions of their co-religionists further south. The Armagh Orangemen were tamed by their magistracy in 1796 but by then rumours of Protestant excesses and government collusion were widespread. Sectarian tensions merged with demands for radical or revolutionary change which led to the communal blood-letting of 1798.[43]

Agrarian protest continued into the nineteenth century with the disturbances in late 1806 associated with the 'Threshers' in the five counties of Sligo, Mayo, Cavan, Leitrim and Longford. Both the Threshers and the Carders' campaign of 1813–16 were associated with Anglican tithes and Catholic priests' dues. Government repression was swift and harsh.

'Ribbonism'

'Ribbonism' added a sectarian and political dimension to movements of popular protest. It was the successor to the Catholic Defenders who had opposed the Orangemen in 1798 and who had subsequently faded from view. Both had been organized for defensive purposes but there was some difference in their aims. Defenders had been concerned primarily with land issues and had included non-Catholics. Ribbonmen were much more pointedly sectarian, excluding everyone who was not a Catholic.

From the Ulster border counties Ribbonmen spread into north Leinster and north Connacht, building up an extensive and sophisticated organizational network. But it was mainly an urban movement, strongest in Dublin but also found in Belfast, Londonderry and the smaller towns of southern Ireland (Limerick, Tarbert, Mountrath, Mountmellick, Cloughjordan and Bandon) where Orangeism was also strong. A similar trend was evident in cities where Irish immigrants settled: Orangeism and Ribbonism were both strong in Glasgow, Manchester and Liverpool. Each group tended to thrive on the sectarianism of the other.

Ribbonmen were largely lower-middle-class and labouring Catholics from a wide range of occupations. They were opposed to mere agrarian protest. As an urban-based organization Ribbonism saw agrarian issues as of secondary importance, though it did try to co-ordinate agrarian protest. As a secret organization Ribbonism was much more formidable than any contemporary agrarian society. It was feared because of its sectarianism, the suspected radical nature of its politics and the widespread belief that it formed a nationwide conspiracy with links with radicals in Britain and America.

In its political aspects Ribbonism provides a link, though a far from clear one, between the United Irishmen of the 1790s and the Fenians of the mid-nineteenth century. It promised much as a conspiracy but without achieving any substantial change in the course of Irish history. It was agrarian, sectarian and political but without achieving that sense of Irish nationalism that characterized later movements. Contemporaries confused Ribbonism with agrarianism even at its most active period in the 1820s and 1830s and as its political and sectarian nature was overshadowed by economic and social aspects it became a general term to describe all forms of agrarian protest, especially after the Famine.

'Rockism'

The most widespread of the pre-Famine agrarian movements was 'Rockism'. Its causes were economic following the partial failure of the potato crops in 1817 and again in 1821. Wages fell, underemployment had increased and legislation passed between 1815 and 1818 made it easier for landlords to evict defaulting tenants. The Rockite movement spread in 1821 from Limerick to Munster and the neighbouring counties of Leinster. Widespread violence, destruction of property and intimidation occurred until 1824. The early 1830s saw widespread disturbances of a sectarian nature in County Clare and Queen's County associated with the 'Terry Alts'. As in much of the other early nineteenth-century agrarian disturbances the struggle was between the labourer and the farmer rather than between landlord and tenant as was the case in the second half of the century. The 'Whitefeet' disturbances in Queen's County and Kilkenny in the 1830s were, unlike the Terry Alts, concerned with tithes. The resultant 'tithe war', plus the Whig government's need for support from O'Connell and his 'party' led to the 1838 Tithe Act which converted tithes into a rent charge payable by the head landlord who passed the charge down to sub-tenants except the lowest class of cottiers and tenants.

CONCLUSIONS

Agrarian protest can, in Ireland as on mainland Britain, be seen as a plea to restore an idealized and 'just' social and economic system. What was different about Ireland was not the level of protest but the psychological construction placed on each outbreak. Irish rural violence may have been motivated largely by economic considerations and those protesting may have been 'political illiterates', but to many in authority their actions constituted a real and potent political threat not simply to public order but to the existence of the British Protestant state. Ireland was a far more fractured society than Wales, Scotland or England. While in the latter much violent protest had already died away by 1850 as the scope for exerting political pressure through an institutional framework developed, violence continued to be used in Ireland as an auxiliary to, or even a substitute for, political dialogue.

Popular protest was the means through which those denied actual political power attempted to reverse policies, at both local and national levels, which were believed to alter the traditional 'balance' within society. Riot, intimidation, destruction of property, physical attacks on people and animals and anonymous letters were seen as legitimate means of restoring a society and an economy in which those in authority had power, duties and responsibilities. Moral indignation and a sense of wrong underlay much protest. As British society became more individualistic and as communities changed – in terms of their total populations as much as anything else – so the expression of a sense of 'injustice' through riot peaked and then declined. The brief solidarity of the crowd was replaced by the more permanent solidarity of the trade union or pressure group. Spontaneity gave way to institutional rationality.

NOTES

1 Evidence of William Dawson, Cambridge Record Office. Information quoted in R. Brown *Change and Continuity in British Society 1800–1850*, Cambridge University Press, 1987, p. 65.
2 *Cambridge Chronicle*, 17 April 1835.
3 There is a variety of studies on collective behaviour at a theoretical level. E. Canetti *Crowds and Power*, Penguin, 1973 is an interesting starting-point and can be supplemented with the more detailed studies of N. Smelser *Theory of Collective Behaviour*, Routledge, 1962, S. Halebsky *Mass Society and Political Conflict – Towards a Reconstruction of Theory*, Cambridge University Press, 1976 and S. Moscovici *The Age of the Crowd: A Historical Treatise on Mass Psychology*, Cambridge University Press, 1985. R. J. Holton 'The Crowd in History: Some Problems of Theory and Practice', *Social History* 3 (1978), pp. 219–33 is particularly useful.
4 Useful studies by historians at theoretical and empirical levels include L. A. and C. Tilly (eds) *Class Conflict and Collective Action*, Sage, 1981 especially Charles Tilly's introduction pp. 13–26, J. Stevenson and R. Quinault *Popular Protest and Public Order: Six Studies in British History 1790–1920*, Allen & Unwin 1974, pp. 15–32, G. Rudé *Ideology and Popular Protest*, Lawrence & Wishart, 1980, pp. 7–38 and *Paris and London in the 18th Century*, Collins, 1971, E. Hobsbawm *Primitive Rebels*, Manchester University Press, 1959 and *Bandits*, Penguin, 1975, A. Fletcher and J. Stevenson (eds) *Order and Disorder in Early Modern England*, Cambridge University Press 1985, pp. 1–40 and J. Stevenson *Popular Disturbances in England 1700–1870*, Longman, 1979, pp. 1–16. M. Harrison *Crowds and Power. Mass Phenomena in English Towns 1790–1835* Cambridge University Press, 1988 provides a useful 'state of the art' synopsis of theoretical studies.
5 In addition to Rudé's work cited above, mention should be made of his *The Crowd in the French Revolution*, Oxford University Press, 1959, *Wilkes and Liberty*, Oxford University Press, 1962, *The Crowd in History 1730–1848*, John Wiley, 1964, *Protest and Punishment*, Oxford University Press 1978 and *Criminal and Victim*, Oxford University Press, 1985 and his study of the 1830 agrarian disturbances, with E. Hobsbawm, *Captain Swing*, Penguin, 1973.
6 G. Rudé *Paris and London in the 18th century*, op. cit. E. Canetti op. cit., p. 17.
7 H. Perkin *The Origins of Modern English Society 1780–1880*, Routledge, 1969, p. 196.
8 Alexis de Tocqueville *The Old Regime and the French Revolution*, Fontana, 1970, p. 214 (translation of 1856 edn).

9 J. C. Davis 'Towards a theory of revolution', *American Sociological Review*, vol. xxvii, (1), 1962, p. 6.

10 G. Rudé 'The Pre-Industrial Crowd', in *Paris and London*, op. cit., p. 19.

11 E. Canetti op. cit., p. 18.

12 G. Rudé op. cit., p. 21.

13 E. Canetti op. cit., p. 23.

14 ibid., pp. 32–3.

15 G. Rudé op. cit., pp. 19–21.

16 E. Canetti op. cit., pp. 47–54.

17 ibid., pp. 55–60.

18 ibid., pp. 60–3.

19 ibid., pp. 63–6.

20 ibid., pp. 66–71.

21 D. Hay 'Property, Authority and Criminal Law', in D. Hay, P. Linebaugh and E. P. Thompson (eds) *Albion's Fatal Tree: Crime and Society in Eighteenth Century England*, Allen Lane, 1975, pp. 17–63.

22 E. P. Thompson 'The Moral Economy of the English Crowd in the Eighteenth Century', *Past and Present*, 50 (1971), pp. 76–136.

23 ibid., p. 78.

24 ibid., pp. 78–9.

25 ibid., p. 80.

26 ibid., p. 88.

27 ibid., p 89.

28 A. W. Coats 'Contrary Moralities: Plebs, Paternalists and Political Economists', *Past and Present*, 54 (1972) and E. Fox Genovese 'The Many Faces of Moral Economy: A Contribution to a Debate', *Past and Present*, 58 (1973) were important contributions to the debate but see also J. Stevenson 'The Moral Economy of the English Crowd: Myth and Reality', in A Fletcher and J. Stevenson (eds) op. cit., pp. 218–38.

29 A detailed discussion of marketing by J. A. Chartres is in J. Thirsk (ed.) *The Agrarian History of England and Wales Vol. V, part 2 1640–1750*, Cambridge University Press, 1985, pp. 406–502.

30 J. Stevenson op. cit., p. 237.

31 The literature on food riots is extremely large: see J. Stevenson *Popular Disturbances in England 1700–1870*, Longman, 1979, pp. 99–112 for a general survey but also of value are A. Charlesworth (ed.) *An Atlas of Rural Protest in Britain 1548–1900*, Croom Helm, 1983, pp. 63–118, and R. B. Rose 'Eighteenth century Price Riots and Public Policy in England', *International Review of Social History*, 6 (1961), pp. 227–92. More detailed studies include W. J. Shelton *English Hunger & Industrial Disorders*, Macmillan, 1973 and D. E. Edwards 'Morals, Markets and the English Crowd in 1766', *Past and Present*, 104 (1984) on the 1760s; J. Stevenson 'Food Riots in England 1792–1818', in J. Stevenson and R. Quinault (eds) op. cit., pp. 33–74, R. Wells *Dearth and Distress in Yorkshire 1793–1802*, Borthwick Papers 52, York, 1977, A. Booth 'Food Riots in North-West England 1790–1801', *Past and Present*, 77 (1977), D. E. Williams 'Were 'Hunger' Rioters Really Hungry? Some Demographic Evidence', *Past and Present*, 71 (1976), J. Bohstedt *Riots and Community Politics in England and Wales 1790–1810*, Harvard University Press, 1983; A. J. Peacock *Bread or Blood*, Gollancz, 1965 on the 1816 riots.

32 J. W. Leopold 'The Levellers Revolt in Galloway in 1724', *Scottish Labour History Society Journal*, 14, 1980.

33 On protest in the Highlands and Wales see E. Richards 'Patterns of Highland Discontent 1790–1860' in J. Stevenson and R. Quinault (eds) op. cit., and *A History of the Highland Clearances*, 2 vols, Croom Helm, 1982, 1986. D. J. V.

Jones *Before Rebecca*, Allen Lane, 1973 considers popular protest between 1793 and 1835.

34 The issue of 'blacking' is best approached through E. P. Thompson *Whigs and Hunters*, Allen Lane, 1975.

35 The standard work on Rebecca is D. Williams *The Rebecca Riots*, first published 1955, reprinted University of Wales Press, 1986 but see also P. Molloy *And They Blessed Rebecca*, Gomer, 1983 and D. J. V. Jones *Rebecca's Children*, Oxford University Press, 1989.

36 For the 1816 riots see A. J. Peacock op. cit. and R. Brown *Change and Continuity in British Society 1800–1850*, Cambridge University Press, 1987, pp. 62–77.

37 E. Hobsbawm and G. Rudé *Captain Swing*, op. cit., is the most accessible study of the 1830 disturbances.

38 Luddism and trade unionism in the early nineteenth century will be examined in more detail in Chapter 12.

39 E. Hobsbawm *Primitive Rebels*, op. cit., pp. 110–11.

40 G. Rudé *Paris and London*, op. cit., p. 318.

41 J. Stevenson (ed.) *London in the Age of Reform*, Basil Blackwell, 1978 contains several important essays but see also G. Holmes 'The Sacheverell Riots', *Past and Present*, 72 (1976), pp. 55–85 and N. Rogers 'Popular Protest in Early Hanoverian London', *Past and Present*, 79 (1978), pp. 70–100.

42 In addition to the general works on Ireland cited in earlier chapters see S. Clark and J. S. Donnelly Jr (eds) *Irish Peasants: Violence and Political Unrest 1780–1914*, Gill & Macmillan, 1983 and the opening chapter of C. Townshend *Political Violence in Ireland*, Oxford University Press, 1983.

43 On Ireland in the 1790s and the 1798 Rising see Chapter 6 for the reactions of Pitt's government and Chapter 12 for the radical position.

12 The radical response 1790–1835

From a historical perspective, despite the obstacles, subordinate groups have tended to move towards greater freedom of expression and action, although this progress varies greatly from one circumstance to another. There were always some slaves who revolted; there were some women who sought greater development or self-determination. Most records of these actions are not preserved by the dominant culture, making it difficult for the subordinate group to find a supporting tradition and history. Within each subordinate group, there are tendencies for some members to imitate their dominants. . . . Some may try to treat their fellow subordinates as destructively as the dominants treat them. A few may develop enough of the qualities valued by the dominants to be partially accepted into their fellowship . . . conflict is inevitable. The important questions, then, become: Who defines the conflict? Who sets the terms? When is conflict overt or covert? On what issues is the conflict fought? Can anyone win? Is conflict 'bad', by definition? If not, what makes for productive or destructive conflict?[1]

INTRODUCTION

This long opening statement makes three important points: society is divided into subordinate and dominant groups; there is an inevitable conflict between these groups; and, that historically this conflict has always existed. Certain aspects of the relationship between dominant and subordinate groups in society have already been examined. This chapter will focus on the ways in which those in British society who lacked political rights, especially the right to vote and the right to use trade unions to safeguard their economic rights, sought to alter radically the balance of power between governors and governed in the period between the outbreak of the French Revolution and the mid-1830s.[2] Five main areas will be considered: the so-called 'revolutionary' decade of the 1790s; the revival of radicalism in the first decade of the nineteenth century; radicalism after 1815; trade unionism into the 1840s and women and radicalism.

THE NATURE OF RADICALISM

In the last chapter a distinction was drawn between traditional popular protest and radicalism. The former was largely a defensive response to economic and social change while radicalism was broadly concerned with a critical examination of the nature and composition of the existing political system and with how that system might be changed, if necessary by 'revolutionary' means. It is generally recognized by historians that there was a radical tradition which dated back to the mid-seventeenth century grounded in the notion of an Englishman's 'liberty'. This rested on the widely held belief that the Old Anglo-Saxon Constitution, overturned by the Norman invasion, had been restored in 1688. It showed remarkable vitality and was not replaced by cosmopolitan French ideas of the 'rights of man' which were absorbed within the older tradition. Much of this radicalism was motivated, as were its more traditional expressions, by concerns over the economy, labour issues and proletarianization, but there was also a growing realization by popular opinion that improved economic conditions necessitated a more democratic constitution and a state which was less in the grasp of the property-owning elite.

This politicization of radicalism, in terms of ideology and organization, was paralleled by the growing consciousness of the working population of its identity if not as a 'class' then as groups of workers with certain interests in common. Contemporaries among both the middle class and the labouring population recognized that, despite the diversity of working experience, it was difficult to deny the existence of a new 'working-class' presence. The question historians need to address is not whether it is possible to identify a 'working class' as such but whether the important differences within the labouring population, for example, between skilled and unskilled workers, men and women, were sufficient to prevent the emergence of either a coherent 'class consciousness' or whether there was enough in common among the labouring population to enable the development of a 'mass platform', an agenda for radical political change.

It has recently been pointed out by J. C. D. Clark that this view of the development of radicalism is flawed in certain respects.[3] First, historians, who may be critical of the 'Whig interpretation' of 'high' politics, seem to accept a 'Whig interpretation' of radicalism. The radicals of the 1790s seem to anticipate those of the 1810s and so on. Secondly, historians have recognized that radicalism emerged from a critique of eighteenth-century society but, Clark argues, this critique had its origins not in economics but theology. By restoring the importance of the Divine Right of kings and questioning the extent to which it had been replaced by the divine right of property owners and a preoccupation with the defence of property following the 1688 'Glorious Revolution', Clark maintains that radicals drew the structure of their arguments not from a materialist analysis of society but from a theological one. There was, he suggests, a logical connection between Dissent and Democracy.

THE 1790s

Reactions to revolution

In 1789 the fall of the Bastille foreshadowed the revolution in France. The reforming movement in England in the 1790s was not a failed 'French revolution' though there are parallels between the artisan movement in Britain and the sans-culotte movement in France in their conceptions of democracy, attitude to leadership, property, social morality, their idea of unity and suspicion of the 'respectable', their continuous expectation of betrayal and above all their feeling for equality and desire for universal brotherhood.[4]

Reactions to the revolution were mixed in Britain but many people were well disposed towards the upheaval. Some favoured change, believing it would be advantageous for France to move towards 'constitutional' monarchy, a view grounded in the 1688 Revolution and its impact on monarchy. Others believed it would lead to reform in England. This can be particularly seen in the case of Dissenters who found encouragement in the revolution for agitating against the Test and Corporation Acts in 1790.

The British believed themselves to be the freest people in Europe, thanks to the 1688 Revolution, and many foreigners flatteringly took the same view. It is not surprising that the opening stages of the revolution looked like a French attempt to copy Britain. William Pitt perceived political advantage to Britain because it weakened France's colonial position. He also believed that sooner or later France would be restored to harmony with 'freedom resulting from good order and good government', though this kind of praise for the revolution was more common from Charles James Fox and the more radical Whigs.

Intellectual debate

First, it is important to examine the intellectual debate on revolution which lasted from the English rejoicing at France's 'new dawn' in 1789 until late 1795 when Pitt's government introduced measures to stop the spread of radicalism by printed and spoken word. The starting point for the debate was a 'political sermon' given by the Unitarian minister Richard Price on 4 November 1789 in which he pointed to the intellectual fissures in the 1688–9 Revolution Settlement as part of the Dissenting agitation for repeal. Many opponents of Dissent feared that much more was involved than mere religion and party political opinion, expressed in the partisan literature produced between 1787 and 1790, tended to harden.

Edmund Burke's change of heart was instructive. He had absented himself from the bitterly fought parliamentary contests of 1787 and 1789 but on 2 March 1790, having heard Fox link repeal with the issue of the French Revolution, he intervened to vote against the Dissenters' third motion. Repeal was wrong, he argued in a speech which anticipated his *Reflections*, because the circumstances had changed; Fox and the Dissenters had become too influenced by the prevailing discussion on political rights in France.

Burke had begun to write on the revolution in October 1789 but was spurred on by Richard Price's sermon and by having heard or read of support for the revolution from Fox and Pitt. He came out publicly against the revolution in February 1790 and in November published his *Reflections on the Revolution in France*. It was an Anglican defence of the state and a denial of Price's contention that 'the people' had acquired important rights in 1688–9, especially the right to choose their own governors, the right to remove them for misconduct and the right to frame a government for themselves. Religion, not some vague contractual notion, was for Burke at the heart of civil society. The ideals which he celebrated were sectarian, the aristocratic concepts of paternalism, loyalty and the heredi-tary principle in which the great social institutions – the Church, the law, even the family – validated the aristocracy as the governing class and the protectors of traditional values.[5]

By fully describing a conservative viewpoint Burke established a back-ground which enabled others to articulate their own thoughts. Thomas Paine wrote the first part of *The Rights of Man* as a riposte to Burke's *Reflections* in three months and it was published in February 1791.[6] Though only one of the thirty-eight responses to Burke, *The Rights of Man* was without doubt the most influential, fusing the intellectual and abstract debate about the revolution with a new, and, from the government's point of view, worrying, practical political realism.

Thomas Paine

Paine put forward a simple populist message denouncing Burke's idea of society as an association between past and present generations and his view of the role of monarchy and aristocracy. His book animated its audience, initiating a new type of reading material and widening the reading public. By November 1792 *The Rights of Man* was, according to Benjamin Vaughan, as much a standard book in England as *Robinson Crusoe* and *The Pilgrim's Progress*. Accounts of sales vary but there is no doubt of its vast circulation. Part One sold 50,000 copies in 1791 at the price of three shillings and was reprinted when Part Two was published in April 1792, both parts selling for six pence. There was also no doubting the impact the book had on people's thinking. William Cobbett wrote his first political pamphlet in 1792 as a result of its attack on corruption.

Richard Carlile, though he did not read the book until the economic hardship of 1816 was led to consider political questions and he grounded his long and eventually successful attack on the legal limitations of freedom of speech on Paine's ideas. But the influence of *The Rights of Man* extended to those who had less spectacular political careers.

The book had a profound impact in the new political clubs and was often distributed in cheap editions, read aloud and debated. To his supporters Paine was both a political ideologist and an heroic figure. To his opponents he became a symbol of the excesses of revolution. He was frequently burned in effigy especially after the beginnings of terror in France at the end of 1792 and the first few months of 1793. In Nottingham, for example, Paine was ritualistically killed, stoned by ladies at a dinner and dance. Between 1792 and 1795 the circulation of Paine's work was one of the main reasons given for the passage of repressive legislation and for the arrests of those charged with high treason. From the Royal Proclamation against Seditious Writings in May 1792, to Paine's trial *in absentia* in December, the Report of the Committee of Secrecy, the suspension of Habeas Corpus, the treason trials and the passage of the Treasonable Practices Act, Parliament attempted to contain the intellectual fervour released by Paine's writings. Conservatives had no means of identifying a popular movement except in terms of conspiracy and treason. If a political activity was not a spontaneous outburst by a section of society which was, by definition, undisciplined, inarticulate and emotive, then it was necessarily disciplined by an externally imposed conspiratorial design. Treason and conspiracy were more acceptable concepts than that of a politically aware labouring population. Repression can be seen as a reassertion of hegemonic control and a denial, through the curtailing of certain intellectual exchanges and the categorization of Paine's design as 'evil' and ironically not worth serious attention, that the movement for political reform was an acceptable and alternative intellectual choice.

The debate was not confined to a dialogue between Burke and Paine but encompassed a whole sequence of works which depended for their meaning on each other, upon the specific historical environment and the audience they were aimed at. Literature and politics were enlisted in the same crusade as never before. Political advocacy set the pace and the fashion of every other kind of composition. Many of the authors knew each other and their work, which stimulated one another, has been seen as a collective political and literary enterprise. Paine, William Godwin and Mary Wollstonecraft produced a number of innovative and utopian proposals between 1791 and early 1793 – the establishment of a human welfare state, the withering away of the centralized state, an egalitarianism in inter-personal relationships to remove the subservience of employees to employers and women to men. But much of the debate was fought at a more humdrum and practical level. Thomas Spence's *Meridian Sun of Liberty* cost only one penny and was aimed at a different audience than

Burke's *Reflections* at three shillings and Godwin's *Political Justice* priced at a pound. The extent to which the debate reached different sections of the public was determined by the price written material was sold for.

Conservative response

Government was concerned that 'informed opinion' was in the hands of a closely knit circle for which the dinner table of the Unitarian publisher Joseph Johnson served as a focus: Joseph Priestley, Anna Barbauld, William Blake, Erasmus Darwin, William Wordsworth, William Godwin, Thomas Paine, John Horne Tooke, Mary Wollstonecraft and Thomas Beddoes. While those individuals were self-evidently addressing each other they represented no threat to established order. But the combination of rapidly spreading political organizations with a supply of radical writings to politicize the masses was another matter. Hence the build-up of a loyalist backlash in late 1792 with John Reeves and his Association for Preserving Liberty and Property against Republicans and Levellers commissioning and circulating popularly written anti-Jacobin pamphlets to ensure the loyalty of the labouring population. The Association maintained pressure on the radical publicists from one side while the government controlled radical publishing, processes helped by the patriotic reaction to the outbreak of war with France in 1793. John Thelwall, the leading radical populist of the 1790s, spoke of 'the massacre of opinion' and William Hazlitt wrote with only the slightest touch of mockery that

> In 1792 Paine was so great, or so popular an author, and so much read and admired, that the Government was obliged to suspend the constitution and go to war to counteract the effects of this popularity.

There was an important change of feeling that began with the mass distribution of *The Rights of Man* and which was exacerbated by the outbreak of war. With the publication of *Political Justice* in February 1793 the expansion of radical thinking came to an end. There were fewer pamphlets published and the new ones were less innovatory, repeating old ideas and trying to reassure a moderate audience rather than developing new theories. The objective of many radical thinkers was to attract and sustain the widest possible support for an anti-government platform. They ceased to be optimistic, extremist and impractical in their thinking. The campaign against radical intellectuals grew after 1795 and was fought in the newspapers and journals, in the cartoons of Gillray, and in the proliferation of 'anti-Jacobin' novels. By 1800, with European societies destabilized and Burke's fears apparently realized, the boldness of the radical vision of communicating with a wider audience in a common language had been established. In practical terms, however, the reforming movement achieved little.

Demands for reform

Parallel to the intellectual desire was the practical possibility of creating a Jerusalem from below and realizing the perfectibility of man. This had its expression in the various movements for political reform of which the Corresponding Societies became the most important. British reformers of all shades of opinion were galvanized into action by the events in France. The campaign for the repeal of the Test and Corporation Acts was stimulated by events across the Channel, the moribund Society for Constitutional Information (SCI), founded in 1780, began to disseminate radical propaganda and in April 1792 some liberal Whig reformers formed the Society of the Friends of the People to campaign for parliamentary reform.

The French Revolution revived the activities of veteran reformers like Richard Price, Christopher Wvyill and John Cartwright and stimulated existing middle-class reform societies like SCI. It also led to the creation of new radical groups, composed of artisans and working men, with more ambitious aims, which rapidly diverged from the more 'respectable' and acceptable forms of agitation associated with earlier movements. By July 1791 tensions in British society over the French Revolution were beginning to emerge. Conflict between reformers and loyalists surfaced and in certain places, like Birmingham, erupted into violence. The bitterness of political divisions was, contemporaries believed, a consequence of the lengthening shadow of the French Revolution, its growing extremism and the Paineite radical critique.

The French Revolution may have aroused people to political action and provided them with an ideology through which to redress their grievances but it was the economic conditions in the first half of the 1790s which have been seen by some historians as the major recruiting ground for the radical cause. The disturbed state of Europe in 1792–3 led to an economic depression in Britain with widespread unemployment and lower wages. War in 1793 seriously interrupted trade and placed an increasing tax burden on the middling and lower orders. Economic distress reached critical proportions in 1795–6 following harvest failure in 1794, pushing up food prices at a time when the labouring population was already faced with higher taxation and lower wages. It is, however, important not to see the reforming movement simply in terms of a response to economic conditions. What was different about the Corresponding movement was that it crossed the threshold from traditional economic grievances to a more fundamental political critique.

Corresponding Societies

During the winter of 1791–2 popular radical societies emerged of which the London Corresponding Society (LCS) was the most important. Founded in January 1792 by a small group led by the shoemaker Thomas Hardy, who became both secretary and treasurer, membership was open to all who paid a penny at each weekly meeting. Though formed to discuss the poverty faced by many of the labouring population and the high prices of the day, the LCS quickly adopted a political programme for remedying their grievances: universal manhood suffrage, annual parliaments and redistribution of rotten boroughs to the large towns. The LCS spread rapidly across London and developed a sophisticated organizational structure of divisions, district committees and general committee.

Two features impressed the opponents of the LCS: its size and its social composition. It is difficult to estimate size with complete accuracy and the 5,000 members claimed by the LCS itself included occasional attenders. By late 1792 about 650 people regularly attended its meetings. This fluctuated between 250 and 1,000 in the next eighteen months before reaching its peak in the second half of 1795. Despite government repression the LCS attracted 1,500 members and the total active membership was perhaps twice this. By the spring of 1796 this had fallen to about 2,000, by the end of the year to 1,000, to about 600 in 1797 and to 400 active members before its enforced dissolution in 1798. LCS membership was confined to a very small proportion of London's working population. To call the LCS a 'working-class' organization neglects the extent to which its membership was made up of individuals from the 'middling' and professional classes as well as artisans and tradesmen. An analysis of 347 activists shows that only half were artisans and the rest were medical men, lawyers, booksellers, clerks, shopkeepers and printers. Though the LCS could fairly claim to speak with a collective voice for London's dispossessed artisans, its belief that it spoke more generally for the dispossessed throughout the nation was more rhetorical. There is no evidence that it ever had much appeal to unskilled labourers or the very poor.

Provincial radical societies had begun to spring up before the LCS was founded. The Sheffield Society for Constitutional Information was formed in late 1791 against the background of antagonism between artisans in the cutlery trade and their masters. Within a few months it had grown from a few members to 2,500 members by mid-1792, though active members accounted for only 600 people. In the autumn of 1792 the Sheffield SCI could bring 5–6,000 people on to the streets to celebrate the French victory at Valmy and a similar number in February 1794 to pass resolutions in favour of peace abroad and liberty at home. Sheffield radicalism seems to have adopted little more than a gesture towards deferential politics. There was an abortive attempt to deal with the Whig Friends of the People and there was frequent impatience with the London radicals in both the LCS and SCI.

Sheffield radicalism had a missionary verve which resulted in the reform argument being taken out into the surrounding villages, besides stimulating the development of radical societies in towns like Leeds, Nottingham, Derby and Stockport. Joseph Gales issued political propaganda through the Sheffield Register and the journal *The Patriot*, a process paralleled in Manchester, Norwich and Leicester. The community in Sheffield showed a sense of self-identification that was unusual in the 1790s. This was the result largely of the social structure of the town where there was a significant degree of antagonism between employers and employees. There were few gentry in the area and though Dissent was widespread it had not led to a distinct Dissenting elite as, for example, in Norwich.

During 1792 the number of societies mushroomed, some of them influenced by the older societies, others by the LCS and the Sheffield SCI. Regional differences became more obvious. Manchester, with its nascent factory proletariat, merchants, entrepreneurs and expanding population, stood at the other end of the scale to Sheffield. It had been rigidly Tory since the 1750s and in the Test Act agitation between 1787 and 1790 a strong Church and State club had entrenched itself. This may account for the slow initial development of the Manchester Constitutional Society founded by Thomas Walker as early as October 1790. Walker, a cotton merchant, and Thomas Cooper, a barrister, were its leading members and they modelled themselves and their society on older reformers like Priestley and on the London SCI. It catered for the emergent middle classes, met once a month and for a year published the *Manchester Herald* weekly. The increase in radical activity in 1792 led to the establishment of the Patriotic Society in May and the Reformation Society in June which became foci for artisans, tradesmen and a few labourers.

In Norwich the radical cause developed along similar lines. A Revolution Society was established in 1788, was dominated by middle-class Dissenters, merchants and tradesmen and gave a lead to the reform movement. It rivalled Sheffield as *the* pacemaker of English Jacobinism. The textile industry sustained artisans of a particularly independent temper and Norwich's Dissent was rooted in a craggy, though surprisingly liberal, tradition. By 1792 forty tavern clubs of shoemakers, weavers and shopkeepers had developed, comprising some 2,000 members. The Norwich organization spread over the area from Yarmouth to King's Lynn, Wisbech and Lowestoft. In marked contrast to Manchester the alliance between the different types of radical society succeeded.

Radical societies developed throughout Britain during 1792 though many had small memberships and disbanded during the powerful conservative reaction in 1793. Birmingham, for example, had a large artisan population but remained quiet. The moribund Constitutional Society led by Priestley was too moderate for men like John Harrison, a Sheffield razor maker, who founded the Birmingham SCI in late 1792 and established links with the LCS. Neither moderate nor radical reformers could achieve political dominance and by 1795 Birmingham radicalism had withered. A similar situation existed in Leicester. Some major provincial centres like Plymouth, Portsmouth, Bristol, Hull and Liverpool could not sustain radical societies at all.

The remarkable feature of this period was not really the growth of organized societies, which were uneven geographically and socially, but the unprecedented diffusion of political ideas, often related directly to the specific local experience. Without an awareness of the wide and deep penetration of ideology and its effects on a minority of the population, which could perhaps at any time of crisis turn into a majority, the apparatus of intimidation and the recurrent explosions of 'loyalty' are meaningless hysteria.

Reform: was it Jacobin?

Was the reform movement 'Jacobin' in its viewpoint? Relatively few radicals were prepared to adopt Paineite principles fully and emphasis was placed on parliamentary reform rather than on the economic and social programme outlined by Paine in the second part of *The Rights of Man*. Radicals were anxious to avoid charges of social and economic levelling, accepted that a degree of inequality was natural and inevitable and recognized that any overt assault on monarchy and aristocracy would alienate the 'respectable' in society for whom order and property were important. Many radicals believed that social and economic injustice was the result of an unjust political system and that parliamentary reform would led to a more just system. The radicals of the 1790s adopted the political platform put forward by earlier reformers, especially that advocated by the Westminster Association of 1780. They were fundamentally 'constitutionalist' but though committed to a radical platform, the vast majority were not republicans like Paine. The revolution provided an impetus and an energy for the British popular movements and little else.

The republicanism and increasing violence of the French Revolution after mid-1792 alienated large sections of British society. For example, Samuel Romilly, the advocate of legal reform, was still looking to France in May 1792 but after the September 'massacres' this ceased. Correspondence between the British Revolution clubs and provincial Jacobin clubs seems to have ended because of the recognition that the doctrines which were gaining currency in France were not those that the Revolution clubs stood for. The only thing which British Jacobins could agree upon in terms of final aims was that a radical reform of Parliament was necessary.

Organization

How did the radical societies attempt to achieve their aims? The organized weekly meetings and the dissemination of printed political propaganda provided the focus for their activities. They corresponded regularly with each other and with groups in France. But their attempt to reach a mass audience remained at the level of political education and consciousness-raising. There was also some recognition of the need for displays of unity and demonstrations of mass support which would put pressure on the governing elite. There was, however, no nationwide petitioning campaign: there were only 36 petitions in support of Charles Grey's motion on parliamentary reform in 1793, 24 of which were from Scotland and none from an English county and they failed to demonstrate any mass overwhelming support for radical change. Some radicals were prepared to urge the calling of a 'National Convention', an 'anti-Parliament' representing the true wishes of the people unlike the corrupt Parliament at Westminster. This too had its origins in radical proposals put forward in the 1770s. The calling of a National Convention in December 1792 when 160 delegates representing 80 Scottish radical societies met in Edinburgh aimed to unite reformers behind an agreed radical programme. This was a significant innovation but the reformers seriously overestimated their degree of mass support and dangerously underestimated the fears it would arouse in the authorities. The Convention was extended to include English delegates but difference between moderate and radical delegates and its commitment to parliamentary reform, its adoption of French revolutionary procedures and its uncompromising defiance of established authority was alarming and it was closed on 6 December.

Radical tactics were very restrained and the reformers used many of the same tactics as earlier reformers in their attempts to achieve political reform. There was a failure to rally the bulk of the labouring population behind parliamentary reform and few radical leaders appreciated the power of organized labour. Some radicals did try to whip up food rioters in Sheffield in 1795 to protest against the war and demand parliamentary reform and similar tactics were used in the north-west in 1800, but these were isolated examples and the radicals made no attempt to co-ordinate popular riots. Most radical leaders, with their middle-class background, were committed to non-violent action. Only a small minority was prepared to conduct an underground conspiratorial movement in which violence, revolution and treason were integral parts. When the governing class refused to concede reform, resorting to repression and persecution, most radicals lost heart or moderated their demands.

Reaction

The attack on popular radicalism in the first half of the 1790s took the form of a three-pronged attack: an attack on its ideology, a populist and loyalist reaction and a legislative attack by Pitt's government.[7] The reform movement collapsed not simply because of repressive actions but because the opponents of reform developed an intellectual and moral defence of the existing social and political system that was convincing not just to those with property but to large sections of British society.

Conservative ideology in the 1790s, even without the elegant defence by Edmund Burke, possessed considerable appeal, endurance and intellectual power. A tradition of firm resistance to constitutional change in Britain had been apparent in the decades leading up to the revolution and events in France, especially after 1791, reinforced this tradition. Radicals at home were seen in the same light as revolutionaries abroad. It did not prove difficult to persuade the public in general that the reforms suggested by the British Jacobins would destroy the established order as the revolutionaries had done in France. French anarchy was contrasted unfavourably with British stability and prosperity.

It was relatively easy for conservative apologists and propagandists to appeal on an emotional level to British hatred of France and fear of radical change. In addition to this there was a more sophisticated intellectual response contrasting the stability of the mixed constitution with the anarchy and clamour of 'mob' rule and democracy. Anti-radical propaganda, subsidized by the loyalist associations, by government and by private individuals, took many forms: pamphlets and tracts like the Cheap Repository Tracts, half of which were written by Hannah More, between 1795 and 1798; pro-government newspapers like the *Sun*, the *True Briton* and the *Oracle*; journals like the *Anti-Jacobin* (1797–8) and its successor the *Anti-Jacobin Review and Magazine*, a monthly which lasted until 1821; political caricatures and cartoons by artists like Isaac Cruickshanks, James Gillray and Thomas Rowlandson; and local newspapers like the *Manchester Mercury* and the *Newcastle Courant*. This concerted propaganda campaign was outstandingly successful and convinced the majority of English people for whom, modern research has demonstrated, living through the French Revolution was a disaster.

Loyalist associations

Loyalist conservative associations emerged initially as a response to the Dissenter campaign for repeal of the Test and Corporation Acts but the number of Church and King clubs was given a major boost by the revolution especially the Royal Proclamation against seditious writings on 21 May 1792. By September 1792 some 386 loyal addresses had been received by the king and in November John Reeves formed the first loyalist Association for the Preservation of Liberty and Property against Republicans and Levellers (APLP) in London. By the end of 1793 the total number of APLPs may have been as high as 2,000 making them the largest political organization in the country. They spread from London first into the neighbouring counties, then to the west, Midlands and finally the north. Active membership was largely confined to men of property, though they were able to enlist support from across society. They have been seen, by Harold Perkin among others, as a far more successful 'working-class' organization than the radical societies.

Loyalist associations adopted the organization and some of the methods of the reformers. They produced and disseminated a great deal of printed propaganda but were not content to rely upon persuasion, resorting to intimidation and persecution in order to defeat their opponents. Many associations had a short life, losing impetus after local radicals had been defeated. The setting up of the Volunteers, authorized by Pitt in March 1794, was largely based on existing loyalist associations and in 1804 they were 450,000 strong. Calls for loyalty and patriotism proved far more powerful with the bulk of the population than demands for radical change.

Government repression

Powerful though the loyalist movement was, Pitt was unwilling to take any chances and used the full powers of the Establishment to destroy the radicals, inaugurating what has been called Pitt's 'Reign of Terror'. The Home Office monitored the activities of the radical societies using spies and informers as well as more conventional methods like tampering with letters, receiving reports from local sources, watching the activities of radicals abroad and infiltrating radical groups.

The government was convinced that it faced a revolutionary conspiracy, a view reinforced by the intelligence received from local magistrates and spies, and consequently believed it was justified in taking firm action. After the success of the Scottish treason trials in 1793–4, Pitt and Dundas decided to move against English radicals. Forty-one men, including Hardy, were arrested in late 1794 and charged with high treason but after he, Horne Tooke and John Thelwall were acquitted further trials were abandoned. The administration had little further success with treason trials during the remainder of the decade but had more success with those for publishing seditious libels. There were less than 200 convictions during the 1790s and whether this constitutes a government-inspired reign of terror is open to debate.

Parliament was prepared to pass legislation in support of the government though, in practice, this often turned out to be far less effective than anticipated. Habeas Corpus was suspended from May 1794 to July 1795 and April 1798 to March 1801 but only a few were imprisoned without trial. The Two Acts of 1795 – the Treasonable Practices Act and the Seditious Meetings Act – proved less than effective weapons despite the wide powers they gave to central and local government. The Treasonable Practices Act was designed to intimidate and in fact no radical was prosecuted under it. The Seditious Meetings Act failed to prevent the increasing number of meetings organized by the LCS. There was only one prosecution under a 1797 Act, rushed through Parliament following the naval mutiny, making it a capital offence to incite mutiny in the armed forces. The banning of the leading radical societies by law in 1799 was unnecessary, largely because they were already in a state of collapse. The Combination Acts of 1799 and 1800, which banned combinations of workers, completed the legislative armoury of repression.

Government legislation was infrequently used but it remained as a threat hanging over radicals and limiting their freedom of action. Its effect was to intimidate and harass, destroying the effective leadership of the radical societies, silencing the ablest propagandists and frightening ordinary radicals into abandoning the reform movement. But the collapse of the radical movement was not simply a matter of repression by government or magistrates. War revived a latent deep-seated patriotism among the bulk of the population for whom radicalism was of only tangential importance.

Wales in the 1790s

Richard Price and David Williams were individuals of international reputation and, although London based, they linked Wales with international events. Price was formally asked to advise the new American republic on finance and Williams was invited to France to advise on its new constitution. The impact of Price's sermon on Wales is difficult to assess. It is likely that few Welsh people read it at first hand, despite the sermon's wide circulation, since no Welsh translation was made. David Williams regarded himself as a teacher of politics and in 1790 published *Observations on the Constitution* though his later response to events in France was more critical. Both writers had more impact outside Wales than inside and the reaction to the revolution was as much a response to economic and social conditions as to new systems of ideas.

The 1790s were difficult years for Wales.[8] There was endemic poverty in the rural areas. There was a radical tradition of Dissent and this had links with the Welsh in America who had been driven to emigrate because of religious persecution. Added to this was a dimension associated with the legend of Madoc, a twelfth-century prince, whose claims to have discovered America were stressed. He epitomized the notion of political freedom and gave legitimacy to Welsh settlement there. Correspondence linked Wales with events in America and ideas of civil equality were widely disseminated throughout Wales in books and pamphlets.

Morgan John Rhys had a more direct impact on Wales because he spent most of his working life there and wrote and preached in Welsh. He was less concerned with ideas and organizations than Price and Williams but sought practical solutions to problems. He founded Sunday schools while Williams wrote an *Essay on Education*. He wrote against the slave trade and was a powerful supporter of the French Revolution seeing it as the judgement of God and overthrowal just retribution for tyrannical power. His *Y Cylchgrawn Cymraeg* was the first periodical of an emergent Welsh radical tradition; five issues appeared in 1793. Rhys was certainly the first to realize the importance of a free press for informing opinion in Wales. But his interpretation of the reforming problem was too narrow – he believed it was the Word of God which set people free and so acted accordingly – and he was quickly disappointed by events in France. As a result he emigrated to America in 1794 to set up a community, Beulah, as a refuge for radicals and Dissenters from government repression.

Political debate in Wales continued through a number of sporadically published periodicals. Thomas Evans' *Trysorfa Gymmysgedig* put forward the ideas of Joseph Priestley, and gave a great deal of publicity to the treason trials which began in 1794, but it lasted for only three issues. David Davies' *Geirgrawn* ran to nine issues in 1796 and was intended to revive the cause of reform after the treason trials. John Jones rendered Paine's ideas into Welsh in the pamphlet *Seren Tan Gwmwl* in which he aired grievances and criticized indolent Welsh MPs, but also condemned the violence against magistrates which had occurred in parts of Wales. The London Welsh societies, especially the Gwyneddigion, played a significant role in supporting the political debate in these periodicals and as a result they suffered government repression after 1794.

Political clubs were less evident in Wales than in England and Scotland. The SCI was particularly active in North Wales and Morgan John Rhys founded a society for distributing bibles to France in 1791. He also formed branches of the LCS and SCI which he addressed on subjects like parliamentary reform, the abolition of class privilege and the reduction of taxation. An offshoot of the LCS existed in Cardiff, a vigorous Jacobin club was said to exist in Brecon and even Bala boasted some Jacobins. However, these were extensions of English clubs and it is not known whether any appeal was made through the medium of Welsh.

Loyalist propaganda stemmed from the gentry and especially the clergy. The Church of England was seen as the only bulwark against atheism and revolution and in 1792 loyalist associations spread through both counties and towns. Pamphlets like Hannah More's *Village Politics* were translated into Welsh and there were widespread demonstrations of loyalty. Radical societies and publications were suppressed and the French who landed at Fishguard in 1797 were not greeted by a spontaneous Jacobin rising, though their landing did provoke a witch-hunt against local radicals. Welsh Jacobinism was a brief phenomenon, a combination of political ideals and the fantasy of Madoc, but it left a living tradition particularly in the textile towns and villages of mid-Wales, in the hinterland of Carmarthen and, above all, on the coalfields of South Wales.

Scotland in the 1790s

The French Revolution certainly helped stimulate political awareness in Scotland.[9] In 1782 there were eight Scottish newspapers: by 1790 there were twenty-seven and more were established in 1791–2. In July 1792 the first Society of Friends of the People in Scotland met in Edinburgh and they quickly spread all over Scotland. These societies were led by radical lairds and lawyers but, with their low subscription, they had more in common with the LCS than with the London Friends of the People. Dundas, whose grip on Scottish political life was reinforced by events in France, shared the general concern among the propertied that a populist movement, which encouraged political mobilization of the lower orders, might lead to effective demands for social and political reform. The official government line hardened into denouncing anyone who wanted reform in any form as a 'Leveller', 'Republican' or 'French Democrat'.

The first National Convention of the Friends of the People in Scotland was held in 1792. Thomas Muir, an Edinburgh advocate, was a prominent member and insisted on reading an address from the Society of United Irishmen, which many considered too violent. Despite the traditional composition and objective of the Convention, from January 1793 a series of sedition trials designed to discredit and intimidate the reform movement occurred. Muir was sentenced to fourteen years' transportation. The increasing violence of the revolution abroad resulted in the original leadership of the Scottish societies retreating towards conformity as in England and Wales. In 1792 its leaders were merchants, lawyers, manufacturers and teachers but by late 1793 skilled artisans, especially weavers, moved to the forefront.

The government systematically persecuted the Friends of the People and warnings of social subversion became a self-fulfilling prophecy. In the industrial towns of west Scotland and in the commercial towns of the east it was the skilled artisans who resisted the government's political offensive and formed the much more militant United Scotsmen. But there was no political mobilization in Scotland as there was in Ireland and the French government persistently deluded itself into believing that Scotland, like Ireland, was eager to shake off the English yoke. In 1799 the United Scotsmen were finally banned. In reality, however, Scotland did not have a politically-motivated opposition to the government during this period.

The revolutionary 1790s?

The leadership of the radical societies of the early 1790s had always renounced any desire to achieve their objectives by force. Nearly all of the radical theorists were cautious about suggesting the violent overthrow of the state. John Thelwall, for example, thought that tyrannical government might result in revolution but always insisted that he wanted to see a gradual transformation of the Establishment. William Godwin utterly rejected violence as the means of achieving political change. Thomas Paine and Thomas Spence were somewhat equivocal, though they never advised the people to take up arms. However, the government remained convinced that there was a genuine threat of revolution, a view buttressed by the mass of evidence given by witnesses to the parliamentary Committees of Secrecy in 1794, 1799, 1801 and 1812.

How valid were the government's beliefs? Much of the evidence given to the parliamentary committees was highly suspect. Spies and informers had a vested interest in exaggerating the extent of the revolutionary threat. Local magistrates often panicked at the first signs of political or social protest, seeing revolution when there was only 'distress'. There is also the problem of trying to examine what was essentially a 'secret' movement: revolutionaries tended to avoid publicity and written records which could, if discovered, be used against them. Even when there is more reliable evidence of revolutionary conspiracies historians have to decide whether they were serious political projects, reflecting a profound disenchantment with contemporary society and its values, or merely the fantasies of deluded individuals or fanatics. Historians tend to fall into three main groups in relation to the extent of the revolutionary threat.[10] Some historians (Veitch, Cannon and Thomis and Holt) have played down the significance of the threat. Other historians (Thompson, Wells), usually from a left-wing perspective, see revolutionary groups as having wider support. Thirdly, there are those (Dinwiddy, Goodwin, Stevenson) who accept the existence of a revolutionary underground, but doubt the degree of its popular support. It is unlikely that there will ever be complete agreement among historians on the issue.

United Irishmen

The government certainly exaggerated the revolutionary threat as a means of justifying its repressive actions but there certainly was domestic conspiracy and foreign undercover activity during this period. Perhaps the most serious revolutionary threat came from the linkage of the conspiratorial wing of the British radical movement from the mid-1790s with the United Irishmen and through them with France. The United Irishmen were established in Belfast in October 1791 by Wolfe Tone, William Brennan and Samuel Neilson and sought to unite both Catholics and Protestants in a campaign for political and social freedom. A society was set up in Dublin a month later but the movement had difficulty in agreeing on a political programme or in enlisting support across the religious divide. Universal manhood suffrage, for example, worried many Protestants in a country where Catholics were in the majority. Initially the United Irishmen sought to achieve their objectives through persuasion and by enlisting mass support but many Catholics put their faith in the Catholic Committee and in the Defender organizations while Protestants responded by establishing Orange lodges.

The United Irishmen were neither republican nor committed to independence from Britain until the mid-1790s when the intransigence of the British government and the willingness of the French to exploit the smouldering social tensions drove the society into the hands of a militant, republican minority led by Arthur O'Connor and Lord Edward Fitzgerald. Between 1796 and 1798 the French sent five naval expeditions to Ireland but lack of co-ordination between Irish revolutionaries and the French Directory, divisions within the militant United Irishmen leadership, lack of coherent strategy and the vigilance of the authorities resulted in complete failure. The 1798 rebellion was largely a popular rising by desperate Catholics determined to protect themselves against the violence of the Orange lodges, and it was bloodily crushed before a small French force made its appearance.

The United Irishmen went into steep decline after 1798. Wolfe Tone and Fitzgerald were dead. Other leaders, like O'Connor, were arrested but on admission of guilt were allowed to go into exile. The government was, as a result, able to prove the existence of a widespread conspiracy without having to bring its informers and spies to court. The French were unwilling to mount any further naval expeditions and the United Irishmen, still worried about the position of Catholics, were unable to secure significant Protestant support; with its leaders in exile, it became increasingly ineffective. The desperation of the United Irishmen can be illustrated by the abortive attack on Dublin Castle by plotters led by Robert Emmet in July 1803. His expectation that the rest of the country would rise was ill-conceived and verged on fantasy.

The United Irishmen were aware that successful revolution in Ireland depended on events elsewhere. French military support was one means of putting pressure on the British government. A successful insurrection on the mainland was another way of gaining concessions for Ireland. In 1796 the United Irishmen had established an underground organization in Britain, attracting support especially in Lancashire, the poorer areas of London and central Scotland. Two United Irish leaders, O'Connor and Rev. James O'Coigley, were active in England in 1797 but in early 1798 the government acted swiftly and effectively against the uncoordinated revolutionary associations, arresting their leadership. O'Coigley was executed for treason. There was no English insurrection at the time of the 1798 Irish rebellion, even though there was some activity by the United Englishmen in London.

The collapse of the Irish rebellion led to many United Irishmen fleeing the country. Some reached London and were soon involved in further conspiracies. By late 1799 there were, according to evidence to the parliamentary Secrets Committee, twenty active United Englishmen divisions in London and similar groups elsewhere. But they lacked co-ordination, strategy and energy and feared, with justification, that many of their groups had been penetrated by government spies. The remnants of these revolutionary organizations revived in 1801–2 in south Lancashire, west Yorkshire, the north-west and London under the impetus of war-weariness, high food prices and economic depression. Government action did not discourage an armed insurrection planned in London by Colonel Despard, an aggrieved Irish officer, in late 1802. Before the full extent of the plot was known the government acted, arresting Despard and his colleagues. Their execution in February 1803 effectively destroyed Anglo-Irish Jacobinism and eroded whatever support there was for violent revolution in England.

Legacies of insurrectionary politics

Certain legacies of this period of insurrectionary politics have been identified.[11] First, it laid the foundations for an Anglo-Irish dimension to radical politics. In both the British and Irish situations there was 'alienation': in Britain this generated forms of class consciousness, in Ireland an increasing sense of nationalism. But the enemy in both cases remained the same: the British system of unreformed, unrepresentative government that denied Catholic emancipation and maintained the privileges of a landed elite against the interests of an increasingly pauperized majority. The Anglo-Irish dimension was reflected in the emancipation crisis of the 1820s, the reform agitation of 1831–2 and especially in the Chartist period. Secondly, government perception placed great emphasis on the potential of revolutionary minorities. Finally, there was no absolute divide between constitutionalists and revolutionaries. The view an individual took depended more perhaps on circumstances than principle. The insurrectionaries of 1797–8 and 1801–2 may have been active as constitutionalists in 1793–5, supported the petitioning movement of 1801 before reverting to insurrection again when this failed. Repression, loyalist intimidation, a war-engendered sense of patriotism and conservative propaganda cut off some constitutional methods of protest. The revolutionary option was all that was open to those who sought change until circumstances were again conducive to open mass movements.

The revolutionary activities of the United Englishmen have been treated separately by some historians to the naval mutinies of 1797, the disorders of 1799–1801, the 'Black Lamp' disturbances of 1801–2 and the Luddite disorders of 1811–13. For these historians the motivation was harsh economic conditions. E. P. Thompson and Roger Wells have argued that on each occasion there was a very real threat of insurrection. In general it seems that the links between political radicalism and economic distress were tenuous and that radical activists did not develop, at this time, any effective strategies for capitalizing on the network of trade societies or the conditions of the labouring population. It does, however, seem difficult to compartmentalize popular activities into those that were purely economic and those that were political.

Mutiny 1797

The alarming growth of disaffection in the Royal Navy, Britain's first line of defence against France, worried government more than any other radical threat during the war years. Inflation in the early 1790s undermined the already low wages of sailors but it was actual conditions on board ship which precipitated mutiny. Bad conditions were not in themselves sufficient explanation for the events of 1797 and there was a degree of political motivation. A significant minority of sailors, some 15,000 out of 114,000 men, were Irish quota men of which many were former United Irishmen pressed into service as a means of repression. Cells of United Irishmen in the Channel fleet sent delegates to incite Irish seamen at the Nore. Mutinies, it was believed, would improve the chances of a French invasion of Ireland.

In April 1797 the Channel fleet at Spithead refused to sail until its grievances had been remedied and in May the North Sea fleet at the Nore followed suit. Concessions swiftly ended the first mutiny but demands at the Nore were greater and the sailors better organized. Two delegates were elected from each ship to a central committee headed by Richard Parker and there was talk of taking the fleet to France if demands were not met. The government acted more firmly in this case and their offer of concessions divided the mutineers. By June the mutiny was over and the authorities executed thirty-six of the leaders, including Parker.

The mutiny shook Pitt's government in two ways. First, it clearly demonstrated the vulnerability of the country. Secondly, there was an intensely felt fear that Jacobin instigators had incited the seamen. Though there is evidence for the activities of United Irishmen and the organization of the seamen at the Nore reflected the influence of the radical societies, there is little doubt that for the vast majority of sailors the mutiny was over conditions and pay and that once concessions had been achieved support for further action quickly collapsed.

1800–15

The 'Black Lamp'

Evidence of a revolutionary dimension for the 'Black Lamp' agitation in West Yorkshire in 1801–2 is also slim. E. P. Thompson argues that while genuine economic grievances lay behind the actions of woollen workers, remnants of the United Englishmen in the area exploited the situation for political purposes. Unfortunately much of his case is based on the reports of a government agent who was subsequently dismissed for sending in alarmist reports. There is little evidence that the nocturnal meetings were concerned with political conspiracy rather than the economic interests of the workers. In both the 1797 mutinies and the 'Black Lamp' agitation it is unlikely that economic motivation was in itself sufficient justification for agitation. Industrial protests and political agitation were often closely associated and could feed on the same grievances.

There is little doubt that an underground revolutionary tradition existed in the early nineteenth century but that, after the collapse of the Despard conspiracy and the 'Black Lamp' agitation, it ceased to play any significant role for at least a decade. Thompson maintains that it was simply driven underground by government repression and erupted again in the Luddite agitation of 1811–13. It is the size, not the existence, of the revolutionary threat that is in question. Thompson and his supporters seem to exaggerate the scale and effectiveness of the revolutionary underground and the degree of support it had among industrial workers. Successive governments had little difficulty, despite the propaganda and the rhetoric, in containing the insurrectionary threat.

Luddism

Luddism has, like the mutinies and 'Black Lamp', been characterized either as a 'quasi-insurrectionary movement' or as an agitation about genuine economic grievances and distress.[12] The difficulty historians face with the Luddite disturbances of 1811–13 is that their peak coincided with the middle-class agitation against the Orders in Council and the most severe food crisis of the war. Government was prepared to capitalize upon this situation in their belief that there was a deep-laid revolutionary conspiracy.

There is little disagreement about the economic causes of the protests in Nottinghamshire, south Lancashire and Yorkshire. Low wages, high rents for frames or looms, the employment of semi-skilled labour on lower wages all contributed to the Luddism of Nottinghamshire and Lancashire. Only in west Yorkshire did the skilled croppers fear the spread of the new technology, the gig mill and the shearing frame. In each area workers' organizations had failed to achieve improved conditions by the conventional means of petitions to Parliament. Parliament had also failed to utilize paternalistic legislation to protect the workers' position. Physical attacks and intimidation were the last resort of men who had exhausted traditional means of effecting change. The protests of 1811–13 were complex and related to changing economic conditions and attacks on traditional living standards. Luddism was far more than hostility to powered machinery.

The 'revolutionary' view of Luddism owes much to the alarmist reports of local magistrates and sources tainted by being supplied to government by spies and informers. Much of the evidence for arms and drilling was based on hearsay or rumour. But arms were occasionally used, mills were attacked and machinery destroyed. The disturbed state of localities in which Luddism occurred encouraged individuals and groups, who had little to do with textile workers, to enrich themselves through armed robbery. The Luddites may have been well organized and had substantial local support but there was no plot to overturn the existing constitution.

E. P. Thompson accepts that Luddism in Nottinghamshire was primarily an industrial dispute motivated by economic grievances but insists that in

Lancashire and Yorkshire a revolutionary underground was active which aimed at political subversion in the manner of the 'Black Lamp' and the Despard conspiracy. Though the scale, effectiveness and extent of support for the revolutionary dimension may have been exaggerated by Thompson and his supporters, they have highlighted the problem of drawing a stark distinction between industrial protest and political agitation. Manchester weavers, for example, unsuccessfully petitioned Parliament in 1811 for redress of their grievances. In a printed address in October 1811 they pointed out the connection between the legislature's refusal to act and the need for a radical reform of Parliament. In the Manchester and Bolton areas there is evidence for political committees, arming and nocturnal drilling and secret oaths in 1812 but these were the result of frustration at the failure of more traditional approaches. It is no longer possible to accept that Luddism, the 'Black Lamp' and the 1797 mutinies were without a political dimension.

Anti-war groups

The war with France had always been opposed by some individuals, despite the patriotism of the majority. For some it was a matter of principle: to many Dissenters and liberals it offended Christian principles, justice and reason. Others opposed it on the more pragmatic grounds of waste and inefficiency. Great resentment was caused by new taxes, vast loans and the massive expansion of the military and naval establishment. The 'Friends of Peace' organized a sophisticated extra-parliamentary movement which drew attention to the costs of the war. Vigorous protest against the war was focused in the manufacturing districts of the north and Midlands and was co-ordinated by leading Dissenting manufacturers including William Roscoe of Liverpool, Josiah Wedgwood of the Potteries, William Strutt of Derby, Ebenezer Rhodes of Sheffield and John Coltman of Leicester. Their motivation may have been as much one of economics as of principle. In 1807–8 they waged a campaign against the Orders in Council but failed to influence government policy. In 1812 another massive protest campaign, largely co-ordinated by Henry Brougham, brought petitions signed by 50,000 people and led to the ending of the Orders. Success was the result of the co-operation displayed by the most important manufacturing regions in England.

There was also considerable criticism of the government's handling of the war and particularly the corruption of some of its agents. This enabled the opposition inside Parliament and extra-parliamentary groups to blame not only individual ministers but the political system itself. The revival of demands for parliamentary reform was undoubtedly stimulated by popular concern about military defeat and government corruption.

Burdettite radicalism

The most prominent advocates of parliamentary reform towards the end of the French wars were Sir Francis Burdett, who became MP for Westminster in 1807, the veteran reformer Major John Cartwright, Francis Place and the journalist William Cobbett. Anxious not to provoke an anti-Jacobin reaction, Burdett was flexible in approach. He argued privately for universal suffrage, but publicly was committed to more limited objectives. He had a rather old-fashioned and patrician attitude to reform, seeing the gentry as the natural leaders of society. However, he attracted considerable support from the working population through his presentation of parliamentary reform as a means of reducing taxation.

In 1810 Burdett was imprisoned in the Tower of London for attacking recent military failures and clashing with the House of Commons over its privileges. This led to widespread rioting in London and to petitions from the provinces. Burdett became a popular martyr for liberty in the manner of John Wilkes and the cause of parliamentary reform was given an important, if temporary, boost. The importance of Burdettite radicalism was more significant and widespread than some historians have suggested but it never amounted to a coherent, nationwide campaign for parliamentary reform. Ideologically moderate and aimed primarily at a middle-class audience, it looked back to earlier radical movements. Many of its leaders' careers dated back to Wilkes and the American Revolution. They revived the notion of the ancient constitution arguing that electoral reform would restore its purity and lead to the recovery of people's traditional rights. Their appeal was to the traditional liberties of Englishmen not to the rights of man. Parallel to this was revival of traditional attitudes towards the growth of executive power and the expansion of government patronage, and it had limited success in these areas.[13]

The reformers were divided in their aims. Some were satisfied by curtailing government patronage. Others, like Burdett and Francis Place, wanted a moderate extension of the franchise. Cartwright, Cobbett and Henry Hunt supported a more radical programme of parliamentary reform. They were equally divided over how to achieve these objectives. Some reformers looked to the prosperous and educated middle classes for support but others sought to devise methods of rousing the whole nation.

The major weakness of radicalism at this time was its failure to devise a strong organizational base from which to generate mass support. There were, however, a few signs that things were beginning to change. Burdett's success in the 1807 election was, in part, a consequence of the work of the Westminster Committee, a group of shopkeepers, artisans and tradesmen led by Francis Place. Though without formal organization and funding, it sought, through extensive canvassing of the 17,000 ratepayers eligible to vote, to restore the 'independence' of the constituency against the established political parties. It marked an important breakthrough, though was not replicated in other urban constituencies.

Hampden clubs

In 1811 a new political society, the Hampden Club, was established in London to work exclusively for parliamentary reform. Encouraged by Burdett, its exclusive propertied membership was criticized by Cartwright who doubted whether such men could have a genuine commitment to radical reform. Cartwright had come to conclusion that mass support was necessary for a programme of radical reform based on universal suffrage and that to confine the movement to the exclusive Hampden clubs was a recipe for disaster. He was unable to convince the leading London reformers and resigned in June 1812 to promote a rival organization (the Union Society) and to take his radical message to the provinces, though he rejoined a year later.

In 1812 and 1813 he stumped round the country visiting most of the major industrial and population centres. He sought out local leaders, who were instructed how to set up a political society and district committees, how to exploit the press for reform propaganda and how to organize mass support for petitions in favour of parliamentary reform. These missionary tours indicated that there was growing dissatisfaction with the unreformed parliamentary system and with its political and economic consequences. He demonstrated the potential for the conversion of severe economic distress into mass political awareness. It was, however, not until after 1815 that the removal of the French threat opened the way for further radical action.

THE POST-WAR CRISIS

The 'mass platform'

In the five years after Waterloo popular radicalism gained a degree of mass support it had lacked since the 1790s. Central to the emergence of the 'mass platform' was Henry Hunt.[14] He broke through the restraints of traditional extra-parliamentary politics and gave popular radicalism its independent, uncompromising, democratic tone. Hunt introduced constitutional mass pressure from without for the restoration of the constitutional democratic rights of all. It proved extremely popular and continued to inform radical agitation until the 1840s. In doing this he upstaged moderates like Burdett and the insurrectionary plans of the 'Spencean' revolutionaries.

The 'constitutional' nature of this mass platform has been misrepresented by many historians. Marxist historians dismiss its popularism as a barrier to the development of a revolutionary perspective while Whiggish writers recognize reformist respectability in its constitutionalism. Both fail to give proper justice to both the physical strength and confrontational nature of the movement. The mass platform drew on popular conceptions of the constitution and the glorious struggles of the past and, through myth and traditions, reached a wide audience, including the normally apathetic. It was, however, not simply a discourse which attracted the crowds and mobilized the masses, it allowed radicals to out-manoeuvre and discredit the government. Through their view of the constitution the radicals were able to portray themselves as the real upholders of the legitimizing ideology of the ruling classes, constitutional freedom and the rule of law. Theirs was a 'moral' force, disciplined, orderly and peaceful until all 'constitutional' channels had been exhausted. In the confrontation of the summer of 1819 each side hoped the other would overstep the mark and so lose public sanction. 'Peterloo' was a tremendous moral and propaganda victory for Hunt and the radicals.

The essential weakness of this strategy was demonstrated in the aftermath of Peterloo. Had the social contract which established government been violated? Should the people exercise their sovereign right of physical resistance to corrupt authority? It was a matter of judgement, rather than a commitment to 'moral' or 'physical' force, which divided radicals at critical moments like the post-Peterloo crisis. As radicals agonized over whether they had constitutional right on their side, they lost their physical momentum: mass support dwindled and the authorities regained the initiative. The Cato Street conspiracy in 1820 was as much an angered response to the collapse of the mass platform and the reimposition of repression as a viable revolutionary threat.

Economic 'distress'

Serious social 'distress' and dislocation of the economy occurred in the five years after Waterloo.[15] Industries like ironmaking and shipbuilding, which had expanded to meet wartime needs, rapidly contracted. Demobilized soldiers and sailors flooded the labour market. Poor rates increased. Standards of living among the working population fell. The 1815 Corn Law provided the pretext for action by both middle-class reformers and popular radicals. To the former the Corn Law expressed the unjustifiable face of the self-interest and political power of the landed interest. To the working population it was to blame for high bread prices.

Mass meetings were held around the country protesting at the bill and 42 petitions were sent to Parliament. For almost a week in March 1815 London was paralysed by a series of riots and the houses of protectionist MPs had to be protected by troops. Despite this, scores of substantial houses were damaged by bands of roving urban bread rioters. In 1816 there were further outbreaks of Luddism in the Midlands, Leicestershire and Yorkshire, food riots in manufacturing centres and 'bread and blood' riots in East Anglia. These were economically motivated, based on direct and often destructive action reflecting traditional forms of protest rather than a mass platform. But the alarms created by the French Revolution and Paineite radicalism had hardened the attitudes of the propertied towards popular violence. The riots were crushed with some severity. Local 'bargaining by riot' over prices and wages was no longer a viable or acceptable means of achieving change: the 'moral' economy was dead.

Why people thought reform was an achievable objective

Why were working men persuaded in large numbers that parliamentary reform was an achievable objective? The readoption of a democratic programme, especially by Henry Hunt, was undoubtedly one reason for this development. A large number of local Hampden and Union clubs sprang up in the provinces, especially in Lancashire and the east Midlands. They were committed to universal rather than household suffrage largely because other strategies had been tried, found to be ineffective or had simply failed. Many workers turned to parliamentary reform because of their weakness in the industrial sphere and because they believed that the state was contributing to that weakness when it should have been protecting them. Handloom weavers were much in evidence in the Lancashire Hampden clubs in 1816 and 1817. Remedial action was called for by handloom weavers and framework knitters. Parliament did not respond.

The radical newspapers, like the *Political Register*, Wade's *Gorgon*, Wooler's *Black Dwarf* and Sherwin's *Weekly Political Register*, were a major influence on the emergence of the reform agitation and focused it on the one issue which all radicals thought reform would relieve: the levels of taxation. Radicals argued that taxation, because much of it was indirect, cut deeply into the budget of the working population, contributed to unemployment and 'distress', reduced demand for manufactured goods and consequently demand for labour. A radically reformed Parliament would reduce taxation and allow the working population to keep the fruits of their labour, reduce privilege and eradicate the 'Old Corruption' of the parasitic classes who lived off the taxes levied on working men. This was essentially a 'consumerist' argument and it was to take the ideological developments of the 1820s to turn this into a critique of the capitalist system with the focus shifted from taxation to profits. Thomas Spence offered a more radical solution in his arguments that land should be transferred from private to communal ownership. They retained a certain influence after Spence's death in 1814 especially for the group of ultra-radicals which centred round James Watson and Arthur Thistlewood. But Spencean ideas, despite the reports of the parliamentary committee on secrecy in 1817, were never widespread in the radical movement.

Reformers faced a major dilemma in 1816 over the tactics and methods they should adopt: 'constitutional' or 'revolutionary', 'moral' or 'physical' force. The starkness of the choices open to reformers was not as simple as this implies. They merged into each other and, for many, the dividing line was a fine one. Though 'divisions' of the Society of Spencean Philanthropists believed that abolition of private property was preferable to parliamentary reform, in 1815 and 1816 they supported Henry Hunt and his mass platform against the rival 'constitutional' approach of Burdett and Cobbett. Hunt appeared to endorse violence while the moral force of Burdett relied on public meetings and petitions.

1816–19

The autumn of 1816 saw a series of mass meetings to petition against distress and for reform planned by the Spenceans with Hunt in the chair. He persuaded the Spenceans not to use the Spa Fields meeting on 15 November as the starting point for a march to Carlton House to petition the Regent. Most people took his advice but a small group did march through Westminster, damaging foodshops in protest against high prices. Government informers convinced the government that some of the Spenceans planned a rising in London and this led to troops and police being stationed at strategic points during a second Spa Fields meeting on 2 December. Thistlewood persuaded a break-away group of a hundred or so to march on the city, plundering shops on the route. The riot was far less damaging than it appeared and the authorities had little difficulty in containing it.

Hunt decided that he had not known of the intended insurrection and Thistlewood claimed that it failed because of Hunt's caution. The ambiguity of the evidence leaves historians in doubt as to whether it was a spontaneous rising or a well-planned conspiracy. It did, however, give the government the opportunity to demand repressive legislation, a position strengthened by the assault on the Prince Regent's coach on 28 January 1817. Claiming a conspiracy existed, Castlereagh introduced bills to suspend Habeas Corpus, banning 'seditious meetings', renewing sections of the Treason Acts of 1795 and making subversion of the armed forces a capital offence.[16]

The 'Blanketeers'

Groups of weavers in Lancashire sympathized with extreme London radicalism and Joseph Mitchell, William Benbow and Samuel Bamford established links with both Hunt and the Spenceans. A meeting of 4–5,000 weavers in St Peter's Field, Manchester, organized by Benbow on 10 March, planned to march to London to petition the Regent to relieve distress. Local magistrates saw it as potentially seditious and 200 'Blanketeers' were arrested at Stockport. Up to 500 marchers reached Macclesfield in small groups, while fewer than a hundred continued further. Government spies inflated radical ideas and the discovery of plots to march on Manchester resulted in the arrest of leading Reformers and the break-up of the Hampden clubs.

There was no rising in Manchester and whether any was ever planned is debatable. In June 1817 actual risings did occur in the Holme Valley, near Huddersfield, and at Pentrich near Nottingham led by Jeremiah Brandreth, areas where Luddite violence occurred in 1812. In both cases W. J. Richards, alias 'Oliver', a government spy, played a central role in exploiting vague talk of insurrection which he confessed was 'weak and impractical'. In both cases the authorities had no difficulty in containing the radical threat. E. P. Thompson sees the Pentrich rising as the first wholly proletarian insurrection and there is evidence that some of the conspirators were skilled and literate men, far from single dupes of 'Oliver'.

The Pentrich rising

The Pentrich rising involved only a few hundred people but the government decided to make an example of it: 45 were tried for High Treason and three, including Brandreth, were executed. This reaction may have been the result of genuine alarm but attempts by historians to demonstrate that there was a genuine conspiracy have provided retrospective justification. However, the sentences were widely regarded as excessive and the exposure of 'Oliver's' role was eagerly grasped by the Whigs and the radical press. The government could be accused not simply of subverting constitutional liberties but of trapping unwary individuals into fatal conspiracy. The revelation of the role of spies helped turn public opinion against the government and it failed to secure the conviction of either the Spa Fields conspirators in July 1817 or the radical printers Wooler and Hone.

The government, though it still commanded a majority in the House of Commons, found itself increasingly isolated. But the reformers were also under pressure and anxiety about spies led to the growing articulation by a majority of radicals of the constitutional and legal route to reform. Spenceans still favoured revolutionary change but they were isolated because constitutional reformers recognized the damage their involvement in the events of 1817 had inflicted on the cause. Thistlewood and his co-conspirators planned a rising in October 1817 but differences between him and Watson over plans to murder Sidmouth and other ministers in February 1818 led to further splits in the Spenceans. Thistlewood was imprisoned for a year in May for challenging Sidmouth to a duel. On his release he planned an insurrection in London but Hunt took the chair at the Smithfield meeting on 14 July 1819 and prevented it becoming the launching pad for revolutionary action.

Towards Peterloo

In early 1818 Habeas Corpus was restored and political prisoners released. A new campaign for reform developed with political unions founded in Yorkshire, Lancashire, the north-east, the Midlands and the West Country. The radical press continued to flourish despite government persecution. In 1819 a series of mass meetings to promote reform was planned and widely publicized by the radical press. Meetings to petition Parliament were held in Manchester on 15 January, Stockport a month later, throughout Lancashire and Yorkshire in the summer, at Oldham on 7 June, Manchester on 15 June, Stockport again in 28 June, Birmingham 12 July, Leeds 19 July and London 21 July. A further proposed meeting in Manchester on 9 August was banned but, following the organizers taking legal advice, was announced for 16 August.

The nature of these meetings, their election of delegates and the language used by speakers led to government, at both local and national levels, thinking that radicals were moving irrevocably towards insurrection. The mass meeting in London resolved that Parliament was not properly constituted and that its Acts would not be binding after 1 January 1820. Many radicals had taken part in quasi-military drilling and the authorities regarded the Manchester meeting as subversive rather than constitutional and peaceful. Attempts to arrest Hunt and other speakers by inexperienced yeomanry cavalry had disastrous consequences. Eleven people were killed and 600 injured in the infamous 'Peterloo Massacre'.

Peterloo was important on several levels. The government had little alternative but to endorse the magistrates' actions but in doing so outraged opinion and exposed themselves to violent attacks from the Whigs and radicals. Meetings condemning the government were held throughout the country and in Yorkshire Lord Fitzwilliam was dismissed from his lord lieutenancy for drafting resolutions, passed at a Yorkshire County meeting, condemning interference with public assemblies and demanding a public enquiry. Peterloo gave the Whigs the opportunity of broadening the basis of their support, converting large sections of middle-class opinion to the view that some reform was necessary. The moral authority of the unreformed order was shattered.

Public opinion may have been outraged by Peterloo but the government went on the offensive providing evidence to the House of Commons of insurrectionary plans from lord lieutenants and county magistrates to support further repression. The resulting 'Six Acts', which became law at the beginning of 1820, gave magistrates extensive powers to restrict public meetings and conduct searches for arms. The radical press was restricted by the Blasphemous and Seditious Libels Act and all cheap publications were deemed newspapers and so liable to the fourpenny stamp duty in an attempt to place them beyond the pockets of working people. The initiative soon moved towards the government. Parliament rejected an enquiry and in March 1820 Hunt was sentenced to two and a half years imprisonment.

The Cato Street conspiracy

The revival of the economy and the restoration of government powers was frustrating to many radicals. In December 1819 Thistlewood resolved that the Spenceans must provide a positive lead for their supporters in the provinces and provoke a spontaneous rising. He planned to assassinate the whole cabinet and then seize the Tower, but the government was fully aware of the plans and arrested the conspirators. Thistlewood was among those executed, despite a widespread belief that he was mentally unbalanced, on 1 May 1820. The abortive Cato Street Conspiracy was followed by a number of small 'risings'. On the night of 31 March groups of weavers collected on the moors above Huddersfield with the alleged aim of capturing the town, but, when no other groups joined them, they melted away. On the night of 11–12 April a party of 300–500 men marched towards Grange Moor outside Barnsley with flags, drums and weapons but dispersed when no additional support arrived and some yeomanry appeared. On 5 April in Scotland, after a strike in Glasgow a group of radicals from Stratheven marched on the city but dispersed when further support failed to materialize. At the same time a small group of weavers left Glasgow for Stirlingshire but were overwhelmed by troops at Bonnymuir. Three men were later executed. Further rumours of a concerted rising came to nothing.

Peterloo and the Six Acts had revived some hope of a nationwide rising similar to those projected in 1801–2 and 1817. E. P. Thompson is right to point to the existence of a revolutionary tradition during the period after Waterloo. It cannot be attributed simply to the instigation of government spies. It is difficult to estimate its real strength or degree of support because of the lack of real leadership and direction, the difficulty of nationwide co-ordination and the unwillingness of the majority to support insurrectionary schemes.

The Queen Caroline affair, 1820

Post-war radicalism reached its climax in 1820 with the return of Queen Caroline to England. It was, according to John Stevenson, a primarily metropolitan affair in the tradition of John Wilkes. Long estranged from the Prince Regent, Caroline returned to England after he became king on 29 January 1820. The hypocrisy of his attempt to divorce Caroline because of her sexual misconduct created a temporary alliance between the Whig parliamentary opposition and popular street agitation behind the 'Queen's Cause'. The government found itself in an impossible situation, could not represent a campaign in support of a member of the royal family as seditious and abandoned the intended trial of the queen in late 1820. Support for Caroline faded rapidly after January 1821 when she accepted an annual pension of £50,000. Humiliated by being locked out of Westminster Abbey at the coronation of George IV her health declined and she died on 6 August. The government hoped to avoid further demonstrations by returning her remains to Brunswick for burial as soon as possible, but was unsuccessful. The Caroline affair was highly personalized and theatrical but, though it roused widespread support and was embarrassing to the government, it lacked the radical substance of the previous five years.

Both Peterloo and the Queen Caroline affair put the government under considerable pressure and politicized the increasingly self-conscious middle classes. They also demonstrated that the mass platform was most effective when moved to action in a charged political climate created by individuals in positions of influence and power. The insurrectionary fiascos between 1815 and 1820 had demonstrated that the working population could not achieve political reform on its own and had scared off possible supporters from among the middle classes.

THE 1820s

The 1820s are frequently seen by historians as the decade when the mass reform movement waned as a result of relative prosperity and economic growth, conditions which lasted, except for a sharp recession in 1826, until 1829. This process was certainly reflected in Parliament: attempts by Lord John Russell to introduce reform in 1822, 1823 and 1827 were soundly defeated. In four important respects, however, the 1820s saw developments which played a formative role in the concerted revival of radicalism in the 1830s and 1840s: an increasing capitalist control over the work process, successful extra-parliamentary campaigns on moral and religious questions, an ideological reappraisal and the beginnings of the 'war of the unstamped'.

The economic climate did not benefit all sections of the working population. Agricultural workers in southern England, urban silk workers and hand workers in the textile trades experienced deteriorating living standards as a result of the extension of technological innovation and the increasing control employers had over the work process, especially in the 'factory'. A sense of exploitation and injustice, stimulated by the failure of Parliament to provide any palliatives, did much to direct underprivileged groups towards finding a political solution for their economic ills. The proletarianization of the working population – Thomas Carlyle saw this as a move from a 'bread' to a 'cash-nexus' – and the increasingly capitalist nature of work relations had some social and political stability built into it. But the degree to which that stability could be maintained was dependent on good economic conditions. The widening of 'distress' from those groups whose economic position had been worsened by industrial change to include those whose conditions had been improved by it could lead to the re-emergence of the mass platform of the 1810s. Industrial change was acceptable to many people only as long as it continued to deliver individual economic benefit. The changed economic climate of the 1830s and early 1840s led to a changed radical climate.

Organizational change

The 1820s saw important developments in the art of organization. The petition was a traditional right, used from the 1760s to express popular opinion. Methodism had used the 'division' or 'class' for organization. William Cobbett and Richard Carlile had shown the power of the press. But, though it embraced all these elements, the characteristic expression of radicalism in the 1830s and 1840s was the mobilization of public opinion through mass organizations. Contemporaries recognized that the models for this form of action were the anti-slavery campaign, which had already achieved some success with the abolition of the slave trade in 1807 and was to succeed in abolishing slavery throughout most of the British Empire in 1833, and Daniel O'Connell's Catholic Association.

After 1815 the arguments about slavery received added momentum through the wider debate about political reform. Increasing numbers of slave revolts and demographic proof that abolition had not dramatically improved the position of slaves persuaded increasing numbers of people that emancipation was the only answer. From 1822 the abolitionists regrouped under younger leaders with a new economic critique of slavery but continued to use well tried tactics. Thomas Clarkson toured the country in 1823 and 1824 stimulating more than 800 petitions and the formation of over 200 local associations. Parliamentary candidates were forced to declare themselves against slavery and by the mid-1820s support for slavery could be an electoral liability. Anti-slavery publications aroused public opinion and female anti-slavery associations grew in number and influence. Public meetings, attended by men and women of all social groups, were held in London and in the provinces. This co-ordinated campaign, the 1833 Act and final abolition in 1838 in most parts of the British Empire provided a model for any group intent on pursuing political change.

O'Connell achieved Catholic emancipation even more rapidly. His agitation was largely middle class, though supported by the Irish peasantry through the medium of the Catholic Church. Between 1823, when the Catholic Association was founded, and 1829, when emancipation was achieved, O'Connell mobilized Irish opinion. The 1826 election saw the transfer of traditional support for landlords to Protestant Emancipationists. In 1828 Vesey Fitzgerald, an emancipationist, could not hold his seat against O'Connell. With civil war a real possibility, Wellington had little option but to concede Irish demands. The Catholic Association had shown that a centrally-organized mass movement, backed with the threat of force, could compel Parliament to change its mind on a basic constitutional issue and to carry legislation to which perhaps a majority of MPs were opposed.

Ideological developments

There were two important developments in radical ideology in the 1820s.[17] First, the failure of the mass platform in 1819 was followed by a period of critical self-analysis, dissension and revision in which Hunt defended the mass platform against revisionism and opportunism. This raised some fundamental questions about the meaning of radicalism and the nature of protest. Hunt saw no need for any revision and directed his energies to reactivating the mass platform through the improved organization of the newly created Great Northern Union. This brought attack from both Carlile and Cobbett.

Carlile turned away from the mass platform, repudiated crowds, constitutionalism, populist slogans and 'respectable' leaders. He argued for individual intellectual rigour in place of futile agitation and opposed maximum participation, mass agitation and political challenge. Paradoxically, Carlile's counter-hegemonic brand of 'infidel-republicanism' led to the mid-Victorian linking of radicalism and liberalism, which acquired social respectability in elite politics and self-help protest. His ultra-radicalism of individualism, rationalism and reasonableness appealed to middle-class liberals. Ideologically and intellectually weak, the constitutional mass platform offered the best protection against the osmotic effects of this improvement ethic and middle-class 'reformism'. Hunt preserved the confrontational nature of the platform, the independence of the radical challenge and the integrity of oppositional values. It was not the ideologists but the orators, agitators and organizers who were the real radicals in nineteenth-century Britain.

The dispute with Cobbett was over tactics not ideology. Hunt was a fundamentalist in his radicalism, refusing to moderate his demands for universal suffrage, annual parliaments and the ballot and dismissing moderate reform as worthless, if not harmful, to the unfranchised. Cobbett, by contrast, was pragmatic in his approach. He frequently trimmed his programme, offering his services to discontented groups in society in the hope of exploiting the situation to gain at least some measure of political or fiscal reform.

The 1820s also saw the evolution of socialist and anti-capitalist theories which, though less immediate than the Hunt debates on the issue of reform, were in the longer term fundamental to the working population.[18] Contemporaries explained popular distress in three different ways. First, it was due to the breakdown of the traditionally balanced relationships between masters and workmen, though this accounted for problems in only a limited number of traditional trades. Secondly, some analyses focused on the expropriation of the people from the land. Again this had a limited application given the self-evident growth of Britain's manufacturing industries. Thirdly, there were explanations which placed the blame firmly on political factors, especially high levels of taxation and, after the return to cash payments in 1819, the manipulation of currency. Parallel to these radical explanations for distress was the orthodox political economy of David Ricardo, Malthus, James Mill, Torrens, McCullogh and Nassau Senior.

From the mid-1810s and especially between 1824 and 1827 an alternative theory grounded in a critique of traditional political economy was developed by Robert Owen (*A New View of Society*, 1813), William Thompson (*Inquiry into the Principles of the Distribution of Wealth most Conducive to Happiness*, 1824), Thomas Hodgskin (*Labour Defended Against the Claims of Capital*, 1825, and *Popular Political Economy*, 1827) and John Gray (*Lecture on Human Happiness*, 1825).

These writers attempted to develop a labour theory of value to explain the exploitation of labour and the recurrent economic crises of capitalism. They argued that the problem was not one of government policies, though they did recognize that economic exploitation was made possible by the legal system, but of processes endemic in the economy. Early socialist writers like Robert Owen were neither anti-industry nor anti-capitalist. Owen was more hostile to competition than to capital. He argued that it was the competitiveness of capitalism which held back the growth of prosperity and caused crises of overproduction. His solution was to establish a rational moral order through co-operative communities in which the interests of workers and employers would be the same. Capitalists, Owen argued, need not be eradicated. Their capital might help to start co-operative enterprises and, despite the higher reward assigned to labour, their profits would rise rather than fall because of the releasing of the forces of growth.

Thompson, Hodgskin and Gray were much more critical of capitalists and their profits, and their alternative economic ideology was widely disseminated through the radical press. Broadly, they argued that both profit and rent were unearned income and that the propertied classes were able to expropriate the whole of what labourers produced beyond what they needed for subsistence. The old preoccupation with political corruption, the state and taxation was abandoned in favour of a new theory grounded in the labour theory of value and exploitation. This 'new' analysis did not succeed in displacing the old radical reasoning until after 1850, resulting in significant contradictions in the radical position in the 1830s and 1840s which contributed to the weakening of its case.

But, whether directed at 'Old Corruption' or at capitalists, for Hunt and other radical leaders the demand remained the same: an end to the system which left labour unprotected and exploited by those who monopolized the state and the law. It was through political power that the inequalities within the economy could be removed and the economic well-being of the working population ensured.

The radical press

The final development of the 1820s was the widespread dissemination of these alternative political ideas through cheap unstamped newspapers.[19] The press was restricted in two important respects – financial and legal. Duties had been imposed on newspapers, paper, pamphlets and advertisements since the Stamp Act of 1712. By 1815 these 'taxes on knowledge' stood at 4d. stamp duty on a newspaper and 3s. on each edition of a pamphlet. Acts in 1798 and 1799 had made the registration of printers, publishers, proprietors and presses compulsory. The courts could limit the free expression of the press through the laws of libel: defamatory libel against individuals, seditious libel against political institutions and blasphemous libel against religious institutions.

There was a hardening of government attitudes to the cheap press after Peterloo and it was virtually driven out of existence during the early 1820s. Magistrates were given greater powers to enforce the law against blasphemous and seditious publications and financial restrictions were increased. In addition to government prosecutions, especially against Richard Carlile, cheap newspapers and especially those who sold them were attacked by the Society for the Suppression of Vice (formed in 1802) and, from 1820, by its secular counterpart the Constitutional Association through private prosecutions. Between 1820 and 1824 there was widespread disruption of the radical press through attacks on booksellers and publishers but repression, though initially quite successful, was self-defeating. As prosecutions continued in London radical volunteers came from the provinces to fill the radical ranks. The Home Office made its final assault in mid-1824 but, largely under Peel's influence, the government began to modify its policies, though the 1819 Blasphemous and Seditious Libels Act remained law until 1869–70.

The use of the courts as a means of repressing the cheap press had been shown by the events of the early 1820s to be ineffective but the radical revival of the 1830s brought a new struggle for a free, cheap press and led to further repression. The 'war of the unstamped' provided an important link between the popular agitation for reform in the early 1830s and the emergence of Chartism after 1836.

'Taxes on knowledge' were opposed by both working- and middle-class reformers after 1830. The emphasis of these two groups was different: the latter sought to change the law, the former to destroy it. Individuals like Henry Hetherington, John Cleave and James Watson were involved in a determined effort to violate the press laws by publishing and distributing hundreds of illegal tracts and newspapers. Newspapers like the *Poor Man's*

Guardian mounted a vigorous assault on the competitive economic system and individual property rights, meeting intense hostility from the ruling elite, the conservative middle class and the Anglican Church. It was widely assumed that, if knowledge was power, the kind of knowledge provided by the radical press could lead to the creation of a more just society.

The unstamped press, however, demonstrated the contradictions inherent in radicalism during this period. There were two rhetorics in these newspapers, reflecting the ideological debates in the 1820s. The older position, grounded in an attack on the whole structure of 'Old Corruption', focused its attacks on taxes, rents, pensions, the aristocracy and the Church with occasional expressions on Spencean views on land nationalization and Owenite co-operative ideals. The newer position was based on a more sophisticated analysis of industrial society.

Government repression of the unstamped press, whose combined circulation far exceeded that of the 'respectable' stamped press, was intensified in 1835–6. But it proved largely unsuccessful and in March 1836 the newspaper duty was reduced to a penny, which ended the agitation. This was a compromise which left sections of the working population with a similar sense of betrayal to that of 1832. Though the agitation did not lead to the removal of all taxes on knowledge – that had to wait until the 1850s – it did play a major role in the development of popular radicalism. It spread information about popular movements, relayed local grievances to a national audience, provided training in journalism and political agitation for many activists who were to become Chartists and, though the old radical analysis of the political and economic system was not displaced, it brought the language and ideas of the anti-capitalist critique to a wider audience.

THE 1830s

The early 1830s saw a deepening of hostility among large sections of the working population in both London and the industrial districts. Popular radicalism advanced on a broad front of which political reform was one strand. There were campaigns against newspaper taxes, the factory movement, trade union activity on an increased scale and the anti-poor law agitation.[20] Historians who seek evidence for the widespread existence of class consciousness during the early nineteenth century base much of their case on the 1830s. There are, however, other areas of debate among historians: was there a genuine threat of revolution between 1830 and 1832? What was the Factory Movement concerned with? How damaging was the collapse of general unionism in 1834 to existing trade societies? Why was the anti-poor law agitation so short-lived? How pervasive was the anti-capitalist ideology peddled by the unstamped press and was it a more suitable critique of industrial capitalism than the increasingly outmoded 'Old Corruption'?

The reform agitation

Severe economic distress in the autumn of 1829 brought widespread suffering to both industrial and agricultural Britain and the French Revolution of July 1830 helped further raise the political temperature. However, political radicalism had to compete with other forms of protest and was not always given priority among the working population. One obvious reason why a few radical leaders, like Hunt and the journalist Henry Hetherington, showed little interest in parliamentary reform in the early 1830s was that the Whig Reform bill offered nothing to them or their supporters. But the Reform bill was so unexpectedly bold that the reaction of leaders like Cobbett and Carlile was initially favourable.

There was a fierce and bitter debate between those radicals who supported the bill and those who opposed it. Cobbett, for example, saw it as a stepping stone, an initial breach in the defences of the *ancien régime*. Henry Hunt was opposed by much of the London-based radical press and directed his attention to the working population of the north. He maintained, as he had done since the 1810s, that universal suffrage not moderate reform was necessary. He argued that the bill would increase Whig control over the political system and that, by extending the vote to the 'respectable' in society, it would split the mass platform. The balance of opinion for or against the bill varied considerably from one area to another.

Divisions within popular radicalism cannot be minimized during the reform agitation. In London there were two radical bodies: the National Political Union (NPU) led by Francis Place and the more radical National Union of the Working Classes (NUWC). The government was persuaded to ban demonstrations by the NUWC so that by late 1831 the NPU had twice as many members. Though members of the NUWC saw Place as a traitor to his own class they were far from united in their attitudes to the Reform bill and their debates exhibited conflict between those who were prepared to accept moderate reform and those who wanted universal suffrage. Divisions in London were paralleled in the provinces. Agitation in Birmingham and Leicester was marked by collaboration between the moderate politically conscious working population and the middle classes. But these were the exception and towns like Manchester and Leeds contrasted sharply with Birmingham and Leicester. The Manchester Political Union, which supported the bill, consisted largely of the lower-middle-class 'shopocracy' rather than working people, though it had little sympathy with the mill-owners. It was opposed by a working-class Political Union, pledged to universal suffrage and with close links with the NUWC. The 'extreme' views of this group undoubtedly inhibited many of the middle class from speaking out in favour of reform as firmly as their counterparts did in Birmingham. These complex social divisions were reproduced in other northern cities like Leeds, Bolton and Bradford, where conditions or work in factories tended to be the dominant issue.

The prolonged Reform agitation was punctuated by outbreaks of violence, though these stemmed more from local circumstances than from any coherently organized revolutionary movement and were centred not in the newer economic centres but in older traditional, manufacturing towns. There were riots in London in April and October 1831 when windows of property belonging to opponents of the bill were smashed. During the 1831 general election there were disturbances in several Scottish towns as well as in England. After the second bill had been rejected by the Lords on 8 October widespread rioting seemed, to those in government, to presage revolution. In Derby, Nottingham and Bristol there were major disturbances and widespread damage to property as well as minor outbreaks at Worcester, Exeter, Tiverton, Blandford, Sherborne, Yeovil and Leicester. During the 'Days of May' in 1832 renewed resistance from the Lords and the threat of a Wellington ministry aggravated the tension within a society threatened by a tithe war in Ireland and by cholera on the mainland. Only in Merthyr Tydfil in 1831 did popular radicalism and community feeling fuse with economic discontent to the extent that the maintenance of the law and order was threatened.[21]

The Whig reform measure was sufficiently radical to make it difficult for critics, like Hunt and Hetherington, to generate sustained opposition to it. It was only in periods of excitement and uncertainty after rejection by the Lords and when the future intentions of the Whigs were undefined that those who were discontented with the measure pressed the democratic case. But neither excitement or Whig indecision was sustained for any significant period of time and the ultra-radicals could offer no credible alternative to the campaign for the bill. To view 1832 as the 'great betrayal' is to underestimate the degree of support among the working population for reform and overestimate the degree of opposition. The threat of revolution was rhetoric not reality.

1832: a betrayal?

If there was 'betrayal' then it occurred in the period after 1832 when the Whigs adopted policies which were seen by many of the working population as against their interests. The 1833 Factory Act was a severe disappointment to the 'short-time' movement. There was an offensive against the working population and their means of economic protection in the action taken against trade unions. The 1834 Poor Law Amendment Act generated widespread opposition, largely unsuccessful in southern England but leading to more flexibility of application in the north. The most significant characteristic of radicalism in the five years after 1832 was that the gap between middle-class radicalism and the reforming agitations of the working population widened. The middle classes, whose political objectives had been broadly satisfied by reform, were largely indifferent to the aspirations of the labouring population. The vocabulary of radicalism became the property of the labouring population, increasing its political consciousness and sense of solidarity. The immediate origins of Chartism can be found in the aftermath of the Reform Act and in the recognition that the moderate and gradualist approach to change did not deliver the required political results.

The Whigs had not changed the system of 'Old Corruption' despite the 1832 Act, the introduction of the principle of election into the poor law and municipal government, the destruction of the old poor law and the introduction of factory inspectors. The positive features of mass platform radicalism, its organization and ideology, which had their genesis in the 1810s and 1820s respectively, flourished in the 1830s. The negative side – conflict – was added in the 1830s especially by the anti-poor law agitation. The contradictions within popular radicalism between 'reformism' and revolution, between the 'old' and the anti-capitalist ideologies, and between co-operation with the middle classes and a movement based on working-class solidarity remained. The major issue facing Chartism was whether it could transcend these contradictions.

TRADE UNIONISM

The Webbs' interpretation

Political reform was given high profile by contemporaries and by later historians but combinations of workers in trade unions to improve their economic conditions was also important, perhaps in retrospect more important.[22] The impression that trade unionism developed as a conse-quence of industrialization has, until recently, led to neglect of the exist-ence of unionism among many groups of skilled workers in the eighteenth century. This neglect owes much to the treatment which Sidney and Beatrice Webb adopted in their classical work, *The History of Trade Unionism*, London, 1920, and to the stark division historians have made between pre-industrial and industrial Britain.

The Webbs defined a trade union as 'a continuous association of wage-earners established for the purpose of maintaining or improving the con-ditions of their working lives.' This definition has important limitations and inclined them to belittle the evidence for early trade unionism, though they traced the movement's 'origins' back to the seventeenth century. The emphasis on the idea of continuous existence – by implication they meant formal, institutionalized organizations – led the Webbs to deny the import-ance of informal, local combinations. It is, however, clear that men regu-larly brought together in the same workforce or area had unofficial leaders and developed their own customs and practices without embodying them in regular institutions. Formal organizations emerge only in times of particular crisis such as a strike but often, as in the case of the north-eastern sailors who struck twelve times between 1768 and 1825, there is little evidence for organizing committees. Informal collective pressures certainly existed, though again there is little specific evidence, and were used to exclude women and other 'outsiders'. Most of the disputes of the eighteenth century – C. R. Dobson lists 386 for the period 1715–1800 – do not seem to have involved formal continuous organizations, but there is little doubt that they involved wages, hours of work and control of the labour supply, which were 'trade union' issues. Some fell into the category of 'bargaining by riot' when workers attempted to secure their collective ends by violence and intimidation. The 1765 northern miners' strike was accompanied by so much violence and systematic destruction of winding gear that arson was specifically proscribed in an amended Malicious Injuries to Property Act in 1768. It is valid to see this sort of action as incipient trade unionism, even if not in the Webbs' sense.

A second major criticism of the Webbs' view of the eighteenth century lay in their efforts to prove that trade unionism was a relatively modern development, a characteristic of an industrialized society. Eighteenth-century Britain, however, was proto-industrial and was already characterized by significant separation of capital and labour. Workers no longer owned the materials on which they worked or sold the product to the consumer. Workers sold their 'labour power'.

Unionism before 1800

It is difficult to get much idea of the scope of trade unionism in the eighteenth century. Certainly by 1800 it involved a very small proportion of workers and it was still a minority movement in 1850. Trade unions were almost exclusively male. There were women in the Manchester small-ware weavers in 1747 and in 1788 as many as 18,500 females made up the Leicester Sisterhood of Female Handspinners. But these were exceptions. Despite evidence for the economic marginalizing of women workers, they had difficulty in organizing and it was not until the 1850s that unionism made much headway among them.

Trade unionism in the eighteenth century was predominantly the preserve of skilled workers who combined to protect their status and economic standing against attacks from employers who sought to cut wages and change customary ways of working.[23] They also combined to protect the 'closed shop' of their 'trade' against incursion from cheap labour and from women. Collective action was commonplace in eighteenth-century Britain among a wide range of workers and there is clear evidence for some continuity of organization through the workplace or village club. Industrial protest may have been sporadic, organization was not.

The degree of organization varied among different groups of artisans. London tailors, for example, had first come to the public's attention in

1720–1 when their actions led to an Act banning combinations in the tailoring trades of London and Westminster and fixed wages by statute. Wage disputes were renewed in 1744–5, 1752, 1764, 1768 and 1778. Similar evidence of what Francis Place called 'perpetual combination' existed for journeymen hatters and the effect of the union's strength was felt by master hatters in London, the Midlands, Bristol and Lancashire. Weavers and combers in the Devonshire serge industry developed effective unionism through town clubs from early in the century, culminating in an Act of 1726 prohibiting combinations among woollen workers. Weavers' combinations in Gloucestershire, Wiltshire and parts of Somerset also dated from the 1720s and in 1757 the employers secured parliamentary approval for ending the principle of wage regulation in this area of manufacture over fifty years before the general repeal of the wage-regulating clauses of the 1563 Statute of Artificers. Woolcombers' organizations existed in the south-west, Essex, Leicester and Yorkshire by the 1740s, among cotton weavers in Lancashire by 1750 and among papermakers, compositors, plumbers, painters, carpenters, shoemakers, bakers and metal workers by the end of the century.

There is widespread evidence for craft unions but the law was clearly on the employer's side and Adam Smith was not alone in dismissing unions' effectiveness. By 1799 there were already more than forty Acts on the statute book which could be used against trade unions, though many of these were confined to specific trades like those banning combinations among hatters in 1777 and papermakers in 1794. These Acts were passed by Parliament in response to pressure from employers for more effective ways of combating trade union organizations of journeymen in their trades. The presumption was that combinations were illegal. This was grounded in the concept of 'conspiracy', under which the fairness of the workers' case was not the issue, only the fact of conspiracy against the employers. It was not the refusal to work by an individual that was illegal but the collective action or conspiracy of the combination. Throughout the eighteenth century there were many occasions when conspiracy proceedings were taken against trade unions: for example, against seven Liverpool tailors in 1783, against Leicester hatters in 1777 and 1794. Though local court records have undoubtedly been lost, between 1710 and 1800 conspiracy proceedings as a weapon against trade unions were used in 29 cases. In Scotland, by contrast, judicial intervention was far more common than recourse to punitive action. Scottish judges regularly set wage rates and regulated hours during the eighteenth century and it was not until after the weavers' strike of 1812 that this legal regulation was swept away.

The law was not a particularly effective weapon against combinations in the eighteenth century. Proceedings could be very slow and costly, employers were disinclined to reopen old conflicts and had to face latent hostilities after their actions were over. Often the threat of legal action was sufficient to get people back to work. But legal action did not always correspond to economic advantage and workers who took action during an upturn in the economy often achieved their objectives as employers did not want to lose the advantages of a rising market. Combinations of employers were as much a part of the industrial scene as combinations of workers and could be just as secretive. Agreements between employers which resulted in wages cuts led to major disturbances in Somerset in 1738–9 and in 1764 a strike took place in the serge industry when weavers learnt that a meeting of masters was about to agree on lower prices. Employers were able to 'police' their own area, through refusing to employ workers who had no 'discharge certificate' from previous work, or by getting workers to sign agreements on wages and, under the threat from combinations, by locking workers out. In these circumstances the use of the legal process was superfluous.

How effective were workers in pressing their claims through combinations? Choosing the right moment for withdrawing labour was of central importance. Serge workers chose the spring when demand for lighter cloth was at its height. The death of Queen Charlotte in 1817 offered the Coventry weavers of black ribbon an ideal opportunity for pressing their wage demands. Part of the strategy of making strikes effective was building up a support fund and there is evidence of this among book-binders, printers, calico printers and others. Violence was frequently used as a means of intimidating employers and 'blackleg' workers, though many contemporaries saw it as an expression of desperation. It was used by skilled as well as unskilled workers and 'collective bargaining by riot' was as much a part of industrial action as the strike in the eighteenth century. It is difficult to estimate the effectiveness of trade union action in the eighteenth century. Skilled workers often saw themselves as protecting the traditions of their trades against interlopers and against their masters whose advantage lay in deregulation. Their effectiveness depended on local support, a sound financial basis, favourable economic conditions and, on occasions, the willingness of magistrates to act as arbiters between them and their employers. By 1800 there was a widespread, vibrant and not ineffective tradition of trade unionism in Britain.

Unionism under the Combination Acts 1799–1824

Trade unionism found itself under concerted attack in the first quarter of the nineteenth century.[24] The Combination Acts of 1799 and 1800 introduced legislative repression. The repeal of the apprenticeship clauses of the Statute of Artificers in 1814 threatened the exclusive 'property of skill' of the craft unions and the 'machinery question' their economic security. War, rising prices and the threat from political Jacobinism provided justification, though Ian Christie has recently maintained that the widespread existence of trade combinations acted as a safety-valve for discontent among the working population, confining revolutionary activity to a minority of the population.

The first quarter of the nineteenth century saw the Combination Acts in force. Passed in 1799 and modified in 1800, they have been represented in trade union mythology as the most outstanding example of the repression of the rights of the working population to combine in their own defence. The Webbs were correct in seeing them as a reflection of government fears of revolutionary ideas but their limited view of eighteenth-century unionism led them to the incorrect conclusion that the Acts marked a 'far reaching change of policy'. It was the general nature of the prohibition of combinations that was new, not prohibition itself.

The Acts were passed very quickly, with encouragement from both William Wilberforce and William Pitt, and took workers' organizations by surprise. They were certainly one-sided and did not treat combinations by employers as harshly as those by workers. The 1799 Act was intended to prevent dislocation of trade during wartime and was partly inspired by fears of revolution. It aimed to secure speedy settlement of disputes by summary proceedings before a single magistrate. Following protests against its unfairness it was modified in 1800 to bring employers' combinations under the law as well as workers' (though this proved inoperable), requiring two magistrates, who could not be masters in the trades concerned, and introducing arbitration clauses (though these never seem to have operated).

The effects of the Acts were exaggerated by contemporaries and subsequently by some historians. They were used infrequently and when used were often ineffective. Summary jurisdiction, their main intention, was largely defeated by appeals to the quarter sessions and convictions were frequently thrown out on technical points. The Combination Acts have been seen as a negligible instrument of oppression and employers continued to rely largely on the older legal controls provided by common law, existing statutes and the contractual law of master and servant. So why has a mythology been manufactured round the Combination Acts? M. D. George, as early as 1936, provided a convincing explanation. She argued that:

> these were the only Acts styled Combination Acts and therefore all the opprobrium attaching to the mass of legislation repealed in 1824 was loosely and vaguely attached to the Act of 1800.[25]

Witnesses to the 1824 Committee were confused as to whether prosecution had been brought under the 1800 Act, or for conspiracy, riot, or for breach of contract. Though E. P. Thompson's statement that it did not matter to workers which law they were prosecuted under is undoubtedly true, it certainly does make a different whether or not the Combination Acts marked a change of policy and whether they made legal repression more severe.

Combinations were certainly subjected to legal repression during this period and many individuals were prosecuted, fined and imprisoned. This seems to have been more widespread in areas of rapid technological growth and in the politically conscious textile areas of Lancashire and Nottinghamshire where outworking was widespread. Cotton spinners struck in 1810 and there were four separate strikes among cotton workers in 1818 by jenny spinners and powerloom weavers in Stockport, mule spinners in Manchester and handloom weavers. The intensity of opposition to the Combination Acts among handloom weavers and the repressive response from employers in Lancashire was a reflection of the struggle to maintain their livelihood; the tendency of modern historians to downgrade the effect of the Combination Acts gains little support from there.

Older skilled trade societies, though occasionally prosecuted, seem to have been more readily accepted by employers as legitimate channels for workers' grievances. Evidence to the 1824 Committee gives many examples of collective bargaining where employers did not choose to take legal action. Printing workers did not come into conflict with the law despite their spreading organization in London and the provinces. London artisans and artisans elsewhere emerged from the French wars more strongly organized then ever before with a new 'trade union consciousness' linking wages to organizational power. Intra-trade networks developed: in 1800 these existed in seventeen trades and by the mid-1820s in at least twenty-eight.

The effectiveness of trade unionism among skilled workers was threatened far more by the repeal, in 1814, of the statutory requirement that a seven-year apprenticeship should be served before a craft should be exercised than by the Combination Acts. The apprenticeship clauses of the Statute of Artificers had fallen into disuse in the eighteenth century, so why did this emerge as an issue in the early nineteenth century? The agitation against repeal was centred in London, but there was widespread support from the calico workers of Lancashire and in the frame-knitting district of the East Midlands. Skilled workers in these areas saw their control of work practices threatened by employers' use of unskilled and untrained labour and by new technology introduced, according to Andrew Ure in *The Philosophy of Manufactures* in his defence of the factory system in the mid-1830s, to break the hold of the trade societies. Employers, by contrast, saw the apprenticeship clauses and the restrictive practices they ensured as a barrier to the further expansion of capitalist practices. In the case of apprenticeship and new machinery employers were successful in trades which were less protected and less well organized. The result was an influx of unskilled and cheaper labour into a trade undercutting the privileged status of skilled men. In trades where manual skills remained an essential feature of production and where well organized artisans could co-ordinate collective action apprenticeship, and with it the closed shop, survived.

By 1824 skilled workers had shown themselves capable of protecting their labour interests against the capitalist interests of employers as they had done in the eighteenth century. The 1814 repeal was in this respect more important for skilled workers than the Combination Acts because it legitimized the twin processes of deskilling and the introduction of cheap labour. But before 1824 there were few signs that unionism had crossed the boundary of skill between artisan and unskilled labour.

The repeal of the Combination Acts was achieved in 1824 as a result of a campaign led by Francis Place and supported by economists like Joseph Hume and J. R. McCulloch. His campaign, masterly in diplomacy, lobbying and argument, was aimed at a Parliament which already accepted the ineffectiveness and unfairness of the legislation. The 1824 Act swept away not only the Combination Acts but also excluded trade unions from prosecution for conspiracy. Many people had been convinced by Place's argument that repeal would bring trade unionism and strikes to an end. The events of 1824–5 quickly led them to rethink their position. Repeal coincided with a boom in trade, releasing a flood of union activity with demands for wage increases accompanied by strikes and violence. Employers demanded the restoration of the Combination Acts and it took all Place's diplomacy to prevent this. The 1825 Act, the result of a report from a select committee, recognized the rights of combination and collective bargaining over wages and hours but restored union subjection to the law of conspiracy. It also made the law on picketing and intimidation more stringent. The Act was a compromise which gave unions the right to exist but limited their effectiveness to act with powerful legal sanctions.

A 'revolutionary decade' 1825–35

Historians have taken different views of trade union developments in the next ten years.[26] Left-wing historians like the Webbs, G. D. H. Cole and E. P. Thompson have characterized the period as one of growing political and class consciousness with the emergence of general unions. Other historians, like A. E. Musson, argue that the 'revolutionary' nature of unionism in this period has been exaggerated and that much trade unionism remained small, sectional and local. General unionism may have been exciting to both contemporaries and to later historians but the organization, collective bargaining and friendly benefits for unemployment, sickness and death of the older trade societies and the superficiality of their response to Owenite and anti-capitalist ideology must be emphasized.

There were, however, two significant developments during these years. The first was organizational: the formation of district and national unions and attempts at general trades' unions or federations. The second was ideological: a broadening of union horizons to include political and social ideas and an anti-capitalist critique. These came together, though far from successfully, in the Grand National Consolidated Trades Union (GNCTU) of 1834. Owenite ideas had a limited impact on most workers, though they often expressed sympathy with Owen's aims and a few started small schemes of co-operative production. District and national unions in specific trades proved to be more enduring than general unions and, though weakened by strikes and lock-outs, often survived to be resuscitated in the 1840s.

The movement towards regional and national unionism in specific trades was evident among cotton spinners. In 1824 Manchester spinners were involved in several local disputes and took up the object of forming a county union for Lancashire, trying to broaden their support by seeking federation with the Glasgow spinners who were also in dispute. Though this proved unsuccessful further strikes in 1825 and 1828 demonstrated the need for better organization. The result was the establishment of a Grand General Union of Operative Cotton Spinners (GGU) led by John Doherty in 1829. He wanted stronger organization than those which had been attempted in 1810, 1818 and 1824 and, despite regional differences between cotton spinners, was able to achieve agreement on a national strike pay level of ten shillings from a central fund and on the need for consent from other districts before industrial action could be taken. Expectations proved too high and in a series of strikes in Lancashire in late 1830 and early 1831 the GGU failed to deliver the goods: strike pay was only half that promised and there was poor support from other areas. The GGU collapsed and further movement towards federation in Lancashire had to wait until 1842.

John Doherty, a practical trade unionist rather than an Owenite idealist, had already shifted his focus to the National Association for the Protection of Labour (NAPL). Formed in late 1829, its inaugural meeting was attended by workers from twenty trades from Lancashire. Although successful in spreading the movement into the Midlands and other northern industrial centres at its peak in the autumn of 1830 its 60–70,000 members came overwhelmingly from Lancashire and Cheshire. The NAPL gained support from declining handworkers like weavers and knitters as well as cotton mule-spinners but also from miners and potters. It lost both strength and momentum after the autumn of 1831, but it persisted in name until 1833. It failed to achieve any of its objectives and never attracted the most highly skilled workers like engineers and printers who kept their craft unions, but had been successful in mobilizing much larger occupational groups.

Similar movement towards national unions was evident among building craftsmen. This began among carpenters and bricklayers in 1827 and soon led towards general unionism. Technology was not the problem in the building trade; innovation in organization was. The issue was one of 'general contracting'. The traditional system of architects employing master craftsmen in the various branches of the trade was being replaced by a tripartite system of architect, middlemen or employers of labour in crafts to which they did not belong, and master craftsmen. The claim was that these general contractors forced down rates and wished to change the working practices of the craftsmen. Demands for an ending of general contracting led to unsuccessful confrontation between the Builders Union and employers in 1833–4. The building industry again split into its separate trades.

Robert Owen's Grand National Consolidated Trades Union (GNCTU) brought the ferment of trade unionism to both its zenieth and its end. It was in part a revival of Doherty's earlier general union and, although it has entered union mythology especially through the connected Tolpuddle Martyrs, it was even less successful than the NAPL, lasted less than a year and never became the vast organization into which it was later inflated by the Webbs. The GNCTU was not London's first attempt at general unionism: the campaign against repeal in 1814 had gone across trades and in 1818 John Gast, leader of the shipwrights, had organized London artisans in the 'Philanthropic Hercules', a formalization of existing inter-trade assistance. There had already been much interest by London artisans in co-operative production which predated Owen. The GNCTU was formed in a period of active unionism in London especially among the carpenters, shoemakers and tailors, who wanted to stop the drift from being skilled artisans towards being 'sweated' into a proletariat along with an expanding population of unskilled.

It is difficult to reconstruct the exact sequencing of events in London in 1833–4 but it is very clear that the formation of the GNCTU came at a time of existing and continuing union activity. The initiative was taken by the tailors and in mid-February 1834 the GNCTU was born. Its main aims represented artisan concerns: mutual support in strikes, provision of sickness benefits, employment of members who were on strike and of unemployed members. The Webbs' estimation of half a million members has been shown to have been ridiculously high. The total paid-up member-ship approached only 16,000 but there were attempts to broaden its appeal and certainly it had tacit support from many more workers. There was some movement towards the unorganized, including women workers, and it was this broadening of the movement which heightened government and employer hostility. The GNCTU failed to attract support from the majority of trade societies – London tailors, silk weavers and shoemakers formed a greater part of it. Though a few labourers, like those at Tolpud-dle, briefly organized, it spread only to a limited extent beyond traditional craft trades. It had no real organization or financial basis and, when faced with employers' lock-outs and prosecutions, including that of the six Dorchester labourers for administering an illegal oath at Tolpuddle, it collapsed.

A. E. Musson has called the GNCTU 'a fascinating phenomenon, but sadly ephemeral' and it is true that movements for general unionism in the case of both the NAPL and GNCTU were very short-lived. Musson

argues that historians have given the GNCTU attention out of all proportion to its significance and that the future lay with district and national
federations within trades not with vast trades federations. Though his
conclusion may be valid he has perhaps overstated his case and historians
from different sides off the political divide, like Thompson and E. H.
Hunt, agree that unionism between 1829 and 1834 did mark an important
move in the direction of working-class consciousness. This was not a
permanent, broad-based or continuous class consciousness out of which a
working class was formed but a consciousness among skilled artisans and
handworkers experiencing dilution into the 'unskilled'. The GNCTU was
neither an aberration nor a radical departure for trade union development.

Developments after 1835

The inflation by the Webbs of both the numerical support for and the
collapse of the GNCTU caused them, according to Musson, to produce a
'warped' interpretation of developments after 1834. This has led to two
ways of looking at the subsequent period. For the Webbs there was an
emphasis on a decline in confrontation and in overt class consciousness.
Others stress the continuity of activity between the 1820s and the 1840s.
Certainly, with the intense depression between 1836 and the early 1840s,
trade unionism was under severe strain in the face of a subsequent
employer offensive. This led certain workers, like handloom weavers, to
seek political rather than economic solutions to their problems. In Scotland the bitterness and defeat of the Glasgow spinners' strike in 1837 and
the subsequent trial of union leaders set back the development of Scottish
unionism for up to a decade.

How valid is the Webbs' claim? There is ample evidence that unions
renounced the language of the class war, improved their organization and
public image and concentrated on sectional, local and limited objectives.
Violence in Glasgow, against blackleg labour during a cotton spinner
strike in 1837, and in Cork and Dublin led to pressure for the government
to reintroduce anti-union legislation. An enquiry in 1838 decided against
this but the threat was taken very seriously and led to united action by
London and provincial unions. The language of craft unions was moderated, at least in public, and the language of accommodation replaced the
conflict rhetoric of the early 1830s. The potters displayed an approving
interest in new technology and the printers distanced themselves further
from the notion of general unionism for which they had always had little
enthusiasm. Strikes were seen increasingly by craft unions as the final
resort, though this did not mark a major alteration in how this strategy
was perceived; flint glass workers declared them to have been the bane
of the union movement and abolished strike pay.

Apprenticeship was, however, still a major issue between skilled trade
unionists and their employers. It meant the closed shop crucial to union

success was preserved in only two contexts: where a skill remained essential for production and could only be achieved through long apprenticeship or an effective closing of entry against unskilled men. New technology and the acceptance by a mass market of ready-made goods of often inferior quality led to changes in some trades but the preservation and survival of apprenticeship remained a key objective of many trades. The main weapon in the armoury of Sheffield cutlers and grinders, for example, lay in their restriction of the supply of labour. Tyneside shipwrights in 1841 still held the ratio of one apprentice to three craftsmen and it was firmly insisted on in the union rulebook in 1850.

There may have been much talk of the need for accommodation with employers and the prospect of achieving more by negotiation and conciliation than by strike action but the context in which this existed was fundamental. There was often little reciprocity on the part of employers who were likely to respond to weakness by increased attempt to break unions. The Miners' Association, which was established in late 1842, had 60,000 members at its peak in 1844 from every major coalfield in the British Isles but was defeated by concerted action by coal-owners.

The Webbs' notion of accommodation should not be overemphasised. There were certainly continuities within skilled craft unions throughout the first half of the nineteenth century but what is important, for developments after 1850, was a shift in the meaning of 'elite' unionism. During the 1830s the leading craft unions were from the 'lower' trades, among weavers, tailors and shoemakers, but from the 1840s this primacy moved to the 'upper' trades. The 'aristocracy of labour' of the 1840s was fundamentally different from the traditional artisan 'aristocracy' of the 1820s. It was grounded in the new technology, new trades and in industrial change. It was necessary for capitalism to reach accommodations with these groups for its own survival and expansion. It is, however, important not to see this as a complete accommodation by all trade unions to the values of liberal capitalism. Struggles for 'workers' control' over the processes of labour and an insistence on apprenticeship remained points of conflict between capital and labour. Women were entirely excluded from accommodation by men, both employers and trade unionists. The unskilled, by far the majority of workers, remained outside and had no place in this *rapprochement*. In 1850 trade unions accounted for only a small proportion of all workers and many would have agreed with Sir Archibald Alison who dismissed them all as nothing more than 'a system of aristocracy of skilled labour against the mass of unskilled labour'.[27]

The interests of trade unions lay in maintaining differentials within the working population, not in promoting the interests of the unskilled from whom they were separated by a chasm of training, education and attitudes.

WOMEN AND RADICALISM

The recognition that women played an important part in the radical movements of the eighteenth and early nineteenth centuries has been a feature of historical research and writing in the last twenty years.[28] This formed part of a feminist critique of a world shaped in the interests of and dominated by men in which women were subordinated and silenced.[29] The emergence of mass feminist politics is often seen as a result of the industrial revolution and the emergence of an ideological hegemony by the middle classes. The former separated work and home. The latter segregated men and women into separate spheres. (i.e. men = public domain, women = private domain). The emergence of a working class as a political as well as a social and economic category was accompanied by an increasing denial of the same categories for women. Women emerged as a social problem.

In what ways did radicalism among women differ from radicalism among men during this period? Women's radicalism was often posed in terms of their perceptions of themselves and their status in relation to men. As a result the starting point for protest was broader: lack of education, male dominance over women and their property in and out of marriage, 'domestic drudgery', restrictions on female labour and the double standard of sexual morality figured as well as exclusion from the franchise. Men saw radicalism almost entirely in terms of the extent to which all men could participate in the existing narrow male decision-making process. The levels of female and male consciousness varied, a consequence of individual and group experience, but for women that experience was always grounded in a shared exploitation, the single feature of this period on which men from all social groups could agree.

An interesting comparison can be made between attitudes to women in England and Scotland during this period.[30] The English ruling class was much less sympathetic to the political claims of women than their counterparts in Scotland. Mary Wollstonecraft was described by Horace Walpole as 'a hyena in petticoats' while the Scottish intelligentsia was examining the reasons behind women's enslavement. English women had no legal status in marriage, Scottish wives often retained their maiden names. English women could not easily obtain a divorce until 1857, ten years later than in Scotland. English men had the legal right to beat their wives but in Scotland a series of legal cases between 1804 and 1850 removed this right. Scottish husbands could not imprison their wives in their own houses, a right which did not end in England until 1891. Patriarchal dominance was more obvious in England than in Scotland.

Scottish working women in the early nineteenth century were regarded as far more independent than their English counterparts. They were, according to Henry Cockburn, 'high spirited' and 'spoke and did exactly as they chose'. They were not subservient to their husbands' political and religious opinions. This militancy can be accounted for, first, by their comparatively more important role in the economy. In 1844 the percentage of female workers in the total labour force in England engaged in coal mining, factory work and agriculture was 1.5, 54.3 and 3.96 respectively; in Scotland the corresponding percentages were 4.53, 70.15 and 11.3. Secondly, there was a strong, distinctive, though 'hidden', matriarchal dimension to popular culture which did not exist in England and through which protest could be defined.

The attacks on popular culture in Scotland and England had different dimensions. In England they were seen in terms of economic efficiency, moral and social order but in Scotland they were part of the attempt by the ruling elite to strengthen patriarchal authority by redefining and restricting the independent role of women. The emergent middle-class notion of 'separate spheres', which was clearly influential in England, met with much more resistance in Scotland. Because capitalism needed a new sexual division of labour, Calvinist clergy and magistrates imposed sexual repression, prudery and censorship on Scottish society. In both countries the new domestic ideal of womanhood defined men as the 'breadwinners' but, while these new ideas were increasingly accepted in England, in Scotland female factory hands and women in the fishing industry refused to accede to the new ideal of domesticity. By 1850, however, in both countries a sexually and socially repressive culture of 'respectability' had emerged in which women were defined in terms of their domesticity rather than for their contribution to the public domain.

At the level of intellectual enquiry the approach of many Scottish thinkers was far more liberal than their English counterparts. In England a series of philosophical and biological arguments was constructed to protect men from the threat of intellectual women but in Scotland the approach was far more questioning and 'open'. From the 1770s middle-class women were admitted to literary and philosophical debating societies in Edinburgh, Glasgow and Dundee in contrast to women's total exclusion from social and intellectual life in England. The Tory witch-hunts of the 1790s brought much Scottish liberal thinking to an end and by the 1840s university teachers were no longer willing to encourage female intellectuals. Progressive middle-class women, unlike those in the working population, found it increasingly difficult to play any part in Scottish radical politics. There was a direct line of repression of women from the suppression of a Female Benefit Society for maidservants in 1798 to the statement by the Whig intellectual Francis Jeffrey in 1833 that the proper sphere for female talent was in the home. By 1850 there was little difference in the roles of middle-class women between England and Scotland.

The first recorded strike of women workers in the world was in the Scottish town of Paisley in 1768. Why Scotland and not England? Throughout this period women played a far more significant role in the Scottish than in the English economy. In contrast to the situation in England there was often a serious labour shortage in Scotland. Scottish male workers did not demonstrate against the employment of women, as English male workers did. Patriarchal attitudes existed in Scotland but they were more strongly grounded in the ruling elite than among the working population. Strikes by Scottish women workers were usually supported by male trade unionists: in 1834, for example, the mass strikes by female operatives in Aberdeen were supported by male workers in the tailors', shoemakers' and weavers' trade unions. In England strikes by working women, especially those associated with the Owenite phase of union development in the late 1820s and early 1830s, were not simply regarded with horror but were seen as a threat to the basis of all authority in society. A strike by 1,500 card-setters in 1835 led Jack Wade to comment that: 'Alarmists may view these indications of female independence as more menacing to established institutions than "the education of the lower orders".'[31] There was a continuity of women's strikes in Scotland during the transition to a fully industrialized society.

Women played a major role in popular disturbances in Scotland between 1780 and 1850. 46.4 per cent of those charged with riot in opposition to lay patronage against the wishes of the congregation were women. This was not a 'bread and butter' issue but was one of a highly sophisticated political and religious nature. Women were very active in the widespread militia riots of the 1790s. Working women throughout Scotland were hostile to the French wars and not only participated in strikes and demonstrations but also led and spoke at them. They took part in disturbances for the same reasons and in the same ways as men did.

By contrast, English working women were 'new' to politics in the early nineteenth century. They had participated in, on occasions precipitated, food riots in the eighteenth century and there are many examples of female friendly societies in the early nineteenth century but they had not been at the forefront of political struggles. Patriarchal authority was strong throughout English society and this was reflected in the ways in which women were involved in the radical movements after 1816. William Cobbett *invited* working women to play a part in the emergent labour movement, an ironic action since he was a consistent opponent of enfranchising women. In 1818 women were allowed to vote at meetings, though radical newspapers like the *Gorgon* continued to oppose women's suffrage, and by 1819 female reform associations were widespread in northern England. Women played a major role in the Peterloo massacre to such an extent that when Castlereagh was introducing the Seditious Meetings Prevention Bill in late 1819 he denounced women with particular venom.

The Short-time Committees of the 1830s, anti-poor law agitations, and Chartism involved English women workers but, unlike Scottish women, they were speaking in support of their husbands and fathers rather than for themselves. When whole communities rebelled against punitive legislation, removal of customary rights, against 'distress' or unemployment, women rioted, attended meetings, formed committees (in which the sexes were usually segregated). They sold the 'unstamped' newspapers in the 1830s and the presence of women in the demonstrations of the 1830s was remarked on by many contemporaries. Active resistance saw radical rhetoric address both sexes. But when it came to negotiation with employers, JPs, government representatives it was men who took leading roles and women were excluded from this specific and, in terms of the distribution of power in society, crucial dimension of public discourse. Edward Royle and James Walvin put it simply:

> overall their role can be compared to that of the womenfolk at a village cricket match. Their place was in the pavilion making the teas. . . . Seldom were they permitted to field a team of their own.[32]

Men saw their authority – sexual, economic and in terms of status – threatened by industrial change. There was no shortage of labour in England and the vocabulary of grievance extended from loss of skill to loss of authority over apprenticeship and over women in the factories. Male workers played as important, perhaps more important, role in the economic marginalization of working women as their employers. Skilled men's unions excluded women and the notion of a 'family' wage was replaced by one in which the man was the 'breadwinner'. Women moved into less well paid employment or 'assisted' their husbands in their trades. Boys came under the proper supervision of their fathers or male relatives in ways that girls seldom did. Skilled labour became a male preserve and a woman's skill was increasingly seen as residing in the household and her property in the virtue of her person. Once separated from the home, the family and domestic occupations, or existing outside the bounds of marriage, a woman was assured of neither skill nor virtue. Deskilled, educated only for domesticity, sexually and politically repressed, English working women were subjugated to popular conceptions of patriarchal authority. Their motivation and their definition as 'persons' came from outside themselves and they seem to have accepted an image of themselves which involved both home-centredness and inferiority.

CONCLUSIONS

How effective was popular radicalism between 1790 and the mid-1830s in achieving its objectives? There were periods of 'crisis' in which government found itself under intense pressure but it was able to sustain its authority either because of divisions within radicalism itself or through its control of the forces of coercion. The 'revolutionary threat' was always a minority alternative though it was convenient for government to suggest otherwise. The effectiveness of popular radicalism must be seen against this back-cloth. Certainly these decades saw considerable conflict as existing structures came under strain because of population growth, urbanization and economic change but there were other forms of social relationship to conflict. Deference, indifference, accommodation and co-operation were present in the working population. Diversity of social and economic experience led to a diversity of responses ranging from the revolutionary, the radical, the conservative to the apathetic. There was no inevitable route to power and dominance for the working population through conflict.

There was some evidence of united action by the working population during this period though there were many indications of a sense of general bewilderment at the speed and scale of change. Responses to rapid social change were many. Some sought solutions through demands for political change. Others tried to protect themselves through trade unions and friendly societies. Opting out of an increasingly uncongenial world and turning to the millenarian sects was the chosen solution for the disenchanted. Others, instead of waiting for divine intervention, responded to industrialization by trying to divert it away from individualism to noncompetitive communalism. Superficially these responses appeared to have little in common, though they were by no means mutually exclusive, and membership was extremely fluid. If there was a common unity it lay in the insecurity produced by changes of an unprecedented nature. Chartism brought these disparate elements together.

NOTES

1 J. Baker Miller *Towards A New Psychology of Women*, 2nd edn, Penguin, 1988, pp. 11–12.
2 There are several general books which cover radicalism between the 1790s and 1830s: E. Royle and J. Walvin *English Radicals and Reformers 1760–1848*, Harvester, 1982, D. G. Wright *Popular Radicalism: The Working Class Experience 1780–1880*, Longman, 1988, M. I. Thomis and P. Holt *Threat of Revolution in Britain 1789–1848*, Macmillan, 1977, E. H. Hunt *British Labour History 1815–1914*, Weidenfeld, 1981, H. Perkin *The Origins of Modern English Society 1780–1880*, Routledge, 1969, J. Stevenson *Popular Disturbances in England 1700–1870*, Longman, 1979, E. P. Thompson *The Making of the English Working Class*, Gollancz, 1963, Penguin edn, 1968 and S. H. Palmer *Police & Protest in England and Ireland 1780–1850*, Cambridge University Press, 1988. R. Price *Labour in British Society*, Croom Helm, 1986 and J. Belchem *Industrialisation and the Working Class*, Scolar Press, 1990 place radicalism in its social and economic context.
3 J. C. D. Clark *English Society 1688–1832*, Cambridge University Press, 1985 provides a valuable critique of historians' perceptions of radicalism; see especially pp. 346–8.
4 At the level of ideas in the 1790s see H. T. Dickinson *Liberty and Property: Political Ideology in the Eighteenth Century*, Weidenfeld, 1977, pp. 232–318, H. T. Dickinson (ed.) *Politics and Literature in the Eighteenth Century*, Dent, 1974, pp. 145–324 and M. Butler (ed.) *Burke, Paine, Godwin and the Revolution Controversy*, Cambridge University Press, 1984 provide the main texts. J. Boulton *Language of Politics in the Age of Wilkes and Burke*, Oxford University Press, 1963 and O. Smith *The Politics of Language*, Oxford Univer-

sity Press, 1985 examine the ideas behind language. J. C. D. Clark op. cit. provides a conservative interpretation.

Good studies of the 1790s include G. S. Veitch *The Genesis of Parliamentary Reform*, 1913 and P. A. Brown *The French Revolution in English History*, 1918 but these have been superseded by A. Goodwin *The Friends of Liberty: The English Democratic Movement in the Age of the French Revolution*, Hutchinson, 1979 though they are still worth dipping into. More specific studies include J. Cannon *Parliamentary Reform 1640–1832*, Cambridge University Press, 1973, I. R. Christie *Stress and Stability in Late Eighteenth Century Britain*, Oxford University Press, 1984, C. Emsley *British Society and the French Wars 1793–1815*, Macmillan, 1979, J. A. Hone *For the Cause of Truth: Radicalism in London 1796–1821*, Oxford University Press, 1982, I. McCalman *Radical Underworld: Prophets, Revolutionaries and Pornographers in London 1795–1840*, Cambridge University Press, 1988, H. W. Meikle *Scotland and the French Revolution*, 1912, R. Wells *Insurrection: The British Experience 1795–1803*, Alan Sutton, 1983 and *Wretched Faces: Famine in Wartime England 1793–1803*, Alan Sutton, 1988. G. A. Williams *Artisans and Sans-Culottes: Popular Movements in France and Britain during the French Revolution*, Edward Arnold, 1968 provides a comparative approach and H. T. Dickinson *British Radicalism and the French Revolution 1789–1815*, Basil Blackwell, 1985 is an excellent short survey. H. T. Dickinson (ed.) *Britain and the French Revolution 1789–1815*, Macmillan, 1989 contains some essential essays.

5 Edmund Burke is discussed further in Chapter 6, pp. 135–6.

6 T. Paine *The Rights of Man*, Penguin, 1969 with an introduction by Henry Collins is a useful edition. M. Philp *Paine*, Oxford University Press, 1988 is a good short study. G. Claeys *Thomas Paine: Social and Political Thought*, Unwin Hyman, 1989, is more detailed.

7 On the reaction to radicalism see, in addition to the works cited above, J. Ehrman *The Younger Pitt, volume two: the reluctant transition*, Constable, 1983, pp. 385–440. H. T. Dickinson (ed.) *Caricature and the Constitution*, Cambridge University Press, 1986 is excellent on the role of visual propaganda. H. T. Dickinson 'Popular Conservatism and Militant Loyalism 1789–1815' in H. T. Dickinson (ed.) op. cit. pp. 103–26 is an up-to-date survey.

8 On Wales in the 1790s see the general works on Wales cited in earlier chapters and the more detailed works by G. A. Williams *The Search for Beulah Land: the Welsh and the Atlantic Revolution*, Croom Helm, 1980 and *Madoc: the Making of a Myth*, 1980; Oxford University Press, 1986. T. Evans *The Background of Modern Welsh Politics 1789–1846*, Cardiff, 1936 is readable but in need of revision.

9 On Scottish radicalism see H. W. Meikle op. cit.

10 The 'revolutionary underground' is best approached through the work of Roger Wells op. cit., M. Elliott *Partners in Revolution: The United Irishmen and France*, Yale, 1982 and 'Ireland and the French Revolution' in H. T. Dickinson (ed.) op. cit. pp. 83–102. See also T. Pakenham *The Year of Liberty*, Panther, 1972 edn. and M. Elliott *Theobald Wolfe Tore*, Yale University Press, 1989. G. Dobree and G. E. Mainwaring *The Floating Republic*, first published 1935, Cresset Press, 1987, J. R. Dinwiddy 'The "Black Lamp" in Yorkshire 1801–1802', *Past and Present*, 64, 1974, M. Elliott 'The "Despard Conspiracy" reconsidered', ibid., 75, 1977 and T. R. Knox 'Thomas Spence: The Triumph of Jubilee', ibid., 76, 1977, H. T. Dickinson (ed.) *The Political Works of Thomas Spence*, University of Newcastle, 1982 contains his major works.

11 R. Wells *Insurrection*, op. cit., pp. 263–5.

12 Luddism is best approached through the debate between E. P. Thompson, op. cit. and Malcolm Thomis *The Luddites: Machine-Breaking in Regency England*,

David & Charles, 1970. R. Reid *Land of Lost Content: The Luddite Revolt of 1812*, Heinemann, 1986 is readable. Charlotte Brontë *Shirley*, Penguin edn, 1981 is a fictional study, first published in 1849, which gives an extraordinarily accurate picture of conditions in 1811–12 but see also A. Briggs 'Private and Social Themes in Shirley', *Brontë Society Transactions*, 13 (1957), pp. 203–19.

13 On the issue of 'economical reform' between 1806 and 1812 see Chapter 6, pp. 156–7.

14 John Belchem has provided a detailed discussion of the 'mass platform' in 'Republicanism, Popular Constitutionalism and the Radical Platform in Early Nineteenth-Century England', *Social History*, 6 (1981), pp. 1–32 and *'Orator' Hunt: Henry Hunt and English Working-Class Radicalism*, Oxford University Press, 1985.

15 In addition to the general works cited above, especially E. P. Thompson, op. cit., for the post-war period see J. R. Dinwiddy *From Luddism to the First Reform Act*, Basil Blackwell, 1986 and R. J. White *From Waterloo to Peterloo*, first published 1957, Peregrine edn, 1968. White should, however, be approached with caution.

On radicalism in London see J. A. Hone op. cit., I. McCalman op. cit., I. Prothero *Artisans and Politics in Early Nineteenth-century London: John Gast and his Times*, Dawson, 1981, A. Calder-Marshall 'The Spa Fields Riots', *History Today*, 22, (1971), pp. 407–15, S. H. Palmer, 'Before the Bobbies: The Caroline Riots of 1821', ibid., 27 (1977), pp. 637–44 and the paper in J. Stevenson (ed.) *London in the Age of Reform*, Basil Blackwell, 1977. On the revolutionary ethos in London see T. M. Parssinen 'The Revolutionary Party in London 1816–29', *Bulletin of the Institute of Historical Research*, 45 (1972), pp. 266–82 and the rather dated J. Stanhope *The Cato Street Conspiracy*, Jonathan Cape, 1962.

D. Read *The English Provinces c. 1760–1960: a Study in Influence*, Edward Arnold, 1964 is useful on radicalism after 1815. More specific studies include A. J. Peacock *Bread and Blood*, Gollancz, 1965 on the 1816 disturbances, J. Stevens *England's Last Revolution: Pentrich 1817*, Moorland Press, 1977; on Peterloo compare D. Read *Peterloo: The 'Massacre' and its Background*, Manchester University Press, 1958 with the revisionist, though not always convincing, D. Walmsley *Peterloo: The Case Reopened*, Manchester University Press, 1969, R. Reid *The Peterloo Massacre*, Heinemann, 1989 is a good narrative. P. R. Berresford Ellis and S. M. A'Ghobhainn *The Scottish Insurrection of 1820*, Gollancz, 1970 and J. D. Young *The Rousing of the Scottish Working Class*, Croom Helm, 1984 provide useful Scottish background. Until OUP publishes its volume on Wales 1780–1880, see D. Smith (ed.) *A People and a Proletariat: Essays in the History of Wales 1780–1980*, Pluto Press, 1980, T. Herbert and G. E. Jones (eds) *People and Protest: Wales 1815–1880*, University of Wales Press, 1989 and D. J. V. Jones *Before Rebecca*, Allen Lane, 1973.

Useful biographies include J. Belchem op. cit. on Henry Hunt, G. Spater *William Cobbett: The Poor Man's Friend*, 2 vols, Cambridge University Press, 1982, D. Green *Great Cobbett: The Noblest Agitator*, Oxford University Press, 1983 and the brief study by Raymond Williams *Cobbett*, Oxford University Press, 1983, G. Wallas *The Life of Francis Place 1771–1854*, Allen & Unwin, 4th edn, 1925 and M. Dudley *Francis Place 1771–1854: The Life of a Remarkable Radical*, Harvester, 1988.

16 For this period from the viewpoint of Liverpool's administration see Chapter 7, pp. 193–5.

17 On the ideological changes in the 1820s see J. Belchem op. cit. and J. R. Dinwiddy op. cit., pp. 38–44 and T. Tholfsen *Working Class Radicalism in Mid-Victorian England*, Croom Helm, 1976, pp. 25–82.

18 On the emergence of socialist and anti-capitalist theories see N. W. Thompson *The People's Science: The Popular Political Economy of Exploitation and Crisis 1816–34*, Cambridge University Press, 1984, especially chapters 2 and 5, E. Halévy *Thomas Hodgskin*, Benn, 1956; on Robert Owen see J. F. C. Harrison *Robert Owen and the Owenites in Britain and America*, Routledge, 1969, S. Pollard and J. Salt (eds) *Robert Owen: Prophet of the Poor*, Macmillan, 1971 and J. H. Treble (ed.) *Robert Owen: Prince of Cotton Spinners*, David & Charles, 1971. S. Yeo (ed.) *New Views of Co-operation*, Routledge, 1989 is useful. G. Claeys *Citizens and Saints: Politics and Anti-Politics in Early British Socialism*, Cambridge University Press, 1989, is a major study.

19 On the role of the 'unstamped' press and the 'war of the unstamped' see J. H. Wiener *The War of the Unstamped*, Cornell University Press, 1969, W. H. Wickwar *The Struggle for the Freedom of the Press 1819–1832*, Allen & Unwin, 1928 and P. Hollis *The Pauper Press: A Study of Working Class Radicalism of the 1830s*, Oxford University Press, 1970.

20 For a discussion of the 1828–32 period from the viewpoint of government see Chapter 8 and for the post-1832 period Chapter 9.

21 G. A. Williams *The Merthyr Rising*, Croom Helm, 1978, reissued by University of Wales Press, should be read on this issue.

22 There is much on trade unionism in the general books cited in note 2 especially E. H. Hunt op. cit., but see also J. Rule *The Labouring Classes in Early Industrial England 1750–1850*, Longman, 1986, pp. 253–349 and K. D. Brown *The English Labour Movement 1700–1951*, Gill & Macmillan, 1982, pp. 28–50. The following more detailed studies of unionism should be consulted: A. Fox *History and Heritage: The Social Origins of the British Industrial Relations System*, Allen & Unwin, 1985, H. Pelling *History of British Trade Unionism*, Penguin, 1963 and in various more recent editions and A. E. Musson *British Trade Unionism 1800–1875*, Macmillan, 1972. C. Wrigley 'The Webbs: Working on Trade Union History', *History Today*, May 1987 is a useful assessment of a classical study of trade unionism.

23 On eighteenth-century unionism see C. R. Dobson *Masters and Journeymen: A Pre-History of Industrial Relations 1717–1800*, Croom Helm, 1980 and J. Rule *The Experience of Labour in Eighteenth Century Industry*, Croom Helm, 1981. W. Hamish Fraser *Conflict and Class: Scottish Workers 1700–1838*, John Donald, 1988 is essential for the Scottish dimension. J. Rule (ed.) *Trade Unionism 1750–1850 The Formative Years*, Longman, 1988 contains important essays.

24 For unions under the Combination Acts see A. E. Musson op. cit. for the historiographical debate. E. P. Thompson op. cit. and M. D. George 'The Combination Laws', *Economic History Review*, 6 (1936) provide contrasting interpretations. A. Aspinal (ed.) *The Early English Trade Unions*, Batchworth, 1949 documents developments. M. Berg *The Machinery Question and the Making of Political Economy*, Cambridge University Press, 1980 is essential on responses to the new technology, and J. Rule op. cit. on apprenticeship.

25 M. D. George op. cit., pp. 176–7.

26 For unionism after repeal see H. Browne *The Rise of British Trade Unions 1825–1914*, Longman, 1979, R. G. Kirby and A. E. Musson *The Voice of the People: John Doherty, 1798–1854, Trade Unionist, Radical and Factory Reformer*, Manchester University Press, 1975, W. H. Fraser 'Trade unionism', in J. T. Ward (ed.) *Popular Movements 1830–1850*, Macmillan, 1970, pp. 95–115. On the GNCTU see the works on Robert Owen cited in note 20 and W. H. Oliver 'The Consolidated Trades Unions of 1834', *Economic History Review*, 18 (1964), pp. 77–95. J. Marlow *The Tolpuddle Martyrs*, Deutsch, 1971 is a popular study.

27 Quoted in K. D. Brown op. cit., p. 50.
28 The role of women in radicalism in this period can best be approached in J. D. Young *Women and Popular Struggle*, Mainstream Publishing, 1985, pp. 37–70, D. Thompson 'Women in Nineteenth Century Radical Politics: A Lost Dimension', in J. Mitchell and A. Oakley (eds) *The Rights and Wrongs of Women*, Penguin, 1976, pp. 112–38 and B. Taylor *Eve and the New Jerusalem*. Virago, 1983. The two classic studies of working women, I. Pinchbeck *Women Workers and the Industrial Revolution 1750–1850*, first published in 1930, and B. Drake *Women and Trade Unions*, London, 1921, have recently been republished by Virago (1985 and 1984). J. Rendall *Women in an Industrializing Society: England 1750–1880*, Basil Blackwell, 1990, places radicalism in context.
29 S. Alexander 'Women, class and sexual differences in the 1830s and 1840s: some reflections on the writings of a feminist history', *History Workshop*, 17 (Spring 1984), pp. 125–49 summarizes the reasons behind the emergence of women's radicalism as a serious study.
30 This discussion relies heavily on J. D. Young op. cit.
31 Jack Wade *History of the Middle and Working Classes*, London, 1835, p. 570 quoted ibid., p. 62.
32 E. Royle and J. Walvin op. cit., p. 186.

Addendum: C. Behagg *Politics and Production in the Early Nineteenth Century*, Routledge, 1990, focuses on Birmingham, a centre of small-scale industry.

13 Class politics? Chartism and the politics of pressure

People who have not shared in the hopes of the Chartists, who have no personal knowledge of the deep and intense feelings which animated them, can have little conception of the difference between our own times and those of fifty or sixty years ago. The whole governing classes – Whigs even more than Tories – were not only disliked, they were positively hated by the working population. Nor was this hostility to their own countrymen less manifest on the side of the 'better orders'[1]

For nearly twenty years after 1837, Chartism was a name to evoke the wildest hopes and the worst fears, like Bolshevism in a later age.[2]

The 1830s saw a combination of circumstances which led to the re-emergence of radical protest by the working population and of the politics of pressure among the middle classes. The 'betrayal' of 1832, the Whig repression of trade unionism, the Tolpuddle 'martyrs', the nature of reforms after 1832 and an awareness that the landed and elitist nature of authority and power was to be maintained created a political environment in which radicalism revived. The 'crisis' of the mid-1830s when, for the first time, the industrialized economy faltered significantly led to the spectre of long-term 'want' and 'distress', falling standards of living among groups for whom economic change had previously been largely beneficial and an enhanced perception of the unfairness of the legislative protection of one sector of the economy at the expense of the rest. This chapter will examine the politics of pressure in its varied forms and will focus on Chartism and the Anti-Corn Law League.

CHARTISM

Historiography of Chartism

The historiography of Chartism in the twentieth century has shown that historians' perspectives of the movement have naturally changed through time.[3] In the early part of the century attention focused on supposed divisions between 'physical force' and 'moral force' wings of Chartism,

with the role of William Lovett in the latter gaining considerable sympathy. By the late 1950s and early 1960s the emphasis had moved to the
diversity of the movement, a result in part of the book *Chartist Studies*
edited by Asa Briggs and published in 1959. Since the localized studies
from different parts of Britain – David Goodway on London and A. J.
Peacock on Bradford, for example – have underlined the local variations
within the movement and the diversity of its strength and character.
The difficulty of making generalizations about Chartism led an American
reviewer to remark in 1962 that it 'was a series of responses, not a
movement'. More recently historians have made attempts to re-examine
the movement as a whole, especially its political nature. Dorothy Thompson, for example, maintains that:

> For a short period, thousands of working people considered that their
> problems could be solved by a change in the political organisation of
> the country. They believed this passionately. . . . The political question
> dominated all others.[4]

This emphasis has been paralleled by the implicit or explicit concern with
arguments about 'class'. Marx and Engels based much of their analysis of
class consciousness and class conflict on their observations of the Chartist
movement and what was happening in England in the 1840s. Was Chartism
the world's first proletarian revolution which failed because of lack of
theoretical clarity and opportunist leadership? Was it a 'class' movement
or were the conflicts of interest between trades, localities and social groupings within the working population greater than any conception of a
working-class national interest? Can historians talk accurately of a working
class in the 1830s and 1840s? Some of these issues have been raised
previously but it is clear to some historians, like E. P. Thompson, that
there was a continuum of working-class experience in the first half of the
nineteenth century and that the Chartist period marked a peak of self-
consciousness and united action. Others have emphasized the extent to
which the working population was not a proletariat in this period. How
far Chartism was a developed class movement is still an issue in need of
solution.

The emergence of Chartism

Chartism first appeared as a formal movement in the spring of 1838
with the publication of the People's Charter, a document produced by
consultation between leading radical MPs like John Roebuck and representatives of the London Working Men's Association (LWMA) which
had been established in 1836 to agitate for 'an equality of political rights'.
The 'six points' of the Charter – annual Parliaments, equal electoral
districts, payment of MPs, universal manhood suffrage, vote by ballot and
the abolition of property qualifications – were necessary to secure this

equality. The origins of Chartism, however, can be traced back to the early 1830s and in particular to the disappointment or 'betrayal' radical activists felt at the outcome of the reform agitation between 1830 and 1832. The 1832 Reform Act failed to meet the demands of radical organizations like the National Union of Working Classes which had campaigned vigorously for change. The franchise remained very restricted. The Commons was elected by only 14 per cent of adult males. The working population was still excluded from Parliament and felt duped by the middle classes. Thomas Cooper wrote of the municipal reform in 1835 that

> the poor and labouring classes . . . now mutter discontent at . . . the recreant middle classes whom municipal honours have drawn off from their hot blooded radicalism, and converted into cold, unfeeling wielders of magisterial or other local power.[5]

This sentiment applied equally to 1832.

The LWMA was one of several organizations created in the course of the 1830s which expressed both disappointment and disillusion. The East London Democratic Association, founded in early 1837 and Feargus O'Connor's and his Irish supporters' Marylebone Radical Association, though more militant, had similar objectives to the LWMA. In May 1837 Thomas Attwood's Birmingham Political Union, which had stagnated after 1832, was re-established and political unions sprang up in other provincial centres like Manchester. These groups, individually and in co-operation, channelled discontent among the working population through the printed and spoken word, a discontent made both more obvious and widespread by growing economic depression.

The emergence of Chartism as a political movement owed much to the policies of the Whig government. Between 1830 and 1836 it had maintained a relentless war against the unstamped radical press. Over 700 sellers of radical journals were prosecuted and this left a residual antipathy towards the government even after stamp duties were reduced in 1836. The LWMA, for example, was formed by William Lovett after the disbanding of the Association of Working Men to Procure a Cheap and Honest Press which had co-ordinated the anti-stamp agitation.

The Whigs also adopted a repressive policy towards trade unionism. Many prominent radicals, including O'Connell and Joseph Hume, who had utilized the support of the working population during the reform agitation, were bitterly opposed to unionism. This helped to exacerbate the growing rift between the middle classes and the working population, already disappointed by parliamentary reform. The prosecution of the Tolpuddle martyrs in 1834 was particularly important in this continuing process. The political union in Bradford, for example, collapsed because of internal disagreement between middle class and workers over the Tolpuddle case. A similar pattern existed in Scotland with a rapid deterioration of the alliance between middle-class radicals and trade unionists.

The arrest of members of the Glasgow cotton spinners' union in July 1837 on suspicion of arson and murder led to a widespread campaign in their support throughout Scotland and northern England. The militancy of this campaign put further strain on co-operation between middle-class radicals and the working population. Many of the men who drew up the Charter were involved in the campaign of protest organized against the sentence passed on the Glasgow men. George Stephens, in an open letter to Lord John Russell, wrote in 1836: 'what remains for the labourer but plunder? There is no law for a starving man – there is no tie of conscience or principle binding on a famished wretch who hears a wife and children clamorous for food.'

The reformed Parliament had failed to provide any substantial improvement in working conditions, one of the main objectives of the factory movement, and this became a further source of political discontent. The 1833 Factory Act, though it regulated the working day of children in the textile industry, left adult hours unaltered. The logical conclusion of this for many working men was that factory reform could be achieved only if Parliament was reformed. The frustrations of factory reformers swelled the rising Chartist tide and many of the northern delegates to the Chartist Convention in 1839 had entered politics through the ten-hour movement.

Many had also gained political experience through the campaign against the imposition of the new poor law, arguably the least popular of all Whig measures. Implementation of the 1834 Act was relatively smooth in southern England but the timing of that process in the north was unfortunate, coinciding with the beginnings of economic slump. It was bitterly resisted. The workhouses became *the* symbol of Whig oppression. Richard Oastler led the attack but he was soon joined by O'Connor, Rayner Stephens and metropolitan radicals like Henry Hetherington and Bronterre O'Brien. The latter attacked the new law in the first issue of his *National Reformer* in January 1837:

> . . . the new Poor Law Act is the last rotten blood-stained prop by which the money-monster hopes to sustain the tottering fabric of his cannibal system . . . and would then bastile and starve you for the fruits of its own barbarity.

By 1838 the campaign was beginning to run out of steam and gradually the north turned to a wider-based radicalism.

Towards the end of the decade resentments over Whig attitudes to the press and trade unionism, the frustrations of factory reformers and the fear generated by the new poor law converged into general demands for political reform as the only way of remedying the specific grievances of the working population. The attitude of the radicals towards the Whigs can be seen in an article published in the *Chartist Circular* in May 1840:

> A Whig is a political shuffler, without honour, integrity or
> patriotism . . . he courts public favour, smiles graciously on the
> people . . . until he gets them to assist him in advancing his selfish
> schemes. But he treats them with ingratitude and contempt, when they
> afterwards remind him of his obligations and request him to perform
> them.

The 'mass platform' was revived. The key figure in the translation of
several separate grievances into a general demand for parliamentary
reform was Feargus O'Connor. He was the natural successor to Henry
Hunt. He founded his own organization, the Great Northern Union, in
1838 and was also, through his charisma and oratory, able to win substantial support in the Birmingham Political Union and the LWMA.

It is, however, important not to exaggerate the organic unity of Chartism. The winter of 1838–9 was spent by many radicals preparing for the
forthcoming convention and the presentation of the Charter to Parliament.
The unity that existed was fuelled by a pervasive sense of resentment, but
at all levels of the movement there were different emphases, tactics and
organizations, which gave Chartism its 'kaleidoscopic appearance'.

Why Chartism was different from earlier radical movements

What made Chartism different from radical movements earlier in the
century was a certain comprehensiveness in both geographical and occupational terms. Chartism was much stronger in certain areas than others
and its real powerbases – in the three textile districts of the East Midlands,
the West Riding of Yorkshire and in southern Lancashire – had seen
substantial agitation in the 1810s. Within these areas Chartism was stronger in industrial villages and medium-sized towns like Ashton, Stockport,
Oldham, Bolton, Halifax and Bradford than in the major provincial centres of Manchester and Leeds. But there were other areas, like South
Wales, the Black Country and parts of the south-west, which had experienced little organized radicalism before. In the first National Petition
London provided 19,000 signatures compared to 100,000 from the West
Riding. Mass support for Chartism in London came only in the 1840s. In
other areas, however, Chartism never secured much support. In Ireland,
cities like Belfast, Cork and Dublin had Chartist organizations but the
general suspicion by O'Connell and the Catholic Church that Chartism
would undermine society, and of the Young Ireland Movement because
Chartism was English, ensured that its impact was limited. This is suprising
given the widespread involvement of emigré Irish in mainland Chartism
and the interest by Chartists in the Irish question. Chartism gained little
support in areas where Wesleyan as opposed to Primitive Methodism
was strong. In Cornwall temperance and Methodist leaders combined to
minimize Chartist influence. In other areas, by contrast, local Noncon-

formists played a central role in the movement and some national leaders like Henry Vincent sought to give the movement a Christian rationale. More generally, Chartism was weak in largely rural areas where deference and traditional forms of protest remained strong. In East Anglia agricultural labourers were not convinced that the vote would remedy their economic position and, threatened by the new workhouses and unemployment, reverted to incendiarism in the 1840s. In rural Wales, where the gap between rural and urban workers was to some extent bridged by their joint opposition to English dominance and their shared Nonconformity, Chartism was accompanied by more traditional protest in the form of the Rebecca riots of 1839 and 1842. Beneath the regional and local diversity of Chartism there was a very real sense of national unity in the movement, especially in the peak years between 1839 and 1842 and in 1848.

An analysis of the occupational support for Chartism also reveals a consistent pattern. A wide range of urban and industrial workers was involved. Economic conditions were only partly responsible for this, though they were of major importance. Of the twenty-three local associations who responded to a questionnaire distributed by the 1839 convention, only two stressed lack of the vote as a general grievance. The majority complained of low wages, dear food, scarcity of work and economic hardship.

Considerable support came from domestic outworkers. They saw Chartism as a means of combating the destruction of their way of life and of the nature and values of the communities in which they lived. Textile handloom weavers, linen spinners and woolcombers in Yorkshire and silk workers in Essex were chronically depressed and continued an earlier radical tradition. It is significant that a characteristic of strong Chartist areas was a rising population which placed additional pressure on occupations in easily learned and labour-intensive industries. In Scotland handloom weavers were the major force behind Chartism. The move to demands for a political answer to their economic grievances was motivated not by the belief that the vote would benefit their conditions but that without it there could never be a solution.

Factory workers played a far more active role in Chartism than they had in previous radical movements. Here too the initial motivation was economic, springing from the widespread unemployment of the late 1830s. Contemporaries like Rayner Stephens and Cooke Taylor were not alone in noting that Lancashire Chartism was a 'knife and fork question'. But it was more than this. The early part of the century had seen long hours offset by relatively high levels of security and wages. This position had been weakened by technological change, especially the introduction of the self-acting mule, which had diluted the level of skill involved and devalued the workers' role in the processes of production. The subordination of labour to capital had become 'real' in the sense that it now rested on both the structure of ownership and the character of the labour process itself.

The larger units of production (factories) were now accompanied by a different technical relationship between workers and the means of production.

The close association between trade unionism and Chartism in some areas has been regarded as indicative of the unity of action among the working population. There was considerable overlap in terms of personnel and leadership between Chartism and trade societies. Factory workers were now less able to protect their interests through trade union action and many turned – temporarily – to political agitation. Miners had also been insulated from broad popular movements but during the late 1830s and early 1840s large numbers, especially in Wales and the West Midlands, became enmeshed in Chartism. The motivation behind their actions was increasing industrial bitterness and the inability of trade unionism to find solutions. In Staffordshire the linkage to Chartism seems to have been superficial. Chartists did play a prominent role in the organization of the strikes in August 1842 but more importance was attached to the specific local grievances of the miners than to the Charter. By contrast, they were able to achieve a genuinely political agitation in South Wales during 1838 and 1839 among both iron-workers and miners, culminating in the abortive Newport rising.

Factory workers and miners appear to have occupied an intermediate position between the rank-and-file outworkers and the artisans and small shopkeepers who formed most of the leadership. In Suffolk and Essex, for example, tailors, shoemakers and building artisans looked to agricultural labourers for mass support. In Bath artisans provided the leadership and the declining cloth trade the rank and file. In the Bradford Northern Union artisan leadership was supported by woolcombers and weavers. In Aberdeen there was a similar balance between handloom weavers and a small, articulate artisan leadership. Craftsmen were prominent partly because of a long tradition of political radicalism. But there were important economic considerations which gave artisan leadership an added edge. In the clothing, furniture and building trades their economic position was deteriorating or at least vulnerable. There was a growing market for relatively low-quality goods and a downward trend in prices which compelled employers to cut costs. These features were responsible for a continuing expansion of a 'dishonourable' or non-unionized sector in traditional trades, the employment of unapprenticed and semi-skilled labour and a downward spiral into 'sweated' trades. Only a few skilled trades, like bookbinding and watchmaking, were able to maintain their status and prosperity and remained aloof from Chartism.

Women were involved in Chartism to an unprecedented extent.[6] This strong female involvement – up to a third of those who signed the First Petition in 1839 and the petition on behalf of the transported John Frost in 1841 were women – was not motivated primarily by the question of women's suffrage. Women participated in the movement in support of men and their communities rather than on behalf of their own sex. In the early years of the movement there were over a hundred female radical associations and as a result of their activities a general commitment to the inclusion of women in the suffrage and the improvement of women's education was accepted by many radicals. By the mid-1840s the increasing rationality and respectability of the movement meant that radical papers mentioned women less. This did not mean that women dropped out of the movement but that the notion of 'separate spheres' and the removal of women from the public domain was an implicit feature of that respectability.

The Chartist localities were bound together by the tourings of the national leaders, by itinerant lecturers, by the Chartist press and by organizations like the network of National Associations and the National Charter Association. But though Chartism was in a very real sense a national movement, the ability of the local leadership to attract and retain the support of the rank and file varied from place to place. In Lancashire it was rooted firmly in the obvious social inequality between workers and employers in the dominant cotton trade. In Coventry the absence of this class dimension kept Chartism ineffective. Ribbon weaving was still organized on a small scale permitting journeymen to become small masters in their own right. City freemen enjoyed privileges which separated them from the working population, thus depriving it of potential leadership. The local variations within Chartism caused by economic and social differences were compounded by political differences. Chartists in different areas stressed different political programmes alongside the Charter, which was frequently the only unifying element. In Lancashire the stress was upon factory and economic improvements but in Nottingham and South Wales hostility to the poor law remained dominant.

Chartism 1838–40

The tendency among historians to view Chartism as a movement in which there were two distinct and conflicting elements – the moral force wing led by Lovett and based among the intelligent skilled artisans of London and a physical force wing led by Feargus O'Connor and the illiterate and violent population of the northern industrial districts – has been effectively undermined. It was not as simple as that. But there were important differences over how the Charter should be put into effect which created local, as well as national, factionalism. The Leeds Working Men's Association, for example, was split into three groups: one favoured O'Connor's strategy of peaceful protest combined with the intimidation of potential violence; a second leaned towards Lovett and the LWMA; and a third group was influenced by Owenite ideas. Julian Harney was later to observe that 'faction has cut the throat of Chartism'.

The Chartist movement did not rise to a peak and then decline; rather it peaked on three occasions: in 1838–40, 1842 and 1848 corresponding to mass petitions to Parliament and popular protest. In June 1836 the LWMA was formed, initially by artisans, with William Lovett as secretary. The six points of the 'People's Charter' were contained within a petition drafted by Lovett and Francis Place in early 1837 and were endorsed in a series of public meetings. The Charter emerged out of a tradition of articulate, politically aware, London artisan radicalism, with the assistance of a small group of middle-class radicals.

Thomas Attwood revived the Birmingham Political Union in 1837, initially to advocate household suffrage but soon supporting universal suffrage. The LWMA and BPU drummed up support for the Charter in various parts of the country, drawing on radical associations which had already come into existence in Scotland and northern England, some at the instigation of O'Connor who had toured the north in 1835. He realized that success for Chartism as a political movement meant the revival of the 'mass platform' and that this would prove difficult for a movement exclusively based in London. O'Connor was effective both as demagogue and organizer and during the winter of 1836–7 he broadened the basis of his support from London–Lancashire–Yorkshire to Nottingham, Newcastle and Scotland. He opposed any alliance with the Whigs or middle-class radicals. By mid-1838 he exercised considerable dominance over northern popular radicalism, which in contrast to the diverse radicalism of London was characterized by a unified communal response, through his newspaper the *Northern Star* founded in November 1837 and by bringing it together in the Leeds-based Great Northern Union in April 1838.

The nature of London's economy, with over 400 different trades, its huge size and its localism, prevented any strong sense of community. The relative unity of Chartism in the provinces contrasted with the rivalries and divisions within Chartism in London. O'Connor was already suspicious of Lovett's continued co-operation with middle-class radicals and the LWMA's less than enthusiastic support for convicted Glasgow cotton trade unionists. In March 1838 Harney and some colleagues expressed their opposition to the LWMA's policies by seceding and forming the O'Connorite London Democratic Association (LDA) to cater for the more depessed London trades like the Spitalfields silk workers. 'In the Democratic Association,' it was stated in its official newspaper, 'the Jacobin Club again lives and flourishes, and the villainous tyrants, who'll find to their cost, that England too has her Marats, St. Justs and Robespierres.'

In September 1838 a major outdoor meeting in the north was held on Kersal Moor, Manchester, the first of a series of regional meetings held to enable the election of delegates to a National Convention scheduled to be held in London early in 1839 to organize the national petition. The electioneering which preceded its meeting exposed the differences within Chartism as the various factions sought to consolidate their positions. This struggle can be seen in the movement's rapidly growing press. In January

1839 the LWMA published the *Charter* to put forward its position. Other London Chartists responded with the rival *Chartist* the following month and the LDA joined in with the *London Democrat*. In Scotland moral force found support in the *Ayrshire Examiner* but in the press battle O'Connor undoubtedly had in the *Northern Star* the strongest weapon at his disposal.

In February 1839 the Convention finally met in London. It consisted of fifty-four delegates of whom twelve, mostly sympathetic to the LWMA, represented London, twenty-five came from the industrial north, eight from Scotland, two from Wales and five from the Birmingham Political Union. About half were working men and the remainder radical gentry or small employers. Divisions emerged over major issues: should the Convention regard itself simply as a means of managing the petition or should it set itself up in opposition to the House of Commons as 'the People's Parliament'? But the crucial question was whether, if the petition was rejected, physical force and insurrection should be adopted. Ideological differences were exacerbated by administrative ineptitude. Lovett was appointed secretary but was not given the necessary clerical assistance and there was consequently failure to give a clear lead on the organization of missionaries and, more importantly, on collecting the 'national rent', the means of financing the Convention's activities. A hostile press was quick to accuse the Chartists of mismanagement and fraud and the methods used to collect the 'rent' were, in some areas, little short of criminal, which alienated middle-class opinion even further.

As the language of militants, like Peter Bussey of Bradford and G. J. Harney, became more extreme many of the moderate members of the Convention, principally those from Scotland and Birmingham, returned home. It was the question of violence and the closely connected issue of co-operation with the middle classes which did most to divide the Convention delegates. Joseph Rayner Stephens put forward a gospel of revolt. Trained for the Wesleyan ministry, he was expelled in 1834 for agitation in favour of factory reform but it was his scathing attacks on the new poor law which endeared him to the working population, who built three chapels for him in the Ashton district. He considered himself 'a revolutionist by fire, a revolutionist by blood, to the knife, to the death'. In May 1839, in a sermon preached at Ashton, he said: 'Down with the House of Commons; down with the House of Lords; aye, down with the throne, and down with the altar itself; burn the church; down with all rank, all dignity, all title, all power . . .'. The government acted against the Chartists by banning torchlight processions and made it clear that it would use the forces of law and order to maintain its position. When Melbourne's government resigned in May, the national petition could not be presented and the remaining thirty-five delegates to the Convention moved to Birmingham. Various strategies were discussed: a withdrawal of bank deposits (like the threatened 'run on gold' in May 1832); withholding taxes, rents and tithes; the use of the general strike advocated in a pamphlet published in 1832 by William Benbow, a militant shoemaker from Middleton who had helped organize the 1817 March of the Blanketeers; and taking up arms. No agreement was reached and the delegates decided to leave the decision on strategies to local associations. Certainly O'Connor and O'Brien had begun to modify their rhetoric when it came to translating militancy into action. This decision was, in part, a response to the hardening of government policy by Lord John Russell, the Home Secretary. Initially he had adopted a conciliatory strategy, resisting those demanding repressive action. Speaking at a dinner given in his honour by the civic authority in Liverpool, Russell said in late 1838:

> There were some, perhaps, who would put down such meetings . . . it was not from the unchecked declaration of public opinion that the government had anything to fear. There was fear when men were driven by force to secret combinations.

But by mid-1839 a harder policy had emerged: drilling was banned, lord lieutenants were given powers to raise and arm special constables and 6,000 troops were stationed in the Northern District under General Napier. The Metropolitan Police, often used as a mobile riot squad in this period, was used to put down rioting Chartists at Llandiloes in Montgomeryshire in May. Leading figures in the London and Lancashire movement were arrested and the tempo of arrests increased after a riot in the Birmingham Bull Ring in July.

The Convention had been reduced by resignation, dissension and now arrests, and it moved back to London. On 12 July, when the Commons rejected the petition by 235 votes to 46, the Convention had finally to face up to the issue of violence and resistance. On 17 July it voted, by 13 to 6, to hold a 'sacred month', despite the fact that letters from local associations questioned the wisdom of calling a general strike during a severe trade depression and pointed to insufficient planning. On 24 July, following consultations with sixty-three Welsh, Scottish and English associations which showed support from only nine, O'Connor got the decision reversed. The national Chartist leadership, decimated by arrests, drew back from nationwide confrontation with the authorities, the Convention was dissolved in September and the initiative moved to the local associations.

There was a revival of the conspiratorial tradition of direct action and armed force. Meetings were held in the early autumn to co-ordinate a national rising but, in the event, this only occurred in South Wales. On the night of 3–4 November 7,000 miners and iron-workers from the South Wales coalfield marched in three columns to Newport with the aim of releasing Henry Vincent from Newport Gaol. There is also evidence that they were launching a massive uprising to create a people's republic in the Welsh valleys which, they hoped, might spread to other parts of

Britain. Troops opened fire, killing at least twenty-two and wounding about fifty. The rest fled in confusion and many, including leaders like John Frost, Zephaniah Williams and Charles Jones, were arrested in the succeeding days. Over 250 people were arraigned in the last mass treason trial in British history. Death sentences were passed on the three leaders, though these were later commuted to transportation for life to Australia. The Newport rising was not a small-scale affair or the work of Whig *agents provocateurs* or simply a 'monster demonstration', as earlier historians concluded, but was the product of a radical political culture in an area when class divisions were clearly demarcated.[7]

Further risings were planned in the wake of Newport. Attempted insurrections took place in Sheffield, Dewsbury and Bradford in January 1840. These towns had, unlike those in Lancashire, been largely untouched by the wave of arrests or the presence of large military and police forces in July and August 1839. Sheffield had a coherent and confident working-class movement and a long tradition of radicalism stretching back to the 1790s. On 12 August a token one-day 'National Holiday' occurred, which led to Samuel Holberry emerging as the leader of the militant Chartists. Widespread planning to co-ordinate a regional insurrection, betrayed to the authorities, led the Sheffield movement to act on the night of 11–12 January 1840. Holberry and his close associates were arrested before they could act but although Dewsbury failed to rise after this débâcle, Bradford went ahead. As in Sheffield, plans were betrayed by a spy and the rising petered out.

The authorities adopted policies which successfully defused the situation. The Chartists assumed that government would be unable to resist overwhelming numbers, as in 1831–2, would move towards repressing policies and that this would spark off an explosion of protest sufficient to engulf the forces of reaction. But government did not act as expected. Initially Russell adopted conciliatory tones giving more extreme Chartists time to alienate middle-class reformers and moderate opinion by their militant rhetoric. The initiative quickly moved to the government and the Chartists found themselves on the defensive, caught between defeat or insurrection. By the end of 1839 it was clear that they had no chance of defeating the state by force and that troops had no compunction about firing on Chartists if ordered to do so. At local level the situation depended on the attitudes adopted by magistrates, military and police. Sympathetic handling could defuse potentially explosive situations. Napier, for example, met Lancashire Chartist leaders and promised to keep troops and police away from a major rally at Kersal Moor as long as it was peaceful. He was frequently angered by the attitude of local magistrates always sensitive to situations where both public order and property seemed threatened, which tended to enflame Chartist anger rather than defuse it.

Chartism 1840–42

By the summer of 1840 Chartism was in considerable disarray. Its survival depended on the ability and dedication of local leaders and the hold which it had over ordinary people. Different emphases began to emerge. The Chartist church movement which began in Scotland began to spread southwards, flourishing in the Birmingham area and in the West Country, the powerbase of Henry Vincent. William Lovett proposed to launch a new organization called the National Association for Promoting the Improvement of the People, stressing education and self-help. Lowery was also convinced that social reform would be ineffective unless preceded by moral reform. Henry Vincent toured the country, after his release from prison in early 1841, on behalf of teetotal Chartism and other leaders like Hetherington, Hill and Cleave shared his enthusiasm. In Leeds and other provincial cities Chartists turned to municipal electioneering. In Nottingham Chartists took up the poor law issue again. But, despite this diversity, some degree of unity and national organization was provided by the National Charter Association (NCA) formed in Manchester in July 1840 largely at O'Connor's instigation.

The NCA remained the major national organization for the next decade and some historians have seen it as the first independent working-class political party. O'Connor encountered considerable opposition to the NCA and growth was slow. Many Chartists, including Lovett, refused to join because they feared that it might be deemed illegal under the Corresponding Societies Act. Because local branches of a national political organization were illegal, the NCA had to be a central body, with localities represented on a general council several hundred strong. Others, especially in Scotland and parts of the Midlands, were suspicious of its centralized focus. It was very much O'Connor's organization and this led to significant personal opposition. By the end of 1840 just under 300 local associations had affiliated. These were concentrated in Lancashire and Yorkshire, the Nottinghamshire–Derby area and in London. During 1841 O'Connor claimed 50,000 members from 401 localities.

The NCA was the only new Chartist departure that O'Connor regarded with any favour, fearing that the rest would lead to the fragmentation of the movement. His fears were not without foundation. Lovett's association had considerable middle-class backing and the success of Chartist municipal candidates in Leeds owed something to the efforts being made to reforge a Chartist–Radical alliance. O'Connor took the view that the Anti-Corn Law League offered working people minimum support to achieve its own ends but the winter of 1841–2 saw agreement reached in several cities between Chartists and repealers.

Some Chartists turned to the Complete Suffrage Union (CSU), launched by Joseph Sturge in Birmingham in April 1842. His objective was to reconcile middle and working classes through the repeal of class-based legislation and a declaration that the exclusion of the bulk of the population from the franchise was both unconstitutional and unchristian. This attracted considerable support from the middle classes, from those Chartists alienated by the violence of 1839–40 and in Scotland, while Vincent rallied the movement in the West Country. Lovett and Francis Place also lent support and at the first meeting organized by the CSU in Birmingham the moderate nature of the movement was emphasized by the systematic exclusion of O'Connorites. By late April 1842 there were fifty local associations and the CSU presented a rival parliamentary petition to that of the NCA.

O'Connor initially conducted a fierce campaign against the CSU, which was obliged to adopt the Charter in all but name, but recognized the tactical advantage of a brief alliance with middle-class radicals and came out in favour of class collaboration in July 1842. By the autumn, under pressure from Chartist hardliners over his vacillation during the Plug Riots, he reversed his position and again attacked the CSU as 'a League job'. At a CSU conference in December, packed with Chartist delegates despite prior agreement, the middle-class radicals insisted on the adoption of a 'New Bill of Rights' for universal suffrage instead of the emotive 'Charter'. Lovett was not prepared to accept this and joined with O'Connor in substituting 'Charter' for 'Bill', leading to the immediate secession of the majority of the middle-class CSU delegates. Class collaboration was ended and O'Connor's grip of the movement was tightened.

The experiment and failure of class collaboration in 1842 took place in an atmosphere of widespread industrial unrest and Chartist activity. The previous September saw the launching of the second national petition and Convention. The latter eventually met in Birmingham in April 1842. It was much better organized than its predecessor with the number of delegates limited to 24 from English constituencies and 25 from Welsh and Scottish ones. They were elected by paid-up members of the NCA rather than at mass meetings. The petition was also better organized and, it was claimed, contained three million signatures. The result was, however, the same: rejection by the House of Commons by 287 to 46 votes on 1 May. This created much bitterness in Chartist localities, a situation exacerbated by the death in York Castle of Samuel Holberry and the worst economic recession of the century.

Up to half a million workers were involved in the series of strikes which swept across many industrial districts in the north and Midlands in July and August 1842. Miners on the North Staffordshire coalfield struck in July, followed by a rash of strikes in the Lancashire textile industry in response to wage cuts. Mobs of strikers travelled through the county enforcing a general stoppage by drawing out the plugs of factory boilers. Within weeks the strike had spread across the Pennines into Yorkshire and north into Scotland. By September fifteen English and Welsh and eight Scottish counties had been affected. In several towns troops were called out to quell civil disturbances.

The extent of Chartist involvement created as much controversy at the time as it has subsequently among historians. It is, however, clear that many of those who spoke at the Manchester meetings were Chartists who had no connection with the textile trades. Chartist leaders seem to have been caught unawares by the strikes but soon exploited the situation for their own ends. The series of regional trade conferences in August gave a further opportunity for Chartist intervention and there was a widespread adoption of the Charter as one of the strike's main aims. In Manchester, Glasgow and London there was some convergence of Chartist and trade union activity. The extent to which Chartists were involved varied regionally. In Yorkshire, for example, where trade unions were weaker and less widespread than in Lancashire, local Chartists exercised strong influence over tactics but generally Chartist leaders were too divided to take full advantage of the strike movement.

The unions themselves had little central machinery capable of co-ordinating the strikes and the different attitudes of Chartists prevented the NCA from taking on this role. Chartists were reacting to a situation rather than playing a central part in determining that situation. Tension eased in September as economic conditions improved. The 1842 harvest was good and trade was already reviving, which led employers to agree to cancel wage reductions. However, the strike movement had two adverse effects on the Chartists. First, the effort made by some to organize the strikes for their own ends led Peel and his Home Secretary, Sir James Graham, to blame them for the strikes. There was a wave of arrests in September, including that of O'Connor, who got off on a technicality. Harsh sentences were handed out: in Staffordshire, for example, of 274 cases tried, 154 men were imprisoned and 5 were transported for life. By early 1843 there was less need for harsh treatment, as the strikes were over and unrest had quietened. Peel and Graham recognized, as Russell had done in 1839–40, that pushing repression too far was counterproductive, alienating public opinion and creating public sympathy. Secondly, though this was by no means a universal reaction, trade union disillusion with Chartism probably increased. At the metal trades conference in Manchester in August one of the resolutions passed was that:

> this meeting deprecates the late and present conduct of those employers who have been reducing labourers . . . but at the same time, we can not, nor do we sanction the conduct of those individuals who have been going about destroying property and offering violence to the people.

To unionists the issue was economic rather than political and, for them, the strikes were not entirely unsuccessful. Wage cuts were restored and in some places increased to the 1840 levels and in the cotton districts trade unionism emerged on a more organized and confident basis.[8]

Confrontational tactics had failed in 1839–40 and in 1842. Mass arrests and imprisonments had sapped the strength of the movement and the relative economic prosperity of the years between 1842 and 1848 helped to dampen the enthusiasm of the rank and file. This meant that Chartism, though still potentially a mass movement, became increasingly fragmented. The agreement between Lovett and O'Connor in late 1842 over the CSU proposals was shortlived. He had no intention of working with O'Connor and gradually he and others of like mind withdrew to pursue their objectives by peaceful agitation. O'Connor emerged firmly in control of the formal Chartist movement which he promptly led off in entirely new directions.

Lovett placed increasing emphasis on educating the working population. Henry Vincent and Robert Lowery continued their work on temperance. Other diversions took the form of increased trade union activity, Owenite Socialism, support for the Anti-Corn Law League and for European republicanism. 'New Moves' like these represented attempts by activists to find alternative solutions, though they generally failed to gain mass support. The relatively wide ratepayer franchise was exploited by municipal Chartists, notably in Leeds and Sheffield, with some success. In Leeds Chartists sought election to borough offices, becoming members of the Board of Surveyors for Highways and of the Poor Law Guardians. Within the Council chamber Chartists made up only a small proportion of the 64 members and tended to be small shopkeepers and tradesmen rather than members of the working population. In Sheffield the Chartist leader Isaac Ironside created a more impressive caucus than that of Leeds and by 1848 there were 22 Chartists on the council. Over the Pennines, in Rochdale, Chartists took control of the Board of Guardians from 1844, ensuring that few of the basic precepts of the new poor law were applied before the 1870s.

Chartism 1843–8

Skilled and prosperous workers, organized in strong trade societies, tended to distance themselves from Chartism but improved trade after 1842 saw a temporary revival of national unions among workers in cotton, mining and other areas. The *Northern Star* gave increased coverage to industrial matters after 1842 and became the official organ of the National Association of United Trades for the Protection of Labour, formed in March 1845. It was composed mainly of the same type of craftsmen who backed metropolitan Chartism but, despite its grand title, it lacked support from Wales, Scotland and Ireland as well as parts of England. O'Connor did not succeed in tapping trade union support, probably because his militancy had scared it off.

Increasingly O'Connor turned his attention to the land question.[9] The Land Plan provided a major outlet for frustrated Chartists, and proved a highly attractive proposition as well as an opportunity for further ridicule from their opponents. The Plan has to be seen in the context of the experiments at community living during the 1830s and 1840s, particularly by Owenites and other socialists. It offered the means of restoring artisan independence and self-reliance and was accepted by a reshaped convention of fourteen delegates in 1845 with NCA backing. The idea was to raise capital for a land company by permitting the purchase of shares at 3d or more a week. With the cash land would be purchased, made into smallholdings complete with the necessary buildings and rented to shareholders chosen by ballot.

The Plan was rooted in land programmes derived from a line of radical thinkers including Paine, Spence and Cobbett. It was popular among those who viewed industrialization and urbanization not as economic progress but as a process by which the individual of the pre-industrial period was dehumanized. It seemed to represent an attempt to reverse the process of industrialization. O'Connor wrote in 1843 that

> I am about to present to the industrious of all classes the means whereby social happiness, political freedom, and the pure spirit of religion may be introduced . . . as a substitute for the misery, the discomfort and the immorality at present prevailing. . . .

O'Connor benefitted from the fact that he launched the scheme when rising unemployment generated considerable interest in emigration and home colonization as a means of absorbing surplus labour. Many trade unions had already started emigration schemes and groups were running allotment societies. Much initial support came from the industrial north and Midlands but enthusiasm soon spread south.

Momentum gathered once O'Connor purchased his first site near Watford and on May Day 1847 the first tenants moved into O'Connorville. Subscriptions soared and the renamed National Cooperative Land Company bought further estates at Lowbands, Snigs End, Minster Lovell and Great Dodford. Over £100,000 was collected from some 70,000 subscribers, though only 250 actually settled on the two-acre allotments. But the company and its associated Land Bank were plagued by legal difficulties. In May 1848 Parliament appointed a select committee to investigate the Land Company, which had come under scrutiny when O'Connor tried to give it legal protection by amending the Friendly Societies Act. At the end of July the committee reported that the company could not be registered as it was illegal. Though there was no evidence for the rumours of fraud, the accounts were confused and inaccurate and this further weakened confidence in the scheme. O'Connor found that the flow of share capital was drying up and, after exploring alternative means of saving the scheme, he finally took the route recommended by the select committee and wound the company up in 1851.

Contemporaries like W. E. Adams, and later historians, have seen 1848 as a watershed in the history of the Chartist movement. It is certainly true that after 1848 Chartism lost whatever unity it had, with even O'Connor willing to accede to household suffrage while leaders such as Jones and Harney moved towards a socialist solution to the issue of the franchise. In his autobiography Thomas Cooper thought that Chartist demands were 'wilder' in 1848 than in either 1842 or 1838, a belief which was accepted by those in authority.

The winter of 1847–8 was a severe one. The *Northern Star* talked of the 'extreme prevalence' of bronchitis, pneumonia, typhus, measles and scarlatina. Smallpox was also widespread. Commercial crisis and growing economic distress was accompanied by increasing Chartist activity. The news of revolution in Paris and elsewhere in Europe which reached England in late February 1848 further exacerbated matters. Meetings in London and in the rest of the country profilerated. Authority was uneasy at the Chartist plans to present a third petition. There were fears that Britain would be infected by the revolutionary spirit sweeping Europe, especially since Harney's Fraternal Democrats, organized in 1845, had been in contact with European radicals. There were also fears that the measures proposed by the Convention which assembled in London in early April would tie down the army at a time when Irish radicals threatened rebellion. The numerous Irish connections of Chartism, not the least O'Connor's own, added credibility to the fears of authority of a possible union between Irish nationalists and Chartists in England.

In March 1848 a middle-class radical meeting in London, which demanded the abolition of income tax, was taken over by Chartists. Attempts by police to break up the demonstration resulted in three days of widespread disturbances. Similar disturbances took place in Glasgow and Manchester. In each case, though there was an important Chartist presence, the disorder, looting and crime that took place was largely by non-Chartists but Chartists were guilty by association in the eyes of the propertied. Forty-nine delegates were elected to the third Convention which first met in London on 4 April and planned a peaceful demonstration on Kennington Common on 10 April to be followed by a procession to present the petition to Parliament. O'Connor's personal position had been considerably strengthened by his election as MP for Nottingham in 1847 and he hoped that the petition would contain five million signatures.

Strong precautionary measures were taken by the authorities, for whom the Chartist threat was very real. 8,000 troops were drafted into the capital to complement the thousands of special constables. The procession was banned but the meeting went ahead. The resolution of government was sufficient to frighten O'Connor into asking his supporters not to confront the authorities and to disperse peacefully. The petition was conveyed to Parliament in three cabs and the 'crisis' was over. The meeting was ridiculed by many as a 'fiasco' and two days later O'Connor faced further criticism when his five-ton, five-million-signatured petition was found to weigh barely a quarter of a ton and contain less than two million genuine signatures.

The Convention continued to sit, undaunted by the rejection of the petition. It organized more mass meetings preparatory to the summoning of a National Assembly which would call upon the Queen to dissolve Parliament and accept only a government prepared to implement the Charter. Internal disagreement, mutual suspicion and recriminations increasingly paralysed the Convention and the National Assembly, neither of which had mass support, and dissolution quickly followed.

On 2 June *The Times* concluded that 'Chartism is neither dead nor sleeping. The snake was scotched not killed on the 10th of April. The advancing spring has brought with it warmth, vigour and renovation.'

The spring and summer of 1848 saw a great deal of activity, arrests and trials and several riots, against the background of imminent revolution in Ireland. The focal points of government concern were the Bradford district in May and London between June and August. Police broke up meetings in the East End on 4 June and the provisional executive of the National Assembly called a day of protest on 12 June. The government responded with a heavy display of force at the mass meeting on Bishop Bonner's Field. Once it had peacefully disbanded, a small committee appeared to be planning a national rising with Irish support and the connivance of the NCA. These groups failed to raise sufficient support, were quickly infiltrated by government spies and, on the day of the proposed insurrection, the police had no difficulty in rounding up the conspirators.

Was the Chartist threat real in 1848? To those in authority it certainly was. They saw the daily meetings and riots – it was often difficult to distinguish between the two. They received reports of drilling and military-style marches from the country. Prompt and firm action put O'Connor in the position of having to translate his militant demagoguery into action or to back away. On 10 April his hold over the movement was broken; other leaders simply did not have his authority and were anyway divided in their counsel. Just as in 1838 and 1842, Chartism was contained from without and critically weakened from within. Yet Kennington Common and the June riots are only 'fiascos' in retrospect. Chartism's failure in 1848 was not one of ideas but of will. The united 'mass platform', already weakened, disintegrated.[10]

Gammage, one of Chartism's first historians, may have been technically a little premature when travelling round the country in the 1850s lecturing on the movement's failure. Chartism lingered on for a further decade, displaying vigour in some areas like Halifax, but it had ceased to be a mass movement. In 1852 Marx observed that the Chartists were 'so completely disorganised and scattered, and at the same time so short of useful people, that they must either fall completely to pieces and degenerate into cliques . . . or they must be reconstituted'.[11]

But its journals still flourished and Ernest Jones and his charter socialism achieved some following, especially in London among lower grades of craftsmen resentful at the growing influence of trade unionism. Chartists continued to be active in local politics but by 1860 organized Chartism was dead. The last convention gathered in 1858 and two years later the NCA was formally wound up.

Why did Chartism fail?

It is important, given the extent of active class consciousness achieved in 1839, 1842 and to a lesser extent 1848, to attempt to explain why Chartism gave way so abruptly to a period of temperate and fragmented activity among the working population marked by a greater reliance on trade unionism. Repeated failure sapped the momentum of Chartism. To sustain the mass platform the movement needed to generate the widespread belief that success was possible. The events of 1839 – confusion of strategies, the abortive 'national holiday', and the suppression at Newport – seriously damaged its capacity to do this. The defeat of the general strike in 1842 and the crushing failure of 1848 completed the process. The authorities inflicted the most damaging psychological defeat on the popular reform movement of the century, bankrupting the long tradition of the mass platform.

In part this was a consequence of the fundamental organizational weaknesses of the movement. Lack of administrative experience and imagination was clearly exposed by the ways in which the conventions were organized and financed. Rejection of the three petitions showed how little parliamentary support the Chartists had. The reforming movement of 1830–2 and the activities of the Anti-Corn Law League, both of which used similar tactics to Chartism to whip up outside pressure, were successful because they could also rely on parliamentary allies. The Chartists could not. With little parliamentary backing or solid middle-class support, the movement found itself either having to give up, raise and maintain public support or opt for less peaceful methods. This divided both leadership and rank and file, creating dissension and lack of tactical direction. In addition, though all Chartists could agree on the Charter, the other aims of the movement were less precise. To Lancashire cotton workers Chartism held out the prospect of economic improvement and factory reform. To the London artisan, it pointed the way to political equality. Nationalism tinged Welsh Chartism while in Scotland it was imbued with the ethics of self-improvement. The Chartist leaders also had different ends in view: Lovett saw the franchise as one element in a general programme of social improvement; for Ernest Jones Chartism was equated with socialism; O'Brien saw it in relation to currency reform and land nationalization; and, for O'Connor the franchise was the political counterpart of his schemes at land reform. Loss of momentum within the movement saw these differences emerge as the various interest groups sought alternative ways of realizing their ends. Chartism could not maintain unity of purpose.

Economic conditions played an important role in this failure. Though there has been a valid reaction against the 'gross economic reductionism' of earlier historians, the fundamental importance of the trade cycle should not be neglected. The difficulty of maintaining momentum, except in periods of more than usual hardship, was universally recognized by contemporaries.

The changes that occurred in the policies and attitudes of the governing classes, in part the result of Chartism, can be seen as evidence of its partial success. The movement focused attention on social problems and the need to tackle them. These efforts often occurred at local level and were motivated by a conscious or unconscious desire to alleviate discontent and reduce divisions within society as well as by genuine Christian compassion. There was some liberalization of state policies in the 1840s and this weakened the Chartist case that *only* a reformed Parliament could improve the conditions of the working population.

A final explanation for the demise of Chartism lies in the consolidation of industrial capitalism that had occurred by the mid-nineteenth century. In the previous fifty years industrial flux and insecurity had created militancy among the working population who believed that political reform could arrest or reverse this process. By 1850 this battle had more or less been lost and Chartism remained relevant only in places like Halifax and Bradford, where the woollen and worsted trades were still fighting a rearguard action against mechanization. Militancy, in this scenario, was associated with the traumas of the early stages of industrialization not with the more mature and settled stages of industrial capitalism, characterized by methods to advance the interests of the working population which did not rely on confrontation. The working population did not become more militant as it became proletarianized. This does not alter the significance of Chartism in the shift from older methods of popular protest to the consideration of new approaches, like the general strike, the exertion of pressure through mass organization and anti-capitalist critiques, more relevant to an industrial urban society.

Chartism was the first organized mass movement of the working population in British history in terms of its geographical and occupational breadth and the unprecedented involvement of women. But it did not draw on trade unionism in any formal way or bridge the gulf between rural and urban workers. It did not mark, as those with a Whiggish view of history believed, a vital stage in the inevitable progress of organized labour. Chartism was motivated by 'knife and fork' issues but was also concerned with the dignity of the individual and the 'rights of man'. It looked back to the campaigns of the 1790s and forward to the emergence of socialism as a political force from the 1880s.

MIDDLE-CLASS PRESSURE

Opening points

The emergence of the middle classes was a product of industrialization and urbanization and between 1780 and 1850 they established themselves as a challenge to the political hegemony of the landed interest. Middle-class radicalism was centred in the professional and manufacturing classes. The growth of new professions outside the traditional areas of the Church, law and medicine was one of the most important aspects of middle-class development during the first half of the nineteenth century. These professions were imbued with the Utilitarian philosophy of Jeremy Bentham and the Mills, father and son, in which value was determined not by tradition but by the 'greatest happiness to the greatest number' and which provided an innovative way of critiquing contemporary society and its institutions. Manufacturers like Richard Bright and Henry Ashworth provided an alternative and extremely successful economic focus grounded not in landed but in manufacturing wealth.

Ideologically and economically successful though the middle classes were, their transformation of the social and political structure was slow and uneven in the first half of the century. They had successes in specific areas but lacked both the power and the will to undermine effectively the political hegemony of the traditional landed interest. There was considerable diversity of economic status among the middle classes which meant that, though historians with some validity have emphasized their homogeneity in contrast to heterogeneity of the working population, they were not as united, or as class conscious or as radical as has frequently been made out. The pre-industrial commercial-financial interest was very conservative in outlook. The new professional classes were concerned with status and upward mobility and were often unsympathetic to radicalism. The northern manufacturing classes, which formed the mainstay of the Anti-Corn Law League (ACLL), proved erratic reformers in the 1850s once their economic grievances had been settled. Middle-class radicals in the first half of the nineteenth century did not represent either the 'nation' or the middle classes as a whole but simply the 'vanguard of the bourgeoisie'.

Like the Chartists, middle-class radicals detested the 'aristocratic ideal' and its social, religious and political domination based on rank, prescription and tradition. They differed from the Chartists in their attack on the aristocracy by expressing that opposition not through the idealized radical 'tradition' of abstract political principles but in terms of specific demands like the abolition of the Corn Laws. It was the 'practical' nature of its radicalism which marked the middle classes off from the millenarian working-class tradition.

'Philosophic Radicals'

In the 1830s and 1840s the Radicals attempted to attack the aristocracy on two fronts – political and economic. The 1832 Reform Act was, in part, a recognition by the Whig leaders of the economic advances of the middle classes in the previous fifty years and an acceptance of their claim to political 'respectability'. Grey argued in 1831 that concession to 'the rational public' was essential if republicanism and the destruction of existing institutions was to be avoided. But the Whigs aimed to strengthen rather than weaken aristocratic power by underpinning it with middle-class support and linked the extended franchise with men of 'property and intelligence'. This strategy successfully split the alliance between middle-class radicals and popular protest, isolating the working population and leaving them politically impotent.[12]

The 1832 Act fell far short of the aspirations of those middle-class Radicals who sought to produce a more democratic and just society by undermining the dominance of the aristocracy.[13] They sought, inside Parliament, to force Grey and Melbourne to introduce further 'organic reform' in government and administration. This objective did not seem remote when the reformed Parliament assembled in 1833. Out of the 500 'reformers' who sat in the House of Commons in that year, the Radicals, including the Irish MPs led by O'Connell, formed a bloc of 100–120 MPs, regarded by the official Whigs as a separate and potentially hostile group. The English group consisted of 60–70 MPs but, though they were all Radicals, they differed widely in temperament, background and ideas and never formed a coherent group. The most important representatives of middle-class radicalism were about twenty 'Philosophic Radicals' – individuals like George Grote, the advocate of the secret ballot, J. A. Roebuck and Sir William Molesworth, a country gentleman. John Stuart Mill, the most important of these Radicals, because of his work at the East India Company, was debarred from Parliament but provided theoretical focus and enthusiastic support from outside especially in his editorship of the *London and Westminster Review*. Mill hoped that a leader would emerge among the parliamentary Radicals who could weld the whole body of radical opinion into a coherent whole. He was to be disappointed.

The potential Radical strength of 1833 was quickly dissipated and there was a steady decline in their influence down to the 1835 general election. The parliamentary events of 1834–5 with the resignation of Melbourne, Peel's minority Conservative administration and the 1835 election, led to a slump in the number of official Whigs but an increase in both Radical and Irish MPs. If all three groups worked together they could defeat the Conservatives and Melbourne would be returned to power. This is what happened in the Lichfield House Compact of March 1835 by which O'Connell, in return for Irish reforms, was prepared to support the Whig government. The real losers of this compact were the English Radicals, who were forced to accept an unpalatable Whig government or see the return of Peel. They had lost their capacity to act as a separate 'party' or to impose their ideas on the Whig leadership. It was O'Connell rather than the Radicals who controlled the direction of Whig policies.

Russell's 'finality' speech in 1837 ruled out further organic reform, though Whig policies on the poor law, church and municipal reform reflected pressure from middle-class and Dissenting interests in the country. The position of the parliamentary Radicals was further weakened by the 1837 General Election. The number of Radicals returned was about fifty and many soon drifted back to mainstream Whiggism. Joseph Hume and Arthur Roebuck lost their seats in Middlesex and Bath respectively to Conservatives. Attwood retired in 1839 and in 1841 Grote gave up his seat for the City of London. This marked the effective end of parliamentary Radicalism.

Why did Radicalism fail to alter the balance of political power or lead to further organic reform in the 1830s? The temperament of individual Radicals, especially their inability to work together as a coherent group with a recognized leader, certainly provides part of the answer. But they also underestimated the strength of the Conservative reaction and the unwillingness of the Whigs to push fundamental reform after 1832. The Radicals have been called 'amateurs in politics' and this provides a third explanation for their failure to achieve anything concrete. As 'amateurs' they had no basis of support in the country. Few sat for popular constituencies and they had little knowledge of the people on whose behalf they claimed to speak. Isolated in Parliament they were soon isolated by the political system they were trying to reform, and effectively emasculated. The future of middle-class radicalism lay with the extra-parliamentary Anti-Corn Law League.

The Anti-Corn Law League

In September 1838 the Manchester Anti-Corn Law Association was formed by a group of local businessmen and Radicals including Henry Ashworth, J. B. Smith, George Wilson, Archibald Prentice, editor of the *Manchester Times* and later historian of the League and Richard Cobden and John Bright.[14] Their aim was the total abolition of the Corn Laws, an objective which alienated the Whigs almost as much as the Tories. Lecture tours in the north of England encouraged the formation of other local associations. Links were established with London free-traders and on 4 February 1839 a delegate meeting of all the anti-Corn Law associations was held in London. It was not particularly successful. Few delegates attended. London radicals were indifferent because they resented the dominance of the Manchester delegates, were anyway less committed to free trade and regarded the anti-Corn Law agitation as a middle-class attempt to divert attention from the Charter. This confirmed Cobden's belief that the focus of the movement must lie in Manchester. When the House of Commons rejected Charles Villiers' motion against the Corn Laws in March 1839 the delegates proceeded to set up the Anti-Corn Law League as a national organization with its headquarters in Manchester. Clearly the ACLL was the product of the concerns of northern business interests.

The movement against the Corn Laws can be traced back to the parliamentary debates of 1815. The controversy has been frequently, and too simply, characterized as one of industrial against landed interests and public opinion against aristocratic government. But agitation against the Corn Laws was endemic in the chief manufacturing centres though dormant in periods of low prices – for example during the period of good harvests and low wheat prices between 1832 and 1836 – and flaring up in periods of dearth or depression. Deteriorating economic conditions after 1836 largely account for the emergence of a national movement. High food prices were accompanied by declining wages and profits and high levels of unemployment, especially in the cotton industry. For Manchester businessmen the major cause of the depression was the decline of the export trade, a decline occasioned by the inability of foreigners to pay with grain or raw materials for imported British manufactured goods. The Corn Laws were, they believed, slowly strangling the economy.

Clearly the ACLL was an economic pressure group with a very specific objective but it has been argued that the League also marked a new and successful phase in the history of Radicalism. With the parliamentary Radicals in disarray and with the working population pursuing the Charter, the ACLL can be seen as an attempt to provide the middle classes with a realistic and achievable goal. Richard Cobden played a major role in the broadening of the economic aim of the League into an emotive and enthusiastic attack on the Corn Laws as *the* symbol of aristocratic hegemony and privilege.

Cobden recognized the strengths and weaknesses of middle-class Radicalism and realized that a direct attack on the aristocratic system would achieve little. He had successfully led the fight to get Manchester incorporated into the Municipal Corporation Act in 1837–8 against the quasi-feudal court-leet. The result was a considerable majority for 'liberals' in the 1838 municipal elections. He felt that an attack on the monopolistic position of the aristocracy had widespread support and that the floodgates of reform could be opened by compelling them to retreat on a fundamental position. The singular emphasis on the Corn Laws focused attention on the aristocracy in a way which heterogeneous radical politics, with their potential for dissension and division, did not. The Corn Laws could, he believed, rally all liberal forces in a way no other issue could.

The League based its appeal on the economic advantages of free trade – cheaper food, more employment, higher exports and greater prosperity – and the first phase of its work was aimed at converting the public to the case against the Corn Law. The practical problem faced by Cobden was the need for an alternative fiscal strategy to that based on protection. The 1840 Whig Select Committee on Import Duties concluded that the chaos of import duties was in need of simplification and that repeal would pose no immediate threat to British agriculture. Cobden believed that repeal was as much in the interests of the working population as of the manufacturers. If he could persuade popular protest of the validity of his argument then he could maintain that the ACLL was advocating a 'national' as opposed to 'sectional' cause and add the weight of numbers to the campaign. In this he was less successful. Chartist leaders were either unimpressed by his case or opposed to it. To them the motives of the League were suspect: employers had opposed the Ten-Hour movement and supported the new poor law. Whatever the merits of the free trade argument, they believed that the interests of the working population could not be safeguarded without the Charter. By 1842 the League had largely failed to win support from industrial workers.

It is important not to overestimate the extent of middle-class support for the League up to 1841. The movement developed on quasi-religious lines and looked to the anti-slavery movement of the 1820s and 1830s as a model for action. Its moralistic character mobilized Nonconformist antipathy towards the Anglican Church: Cobden in 1841 claimed that protection was 'opposed to the laws of God' and was 'anti-scriptual and anti-religious'. These demagogic and crusading characteristics alarmed the more conservative among the middle classes.

Propaganda, however, though it influenced opinion, had little direct effect on achieving repeal. Russell suggested in 1839 that the Whigs might support repeal by publicly supporting the replacement of the sliding scale with a small fixed duty on corn, a policy used as an electoral gambit in 1841. Peel remained silent on the issue. Cobden recognized that repeal would be achieved only through electoral activity with the ultimate aim of forcing the House of Commons to concede. This marked the beginning of the second phase of the League's activities. The Walsall by-election in 1841 showed the potential of the League as a third force in politics and in the general election later that year the strategy was applied in a number of favourable constituencies. Eight Leaguers, including Cobden for Stockport, were elected and this gave them an important parliamentary base, which the Chartists lacked. But the outstanding victory in 1841 lay with Peel and the Conservatives.[15]

The victory for the protectionist party put the ACLL in an awkward position. Peel's 'frightful majority' meant an electoral rebuff for the arguments of the League, though the 1842 budget showed that this was more apparent than real. It also led to a revival of demands by some middle-class Radicals for organic reform in conjunction with the Chartists. This precipitated a crisis of confidence for Cobden, Bright and the other leaders of the ACLL, a crisis exacerbated by the deepening of distress in the northern manufacturing districts in the winter of 1841–2.

The League Council split into two parties: a moderate element associated with R. H. Greg advocated a cautious and entirely law-abiding policy and a more extreme group led by Prentice, who talked of forcing Peel's hand by closing factories or refusing to pay taxes. The League was also faced by a formidable rival in the form of the Complete Suffrage League which attempted, unsuccessfully, to unite all radicals behind a common programme of reform. Peel's 1842 budget made matters even worse since it appeared that he had to some extent stolen the thunder of the free-traders.

The summer of 1842 saw the League at its lowest ebb with no policies and increasing lack of confidence. Cobden thought of opposing Peel's proposals but recognized that their popularity would have destroyed both the League and himself. He took the dangerous step of trying to shake public confidence in Parliament by comparing the immorality and sectionalism of the Commons with the moral righteousness of the League. A lock-out of workers was seriously considered but workers pre-empted this in the series of strikes in mid-1842. The League was rightly blamed by government for contributing to an atmosphere in which widespread industrial discontent occurred. Moderation, however, prevailed. The decline of the Complete Suffrage League, actions against Chartism and a resolution of its internal crisis pushed the League back on course. By the end of 1842 it emerged stronger and more confident than before.

The ACLL's capacity for intensive agitation was increased by a thorough overhaul of its organization. Joseph Hickin, the leader of the Walsall Radicals, put the League's office in Manchester on a more businesslike footing. J. B. Smith retired and George Wilson became administrative head of the ACLL organization. In March 1842 the League Council divided the country up into twelve areas each with its own organization, improving both the collection of money and the enrolment of new members. The League's propaganda machine was expanded. From December 1842 its paper the *Circular* began to appear weekly, the *Economist* was founded in 1843 and became the medium for free-trade ideas, Cobden and Bright undertook widespread lecture tours and anti-Corn Law tracts were sent to every elector using the new 'Penny Post' system. Norman McCord says that

> The collection of the fund, the registration of members and the distribution of tracts to electors, marked the infusion of new life into the agitation after the crisis of 1841–2 and the end of internal disagreement and indecision.[16]

From 1842 to 1845 the League directed its energies towards preparing for a decisive struggle at the expected 1848 general election. It could not have foreseen the 1845–6 crisis and, having rejected extreme measures, turned towards electoral politics. Attempts were made to win over tenant farmers to free trade. They were regarded as the key to control of the county seats and Cobden hoped to use their antagonism towards their landowners. This direct assault on the shires failed because many tenant farmers supported protection and may even have influenced their land-lords into a protectionist stance rather than the other way round.

The League then adopted more indirect methods. It organized extensive postal objections to hostile county votes. It sought to create new free-trade votes by buying up the freeholds in key constituencies, achieving some success in south Lancashire and the West Riding. Free-traders inter-vened as a third party in by-elections. By the summer of 1846 only a small number of seats had been made safe in this way and it is unlikely, as John Prest maintains, that Peel was scared into repealing the Corn Laws to avoid an anti-Tory landslide in the counties. McCord doubts whether free-traders would have emerged electorally victorious had such a trial of strength proved necessary.

The stimulus for repeal came not from extra-parliamentary agitation but inside the Cabinet and Parliament as a result of the Irish crisis of 1845–6. The League can perhaps take credit for the conversion of the Whig leader in his 'Edinburgh Letter' of November 1845. But it is more doubtful whether the same can be said of Peel's decision. He had come to the conclusion that the Corn Laws could not be defended before the Irish crisis, but for reasons which were more complex than the League's. He saw the Corn Laws as divisive and that retreat by the aristocracy was necessary. But it was an ordered, strategic retreat, a sacrifice in order to keep intact the main strongholds of aristocratic power made by a Prime Minister and Parliament and not as the result of an electoral contest or 'pressure from without'.

What was the significance of the ACLL in middle-class Radicalism in this period? Both the economic and political consequences of repeal have been exaggerated. Certainly neither proved immediately disastrous to the landed interest and aristocratic government easily survived the crisis of 1846. The realities of political power remained unaltered and no organic reforms were passed until after 1865. The resilience of the aristocratic elite after 1846 is a measure of the real political weakness of the ACLL and the middle classes in the 1840s.

The League claimed to act as the spokesman for the middle classes but, though it received strong support from northern manufacturers, not all members of the business community were prepared to give it unlimited support and some, like the financial elite in London, were actively hostile to free trade. It is important not to oversimplify the agitation into a straight urban/manufacturing versus rural/landed conflict. The League fought a national campaign and yet the strength of the middle classes lay in local not national politics, in their businesses and the status acquired through local office. This parochialism, and many businessmen's support for the

League, reflected this parochialism, was reinforced after 1846 with the growing acceptance of free trade and the 'entrepreneurial ideal' and they abandoned national politics. The difficulty in providing any focus for the formation of a new united Radical party in the late 1840s and 1850s was a reflection of the League's success in achieving its economic objective. In terms of its organizational structure, its use of propaganda and its tactics the ACLL looked forward to the radical politics of the second half of the nineteenth century. But in the late 1840s middle-class Radicalism lacked, as it had in the mid-1830s, leaders, unity and coherent policies.

Pressure group politics

In the first half of the nineteenth century pressure groups fell into two main types.[17] First, there were those groups which spoke on behalf of recognized corporate or community interests which generally had a common economic base like the emergent railway lobby or the declining West Indian interest. Secondly, there were groups which crusaded for a particular cause and whose unity came from their common goal. The status of each group in British society varied. Interest groups, simply because they were rooted in property, could legitimately claim to be consulted within the political community. Crusading pressure groups remained politically ambiguous because they disturbed the deliberative role of Parliament and spoke for no recognizable corporate interest. They have been defined in the following terms:

> Pressure from without, then, is used here in the sense that contemporaries used it, to refer to those more or less radical and mainly middle class pressure groups, pursuing specified goals and working for legislative change by putting pressure on parliament and government; possessing a sophisticated language, by claiming to speak for the People, the Nation or the Country.[18]

This definition excludes movements like Chartism and the ACLL as too diverse and the protectionist lobby as too limited and defensive.

Certain key questions emerged from the development of pressure from without. What did 'public opinion' mean in this period and how was it related to formal and 'informal' politics? How did pressure groups operate and how effective were they? What was their social and religious composition and their regional roots? What were the wider implications of pressure from without for the political community? Finally, can pressure from without be said to have radicalized politics, contained class conflict and made the political structure more pluralistic?

Before 1832 the role of Parliament rested on certain principles which pressure from without offended. Parliament was the deliberative assembly of the nation and unruly unions were felt to intimidate this role. It was Parliament's role to consider not the wishes of the people but their well-being, of which the people were not true or fit judges. Two further arguments were used to buttress this position. First, the so-called voice of the people was often stimulated by demagogues who sharpened social antagonism and undermined good order. Secondly, that even when it was genuine, the *vox populi* was often unsure and temporary so that the sluggishness of parliamentary reaction was a fair test of its significance and staying power.

This position was denied by radicals. They did not see themselves as a mob encroaching on the proper role of Parliament but as speaking for the People, for the common interest against the exclusive interest of the ruling elite. 'The People' were not rootless, changeable and individualized, as Canning among others maintained, but bound, though not by property, by a morality of a 'national mind' – stable, reflective, self-educating and self-disciplined. They were 'respectable' and sought to direct legislation towards moral reform.

Pressure groups maintained that without extra-parliamentary agitation social and political progress in terms of Catholic emancipation, parliamentary reform, the end of slavery and the repeal of the Corn Laws would not have occurred. During the 1830s and 1840s three main groups of reformers can be identified – parliamentary reformers, the Manchester free-traders and Dissent – which sought to put pressure on government.

The parliamentary reformers, led by Joseph Hume and Arthur Roebuck, derived their intellectual authority from the philosophic radicals of the 1830s. Parliament, they argued, was dominated by the aristocracy which legislated for its own sectional interests and that reform must give power to the People. They were London-based, secular and rationalist, drawing their support mainly from artisans and the small shopkeepers. Their concept of the People was not based on a distinct class language. They maintained that parliamentary reform (the ballot, household suffrage and triennial parliaments) must be accompanied by governmental reform as a means of further reducing aristocratic patronage and corruption. This led to Hobhouse's Vestries Act of 1831, municipal reform in 1835 and administrative reform in the 1850s. They also maintained that popular education was necessary so that the people could use their votes properly and not succumb to aristocratic influence. This led to Roebuck's motion on national education in 1833 and spilled over into Brougham's Mechanics Institutes, Charles Knight's Society for the Diffusion of Useful Knowledge, Rowland Hill's Post Office reform in 1840, Ewart's campaign for public libraries and Collet's work for the removal of last vestiges of stamp duty on newspapers in the 1850s.

The difficulty this group faced was that parliamentary reform required positive legislative action, unlike the free-traders who sought the more negative dismantling of monopoly. They attacked landlords as a parasitic class, following Ricardian political economy, and denied the morality and legitimacy of an idle landed class living off unearned income. Parliamentary reform, they maintained, would merely change the superstructure of political power, but land reform would destroy its economic basis.

For Dissent the 1830s was devoted to the removal of civil disabilities and church tithes. The 1833 decision on matching building rents for school was largely uncontroversial but the 1843 Factory Bill, with its proposal that new factory schools should be supervised by the Established Church, led to a wave of militant dissent. Edward Baines, editor of the *Leeds Mercury*, provided the lead but its pressure group organization was mainly the word of Edward Miall, who favoured the disestablishment of the Anglican Church and who formed the Anti-State Church Association in 1844 to campaign for this end.

How did pressure from without operate? The first step was usually to try and persuade from within Parliament. The anti-slavery committee, headed by Thomas Buxton, had its own parliamentary voice. Other reformers like Attwood, Miall and Baines, became MPs as a way of bringing pressure from without within, though Cobden alone possibly managed this successfully. Without such a voice pressure needed to be more oblique. The Anti-Corn Law League sought to put pressure on MPs to speak up in the House of Commons and only when this failed did it develop a strategy of pressure from without.

Extra-parliamentary pressure developed in two ways. First, pressure groups sought to raise awareness of the particular issue through education, propaganda and journalism. Cobden founded the *Economist*, the philosophic radicals used the *Westminster Review*, Miall founded *Nonconformist* and Edward Baines used his editorship of the *Leeds Mercury*. Secondly, pressure groups needed to provide evidence of a 'national voice'. Regional coverage was through networks of local branches which circulated petitions and subscribed funds and were provided with lecturers, propaganda and research material from the central organization. These local branches put electoral pressure on MPs, through close examination of the electoral register and extracting pledges of support.

Sometimes pressure groups toyed with more direct methods. The Catholic Association intervened in the County Clare election in 1828 and the political unions threatened to 'go for gold' in 1832. The League, following the Conservative victory in 1841, contemplated closing mills and refusing taxes. Reformers also sought a union between middle-class and working-class groups – in 1831 the National Political Union; in 1840 the Leeds Parliamentary Reform Association formed by Samuel Smiles; the Complete Suffrage League in 1842, and the Parliamentary and Financial Reform Association in the late 1840s – as a strategy for increasing pressure on the aristocracy.

When unions between the middle classes and the working population broke down, as they frequently did, separate but parallel organizations re-emerged. The campaign against newspaper duties in the 1830s was essentially a middle-class affair through a parliamentary lobby but it was aided by the separate, extra-parliamentary agitation through the unstamped press. The Health of Towns Association of 1844 with its central committee and provincial branches led to the emergence of the Metropolitan Working Class Association in 1845. After 1848, with the demise of Chartism, it became easier to co-opt working people into pressure group activity.

Impact of pressure group politics

It is difficult to assess the impact that extra-parliamentary pressure had on central government in this period. Certainly many groups highlighted particular issues on which government was prepared, eventually, to legislate. Contemporaries were certainly confident that pressure groups did provide an impetus for social progress. But it was always easier to repeal legislation – the Test and Corporation Acts, the church rates, the Corn Laws – than to introduce new legislation. Viscount Morpeth introduced his sanitary legislation in 1847 and 1848 under the aegis of the Health of Towns Association but legislation was acceptable to the House of Commons only because of the return of cholera. Pressure groups recognized that, though they could influence, even intimidate, the legislature, the last word lay with Parliament. It could legislate but it could also refuse to do so. The difference between 1830 and 1850 was that pressure groups were recognized as a legitimate channel through which opinion had access to government.

Collective associations like trade unions and popular protest like Chartism had ambivalent effects on the lives of the working population. They sought to improve conditions through demands for economic and political change but the extent to which they succeeded, at least in the short term, was limited. There were other approaches open to working people through which they could protect themselves against distress.[19]

'SELF-HELP'

In the 1866 edition of *Self-Help*, Samuel Smiles regretted that some had misunderstood and criticized him for eulogizing selfishness. This was, he maintained, the antithesis of self-help. He said that 'the duty of helping one's self in the highest sense involves the helping of one's neighbours'. Smiles reserved the highest praise for mutual aid associations. Co-operative and friendly societies cultivated the habits of prudent self-reliance among the people. Mutual assurance was 'economy in its most economical form'.

Friendly societies

Voluntary associations or friendly societies had their origins in the late seventeenth century when groups of people entered into a mutual compact to help each other in case of problems or disasters. During the first half of the nineteenth century the main form of organization was the local society. In 1801, it has been estimated, there were about 7,200 societies with 648,000 members and by 1818 this number had risen to almost a million people. The geographical distribution of friendly societies shows that they developed more rapidly where there was at least some industry: in 1821 Lancashire, for example, had 147,029 individuals in friendly societies, some 17 per cent of its population, while in rural counties the figure was as low as 5 per cent. This can be explained by the higher industrial wages but may also be because industrial workers felt greater need to make provision against sickness than those who worked on the land. There was also a difference between rural and industrial areas in the variety of occupations from which members were drawn. In 1840 the seven well-established societies in Sheffield drew their members from seventy-nine trades. In rural areas there was less variety in the occupations of members. Recent research had questioned this, arguing that in some northern rural areas agricultural labourers contributed in large numbers. But the experience of the rural north was not paralleled in the south. Some societies were confined to men of one particular trade and, at times, these developed into trade unions. Women were generally excluded from friendly societies.

The main financial benefits expected by a member of a local friendly society were a weekly allowance when he was sick and a funeral payment for his widow. The inability of societies to pay the promised benefits and their collapse was the aspect of their activities which attracted most attention in this period. The main reason for this was the competition between local societies which led them to offer benefits larger than the contributions could support. The development of affiliated orders – national or regional societies – from the late 1830s was, in part, a response to this weakness. The orders which stood out were the Independent Order of Oddfellows, the Royal Order of Foresters, and Manchester Unity formed in the 1810s, around 1813 and from 1827 respectively. The Royal Order of Foresters, with its centre in Leeds, had over 350 courts or local societies by 1834 spread over the West Riding, Lancashire and Cheshire but resentment at the autocratic control of Leeds led to a secessionist movement and the establishment of the Ancient Order of Foresters in August 1834.

The attitude of government to friendly societies was coloured in the early part of the century by fears that they might become centres for revolutionary subversion. The early affiliated orders did little to dampen this fear with their secret rituals, passwords and widespread coverage in industrial areas where government believed the revolutionary underground was situated. Between 1793 and 1829 a series of Acts were passed designed to encourage friendly societies to relieve demands on the poor rate and ensuring registration and supervision by local magistrates to check any tendency towards illegal combinations. From the 1830s the attitudes of the state generally towards societies changed markedly. Increasing emphasis was placed on the need to encourage independence and self-help, the need to persuade societies and their members to stand on their own feet and not to expect the state or local authorities to prop them up. In 1834 and 1846 Acts dealt with the registration of societies but it was not until 1850 and especially 1855 that they received legal protection.

Building societies

Building societies emerged alongside friendly societies, though their appeal was always more limited in the nineteenth century. Friendly societies were generally able to offer subscription rates sufficiently low to attract most sections of the working population. Building societies did not. They attracted support from tradesmen and other members of the lower middle class rather than from poorer working men. By 1825 over 250 building societies had been founded, with a significant increase in the number of foundations after 1815. The legal standing of early building societies was confused but in 1836 the Benefit Building Societies Act provided protection similar to that given to friendly societies.

Savings banks

A third way by which working men could safeguard their position was through savings banks. Legal protection was provided in 1817 which led to 132 savings banks being founded in 1818 and a further 39 the following year. These banks appealed to artisans and the lower sections of the middle classes. The 1834 Poor Law Amendment Act stimulated an expansion of savings bank activity in the late 1830s, particularly in some southern agricultural areas, though the number of potential candidates for 'able-bodied pauperdom' who became clients was comparatively small. The Sussex Savings Banks, for example, had deposits of £43,466 in 1834, which had increased to £51,409 by 1837. Savings banks were more attractive in rural than industrial areas, the reverse of the case with friendly societies. This attractiveness may be a reflection of rural social attitudes since many banks were established by landlords, squires, parsons or other notable figures.

The legal and financial position of the banks was clarified in the 1828 and 1844 Savings Bank Acts. But a series of frauds in the middle years of the century exposed the shortcomings of the legislative framework within which the banks operated and served to moderate the growth of deposits. Between 1847 and 1850 withdrawals exceeded deposits by a considerable margin. The Cuffe Street Savings Bank in Dublin finally collapsed in 1848 and there were cases of fraud and theft in the savings banks at Tralee and Killarney. Demands for legislation were resisted: passing laws because of Ireland, it was maintained, reflected unfairly on the management of English banks. But the fraud revealed after the death of George Howarth of Rochdale showed that English banks were open to the same criminal practices as those in Ireland.

Doubts have long been expressed over the extent to which savings banks attracted and met the needs of working men. In 1840 the Sheffield Savings Bank had 5,022 depositors. Of the 2,716 men involved only 967 were engaged in manufacturing trades and of an estimated 5,000 cutlers in the town only 221 had accounts. Recent work has, however, moderated this view. Many of the depositors in savings banks had only small accounts which, it has been argued, indicated that they were probably from the wage-earning class. However, nationally the two largest identifiable groups were domestic servants and children and, in general, industrial wage-earners were not attracted.

Contemporaries were aware that savings banks did not meet the needs of the poorer groups in society but believed that the frittering away of wages by the working population was one of the greatest social evils. The result of this was the emergence in the late 1840s and particularly the 1850s of the penny bank movement. The contemporary temperance movement supported savings banks as a means of preventing intemperance. Some temperance societies established penny banks: for example, the Small Savings Bank at Banbury founded in 1847 sought to accommodate the savings of those who could not use normal savings banks but who might otherwise have drunk it away. Considerable numbers of penny banks were established in the 1850s often centred on a church or chapel, a club or a workplace.

Co-operatives

Co-operative societies were considered by Smiles to 'have promoted habits of saving, of thrift and of temperance'. There were isolated attempts at co-operative societies before 1844. Some were the initiative of philanthropists, others the result of the influence of Robert Owen. The transition from the earlier to the later co-operative movement can be traced in the development of the Rochdale Equitable Pioneers Society and the opening of their store in Toad Lane in 1844. The original rules of the Society were as idealistic and Owenite as those of other early societies and the founders were also concerned with political issues such as the best means of achieving the Charter. What made the Rochdale Society different was its decision that the profits from sales should be divided among all the members who made purchases, but who would not have to find capital for the society out of their own pockets. If the Society failed members would lose nothing, but if it flourished they would obtain further shares of the profit. The strong appeal of the trade dividend kept members loyal to the store and gave them an immediate interest in its success.

Success led to widespread imitation and by 1850 more than 200 societies had been established, largely in northern England. Some of the older co-operative societies changed to the new system: for example, the Stockport Great Moor Society, founded in 1832, adopted the Rochdale model in 1847. Though the Rochdale Pioneers stressed the earlier ideas of the co-operative movement into the 1850s increasingly the stores saw themselves as a way of improving the economic position of working people in the existing social system whose continuance was taken for granted. Co-operative stores were no longer seen as a means of abolishing the existing social and political system and replacing it with an idealistic society.

How successful were friendly societies, building societies, savings banks and co-operative societies in improving the social conditions of the working population? It is important to distinguish between the realities of the first half of the nineteenth century and the rhetoric of Smiles and other self-help ideologues. Hard work was a basic fact of the lives of working people from childhood to old age. It was imposed by economic necessity and generally was not seen as the cheerful pursuit of the ideal of self-improvement advocated by their social superiors. So if hard work was an implicit part of life for people, why place such emphasis upon it? Self-helpers maintained that the economic prosperity of the industrial revolution was the result of personal effort by entrepreneurs and the bourgeoisie and that working people could achieve similar success and material progress by the same means. There were, of course, examples of working people who had succeeded. But the obverse was also true: for millions of people a lifetime of hard work petered out in the poverty of old age and the spectre of the workhouse.

Hard work was wedded to the belief that human behaviour had its roots in personal, not social, explanations. Social problems were the result of personal weaknesses not prevailing economic conditions. There is ample evidence for the appeal of self-help organizations in this period: friendly societies had more members than trade unions into the 1870s. But the appeal was to those who could afford membership and it was not possible for an individual on inadequate wages to be won over to thrift as a way of life.

CONCLUSIONS

The extra-parliamentary agitation and the movement towards self-improvement were about conflict and compromise, revolution and accommodation and collective and individual aspirations. Through them the working population and the middle classes sought differing levels of empowerment. Control of the political system for the Chartists would have opened the way to the development of an economic system in which the needs and aspirations of the working population could be met. 1832 and 1846 marked key points in the recognition by the aristocratic elite that the objectives of the middle classes could not be ignored and that they could be accommodated within the existing social system. Different aspirations meant that the working population and the middle classes were rarely, if ever, united in their campaigns for economic and political equality. E. P. Thompson argues that, having failed to overthrow the capitalist system, the working population proceeded to 'warren' it from end to end. By the warrening process Thompson means the development of those socially useful and emotionally satisfying organizations like trade unions and co-operative societies which had their origins in the decades before 1850. This can account for the apparent smoothness of their transition from the turbulent 1840s to the less disturbed 1850s. Independent and radical politics at a national level for the working population and, to a lesser extent, among the middle classes no longer appeared practical, at least for the moment.

NOTES

1 W. E. Adams *Memoirs of a Social Atom*, London, 1903, Vol. I, p. 237.
2 J. F. C. Harrison *The Common People*, Flamingo, 1984, p. 261.
3 The literature on Chartism is immense. J. F. C. Harrison and D. Thompson (eds) *Bibliography of the Chartist Movement 1837–1976*, Harvester, 1976 provides a detailed statement and E. Royle 'Reading History: Chartism', *History Today*, December 1985 provides a useful update. The best narrative accounts of the movement are M. Hovell *The Chartist Movement*, Manchester University Press, 1918 and J. T. Ward *Chartism*, Batsford, 1973. D. Jones *Chartism and the Chartists*, Allen Lane, 1975 and D. Thompson *The Chartists*, Temple Smith, 1984 are more analytical, the latter being the outstanding general work on the subject. J. Epstein and D. Thompson (eds) *The Chartist Experience: Studies in Working Class Radicalism and Culture 1830–1860*, Macmillan, 1982 is an important collection of recent essays and contains G. Steadman Jones 'Rethinking Chartism', which is reprinted in an extended form in his *Languages of Class: Studies in English Working Class History*, Cambridge University Press, 1983.

A. Briggs (ed.) *Chartist Studies*, Macmillan, 1959 contains both local and more general studies, A. F. J. Brown *Chartism in Essex and Suffolk*, Essex Record Office Publications 1982, A. J. Peacock *Bradford Chartism 1838–1840*, York 1969 and D. Goodway *London Chartism 1838–48*, Cambridge University Press, 1982 provide valuable local insights. A. Wilson *The Chartist Movement in Scotland*, Manchester University Press, 1970 and D. Jones *The Last Rising: The Newport Insurrection of 1839*, Oxford University Press, 1985 are standard on Scotland and Wales. J. Saville *1848: The British State and the Chartist Movement*, Cambridge University Press, 1987 looks at a particular year and F. C. Mather *Public Order in the Age of the Chartists*, 1959 is an invaluable study of the reactions of authority. G. D. H. Cole *Chartist Portraits*, Macmillan, 1941 is dated but still readable. J. Epstein *The Lion of Freedom: Feargus O'Connor and the Chartist Movement 1832–1842*, Croom Helm, 1982 is an important revisionist study. J. H. Wiener *William Lovett*, Manchester University Press, 1989, is a brief study. A. R. Schoyen *The Chartist Challenge:*

A Portrait of George Julian Harney, Heinemann, 1958 is one of the best biographies.

Short studies of Chartism include A. Wilson 'Chartism', in J. T. Ward (ed.) *Popular Movements c. 1830–1850*, Macmillan, 1970, pp. 116–34, K. D. Brown *The English Labour Movement 1700–1951*, Gill & Macmillan, 1982, pp. 91–127, E. Royle and J. Walvin *English Radicals and Reformers 1760–1848*, Harvester, 1982, pp. 142–80, E. H. Hunt *British Labour History 1815–1914*, Weidenfeld, 1981, pp. 219–37 and M. I. Thomis and P. Holt *Threats of Revolution in Britain 1789–1848*, Macmillan, 1977, pp. 100–16. F. C. Mather *Chartism*, The Historical Association, 1965 and J. R. Dinwiddy *Chartism*, The Historical Association, 1987 are brief synoptic studies. E. Royle *Chartism*, 2nd edn Longman, 1986 and R. Brown and C. Daniels *The Chartists*, Macmillan, 1985, D. Thompson *The Early Chartists*, Macmillan, 1972 and F. C. Mather *Chartism and Society*, Bell & Hyman, 1980 provided documentary studies.

4 D. Thompson *The Chartists*, op. cit., p. 1.

5 Quoted in D. Thompson *The Early Chartists*, op. cit., p. 8 but see also J. Saville (ed.) *The Life of Thomas Cooper*, Leicester University Press, 1971, pp. 136–7.

6 On the role of women in Chartism see D. Jones 'Women and Chartism', *History*, 68, 1983 and D. Thompson *The Chartists*, op. cit., pp. 120–51.

7 A more detailed account of Newport can be found in D. Jones *The Last Rising*, op. cit.. His account should be compared with the earlier work of David Williams in *John Frost: A Study in Chartism*, University of Wales Press, 1939 and 'Chartism in Wales', in A. Briggs (ed.) op. cit., pp. 220–48.

8 On the events of 1842 see the contrasting perspectives of M. Jenkins *The General Strike of 1842*, Lawrence Wishart, 1980 and F. C. Mather 'The General Strike of 1842', in R. Quinault and J. Stevenson (eds) *Popular Protest and Public Order*, Allen & Unwin, 1974, pp. 115–40. J. Rule *The Labouring Classes in Early Industrial England 1750–1850*, Longman, 1986, pp. 120–51 is excellent on trade unionism and Chartism while A. Wilson 'The Suffrage Movement', in P. Hollis (ed.) *Pressure from Without*, Edward Arnold, 1974, pp. 80–104 gives a brief account of the CSU.

9 On the Land Plan see J. MacAskill 'The Chartist Land Plan', in A. Briggs (ed.) op. cit., pp. 304–41 and A. M. Hadfield *The Chartist Land Company*, David & Charles, 1970, a descriptive account.

10 On 1848 see D. Goodway, op. cit. and J. Saville *1848*, op. cit.

11 K. Marx 'The Chartists', *New York Daily Tribune*, 25 August 1852.

12 For a discussion of 1832 see Chapter 9.

13 W. Thomas provides the most recent accounts of the parliamentary Radicals in the 1830s in his 'The Philosophic Radicals', in P. Hollis (ed.) op. cit., pp. 52–79 and the more detailed *The Philosophic Radicals: Nine Studies in Theory and Practice*, Oxford University Press, 1979.

14 P. Adelman *Victorian Radicalism: The Middle-Class Experience 1830–1914*, Longman, 1984, pp. 11–28 and W. H. Chaloner 'The Agitation against the Corn Laws', in J. T. Ward (ed.) op. cit., pp. 135–51 are good summaries of the work of the Anti-Corn Law League.

N. McCord *The Anti-Corn Law League 1838–1846*, Allen & Unwin, 1958 is the standard modern work but Archibald Prentice *History of the Anti-Corn Law League*, 2 vols, 1853, new edn with an introduction by W. H. Chaloner, Cass, 1968, is still a valuable source. The political strategies of the League can be approached through D. A. Hamer *The Politics of Electoral Pressure*, Harvester, 1977, pp. 58–90 and J. Prest *Politics in the Age of Cobden*, Macmillan, 1977, especially chapters 5 and 6. Recent biographies are D. Read *Cobden and Bright. A Victorian Political Partnership*. Edward Arnold, 1967,

K. Robbins *John Bright*, Routledge, 1979 and the different perspectives of W. Hinde *Richard Cobden: A Victorian Outsider*, Yale, 1987 and N. C. Edsall *Richard Cobden: Independent Radical*, Harvard University Press 1986.

15 On the 1841 election and Peel's free-trade policies see Chapter 10.
16 N. McCord op. cit., p. 135.
17 P. Hollis (ed.), op. cit., contains much of value on the nature of pressure group politics.
18 ibid., p. viii.
19 P. Gosden *Self-Help. Voluntary Associations in Nineteenth Century Britain*, Batsford, 1973 gives an excellent coverage of 'self-help' among the working population.

14 Church and chapel – religion under pressure

The Church of England system is ripe for dissolution. The service provided by it is of a bad sort: inefficient with respect to the ends or objects professed to be aimed at by it: efficient with respect to the divers effects which, being pernicious, are too flagrantly so to be professed to be aimed at.[1]

So, in the nineteenth century religion was itself a major source of conflict in west-European societies; it also reflected the other fundamental lines of division. The battles between the official churches and their opponents initially brought together coalitions of those from different social classes.[2]

In the first half of the nineteenth century British society became increasingly polarized and in that process religious persuasion played an important part. British society was undoubtedly religious in 1800 and, despite the somewhat pessimistic conclusions contemporaries read into the Religious Census of 1851, it remained so. This did not mean that religion was unpressurized. The two state religions – Presbyterianism in Scotland and Anglicanism in England, Wales and Ireland – were under pressure from inside and out, and sought to broaden their appeal and strengthen their defences against hostile forces. The eighteenth century saw the beginnings of a popular Protestantism grounded in evangelicalism. This revitalized both Anglicanism and the existing Dissenting sects and, after 1800, led to the emergence of Nonconformity. The third type of religion was grounded in Catholicism.[3] All these types of religion made absolute claims for themselves and attempted to mark out sharp and clear boundaries between their own community and the world beyond. This was, as Hugh McLeod has rightly said, 'the age of self-built ideological ghettos' which were able to maintain over several generations a network of institutions, a body of collective memories, particular rites, hymns and legendary heroes. As the authority of the state churches was challenged, these groups sought to impose a similar degree of control within their own sphere of influence to that which the state churches had once exercised. This chapter is concerned with the pressures each kind of religion faced, how they responded to these pressures and what effects this had.[4]

THE CHURCH OF ENGLAND AND ITS REFORM

A catalogue of problems

The Church of England was in an uncomfortable position at the turn of the century.[5] It had been fully integrated into the social environment of the eighteenth century with village and parish normally coterminous. Its great strength lay in southern England as it was there that the bulk of the population and wealth was located. Every settlement had its own church and the population of each parish was of a manageable size. The situation in northern England was less favourable. Parishes were large and badly endowed. Consequently they attracted few clergy and many livings were held in plurality or by non-resident incumbents. As early as 1743 out of the 836 parishes in the York diocese, 393 had non-resident clergy and a further 335 were held by pluralists. The demographic upswing from the 1740s radically altered the settlement patterns in the north and had a disastrous effect on the Church's ability to maintain proper pastoral oversight. For example, in 1831 Leeds, with over 70,000 people, had only three places of Anglican worship.

The Anglican Church was slow to recognize the full significance of the changes taking place in the population structure of the country. The elaborate legal procedure for creating new parishes further hindered its ability to cope with the changing situation. The diocesan system of the north was equally inflexible and unable to meet the new situation. Until 1836 the whole of Lancashire, large parts of Cumberland and Westmorland, and the north-west part of Yorkshire were all included in the unwieldly Diocese of Chester. There was no bishop based in Lancashire and the West Riding until the Dioceses of Ripon and Manchester were established in 1836 and 1847.

It was not just in the large towns that the Anglican Church's position was serious. Excessive emphasis has been placed on the alienation of urban society and this has tended to deflect attention from the situation in the countryside. The real tragedy for the Church was not in the growing cities but in the countryside where all its resources were concentrated. Absenteeism and pluralism were rife and many church buildings were in disrepair. Where Dissent could establish a foothold in the village, the competition from the Church was often minimal. Enclosure had the effect of reducing the popularity of the Church. Improvements in farming led to the commutation of tithes for land and many contemporaries believed that the increase in the clergy's land was at the expense of the small tenant farmer. An even worse reaction against the Church of England resulted from the collection of the tithe in kind.[6] It was generally regarded as the ideal way of alienating the parson from his flock.

An unresponsive and inefficient pastoral system was exacerbated by a widespread belief that the Church must be defended at all costs. Unlike the unreformed Parliament, the unreformed Church had its own elaborate defence of the status quo. The French Revolution deeply frightened the propertied classes and strengthened their belief that the society under their control must be defended as a divinely ordained hierarchy. In this situation suggested reforms, including those of modest dimensions, could easily be identified with revolution and revolution with the destruction of Christianity. Even those who avoided the extremes of reaction felt it was their religious duty to preserve the constitution, the social order and the morality now under threat. In 1834 a fifth of the magistrates in England were Anglican clergymen, embodying an enormous investment in social stability. Peter Virgin's monograph, *The Church in an Age of Negligence*, Cambridge University Press, 1989, shows that clerical abuses were as bad as the Victorians supposed. In 1813 only 40 per cent of parishes had resident clergy. But he demonstrates that the problem was not simply the poverty of livings. Clerical incomes had greatly increased between 1700 and 1840: allowing for inflation, on average by over three times. The social status of clergy had also risen, persuading many from the gentry to take the cloth and producing a phalanx of clerical JPs. The problem was that the Church of England was utterly enmeshed in the patronage system of English society. Pluralism was the established method of rewarding friends and dependants. Bishops were too inefficient to reform their dioceses and anyway had a vested interest in the free exercise of patronage. It was the reform of the ramshackle structure after 1830 and especially the breakup of clerical patronage which made the Church into a more efficient institution.

To critics like the journalist John Wade, whose polemic the *Black Book* appeared in 1820 and in a revised form as *The Extraordinary Black Book* in 1831, the abuses of the Church, its ineffective organization and its conservative views were in need of reform. This was not the view of the Church: its property and patronage rights had to be defended; it was not accountable to the public; it had, as an established institution, a prescriptive right to authority. By a series of instinctive, but ill-judged actions, the Church identified itself with extreme Toryism and alienated opinion further in the 1820s and early 1830s. Abused by the radicals from outside Parliament, the events of 1828–9 showed how little the Church could expect from its political friends. The repeal of the Test and Corporation Acts and Catholic emancipation ended the special relationship between the Church and Parliament. Dissenters and Catholics would now participate in legislation affecting the Church. The attitude of the bishops during the reform agitation of 1830–2 further tarnished its reputation and completed the Church's identification with reaction.

The difficulties of resisting reform

The Church could not resist the pressures for reform. First, it was not united in maintaining its authoritarian and conservative position. Critical opinion from evangelicals and from the laity led to concentration on the reform and reinvigoration of the parish. Secondly, the Church of England and the Church of Ireland had been joined by the Act of Union. It became increasingly necessary to reform the gross abuses and alter the political position of the Church of Ireland and this, by extension, raised the same question in relation to the Anglican Church. Finally, since it had no governing body of its own, the Church had to depend on Parliament and party politicians for support in its reactionary attitudes. The Church might claim to be aloof from public opinion, but after 1832 politicians could not afford to be.

Charles Simeon

Initially reform of the Church was left to individuals. Charles Simeon,[7] the evangelical Vicar of Holy Trinity, Cambridge, sought to improve the quality of those entering the Church. Professional training for clergymen was non-existent in the late eighteenth century and Simeon supplied the need at Cambridge with instruction to improve the quality and delivery of sermons. His example probably encouraged the establishment of the first specialist theological colleges, at St Bees in 1816 and Lampeter in 1828.

Good evangelical clergymen were necessary, Simeon maintained, but he also believed in the need to ensure continuity of 'gospel ministers' in livings if the work of the Church was to be maintained. The idea of a corporation or trust to secure advowsons had already been operated but in 1817 Simeon began his trust with the purchase of the patronage of Cheltenham. His most important successes came as a result of the Municipal Corporation Act of 1835 which compelled the corporations to give up their patronage. He and, after his death in 1836, his successors secured Bath, Derby, Macclesfield, Bridlington, Beverley and two parishes in Liverpool. He was perhaps more aware than many of his contemporaries of the need to secure a foothold in the growing industrial towns.

Simeon was very conscious of the need to operate within the framework of the Church of England. He disliked the insistence of evangelicals who argued that the commission to preach the gospels meant that they could override parochial boundaries. He insisted on church order and it was by this, Charles Smythe argues in his *Simeon and Church Order*, Cambridge University Press, 1940, that Simeon probably averted many Anglican evangelicals leaving the Church of England.

Other evangelical influences

Lay influence on the Church of England was felt from the systematic nationwide penetration of the Anglican evangelicals associated loosely with William Wilberforce.[8] The British and Foreign Bible Society and the Church Missionary Society, founded in 1803 and 1811, independently of the success they enjoyed abroad, played a major part in extending evangelical influence in Britain. The Bible Society too disseminated copies of the Bible – by 1825 it had issued over four million – without note or comment. Many non-evangelical clergymen disliked this since they emphasized the importance of the Book of Common Prayer as well as the Bible and were suspicious of the co-operation with Dissenters which the Society encouraged. The campaign of the Church Missionary Society in 1813–14 was also successful in attracting support for the evangelicals, particularly in the cities of the West Riding.

The evangelical campaign sought to bring the working people within the orbit of the Established Church with the aim of keeping them in their place. Evangelicalism was seen as an antidote to revolution from the 1790s. Hannah More (1745–1833) and her sister Martha played a considerable role in educating people for their place in society. In 1795 she started the Cheap Repository Tracts in response to cheap radical literature, especially Paine's *Rights of Man*. All the tracts – there were 114 in all with an annual circulation of over two million copies – had the same evangelical and conservative intention.

By 1815 the evangelicals had directed their attention at all sections of society. Wealth, social and political contacts, and the crisis occasioned by the French Revolution, helped them to spread their ideas among the aristocratic elite. The anti-slavery campaigns mobilized middle-class opinion and the Cheap Repository Tracts provided 'proper' reading for the working population.

Church-building

Joshua Watson (1771–1855) was concerned to improve the ability of the Church to appeal to the growing urban population. A wine merchant with wide commercial and financial interests, he retired from business in 1814 to devote himself to good works.[9] He appealed to High Churchmen, in contrast to the evangelicals, and the group that gathered at his house in Hackney became known as the Hackney Phalanx and publicized their activities through the *British Critic*.

Watson was prominent in the formation of the National Society for Promoting the Education of the Poor in the Principles of the Established Church in 1811. Its purpose was to encourage parishes to start their own schools: within three years it had raised sufficient contributions to establish 360 schools in which there were 60,000 pupils, and nearly a million twenty

years later. The society was not supported by the state until the government introduced annual grants in 1833. Though the 1839 Whig educational
proposals were mangled by Anglican opposition a committee of the Privy
Council did take over the supervision of education and Watson's resignation in 1842 coincided with the assertion of the authority of the state
in education.

The other charitable effort which Watson led was the movement to
build new churches. There was little point in educating children into the
Anglican faith if, when they grew up, they could not become regular
churchgoers. This was a very difficult enterprise for private charity, even
if money could be found. Until 1818 a new parish had to be created by
Parliament and to build a new church in an existing parish required the
consent of the patron and the incumbent, either of whom might feel their
rights were being infringed. In 1818 Watson formed an Incorporated
Church Building Society and in the same year Lord Liverpool established
an official commission with a grant of £1 million with a further £0.5 million
added in 1824. Parliamentary grants were virtually used up by 1828 and
were not renewed, but such was the stimulus given to private subscribers
that the commission did not finish its work until 1857. It had then built
612 new churches accommodating 600,000 people and this figure does not
exhaust the total number of churches built. Many were built or rebuilt by
private means.

Reform by legislation

By the early 1830s, despite the work of these individuals and groups, there
was a feeling that the Church was faced with the alternative of thorough
reform or 'complete destruction'. This was sufficient to break through the
obstacles to organizational change and pastoral renewal which had long
prevented its adjustment to industrial and urban society.[10] The ecclesiastical and political crises of 1828–32 were closely connected. The repeal of
the Test and Corporation Acts, though they altered the daily lives of
Anglicans and Nonconformists little, gave legitimacy to the *de facto* situation. But, combined with Catholic emancipation in 1829, they symbolized
dramatically the failure of the old monopolistic conception of the Establishment. The blind conservatism of the Church of England's leadership
during the reform agitation, a conservatism motivated by a fear that the
country was near revolution and that the Church faced disestablishment,
the 1832 Reform Act and the Whig electoral landslide meant that moderate reform could no longer be avoided. This 'metamorphosis' and the
initiative for reform passed to the state. The restructuring of the Establishment was something imposed by a Parliament which could not afford to
wait for some consensus to emerge within the Church itself.

In June 1832 an Ecclesiastical Revenues Commission was established,
but for two and a half years little concrete occurred. The Commission

investigated the entire financial structure of the Establishment but, as the debate about the Church intensified outside Parliament, proposals for reform were either defeated or allowed to lapse. The breakthrough came with the setting up of a new Commission to 'consider the State of the Established Church' during Peel's minority administration. In 1836 Melbourne established it on a permanent basis as the Ecclesiastical Commission and, under the chairmanship of Charles James Blomfield, Bishop of London, it quickly became the main instrument of organizational improvement in the Church. It never became a government department answerable to Parliament through a minister and retained a degree of independence thought necessary if reform was to triumph over the opposition of vested interests in the House of Lords and in the Church at large. But, since the Church possessed no effective assembly or courts of its own, the initiative had to come from government.

Major reforms of the Church's structure occurred in the second half of the 1830s and during Peel's ministry: the boundaries of existing dioceses were modified and new dioceses created in 1836; severe restrictions were placed on pluralism in 1838 and excess revenues from cathedrals were distributed to those with greater needs in 1840. In addition the Whigs introduced the Registration Act in 1836 which put the registration of births, marriages and deaths in the hands of a civil official and not the Church and in 1838 the Dissenters' Marriage Act ended the obligation of Nonconformists to marry in Anglican churches.

Of crucial importance in re-establishing the popular position of the Church was the need to resolve its financial problems. Both church rates and tithes were unpopular. Though compulsory church rates were not abolished until 1868 legal judgments made it clear that they could only be collected when authorized by the churchwardens and a majority of the vestry. As Dissenters were eligible to vote for both, in some towns, like Birmingham, the rate lapsed. This was preferable for Nonconformists to the scheme which the House of Commons seriously considered to repair all parish churches out of taxes. On tithes, the Whigs did something. The Tithe Commutation Act of 1836 ended tithes in kind and replaced them with money payments based on the average prices of corn, oats and barley over the previous seven years.

The approach of the Commission was both radical and realistic. The decision to use excessive endowments to help poorer parishes resulted in 5,300 parishes being assisted in this way between 1840 and 1855. Church-building and renovation increased after 1835 and by 1850 the numbers of non-resident clergy had fallen significantly, strengthening greatly the work of the Anglican ministry. The increase in the pastoral efficiency of the clergy was accomplished by a decline in their status relative to other professions. The number of clergymen on the County Bench fell. The Church was saved in the 1830s and 1840s by giving up some of its social and secular administrative functions and by a further surrendering of its autonomy to the state. The religious dimension of the priestly office had become paramount.

The High Church 'party' had been in the vanguard of the Church's reaction to change since the 1790s and may well have inhibited reformist tendencies before 1830. Its members distrusted their more evangelical colleagues, whose pastoral concerns seemed to threaten the norms of the unreformed Establishment, and were horrified by the structural and administrative reforms of Blomfield and Peel. But it was the problem of the Church of Ireland which led to the emergence of the Tractarian or Oxford movement.[11]

The Church of Ireland

In 1800 the Church of Ireland was a weak and ineffective organization.[12] The episcopal hierarchy was government appointed and frequently non-resident. Many lower clergy were pluralists, churches were in poor repair and one benefice in ten had no church at all. Irish Anglicans were a small minority of the total Irish population; 56 per cent of their total lived in Ulster, 25 per cent in Leinster, 12 per cent in Munster and 6 per cent in Connacht. In all parts of Ireland Anglicans were heavily represented among the landowning classes. In the three southern provinces they were also heavily overrepresented among the professions and at the upper levels of financial and commercial life. Ulster Anglicans were represented at other levels of society as well as among the landed classes.

Between 1800 and 1830, the period Akenson calls 'the era of graceful reform', there was a general tightening of ecclesiastical discipline and organizational change curbing the most serious abuses. Between 1787 and 1832 the number of churches rose by nearly 30 per cent and, with the division of over-large parishes, the total number of benefices rose by a quarter. Pluralities were discouraged and ministers encouraged to live in their parishes. This general improvement continued after 1830 but internal renovation was increasingly combined with reforms imposed from outside. 'Graceful Reform', in Akenson's words, gave way to 'Reform by Critical Strangers'.

The movement for reform came from more than one source. Irish evangelicalism had been growing since the late eighteenth century and there is little doubt that it played a significant role in encouraging both clergy and laity to adopt a more conscientious attitude to religion and its duties. But its influence should not be overstated. Evangelicalism grew in strength between 1800 and 1850, by which time the Church was predominantly evangelical. It was not until 1842 that the first avowed evangelical bishop was appointed. The evangelicals are perhaps best seen as the extreme wing of a wider shift in outlook by both clergy and laity in this period.

Much of the reform of the first half of the century was the work of conservative reformers like John Beresford, Archbishop of Armagh (1822–62) who were deeply committed to introducing higher standards into the Church. They received important support from government in this task. Considerations of patronage and political interest continued to play a role in the appointment of bishops but they were increasingly weighed against the claims of merit and character. There was also legislative action: the Board of First Fruits and Tenths was reorganized and its income supplemented by parliamentary grants; and the Acts of 1808 and 1824 provided for more effective punishment of non-resident clergy.

Parallel to these reforms was the progressive reduction in the privileges of the Church of Ireland from the 1830s. In 1831 the creation of a non-denominational elementary education system was seen by many churchmen as setting aside one of the exclusive prerogatives of the Established Church. The 1833 Church Temporalities Act imposed drastic reforms, reducing the archbishops from four to two and the number of bishops by ten and creating a body of ecclesiastical commissioners to control a substantial part of the Church's revenue. On the question of tithes, the major grievance of the Church's opponents, an Act of 1838 offered a compromise, converting tithes into a concealed payment, set at a lower level than previously and subsumed into the tenant's rent. This has been seen as part of the process of establishing a 'neutral state' in Ireland, a recognition that in part is a response to the growing political assertiveness of Irish Catholics that Ireland could no longer be effectively governed as long as this remained the preserve of any single group. The most visible indication of this was the willingness of government, beginning with the Whigs but continued by Peel after 1841, to distribute a reasonable share of patronage to all religious denominations.

These reforms certainly did not spell disaster for Irish Anglicanism and it remained the religion of a socially advantaged but numerically weak minority. However, in the 1830s many Anglicans were outraged by these reforms and it was the imminent passage of the Irish Temporalities Bill that prompted John Keble to preach his sermon on 'National Apostasy' on Sunday 14 July 1833. This marked the formal beginnings of the Oxford or Tractarian movement.

The Oxford movement

The origins of the Oxford movement lay in the casual discussions between John Keble, Edward Pusey, John Henry Newman and Richard Hurrell Froude in the senior common room at Oriel College, Oxford in the late 1820s. All were traditional High Churchmen though there were significant differences between them. Keble was the most conservative, with a position similar to that of most eighteenth-century High Churchmen. Pusey was much attracted by German biblical criticism and theological liberalism in the 1820s, though he later adopted a more conservative stance. Froude believed that if the Church of England was to recover its Catholic heritage then some sort of accommodation with Rome was unavoidable. Newman, unlike the others from an evangelical background, had become dissatisfied by the 1820s with evangelical theology and was much influenced by Froude.

The so-called Hadleigh conference in late July led to agreement over the principles of the new movement: to proclaim the doctrine of the apostolic succession; the belief that it was sinful to give the laity a say in church affairs; the need to make the Church more popular; and to protest against any attempts to disestablish the Anglican Church.[13] The Oxford movement was a reaction against prevailing religious attitudes. It was part of the general and widespread revival of the 'corporate' against the 'individual' evangelical spirit of the day. It was a reaction against the Church as a department of state – as Keble said 'let us give up a national Church and have a real one'. It was essentially a spiritual movement, concerned with the invisible world and was thus not only anti-liberal but paradoxically intensely political. Newman opposed liberalism and Erastianism as both struck at the spiritual dimension, the former by enslaving its spiritual guardian, the latter by destroying its dogmatic foundations. The Tractarians diagnosed the age as one blighted by worldliness and maintained contemporary Protestantism was incapable of rescuing from spiritual decay.

The method of the Tractarians was to concentrate on a single article of the Christian creed: 'I believe in one Catholic and Apostolic Church', by which they meant the maintenance of apostolic order in the Church through the episcopacy. They used *Tracts for the Times* to disseminate their views. The first was published in September 1833. By the end of 1833 20 tracts had been published; 50 by the end of 1834 and 66 by July 1835. Tracts were nothing new. Wesley had used tracts and the evangelicals had their Religious Tract Society. What was novel about the Tracts of the Oxford movement was that they were products of the High Church, written and circulated by dons and addressed not to the poor but to educated minds.

The reaction of many to the Oxford movement was to raise the spectre of popery. The papist and bigoted nature of the movement was partially confirmed by the Hampden case of 1835 when leading Tractarians opposed the appointment of Hampden as regius professor of divinity. Their attack had two strands: their opposition to the appointment of a clergyman with what they saw as suspect rationalist views, and their opposition to his appointment by the patronage of a Whig prime minister. Hampden symbolized both the liberal and Erastian face of the Church of England. By the end of 1837 Newman in effect led a 'party' within the Establishment and this gave anti-Catholic groups further evidence of the increasing Catholicity of the Tractarians.

The movement had several limitations. First it was the *Oxford* movement, academic, clerical and conservative. Its appeal was restricted to the educated, not deliberately but as a result of the interests and sympathies of its protagonists. It was not until after 1845 that the Anglo-Catholic revival reached out to the poor and got a footing in the slums. It was predominantly clerical and, though it did acquire some support from eminent laymen, the Tracts were addressed to clergymen. The movement had to be clerical because if the clergy did not accept its message it was certain no one else would. Its success in interesting the country's clergy in theological questions and church principles was one of its major achievements. It was inevitable that the standpoint of the movement was backward-looking. For Newman the problem started with the Reformation – 'a limb badly set – it must be broken again in order to be righted'. This retrospection could, and was, seen by many as conservative if not reactionary.

By 1840 the question arose as to whether the movement was leading towards popery or away from it. Pusey was putting forward a High Anglican policy within the Church. The publication by Newman of *Tract XC (90)* was a turning point both for himself and the movement. His analysis of the Thirty-nine Articles led him to emphasize their catholicity. They did not condemn, he maintained, many Catholic practices and means of grace, which they were generally supposed to do. The hostile reaction to *Tract XC*, especially from the bishops, made Newman increasingly suspect that Anglicanism was not doctrinally a 'middle way' between Roman Catholicism and pure Protestantism but merely a pragmatic legislative solution introduced by Elizabeth I in 1559–60 to resolve religious uncertainty and prevent religious strife. This ended his usefulness to the Anglican Church. He still regarded himself as an Anglican but his assurance was gone. In the following years he worked out his theory of development in order to satisfy himself that the contemporary Church of Rome was the legitimate heir of the Church of the New Testament.

The movement increasingly looked to Keble and Pusey for leadership but from 1842 to 1845 they were under severe attack. In 1842 Isaac Williams did not get the Chair of Poetry because of anti-Tractarian sentiments. Pusey was suspended from preaching for two years in 1843 and in 1845 Ward was censured. The secession of Newman, Ward and Faber in 1845 and the attitude of the Puseyites weakened the Church of England in politics and public esteem but the movement as a whole gave substance once again to the idea of the Church as a divine society and a sacred mystery.

The crisis of 1845 was regarded at the time as a great watershed but it was only one of a serious of crises that the movement passed through after the publication of Froude's posthumous *Remains* in 1838–9 and with each new crisis there was a number of secessions. In the early 1850s there were major secessions over the Gorman case. Bishop Phillpotts of Exeter, the Tractarians only openly episcopal supporter, refused to institute the Revd G. C. Gorman, an evangelical, in a parish in his diocese on the grounds that he denied the doctrine of baptismal regeneration. For most evangelicals infant baptism was a meaningless symbol; the real test of true Christianity was the conversion experience. A complicated legal dispute followed with Gorman eventually appealing to the Judicial Committee of the Privy Council, a court of appeal established in 1833. There was an attempt to fudge the issue but Phillpotts still refused to institute Gorman and in the end this was carried out by the evangelical Archbishop of Canterbury, J. B. Sumner. What angered many High Churchmen was not the actual judgement but that it was a secular rather than an ecclesiastical court which had made a doctrinal decision. Newman's secession may have been a profound psychological blow but to consider that the Oxford movement ended in 1845 is as meaningless as to see 1832 as the end of political reform.

The impact of the Oxford movement was essentially ecclesiastical. The Tractarians played an important role in the provision of theological training for the clergy. Chichester (1839), Wells (1840), Cuddesdon (1854) and Salisbury (1860) were all founded on definite High Church principles. Before 1830 the role of clergymen within society can perhaps best be described as 'social' rather than 'spiritual'. The Oxford movement provided clergy with a new concept of their social role which was not quasi-political but profoundly spiritual. This new concept of priestly vocation goes a long way to explain clerical support for Tractarianism. Evangelical assertions that the laity were becoming priest-ridden were not without foundation.

The Established Church in Wales

The position of the Established Church in Wales was very similar to the situation in northern England. Parishes, especially in upland Wales, were large. Its organization and finances were designed for a rural, not an industrializing society. In South Wales there was increasingly insufficient church accommodation. Merthyr Tydfil had seating for only 2,500 out of its population of over 50,000 in the early nineteenth century.

Lay control over the Church was widespread. Funds had been diverted into lay hands since the Reformation and by the 1830s over 20 per cent of Church income went into lay hands. Laymen often had the right to appoint clergy and, because they were unwilling to spend much on clerical stipends, pluralism and absenteeism was common. In North Wales the bishops of St Asaph and Bangor kept much of their revenues and there the traditional problems of pluralism and lay impropriation were less evident. They were not faced with industrialization on the same scale as those bishops in the south. Financially secure and not faced with the major problems of social change, the Church lost ground to Nonconformity just as in the industrialized south.

After 1832 the Ecclesiastical Commission was empowered to create new parishes but none were created in Wales until 1920. There was some attempt to meet the challenge of changing population patterns with new churches after 1840 but no Welsh-speaking bishop was appointed until 1870. But there was some improvement in the quality of clergymen as a new breed of men, more dynamic, often evangelical, emerged from the Lampeter theological college and the worst abuses of pluralism, non-residence and lay patronage were gradually eradicated.

The Established Church retained its role as the religious arm of the state and as a political force in Wales during the first half of the nineteenth century. But it was an alien Church and a focus of national resentment linked to the landowning class. It was divorced from community and nation. The educational monopoly of church schools, the exaction of tithes from a poor population to maintain a Church to which it did not belong and the banning of Nonconformist burials in church precincts fuelled this resentment. It was easy to identify the Church as alien and Nonconformity as Welsh and in that climate demands for disestablishment flourished.

Conclusions

While unreformed the Anglican Church claimed the allegiance of the whole society. It was thoroughly integrated with the mainstream culture and social structure and monopolistic in its attitude to religious rivals. As long as political sanctions against religious deviance were firmly upheld widespread support for alternative religious perspectives could be held in check. But from 1689 British society moved gradually towards a pluralist, religious voluntarism. By the 1830s Britain was well on the way to becoming a pluralistic society containing not one but a plurality of cultural systems. The reforms of the 1830s and 1840s represented a decisive turning point. Though still the Established Church in England, Wales and Ireland it had accommodated itself to the reality of permanent competition with other 'churches' within its boundaries. The state might intervene to support the Establishment but there was no chance that it would restore the Church to its constitutionally prescribed role as a monopolistic religion. Like the landed elite, the Church, though it fought a skilled rearguard action for the remainder of the century, was increasingly prepared to compromise to preserve its remaining privileges. This was metamorphosis, not restoration. The result was a change in the character of the Church to being one denomination among several.

CRISIS IN THE SCOTTISH PRESBYTERIAN CHURCH

At the same time as, though quite independently of, the Oxford movement there was a crisis within the established Presbyterian Church of Scotland which led not to a secession but to a disruption.[14] The issue the Presbyterian church faced was whether parish ministers should be nominated by lay patrons or only elected by the Church itself.[15] Patronage, abolished in 1690, had been restored in 1712 and, throughout the eighteenth century, had been a cause of dissension in the Church. Presbyterians directed their controversial energies not to fundamental questions of theology but to church government because, unlike in Anglicanism and Catholicism, there was little latitude of belief in the Church of Scotland. Ministers dispensed the same minutely detailed creed and consequently there were few direct challenges to the nature of religious belief.

Moderates and evangelicals

By 1800 there were two parties in the Church of Scotland, the moderates and the evangelicals and the moderates were in the ascendancy. Though the main ostensible reason for their difference was patronage, behind this lay a contradiction between a cultured, rationalist and somewhat worldly conformity and a zealous, evangelical and missionary fervour of stricter Calvinist orthodoxy. The moderates stood for the absolute rights of patrons, strict obedience to both civil and ecclesiastical law, opposition to anything in the way of popular government or parochial reform. As a result evangelical desires to extend the Church into the new centres of population were frustrated.

Thomas Chalmers (1780–1847) led the evangelicals. He considered that control by the moderates had prevented the Church from fulfilling its mission. In 1833–4 the evangelicals achieved a majority in the General Assembly. The 'Ten Years' Conflict' began with an attempt in 1833 to pass a Veto Act in the General Assembly designed to secure the rights of parishioners to reject a patron's nominee. Though the moderates were able to stop this measure it was their last victory and in the following year the Veto Act was passed along with a Chapels Act which enabled the Church to develop and adapt its parochial system to meet existing and future needs. Within months the Veto Act was challenged in the civil courts by patrons seeking to use their rights. The Scottish Court of Sessions pronounced the Veto Act to be *ultra vires* and the claims of the Church of Scotland to be free of state jurisdiction were rejected. The House of Lords, in a somewhat casual judgement, confirmed this view. Chalmers and other evangelical leaders made repeated attempts to persuade Whig and Conservative governments to secure the rights of the Church of Scotland but they were unsuccessful. By 1842 the evangelicals had come to the conclusion that the Church would not be given the freedom they considered essential. They had widespread support among the laity as well as in the ministry and, convinced that Parliament offered no redress, they made preparations to break with the State and set up a Free Church.

'Disruption', 1843

When the General Assembly met in Edinburgh on 18 May 1843 470 out of the 1,200 Church of Scotland Ministers left the Establishment. This 'Disruption' led to the setting up of the Free Church, with Chalmers as its first Moderator. He did not believe that this marked a secession from the Church since he regarded the Free Church as the true national church. The Free Church at once directed its energies to providing a national organization to cover all of Scotland. The 'Ten Years' Conflict' was followed by the 'Ten Years' Rebuilding' as new churches were opened. Between 1843 and 1845 500 places of worship were opened and £320,000 raised for their construction; £100,000 was raised for the building of new manses.

The Disruption weakened the Presbyterian Church in the long term. The poor law could no longer be left to the depleted Church of Scotland and was put on a new basis by Peel's government. The educational system was now split between those who went to Church of Scotland or Free Church schools. The late 1840s and 1850s saw the nature of Presbyterian faith being called into question through anti-Calvinist feeling and criticism. The formation of the United Presbyterian Church in 1847 by the union of the Relief Church and the Secession Church seemed to anticipate this threat. Presbyterianism was now a three-cornered affair – the Church of Scotland, the Free Church and the United Presbyterian Church – and this proved a weak basis on which to resist new theological and cultural challenges. Patronage, the issue which led to split in 1843, was abolished by Parliament in 1874. But the issue of the disestablishment of the Church of Scotland was kept alive by the Free Church. The Church was no longer the great unifying institution of the Scottish nation.

EVANGELICALISM WITHIN THE ESTABLISHMENT

The evangelical revival of the eighteenth century was partly a consequence of the increasing frustration felt by individuals like the Wesleys with the intense conservatism of Anglican High Churchmen.[16] Not all of those who supported Wesleyan Methodism followed them out of the Church of England in the 1790s. From the mid-eighteenth century groups of rather more evangelical clergy and laity also began to attack the conservatism of the Established Church from within. They took a considerable initiative in missionary work and campaigns for social and 'moral' reform and by the 1820s were beginning to establish a foothold in the parishes of some larger towns. By 1830 three evangelicals had been made bishops. Despite their emphasis on spiritual conversion and the absolute supremacy of Scripture over the traditions of the Church, they were not anti-sacramental and encouraged more frequent communion services.[17] Theirs was a simple and unmysterious form of worship. People are all in a state of natural depravity, weighed down by sin, and life is an arena of moral trial in which people are tempted, tested and ultimately sorted into saints and sinners. There is a sort of spiritual contract between each soul and God in which intermediaries like the clergy are of relatively little importance. Redemption comes through the faith of the individual in Christ's Atonement on the Cross. This was an evangelical 'scheme of salvation'. Within the Anglican middle classes evangelicalism spread rapidly from the mid-1820s because of economic alarms, Catholic emancipation, constitutional crises, cholera and other signs of an impending divine intervention.

By the 1820s Anglicans were speaking about Anglican evangelicals as 'the Evangelicals' as if they were the only ones. This division between Anglican and non-Anglican evangelicals had not been the case during the first phase of evangelicalism before the 1780s when people moved freely across the formal boundaries between denominations. The reason why this division grew up was in part a result of Wesleyan Methodists leaving the Established Church and in part because the Anglican evangelicals were the only ones who mattered socially and politically.

The second phase of Establishment evangelicalism was inaugurated by the conversion of William Wilberforce and Hannah More in the 1780s and these individuals brought a social distinction and respectability that evangelicals had not previously enjoyed. Under their banner of the 'Evangelical Party' – in itself a somewhat ambiguous term given the diversity of Anglican evangelicalism – this group became the most dynamic and ambitious element in the Established Church. Evangelical Anglican clergy worked within the Establishment claiming, much to the annoyance of bishops during the early nineteenth century, that they represented the central Anglican tradition established during the mid-sixteenth century. By the 1820s evangelicals were in control of most of the national and local religious societies, though the latter were more interdenominational than their national headquarters. They published the bulk of the popular Christian literature of the period: the Bible in all languages; classics of the evangelical point of view like *The Pilgrim's Progress*; soul-arousing works of every kind, and, periodicals like the *Christian Observer* and the *Eclectic Review*. It was developing, through the work of Charles Simeon, parochial organization designed to maintain an intense religious life and to channel the charitable impulse to promote social and religious discipline. By the 1830s its national leadership was consolidated among peers, MPs, bishops and the leading figures of the ecclesiastical and business world.

This diffusion of Anglican evangelicalism was not achieved without some loss of vigour. This process has been called one of 'accommodation' making evangelicalism palatable and manageable for the cultivated classes, an attractive and exemplary model for a combination of piety and social position. It is difficult to estimate the extent to which this was a conscious aim of Wilberforce and his supporters, or the level of its success. But there is little doubting its influence throughout British society touching those who were not evangelically minded and who may not have liked its theology: for example, Sunday observance, the enforcement of the blasphemy laws, especially in the 1820s, and the encouragement of Sunday and day schools. The moral revolution was accomplished and overt sexuality was driven into the underworld or into lower-class life. Victorian respectability predates the accession of the queen in 1837.[18]

The existence of Establishment meant that the relation between the Anglican and non-Anglican evangelicals became increasingly difficult after 1820. During the 1820s and 1830s the Dissenters moved from a reluctant acceptance of Establishment to an attitude of general dislike. By the 1840s disestablishment was raised as a major issue, with Dissenters wishing to reduce the Church of England to an equality of status with their own denominations, competing freely in an open 'religious' market. This view of the Establishment was known as 'voluntarism' and was an attitude increasingly sympathized with by Methodists of every kind, by many Presbyterians in England as well as Scotland and by Irish Roman Catholics. Though some evangelicals like Lord Shaftesbury never hesitated to co-operate with Dissenters and a few left the Church, most Anglican evangelicals persisted in looking on the Establishment as an advantageous and necessary condition.

While the existence of an Establishment was a ground of division within evangelicalism, the principle of 'No Popery' was a ground of union. This has been seen as one of the causes of the lowering of the tone of evangelicalism and a resurgence of anti-Catholic feelings in the 1840s and 1850s. Some change in the relationship between public men and public opinion may partially explain what happened to evangelicalism after 1830. Post-reform politics saw the emergence of a more politically conscious public with worries, real or imaginary, about which that public wanted something done. By 1836 Wilberforce, Hannah More and Charles Simeon had all died. The successors to the Clapham leaders – Shaftesbury and Fowell Buxton – were not personally inferior but evangelicalism seems to have moved into a lower gear. Best argues that:

> It is almost as if its greatest contribution had by then been made and as if it was felt to lack the breadth and tone of distinction which could satisfy many of its natural leaders in the post-revolutionary age. . . .[19]

Evangelicalism was a religion of duty, placing service above doctrine, and appealed particularly to women.[20] Wilberforce argued in *A Practical View* that women were more favourably disposed to religion and good works than men. The activities and restrictions of nineteenth-century family life and female education tended to focus the affections and raise philanthropy to the level of obedience to God. Though some women found Christianity restrictive, most female reformers saw it as an emancipatory influence heightening women's self-esteem and giving them a sense of place and direction. Christianity confirmed that women had a rightful and important place in the charitable world, a place which particularly to men was a subordinate one. Female evangelical piety did not threaten the social order. Clare Lucas Balfour wrote in 1849 that:

> the history of every religious and benevolent society in the civilized world shows the female sex pre-eminent in numbers, zeal and usefulness, thus attesting the interest women take in Christian labours for the welfare of society.[21]

Historians acknowledge the role of evangelicalism in shaping the mentality of the first half of the nineteenth century but recognize the difficulty of defining that role precisely. Evangelicalism's middle-class piety fostered concepts of public probity and national honour based on the ideals of economy, professionalism and 'respectability'. Though many prominent evangelicals were paternalists and bitterly opposed to the prevailing *laissez-faire* ethos of the period, many contemporaries thought of evangelicalism as synonymous with philanthropy. Boyd Hilton argues that evangelicals helped to create and buttress the very capitalist philosophy that was under attack. They wanted society to operate as closely to 'nature' as possible by repealing interventionist laws, leaving people to work out their own salvation and spiritual life in the course of their ordinary lives. In that evangelical ethos suffering seemed to be part of God's plan and government took a harsh attitude to social underdogs in order not to interfere with such dispensations of providence. 'Self-help' was both an economic and spiritual means of achieving salvation.

NONCONFORMITY

The metamorphosis within the Established Church was bound to have significant effects on the Dissenting churches after 1830. But Anglicanism was not the only form of organized religion to undergo fundamental changes in the first half of the nineteenth century. There was a shift within Methodist, Congregational and Baptist communities away from the sect-type religious culture of the eighteenth century towards a new and patently denominational orientation to the wider society. Methodism in particular ceased to be a movement and became an organization. The term 'Dissent' was gradually replaced by 'Nonconformity', 'dissenters' by 'Nonconformists'.[22]

Towards denominationalism

The movement towards denominationalism among the nonconformist churches had its origins in the late eighteenth century. It was both organizational and 'clerical'. Denominationalism was the result of the need and desire to pursue new goals. It arose out of the evangelical revival in the eighteenth century and was not a reaction to it. The new goal was evangelicalism – missionary activities both abroad and at home – and it was possible because of the theological shift away from the Calvinist doctrine of the elect (people are either born to go to heaven or not) which would have rendered such activity pointless. In this situation the Church could and should be open to all. The formation of the Northamptonshire Association in 1764 among Particular (Calvinistic) Baptists marked a turning-point. In 1797 the (Baptist) Home Mission Society was formed in London. County or Area Associations of Churches were formed among the Independents, but generally later than among Baptists, in Warwickshire in 1793, Wiltshire and East Somerset in 1797, Hampshire in 1797, Lancashire in 1806 and Hertfordshire in 1810. In due course a (Congregational) Home Missionary Society was formed in 1819 to work in those areas where County Associations were weak or non-existent.

Village preaching depended on support from elsewhere and united action by a number of churches was an obvious way of doing this.[23] Itinerancy challenged isolationism and undenominationalism and, during the second and third decades of the nineteenth century, the freedom enjoyed by the early itinerants succumbed to the process of institutionalization. Evangelism became increasingly a denominational rather than a local responsibility. Despite this positive development, the 1820s saw the first signs of formalism and stagnation, forces which later sapped the dynamic strength and recruiting power of English Nonconformity.

The movement towards denominationalism can also be seen in terms of academies, buildings and fund-raising. The academies at Hoxton and Hackney both had their origins in the new evangelist missionary spirit. Both Hoxton, founded in 1783, and Hackney, founded thirteen years later, to provide preachers for the Village Itinerancy, were largely staffed by Independents. The Particular Baptists' College founded in Yorkshire in 1805 and the New Connexion General Baptists' Academy founded in 1789 were also products of the revival, taking a clearly denominational form. Successful preaching made new buildings necessary. In the past they had usually been provided by the generosity of one or two leading members but where new causes had been established through iterancy this proved more difficult. This problem of regulating 'chapel cases', where ministers wished to beg for funds in London, was tackled by the first General Congregational Union in 1809 – an attempt which certainly contributed to its demise. The Baptist Building Fund was established with the same object in 1824. It was possible for the central organization of the different churches to exert, if they chose, control and discipline.

Denominationalism also had expression in an increasingly 'clerical' approach. Jabez Bunting and his Wesleyan colleagues gradually strengthened the distinction between travelling and local preachers, by developing the doctrine of the 'pastoral office' and enforcing the commitment to permanent itinerancy and corporate discipline among the travelling preachers. Excessive spontaneity – too much lay initiative – was seen as a threat to the integrity of Wesleyanism and a theological basis for the differentiation of roles and functions between ministers and laymen was elaborated. This redirection of the Methodist movement under ministerial initiative created immense strains and resulted in a prolonged period of conflict and schism, beginning with the New Connexion breakaway in 1797 and ending with major disruptions and realignments between 1849 and 1857. 'Primitive Methodists', 'Bible Christians', Tent Methodists' and 'Wesleyan Reformers' were significant in capturing an element of protest against consolidation and institutionalization which underpinned the fragmentation of the Methodist strain of evangelical Nonconformity. Other Nonconformists lacked both the will and the machinery to sharpen the clerical–lay distinction in this way.

The movement from undenominationalism to denominationalism, from a 'unity of experience' to a 'unity of organization', can be seen as a response to the need for some form of social control. In this view denominationalism reflects the failure of Nonconformity to respond to popular religion and of the anxiety and potential dangers to the country if it got out of control. This view seems to draw too stark a distinction between lay/undenominational and clerical/denominational. It seems more likely that the move to denominationalism was occasioned by the need to maintain the social constituencies of the different Nonconformist groups. Between 1780 and 1815 Nonconformity was marked by its preoccupation with rural society. County associations among Congregationalists and regional bodies among Baptists devoted their energies to the hinterlands rather than the larger centres of population. Even national bodies pursued similar aims. By 1823 the Baptist Western Association numbered 78 member churches, an increase of 44 since 1780. There was little awareness during the French wars of the developing scale of urban irreligion.

With the spread of urban awareness came a recognition of the problems involved in establishing effective contact over urban populations. Neither the individualism of the pioneering preachers or the rudimentary organization of the regional societies could cope with the scale of the problem. The result was a move to national networks of evangelism under the control of denominational bodies which were, alone, capable of integrating planning and direction. Denominationalism was a consequence of the need to mobilize resources effectively to deal with the urban problem.

The impetus for structural definition stemmed from the need for more efficiency and a growing sense of denominational identity accompanied the return to peace after 1815. There was an increasing demand for religious accommodation with the attendant financial problems of their provision and maintenance. By the 1820s this material interest had combined with rising ministerial status to accentuate contemporary concerns for 'respectability', hastening the change from individual spontaneity to a more formal assumption of responsibility for further expansion. By 1830 the shape of the movement had visibly altered with the old emphasis on free-ranging, outdoor evangelism supplanted by indoor, more controlled, gatherings.

The diversity of Nonconformity

The diversity of Nonconformity makes it difficult to generalize about its development and some consideration of each of the major groupings is necessary.[24] Presbyterianism had slowly moved away from the doctrine of the Trinity and by 1830 a majority of its members were Unitarian in creed. Unitarianism had developed from the 'rational theology' of the eighteenth century but its association with free thought, radicalism in politics and its defence of people like Richard Carlile made orthodox Dissent suspicious. Increasingly the doctrinal differences between Unitarians and Trinitarians mattered.

Unitarians and Trinitarians

In 1816 the minister of the Wolverhampton Unitarian chapel was discovered to be a Trinitarian and his congregation dismissed him. In the ensuing legal case the vice-chancellor held that the chapel was built when it was illegal to be a Unitarian and that the law could therefore have upheld no endowment to support Unitarian worship. The Wolverhampton case put in jeopardy the chapel and endowment of every Unitarian congregation founded before 1813, when Unitarian opinion ceased to be illegal. A similar decision in favour of Trinitarians occurred over the fund left by Lady Hewley in 1704 to provide endowments in the six northern English counties. The vice-chancellor's court confirmed that only Trinitarians were eligible for endowments from the fund in 1833 and this judgement was maintained by the Lord Chancellor and the House of Lords in 1836 and 1842 respectively. These cases divided English Dissenters and in March 1836 a majority of Unitarian congregations in London separated themselves from the Protestant dissenting deputies, splitting the alliance of 'Old' Dissent.

The legal uncertainty for Unitarians created by the Lady Hewley case was exacerbated by a suit over the richly endowed Eustace Street chapel in Dublin in 1843–4 when Irish Trinitarians sought to acquire the chapels and endowments of Irish Unitarians. The result, which followed the 1836 precedent, meant that every Unitarian chapel might now become the subject of litigation. Peel attempted to resolve the problem by introducing a Dissenters Chapels Bill which said that where there was no trust deed determining doctrine or usage the usage of a certain number of years (twenty-five was agreed on) should be taken as conclusive evidence of the right of any congregation to possess a chapel and its endowments and that any suits pending should have the benefit of the Act. Peel was surprised by the depth of opposition to the bill from Wesleyan and orthodox Nonconformists and the evangelical clergy of the Church of England. Its passage was important as a further extension of the 1813 Toleration Act to others besides orthodox Trinitarians.

Presbyterians in England

The few surviving Trinitarian congregations looked to Scotland for aid but the established Church of Scotland was reluctant and in 1839 the General Assembly acknowledged the independence of the Presbyterian Church of England. The Unitarians were not an expanding religious grouping but the Trinitarians, their numbers swelled by Scottish immigration into England, were. In 1836 the congregations of Lancashire and the north-west agreed to form a synod of two presbyteries and adopted the Westminster confession of faith. The synod expanded during the late 1830s and 1840s: London and Newcastle were brought in in 1839; Berwick in 1840; Northumberland in 1842 and Birmingham in 1848. The changing attitude of the synod was reflected in the change of name: in 1839 it was the 'Presbyterian Church of England in connexion with the Church of Scotland' and in 1849 the 'Presbyterian Church in England'. Not until 1876 did it become the Presbyterian Church of England.

The 1851 Religious Census showed that the distribution of Presbyterianism was almost entirely a reflection of Scottish immigration into England. Half of the total number of attendances were recorded in the three northern counties of Northumberland, Durham and Cumberland. Lancashire and London each accounted for about 20 per cent and the remaining 10 per cent was made up of isolated congregations in Westmorland, Yorkshire, Cheshire, Staffordshire, Warwickshire and Worcestershire.

Congregationalists

Between 1830 and 1860 the Congregationalists turned from a loose federation into something like a modern denomination. This was a major achievement since a denomination meant some form of central authority and Independents had always held that each chapel was sovereign. The force which moved Independents towards some form of central authority was the recognition that Dissenters' rights to marriage or burial or church rates were better protected by county associations than by small sovereign units and the need for central support to support colleges and to make stipends adequate for ministers. An attempted union in 1811 failed but in 1831 a Congregation Union was tentatively established.

During the 1830s the Union survived uneasily. County associations joined slowly – Oxford and West Berkshire in 1841, Cornwall in 1846 and Hampshire in 1848 were among the latest to join – but they sent no money. The Union was saved by the skill of Algernon Wells, secretary from 1837 until his death in 1850. He put it on a sound financial and organizational footing with profits from its publications. After 1845 the Union ran into difficulty because of the problems within Wesleyan Methodism which brought central government into question. Many Independents sided with Bunting's opponents and the death of Algernon Wells removed an important force for moderation within the Union.

The Union reduced the variety of uses in chapels but there had always been pressure towards free worship and the breadth of Independent doctrine. Congregational churches were faithful to Calvinism but could not observe the advances of Methodism without adopting some of its devices and its missionary enthusiasm. They gained from Sunday schools and village preaching but there was a thinning in the upper and educated ranks of society. The political disputes between Church and Dissent in the 1830s and 1840s raised fears that Independents were natural allies of Irish and radicals and this meant that by 1850 Congregational churches had a more broadly lower-middle-class composition than they had in 1800, though they housed more worshippers.

The 1851 Religious Census revealed the same basic geographical pattern that had existed at the end of the seventeenth century. Congregationalism was strongest in a line of counties stretching eastwards from Devon to Essex and Suffolk. The Census shows that whatever hold Dissent had in the largest urban complexes was due largely to the Wesleyan Methodists. The exception was London, where Congregationalists took the leading role. But even here the picture was patchy. There were few congregations in Kensington, Chelsea and Bayswater where Anglicanism was dominant. The East End also proved poor soil and apart from a number of missions supported by wealthy suburban congregations there were few Congregational chapels. In the ordinary lower-middle-class suburbs, especially south of the Thames, the field was left clear for the Baptists and the Methodists. It was in the prosperous and expanding suburbs like Hampstead, Brixton, Highbury and Clapham that Congregationalism had its real base.

Baptists

Baptists were Independent congregations which practised the baptism of believers and there was little to distinguish them from Congregationalists. But this outward harmony concealed considerable diversity. Congregational chapels contained few labourers, but many Baptist chapels consisted of people from the lower levels of society. Baptist congregations had less educated pastors, more illiterate members, held their Calvinism more rigidly, were doctrinally more conservative and maintained their independence more vehemently. Baptists were divided into three groups: General or Arminian Baptists; Particular Baptists who were moderate Calvinists, and Strict and Particular Baptists who were Calvinist but not moderate. Most of the General Baptist congregations went back to the seventeenth century and had faded into Unitarian belief but since 1770 a small group, the General Baptists of the New Connexion, preserved the orthodox Arminian faith.

The nineteenth century was marked by a period of coming together among Baptists and as early as 1813 a Baptist Union was created to provide a common meeting ground for Particular and General Baptists. To create a 'union' proved more difficult than among Congregationalists even though the same needs for union existed – a missionary society in need of money and direction, training of ministers, stipends for pastors and chapels in debt. The General Baptists were lukewarm in their support for the 1813 union which, though it was reorganized in 1832, grew more slowly than support for the contemporary Congregational Union.

The 1851 Religious Census showed that about 366,000 Baptists attended services. Particular Baptists had 1,491 chapels in England and 456 in Wales. The New Connexion of General Baptists had 179 chapels in England and three in Wales. Old General Baptists had 93 chapels. The Baptists' main strength lay in the block of counties from the East Midlands to the coast of East Anglia. Except in Dorset and Methodist Cornwall, Baptists increased in all the southern counties of England after 1800. By contrast there were few Baptists in the northern counties apart from the West Riding.

The Quakers

The major expansion of the Society of Friends (the Quakers) took place in the eighteenth century and they were numerically strongest in the north (Lancashire, Yorkshire and Westmorland), in the south-west and in London, Bristol and Norwich. Most Quakers came from the rural and urban *petit bourgeoisie* with correspondingly few among the upper classes or the lower orders. But this trend was reversed in the first half of the nineteenth century. Three major causes of this were identified by contemporaries. First, the evangelical revival had the effect of dividing Quakers into those who adopted an evangelical approach to their belief and those for whom discussion of the Bible (its reading aloud at meetings did not occur until 1860) was unthinkable. The dispute came to a head in 1835–7 and led to about 300 Friends of Lancashire and Kendal leaving the Society. For a time they maintained a separate denomination as Evangelical

Friends but soon found little to divide them from other denominations; some joined the Church of England and others the Plymouth Brethren.

Secondly, Quaker religious education was extremely poor. It was seen as secondary to simply waiting upon the Word and was consequently undeveloped. Quaker Sunday schools were not begun until the 1840s. Thirdly, marriage discipline was strict and if it was broken then the individual was bound to be expelled. John Bright's brother and two sisters were expelled for marrying outside the Society. Perhaps a third of the Friends who married between 1809 and 1859 were, according to one contemporary, expelled for marrying outside the Society. The conservatism of the Quakers led to decline and this was not arrested until the 1860s when marriage discipline became less draconian, religious education was improved and there was a recognition of the positive value of evangelism.

The Mormons

During the nineteenth century a number of religious movements grew up in the United States and were then brought to Britain. Before 1850 only the Church of Jesus Christ of Latter-day Saints or the Mormons was of any significance. Founded in the 1820s, the Mormon Church claimed to be the only true and valid church. It first appeared on the English religious kaleidoscope in 1837 when seven Mormon missionaries landed at Liverpool. A second mission in 1840, led by the leader Brigham Young, proved equally successful. Based in Liverpool, Mormon missions were sent round the country and it is small wonder that many of the early converts were the poor, for whom the 1840s was a period of intense hardship. Furthermore the Mormons organized a very efficient emigration system from Liverpool. Between 1841 and 1843 nearly 3,000 emigrants left Liverpool and, despite the suspension of all emigration in 1846 and 1847, by 1850 the number of emigrants had risen to nearly 17,000. In the 1851 Religious Census 16,628 Mormons attended the evening service on Sunday. The 1850s saw Mormonism in decline throughout Britain. In part this was the result of improved conditions for the working population. More important was the announcement by Brigham Young in 1852 that polygamy was God's will. Outside the Mormon mission house in Soham (Cambridgeshire) 1,200 people watched as village youths enacted a Mormon wedding, to which seven brides rode on donkeys. Polygamy exposed Mormonism to charges of immorality and vice and was fatal to evangelism in Britain. The number of Mormons sank back slowly to 2,000 by the 1860s.

Welsh Nonconformity

The 1851 Religious Census showed that both traditional Dissent, in the shape of the Baptists and the Independents, and the Methodist groups which had emerged in the eighteenth century, had assumed positions of considerable strength in Wales.[25] The dominant Welsh denomination was the Calvinistic Methodists who could claim some influence throughout Wales and had a virtual hegemony in the north. The Baptist and Independent strongholds were in South Wales. Despite constant theological disputation – less of a problem than in England because only the Wesleyan Methodists were not Calvinist – there was a fundamental strength in a shared evangelical theological base and in an embryonic, if ambiguous, notion of nationality expressed through Welsh. Welsh Nonconformity was able to escape the damaging denominational splits that occurred in England and maintained a common religious and social commitment towards, and in a sense against, the world outside. Its religious coherence made possible the impact which it had on Welsh society.

The period between 1800 and 1850 was one of unrestricted expansion for Welsh Nonconformity. Preachers were largely itinerant. The emphasis was upon evangelism and preaching was frequently inspirational bringing congregations to a high pitch of emotional excitement. Within this period there were years of particular growth which were usually, though not exclusively, periods of religious revival. Revivals seemed to occur with regularity at the end of each decade and nourished Welsh congregations in three ways. Revivals preserved the future of congregations by attracting new members or by converting 'hearers' into full members. They injected a new spiritual dynamic into those who already attended. They had not occurred in the eighteenth century when Nonconformity was not the church of the poor. Revivalism enabled it to become the church of the working population in the nineteenth century. In the industrial south there were revivals in 1810, 1815 and 1829 centred on the Calvinistic Methodists, between 1841 and 1843 among Independents and 'cholera revivals' in 1831–2 and 1849–50 in the badly affected urban centres.

Scotland's Nonconformity

In Scotland Presbyterianism was increasingly under pressure in the first half of the nineteenth century both from within and from dissenting churches without. The Scottish Episcopal Church was in sharp decline in the northern half of the country, losing members from the lower ranks to Presbyterianism, especially in its evangelical form. It became increasingly 'High Church' in its services and this attracted the majority of the aristocracy and large landowners. But there is considerable evidence from 'Low Church' Episcopalians, who came from other parts of the British Isles, especially Ireland, that the church was doing little for the growing urban population.

Scotland was an increasingly pluralistic society in terms of religion, with a variety of smaller sects and churches. Many were the product of schism within indigenous Presbyterianism. However, Congregationalist and Baptist churches developed strongly localized support in the larger towns of the Central Lowlands and in fishing communities throughout Scotland. The Methodist message proved popular in the late eighteenth century but the Methodist Church did not. Native Presbyterian churches increasingly provided the same evangelical message and, with a few exceptions like Shetland fishermen and migrant English and Irish workers round Glasgow and Airdrie, Methodist membership stayed quite low. There were less than 1,400 adherents in 1790 and under 4,000 forty years later.

Revivalism played a significant role in maintaining religious intensity though its impact was less widespread but lasted longer than in Wales. Emotional revivals great and small punctuated the eighteenth century. The most famous was the 'Cambuslang Wark' of 1742 which brought burning religious fervour to Lanarkshire. The 1840s saw revivals in Kilsyth and Aberdeen, 'awakenings' which centred on mass communion after highly charged preaching. But all areas of Scotland seem to have been susceptible and any explanation based on class or occupation is unconvincing. Perhaps most important was the Calvinist doctrine of not knowing whether one was of the elect or not. Religion remained the means by which many people expressed their values, aspirations and grievances in Scotland during the changes wrought by economic and urban development.

Nonconformity in Ireland

Protestant Dissent was both dynamic and expansive in Ireland in the first half of the century. Presbyterianism was heavily concentrated in Ulster, where 96 per cent of its members lived. In the counties of Antrim and Down and in Belfast and Carrickfergus, Presbyterians were the largest single religious group, while they were also well represented in Co. Londonderry. In the countryside Presbyterians held larger and more profitable farms than any other religious group and were less likely to be found among the ranks of landless labourers. In the towns, they were overrepresented among skilled workers and in middle-class occupations. By 1850 there were over 70,000 members of small Nonconformist denominations. The Methodists accounted for over half the combined membership of these groups followed by Congregationalists, Baptists and Unitarians.

Irish Presbyterianism did not suffer the same problem of low morale and weak internal discipline which afflicted both Irish Catholics and Anglicans. The effects of the evangelical revival in the early nineteenth century were seen, not in the area of religious discipline but rather in matters of religious orthodoxy. Differences between Unitarian and Trinitarian doctrines had led to division within the Synod of Ulster in the eighteenth century but it was not until the 1820s that these long-standing theological differences became a source of major conflict. In 1822 Henry Cooke launched an attack on Unitarian views which led to the Synod firmly declaring itself in favour of Trinitarian belief in 1827. Two years later those who did not agree with this decision, led by Henry Montgomery, seceded and set up their own body, the Remonstrant Synod. In 1840 the Synod of Ulster, purged of its heterodox elements, came together with the Secession Synod, a group which had seceded in the 1730s, to form the General Assembly of the Presbyterian Church in Ireland.

These theological disputes reflected wider social and cultural divisions within Presbyterianism. 'Liberal' views, which accepted a looser definition of belief, were stronger in the eastern part of Ulster, among the urban population and the wealthier congregations, while more doctrinaire and conservative views predominated in the west of the province, among rural Presbyterians and among the less affluent. Some historians have noted a political dimension to the dispute with Cooke openly allying himself with the leaders of Irish Toryism while Montgomery was a leading spokesman for Ulster Liberalism. Though political differences may have given the theological debates added edge, there is little doubt that the main impetus to division was the rise of evangelicalism and the resulting demands for a firmer definition of doctrinal certitude.

METHODISM

The 1790s was a decade of internal crisis for Wesleyan Methodism as it sought to find solutions to problems left unresolved on John Wesley's death in 1791.[26] The result was the 1795 Plan of Pacification which permitted the sacraments to be given in chapels where the trustees, stewards and leaders agreed to it, and the secession of the Methodist New Connexion in 1797 over the form of church government. Between 1800 and 1820 Wesleyan Methodism faced threats from outside and from within as it sought to find 'respectability' and acceptance throughout British society.[27] Three problems dominated discussions: the problem of Methodist loyalty; how and in what directions Methodism should grow; and how Methodism should respond to popular radicalism.

The question of loyalty

Methodism seemed particularly revolutionary. Enthusiasm and evangelism tapped strong emotions and were believed to have genuinely dangerous potential. Methodists were therefore suspected of radical tendencies, even when their leaders went to great pains to demonstrate their support for the Tory Establishment. Within Methodism the struggle was between conservative and broadly 'liberal' wings both convinced they were being faithful to Wesley's principles and intentions. On Wesley's death 'Church Methodism' was still an option and those who advocated it could use his refusal to separate himself from the Church of England as a conclusive argument. Though theoretically an alternative it was soon replaced by the determination to build a church more strongly organized than the Church of England. The Methodist Conference of preachers only was to be the 'living' Wesley, entitled to govern autocratically as he had governed but delegating its power to local superintendent ministers appointed by it. With this hierarchical conception of church government went a 'no politics' rule which in practice meant no radical politics. A 'liberal' wing opposed this conception of government, arguing that they were faithful to Wesley's own impatience with rules, loyal to his appeal to the poor over the heads of the existing dominant aristocratic elite. Ministers were regarded as servants rather than masters and laymen had to be included at every level of government from national to local level. The minister's function was to evangelize and bring new recruits into the Christian family where all were equal. Implied in this alternative view of Methodism was a revolutionary vision of Britain not, as the conservatives maintained, an acceptance of the existing social structure.

Between the 1790s and 1820s the aristocratic elite suffered from growing paranoia and political radicalism and widespread economic distress caused government to be apprehensive. This was also the period when Methodism, which was about 100,000 strong in 1791, reached its point of organizational take-off. Methodists claimed, though probably with some exaggeration, that there were 200,000 members by 1802, 270,000 by 1806 and 367,000 by 1812. A more moderate, and more reliable, claim was 167,000 members in England alone in 1815 with 631 preachers, 1,355 chapels and over half a million members and hearers combined. Figures apart, there is evidence of the Connexion moving boldly into the more settled towns and villages of rural England and directly challenging the Established Church.

To many, Methodism seemed a great threat to stability and Anglican clergy were especially disconcerted by its 'levelling principles'. Popular religious feeling was, to those who governed, synonymous with fanaticism and fanaticism was an enemy to stability. The response from the Connexion was twofold. First, Methodists continued, following Wesley, to insist that their religious beliefs made loyalty to the established order a spiritual imperative. Methodist sermons, conference resolutions and tracts continually emphasized loyalty, for conscience' sake, to the government and the Crown. Secondly, the preachers of the Connexion proclaimed that Methodism served to dampen the discontent of the lower orders and that its influence was consciously exerted to bring about 'peace and good order'. By the early nineteenth century these arguments, which corresponded with Wilberforce's views on the practical, political effects of 'vital Christianity', were becoming more widely accepted outside Methodism but it was a slow process.

In 1803 the Methodists formed a Committee of Privileges to defend their interests in Parliament and in the courts and in 1811–12 they faced a challenge from both. In 1811 Lord Sidmouth, the Home Secretary, began an attempt to secure legislation which would have placed restraints on the system of preaching central to the Methodist system. For three years Sidmouth had been collecting information on the number of licensed teachers and places of worship in Great Britain and the result of this survey seemed to contrast the strength of Methodism with the weakness of the Established Church. In May 1811 he introduced a bill which specified that licences were required by dissenting preachers and that these would only be granted, a discretion given to local justices, to those preachers whose 'respectability' could be vouched for. Widespread opposition – some 500 petitions were placed before the House of Lords – led to the bill being withdrawn.

In 1812 the Methodist conference led by Adam Clarke noted a 'new spirit of hostility', petitioned for and received protection from Parliament. In July 1812 Lord Liverpool introduced a government bill by which both the Conventicle and Five Mile Acts – legislation of the 1660s directed against Dissenters – were repealed and Methodist preachers were given the legal privileges of clergymen. The New Toleration Act provided Methodists with the legal protection they had previously lacked and they argued that Parliament had patently concluded that Methodism was a force for stability not upheaval. This was over-optimistic and, though the Wesleyan conference sent out the first of many circulars emphasizing the need for continued support for the Establishment, it was still possible for Methodists to be accused of spreading 'confusion and anarchy'. Methodists recognized that their preaching privileges depended on continued loyalty and good order in a period of radical ferment.

The direction for growth

The second problem Methodists faced was how they could increase the number of members and what direction that growth should take. There was a fine line between acceptable mass evangelism and revivalistic excesses which had on occasions worried Wesley and increasingly concerned Wesleyan preachers in the 1790s and 1800s. Though some expressed theological doubts about revivalism, more important was the political pressure from government and the Church of England about growing Methodist extremism. The great Yorkshire revival of the mid-1790s by Joseph Entwistle was admired by many for its simple devotion but others were disturbed by its nature. By 1800 many Methodist preachers realized the extent of the evangelical energies they had released.

The problem was made worse by two things. First, American Methodism which was trying to introduce frontier-style revivalism into eastern cities was introduced into England by Lorenzo Dow. Secondly, Methodist revivalist offshoots in Britain began to organize themselves into some kind of connexional system. Arriving in England in late 1805 Dow soon made contact with revivalistic Methodists in Lancashire, Cheshire and the Potteries. Under his influence Hugh Bourne and William Clowes adopted the 'camp-meeting' technique of the American frontier. Camp meetings were condemned by the Methodist Conference and many chapels were closed to Dow and his followers but they won considerable support. The result, in 1811, was the formation of the Primitive Methodists which seceded from the parent body. It spread quickly through the Midlands and its membership of 7,842 in 1819 more than quadrupled, to 33,507, by 1824. A roughly similar movement – the Bible Christians – flourished in Devon and Cornwall with revival meetings which lasted several days and nights and its application to join the Wesleyan Connexion was refused.

Foremost among those opposed to revivalism was Jabez Bunting. What Bunting wanted was a marriage between vital religion and educated opinion, because in his view revivalism was not only divisive but also silly and degrading. In their opposition to revivalism Bunting and others failed to distinguish between the temporary outbreaks of zealous revivalism in some northern towns and the massive rural support for the brand of Methodism offered by Bourne and Clowes. Revivalism was not the monolithic entity which Bunting identified but had within it degrees of acceptability and unacceptability. As in 1797, the Wesleyan leadership decided that the best method of control was expulsion.

Between the 1780s and 1813 Methodists did what they could to set up missions abroad, largely under the inspiration of Thomas Coke, Wesley's most able associate. Coke's departure for a mission to India and his death on the voyage in 1813 meant that there was an opportunity to bring foreign missions under stricter denominational control. The first Methodist Missionary Society was established in Leeds in 1813 and the motivation behind this has been disputed by historians. Semmel maintains that it was a quite deliberate redirection of Methodist energies overseas because it was politically unsafe and connexionally undesirable to allow uncontrolled expansion at home. By redirecting Methodist enthusiasm abroad the threat posed to domestic stability might be overcome. Sidmouth's threats and undisciplined revivalism convinced Bunting and others that foreign missions were a politically desirable alternative to popular radicalism. Though Semmel's interpretation may have some validity, far more important was an expansive optimism occasioned by Napoleon's disaster in Russia and Wellington's victories in Spain. The non-denominational, but Calvinistic, London Missionary Society and the Anglican Church Missionary Society, founded in 1794 and 1799 respectively, sensed the mood of the nation and put their local machinery into operation. In 1813 clergymen known to be hostile to Anglican evangelicals as no less subversive than Methodists made their pulpits available to those preaching missionary sermons.

The question of the foreign missions brought Jabez Bunting to the fore within Wesleyan Methodism, a position he retained until his death in 1858. In 1813, Bunting, then only 34 years old, was stationed in Leeds as an itinerant preacher serving under the superintendency of George Morley; stationed nearby was Richard Watson. There was no doubting

Bunting's orthodoxy. But Richard Watson, born in 1781, though briefly a Wesleyan itinerant, had joined the New Connexion in 1804. Watson met Bunting in 1811 when the latter was helping organize opposition to Sidmouth's bill. They formed a close friendship and Bunting urged Watson to apply for readmission to the Old Connexion which, because of Bunting's considerable exertions, occurred in 1812. Bunting, Watson and Morley planned the organization of the Leeds Missionary Society as a model for the Connexion. The usefulness of this initiative in its appeal to the rank-and-file was recognized at the 1814 Conference and led to the introduction of a new rule in relation to the Legal Hundred, the 100 senior ministers who could veto the decisions of the Conference. Previously ministers were received into that body by a system of strict seniority but from 1814, though three out of four vacancies were filled by seniority, the fourth could be a nominee of all the preachers of the Conference. Bunting was the first minister to benefit from the new system and the extent of his success may be seen in his election as Secretary of the Conference as well.

The revival of missionary activity was part of the denominational rivalry which affected all aspects of religious life in the first half of the nineteenth century. The formation of the Leeds Missionary Society and its replication in other areas can be seen as a continuance of the missionary work of Methodism but also as an alternative to the work of the Calvinistic London Missionary Society. Methodism did not want to be elbowed out of the international missionary movement.

Methodism and radicalism

The final problem which Methodism faced was popular radicalism. The Conference and the Committee of Privileges were vocal in their support for the existing social order, but the number of circulars they issued testifies to their ineffectiveness among rank-and-file members. In 1812 preachers, including Bunting, fought a hard and potentially dangerous campaign against Luddites, refusing to conduct Luddite funerals and closing chapels to Luddite orators. The ineffectiveness of institutional solutions came home to Bunting when six Luddites, whose fathers were Methodists, were hanged at York in 1813. Throughout the Midlands and the north Methodism faced competition from, and was influenced by, the new generation of political clubs. Also, in 1812, Wesleyans in the hosiery districts of the East Midlands became involved in the anti-war petitioning of the Friends of Peace. The changing fortunes of war in late 1812 and 1813 spared the Conference from further embarrassment.

After 1815 Methodism came under attack on two fronts. The radical press claimed it was too reactionary, while the government accused it of harbouring radicals. Wesleyan leaders transferred responsibilities to local preachers and the result was a squeeze on membership as individuals were expelled for radical actions. Growth in the northern manufacturing districts came to a halt and even went into temporary decline in 1819 and 1820. In Rochdale, for example, there was a 15 per cent decrease in members between 1818 and 1820.

Richard Watson warned Methodists in the Annual Address of the 1819 Conference of 'wicked men' who used 'the deprivations of the poor' and urged them not to be 'led astray from your civil and religious duties by their dangerous artifices'. The same message was found in a tract by John Stephens, the tough circuit superintendent in Manchester, who expelled 400 from the membership roll in his first year. A Methodist pamphlet of 1821 denounced perverters of the poor like Cobbett, Paine and Carlile and encouraged patriotism in opposition to liberal radicalism. Official Methodist statement made it absolutely clear to the working population of the north that it could be radical or Methodist but not both.

Events between 1800 and 1820 had led to a closer definition of Methodism in both a denominational and social sense. Government pressure, revivalism and radicalism and administrative and financial difficulties led to changes in the structure and organization of the Methodist movement. John Stephens reported in a letter to Bunting in 1821 that radicalism was no longer rampant in Manchester and that as radicalism 'dies religion will revive'. Wesleyan conservatism was now well rooted, at least among those with influence. Methodism was becoming respectable.

Jabez Bunting

Jabez Bunting was undoubtedly sincere in his own support for the Methodist mission at home and abroad, but he was also convinced that he was indispensable to that mission's success. Though the formal basis of his power was limited, the control he exerted over the direction which Methodism took after 1820 was both absolute and clerical. He was often called the 'Pope of Methodism'. He was secretary of the Methodist Conference after 1814 and of the missionary society which emerged on a nationwide scale. He was president of the Conference for the first time in 1820 and again in 1828, 1836 and 1844. He was a member of every important committee, weighty speaker at every Conference, edited the *Wesleyan Methodist Magazine*, and had a decisive influence on the 'stationing' of ministers. He managed Conference because the majority supported his policies, because he mastered every subject, because he was more moderate in proposals than in manner and because he was a realist. He persuaded the Wesleyans to open a 'theological institution' with himself as active president in 1834. Bunting established both a spiritual ideal and a disciplinary system, ruthlessly punishing any who dared to criticize him.

Bunting redefined the government of the Connexion. The Conference, which consisted of the Legal Hundred and other preachers, had to some extent been reformed in 1814. Under Bunting, government by senior churchmen and Conference aimed at strong central directing as the only way of focusing Methodist expansion. The burden and responsibility for the local Methodist societies and chapels was carried by local laymen though Conference chose district committees to act during the year. To overrule a decision by determined local officers who controlled the money invited collision between Conference and its congregations, between central and local government, between high clerics and low laymen. Bunting's control over the Stationing Committee enabled him to press the authority of itinerant ministers and diminish that of congregations. In 1818 preachers were authorized to entitle themselves 'the Reverend'. In 1836 Conference approved the laying on of hands in all ordinations of ministers. High Methodists preferred clerical costume but opposition from anti-ritualists in the northern congregations resulted in the 1842 Conference banning it.

As Conference met for only a few days a year and most of the preachers who attended lacked experience of business, real power lay with a permanent executive dominated by Bunting. When Bunting was absent from sessions of the Conference it was unable to conduct sensible business. The problem with this control was that it allowed little room for opposition or independence. Conference tended to agree with what the executive proposed.

The consequence of this was a growing conflict between central government and local initiative. In any local dispute Bunting upheld the right of ministers to instruct and discipline their members. In 1827, for example, he insisted that the Brunswick Chapel in Leeds should have an organ, though most of the Methodists there considered it a symbol of clericalism, if not popery, and in protest formed their own denomination, the Protestant Methodists. In 1835 one of his opponents, Samuel Warren of Manchester, was expelled by the Conference, a decision upheld by the Lord Chancellor. Warren and his supporters wanted local societies to be given more independence, Methodist money to be controlled by laymen, no legislation without the consent of a majority of the local societies and the theological institution to be abandoned. These two groups joined together as the Wesley Methodist Association.

For those who did not wish to be expelled from Methodism it seemed safer to let Bunting dominate and define Wesleyanism. Teetotalism posed a further threat to the unity of the Connexion in the late 1830s and early 1840s. In England it was usually led by Methodists and old Dissenters and in Cornwall it resulted in members deserting ministers who would not sign the pledge and give the sacraments with unfermented wine. Conference in 1841 prohibited unfermented wine but a prudent Cornish superintendent prevented worse schism by turning a blind eye to some usage of the banned wine. In 1842, however, a group of about 600 separated from Conference and organized as the Teetotal Wesleyan Methodists.

Ways of worship within Methodism were as diverse as those in the Established Church by the 1840s. At one extreme some chapels were solemn and liturgical and used the Book of Common Prayer. At the other end the worship was revivalist. Irrespective of the type of worship, women did not become eminent as local preachers in Wesleyan, though they did in Primitive, Methodism. Bunting, though he stood for order, recognized the rightfulness of revivals. It was the extent of revivalism which, by the 1840s, he questioned. He disapproved of ranting and sought to repress it and was careful to dissociate himself from the emotionalism of Primitive Methodists.

The most serious opposition to Bunting and the most serious secession came in the 1840s. Both the *Wesleyan Times* and anonymous pamphlets or 'Fly Sheets' attacked Bunting's personality and policies furiously. Though he never acknowledged authorship, James Everett, a disgruntled preacher and satirist, was accused and in 1849 was expelled along with two contributors to the *Wesleyan Times*. The venom of the dispute between Conference and Everett was intense and was a reflection of discontent with Bunting's regime. The result was the formation of the Wesleyan Reformers, which led to up to a third of Wesleyan Methodists leaving the Conference. Some seceders formed the Wesleyan Congregationalist churches, others gravitated towards the Primitive Methodists and in 1857 Everett succeeded in joining with those who had walked out with Warren in forming the United Methodist Free Church, Liberal in politics and lay in emphasis. Everett became the first president of almost 40,000 members.

The Wesleyan splits left the seceders more radical and those who remained more conservative. But they also aroused many feelings of bitterness and disillusionment. Wearmouth called it a 'spiritual earthquake that shook the very foundations'. They may also have diverted Methodism from evangelism among the working population, though even at the nadir of the reaction against Bunting in 1855 there were still some 260,000 adult Wesleyans who accepted his control of their national life and the local rule of ministers acceptable to him. Bunting's policies of establishing Wesleyan Methodism as a religious grouping between Dissent and the Established Church had been bought at the cost of theological repression and expulsion but in the Methodism he had refashioned many people found an acceptable spiritual home.

Methodism in the 1851 Religious Census

Methodism accounted for nearly a quarter of the total attendances in the 1851 Religious Census. It was most dominant in the belt of open arable country stretching from the south Midlands into Lincolnshire and York-shire, and in Cornwall and the Isle of Wight. Its influence was felt least in three regions: everywhere south-east of a line from Bournemouth to Great Yarmouth; in the three northern counties of Northumberland, Westmorland and Cumberland; and in the counties bordering the Bristol Channel (Devon, Somerset and Gloucestershire) and extending north across the Welsh Marches.

The south-eastern counties of Sussex, Surrey, Hampshire and large parts of Wiltshire and Berkshire were devoid of Wesleyan Methodism in 1851 and no sustained effort was made to introduce it until 1865. Why was this area a 'Methodist Desert'? In part this was a result of Wesley's policy of concentrating on urban areas where the Church of England was failing in its functions and in areas which would readily accept his message. The south-east was unresponsive since the Anglican parochial system had not broken down as it had in the north. By contrast, Methodism was highly successful in the Isle of Wight after 1800 when it stepped in to fill the vacuum left by the Church of England. Methodism capitalized on a similar situation in Cornwall. By 1851 Methodist influence was at its height and all the various branches of the original Connexion were represented. Wesley also paid frequent visits to Devon but it was not until after 1850 that Methodism took off, and never to the same extent as in Cornwall. The strong position of Dissent in Devon before 1740 helps to explain this while the existence of few Dissenting chapels in Cornwall explains the obverse.

Divisions within Methodism

Methodism was not a monolithic denomination and the period between 1790 and 1850 saw it split internally in ways that mirrored divisions in society. During Wesley's lifetime the only division within Methodism was between those who subscribed to a Calvinist theology led by Whitefield, and the Arminian Wesleyans. The development of Calvinistic Methodism had two main strands in the late eighteenth and early nineteenth centuries. First, Whitefield had, with the patronage of Selina, Countess of Huntingdon, been able to preach to sections of the aristocratic elite. On his death in 1770 the Calvinistic Methodists finally split away from Wesley and formed 'Lady Huntingdon's Connexion'. The nineteenth century saw its progressive decline as individual churches either rejoined mainstream Methodism or became Congregational churches. In England one concentration of Calvinistic Methodists was an expression of the Countess' own sphere of influence and extended in a belt from Cambridgeshire and Huntingdonshire, south through London into Kent and Sussex. It was here that aristocratic support was most numerous. Secondly, Calvinistic Methodism had a strong appeal in Wales, where it had developed separately in the 1730s. The second concentration in 1851 was a reflection of the power of Calvinist doctrines in Wales and extended from Somerset northwards along the Welsh Marches to Lancashire.

The Methodist New Connexion, formed into a separate denomination in 1797, was virtually identical to the parent body, except for the power it gave to the laity. It drew its membership almost exclusively from north of the Severn–Wash line and in 1851 there were only nine churches south of that line: five in London, three in Cornwall and one in Norfolk. The

New Connexion was essentially a phenomenon of the Midlands and the north and its greatest strength lay in the complex of counties formed by Worcestershire, Staffordshire, Cheshire, Nottinghamshire, the West Riding and into the north-east.

Primitive Methodism arose as a result of attempts to stifle enthusiasm which were taking place in the main body of Methodism. Originating in Staffordshire, it spread quickly between 1810 and 1850. From its original home it expanded along the line of the River Trent, encountering considerable success in the East Riding, and then it spread northwards into Durham and south through Lincolnshire into Norfolk. On reaching the Bible Christian strongholds in south-east and south-west England Primitive Methodism lost its impetus. By 1851 it was firmly established as a denomination, accounting for over 20 per cent of all Methodists, and was the second largest Methodist group.

Primitive Methodism was largely rural in character and, with the exception of Durham and the Potteries, its main strength was in the predominantly agricultural counties of England. It was not until after 1850 that its appeal to the urban worker became obvious. Primitive Methodism was used, to a certain extent, by nineteenth-century agricultural labourers as a means through which they could fight for social and economic recognition and the Primitive Methodist chapels provided the rural worker with a symbol of independence and defiance of the established social order.

The Bible Christians were a product of the West Country and, unlike the other branches of Methodism, they were not a breakaway body. Though they adopted features similar to Methodism when they applied for membership of the Wesleyan Connexion this was rejected because of the independent character of its charismatic leader William O'Bryan. The Bible Christians opened their first chapel at Shebbear in north Devon in 1815 and four years later held their first Conference. In the early 1820s the leaders of the movement sent a mission to Kent and London and also accepted an invitation to take their cause to Somerset. By 1851 there were small groups of Bible Christians all along the south coast from Cornwall to Kent. However, over large parts of England there was little success. The appeal of Bible Christianity, like Primitive Methodism, was in rural society and provided a religious position from which to attack the economic system symbolized by the Church of England and Anglican landowners. It is no surprise that the Bible Christians found industrial towns difficult to evangelize.

Both Primitive Methodism and Bible Christianity arose in response to the need to fill the religious vacuum left by the Church of England among rural workers. The south and westward spread of the Primitive Methodists was halted when they reached the Bible Christian strongholds, and the converse was true. The similarities between them made it unlikely that both groups could flourish in the same locality. Only in Hampshire and Cornwall did this occur.

The Protestant Methodists, formed in 1827, united with the followers of Samuel Warren to make the Wesleyan Methodist Association in the 1830s. It was, with the exception of Cornwall, weak everywhere south of the Severn–Wash line. The main concentrations were in the north-western counties of Cheshire, Lancashire, Cumberland and Westmorland, with eastern extensions into Durham and Yorkshire and then south in Nottinghamshire and Leicestershire. It made little headway in the strongly revivalist counties of the east: Norfolk, Lincolnshire, the North and East Ridings of Yorkshire. The Wesleyan Methodist Reformers, formed when James Everett was expelled in 1849, were barely organized by 1851. To a large extent the Reformers complemented the Association in geographical distribution and in 1857 they joined with the Association to form the United Free Methodist Church with an initial membership of around 40,000.

Conclusions

The 1851 Religious Census appeared to show a resurgent Nonconformity and a defensive Anglicanism. This was accepted by most contemporaries but it is deceptively simple. By the 1840s Nonconformity was beginning to enter a phase of decelerating growth that eventually led to decline. The economic, demographic and cultural conditions of the previous hundred years had been highly receptive to Nonconformist recruitment. But three separate circumstances began to alter this situation. First, effective Anglican competition emerged with the resurgence of the Church of England after 1832. Secondly, society was changing in ways unfavourable to Nonconformity. The decline of traditional supporters like the urban artisan and the tenant farmers and agricultural labourers meant that Victorian Nonconformity depended heavily for support on those social groups, like the middle classes, least insulated from the influence of the religious Establishment. Finally, Nonconformist religious culture was evolving institutional and denominational priorities which slowed down its rate of growth. By 1851 Nonconformity had just passed the zenith of its power.

ROMAN CATHOLICISM

The period between 1780 and 1850 has been characterized by John Bossy as representing the 'birth of a denomination' for Catholicism.[28] As with Protestant Dissent, Catholicism went through a period of growth in membership, conflict between lay and clerical influences and organizational change. Bossy has called into question two ideas about nineteenth-century English Catholicism. First, he maintains that the notion propagated by Newman, Wiseman and others in mid-century of a 'Second Spring', a miraculous rebirth of Catholicism dating from about 1840, is a piece of tendentious ecclesiastical propaganda. Secondly, he argues that, though commonly accepted by historians, the view that modern English Catholicism was 'a cutting from the Catholicism of Ireland transplanted by emigration into an alien land which had long ceased to have anything worth mentioning to offer in the way of an indigenous Catholic tradition'[29] is a respectable historical opinion in need of substantial modification. It neglects the evidence of a vibrant, if not always successful, tradition of English Catholicism which went back to the sixteenth century.

Increase in numbers

In 1770 there were about 80,000 Roman Catholics in England. By 1850 this had multiplied ten times to about three quarters of a million. This represented a radical numerical transformation. Geographical distribution was also transformed, though less radically. Catholicism developed in areas which had been barren since the Reformation: in the industrial areas of the West Riding and south-east Lancashire, in the east Midlands, in South Wales and, to a certain extent, in London. Its focus in its areas of traditional strength – the rest of Lancashire, the north-east and west Midlands – moved from the countryside to towns and manufacturing districts. This numerical and local transformation brought about social transformation and congregations of labourers, artisans, tradesmen and the poor topped up with a stratum of business and professional families replaced congregations of gentry, farmers, agricultural labourers and rural craftsmen.

Bossy argues that this was in the first place a transformation of the English Catholic community and would have occurred had no Irish immigrants arrived. By 1770 English Catholicism was already expanding because of demographic growth and the efforts of Catholic clergy and its social structure was already in the process of change. Irish immigration reinforced trends already evident. By 1851 urban Lancashire had a ratio of three Irish-descended to one English-descended Catholic and though English Catholics were a minority in the movement they were a considerable minority.

Irish immigrants and English Catholics were initially divided to a certain extent by language, economic status – this should not be exaggerated since both groups contained people of a wide range of incomes and occupations – by social and political attitudes, attitudes to the clergy and simple mutual dislike. They were unified by intermarriage, common schooling and the process of assimilation. In some areas – Cardiff and South Wales, Cumberland and the West Riding – purely Irish communities, with Irish priests and a nationalistic self-consciousness did not have any real contact with English Catholicism until after 1851. They were, however, the exception; the norm, especially in larger cities, was a mixed and stratified community.

A changing balance of power

Numerical transformation upset the balance of power within the Catholic community. In 1770 it was still dominated by its secular aristocracy but by 1850 its clergy had gained control. It was a paradox of the movement for Catholic emancipation that although the lay Catholics who conducted the campaign went to considerable lengths to emphasize their detachment from papal jurisdiction it was the clergy who really gained in authority. Appeals to Rome to decide on the acceptability of new oaths, the need for organization and the emergence of a Catholic middle class divorced from the old landed families, all tended to give the clergy an enhanced role and prepared the way for the centralization of the Church in the mid-nineteenth century.

Between 1778 and 1829 a series of bodies were established to represent the interests of English Catholics in the debates on the dismantling of anti-Catholic legislation. They showed an increasing tendency to come under clerical control. The first Catholic committee, set up in 1778, organized a petition which led to an Act giving Catholics access to the armed forces and abolishing some of the penal legislation against priests. The committee itself and those who petitioned were exclusively from the aristocracy and gentry and the clergy were intentionally not consulted. The second committee, set up in 1782, was similarly composed, though in 1787 when the way was becoming clear for a more comprehensive Relief Act three clerical members were elected. This concession was apparent rather than real since all three were as much respresentatives of the aristocracy and gentry as of the clergy. An Act in 1791 gave legal existence to registered Catholic places of worship and admitted Catholics to the professions.

The 1780s saw the beginnings of opposition to lay domination under the leadership of the northern and western Vicars Apostolic, William Gibson and Charles Walmsley, and the untiring efforts of John Milner (1752–1826), later Vicar Apostolic of the Midland district. They condemned those prepared to compromise to achieve a satisfactory Emancipation Act involving very large denials of papal power in order to declare their loyalty to the Crown and the constitution. In 1789 the Vicars Apostolic met at Hammersmith and claimed the right of scrutiny over proposals for emancipation before lay assent could be given. Their claim to a decisive voice in the emancipation debate amounted to a break with the immediate past.

The Cisalpine Club, formed in 1792, was the high point of lay influence. It stressed the benefits of the British constitution and loyalty to the Crown. It was anti-papal in that its members did not want 'foreign' interference in either the life of English Catholicism or of the nation generally. The Club was, in reality, the last expression of gentry management of the Church and early in the nineteenth century it became of social rather than political importance. For most English Catholics the degree of toleration achieved was acceptable and they were not involved in the abortive attempts at further legislation following the Irish Act of Union.

In 1808, with Whig support, a Board of British Catholics was set up as a propaganda organization to present the Catholic case. It soon fell under clerical control. All four Vicars Apostolic were members, though Milner was expelled in 1813 for his unwillingness to compromise over the terms of the proposed emancipation. The issue which the Board faced internally was whether laymen were entitled to a voice in the appointment of bishops and, if so, how that voice should be heard. Milner opposed all lay interference but William Poynter, Vicar Apostolic of the London district, though he objected to it in theory, was prepared to negotiate about it in practice. This had an external effect on the question of 'securities' which bedevilled the emancipation debate through the 1810s and early 1820s. What checks, if any, should be placed on Catholics as a safeguard to the constitution if they were admitted to Parliament? The first problem was the parliamentary oath. It denied the spiritual jurisdiction of the Pope as well as his temporal powers and was clearly unacceptable. The next difficulty was the 'veto', the right of the Crown to delete the names of candidates for vacant sees. Then there was the right of the Crown to scrutinize documents arriving from Rome. Each of these securities was found in other European countries and, as in England, they were a source of controversy as the state sought new measures of control over the Church and the Church sought to retain its spiritual independence.

Grattan's 1813 Relief Bill would have vested the veto in a Royal Commission of Catholic peers and gentry, a position similar to that claimed by the Catholic Committee in 1790. Three Vicars Apostolic accepted this proposal but Milner was against it. Appeal to Rome resulted in a decision in favour of the majority decision in 1814 but this was reduced to endorsing a limited veto the following year. Milner continued to oppose any proposed legislation – the 1821, 1823 and 1825 bills – which contained the veto. The 1825 bill was largely drawn up by O'Connell and English Catholics were not consulted. Emancipation in 1829 was the result more of the efforts of Irish than English Catholics.

In 1820 the English Catholic clergy was a small body, only 400 strong. There had been little increase in the number of priests since 1770 with the disintegration of the continental training establishments. Three secular-clergy seminaries – at Ware, Ushaw and Oscott – were functioning by 1810 but they were unable to provide more than a trickle of new priests. The years after 1829 saw a new mood of self-confidence among Catholic seculars as they sought a return to ordinary government of the Church by canon law and territorial episcopate and some degree of independence from the rule of Rome. The first half of the century was marked by continued antipathy between the seculars and the regular orders, priests who were members of one of the Catholic religious orders. In 1838 Rome issued two decrees which gave new privileges to the regular clergy operating in England and allowed them to open chapels without the permission of bishops. Two years later the seculars petitioned Rome, requesting that in future no regulars should be appointed as Vicars Apostolic. There was a widespread belief among seculars that regular clergy were anti-episcopal. The dispute between them was not resolved until 1881 when the regulars had to conduct their missions on the same basis as others and their chapels and schools were placed under episcopal control.

The movement towards the 'restoration of a hierarchy' in England can be seen, in part, as an attempt by seculars to gain full control over the English Church. In 1837 the Vicars Apostolic approached Pope Gregory XVI but, though he was willing to increase the number of vicariates to increase efficiency, he was unwilling to re-establish a hierarchy for fear of Crown interference in appointments. In 1840 the Eastern, Central, Welsh and Lancastrian districts were established: the number of vicariates was doubled. Full restoration was still sought by English bishops because of the need to bring Roman discipline and influence to bear on the centralizing of missions and because of the need for additional armour against the regulars. In 1847 Pius IX was persuaded of the case but it was not until 1850 that the hierarchy was restored. The following year the government passed the Ecclesiastical Titles Act, which reinforced the existing prohibition on Catholics assuming territorial titles held by the clergy of the Church of England. For 'Old' Catholics and the remnants of the Catholic gentry the restored hierarchy marked the final eclipse of their power over the Church. It was the symbol of Roman hegemony.

Scottish Catholicism

Scottish Catholicism was reinforced by Irish immigration from the 1790s. Previously it had been largely confined to the Highlands and did not exist to any real extent in the Central Lowlands. The movement of Highland and then Irish Catholics to the west Central Lowlands created a major logistical problem. In 1770 priests travelled from Perth and Edinburgh to Glasgow to minister to the twenty or so Catholics in Glasgow, but in the 1790s priests migrated with their congregations to the city and its environs. The number of Catholics in Glasgow increased accordingly; 60 in 1791, 2,300 in 1808 and 27,000 in 1831. By the 1830s Catholics made up about 13 per cent of Glasgow's population with higher concentrations developing in nearby industrial districts like Old Kilpatrick, Renfrewshire and Monklands. Lacking an official hierarchy, the Catholic Church found organization and finance difficult. Priests were settled and chapel-schools started but the task of erecting proper chapels did not begin until after 1840. Many priests came from the same background as their congregations and were thus free from the barrier of middle-class social status that encumbered Presbyterian ministers. A Roman Catholic hierarchy was not restored to Scotland until 1878.

Catholic emancipation was met with stiff resistance in Scotland. Twice as many Scots petitioned against it as for it. The ministers of the Church of Scotland and most of their congregations were against it. Support came from the Whig middle class, together with the congregations of the Relief and United Secession churches. The bulk of opposition, however, came from the uneducated working population, motivated partly by their fear and distrust of Irish labour often used by empoyers to make effective unionism impossible. Anti-Catholic feelings were greatest in the industrial west and faded towards Edinburgh and the east.

Scottish sectarianism after emancipation gained in vigour. 'No Popery' was inextricably linked with anti-Irish feeling. Though emancipated in 1829, the immigrant Irish were denied participation in political power until the 1884 Reform Act. Scottish Catholicism remained distinct from the English, with its own character and outlook. But Presbyterianism had its own internal tensions deriving from differences between the continuing Scottish tradition and that of the Irish Catholics.

Ireland's Catholicism

In Ireland the late eighteenth and early nineteenth centuries saw the beginnings of a dramatic change of outlook in the Catholic Church. A new generation of reforming bishops imposed higher standards on the behaviour and performance of the clergy and there was a growing separation between the clergy and the laity. Initially these reforms took place within individual dioceses and the extent and pace of change varied. Increasingly, individual efforts were supplemented by a degree of cooperation. In 1831 the bishops of Leinster worked out a uniform code of ecclesiastical discipline for the whole province and in 1850 the Synod of Thurles, the first national assembly of the Irish Church for almost 700 years, introduced a comprehensive code of law, summarizing and consolidating the reforms of the previous half-century.

The growth in Catholic cohesion was accompanied by growing sectarian conflict. After 1820 three separate features led to the intensification of religious divisions. First was the launching of the so-called 'Second Reformation', the missionary activities of the different Protestant denominations directed not just against the heathen overseas but also at the Catholic population. The impact of the Protestant missionary societies was limited and resulted in a determined Catholic counter-attack, poisoning relations between Catholics and Protestants who had previously been willing to work together. Secondly, Irish Catholicism was itself becoming more combative. Thirdly, the emergence of a new style of popular politics further divided Catholics and Protestants. O'Connell's campaign between 1824 and 1829 employed a range of techniques of mass agitation to build up popular support behind Catholic emancipation. A popular movement of this kind challenged the basic assumptions of a political system based on the deferential acceptance of rule by an elite. Protestant concerns were compounded by the direct attack on the privileges of the Established Church, in the shape of the campaign for the abolition of tithes between 1830 and 1838. When after 1840 popular attention turned to a nominally secular issue – the repeal of the Act of Union – Irish political divisions had taken on a clear-cut religious character. Repeal was an overwhelmingly Catholic demand, bitterly opposed by the great majority of Irish Protestants. By 1850 the bloodshed and repression of the 1790s, the tensions created by the Second Reformation and the fears aroused by the new style of political agitation had combined to produce deep religious division at all levels of society.

THE 1851 RELIGIOUS CENSUS

In his report on the 1851 Religious Census Horace Mann noted that 'a sadly formidable proportion of the English people are habitual neglecters of the public ordinances of religion'.[29] There were major difficulties of interpretation in the census but some firm observations were made. First, vast numbers of people stayed away from formal religious services, especially the working population in the large industrial and manufacturing cities and towns which were apparently altogether outside the range of church and chapel influence. Secondly, the Church of England could no longer claim to be the 'national' church. It remained strongest in the counties round London and in eastern England, but in some northern and western areas and in Wales chapelgoers were in the majority.[30]

There seems to be almost complete disagreement among historians about the role and significance of religion in the lives of the working population. One reason for this confusion lies in the difficulty of interpreting the sources. The 1851 Religious Census is frequently quoted as evidence for widespread religious apathy. But what constituted 'high' as opposed to 'low' attendance? How far can people's religious beliefs be deduced from whether they attended on a particular day or not? Religious apathy was highlighted by many middle-class or clerical observers, whose definition of religiosity included regular church attendance, but working-class autobiographies suggest that their authors were strongly interested in religion. It has been argued that the working population had its own different, but equally valid approach to religion, which was strongly practical and concerned especially with mutual aid and with maintaining standards of 'decent' behaviour. However, historians' views on this issue are still largely influenced by the work of E. R. Wickham, on Sheffield, and K. S. Inglis with their rather negative treatment of religion among the labouring population with their stress on 'indifference' and 'apathy'.[31]

Religion and the working population

The impact of religion on the working population in the first half of the nineteenth century was multi-faceted. Any interpretation has to deal with the contradictory notions of secularizing trends and the continuing strength of working-class religiosity. In 1846 Austin Freeman wrote of the spiritual effects of industrialization: 'it has destroyed social unity and replaced it by social disintegration and class antagonism . . .'

The building of new churches failed to keep pace with growing population and people grew up outside the 'dependency system' of squire, parson and the traditions of the community that existed in English rural society. The weakness of the Established Churches left a religious vacuum which was sometimes filled by Nonconformity or by militant secularism.

The weakening of the hold of the Established Churches throughout Great Britain can be clearly seen in the eighteenth century before many of the developments which those who analysed the 1851 Religious Census used to explain religious attitudes. The prevailing style of religion tended to be rational and moralistic and the level of commitment required was fairly low. Indifference and scepticism were widespread and 'enthusiasm' was viewed with suspicion. Religion failed to satisfy the emotional needs of large sections of society who either conformed because it was expected of them or who left the parish church to form their own religious groups, sometimes with a separate place of worship. From the 1730s throughout Britain there was a steady stream of defections from the church, as people questioned both its latitudinarianism and Erastianism and its rationalistic and unemotional nature. Evangelism and the emergence of groups within the Church and outside it raised the level of religious awareness and emotional commitment.

Parallel to this revolution in sentiment was a failure on the part of the Establishment to provide sufficient new churches to keep pace with the growth of population, especially in urban centres. This was believed by contemporaries to have encouraged the spread of Nonconformity and decline in churchgoing. The 1790s saw a polarization of religious attitudes with the addition of a political dimension. The Established Churches were seen as vital agencies for the preservation of a paternalistic, hierarchical society, a conservatism which discredited them in the eyes of those who favoured radical reform. Nonconformist growth was spectacular and millenarianism evoked a widespread, though less permanent, interest.

Both Nonconformists and millenarians reflected the hopes of those who believed that events in France heralded a new era of equality and social justice. But was the impending revolution the work of God or of man? Radicals were often interested in prophecies and many church reformers were also political reformers. It is not surprising that religion and revolution were closely linked in the conservative mind. Millenarians like Richard Brothers, a naval officer living in London who was imprisoned as a lunatic after 1795, and Joanna Southcott, who from 1801 until her death in 1814 enjoyed a widespread following, maintained that the violent events of the 1790s and 1800s had their place in God's plan for the salvation of mankind and that the millennial kingdom was coming soon.

Millenarianism was a very old tradition but the 1790s saw the emergence of a new phenomenon, organized irreligion. Paine's *Age of Reason*, published in 1794, was a leading influence, but less than his other works, and led to resignations from the London Corresponding Society when it decided to publish it. In London the 'infidels' seem to have won some support among the radicals. Non-churchgoing was seen by many clergy in the 1790s and 1800s as evidence for 'infidelism' but this neglects the extent to which there were simply insufficient places in churches.

Declining support?

So did the involvement of the working population in religion increase or decline after 1800? The various splits within Methodism, the church-building programmes of the various denominations and the growing confidence of the Established Church calls into question the view often expressed that religious adherence was in decline. The problem of numbers is exacerbated by the lack of accurate figures for most denominations until 1851. For A. D. Gilbert, the first half of the nineteenth century saw that involvement at its highest. He suggests that the great expansion of Nonconformity ground to a halt in the 1840s and that there was a large number of 'crisis points' when individuals turned to religion because of the widespread belief that many human problems could not be solved by natural means.[32] After 1850, he argues, both church and chapel appealed to the middle classes. E. R. Wickham, by contrast, defined the second half of the nineteenth century as a 'religious boom' in Sheffield with the building of new churches and chapels. He stressed the middle-class character of most congregations but implied an increase among congregations composed of working people. Gilbert's analysis overstates the degree to which the third quarter of the nineteenth century was one of decline but there is no doubt that important changes were taking place in the religion of the working population.

If the statistical argument is inconclusive how far does 'identity' with established denominations provide a solution? Membership of the Established Churches symbolized membership of civil society. The parish church, where the overwhelming majority of the population were baptized, married and buried, was the main symbol of community. The bitter disputes over lay patronage in Scotland and over ritual in nineteenth-century England were a reflection of the feeling that the parish church belonged to the people and that what went on there was everyone's concern not just the concern of an elite whose rights may have been legal but were of questionable morality. Orthodoxy meant citizenship and to deliberately cut oneself off from the parish church was viewed with intense suspicion and meant limiting oneself to the status of a second-class citizen. Orthodoxy was a public affirmation of belief in the existing social system, even if beliefs were private.

The emergence of legitimate religious pluralism and the movement away from legislative limitations on nonconforming groups had a deeply divisive effect. In the nineteenth century sectarian identity influenced most areas of life and even those less interested in religion found themselves in situations where an identity was forced upon them. Sectarian conflict took two major forms in Britain. First, it was the result of the decline of established social systems and the transition to more open and pluralistic society. Secondly, it was the product of the mixing of different populations following social movement from rural to urban environments. Antagonism between church and chapel belonged to the first category, that between Catholics and Protestants to the second.

Catholicism was an essential part of the national identity of Irish immigrants and in areas where they settled Protestantism tended to be equally self-conscious and, of necessity, competitively aggressive. Individuals tended to regard adherents of the rival religion in terms of hostile stereotypes. By 1850 most British cities had distinct Irish Catholic neighbourhoods and anti-Catholicism reinforced the inner cohesion of these communities and the Catholic identity of their members.

The division between church and chapel was less clear-cut, at least in England, and was far more widespread than the localized Catholic–Protestant conflicts. Increasingly between 1800 and 1850 church and chapel symbolized the identity and aspirations of rival elites in their struggle for power. Divisions between the upper and middle classes were reflected in membership of different religious denominations. The issue was not a theological one – there were no clear-cut doctrinal differences between the Established Churches and the larger Dissenting bodies – but one of church government. Membership of a Dissenting congregation was a criticism not simply of the Church of England but of the whole sociopolitical system of which it was an integral part. In Wales the 'chapel' provided an identity grounded in nationality and language which the Established Church could not provide. It symbolized a rejection of anglicization.

Religious identity and political identity were two sides of the same coin. The clergy of the major denominations were deeply involved in the party political system. Between 1832 and 1850 surviving poll books show that Anglican clergy overwhelmingly voted for Tory candidates while Nonconformist ministers and Roman Catholic priests voted for Whigs, Liberals or Radicals. Their voting behaviour was often paralleled by their congregations and these patterns of behaviour had deep roots. The only major change in the first half of the nineteenth century was the decline of Toryism within the Wesleyan Connexion in the 1840s.

The clergy tended to determine the official stance of their denomination but they did not necessarily always speak for all their congregation. There were frequently tensions between the clergy and the laity, between higher and lower clergy and between lay leaders and the rank and file between 1800 and 1850. However, holding a political position at variance with that of the church's leaders could be extremely difficult, especially in centralized denominations like Methodism, Roman Catholicism and Scottish Presbyterianism. Radical Methodists were expelled from the Wesleyan Connexion.[33]

An 'infidel' tradition

Political radicalism often grew out of religious heterodoxy. Unitarians with their congregational autonomy and non-Trinitarian doctrines developed a number of working-class chapels. In Oldham, for example, these appear to have played a significant role in the emergence of radicalism among the working population between the 1790s and 1810s. The most important aspect of the political implications of religious heterodoxy was the role of secularism from the 1790s onwards. The freethinking tradition established in the 1790s largely through Paine's writings raised the issue of the freedom of the press to publish anti-Christian or radical literature and newspapers. Pitt's action against the radical press in 1798 and 1799 as well as the more general conservative backlash forced freethinking underground. It re-emerged as a vibrant force after 1815. The leading figure in the revival of freethinking was Richard Carlile and between 1817 and 1825 he fought a campaign against Liverpool's administration and moral reformers.[34] He claimed that the press had the right to criticize the institutions of Church and State and the government had found that its policy of legislative and judicial repression was self-defeating.

By the early 1830s Carlile's influence on the 'infidel' tradition was declining and the anti-Christian component of Owenism came to the fore. Owen's opposition to Christianity was grounded in the argument that it seemed to produce division rather than harmony in society. Denominations were 'competitive' rather than 'co-operative' and for Owen prevented the creation of his 'new moral world'. Two of Owen's ideas were regarded by contemporary society with particular suspicion. First, Owen questioned whether people were 'bad' by nature, arguing that character was determined by environmental factors. Secondly, his views of marriage and divorce involved Owen in early campaigns for birth control.

The growth of secularism from the late 1830s was the result of a split within Owenism. The break was precipitated by Charles Southwell who attacked Owen as a wrong-headed dreamer and in 1841 began the *Oracle of Reason* in which he proclaimed the rational truths of atheism. Southwell's arrest and prosecution led Malthus Ryall and George Jacob Holyoake to set up the Anti-Prosecution Union. The 1840s resembled the

1820s in many respects and with the same results. Peel and Russell could use the courts to punish freethinkers but they could not silence them. In London intense activity led to the development of the London Atheistical Society to agitate for a change in the law as it affected 'infidels' and a Free Thinkers Tract Society was formed to disseminated radical literature. By 1850 there had been a significant weakening of infidel organizations, as much a result of internal disagreement as external pressures, and this led Holyoake to set up a new movement which in 1852 he called 'Secularism'.

The appeal of freethinking was never very wide and in the first half of the nineteenth century the choice for the working population was between 'orthodox' churches and none at all. There was, however, nothing new about this. The 'indifference' of the working population to organized religion was increasingly defined in middle-class terms. The social crisis of the 1830s and 1840s instilled in the middle classes and aristocratic elite an intense fear of revolution, coinciding with a renewed evangelical concern on the part of the clergy of the Established Churches and they combined to give urgency to an endemic problem. Developments in the first half of the nineteenth century led to an increasing sense of alienation of the working population, especially the poor, from the Established Churches and from many Nonconformist congregations. Acceptable social identity was defined in terms of 'respectability' and the middle classes were busily distancing themselves from everything that seemed uncultivated and vulgar. The hierarchical seating arrangements in churches and chapels, the system of pew-rents and the language and religious tone set by their social superiors emphasized the inferiority of the working population, many of whom were becoming less ready to accept humiliating social distinctions.

CONCLUSIONS

By 1850 organized Christianity had become the religion of the successful. Material rewards were reserved for those who followed a Christian life. Middle-class domination of the major denominations led to attacks on popular culture which provided the working population with a sense of identity. The indifference to organized religion which the middle class perceived among the working population reflected not so much indifference as a lack of interest in the kinds of religion on offer. Evangelicalism appealed to the emotions of the working population but church government and centralized control was seen as an attempt to impose middle-class values and remote control from the congregations. A. D. Gilbert concluded that:

> in the long term the Industrial Revolution was instrumental in diminishing the cultural and institutional role of religion in English society . . . by accelerating the disintegration of the old prescriptive order and

abetting the rise of a pluralistic society . . . [it] produced a basic religious division between Church and Chapel to mirror the emerging complexities of the industrializing nation. But denominational religion was a midwife of the new, urbanized society, not an offspring. For the long term concomitant of industrialization was secularization and modern English society is a context in which significant religious commitment is a subcultural phenomenon.[35]

NOTES

1 Jeremy Bentham *Church of England and the Catechism Examined*, 1818, pp. 198–9, quoted in D. L. Edwards *Christian England*, Vol. 3, Collins, 1984, p. 102.

2 H. McLeod *Religion and the People of Western Europe 1789–1970*, Oxford University Press, 1981, p. 22.

3 A full discussion of the eighteenth-century background can be found in Chapter 5.

4 The following general works cover the 1800–50 period: D. L. Edwards op. cit., pp. 95–130, 155–94, A. Armstrong *The Church of England, the Methodists and Society 1700–1850*, London University Press, 1973, pp. 159–220, O. Chadwick *The Victorian Church*, Vol. I, Black, 1966, G. Kitson Clark *The Making of Victorian England*, Methuen, 1972, pp. 146–205, J. D. Gay *The Geography of Religion in England*, Duckworth, 1971, valuable especially for its maps, A. D. Gilbert *Religion and Society in Industrial England 1740–1914*, Longman, 1976 and W. R. Ward *Religion and Society 1790–1850*, Batsford, 1972. H. McLeod op. cit. and A. Vidler *The Church in An Age of Revolution*, Pelican, 1961 provide a broader perspective. G. Parsons (ed.) *Religion in Victorian England*, 4 vols, Manchester University Press, 1988, contains many valuable articles. R. R. Currie, A. D. Gilbert and L. S. Horsley *Churches and Churchgoers: Patterns of Church Growth in the British Isles since 1700*, Oxford University Press, 1977 provides a statistical treatment of national religious trends but does little on trends for regions and localities.

5 On the Church of England see A. Smith *The Established Church and Popular Religion 1750–1850*, Longman, 1971 and E. R. Norman *Church and Society in England 1770–1970*, Oxford University Press, 1976. On social attitudes see R. A. Soloway *Prelates and People: Ecclesiastical Social Thought in England 1783–1852*, Routledge, 1969 and G. Kitson Clark *Churchmen and the Condition of England*, Allen & Unwin, 1973.

6 On this issue see E. J. Evans *The Contentious Tithe: The Tithe Problem and English Agriculture 1750–1830*, Routledge, 1976, especially pp. 16–41 and 94–114.

7 Charles Simeon is placed in an eighteenth-century context in Chapter 5 pp. 102–3.

8 For Wilberforce before 1800 see Chapter 5 pp. 104–5.

9 A. B. Webster *Joshua Watson. A Story of a Layman 1771–1855*, SPCK, 1954 is a useful biography.

10 For the role of the state see O. Brose *Church and Parliament: The Reshaping of the Church of England 1828–1860*, Cambridge University Press, 1959, K. A. Thompson *Bureaucracy and Church Reform: A Study of the Church of England 1800–1965*, Oxford University Press, 1970 and G. I. T. Machin *Politics and the Churches in Great Britain 1832 to 1868*, Oxford University Press, 1977.

11 On the Oxford movement N. Yates *The Oxford Movement and Anglican*

Ritualism, The Historical Association, 1983 is a brief summary. G. Faber *Oxford Apostles*, Faber, 1933 and R. W. Church *The Oxford Movement*, 1891, a classic in a modern edition edited by G. F. A. Best in 1970, are both valuable. O. Chadwick *Newman*, OUP, 1983 is a brief biography focusing on his ideas. I. Ker *John Henry Newman: A Biography* Oxford University Press, 1990 is a definitive study. O. Chadwick *The Spirit of the Oxford Movement: Tractarian Essays*, Cambridge University Press, 1990 is extremely useful.

12 On the Church of Ireland S. Connolly *Religion and Society in Nineteenth Century Ireland*, SIESH, 1985 is brief and very useful. D. H. Akenson *The Church of Ireland: Ecclesiastical Reform and Revolution 1800–1885*, Yale University Press, 1971 is more detailed.

13 On the ideas behind the Oxford movement see B. Willey *Nineteenth Century Studies*, Penguin edn, 1969, pp. 73–101.

14 Some discussion of the Disruption in its political context can be found in Chapter 10 pp. 285–6.

15 C. G. Brown *The Social History of Religion in Scotland since 1730*, Methuen, 1987 is the best general introduction. A. L. Drummond and J. Bullock *The Scottish Church 1688–1843: The Age of the Moderates*, St Andrews Press, 1973 and *The Church in Victorian Scotland 1843–74*, St Andrews Press, 1975 are standard works.

16 For a discussion of the theological problems of evangelicals and their emphasis on 'conversion' see Chapter 5.

17 On evangelicalism see G. Best 'Evangelicalism and the Victorians', in A. Symondson (ed.) *The Victorian Crisis of Faith*, SPCK, 1970, pp. 37–56 and C. Smyth 'The Evangelical Movement in Perspective', *Cambridge Historical Journal*, 7 (1941–3), pp. 160–174. Boyd Hilton *The Age of Atonement. The Influence of Evangelicalism on Social and Economic Thought 1785–1865*, OUP 1988 is fundamental. D. W. Bebbington *Evangelicalism in Modern Britain*, Unwin Hyman, 1989 pp. 75–151 covers the early nineteenth century.

18 On the moral revolution see M. Jaeger *Before Victoria: Changing Standards and Behaviour 1787–1837*, Chatto & Windus, 1956.

19 G. Best op. cit., p. 48.

20 On women and evangelicalism see F. K. Prochaska *Women and Philanthropy in 19th Century England*, OUP, 1980.

21 C. L. Balfour *Women and the Temperance Reformation*, London, 1849, p. 6.

22 D. M. Thompson *Denominationalism and Dissent 1795–1835: a Question of Identity*, Friends of Dr William's Library, 1985.

23 On itinerancy D. W. Lovegrove *Established Church, Sectarian People: Itinerancy and the Transformation of Dissent 1780–1830*, Cambridge University Press, 1988, especially pp. 142–65 is valuable.

24 On Nonconformity apart from Methodism see I. Sellers *Nineteenth Century Nonconformity*, Edward Arnold, 1977 for a general survey and D. M. Thompson *Nonconformity in the Nineteenth Century*, Routledge, 1972 and J. H. Y. Briggs and I. Sellers *Victorian Nonconformity*, Edward Arnold, 1973 for documentary studies. R. Jones *Congregationalism in England 1662–1962*, A. C. Underwood *A History of the English Baptists*, London, 1947, C. G. Bolan et al. *The English Presbyterians*, London, 1968 and E. Isichei *Victorian Quakers*, OUP, 1970 cover the major groups. R. Helmstadter, 'The Noncomformist Conscience', in P. Marsh (ed.) *The Conscience of the Victorian State*, Syracuse University Press, 1979 pp. 135–72 contains much of value. R. G. Cowherd *The Politics of English Dissent*, New York University Press, 1956 is still worth considering on the political dimension of Dissent after 1815.

25 G. E. Jones *Modern Wales*, Cambridge University Press, 1984, pp. 276–80 provides a good general overview. It can be supplemented with T. Herbert

and G. E. Jones (eds) *People & Protest: Wales 1815–1880*, University of Wales Press, 1988, pp. 73–112 and E. T. Davies *Religion in the Industrial Revolution in South Wales*, University of Wales Press, 1965, pp. 44–96 and *Religion and Society in the Nineteenth Century*, Christopher Davies, 1981.

26 For Methodism in the eighteenth century see Chapter 5 pp. 114–26.

27 Methodism between 1800 and 1850 can be approached in the following general works: R. E. Davies, A. S. George and E. G. Rupp (eds) *A History of the Methodist Church in Great Britain*, Vol. II, Epworth Press, 1978 and the documentary Vol. IV, Epworth Press, 1987, B. Semmel *The Methodist Revolution*, Heinemann, 1974 and D. Hempton *Methodism and Politics in British Society 1750–1850*, Hutchinson, 1984. More specific older studies include M. Edwards *After Wesley*, 1948, E. R. Taylor *Methodism and Politics 1791–1851*, Cambridge University Press, 1935 and R. F. Wearmouth *Methodism and the Working Class Movements of England 1800–1850*, Epworth Press, 1937. R. Currie *Methodism Divided*, Faber, 1968 gives full weight to the secessions. H. B. Kendall *The Origins and History of the Primitive Methodist Church*, 2 vols, E. Dalton, revised edn, 1919 and J. T. Wilkinson *Henry Bourne 1772–1852*, Epworth Press, 1952 examine the major secession, T. Shaw *The Bible Christians*, Epworth Press, 1975 a less important one.

J. Vickers *Thomas Coke: An Apostle of Methodism*, Epworth Press, 1969 is a good biography of a neglected figure. W. R. Ward has edited *The Early Correspondence of Jabez Bunting*, Royal Historical Society, 1972 and *Early Victorian Methodism: The Correspondence of Jabez Bunting 1830–1858*, Oxford University Press, 1976. J. H. S. Kent *Jabez Bunting: The Last Wesleyan*, Epworth Press, 1955 and his defence of Bunting in *The Age of Disunity*, Epworth Press, 1966 puts one side of this leading figure while R. Currie op. cit. is more hostile. J. C. Bowmer *Pastor and People. A Study of Church and People in Wesleyan Methodism*, London, 1975 recognizes Bunting's arrogance but regards him as essentially a defender of 'classical' Wesleyan church order. A full-scale modern biography is needed.

On Methodism in Wales see A. H. Williams *Welsh Wesleyan Methodism 1800–1858*, Bangor University Press, 1935 and the works cited in note 25. For Ireland D. Hempton op. cit. is invaluable.

28 On Catholicism in the first half of the nineteenth century see E. R. Norman *Roman Catholicism in England*, OUP, 1985, pp. 57–82 and J. Bossy *The English Catholic Community*, Darton, Longman & Todd, 1975, pp. 295–390. E. R. Norman *The English Catholic Church in the Nineteenth Century*, OUP, 1984 and his *Anti-Catholicism in Victorian England*, Allen & Unwin, 1968 are more detailed. Catholicism in Ireland can be approached in S. Connolly op. cit. and D. A. Kerr *Peel, Priests and Politics*, OUP, 1982, especially pp. 1–67. On Scotland see C. Johnson *Developments in the Roman Catholic Church in Scotland 1789–1829*, John Donald, 1983 and the older P. F. Anson *The Catholic Church in Modern Scotland 1560–1937*, London, 1937.

29 H. Mann *Religious Worship in England and Wales*, London, 1854, p. 93.

30 J. Bossy op. cit., p. 297.

31 K. S. Inglis *Churches and the Working Classes in Victorian England*, Routledge & Kegan Paul, 1963; E. R. Wickham *Church and People in an Industrial City*, London, 1957.

32 A. D. Gilbert *Religion and Society in Industrial England 1740–1914*, Longman, 1976.

33 On the issue of working-class 'indifference' and antagonism towards the churches see H. McLeod *Religion and the Working Class in Nineteenth Century Britain*, Macmillan, 1984 for a brief bibliographical study. K. S. Inglis *Churches and the Working Classes in Victorian England*, Routledge, 1963 is a 'classic'

study. On the position of the Church of England see B. I. Coleman *The Church of England in the Mid-Nineteenth Century: A Social Geography*, The Historical Association, 1980 and 'Religion in the Victorian City', *History Today*, August, 1980. For the 1851 Religious Census see the chapter by D. M. Thompson in R. Lawton (ed.) *The Census and Social Structure*, Cass, 1978, pp. 241–86.

On 'infidelism' see E. Royle *Victorian Infidels*, Manchester University Press, 1974 and his documentary collection *Radical Politics 1790–1900: Religion and Unbelief*, Longman, 1971. S. Budd *Varieties of Unbelief*, Heinemann, 1977 takes the 1850s as its starting point. J. F. C. Harrison *The Second Coming*, Routledge, 1979 is standard. J. K. Hopkins *A Woman to Deliver Her People*, University of Texas Press, 1982, considers Joanna Southcott. O. Chadwick *The Secularization of the European Mind in the Nineteenth Century*, Cambridge University Press, 1975, broadens the argument.

34 A more detailed study of Carlile can be found in Chapter 12, pp. 360–1.
35 A. D. Gilbert op. cit., pp. 206–7.

15 The changing role of the state

... the sovereign has only three duties to attend to ... first, the duty of protecting society from the violence and invasion of other independent societies; secondly, the duty of protecting, as far as possible, every member of the society from the injustice and oppression of every other member of it, or the duty of establishing an exact administration of justice; and thirdly, the duty of erecting and maintaining certain public works and certain public institutions which it can never be for the interest of any individual, or small number of individuals, to erect and maintain ... institutions of this kind are chiefly for facilitating the commerce of society ... such as good roads, bridges, navigable canals, harbours etc ... and those for promoting the instruction of the people. . . .[1]

The state is a system of relationships which defines the territory and membership of a community, regulates its internal affairs, conducts relations with other states (by peaceful and by warlike means) and provides it with identity and cohesion. It consists of institutions and processes which are extremely various and complex, presiding over different spheres of the community which distribute different social goods according to different principles ... the state is not a monolithic body ... in fact it is not a body at all. From one point of view, the state is society's way of controlling itself, and making sure that others do not control it. From another, it is a sort of protection racket which claims a monopoly over the use of force.[2]

Alexander Pope, writing in the early eighteenth century, maintained that 'whate'er is least administered is best', a view expressing contemporary opinion. Adam Smith, writing some fifty years later, maintained a similar position, arguing that the numerous restrictions and duties which government placed on commerce should be abandoned and that only certain basic necessities for the stable functioning of society should be provided. By the 1830s, however, the scope of state intervention in the lives of ordinary people had begun to expand, a process occasioned by demographic and economic growth and the proliferation of social problems in need of solution.³ This chapter is concerned with what the nature of this change was, how and why it occurred.

WHAT IS 'THE STATE'?

There is no one accepted definition of the 'state'. A fundamental divide separates those who hold that the state should be seen in terms of the rights of individuals and their preservation and those who adhere to a theory in which power is emphasized. This is often reflected in definitions of the state. Hegel, for example, saw the state as the actuality of an ethical ideal while to Max Weber it was the organization which monopolized legitimate violence over a given territory. Marxists have been inclined to comprehend the state simply as an organ of coercion, a reflection of the economic power of the dominant social class and a product of society at a certain stage of development. Lenin spoke of it as consisting of 'bodies of armed men'. These definitions, though they have theoretical credence, often fall down when applied to actual situations. In this chapter the state in eighteenth- and early nineteenth-century Britain is taken to mean the reciprocal framework of regulation and rights encompassing both lay and spiritual aspects of the society in which people lived. The balance between regulation and rights was firmly weighted towards the former. Rights were grounded in often ill-defined and obscure notions like 'the liberties of the people' and the 'moral economy' and, after the 1790s, the 'rights of man'. These had great emotive power, especially when perceived to be under threat, and could be used to legitimate direct action. But, when faced by the authority of the state, they proved no real match. Regulation focused on the real and legitimate forces of coercion that existed in society to protect the coherence of the state and the economic and political authority of the aristocratic elite.

There may also be confusion between the concepts of the state and government and, though less so, between government and administration. For most people living in the eighteenth and nineteenth centuries the state was an abstraction, Marx called it 'an illusion', something which provided unity, structure and justification for the practice of government. By contrast the institutions of government were very real. Local, and to considerably lesser extent, central government provided the framework of legislative and especially coercive instruments which affected people's lives. They dictated what legitimately individuals could and could not do, what they could believe and not believe and how they could act. They 'encouraged' certain forms of social life while suppressing, marginalizing, eroding and undermining others. Schooling comes to stand for education, policing for public order, voting for political participation. Social classifications, like gender and religious conformity, were enshrined in law, embedded in institutions, made routine by administrative procedures and symbolized in the rituals of government. Certain forms of behaviour were given the official seal of legitimacy, others were not. Through them individuals identified – in fact, *had* to identify – themselves and their 'place' in their worlds. Government, to paraphrase Weber, converted the theoretical claims to legitimacy by the state into practice. Government is the state made visible and administrative procedures make government work.

THE STATE: A VIEW FROM 1688

The 1688 Revolution and the consequent 'settlement' were seen in terms of the control of central and arbitrary power and its subjection to the will of Parliament. The aristocratic elite constructed a defence of their economic position, symbolized by their property, against the arbitrary will of the state in the form of the Stuart monarchy and created a system that became, albeit inadvertently, a defence of liberties for all. Through the supremacy of Parliament, the 'rule of law' and the requirement of due process, the independence of the judiciary and a relatively free press all symbolized the power of the aristocratic Establishment. In this analysis though monarchs still chose their ministers, they needed a majority in Parliament, and especially the House of Commons, to govern. This view of 1688 and its aftermath has recently been called into question. There has been a re-evaluation of the practical as opposed to the theoretical position of the first two Georges and a reassessment, and downgrading, of the importance of the archetypal 'bourgeois' theorist, John Locke.

The state was firmly in the hands of an aristocratic elite which dominated Parliament, the emerging bureaucracy, the armed forces, the Established Church, the educational system and local government in the shires. Its concern lay with the land rather than with industry and commerce and it is hardly surprising that the protection of private property and its privileges was one of its primary concerns. Throughout the eighteenth and early nineteenth centuries central control was weak and the impact of government was felt largely at county and parish levels. Differences between Whigs and Tories, a division grounded in familial and factional interests and sustained by tradition and habit, created political contest but it was a contest for power within a single landowning class.

Commercial and financial interests were not excluded from state power. The 'financial revolution' of the seventeenth century had spawned individuals who were capitalists involved in buying and selling, borrowing and lending and risk taking. They provided credit for the 'state at war' but aspired to become members of the aristocratic elite and so participate more fully in the perks and patronage of the state. Upward social mobility had long ensured the survival of the aristocratic elite. Absorbing 'new' wealth into 'old' helped reduce potential social tensions by satisfying bourgeois aspirations.

The public sector in the eighteenth century was small. The state owned substantial army and naval establishments – ships, armouries, dockyards and barracks. There were public buildings under state administration. The Mint had a clear identity. But the only state-provided public utility service was the Post Office. Beyond this the British state did not own or operate utilities. The Bank of England, for example, was a private corporation run by businessmen. The state, however, used market control in order to sponsor improvements in the infrastructure. The West India Dock, for example, was made possible by legislation in 1799 which compelled all vessels coming or going to the West Indies to use the new docks for twenty-one years. The same principles applied to the East India Docks in 1806.

THE STATE AND THE ECONOMY

The public sector may have been small but the state was not without a role in economic development.[4] The pre-industrial economy was closely regulated by government and was criticized by Adam Smith for impairing the workings of market forces. Whether this constituted an economic 'policy' is questionable. There seems to have been little overall guidance of the economy in certain, predetermined directions by eighteenth- or early nineteenth-century government. However, historians cannot ignore the influence of ideas on economic legislation or the belief, held by practically all thinkers, that government had the right, even the duty, to regulate the economy in the national interest. Economic policy – in the sense of 'what was done' – arose in order to secure peace, stability, prosperity and money.

Adam Smith's critique

Certainly Smith's critique of existing economic regulation in 1776 was devastating. The mercantilist 'system', a term which neglects the piecemeal nature of its development, was grounded in a philosophy which suggested that there was a fixed amount of gain from trade and that when one country gained another must lose. Smith took the opposite view, arguing that a free and open exchange of goods within and between countries would lead to an increasing amount of gain and that this would benefit all. He maintained that the state had a duty to remove all 'impertinent obstructions' which, he believed, were the result of a merchants' conspiracy against the nation. But, because 'defence is prior to opulence', Smith approved of regulation to protect the nation from foreign attack, a position which led him, in principle, to approve the Navigation Acts. Protection could, however, be a two-edged sword. For example, the state encouraged inventors by giving them the protection of the patent laws but this could, as in the case of James Watt and his suspicion of 'high-pressure' steam, result in individuals obstructing further developments. The Corn Law of 1815 reflected the commitment of the British state to the perpetuation of particular patterns of economic and political power which, though defensible perhaps a century before, neglected the changed economic environment. Corn laws were no longer universally justified.

Control of the labour supply

There was some control of the labour supply during the eighteenth century. Skilled workers were not allowed to emigrate without permission and internal migration was restricted by the 1662 Act of Settlement. Wage regulation was falling into disuse by 1750 but Parliament was still willing to act. There was regulation covering journeymen tailors in 1768 and London silk workers in the 1773 Spitalfields Act. State regulation of wages was not finally ended until 1813 and this left the price of labour wholly free from official intervention, except for the regulation of trade unions. The Combination Acts of 1799 and 1800 forbade actions in restraint of trade from both workers and employers, though the Acts favoured the latter. The 1563 Statute of Labourers imposed a seven-year period of training for journeymen, giving state recognition to the rights of masters to control recruitment and impose conditions on training. In 1803 some masters petitioned for more effective enforcement of the law but there was counter-petitioning by other masters who wanted to increase their workforce and output by using less skilled workers. Though this process of 'dilution' was given sanction by the repeal of the apprenticeship laws in 1814 it was vigorously resisted by trade societies until after 1850.

THE STATE AND SOCIETY

The consumer

Consumer protection was progressively abandoned during the eighteenth century parallel to the increasing 'commercialization' of society. Laws controlling regional grain markets had fallen into disuse as markets expanded into a national system. There were still controls on quality of production in Yorkshire worsted cloth and Scottish and Irish linen but these became obsolete. The ending of the Assize of Bread in 1815 removed the last price and quality control over basic needs. By 1800 the state had formally withdrawn from consumer control, a process E. P. Thompson sees as the destruction of the 'moral economy'.

Social regulation

Social regulation was justified on similar grounds to economic regulation. It provided stability, order and prosperity. No government can avoid involvement in the behaviour of the governed. Standards of belief and conduct need to be established. England was a society in which, theoretically at least, religious belief and civil obligation were unified. People were free to choose their own religion and were not widely persecuted for their beliefs. But failure to subscribe to the state religion meant foregoing full citizenship. Throughout the eighteenth century and for the first quarter of the nineteenth century this meant that Dissenters, Roman Catholics and Jews were subject to substantial discrimination enforced by the state and reinforced by popular prejudice. These disabilities were deeply resented, creating real social division.

Attitudes to social conduct resulted in similar divisions, with Anglicans seeming to favour a lax morality while Dissenters sought to use the state to regulate the conduct of both the wealthy and the mass of society. Most people did not stand at the extremes but they did incline in one direction or the other. Anti-social behaviour led to state intervention as much on public order as on moral grounds. Prostitutes were controlled under the 1744 Vagrancy Act, together with disorderly persons, rogues and vagabonds. Profane swearing was dealt with under a 1745 Act and stage performances were subject to censorship after the Licensing Act of 1737. In general, however, regulation of conduct was left to the local magistrates and to the discretion of the courts.

Education was largely financed by voluntary contributions, often through the churches. This reflected its importance as a means of socialization. It therefore had little to do with forming the minds of the population, all to do with the inculcation of acceptable attitudes and standards of behaviour. Those who held power in the state did not accept the view of Adam Smith and others that education was necessary to economic development. They asked whether labourers' children needed schooling and also whether it would be dangerous to widen people's horizons through education, a process which might prompt them to question the existing social system. Education for conditioning was acceptable, education for subversion was not. It is not surprising that attempts to introduce legislation to benefit the mass of the population, like Samuel Whitbread's Parochial Schools Bill of 1807, were rejected by Parliament.

A BRITISH STATE?

The British state was not a homogeneous entity but embraced people of widely different traditions. Wales, though the eighteenth century saw a revival of its national consciousness, had come closest to England. There was little distinction of institutions between the two countries, common access to markets and personal status and Wales had representation in Westminster. Scotland, by contrast, had different attitudes to social issues than England though in economic matters it was increasingly brought under English influence after 1707. The Scottish state took a far more authoritarian view, largely through the parish mechanism of the Kirk Session, of its role in regulating the life of the people. Education was seen as an essential social function to be provided under the law of the land. The state made landowners responsible for providing parish schools by placing a levy on them. In spite of attempts to modernize it, the Scottish education system was put under great strain by the impact of urbanization and, by 1800, was losing direction. In rural Scotland the tradition of schooling remained and levels of literacy were as high there as anywhere in Europe. England was not subject to the same moral surveillance that was practised by the Kirk.

Education was seen as a means of strengthening character and improving employment opportunities and consequently providing a solution to the problem of poverty. The Scottish state did not require legal provision for the able-bodied poor, though landowners assisted voluntarily in the relief of the 'deserving' poor. In England the same connection between education and poverty was not made. The poor law provided relief for both the able-bodied and the indigent, funded by parish taxation.

The eighteenth century saw wide-reaching governmental initiatives in Scotland especially in the Highlands. In part these resulted from the need to re-establish law and order following the Jacobite risings of 1715 and 1745. The 'heritable jurisdictions' of the clan chiefs was ended in 1747 and a system of legally enforceable property rights set up. Road building followed the 1715 rising and in 1803 two parallel Commissions were set up to build roads, bridges and canals. Other developments were designed to assist market forces, hasten the end of the economic basis of the clans and modernize the Highland economy. The Board of Trustees for the Improvement of the Fisheries and Manufactures was established in 1727. Its special Linen Committee encouraged manufacture, establishing spinning schools and giving bounties for production. Bounties were made available for the fishing industry and the Fisheries Act of 1808 created an official organization for the industry. The Scotch Distillery Act of 1786 gave Scottish producers more favourable fiscal treatment than those in England. The Commissioners of the Forfeited Estates tried to rationalize and develop lands taken from rebels after 1745 and to demonstrate better farming methods. Economic regulation was used both to control the Highlands and to encourage market growth but not on a sufficient scale to prevent widespread emigration from the Highlands after 1800.

The state and Ireland

Attitudes to Ireland in the eighteenth century fell into two major categories. There were those who argued that Ireland should be treated as an integral part of Britain, a view which in 1801 led to union. However, an alternative perspective regarded Ireland as a colony and felt that its economic initiatives should be restrained when they threatened to damage England's interests. The result was legislative restraint on economic development which confined activity very closely to agriculture. The largest Irish industry, the manufacture of woollen cloth, was destroyed after 1699 by banning exports. Irish cattle could no longer be shipped to England. The linen industry, in which England had no great interest, was the exception.

From the mid-eighteenth century population growth and the impact of revolutionary ideas, initially imported from America, aggravated the tensions caused by the restrictive economic, political and social framework. The options open to the British state were limited. Fundamental reform, like the imposition of a reallocation of land, was not possible without destroying the structure of a society based on landlordism and the Protestant Ascendancy and, by extension, could have put English society under strain. Government was limited to operating within the existing social structure on two fronts. First, it could seek to redress grievances and remove legal disabilities from Irishmen. Secondly, it could sponsor some kind of development programme to relieve economic pressures. In 1782 the Irish Parliament was given greater autonomy and in the early 1790s Irish Catholics were freed from some of their legal disabilities. Pitt's attempts at economic assimilation in 1784–5 failed. The 1798 Rebellion showed that the Irish problem was more pressing than ever. Pitt's programme after 1798 focused on three areas: a union of parliaments, economic assimilation of the two countries and Catholic emancipation. The Act of Union of 1800 brought Ireland into the same constitutional and economic relation with England as Scotland had in 1707. But Catholic emancipation could not be carried.

The intentions behind legislative union were complex. Pitt, though immediately concerned to pacify Ireland in order to be able to wage effective war, intended that union would break down both the sense of Irish separateness and the barriers between the component parts of Irish society. The disappearance of the Irish Parliament would also reduce the direct power of the Anglo-Irish Ascendancy. Free trade could foster Irish commerce and agriculture. But in two important respects Pitt failed. First, the agitation for Catholic emancipation continued with the focus for action on Westminster rather than Dublin. Ireland had become an integral part of the British political agenda. Secondly, the existing land tenure system remained unchanged. Landlords and labourers increasingly saw each other as perverse. The breakdown in effective communication between the different parts of Irish society, evident long before 1800, meant that coercion not consensus was to be the prime characteristic of social and political relationships.

THE 'OLD CORRUPTION' UNDER ATTACK

Contemporaries and later historians

Contemporaries and especially radicals in the early nineteenth century condemned the 'Old Corruption' of the eighteenth-century state. Corrigan and Sayers argue that

For much of the century, 'the State' was, not to put too fine a point on it, a racket, run by particular groups within the ruling classes largely for their own benefit . . . it is not enough . . . to see capitalist development as something that occurred entirely independently of this 'parasitism'. Old Corruption was conducive to capitalism, if in complex and contradictory ways.[5]

Some historians have used the notion of Old Corruption to portray the British state as 'weak', comparing it with the strongly centralized and bureaucratized European monarchies. E. P. Thompson, for example, points to the 'non-intervention' of the state and the licence this afforded agrarian, mercantile and manufacturing capitalism to get on with its own development. In many senses this is an accurate conclusion. Certainly during the eighteenth century economic activity was less hamstrung by state regulation than earlier and what regulation there was 'protected' the economic interests of individuals and groups as well as the state itself.

Corrigan and Sayers maintain that, from the late seventeenth century until the economical reforms of the 1780s, there was a redefinition of landed property and labour discipline through existing state institutions symbolized respectively by Old Corruption and the 'gallows tree' at Tyburn and which led to the emergence of political economy and capitalist, contractual labour relations. Eighteenth-century society can be characterized as one of 'masters and servants', of property (owning and being owned) and propriety (correctness of behaviour or morals).

The law as a tool of property?

There seems little doubt that the state's administrative system, and especially the law, was used to legitimize the rights of property and to direct the labouring population into a proper appreciation of their 'station' in life. The poor law, apprenticeship, regulation of hours and wages of work and a more diffuse moral regulation all provided means of state control over the lives of individuals. The 'morality' of regulation meant that rights were seen as reciprocal by the working population for whom notions of 'just' wages, 'fair' prices and the 'moral economy' were routes through which criticisms of Old Corruption were translated into direct action.[6]

The law was used to privatize what had previously been customary rights. Resistance brought widespread regulation; between 1688 and 1820 the number of capital statutes grew from around 50 to over 200, mostly made up of offences against property. Food rioters and machine-breakers faced the death sentence, and enclosure rioters transportation. The Black Act of 1723 created 50 additional capital offences at a stroke. Violence in labour disputes carried a sentence of 14 years' transportation after 1726. Combinations were outlawed in tailoring in 1720, weaving and wool-combing in 1726, silk, linen, iron, leather and other industries in 1749 and hat-making in 1777.

Whether viewed from Locke's viewpoint that 'government has no other end but the preservation of property' or from a patriarchal position, the majesty of the law was a naked representation of the landed interest. Enforcement at the local level lay in the hands of JPs acting singly, in pairs or in quarter sessions. The Assizes, where centrally appointed judges sat, was the only point of contact for most people with the central state, with the ritual surrounding pronouncement of the death sentence as its awesome centrepiece. The majesty of the law and the public nature of executions was, according to Thompson, a necessary part of a system of social discipline where much depended on theatre. Until 1790 women found guilty of high treason could be burnt: the last recorded case took place in 1789. The punishment for high treason was hanging, drawing and quartering; for petty treason hanging and drawing and for felony simply hanging. For smaller crimes individuals could be branded, whipped, fined or placed in the pillory. Transportation was widely used as an alternative for capital crimes. The rule of law had ritualized terror at its core.

The majesty of the law was central to the power of the state. But the tradition, with deep historical roots, that the law was the guardian of all Englishmen was widely believed. The illusion that the law was The Law was buttressed by the strict procedural rules of trial before which all were equal and all equally powerless. The execution of Lord Ferrers at Tyburn in 1760 for murdering his steward and the acquittal of the leaders of the London Corresponding Society in 1794 have been often evoked to confirm the dispassionate quality of the law. More important, in practical terms, was the extent to which mercy was integral to eighteenth-century law. Since prosecutions were mainly private, gentlemen could decide not to prosecute, could influence juries not to convict or judges to recommend pardons. This control was far stronger than coercion alone. Justice and mercy were both highly personalized, a central feature of paternalism.

There is ample evidence of the slowness of reform and the rationaliz-ation of administration as, for example, with the inquiries into the Chan-cery courts begun in the 1730s and the absence of inquiries, except into the East India Company, between 1740 and 1780. The 'Old Corruption', however, should not be seen as a static state system. Marriage and wealth were an entrée into the governing classes and some of these 'new men' were at the forefront of demands for 'economical reform' from the 1780s, the ending of an 'inefficient' system of government based on patronage and its replacement with efficient and economical activities. This notion of an 'ineffective' system of government has, however, been called into question by John Brewer in *The Sinews of Power: War, Money and the English State 1688–1783*. He asked how did a small island which had played, for the most part, an insignificant role in seventeenth-century Europe, transform itself within sixty years into a great naval power with an immense empire? His analysis of the development of government departments and taxation systems gives a very different picture of the quality of eighteenth-century administration to that painted by nineteenth-century reformers and critics. But neither economic growth nor administrative expertise seem a sufficient explanation, especially since Britain's performance in the former is now considered less remarkable than previously. That Brewer's solution is a political one, is an unintended consequence of 1688. Britain's monarchy proved more efficient than continental absolutism. The Crown retained considerable power while the enlightened despots were much less powerful in practice than in theory. The need to command parliamentary majorities after 1688 and the obligation to justify themselves to Parliament forced ministers to pursue policies in harmony with the 'national interest'. There is a clear contrast between the policies pursued by Walpole, Pelham and Chatham and the amateurish courses followed by early Stuart ministers. Brewer's conclusions are not congenial to those revisionists who have been chipping away at the importance of 1688 – he calls it 'a watershed' – but there is no doubting that the British state of 1760 was different from the English state of 1680.

THE STATE AND REPRESSION 1790–1830

For the working population the period between 1790 and 1830 was marked by repressive legislation aimed at reducing revolutionary tensions and socializing workers into acceptable forms of behaviour. Government guaranteed the rights of property against the claims of labour. Political expression was curbed by the repression of political associations and, when thought necessary, the suspension of fundamental legal rights. The Unlawful Oaths Act of 1797 carried a penalty of seven years' transportation. Following the Peterloo Massacre the 'Six Acts' restricted rights of public assembly and demonstration. Economic freedoms were limited by the Combination Acts of 1799 and 1800 and the remaining elements of paternalist and protective legislation were repealed. Those for the woollen trade were removed in 1809, the apprenticeship clauses of the Statute of Artificers in 1813 and those allowing JPs to fix minimum wages the following year. Trade union rights were restored in 1824 but the 1825 Act narrowly circumscribed permitted forms of organization and activity. Culturally the working population saw its activities restricted by the moral evangelism of Anglicanism and Methodism and the growing identification of its culture as 'crude' and 'primitive'. It responded to this pressure in two different ways. According to some historians, a collective strategy was adopted and a new working class was established. Alternatively, sections within the working population adopted the new moral code with its individualized character and were admitted into 'respectable' society.

A 'REVOLUTION IN GOVERNMENT'

A political economy

The first half of the nineteenth century, and especially the 1830s, saw a substantial expansion in the role of government. This 'revolution in government' has become an area of historiographical controversy.[7] People sought to understand the dramatic economic changes that were occurring. The result was new ideas in economic and social affairs. Industrial capitalism was justified by the 'political economy' of a group of thinkers known collectively as the 'classical economists'.[8] Eighteenth-century thinking – the mercantilist approach – was comprehensively undermined by Adam Smith in his *Wealth of Nations*, published in 1776. He asked for the liberation of the economy from regulation either in the form of restrictive tariffs or of the anti-social monopolies which had been created. He wanted free trade and economic forces to work in a free market which, he maintained in a wider context, allowed individuals to fulfil their full potential. Smith's conception of society as a collection of individuals for whom self-interest was the driving force marked a significant move from the reciprocally structured hierarchy based on land. He did, however, envisage a positive role for the state in providing public services which no individual alone could maintain.

Later writers like Malthus and Ricardo built on Smith's work. Malthus was concerned with the pressure on resources occasioned by population growth while Ricardo demonstrated the central role of capital to a society. Ricardo has been seen as the high priest of the capitalist middle classes, contrasting their position with the image of the parasitic privileged landlord. He strengthened the case for freeing the commercial classes from a protected market in which agriculture had a self-perpetuating dominance.

Benthamism

Parallel to economic theories was the emergence of an alternative philosophy of government associated with Jeremy Bentham.[9] Bentham accepted the broad basis of a free market economy but, like Smith, recognized that the state might have to ensure that a real community of interest was catered for. He and his followers wished to apply the test of utility to all institutions: were they economical, efficient and above all conducive to 'the greatest happiness to the greatest number'? His supporters were consequently called Utilitarians and, though they envisaged collective state action, it was to be geared to the needs of individuals. The issue for Bentham's disciples, especially James Mill and his son John Stuart Mill, was how far *laissez-faire* should go and what degree of intervention by the state was acceptable. To the Mills *laissez-faire* was an ideal and every intervention by the state was a step away from that ideal. In his *Principles of Political Economy*, published in 1848, J. S. Mill maintained that government intervention was only justifiable in exceptional cases where an overwhelming need existed for state action.

Towards a self-help ideology

Gradually the ideas of the political economists and Utilitarians were popularized and percolated through all levels of society. By the 1850s they had been synthesized into that body of attitudes and values often known as 'Victorianism'. Samuel Smiles and others crystallized this social philosophy into four main parts: work, thrift, self-help and respectability. This was not a static social philosophy but a justification for individuals climbing the social ladder through industry and initiative. In the third quarter of the century this was extended into a social theory in which people found their place in society in proportion to their talents: the fittest reached the top, while the inferior remained at the bottom. In this context a deterrent poor law had both a logical and justifiable place.

This social ideology was certainly middle class in both its origins and application but its impact was across society. Service, respectability and, at least in public, a stricter religious observance and moral code permeated upwards into the ranks of the landed elite. The spread of middle-class attitudes was paralleled by important political changes in 1832, 1835 and 1846. There is some disagreement about the extent of middle-class hegemony. Harold Perkin argues for the triumph of the middle-class entrepreneurial ideas while W. L. Burns maintains that it is 'extravagant' to maintain that England was being governed by and in the interests of the middle classes.[10] But there is no doubt that there was a fusion in politics and society of aristocratic and middle-class interests, of property and capital to form a new dominant ruling class.

The self-help philosophy moved downwards as well as upwards. Given the unequal distribution of wealth in nineteenth-century society it is surprising that a shared social philosophy became dominant. There were alternative anti-capitalist theories, associated with Thomas Paine, Thomas Spence and Charles Hall and, in the 1820s Robert Owen and Thomas Hodgskin, which challenged Smith's concept of equal individuals pursuing their own self-interest.[10] Many of these theories were evident in the Chartist movement but after the mid-1840s some working people were affected by middle-class values as they became concerned to get a better deal from capitalism rather than overthrow it. By 1850, whether a conflict or a consensus model is more appropriate to explain social change, there was much in the behaviour and attitudes of the working population that impressed the middle classes. 'New model' trade unionism, adult education, friendly societies and co-operatives among the working population suggest a shared value system.

Laissez-faire and collectivism: a historiographical conundrum

In the simplified 'self-help' view of the ideal society the state had a purely negative role. A. V. Dicey, the late nineteenth-century jurist and Samuel Smiles could have agreed that the period from 1825 to 1870 was one dominated by Benthamism or individualism. But their view of the limits of state activity is difficult to reconcile with the activities that state had adopted. The age of *laissez-faire* and individualism apparently saw the emergence of the centralized administrative state. How can this seeming paradox be explained?

Alternative explanations

Derek Fraser suggests that the paradox can be resolved in a variety of ways but argues that the solutions fall into five overlapping categories. First, he suggests that there was a difference between theory and practice. *Laissez-faire* may have been the ideal but the problems posed by urban and industrial society necessitated an extension of the activities of the state. A second explanation notes the discrepancy not between theory and practice in general terms but between theory and practice in one area or another. There was an inconsistency between the Utilitarian approach to law and politics, in which intervention was justifiable to ensure a harmony of interests, and the call for the free play of market forces in economic matters. So intervention in social matters but *laissez-faire* for the economy. The problem with this explanation is that the line between social and economic issues was far from clear. The poor law, public health and factory reform involved economic as much as social questions. Even in overtly economic matters, like the development of the railways and the nature of companies, the state was taking a major initiative. There was certainly a greater reluctance to interfere in economic matters, but the distinction is far from satisfactory.

A misunderstanding of Benthamism

A third explanation sees Benthamite Utilitarianism as a synthesis of *laissez-faire* and state intervention rather than an exclusive form of individualism. Some historians go further and argue that Bentham was the archetype of British collectivism. Harold Perkin maintains that there was a synthesis of the entrepreneurial and professional ideals and that while the former roughly corresponds to the self-help ideology, the latter involved the professionalization of government, the solution of problems by the application of reason and the creation of the administrative state. The root of the tension between these two ideals lay in the conflict between Smith's natural harmony of interests in the market and the need in certain circumstances to create an artificial harmony through intervention. *Laissez-faire* or intervention, in this explanation, could be equally Benthamite depending on the specific context.

The MacDonagh thesis

These three explanations are all concerned in some way with the implications and contradictions of Benthamite theory, but in the fourth solution, associated with the viewpoint of Oliver MacDonagh, Benthamism has no central role.[12] MacDonagh examined the growing involvement of government in emigration and shipping in the first half of the nineteenth century and produced a five-stage model of government expansion. The first stage involved the recognition of some 'intolerable evil' which, it was believed, could be legislated out of existence by a prohibitory Act. The second stage involved the recognition of the deficiencies in this Act and its replacement with new legislation involving inspectors in enforcement. Thirdly, the momentum created by a body of professionals, with intimate knowledge of the problem, led to growing centralization and superintendence by a central agency. Fourth, growing professional awareness brought an awareness that the problem could not be swept away and that slow regulation and re-regulation was needed. Finally, a bureaucratic machine pursued research to produce preventive measures which passed almost unnoticed into law.

MacDonagh's thesis centres on two main principles, the pressure of 'intolerable facts' and an exponential administrative momentum. Benthamism was incidental to the process and this led to an intense debate among historians over what was meant by the term 'Benthamite' over which, as outlined earlier, there was considerable disagreement. Are historians talking about people who had read Bentham, or his followers, or who were influenced directly or indirectly by him or them, or who had even heard of Bentham? The other point of debate concerns the validity of MacDonagh's five-stage model. It has been suggested that the model breaks down when examining other areas of social policy. Even so, there is much of value in its basic concepts.

Traditional and incrementalist views and tensions

The final explanation takes the MacDonagh thesis a stage further and argues that the evolving administrative state had little to do with concepts of individualism and collectiveness but with a conflict between two views of the role of government, a traditional and a so-called incrementalist view. William Lubenow suggests that the response of the state to intolerable evils was conditioned by these two models of government.[13] The traditional model put great faith in the historic rights and customs enshrined in past constitutional practice, with a particular emphasis on local self-government. It assumed an attack via growing centralization on the traditional freedom of English institutions. The incrementalist model faced up to problems without any clear-cut or predetermined programme of action, but hesitantly and pragmatically. Lubenow focused on the poor law, public health, railways and the factory question and though his model fits public health, it is less certain for other areas. However, his approach does highlight the importance of the local perspective in the growth of the administrative state.

AN EMERGING STATE

Despite the complicated and contradictory views of historians it is possible to highlight four aspects of the emerging administrative state. First, the response of the state to social and economic matters was largely ad hoc, practical, unplanned and pragmatic. It was the pressure of the real world rather than abstract theories which produced administrative growth. Secondly, the relationship between central and local government cannot be ignored. The problem was not whether the state should act to deal with human problems like public health, but what the agency of intervention should be. Centralization was regarded not simply as leading to the end of real local government but as an evil to be feared more than the problem it was attempting to overcome.

When it was clear that intervention was justifiable there was an alliance between central and local government but, when doubt existed, then there was also an alliance between voluntary and state action. Many contemporaries saw intervention as a means for individuals to duck their responsibilities. Combining voluntary and state action was the only way many felt that progress could be made. Any explanation which fails to take into account the interconnectedness of government and voluntary action in the administrative expansion of the state is seriously deficient. Finally, there was the vital element of self-generating, administrative momentum, irrespective of whether it was or was not grounded in Benthamism. The bureaucracy grew and attracted extended powers because of the growing realization of how much needed to be done to create a state in which meaningful natural liberty could flourish. Many contemporaries recognized that there was a case for intervention to create the conditions in which mutual self-help and competition could operate freely. *Laissez-faire* was the ideal, state intervention the pragmatic reality.

Bureaucracy and inspection

The 'revolution in government' had two further dimensions: the creation of an effective and efficient machinery of government and the emergence of inspection as the means of ensuring bureaucratic control. The administrative revolution made much use of the executive powers and devices created before 1830, especially the legitimacy of Parliament. Innovation and regulation by the Privy Council through Orders-in-Council remained important, sometimes legitimized by statute. The new Board of Trade, replacing that abolished in 1782, developed from a Committee of the Privy Council on trade and plantations formed in 1784, reorganized by an Order-in-Council in 1786. But its officers – vice-president 1817, president 1826 – and its responsibilities were established by statute law. From 1839 education was 'organized' by a committee of the Privy Council but its single officer and some of its responsibilities and financial regulation were established by statute. A similar process of statutory definition occurred in the Treasury and the Home Office. The Foreign Office, by contrast, owed as much of its empowerment to prerogative and privilege as to powers-by-statute. By the late 1830s it is possible to talk sensibly of a machinery of central government in ways that were not possible a century earlier.

What are the 'facts'?

The emergence of the statistical ideal, the collection of 'facts' which were used to justify centralist policies, was essential to the transformation of the relationship between local and central government. Commissions of inquiry increased rapidly after 1800, in part result of the movement for economical reform, in part the needs of war. Between 1832 and 1846 over a hundred Royal Commissions were established. Commissions and committees of inquiry operated with a set agenda, controlled membership, definite form of inquiry, relationship between gathered evidence and the legitimation of certain 'facts' which formed the basis for reports and recommendations. This collection and legitimation of 'facts' was paralleled by the emergence of state inspectors – for factories from 1833, the poor law from 1834, prisons from 1835, schools from 1839, for the mining population from 1842 and for mines from 1850 – who in their annual reports generated further legitimate 'facts'. They were charged with inspecting and reporting on the implementation of Acts, the legitimate operation of local institutions and the 'efficiency' of those in receipt of central funding. The state inspectors were the vanguard of central intervention in two important respects. First, they sought to secure a national minimum provision in their different areas. Secondly, they acted to establish and standardize a range of civic institutions which symbolized the extension of the state beyond the efforts of either individuals or local groupings. These civic institutions were either 'objects of terror' like union workhouses or police stations or new public institutions including parks and gardens which celebrated local civic character and pride and characterized respectable and cultured citizenship.

The emergence of the modern state was largely the result of the demographic and economic changes that occurred in Britain in the eighteenth and early nineteenth centuries. The reasons behind the 'revolution in government' are far less clear. Contemporary perceptions of particular policies and the consequent extension of the role of the state varied. It was possible for the same policy to be regarded simultaneously as benevolent, a solution to a practical problem, an effective bureaucratic expedient, a prop to the existing social and political order, an asset to the middle classes and yet also as a legitimate popular demand. Social reform in the eighteenth and nineteenth centuries, the emergence of the 'policing' and 'inspectorial' functions of the state and the parallel centralizing of bureaucratic control, was rarely motivated by one thing. Policies were the result of the consideration of different, often conflicting, perspectives.

NOTES

1 Adam Smith *Inquiry into the Nature and Causes of the Wealth of Nations*, 1776, Everyman edn, 1910, Vol. II, pp. 180–1.

2 B. Jordan *The State: Authority and Autonomy*, Blackwell, 1985, p. 1.

3 For the development of the 'state' see G. Poggi *The Development of the Modern State: A Sociological Introduction*, Hutchinson, 1978, especially Chapters 1, 4 and 5 and P. Anderson *Lineages of the Absolutist State*, Verso, 1975. P. Dunleavy and B. O'Leary *Theories of the State: The Politics of Liberal Democracy*, Macmillan, 1987 and B. Jordan op. cit. provide valuable modern critiques. P. Corrigan and D. Sayer *The Great Arch: English State Formation as Cultural Revolution*, Blackwell, 1985 is a contentious, difficult but fascinating study.

4 On economic 'policy' in the first half of the eighteenth century see L. A. Clarkson *The Pre-Industrial Economy in England 1500–1750*, Batsford, 1971, pp. 159–209.

5 P. Corrigan and D. Sayer op. cit., p. 89.

6 For a fuller discussion of a 'moral economy' see Chapter 11.

7 On the nineteenth century 'revolution in government' see V. Cromwell *Revolution or Evolution: British Government in the Nineteenth Century*, Longman, 1977 and A. J. Taylor *Laissez Faire and State Intervention in Nineteenth Century Britain*, Macmillan, 1972 for the historiographical debate. The following works are worth consulting: D. Fraser *The Evolution of the British Welfare State*, Macmillan, 2nd edn, 1984, U. Henriques *Before the Welfare State*, Longman, 1977, N. Chester *The English Administrative System 1780–1870*, Oxford University Press, 1981, W. C. Lubenow *The Politics of Government Growth*, David & Charles, 1971, O. MacDonagh *Early Victorian Government*, Weidenfeld, 1977, H. Parris *Constitutional Bureaucracy*, Allen & Unwin, 1969, D. Roberts *Victorian Origins of the British Welfare State*, Yale, 1968 and G. Sutherland (ed.) *Studies in the Growth of Nineteenth Century Government*, Routledge, 1972. Much work is contained in published articles for which see D. Fraser op. cit.

8 On the 'classical economists' see W. J. Barber *A History of Economic Thought*, Penguin, 1967, R. Heilbroner *The Worldly Philosophers*, Penguin, 1983 and J. Robinson *Economic Philosophy*, Penguin, 1970. Penguin have published convenient editions of Smith, Malthus, Ricardo and Mill and there are good studies of Smith, Malthus, Bentham and Mill respectively by D. D. Raphael, D. Winch, J. Dinwiddy and W. Thomas in Oxford University Press 'Past Masters' series. On the 'influence' of economists see F. W. Fetter *The Economist in Parliament 1780–1868*, Duke University Press, 1980.

9 On changing philosophies of government see R. Pearson and G. Williams *Political Thought and Public Policy in the Nineteenth Century: an Introduction*,

Longman, 1984. E. Halévy *The Growth of Philosophical Radicalism*, Faber, 1952 still contains much of value on Benthamism.

10 H. Perkin *The Origins of Modern English Society 1780–1800*, Routledge, 1969, W. L. Burns *The Age of Equipoise*, Allen & Unwin, 1964.

11 For a fuller discussion of anti-capitalist ideas see Chapters 11 and 12 especially pp. 360–2.

12 O. MacDonagh *A Pattern of Government Growth 1800–60: The Passenger Acts and Their Enforcement*, 1961 puts forward one explanation of government growth and led to a debate with H. Parris who put forward an alternative explanation in *Government and the Railways in Nineteenth-Century Britain*, Routledge, 1965. O. MacDonagh *Early Victorian Government 1830–70*, Allen & Unwin, 1977 provides a useful synthesis.

13 W. Lubenow *The Politics of Government Growth. Early Victorian Attitudes Towards State Intervention, 1833–48*, David & Charles, 1971 uses four case-studies of poor relief, public health, railway expansion and factory legislation to suggested a piecemeal response to particular crises as an explanation for government intervention.

16 Policy abroad 1815–51

And if I might be allowed to express in one sentence the principle which I think ought to guide an English Minister, I would adopt the expression of Canning, and say that with every British Minister the interests of England ought to be the shibboleth of his policy.[1]

British Foreign Ministers have been guided by what seemed to them to be the immediate interest of this Country without any elaborate calculations for the future.[2]

In 1815 Britain, that 'nation of shopkeepers', had emerged as one of the arbiters of the fate of Europe. By 1851 Britain had a global commercial role: the decisions in Westminster affected countries as diverse as China, Canada and India. This chapter examines how that transformation occurred through a consideration of the principles or, as Edward Grey would have it, the pragmatism underlying foreign policies and the roles of Castlereagh, Canning, Aberdeen and Palmerston, who were Foreign Secretaries for the bulk of the period.[3]

FOREIGN POLICY: UNDERLYING PRINCIPLES

Attitudes to Europe

What were the considerations which underpinned British foreign policies after the defeat of Napoleonic France in 1815? Direct or indirect intervention in the affairs of continental Europe and of European countries' colonial possessions, for dynastic or strategic reasons, to maintain a balance of power had been the *raison d'être* for Britain's foreign policy since the mid-seventeenth century. It has been amply demonstrated that 'splendid isolation' was never a preferred or for long a practical option for British Foreign Secretaries. But there were important respects in which Britain's history in the eighteenth and early nineteenth centuries differed from continental experiences. By 1815 Britain was already well advanced industrially and commercially. Economic and demographic growth meant that Britain could no longer feed its own population and was increasingly dependent on international trade for both food and industrial raw materials. Britain had no large army but to protect trade routes Britain felt that she must be supreme at sea, though there was always the insistence that this was a primarily defensive priority. What was seen by Britain as the pursuit of a vigorous trading position was seen differently by foreigners. To them it was downright aggressive. Commercial imperialism, they perceived, led to formal or informal political control over large parts of the world.

'Public opinion'

Economic change in Britain had resulted in social transformation, in particular the emergence of an articulate 'public opinion' associated with the middle classes. In no other European power was foreign policy so systematically and publicly scrutinized. The collection of printed diplomatic correspondence, known as the *Blue Books*, could always be edited by the government of the day but they contained an enormous amount of detailed information which provided a basis for criticism on a wide scale. Castlereagh recognized as early as 1820 that there was a public opinion in Britain which could not be ignored or flouted. Canning and Palmerston made conscious efforts to woo and direct public opinion by the publication of the documents explaining their policies and by a judicious use of the press. Public opinion was, however, frequently uninformed, prejudiced and xenophobic. It was firmly convinced of the superiority of Britain and its institutions to other countries in the world. This enabled both Canning and Palmerston to appeal to public sympathy when acting in defence of 'constitutional states'.

A 'balance of power'

Contemporaries liked to see Britain as the greatest power in the world in the first half of the nineteenth century. This is clearly an overestimation. Commercial interests often compelled Britain to assume a role in the world which politicians did not always seek but in terms of the continent she was always only one among five great powers: Britain, France, Austria, Prussia and Russia. It was the 'balance' between these five powers which dominated much of Britain's foreign policies.

This 'Concert of Europe' became an important concept in the course of the nineteenth century. Initially it meant the coalition against Napoleonic France but gradually it came to define the permanent relationship between the great powers of Europe. Its development and acceptance was, however, a slow process. It frequently reverted to being a coalition for specific purposes. In the 1820s, for example, when the government of most European countries was in the hands of conservatives, the Concert tended to be the means through which the status quo was maintained, an attitude which brought it into conflict with the growth of the idea of nationalism. Austria, Russia and Prussia certainly had a more interventionist view of the Concert than Britain. They wished to use it as the basis for the defence of the whole existing structure of society and of 'legitimate', by which they meant 'conservative', authority. Britain could agree with this position when it came to the containment of France and was quite prepared to support the Bourbon restoration in 1814. But the principle of legitimacy did not have the same ideological appeal to the British government as it did to the east European powers. In fact all the great powers were prepared to depart from the principle when it conflicted with other national interests or ambitions. British statesmen believed that the Congress of Vienna had created a desirable territorial 'balance of power' in Europe and that peace could be preserved as long as no power seriously diverged from it. Consequently there were no permanent blocs of power in this period. France sided with the eastern powers over Spain in 1822 but with Britain twelve years later. Britain sided with Russia over the Eastern Question in 1840 but with France against Russia in 1854. All British governments found it inconvenient to seek an ally. It was more flexible and more valuable to support a 'balance of power' policy in Europe and participate only when that balance seemed threatened by an actual or potential aggressor from among the great powers. Pragmatism and the specific interests of the great powers rather than adherence to a particular ideology marked foreign relations after Waterloo.

As far as Britain was concerned the Congress of Vienna defined the limits of her continental ambitions and, while a general peace was maintained, British trade could expand unhindered. Britain was quite willing to see the Vienna Settlement altered if its basic aims were still fulfilled. In the 1830s Britain was prepared to see an independent Belgium as long as its neutrality was guaranteed. Palmerston would have liked to see Austrian influence removed from Italy so long as French ambitions did not fill the political vacuum. By 1848 he clearly regarded some parts of the 1814–15 Settlement as obsolete but he, like his predecessors at the Foreign Office, did not adopt a 'revisionist' approach to European affairs.

'National interests': continuity not change?

British foreign policy throughout the nineteenth century has been criticized for being pragmatic, that it was not based on any long-term ideological or systematic considerations. It is, however, possible to identify two general principles which did underlie the actions of successive Foreign Secretaries: security and trade. These tended to be implicit in policies, underpinning and, on occasions, determining action. Castlereagh, Canning, Aberdeen and Palmerston all accepted that they had a responsibility for ensuring that British trade could be carried on throughout as much of the world as possible without interference. Free trade was not simply an economic dogma. It was also seen as a means of achieving international peace. Destructive economic competition, a prime cause of war, would be replaced, according to members of the Manchester School like Richard Cobden, by trade to mutual advantage.

There was an essential continuity between Britain's foreign policy before and after 1815. The French Revolution and Napoleonic Wars did not induce Britain to abandon the balance of power, though it sought to eliminate meddling and ineffectiveness. William Pitt provided the foundations for this development in the plans he made for peace, guidelines put into practice by Castlereagh and Canning. Pitt planned for the creation of a concert among the Powers to provide a more effective system of European security, with a new distribution of power in order to contain future French aggression and a guarantee between the Powers to maintain it.

CASTLEREAGH AND CANNING

The Vienna Settlement 1814–15

Castlereagh[4] applied Pitt's 'legacy' to the great peace settlement which was made at Paris and Vienna in 1814–15 after Napoleon's defeat. He had become Perceval's Foreign Secretary in February 1812 and continued with the post, which he combined with the Leadership of the House of Commons, under Lord Liverpool. Napoleon's débâcle in Russia in 1812 and Wellington's victories in Spain and Portugal in 1813 brought victory within Castlereagh's grasp. The Anglo-American War between 1812 and 1814, in part a consequence of Britain's enforcement of a European blockade, was less successful. Neither side gained much from the war which was memorable only for the burning of the President's residence which was then whitewashed to hide the signs of the British attack and the British defeat at New Orleans after peace had been signed at Ghent in early 1814.

The Vienna Settlement (Figure 16.1) brought Britain few territorial gains though their location emphasized Britain's major preoccupations: the Cape of Good Hope, Ceylon, Heligoland, Malta, Mauritius, St Lucia, Trinidad, Tobago and, as a protectorate, the Ionian Islands. The Cape, Ceylon and Mauritius were of strategic and commercial importance in relation to India. Britain's special interest in the Low Countries, central to her trade with Europe and a potential base for an invasion of England, was safeguarded by the possession of Heligoland and by Austria's decision not to take back the old Austrian Netherlands which were united with Holland. This ensured that no great power controlled the Low Countries. Malta and the Ionian Islands provided strategic bases in the Mediterranean and guarded against the advance of Russia into that area. The West Indian islands reinforced Britain's commercial control over the Caribbean. France

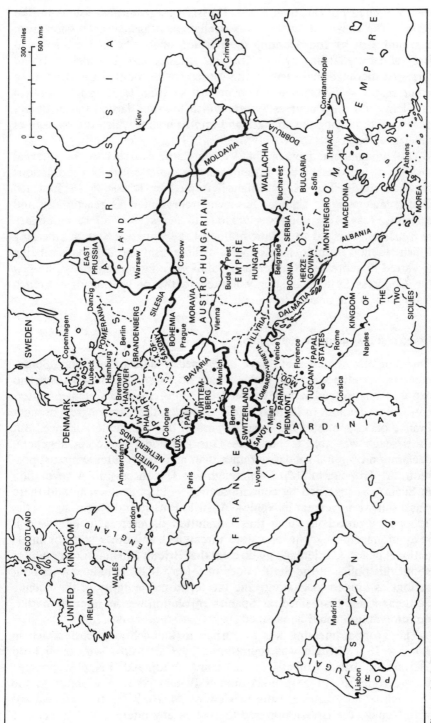

Figure 16.1 Europe in 1815

was contained but not humiliated. Prussia was given possessions on the Rhine. The centre of Europe was strengthened against aggression from east and west by consolidating the position of Austria in Germany and Italy and by guarding against Russian advance into Europe. In broad terms Castlereagh had secured the settlement he wanted for Britain. In other respects Vienna was not a perfect solution to Europe's political problems and the Congress System which followed lacked the flexibility necessary to making the changes and improvements which the passage of time revealed.

The fundamental flaw of the Vienna Settlement lay in the internal systems of individual states rather than the direct effect on the relations between states. The 'Holy Alliance' formed by Russia in 1815, which Castlereagh avoided signing, has been represented as reactionary and certainly Tsar Alexander was anxious to act against all revolutionary movements. This led to a static notion of the Congress System emerging which resulted in the dynamic forces of liberalism and nationalism being thwarted or repressed. Castlereagh's aims were far more modest: he saw the Congress System as strictly limited to the prevention of a French disruption of the peace settlement.

Congress: a system for repression?

The Congress system could have been used to adjust the Vienna Settlement to accommodate the needs which liberalism and nationalism had exposed but instead it was devoted to reinforcing the system of international repression. In 1818, at Aix-la-Chapelle, the first Congress brought France back as one of the great powers in the Quintuple Alliance. But Castlereagh was able to persuade Tsar Alexander to accept a general declaration of moral solidarity rather than an actively interventionist position. At Troppau in 1820 Castlereagh was less successful. A revolution in Spain was regarded by contemporaries as ultra-democratic and there was a similar movement in Naples. Austria, Prussia and Russia signed the Troppau Protocol in which they committed themselves to intervene if revolutionary changes in any state threatened any other state or international peace. Castlereagh made clear that Britain had major reservations about this policy in the State Paper of 5 May 1820. Britain saw its obligations as limited to guaranteeing the territorial integrity of the Vienna Settlement and that, since the Spanish revolution was an internal matter, no intervention could be justified.

The Troppau meeting was adjourned to Laibach and reassembled in January 1821. Britain was represented by Castlereagh's brother, Lord Stewart the British Ambassador in Vienna. Ferdinand of Naples appealed to the congress for help and, though Britain could not object to the dispatch of an Austrian army in view of Austria's treaty arrangements with Naples, the British opposed the use of any international force. The outbreak of a revolt in Wallachia and Moldavia which was followed by the Greek revolt had the effect of uniting British and Austrian policy as both were anxious that the Russians should not profit from the situation at the expense of Turkey. Laibach settled little and a new congress was arranged to meet at Verona in 1822. The threat to British interests in the Near East obliged Castlereagh to consider attending in person, but on 12 August 1822, in a fit of depression, he cut his throat.

Castlereagh and Canning: a comparison

His successor at the Foreign Office was George Canning. He had already held the post between 1807 and 1809 and only his unwillingness to serve with Castlereagh prevented his reappointment in July 1812. In 1814 Liverpool suggested that he might go to Lisbon as British Minister and from June 1816 to December he sat in the cabinet as President of the Board of Control for India. Canning and Castlereagh appeared to have made up their differences, at least outwardly, and Canning was able to exert some influence over Castlereagh's policies. It is possible that Canning had a hand in the drafting of the 1820 State Paper and, once he came to office, he publicly accepted it as the basis for his own policies.[5]

The real contrast between Castlereagh and Canning was not in policy but in personality and the public image they presented. Castlereagh was shy and often clumsy; Canning was bold and eloquent, a public speaker in the rhetorical tradition of the period with a strong sense of humour. Castlereagh was popular at Court but, largely because as Leader of the House of Commons he had had to defend the government's repressive policies against radicalism, unpopular in the country. Canning was disliked by the king and many of his cabinet colleagues but was extremely popular among the general public. Castlereagh was cautious and was only pushed into disagreement with Britain's allies by the pressure of public opinion. Canning was more flamboyant, setting himself vigorously in the van of public opinion and ruthlessly pursuing British interests. Castlereagh was regarded by the statesmen of Europe as one of them while Canning gained a reputation as a crusader for liberalism and nationalism and Metternich saw him as the devil incarnate and the evil genius of revolution.

This contrast exaggerates differences between Castlereagh and Canning. Both were well aware of the limitations of both British interests and British power. Both were pragmatic in approach. The thesis, advanced by H. W. V. Temperley, that Canning's main work at the Foreign Office was to destroy the 'Neo-Holy' Alliance, the use of international force to crush revolution and liberal change throughout Europe, now has little support.[6] Canning was a Tory, albeit a 'liberal' one and like Castlereagh he had little liking for what he saw as the selfish and shortsighted ends of the legitimist status quo. Canning, like his mentor William Pitt, did not want Britain deeply involved in the politics of the continent and sought to regain the freedom of action which he thought would allow Britain to pursue its proper interests. He did not go to Verona and quickly withdrew Wellington, who had gone in his place. Though Canning maintained that this brought the Congress System to an end he overestimated his achievement. Doubts on the part of the Tsar, reinforced by Metternich's arguments, prevented Russia from intervening on behalf of revolution in Greece and against it in Spain. Wellington's argument against French intervention in Spain was also unsuccessful and the Bourbon army found little difficulty in subduing the country in mid-1823. Autocracy was restored.

Canning was reminded that England had waged war in the seventeenth and eighteenth centuries to prevent the union of French and Spanish power under the Bourbons and feared the extension of the forces of reaction to Portugal and Spanish America. Castlereagh had been anxious about this but for Canning, spokesman for Britain's commercial interests and MP for Liverpool, it was of central importance. The United States had already recognized the rebel governments in Latin America but Canning moved more cautiously. He had to take into account opposition from the king and from Wellington but was able to exert sufficient diplomatic pressure on France to get agreement that intervention should not be extended to the rebel Spanish colonies. Canning also entered into negotiations with the United States in an attempt to produce a joint declaration against European intervention. The uneasiness of Anglo-American relations and American suspicions of Canning's motives led President Munroe to issue his famous message (the Munroe Doctrine) in December 1823 prohibiting European assistance to Spain in her struggle against the rebels and any transfer or extension of European possessions to the New World.

Canning's motivation for his defence of the rebel colonies and his pose as a true friend of the United States were not particularly convincing. By mid-1823 he was isolated both from the European powers and very largely at the English Court. His attacks on French intervention met with considerable criticism at home and he needed to drum up popular support against the reactionaries in his own party. Support for the rebels had commercial and political advantages for Canning. His claim that he had 'called the New World into existence, to redress the balance of the Old' must be seen in this domestic context.

Canning and Portugal

The Royal Navy, threat of which had been sufficient to deter European intervention in the New World, was used to enable Britain's strength to be felt in Portugal. Revolutionaries and reactionaries were struggling for dominance and Canning argued that intervention was necessary to maintain the 'special relationship' that had existed between the two countries since the seventeenth century. Canning maintained British influence by sending the fleet to Lisbon to support King John VI in 1824 and by helping to arrange the peaceful separation of Brazil from direct Portuguese rule. King John's death in 1826 led to the accession of the eight-year-old Donna Maria – her father Pedro renounced the throne preferring to remain an Emperor of Brazil. This led to a revival of the absolutist claims of her uncle Miguel. Spanish interference in Portuguese affairs in support of Miguel resulted in direct British intervention. Canning rushed 5,000 troops to Lisbon and threatened Spain with war. This ensured Maria's succession and the acceptance of the 1826 liberal constitution. British naval power played a major role in the success of Canning's actions and a respectable naval presence was usually kept in Lisbon to maintain British influence.

Britain's exit from the Congress System made the weaknesses and strengths of her position very clear. Naval power allowed her to operate effectively only where water dominated communication. This was clearly illustrated by the issues of the New World and Portugal. But Canning's influence on the great European powers was limited while Britain remained isolated and the conservative alliance was united. The Greek revolt against the Turks led to disagreement between Austria and Russia.

Canning and Greece

Greece posed a major problem for Canning. Britain's main interest in the Near East was clear enough: to check Russian expansion, to prevent Russia becoming a Mediterranean naval power and to secure the stability of the Ottoman empire, making it susceptible to British economic penetration. The Greek revolt roused mixed feelings in London. Canning would undoubtedly have agreed with Castlereagh that the preservation of the Ottoman empire was a necessary evil since it offered the best hope of stability in the area. There was, however, a great deal of sympathy for the Greeks among the educated classes, and Turkey's refusal to compromise on the Greek issue combined with a growth of popular philhellenism in Britain, personified by Lord Byron who was to die in Greece in 1824, threatened to undermine British policy in the Near East.

Russia was sympathetic to the Greek struggle and had an interest in eroding the boundaries of the Ottoman Empire. This broke down the conservative alignment with Austria against revolution. Canning recognized the Greeks as belligerents in March 1823; previously they had simply been 'rebels'. Tsar Alexander tried first to get the British to agree to joint intervention but by the end of 1824 he abandoned this strategy. The Greeks suffered from Ottoman military victories and in July 1825 appealed for protection and mediation not to Russia but directly to Great Britain.

In early 1826 Canning sent Wellington to St Petersburg to congratulate the new Tsar Nicholas on his accession and to concert policy over Greece. Canning was concerned to avoid a Russo-Turkish war and the possibility of Russian territorial expansion. The St Petersburg Protocol of April 1826 gave him roughly what he wanted. Nicholas and Wellington agreed that Greece should become an autonomous state, nominally under the sovereignty of the Sultan, and that Russia should support Britain's mediation to achieve this. Austria and Prussia refused to agree to the Protocol but France did and this was formalized in the Treaty of London the following year. The Turks, buttressed by further victories over the Greeks, refused to accede to the demands of the great powers and squadrons of British, French and Russian ships were sent to the east Mediterranean. On 20 October 1827 Turkish irritation at the presence of this fleet led to direct confrontation at Navarino and within two hours a combined Turkish and Egyptian fleet was annihilated. This was followed by the outbreak of war between Russia and Turkey in April 1828.

Canning did not live to see the breakdown of his Near East policy. Navarino changed the balance of power in the eastern Mediterranean and the outbreak of war between Russia and Turkey marked an end to policies pursued since 1826. Canning would probably have been able to limit the effects of this situation but under Wellington's administration Britain's Greek policy simply drifted. Domestic issues rather than foreign policy dominated parliamentary sessions and Lord Aberdeen, who became Foreign Secretary in June 1828, though sympathetic to Greek demands, believed that a narrowly defined state would limit Russian influence. Russia made small territorial gains as a result of the war with Turkey which ended with the Treaty of Adrianople in September 1829. Russian caution proceeded from an assessment of their military and diplomatic strength which concluded that their power was, as yet, limited. Greek independence was achieved the following year. Little of the limited success that Wellington and Aberdeen had between 1828 and 1830 was the result of their efforts. They badly bungled the situation in Portugal by withdrawing the British naval presence thus giving the initiative to the reactionaries. They almost destroyed Canning's achievement in dismantling the conservative alliance and, over the Greek issues, came close to restoring Britain's isolation.

PALMERSTON 1830–41

Henry John Temple, Lord Palmerston, became Foreign Secretary of the Whig administration which was formed in late 1830.[6] Born in 1784, Palmerston entered Parliament in 1807 and there were only two administrations between then and his death in 1865 in which he did not hold office. In 1809 he became Secretary at War, without a seat in the cabinet. He remained at the War Office until 1828, though he was brought into the cabinet by Canning in 1827. He was generally regarded as hard-working and competent but in the late 1820s he seemed destined to be only a minor political figure.

Political apprenticeship

Canning's decision to bring Palmerston into the cabinet in April 1827 seemed to spark a new interest in him. He had rarely spoken on foreign policy though his maiden speech in the Commons had been on the defence of the Copenhagen expedition in terms of a government's right to regard Britain's vital interests as its first consideration and he had made a spirited defence of the British empire when he presented the army estimates in 1816. Canning's unexpected death in August 1827 led to political disarray. The Canningites led by Huskisson and Palmerston remained in office under Goderich and continued under Wellington until May 1828. The five months the Canningites remained in Wellington's cabinet was a period of complete frustration for Palmerston and, freed from the constraints of office, he attacked government policy over Greece and Portugal vigorously, arguing for an extension of Greek territory and against Wellington's support for the absolutist Miguel. His speech of 1 June 1829 was a comprehensive denunciation of foreign policy on both these issues, in which he presented his interpretation of Canningite foreign policy.

The speech did not make any real impact at the time and Wellington, who continued trying to bring Palmerston back into his ministry, did not take it too seriously as an attack on his policy. This was clearly not Palmerston's view. He circulated copies to the press and later provided a version for inclusion in Hansard. Palmerston may have regarded himself as Canning's true successor – a view which should not be overemphasized given that he had not really allied himself with Canning until the early 1820s – but his emphasis was different. Canning had relied on rather vague appeals to constitutionalism and nationalism to persuade Parliament and the general public of the validity of his policies but at heart these policies remained cautious. Palmerston was potentially more abrasive arguing, as he had in his maiden speech, for the right to 'interfere' in support of Britain's vital interests. Palmerston's reasons for proclaiming a Canningite doctrine in foreign policy were rooted in part in domestic politics. In 1829 and 1830 it was important that the Canningites should maintain a clear identity, and foreign policy issues were less divisive among potential supporters than domestic issues. Palmerston had given the foreign policy debate a distinctly ideological slant, insisting that Britain stood for the maintenance of constitutional rights in other countries and for the extension of 'liberty and civilization'. There is little evidence to support Donald Southgate's assertion that Palmerston was making a play for the Foreign Office in preference to any other office[8] and his appointment as Foreign Secretary came only after he had been considered for Leader of the House of Commons and Chancellor of the Exchequer and Home Secretary by Lord Grey.

Palmerston did not take a prominent part in the domestic controversies of the early 1830s. He still had reservations about parliamentary reform, though he did believe that 'piecemeal' reform could prevent revolution and remedy obvious abuses. Grey's handling of Palmerston in this period was very tactful and the latter never seriously contemplated resignation. There is little doubt that Grey had a major influence on foreign policy between 1830 and the summer of 1834 and that his support and often detailed guidance were central to Palmerston's success but the suggestion that he effectively controlled Palmerston's actions has been disproved by the detailed researches of C. K. Webster. Kenneth Bourne's work using the evidence from the Broadlands Papers suggests that a kind of inner cabinet consisting of Grey, Landsdowne, Holland and Palmerston was largely responsible for decisions. Certainly Palmerston did not have the free hand or the prestige he enjoyed later but even under Melbourne from 1835 to 1841 he was still engaged in trying to balance often contradictory opinions. The period between 1830 and 1841 was one of learning and establishing reputation for Palmerston.

In the 1830s Palmerston was faced with the results of a number of challenges to the Vienna Settlement.[9] The July Revolution of 1830 in France was seen by Palmerston, and ironically by Wellington and Aberdeen, as a limited political revolution which the Bourbon king had brought upon himself, that the government of Louis Philippe did not intend to be aggressive and that the best way of maintaining stability in Europe was to recognize the *fait accompli*. Revolution had, however, spread from France into Belgium, where disorder broke out in August.

The Belgian problem

The decision to unite Belgium and Holland in 1815 under the House of Orange did not seem unreasonable as it provided a strong barrier to French expansion into the Low Countries. The two countries had economies which were potentially complementary and religious and linguistic divisions did not correspond to existing boundaries. But it proved a union fraught with difficulties and the Belgians increasingly felt repressed by Dutch attitudes and actions. In 1830 Wellington's government had acted pragmatically on the issue, establishing an ambassadorial conference in London which Palmerston inherited in November. Circumstances favoured Palmerston. The outbreak of revolution in Poland distracted the eastern powers who would have supported Holland had France intervened and Louis Philippe's government was too insecure to risk a serious quarrel with Britain.

The Belgians drew up a new constitution and in February 1831 elected the Duke of Nemours, the son of Louis Philippe, as their king. Knowing that this would prove unacceptable to the other Powers, Louis Philippe vetoed it and instead Leopold of Saxe-Coburg became Leopold I of the Belgians. William I of Holland had reluctantly accepted Belgian independence in January 1831 but claims over the Duchy of Luxembourg led to a Dutch invasion in August 1831. Leopold appealed for aid and while the British fleet blockaded the coast, the French army compelled the Dutch to withdraw. This resulted in the Tory opposition putting Palmerston's policy under severe pressure. It was his ineptitude that had allowed the French to occupy Belgium.

The Powers had agreed as early as January 1831 that Belgium should become an independent state and that they should guarantee its neutrality. The details of the agreement were modified in June and again in October 1831. The terms were acceptable to the Belgians but not to the Dutch. William I, who still controlled Antwerp, refused to withdraw and military measures were again resorted to in 1832. Palmerston argued that it was William I's intransigence that prevented a solution to the Belgian problem and was prepared to accept limited French military intervention. However, he had considerable difficulty in persuading both the king and Parliament of the validity of a policy which seemed a complete reversal of the 'containment' of France agreed in 1815. A new armistice was agreed in 1833 but the final settlement was delayed until the Treaty of London of 1839.

Revolutions in 1830–2

Revolution also erupted in Poland, Germany and Italy in 1830. Public opinion in Britain was generally on the side of the Poles and radical groups urged Palmerston to take action. In practice there was little that he could do other than assert that as a signatory of the Treaty of Vienna Britain had the right to be consulted before Poland's status was changed. By 1832 the Poles had lost their position as a quasi-constitutional monarchy and became yet another Russian province. Palmerston did little to support liberal groups in Germany and by 1832 the conservative status quo had generally been restored.

He was scarcely more successful in the representations he made in Italy. In 1831–2 there were a number of unsuccessful risings in the Papal States and in Modena and Parma. Anti-papal feeling in Britain ran high and again the radical groups urged Palmerston to take action. From the Foreign Office viewpoint the important thing was to prevent conflict between France, which showed some gestures of support for the rebels, and Austria, which gave military aid to the recently elected conservative Pope, Gregory XVI. Palmerston was mainly anxious that the Italian problem should end without further complications and argued that moderate reform would stave off revolution. The Pope took no notice and absolutism was re-established throughout Italy. War between France and Austria had been averted but the cause of liberalism here, as in Poland and Germany, had not been furthered.

The Iberian peninsula

Palmerston's public reputation was improved by his handling of problems in Portugal and Spain where, as in the Low Countries, Britain had long-established strategic and commercial interests. In Portugal British support for Maria had collapsed with Canning's death and by November 1830 Miguel was in control of the whole of the country. Maria's supporters held only Terciera in the Azores. In 1831 the French, with British approval, sent a fleet to Lisbon. As this coincided with the French invasion of Belgium Palmerston again came under attack from the Tory opposition. British opinion was better pleased when he extended his diplomatic support to Pedro, who abdicated his Brazilian throne to come to the assistance of his daughter. He landed at Oporto in July 1832 and Palmerston made little attempt to stop British volunteers, notably Charles Napier, from enlisting under Pedro. Napier defeated Miguel's fleet off Cape St Vincent in July 1833 and took possession of Lisbon three weeks later.

Spain was also rent by conflict between liberals and absolutists in the 1830s. King Ferdinand VII died in September 1833 and the succession was disputed between the supporters of his young daughter, Isabella, and her mother Christina who had been proclaimed Regent, and the supporters of Ferdinand's younger brother, Carlos, who argued that the Salic Law forbade the accession of women to the throne. Carlos had the support of the absolutists and the clerical party while Isabella was supported by the liberals. For Palmerston the attitude of the three Eastern Powers was more disturbing. They had signed an agreement at Munchengratz in September 1833 pledging themselves to uphold the absolutist cause and one effect of this was the sending of financial aid to Carlos.

Palmerston sought to counter this action by establishing, in April 1834, the Quadruple Alliance of Britain, France and the governments of the queens of Portugal and Spain. This prevented the intervention of the Eastern Powers and established, in an embryonic form, the idea of two balancing power blocs, the absolutist powers of eastern Europe and the constitutional powers of the West. Despite this, the conflict between Christina and Carlos continued until late 1839. Palmerston's influence on Spain was much less than in Portugal, but in both countries he had prevented unilateral intervention by France.

Palmerston's actions in his early years as Foreign Secretary were dominated by either revolutions which had swept Louis Philippe to power in France and then spread to the Low Countries, to Poland, Germany and Italy or by the conflict between 'liberals' and reactionaries in the Iberian peninsula. His degree of success was, however, limited to the western periphery of Europe where French military and British naval power and influence could be exerted. In eastern Europe Palmerston could do little more than protest at the suppression of the Polish Revolt and in Italy

Austria and the Pope were able to restore the status quo. Only in Belgium was a solution found that was completely in line with his plans.

The Eastern question

Palmerston, however, took a more decisive stand on the Eastern question than he did on many European issues and here his influence on the course of events was undeniable. The basic questions remained as they had done under Castlereagh and Canning: could the Ottoman empire survive and, if not, what would take its place? Though he hoped, like Gladstone later in the century, that the Turks would leave Europe the political vacuum which would have been created resulted in a commitment to the policy of bolstering up the empire. The Turks had barely reconciled themselves to the loss of Greece when they found themselves under serious attack from the rebellious Pasha of Egypt, Mehemet Ali. Palmerston deeply distrusted him as a French protégé. Mehemet Ali, ruler of Egypt since 1805, had a deep admiration for Napoleon Bonaparte and had been busily modernizing Egypt's educational and legal systems on French lines with the assistance of French advisers.

Mehemet Ali had a good army which he had used to good effect on behalf of the Sultan in Greece in the 1820s, aid which would probably have been successful but for the intervention of the Great Powers. In return for his assistance the Sultan had promised him Syria and Crete. After the Greek settlement Mehemet Ali demanded his reward but, in view of his limited success, the Sultan refused to give him Syria as well as Crete. In 1831 he invaded Syria and the following year defeated the Turkish army at Koneih. The threat to Constantinople led the Sultan to appeal to Britain for assistance. Palmerston would have been willing to provide aid but he was overruled by the cabinet which was in the middle of an election campaign after the Reform Act and was unwilling to accept possibly expensive commitments where British interests were not directly affected. The cabinet also rejected French offers of joint intervention.

In desperation the Sultan turned to Russia. A Russian squadron entered the Bosphorus. Mehemet Ali's forces retreated and with the worried British and French pressing him to compromise, peace was made at Kutahiya in May 1833 which gave the Egyptians what they wanted in Syria. Russian influence in Constantinople was formalized by the Treaty of Unkiar Skelessi in July 1833. It was an agreement which aroused considerable suspicion in Britain and France, though it was essentially defensive. There were, however, secret clauses of which the most important was a Turkish undertaking to close the Dardanelles to all foreign warships if the Russians requested it. The Tsar followed this up in September with the Convention of Muchengratz to which Prussia adhered the following month in the separate Berlin Convention. The three Eastern Powers agreed publicly to maintain the integrity of the Sultan's dominions and in secret clauses to oppose any further advance by Mehemet Ali.

Central Asia

Russia had established a dominant influence at Constantinople and the revival of the conservative alliance provided sufficient justification for Palmerston's alarm. What concerned Britain was the direct threat to India and India's communications with the Mediterranean which it was believed Russian victories in Persia and Turkey in 1826–7 and 1828–9 created and which Unkiar Skelessi reinforced. Between 1833 and 1839 Palmerston pursued a policy in Central Asia which aimed at the containment of Russia. In Persia British policy was concerned to prevent Russia's advance both on her lines of communication with India and upon the frontiers of India itself. In 1809 Britain had secured treaties with Persia, Sind and Afghanistan to hold off the Russian advance but the 1828 victories against Persia had upset this arrangement and Russian influence in Teheran was as powerful as in Constantinople.

Both Tories and Whigs were worried by this development and under Wellington, Grey and Melbourne there was a conscious policy of counter-penetration into Central Asia which led to the first Afghan War (1838–42) and the annexation of Sind. Palmerston pursued this policy with some vigour, opening up the River Indus to British trade and influence as a counter to Russian advance. Though Britain and Russia co-operated in the Persian succession in 1834, Palmerston remained suspicious of Russian intentions and believed that their representatives were pressing the Shah to renew his attack on the strategic fortress of Herat, which he did in July 1837.

By 1836 Palmerston wanted to retaliate against Russian policy but the internal chaos in Afghanistan proved a major difficulty. Despite their encouragement of the Persian attack on Herat, the Russians had also gained ascendancy in Kabul. British intervention in support of a favourable candidate occurred in 1839 but it proved impossible to maintain his position and in 1841 the British suffered a series of shattering military defeats. It was not until late 1842 that prestige was restored by a reoccupation of Kabul, though Britain eventually accepted a compromise which restored the former pro-Russian candidate to power. The events of 1837–42 demonstrated the magnitude of the Russian threat in Central Asia and the difficulty of dealing with it diplomatically and militarily. St Petersburg had little control over the actions of over-zealous agents in Teheran or Kabul. But the real aims of Russian expansionism, whether determined from the centre or locally, were incompatible with Britain's quest for security for India.

The Eastern question revived

An uneasy peace prevailed in the Near East until 1839. The 1833 compromise left much unanswered. Neither the Sultan nor Mehemet Ali were content to leave things as they were. The former wanted revenge against his ambitious subject while Mehemet Ali continued to press, if not for complete independence, at least for hereditary possession of Egypt under nominal Turkish sovereignty. By 1839 the Sultan's army had been reorganized and, recognizing that he was a dying man, he invaded to drive the Egyptians out of Syria. Mehemet Ali's son Ibrahim had little difficulty in defeating him and once again the road to Constantinople lay open. On 1 July 1839 the Sultan died and was succeeded by a sixteen-year-old boy, Abdul Mejid. The Ottoman Empire seemed on the point of total collapse and the Great Powers were seriously alarmed.

Palmerston was in a difficult position. He recognized that the crisis afforded the Russians further opportunity to strengthen their position in Constantinople but by 1839 he was more suspicious of France than Russia in the Mediterranean. Mehemet Ali posed a real threat to British economic and strategic interests. He directly threatened British routes to the River Euphrates and the Persian Gulf, which his forces reached in 1838, and at the same time he was also threatening the Red Sea route to India. To offset this British forces had occupied the important strategic position of Aden in 1839. The unanimity between Britain and France in the 1834 Quadruple Alliance had gradually been eroded. The French had consolidated their hold over Algeria where they had intervened in 1830 and favoured the granting of considerable concessions to Mehemet Ali. The Eastern question involved the direct conflict of Britain and France for trade and in particular for control of communications with India. The means of defending Britain's interests in the Near East and of resolving the contest for supremacy in Constantinople were not to be found in the Western Alliance.

Palmerston did make an attempt to co-ordinate his policy with that of France, as he had done over Belgium, but during 1839 and early 1840 he moved closer to Russia. The increasing divergence between Britain and France was reinforced by the appointment of Thiers as French Prime Minister in March 1840. French defence of Mehemet Ali now became more open. Palmerston did not hesitate to join with the Eastern Powers and Turkey in an agreement to which France was not a party, the Convention of London, on 15 July 1840. Mehemet Ali was offered the hereditary possession of Egypt and the possession of Syria only during his lifetime. He failed to respond in the twenty days given and on 3 November a British fleet bombarded Acre.

Palmerston found himself in a difficult position in the Whig party which had traditionally been pro-French. The French were extremely indignant about the attack on Acre and began to speak in warlike terms but the

French cabinet was equally divided between peace and war parties. Though Palmerston was criticized by contemporaries for his threatening approach to French attitudes, Thiers' policy in Egypt was a direct menace to British interests. Just before the bombardment Thiers had been replaced by Guizot, who was regarded as a more pacific individual and had been recalled from London to head the ministry. Instead of ending the crisis without directly involving the French Palmerston allowed them to rejoin the Concert once Mehemet Ali had submitted in early 1841. The agreement of July 1840 was superseded by the Straits Convention of 13 July 1841 which related to the Dardanelles and the Bosphorus. This forbade the passage of foreign warships through the Straits while the Ottoman empire was at peace and ended the advantages which Russia had gained in 1833.

Palmerston regarded his Near East policy as a triumph. He had successfully resolved the crisis in conjunction with the Eastern Powers and had not humiliated France by involving her in the 1841 Convention. The Conservatives were willing to back him but his own party and the cabinet were divided. The press was very critical and ironically it was the Conservative Lord Aberdeen's influence which resulted in *The Times* calling off the attacks. In the summer and autumn of 1840 few people, apart from Palmerston, believed that war between Britain and France could be avoided. Thiers, however, proved no real match for Palmerston.

China and opium

The assertiveness Palmerston displayed was not confined to his handling of France in the Near East and Russia in Central Asia. His approach to the Chinese question demonstrated the same bluffish attitude. Trade with China had always been difficult and was, until the abolition of its monopoly in 1833, under the control of the East India Company. After 1833 the protection of British trade and British citizens fell to the British government. The result in 1839 was war, though wider issues were involved than the opium trade. Britain was determined to open up the Chinese trade and to compel Peking to adopt normal western diplomatic conventions. But opium smuggling was the flashpoint.

There was a considerable demand for opium in China and the East India Company found that it could make a good profit by growing it in India and exporting it in return for Chinese merchandise. The Chinese authorities in the 1830s vacillated between banning opium imports or simply regulating them. In the late 1830s those advocating a ban won the argument. The authorities in southern China were unable to board British ships to search for opium and placed the small British trading community at Canton under virtual house arrest. They then attacked a British warship and ordered the suspension of all trade with Britain. Banning trade was one thing but the arrest of British citizens and attacks on British shipping was another. Palmerston found himself in the position of having to endorse policy being determined on the ground but he did so whole-heartedly. The British government in India had already sent naval assistance to Canton, which had little difficulty in defeating the junks sent against it.

Palmerston's handling of the Chinese question was criticized by contemporaries, though given the limited extent to which he determined the direction of policy, much of this criticism was unfair. Gladstone raised the question of the morality of the opium trade but his attack was exceptional. To Palmerston the issue was not whether Britain should protect opium smugglers. He did not question the Chinese government's right to ban the trade. The issue was that the peaceable trading community in Canton, none of whom were implicated in the opium trade, had been unjustly molested and intimidated. Palmerston, like all his contemporaries, did not recognize that there was a conflict between two conceptions of the law: the Chinese maintained that the community to which criminals belonged could properly be held accountable for their actions and this notion of collective responsibility was alien to the British concept of individual innocence or guilt.

The war was still in progress when the Whigs were defeated in the 1841 election but the incoming Conservative government made no significant change in policy. The war continued until the Chinese made valuable concessions, which they did in the Treaty of Nanking of 1842. Five 'treaty' ports were opened up to foreign trade, and not merely to the British, though they did get a special grip on China by the annexation of Hong Kong. Nothing was said about opium, the initial cause of the conflict.

Britain and the United States

Britain had a number of outstanding disputes with the United States of America and the end of the Whig government saw considerable disagreement between the two countries. Three issues caused this situation: slavery and the slave trade, the Canadian boundary, and the problem of Texas which derived from the breakup of Spain's American empire.

Both Britain and America had declared the slave trade illegal in 1807, and in 1815 the Congress of Vienna, under pressure from Castlereagh, had also outlawed it. Enforcing the ban proved a more intractable problem. Britain had signed a number of 'right of search' treaties with the smaller nations of Europe, permitting British ships to arrest slavers flying their flags. Larger nations were more difficult to convince. Palmerston negotiated treaties of this type with France in 1831 and 1833 and in 1838 he almost secured the agreement of all the Great Powers of Europe to one treaty which would have allowed a common right of search over all slavers. French anger at Palmerston's handling of the Eastern question led them to withhold ratification and the treaty never became as effective as intended.

The United States had consistently refused to enter any right of search agreement with Britain. This was partly the result of Britain's action against American shipping during the Napoleonic War but largely because of the powerful lobby of the slave-owning southern American states. Palmerston accepted that Britain could not, in the absence of a treaty, stop and search American shipping but was concerned that slavers of other nations hoisted the American flag to escape capture. He therefore argued for a more limited 'right of visit' to check whether a suspected ship was entitled to the colours she was flying. Palmerston inflamed Americans by saying that they would not want slavers to escape simply by hoisting a 'piece of bunting'.

The most likely cause of war between Britain and America, however, seemed to be the continued existence of Canada and the failure to settle the boundary between the two countries west of the Rocky Mountains and in the east between Maine and New Brunswick. The 1814 Treaty of Ghent had left the matter to be settled by independent arbitration and in 1831 the disputed territory was arbitrarily divided between the two claimants. As settlers penetrated the disputed areas clashes of jurisdiction were inevitable. In 1837–8 there were two small-scale rebellions in Upper and Lower Canada (present-day Ontario and Quebec) caused by local disputes. This embroiled Britain and America in a series of incidents on the disputed borders. Some Americans ran guns into Canada and the defeated rebels found safe refuge in Maine. In the north-east, British and American settlers and trappers clashed violently over the disputed border.

A major crisis was initially avoided by the pacific overtures of the American government, despite bellicose pressure from public opinion, and by Palmerston's preoccupation with the Eastern question. But in December 1837 a band of Canadian volunteers crossed into American territory and sank the American steamer, the *Caroline*, which had been involved in gun-running, and killed an American citizen. In November 1840 a Canadian, Alexander McLeod, was arrested and charged with the murder. Palmerston made it clear that he would regard McLeod's execution as an occasion for war. Matters were still in a precarious state when Palmerston gave way to Aberdeen in September 1841.

Palmerston also became involved in the problems of Texas which had broken away from Mexico and formed an independent republic in 1836. The Texans, many of whom were American immigrants, initially sought entry into the American Union. This was refused, largely because of the opposition of the northern states, and in 1837 the Texans sent agents to all the leading commercial powers in Europe to obtain commercial treaties and loans. Palmerston recognized the value of an independent Texas as a balance to American power in the Caribbean and, since Texas was a major cotton producer, she might free Britain from dependence on American cotton. British abolitionists also hoped that Texas might abolish slavery, which was not highly developed, in return for commercial concessions.

In November 1840 Palmerston signed three treaties with Texas: a commercial treaty; a treaty offering British mediation between Texas and Mexico which still claimed jurisdiction over Texas; and a mutual 'right of search' treaty.

Palmerston 1830-41: a success?

The period between 1830 and 1841 has generally been regarded by historians as the most consistently successful part of Palmerston's career. He believed that bluff was an essential part of diplomacy and perhaps he not only bluffed his contemporaries into believing his successes were greater than they were but also later historians. This period showed Palmerston more as an opportunist than as a man of principle. He lacked the profound intellectual conception of foreign policy which characterized Canning. His pragmatism gave him room for manoeuvre but it also meant that he embarked on policies without seeing where they could lead. He desired, like Castlereagh and Canning, peace and stability in Europe and some sort of 'balance of power', though this meant different things at different times. But his achievements in the 1830s were modest. He did little for Poland, Germany and Italy. His plans in Spain and Portugal were of limited success. He sought to contain Russia in the Near East and Central Asia. His actions against America could have led to war and in China they did. Only in Belgium was he entirely successful in achieving his aims. It is important not to judge Palmerston's role as Foreign Secretary in the 1830s in relation to his subsequent career.

LORD ABERDEEN 1841-6

Peel appointed George Gordon, Fourth Earl of Aberdeen, who had already held the post between 1828 and 1830, as his Foreign Secretary in 1841. His first choice would have been Wellington, who had held that office during the minority Conservative administration in 1834-5, but a stroke in 1840 prevented this. There was a marked contrast between Aberdeen and Palmerston. Aberdeen, with his experience of diplomacy, took a more European outlook than the more insular and nationalistic Palmerston. He was a more rational politician than Palmerston, looking instinctively for compromise solutions to problems. There was little bluff in his thinking and Palmerston commented in despair that Britain's foreign policy was 'on a sliding scale'.

Relations with America and France were the two most pressing problems facing Aberdeen in 1841. The hostility of both, especially their combined maritime power, posed a real threat to Britain. Three courses of action were open to Aberdeen. First, he could continue Palmerston's policy of riding out the storm, relying on Britain's strength and the unwillingness of other powers to challenge it. This position had attractions for

Wellington, and to a certain extent Peel, but not Aberdeen. Secondly, he could forge closer links with the Eastern Powers, though he doubted the strength of Austria and Prussia and recognized the unpredictability of the Tsar. Thirdly, he could attempt reconciliation and seek a return to normal diplomatic relations. This attracted Aberdeen intellectually and the opportunity was presented with the replacement of Thiers by Guizot and the election of the equally moderate John Tyler as American President.

A resolution of the American problem?

The acquittal of Alexander McLeod and his arrival in England in November 1841 opened the possibilities of settling outstanding disputes. The American press had openly been canvassing the idea of a general settlement and an informal approach was made to the British government through the banking firm of Baring Brothers, which conducted much American business. Lord Ashburton, a member of the firm, was sent to negotiate. With a sense of moderation on both sides agreement on the Maine frontier was not too difficult to achieve. Aberdeen and Ashburton accepted less than they had been granted in 1831 and a not particularly vital issue had been safely disposed of. Palmerston, however, was vitriolic in his condemnation of the 1842 treaty which he saw as appeasing America, though he received little support from the Whig leadership or from public opinion. Aberdeen would have been in a stronger position to head off this attack had Ashburton been able to deal with all the issues of disputes with America. In particular the Oregon boundary and Texas questions remained unresolved.

Right of search issues continued to be intractable though the Americans agreed to maintain a squadron off the West African coast to police their own ships. The squadron was never very powerful and the slave interests in America were strong enough to ensure that America's suppression of the trade remained half-hearted. American opinion was disturbed by the action Britain took against Brazil over the slave trade. The right to search agreed between Britain and Brazil in 1826 was ended in 1845. Britain ignored the Brazilian decision and continued arresting ships. Aberdeen proved, on this issue, as willing as Palmerston to coerce a weaker power when he believed in the justice of the cause.

Texas still continued to cause problems. Mexico and Texas had gone to war and Mexico ordered two warships from British shipyards. Texas protested but Aberdeen maintained that British neutrality meant that it was just as proper for Mexico to buy in Britain as it was for Texas to buy arms in the United States. Palmerston's three treaties were ratified in June 1842 but joint Anglo-French mediation between Texas and Mexico failed. Britain did not want Texas to join the United States and Aberdeen, urged on by the abolitionist lobby, spoke in Parliament on this in mid-1843 causing much indignation among Americans. The problems proved intractable, largely because of lack of Mexican co-operation, and in 1845 President Tyler secured the passage of resolutions through Congress in favour of the annexation of Texas.

In 1818 a convention recognized the 49th parallel as the boundary between the United States and Canada as far west as the Rocky Mountains. But west of the Rockies the boundary was still undetermined and the lack of urgency about resolving it was demonstrated by Ashburton not negotiating on the question in 1842. By the early 1840s, however, elements of American opinion were looking to the west, to California and Oregon. Several opportunities to negotiate with the Tyler administration were lost and the 1845 presidential campaign was won by James K. Polk, an unknown westerner. He made it clear that he intended the speedy incorporation of Texas and Oregon into the United States. Peel and Aberdeen were sufficiently concerned to take military precautions but negotiations succeeded in resolving the boundary on the 49th parallel.

Restoring relations with France

The restoration of good relations with France did not go smoothly either. Palmerston's departure had brought a better atmosphere but nobody, least of all Aberdeen, felt that an entente had really been restored. Outwardly there certainly was an improvement in relations – Guizot and Aberdeen proved compatible colleagues and Queen Victoria made private visits to the French royal family in 1843 and 1845 – but beneath the surface serious tensions remained.

Britain and France had differences over Greece, Spain and in North Africa. In Greece there were three groups competing for power: a pro-Russian party led by Metaxa, a pro-British party led by Mavrocordato and a pro-French group headed by Coletti. King Otto of Greece had still not granted a constitution as promised by the three guarantor powers, Britain, France and Russia, ruled incompetently and was in financial difficulty. The French were more accommodating than the other powers to these financial problems and Aberdeen suspected that this was a ploy to establish their influence. A revolution in September 1843, headed by the Greek army, led to several months of co-operation between Britain and France until the new constitution was drawn up. Mavrocordato became Prime Minister but Coletti and Metaxa co-operated to bring down his government. Aberdeen felt that he had been betrayed by the French but was unable to alter the situation. Palmerston was later, at the time of the Don Pacifico affair, to argue that Aberdeen had not maintained Britain's proper influence in Greece.

In Spain Aberdeen insisted that he did not want to maintain any 'British party'. Internal problems did not end with the final defeat of Carlos in 1839 by General Espartero, who had allied himself with the Radicals. In 1840 Queen Christina failed to remove him and was forced to flee to

France. Until July 1843, when Queen Isabella was declared of age, Espartero ruled as Regent. But the marriage of Isabella and her sister, the Infanta Louisa Fernanda, remained an outstanding political problem to be settled. Aberdeen was particularly concerned that a French prince should not become the Queen's consort. In September 1845 Aberdeen indicated that once Isabella was married and had children he could see no objection to her sister marrying a French prince.

The revival of French activity in North Africa in the early 1840s ended Algerian resistance and in 1844 the French extended their activities into Morocco. The extension of the North African conflict was taken very seriously by Aberdeen, especially as it coincided with a serious Anglo-French clash in the Pacific. Public opinion had been alerted to rivalry in Tahiti when the French attempted to annex the island in September 1842. British protests led the French to back down but they maintained their protectorate in spirit and trouble became more acute in 1844 when the French annexed the island and briefly imprisoned the leading British missionary, George Pritchard, who was also British consul. Public opinion was enraged and war seemed likely but Aberdeen and Guizot allowed tempers to cool and compromises were found.

By mid-1844 Aberdeen's French and American policies were in ruin. The entente with France, in which Peel had always had less faith than Aberdeen, was seen to be hollow. Peel and Wellington began to look at strengthening Britain's coastal defences. Aberdeen saw this as a negation of all his policies, was isolated in the cabinet and in late 1845 offered his resignation. Peel refused. However, for the rest of the administration Aberdeen pursued conciliatory policies as well as co-operating with Wellington in military preparations.

In any comparison between Aberdeen and Palmerston it has been Aberdeen who has come off worst. Aberdeen could not project himself in public and in this he bears comparison with Castlereagh. Palmerston could. But the differences went deeper than that. Palmerston had a 'little Englander' mentality while Aberdeen had a genuinely internationalist outlook. He could see both the French and the American points of view and was prepared to accommodate them in his policies. It left him open to criticism of weakness from Palmerston. Yet Aberdeen was more successful in coming to terms with the United States and, to a lesser extent, with France.

PALMERSTON RETURNS

Palmerston returned to the Foreign Office in the ministry Lord John Russell formed in mid-1846. This had not been a foregone conclusion. Whig opposition to his return to the Foreign Office had been so strong in December 1845 that Russell had been unable to form a government. By June 1846, when Peel resigned, Russell was able to convince his colleagues and the Queen that the crises with America and France were over and that he would keep close control over the Foreign Office.

Deteriorating relations in Europe

This proved a hollow promise. There was almost immediate deterioration of relations with France. Palmerston was aware of the accommodation reached by Aberdeen the previous year and included Leopold of Saxe-Coburg in a list of suggested marriage partners for the Queen of Spain. The French had insisted to Aberdeen that Leopold's candidacy would be regarded as releasing them from their previous undertaking. They now vigorously attacked Palmerston and took up their own cause in Spain, pressing the marriage of the Queen with the Duke of Cadiz and her sister with the Duc de Montpensier, both members of the French royal family. In the long run the marriages had little effect on Franco-Spanish relations but there can be little doubt, though much of the anger rebounded on Aberdeen, that Palmerston badly mishandled matters.

He was equally adroit at avoiding blame for the situation that developed in Portugal. In 1845 a general election returned the radical Septembrist party and Queen Maria annulled the constitution and appointed Marshal Saldanha as dictator. Civil war seemed possible and the Queen appealed to the signatories of the 1834 Quadruple Alliance. Palmerston, much to the annoyance of Queen Victoria, expressed public sympathy with the Septembrists but in May 1847 he allowed the British navy to aid the Portuguese government in blockading Oporto. Maria was persuaded to restore constitutional government but this was largely cosmetic as Saldanha and his conservative supporters remained in power. Palmerston had kept intact, just, his reputation for supporting constitutional government.

After 1846 poor harvests and revolutionary outbreaks occurred throughout Europe and Palmerston gained a reputation as a successful defender of liberal causes and a command of public opinion which remained with him for the rest of his life. Closer examination of his views, however, shows that he was very cautious in his support of revolutions. His guiding principle was always Britain's interests and he was sympathetic only to moderate and 'constitutional' reforms.

In the autumn of 1846 the Austrians annexed Cracow, all that remained of a free Poland. Britain and France protested separately at this breach of the Treaty of Vienna but were unable to concert their policies because of difficulties over the Spanish Marriages. Neither could they develop a united policy on Switzerland. Here the dispute was between the Protestant, liberal cantons and the conservative cantons or the Sonderbund. Threats to Austria, Prussia, Piedmont and France led the Protestants to appeal to Britain for aid. Palmerston, aware that the continental powers were ranged against him, could do little and throughout 1847 played for time by suggesting an international conference to settle the dispute. Civil war broke out in November 1847 and, though isolated, Palmerston demonstrated his diplomatic skills. The Sonderbund largely collapsed but intervention by the other Powers was overtaken by their own internal problems in 1848.

1848

The Italian revolutions began with a rising in Sicily in January 1848. In the last week of February Louis Philippe abdicated. By the end of March Metternich had fallen and revolution and constitutional change had spread to the Austrian Empire, Prussia and the other German states. Only Russia and Britain stood outside the revolutionary turmoil that engulfed the rest of Europe, though the potential threat from Chartism was ever present. By the summer of 1849 the status quo had been restored in Italy and, although he would have preferred the withdrawal of Austria north of the Alps, Palmerston had prevented French encroachment. The public was pleased to see him as the champion of Italian nationalism in 1848–9, but the Court was not. His apparently anti-Austrian policy was seen as a dangerous threat to the stability of Europe, despite the fact that he regarded Austria as essential to the European balance of power. Palmerston believed that Austria would be better able to fulfil her real role in Central Europe without Italian commitments and to counteract Russian aggression. European conservatives saw him as the defender of revolutionary causes. In reality balance of power meant more to him than nationalism and while he might approve of constitutional change he did not approve of the potential for social upheaval.

Palmerston certainly displayed little enthusiasm for revolution in Germany, where he maintained it threatened international order. He showed little understanding of events in Germany and only intervened when the Schleswig-Holstein question threatened a European war. His attitude towards the Hungarian revolt was ambiguous. Though he sympathized with the aristocratic Hungarian leadership Palmerston recognized that the breakup of the Austrian Empire would have given Russia increased power in central Europe. Only when the Hungarians had plainly lost did he indulge in condemnation of Austrian and Russian brutalities.

Palmerston versus the Court

Relations between Palmerston and the Court were becoming dangerously strained. Victoria and Albert believed that the Crown still had an active role to play in foreign affairs. They increasingly distrusted Palmerston, several times suggesting to the Prime Minister that he might leave the Foreign Office. Two incidents reinforced their views. In 1850 General Haynau, an Austrian who had been responsible for some of the brutality of the defeat of the Hungarian rising, visited London and was assaulted by workers on a visit to Barclay's Brewery and thrown into a horse trough. Palmerston did not take the incident seriously and was only with difficulty persuaded to send an apology to the Austrian government. The following year, Louis Kossuth, the Hungarian nationalist leader, came to London and was awarded a hero's reception. Palmerston wished to meet him and was dissuaded from doing so by the Queen and various cabinet colleagues.

By 1850 Palmerston was under considerable pressure. The Court was antagonistic, though it undoubtedly exaggerated Palmerston's hostility to Austria. The Conservative opposition was suspicious of his policies and his own Whig colleagues were increasingly doubtful of his benefit to the government. The Don Pacifico affair provided the opportunity to destroy him. At Easter 1847 the house of Don Pacifico, a Portuguese Jew who claimed British citizenship because he had been born in Gibraltar, was burnt down in Athens during an anti-Semitic riot. Failing to obtain redress from the Greek authorities he appealed to Britain for assistance. Britain had a series of genuine and long-standing grievances with Greece, especially over the failure to pay the charges on loans guaranteed by Britain and the other powers after she became independent in 1830. The attack on Don Pacifico was also the latest in a line of outrages against British subjects which the Greek government had shown itself unwilling or unable to remedy. Palmerston protested to the Greek government but nothing was done and in January 1850 a British squadron was sent. It established a blockade and this was maintained until a number of British claims, including that of Don Pacifico, were settled. The Greeks gave in but Britain's co-guarantors of Greece, Russia and France, protested.

This incident provided his critics at home with an excellent opportunity to launch a full-scale attack on his foreign policy. Palmerston's case was weakened by the fact that Don Pacifico was of dubious honesty and by the provocative nature of his response. On 17 June 1850 Lord Stanley, the Conservative leader, moved a vote of censure on the government for its policy towards Greece in the House of Lords. Two days later the vote was carried by 169 to 132. Palmerston offered to resign but Russell preferred to test the matter in the House of Commons. The Commons debate lasted from 24 to 28 June and was a comprehensive attack on Palmerston's foreign policy. The issue was not simply Don Pacifico but the policies Palmerston had pursued since 1847. The outcome was a government victory by 310 to 246 votes. Palmerston had won the support of the general public by his famous *civis Romanus sum* argument:

as the Roman, in days of old, held himself free from indignity when he could say, *civis Romanus sum*; so also a British subject, in whatever land he may be, shall feel confident that the watchful eye and strong arm of England will protect him against injustice and wrong.

Palmerston's triumph in the Commons and in the country was great but it was also brief. The government could hardly do more than rally to the support of their own Foreign Secretary but Russell and other members of the cabinet began to share the Court's opinion that Palmerston was a dangerous man. Russell sought the opportunity to remove him from the Foreign Office and the final crisis came over France.

The Queen had continually complained that dispatches were sent out before she had looked at them. Though she could not have overruled her cabinet this did give her a useful opportunity to make her views known. In August 1850 Palmerston had promised to submit dispatches but on 3 December 1851 he commented approvingly to the French ambassador on the coup of Louis Napoleon. He disapproved of French republics because they tended to be adventurous in their foreign relations, though he had co-operated with the French republic established in February 1848. It is not surprising that Palmerston acted as he did but he had not obtained cabinet approval for his action nor did the Queen know. Russell decided to act and, after Palmerston had refused the Lord Lieutenancy of Ireland, he was curtly dismissed. Palmerston had his revenge in February 1852 when Russell's ministry was brought down on a motion he proposed.

OVERSEAS EXPANSION AND BRITAIN'S 'INTERESTS'

International trade and the protection of Britain's 'interests' played a major part in determining the direction of foreign policy and were influential in Britain's overseas expansion. In 1815 Britain was still a protectionist power and the state played a major role in directing foreign trade and overseas expansion. Tariff protection applied to agriculture and the growing manufacturing industries. There were limitations on the emigration of skilled labour and the export of machinery. The Navigation Act ensured that as much British trade as possible was carried in British ships with British crews. The East India Company had monopoly trading rights in the subcontinent. A colonial empire was considered by most statesmen to be important both as sources of resources and as secure markets.

By 1815 this state-directed policy was being called into question in favour of a global system of free trade. It would be useful to Britain to abandon protection and to persuade others to do the same because, given Britain's technological lead, free trade would ensure that her rivals did not develop in the same way and would remain dependent producers. Colonialism and protection could be abandoned and Britain could still retain economic and political control as the chief centre of industrial wealth through 'free trade imperialism'.

'Free trade imperialism': a historiographical debate

What then was 'free trade imperialism'? Gallagher and Robinson argue that Britain's main interest overseas was in extending informal control sufficiently to integrate as many areas as possible into her expanding economy. Control was extended beyond economic development only when it was considered vital to strategic considerations. Intervention in the internal affairs of smaller, weaker states occurred only to ensure the right conditions for maintaining commercial hegemony, a process facilitated by Britain's naval strength. By contrast, D. C. M. Platt maintains that Britain was not inclined towards imperial expansion in the early part of the nineteenth century.[10] He believes that Gallagher and Robinson overestimated the extent to which Britain interfered on commercial grounds. Platt argues that the main concern of government was the negotiation of reciprocal treaties which would prevent discrimination against British produce, persons and property. This 'opening up' of trade did sometimes, as in China, lead to military or naval intervention but was generally limited to protecting lives and property through the existing countries' legal and diplomatic systems. Traders abroad were often hostile to government interference, which they maintained could alter relationships with local elites and mean formal taxation and control. If the boundaries of empire expanded it was not because government thought it necessary but because of problems on the frontiers which threatened existing economic interests. In broad terms, he argues, there was neither the need for nor the ability to acquire an informal economic empire after 1815. Gallagher and Robinson assume too readily the existence of a free trade system in 1815, while Platt does not appreciate the extent to which the traditional economic system was breaking down in the aftermath of Waterloo.

An extension of empire

In what ways were existing colonies treated after 1815 and in what ways was the British Empire, formal or informal, extended? In the first half of the nineteenth century continuous interest was shown in trying to stimulate the growth of colonies in North America, Australasia and Africa by diverting emigrants to them and away from the United States. Emigration policies took on a new dimension when Robert Wilmot Horton became parliamentary under-secretary at the Colonial Office in 1821. He argued that the post-war economic crisis was largely the result of labour surpluses and that the promotion of emigration to the colonies could reduce the excess. Horton suggested that government should lend local authorities money to provide funds for pauper emigrants. The loans would be paid back by the local authorities and by the settlers from the produce of their land. Emigration was seen as a means of social control, of reducing the cost of poor relief in Britain and of expanding an empire controlled from the centre.

Several small schemes were promoted using Horton's ideas but they did little to divert attention from the United States. By 1830 the economist E. G. Wakefield was claiming that he could solve Britain's oversupply of capital by a better use of colonial lands. His views reflected a shift away from state intervention and towards a 'freer' trading policy. He wanted a better exploitation of Britain's colonies, making them into Britain's granaries which could absorb manufactured goods, surplus labour and capital. Wakefield believed that private companies rather than the state should be the primary agents of change but his scheme was still a deliberate attempt to use colonial possessions to enhance Britain's wealth and power.

Robert Torrens, a fellow economist, went further than Wakefield and argued, in the 1830s and 1840s, that there was a symbiotic relationship between colonial economic development and the maintenance of British economic hegemony. Torrens appreciated the growing economic power of European industry and suggested that the colonies should be brought into a customs union with common tariffs against foreign competition but with free trade in all parts of the empire.

Implicit in Wakefield's ideas was the suggestion that the economic development of the colonies could not take place without some degree of local political autonomy. This autonomy was, however, in practice severely limited. Control of land policy, tariffs and foreign policy remained in British hands, leaving the colonies what Wakefield called 'municipal self-government'. By 1850 it was recognized that the means suggested by Wakefield to retain control over colonies was redundant. Free trade meant the end of colonial privileges and made close political control by Britain impossible to maintain. By the 1850s Canadian provinces were operating tariffs against Britain and the Crown's power of land disposal was gradually abandoned. Self-government was granted to white-settled territories whenever London felt that they were able to provide stable government. Formal control was abandoned in favour of an informal relationship in which economic control was maintained through cultural imperialism.

There was, however, a considerable expansion of the areas of the world under British sovereign control after 1815. Some, like the occupation of Sind and the Punjab on the North-West Frontier of India in 1843 and 1849 respectively, and the annexation of territories in Burma in 1824, were the direct result of the need to preserve the 'frontier', where decisions were taken by local officials and forced on an often reluctant home government. In other cases, like the creation of the Australian state of Queensland in 1850, expansion was the result of local economic conditions. The incorporation of New Zealand in 1840 was a response to a perceived breakdown of law and order. The problem with 'frontier' expansion was that it soon became a form of 'creeping imperialism'. This was clearly evident in West Africa after 1850.

In other areas of the world economic considerations explain colonial expansion. Berar and Nagpur were added to the Indian empire in the 1840s because of their importance as suppliers of raw cotton. The British also took control of a number of small coastal territories across the globe, which suggests that there was a connection between commercial expansion and strategic and naval defence. Singapore was occupied in 1819 to protect the growing trade between Britain, India and China and to counteract Dutch attempts to extend their control in South-East Asia. The extension of control to the port of Labaun on the North Borneo coast in 1846 had the same objective. The occupation of Hong Kong in 1841 reinforced British entry into the Chinese trade. The occupation of Aden in 1839 provided a naval base on the route to India and brought a degree of stability to the Persian Gulf. Lagos had the same role in the more limited area of West Africa and in 1851 the British provided the local ruler with a resident adviser.

The 'informal empire' was also extended after 1815. The debate on this issue lies between those who see Britain as trying to gain economic hegemony through free trade and those who see Britain as simply bargaining with other countries for entry into their markets on a basis of equality. A great deal of the controversy has centred on Britain's relationship with Latin America.

In Peru and Argentina there is evidence of the anti-imperialist case. In Peru Britain did not attempt to gain exclusive trading privileges and Peruvian autonomy was demonstrated in several ways. Tariffs were persistently raised after 1830, despite British protests, and a monopoly was maintained over the guano trade. In Argentina, a similar attempt by Britain to negotiate as free an entry into their markets as was possible by diplomatic means can be seen. In Brazil, however, a different picture emerges. Portugal was largely dependent on Britain for her political survival and the British exploited this dependence to obtain a significant economic hegemony in Portuguese markets. In 1810, in return for further support, Portugal allowed Britain into the Brazilian markets with low tariff concessions and certain legal privileges for shipping and British citizens. These privileges were confirmed in 1827 as the price paid for British support for Brazilian independence. Until 1842, when the Brazilians refused to agree to the extension of the treaty, Britain maintained control over tariffs and penalized Brazil's exports of coffee and sugar in favour of her own colonies. After 1850 attempts at privilege and control became unnecessary as the elites of latin America organized their countries to encourage trading contacts with Britain.

CONCLUSIONS

Foreign and colonial policies between 1815 and the 1850s were based on few principles other than the protection of Britain's interests in economic and strategic terms and in terms of an ambiguous and changing notion of a 'balance of power'. Poor communications and the need for immediacy in responses meant that policy was often 'made' by people on the spot, and later confirmed by the Foreign and Colonial Offices. Policies were reactive rather than proactive, responding to situations rather than having an already determined direction. They were more about means than ends.

NOTES

1 Extract from Palmerston's reply to his critics in the House of Commons, 1 March 1848, Hansard, 3rd series, xcvii, p. 123.
2 Viscount Grey of Falladon *Twenty-Five Years*, 1925, Vol. I, p. 6.
3 Textbook coverage of foreign policy can be found in A. Briggs *The Age of Improvement*, Longman, 1959, pp. 344–93, E. G. Evans *The Forging of the Modern State: Early Industrial Britain 1783–1870*, Longman, 1983, pp. 196–203 and N. Gash *Aristocracy and People: Britain 1815–1865*, Edward Arnold, 1979, pp. 283–318. More specific texts include P. Hayes *The Nineteenth Century 1814–80*, A. & C. Black, 1975, K. Bourne *The Foreign Policy of Victorian England 1830–1914*, Oxford University Press, 1970 and M. E. Chamberlain *British Foreign Policy in the Age of Palmerston*, Longman, 1980. M. E. Chamberlain *Pax Britannica: British Foreign Policy 1789–1914*, Longman, 1989 and J. Clark *British Diplomacy and Foreign Policy 1782–1865*, Unwin Hyman, 1989 provide up-to-date studies. A. Sked (ed.) *Europe's Balance of Power 1815–1848*, Macmillan, 1979 is a useful collection of papers from a European perspective.
4 On Castlereagh C. K. Webster *The Foreign Policy of Castlereagh 1815–1822*, G. Bell, 1931 is still valuable. C. J. Bartlett *Castlereagh*, Macmillan, 1966 and J. W. Derry *Castlereagh*, Allen Lane, 1976 are useful biographies.
5 For Canning's policies see H. W. V. Temperley *The Foreign Policy of Canning 1822–27*, G. Bell & Sons, 1925, reprinted with an introduction by Herbert Butterfield, Cass, 1966 and the biography by Wendy Hinde, Collins, 1973.
6 For Palmerston see J. Ridley *Lord Palmerston*, Constable, 1970, for a readable biography; K. Bourne *Palmerston. The Early Years 1784–1841*, Allen Lane, 1982 for a recent scholarly account and M. E. Chamberlain *Lord Palmerston*, University of Wales Press, 1987 for a shorter, accessible study. C. K. Webster *The Foreign Policy of Palmerston 1830–1841*, 2 vols, G. Bell, 1951 is the standard if somewhat dated, study. M. E. Chamberlain *Lord Aberdeen: A Political Biography*, Longman, 1983 is fundamental for Tory attitudes.
7 Specific studies of different aspects of foreign policy include: K. Bourne *Britain and the Balance of Power in North America 1815–1908*, Longman, 1966 for relations with America; M. S. Anderson *The Eastern Question 1774–1923*, Macmillan, 1966 is the comprehensive study; D. Gillard *The Struggle for Asia 1823–1914: a Study of British and Russian Imperialism*, Methuen, 1977, on Central Asia: and E. Parry-Jones *The Spanish Marriages 1841–46*, Macmillan, 1936, reprinted Oxford University Press, 1968 on Spain. C. J. Barlett *Great Britain and Sea Power 1815–1853*, Oxford University Press, 1963 and D. C. M. Platt, *Finance, Trade and Politics in British Foreign Policy 1815–1914*, Oxford University Press, 1968 are fundamental on British 'interests'.
8 P. J. Cain *Economic Foundations of British Overseas Expansion 1815–1914*, Macmillan, 1980 provides an excellent bibliographical study of this issue.
9 J. Gallagher and R. Robinson 'The Imperialism of Free Trade 1815–1914' *Economic History Review*, 4 (1953–4) reprinted in A. G. C. Shaw (ed.) *Great Britain and the Colonies 1815–1865*, Methuen, 1970, pp. 142–63. This collection of essays contains the major writings of the protagonists on the 'imperial' versus 'anti-imperial' debate apart from D. C. M. Platt.
10 D. C. M. Platt, op. cit., argues that policy was determined by political rather than economic considerations.

Addendum: C. A. Bayly *Imperial Meridian*: The British Empire and the World 1780–1830, Longman, 1989, places the imperial developments in their context.

17 1845–51 – A mid-century crisis?

> Forty-five is a critical age for men, maidens and centuries. . . . Our
> expectations . . . are not excessive. Perhaps it is well that they are not.
> 'Blessed', says a supplementary beatitude, 'are they who expect little,
> for they shall not be disappointed.'

Despite the warnings of *The Spectator*, 1845 began with some optimism.
The economy appeared to be working well: trade was good; the cost of
living was down, with wheat, which had reached 64 shillings a quarter in
1841, selling for 46 shillings; railway construction continued to expand,
absorbing surplus labour. Both crime and pauperism had declined in 1844.
Yet the next six years were years of fundamental change. In almost all
branches of life the situation in 1852 was different from that in 1844. In
the economy, in society, in politics and government and in spiritual and
cultural matters the years between 1845 and 1851 were ones of 'crisis'.

IRELAND: AN OBVIOUS 'CRISIS'

The obvious crisis was in Ireland, though north-west Scotland also experienced demographic devastation.[1] By mid-1845 it was evident that a wet
spring and summer would result in a lower-than-average potato harvest
in Ireland. By September potatoes were rotting in the ground and within
a month blight was spreading rapidly. In Tipperary and Cork it made
some fearful ravages and extended into other counties. The chief food for
some 6 million people was being wiped out. The following year blight
caused a total crop failure. In 1847 it was less virulent but in 1848 a poor
grain harvest aggravated the situation further. Both 1849 and 1850 saw
blight, substantial in some counties, sporadic in others. The contemporary
image of death was graphic. *The Times* carried the following reports in
December 1846

> A mother, herself in a fever, was seen to drag out the corpse of her
> child, a girl of twelve, perfectly naked and leave it half covered with
> stones. In another house, within 500 yards of the cavalry station at
> Skibbereen, the dispensary doctor found seven wretches lying unable

to move, under the same cloak. One had been dead for many hours, but the others were unable to move either themselves or the corpse.

I entered some of the hovels . . . and the scenes that presented them-selves to me were such as no tongue or pen can convey. . . . In the first six famished and ghastly skeletons, to all appearances dead, were huddled in a corner on some filthy straw, their sole coverings what seemed a ragged horse-cloth, and their wretched legs hanging about, naked to the knees. I approached in horror and found by a low moaning they were alive. They were in fever – four children, a woman and what had once been a man. . . .

A demographic crisis certainly. Between 1841 and 1851 the population of Ireland fell from nearly 9 million to some 6.5 million. Emigration accounted for perhaps 1.5 million and became an accepted part of Irish life. This leaves about a million deaths as a result of the Famine. Actual starvation rarely caused death but weakened people sufficiently for diseases like typhus and fever to take their toll. In early 1849 a serious outbreak of cholera added to the problem. The impact of famine was felt differently in both regional and social terms. Death and emigration were greatest in areas where dependence on the potato was greatest, subdivision of land most acute, trade and communications least developed. Western and south-western counties were hardest hit, though even here there were differences within local areas. Counties on the east coast, where food could be more easily imported, were least affected. The north-east did not suffer a crisis, despite its high density of population, because of the more industrial nature of its economy. But it was not unaffected. Many disease-ridden migrants crowded into Belfast, where poor living conditions helped spread disease, but this was a public health not an economic crisis.

Labourers and small farmers were the chief victims of the Famine. There was a considerable thinning of those who farmed less than 15 acres by death, disease, emigration and the workhouse. In 1841 71.5 per cent of holdings fell into this category but by 1851 the figure was 49.1 per cent. There was a consequent increase in the number of holdings over 15 acres from 18.5 to 50.9 per cent. Livestock farming expanded on these larger farms, encouraged by attractive prices in Britain and by reductions in transport costs. In 1851 the agricultural economy was apparently still in a state of crisis: the potato had lost its potency, low agricultural prices gave little promise of recovery to those who had survived, and slightly larger holdings hardly made up for increased poor law rates. But from the 1850s change was rapid: livestock increased in value and numbers, tillage declined slowly and a prosperous stability was enjoyed by tenant farmers, whose numbers remained relatively stable for the next fifty years.[2]

The scale of response by government marked a change in policy. There is no evidence to support the rhetoric of nationalists like John Mitchel that it was genocidal in intention. Peel's response was rapid and, within limits, imaginative. The crisis convinced him finally of the necessity for dismantling the Corn Laws but he realized that this would, because of its contentious nature, take time. Immediate palliatives were needed and in November 1845 a special commission was established to co-ordinate relief efforts. Its policy reflected two objectives. First, it was necessary to prove employment so that labourers could afford to buy food. The government established public work schemes but on a much larger scale than before. These were the boom years of Irish railway construction. Secondly, food had to be kept at a level which prevented profiteering. Some £185,000 was spent on supplies, chiefly Indian meal. These measures met the immediate crisis and none died of actual starvation in the season of 1845–6. Peel was succeeded by Lord John Russell in mid-1846 but he lacked Peel's judgement or Irish experience. Economy and efficiency replaced Peel's more humane policy. The full extent of the Famine was seriously under-estimated in official circles. The problem, however, was not the shortage of food in Ireland – between September 1846 and July 1847 five times as much grain was imported as was exported – but of ensuring that those in need had access to those food supplies. The failure was one of comprehension, not compassion. The crisis lay not just in Irish conditions but in government failure to contain famine. What was needed was synchronized intervention but this had not yet been developed either intellectually or physically by the Victorian state.

The Famine marked a watershed in the political history of modern Ireland. The Repeal Association of O'Connell was dead. The Young Irelanders made their separatist gesture in 1848. A sense of desolation, growing sectarian divisions, the rhetoric of genocide and the re-emergence of some form of national consciousness were to lead to the emergence of a movement dedicated to the independence of Ireland from English rule.

AN ECONOMIC 'CRISIS'

This crisis was paralleled by one in the British economy. 1842–5 had seen a revival in economic confidence, largely the result of Peel's fiscal policies. The rate of interest was lowered in 1843; the Bank Charter Act of 1844 renewed confidence in currency; foreign trade recovered with China, America and Brazil. William Gladstone commented in 1844 that 'unemployed capital abounded to an unprecedented degree and there is no doubt that its investment would take a direction towards railways'.

1844 saw 48 railway acts with 120 the following year. The domestic investment boom reached its peak in July 1845 when Parliament decided that cash deposits for railway stock should be raised by 5–10 per cent. This hit investment. Harvest failures in 1846 created world shortages of wheat. The cotton crop also fell short, sending prices up. In order to check speculation in cotton and wheat supplies the Bank of England raised discount rates from 4 per cent in January 1847 to 5.5 per cent in August.

A good harvest in 1847 brought prices down with disastrous consequences for corn dealers who had bought at the old prices. Eleven stock-banks went down. Despite the deprecations of free-traders, the government intervened on 25 October allowing the Bank to make loans on adequate security at 8 per cent interest. This ended the financial crisis which has been described as 'one of the sharpest and also shortest on record, and essentially a domestic crisis, relatively unaffected by external influences'.[3]

But it was more than a financial crisis. The economy certainly continued to grow but after 1847 the rate of growth in some sectors decelerated. The iron industry, for example, had been stimulated by the demand for railway iron. A general depression in 1841–2 was followed by the boom of 1843–5 when iron output topped 2 million tons per annum. But by 1847 the railway boom was over and the United States had developed facilities for making heavy iron rails. The result was wage cuts, unemployment and strikes: 62 per cent of the South Staffordshire furnaces were out of blast; 22 per cent in Wales and 31 per cent in Scotland. Though the upward climb was resumed in 1849 the effect of this slump was to check the growth of the industry. The same deceleration can be seen in the cotton industry which, before 1846, had an annual growth rate of between 5 and 6 per cent but which fell to about 3.5 per cent after 1848. Between 1844 and 1846 textile exports were £38.7 million accounting for about two-thirds of Britain's total exports. By 1854–6, though the cost had increased to £47.6 million this accounted for only 46 per cent of total exports. Of the 'leading sector' industries of the industrial revolution only coal was cushioned from the full effects of the slump by the demands of the growing railway network.

Up to the mid-1840s overseas trade and industrial production increased at about the same rate. But between 1845 and 1850 Britain finally became committed to an official policy of 'free trade'. Peel abolished or reduced many duties in 1845 and the following year repealed the Corn Laws except for a registration duty of a shilling a quarter. In 1849 the Navigation Laws were repealed for foreign trade. Though this process was not completed until 1860 there was a sustained growth in trade which soon outran growth rates in industry. British export industries were able to undercut the rest of the world in cheap cloth and basic iron products. The industrial sector after 1850 became dependent on foreign trade to a much greater extent than before 1845. Peter Mathias has argued that Britain had a 'distorted' industrial structure in 1850 and that the mid-nineteenth century 'bristled with ironies'. British industry was dominated by a few industrial giants – textiles, coal, iron, shipbuilding – which had all responded positively to world demand. Free trade aided that process. But the emergence of industrial competitors like the United States and the eventual development of home-based textile and iron industries in countries which had previously been Britain's foreign markets was to lead to 'these few successful giants of the nineteenth century . . . find[ing] themselves the gasping dinosaurs of the twentieth'.[4]

The repeal of the Corn Laws marked a psychological rather than an actual crisis for the landed interest. In the short term, for at least twenty years, it did not result in the much published demise of English cereal farmers who seem to have prospered in the 1850s. But this vision has been criticized by E. L. Jones for being 'too rosy'.[5] Agriculture was not a monolithic industry in which cereal production overrode all other interests. In fact cereal prices did not show any sustained disposition to move upwards: prices were 7 per cent lower in 1870 than 1850. The 1840s and 1850s saw 'revolutions' on the heavier clay soils made possible by effective cheap drainage and government grants and by the process of mechanization. This left the farm labourer with few tangible improvements in living standards, and increasing numbers moved off the land. The total engaged in agriculture and those living in rural areas began to dwindle in absolute terms. After 1846 there was a shift in many areas away from purely cereal farming to investment in livestock rearing and especially in mixed farming. Both protected farmers, to some extent, against foreign competition. The 'Golden Age' of farming is as much a myth as any other.

The late 1840s saw a crisis in the British economy relative to other economies. The annual rate of growth was slow, at most 3 per cent. This compared unfavourably with the United States which from the 1840s was growing at between 4 and 5 per cent per annum. This can be seen in the three areas on which the overall rate of growth of any economy depends: the growth rates of the labour force, of capital accumulation and in technology. Up to 1841 Britain's population was growing at about 1.5 per cent annually but from 1851 this had fallen to less than 1.25 per cent. The population dynamic begun in the early eighteenth century was not sustained after 1850. By contrast, the United States expanded at over 2.5 per cent per annum through a combination of high rates of natural increase and immigration. There were no high level of investment in the economic infrastructure after the railway booms of the 1830s and 1840s but at no stage of industrialization had capital formation been a high proportion of the national income. By 1850 the average rate was about 10 per cent of the net national product but an increasing proportion of new investment was going abroad. Foreign investment created dividends for investors and markets for exports but did not increase the physical stock of capital in British industries. Britain's lead in technological advance must be seen in the context of the slowness with which inventions were adopted. The United States developed and applied inventions far more quickly. Sir John Clapham commented that by 1851 'The well-informed knew that an American was more likely than an Englishman to get tiresome and expensive handicraft operations done for him by machinery'.[6] The Great Exhibition of 1851 marked the zenith of Britain's industrial and technological superiority. The depression of 1836–42 and the crisis of 1845–51 changed the British economy. Rival countries were now growing faster.

A SOCIAL 'CRISIS'?

In 1843 Robert Vaughan wrote that

> Our age is pre-eminently the age of the great cities. . . . This increase in the magnitude and power of cities . . . is nowhere more conspicuous than in Great Britain. . . . Our country has become emphatically a land of great cities. Our metropolis has become such as the world has not seen. Our leading towns in the provinces equal the capitals of ordinary kingdoms. Whatever, therefore, of good or evil may pertain to the character of modern civilisations, must pertain in an eminent degree to Great Britain, so that if any nation is to be lost or saved by the character of its great cities, our own is that nation. . . .[7]

This prognosis was confirmed by the 1851 Census which found that Britain's population was roughly divided between country dwellers and town dwellers (in communities of over 5,000). The 15 'cities' with over 200,000 people in 1801 had risen to 63 by mid-century and contained 35 per cent of the total population. The impact of urbanization was profound whether in physical terms, expressed in such problems as sanitation, housing and water supplies; in social terms, through the changing nature of society and the impact on the family; or in economic terms through the problems resulting from new systems of commercial and industrial organization. Disraeli was not alone when he wrote of Manchester in 1844 that

> The feeling of melancholy, even of uneasiness, attends our first entrance into a great town, especially at night. Is it that the sense of all this fast existence with which we have no connection, where we are utterly unknown, oppresses us with our insignificance?

Despite the dominance of *laissez-faire* ideas government was not unaware of conditions for the mass of the population but it had not kept pace with the changes in society as a whole and until 1830 central reform was meagre. The 1830s saw the relationship between central supervision and local administration of social legislation begin to be defined but it was not until 1844–51 that responses to social problems began to move from remedial to more positive actions.

Factory inspectors did not possess undisputed powers to enter factory buildings or the right to penalize those who obstructed them in their duties until 1844. In 1850 the mining inspectorate was given extended powers. What was being remedied here was a failure by government to supply the means to enforce its legislation. The 1844 and 1847 Factory Acts, with the clarifying legislation of 1850 and 1853, brought enforceable powers on hours, ages of work and working conditions in most textile industries.

The poor laws and their operation were carefully scrutinized throughout the 1830s and 1840s. The dilemma that existed was neatly expressed in *The Times* in May 1842 when it asked 'Is there no via media, no middle path, between tyrant centralisation and a recurrence to the maladministration of the Poor Laws which existed after 1795?'

The 1834 Poor Law Amendment Act was carried further by legislation in 1844. The central board was given powers over auditing union accounts, providing school districts for children under sixteen and for providing and managing asylums. Government intervention, in the view of the Home Secretary Sir James Graham, was becoming more, not less, necessary because the numbers of the poor were constantly increasing. But there were also significant limitations placed on the powers of the central board. The bone-crushing scandal at Andover where inmates of the workhouse were treated so harshly that some ate the marrow from bones they had been given to pulp resulted in publicity and initiated a debate which led to the reconstitution of the central board under a President sitting in Parliament and accountable to parliamentary scrutiny. This marked a major change in social legislation: direct responsibility and accountability to Parliament.

Developments in both factory and poor law legislation extended reforms begun in the 1830s and earlier, but this was not the case with public health. The 1840s saw Edwin Chadwick's *Report on the Sanitary Conditions of the Labouring Population* and the Royal Commission on the Health of Large Towns. Both confirmed the dreadful nature of urban conditions and roused considerable popular sympathy. Yet it was local initiatives responding to local conditions, like those of Liverpool from 1846, that really achieved success. The 1848 Public Health Act was as much a response to the recurrence of cholera as it was a recognition by government of its responsibilities. Yet the case for the state increasing its role in the area of national health was being expressed even if the rights of private property were violated. But there was widespread and sustained opposition. *The Times* in June 1847 had said that

> All England is afraid of being put under a central board in London. . . . The parochial soul is on fire – provincial patriotism is big with indignation at the project of a central despotism. But the cry is too hasty; the alarm and indignation are premature. The administration will still be local.

David Urquhart, Conservative MP for Stafford, regarded the 1848 Act as

> un-English and unconstitutional – corrupt in its tendencies – it was an avowal of a determination to destroy local self-government . . . destroying every vestige of local pre-eminence and reducing all to one dull and level monotony.

In 1854 the 'experiment' was ended though there was no real return to local anarchy in dealing with public health issues.

Between 1845 and 1851 a dialogue took place between those who argued that social problems required centralist solutions and those who believed localities could respond better to the needs of their populations. Public health legislation and, to a lesser extent, poor law and factory reforms demonstrated that the interests of all were beginning to take priority over the rights of individuals and groups. But there were still limitations. The railway legislation of the 1840s demonstrated the ability of the railway lobby to prevent radical state intervention. The crisis for government on social questions was a choice between 'public' or 'private' interests. Though the debate was frequently conducted from entrenched positions and was far from over, between 1845 and 1851 the pendulum began to swing decisively in favour of the 'public's' interest.

A POLITICAL 'CRISIS'?

There is no doubt that there was a party political crisis between 1845 and 1851. This crisis centred round 'the revolution of 1846'. In the Maynooth Grant of 1845 and the repeal of the Corn Laws the following year Peel attacked the triple Tory orthodoxies of Protestantism, Protection and Landed Property. Peel and his supporters certainly ceased to be Tories, though whether they stopped being Conservatives was another matter. From 1846 until the formation of Aberdeen's administration in 1852 these Peelites were an independent force in Parliament. Not all politicians mourned the end of the party system which had dominated Parliament since 1830 and *The Economist* in early 1847 announced that parties had been 'dissolved'. But the crisis of 1845–51 was one of the redefinition of the party system, not its eclipse.

The Peelites were left-of-centre Conservatives whom circumstances had alienated from the main body. Their 'liberalism' was generally conservative for they believed that the status quo could only be conserved by policies that took into account the principles of natural justice and political economy. It was their instinctive contempt for reaction that cut them off from the old Tory party which clung to Protection by instinct, though it was eventually dropped as a principle in 1852. The land was still a major interest but, as Peel recognized, it was no longer a bond of union, still less the basis for a political party. The Protectionists were a political grouping rather than a political party in the sense of one able to provide or sustain a government. By 1850 British society had become too diversified, too pluralistic to sustain a Tory-Protectionist, a Peelite or a purely Whig aristocratic party in power for long. Until the Conservatives changed from being a party of reaction to one of conservation they were no viable alternative to the Whig-Liberal party.

In 1845 the Whig-Liberals lacked both policies and a leader. The paradox of Whiggery had been stated by Lord Beauvale in 1839

> The truth is that the whole of the Whig doctrine rests on an unsound basis. Their doctrine is to govern by means of the masses, whereas in practice the Govt must come from above, and be conducted in the interests of the masses but not depending on them for support.[8]

The fundamental problem facing them was that they had not made up their mind after 1832 whether to be an aristocratic or a popular party. This was not really resolved between 1845 and 1851 since further electoral reform was necessary before popular strength could be translated into parliamentary power. The Whigs were caught between the pressure of public opinion and the limitations of a narrow parliamentary constitution. Russell's acceptance of free trade and repeal in his Edinburgh Letter of December 1845 may have pleased the liberal wing within his party but it worried the Whigs. Repeal allowed him to resurrect the Whig-Liberals as a party with popular appeal but the 1847 General Election did not translate this into actual seats. Whig-Liberal strength was estimated as 336, though only 316 were dependable, out of the total of 640 MPs. Russell relied on the goodwill of the Peelites, whom he hoped to persuade to join a centre bloc of conservative Liberals, to govern. But the Peelites were unwilling to decide where they stood and this paralysed his strategy. By 1850 the Whigs were again out of policies and Russell was increasingly bankrupt as their leader. The years between 1845 and 1851 confirmed that there was a future in Liberalism but a less certain one in Whiggery.

Between 1845 and 1851 only the Conservatives really underwent a 'crisis'. The problems of the Whig-Liberal party had their origins in the 1830s and were not to be resolved until the early 1860s. But Gladstone overstated the case when he wrote in 1855 that

> The Session of 1845 was the last of those that witnessed party connections in their normal state. Throughout the decade which preceded that year it had been in full and brilliant blossom. Since then we have had properly speaking no parties: that is none in the best sense of the term: none compact and organised after the ancient manner.

EXTRA-PARLIAMENTARY 'CRISIS'

Extra-parliamentary politics underwent something of a 'crisis' during this period. The success of the Anti-Corn Law League has often been set against the failure of Chartism but this is too simplistic an interpretation. Had there not been famine in Ireland it is possible that repeal would not have taken place in 1846. But pressure on Parliament was much broader than these two movements which, until recently, dominated much historical writing. W. R. Greg wrote in 1852 that

Parliament is no longer the only, nor the chief arena for political debate. Public meetings and the press are fast encroaching upon and superseding its original exclusive functions. Every man has become a politician. . . . Public opinion is formed out of doors; and is only revised, ratified and embodied within. . . . The functions of Parliament are no longer unitary. . . . The independent thinker originates; the Country listens, disputes, sifts, ripens; and Parliament revises and enacts.[9]

Between 1845 and 1851 middle-class pressure came of age. It presented a diverse as well as coherent front against aristocratic privilege. The Financial Reform League had ties with the Anti-Corn Law League, the Freehold Land Society, Joseph Hume's Little Charter and national education; and the public health movement with evangelical paternalism, administrative reform, with the Social Science Association, with poor law and national education as well as orthodox free trade.

W. J. Fox, Unitarian MP for Oldham, wrote in 1849 that the reunion of the middle and working classes would rest upon

the combination of fiscal reform, the revision of taxation, the principles of economy and peace, and the reform of the representation, as objects of the same movement. These are the people's objects – the legitimate claims of the many as opposed to the sinister interests of the few.[10]

But his optimism was premature and further parliamentary reform had to wait until 1867. The 1850s and early 1860s have been seen by historians as a period of relative stability, but though the nature of society had changed human nature had not. Violence did not cease being a powerful, almost instinctive, popular force. Food riots had largely died out though there were widespread disturbances in north-east Scotland and in Cornwall and Jersey in 1847. Threatening letters and arson attacks increased after 1845 as did sheep-stealing and egg-stealing. In Ireland, particularly the southern counties, robbery of arms, forcible possession of property, armed assembly, attacks on houses, land and policeman played a far more important part than in England. But only in Scotland and Ireland did the face of rural protest and rural resistance remain largely unaltered.

The level of committals for all indictable riotous offences before 1845 stood at over 2 per cent of all committals, and after 1851 was generally below 1 per cent. Violence and urban disturbances were blamed on a well-defined 'criminal' or 'dangerous' class. In the country the persistence of protest was blamed on specific groups, particularly the Irish, giving rise to ethnic and sectarian conflict. In 1852 the Rev. Thomas Beames described St Giles, Westminster, as

inhabited by the various classes of thieves common to large cities . . . they are the fuel on which agitation feeds, ready to take fire the moment the flame is kindled by great party feuds . . . when rebellion recruits her forces she is fed by the denizens of these retreats. . . . [11]

Political disturbances were seen less as a threat to the established order than as a 'social problem' like any other. Protest was dealt with through the medium of criminal law. Revolution was legislated away.

A SPIRITUAL 'CRISIS'?

Between 1845 and 1851 there was a spiritual crisis within Anglicanism, Nonconformity and Catholicism. The Church of England had been on the defensive for much of the century. Its position as *the* church of the English people was under severe strain and the 1851 Religious Census provided statistical confirmation of this. It had never been the church of the Scots, Welsh or Irish. It lacked evangelical verve, despite the work of the Clapham sect, and had failed to respond positively to the challenge of demographic and urban growth, relying on its symbiotic relationship with the state to maintain its religious and social hegemony. The repeal of the Test and Corporation Acts and Catholic emancipation demonstrated dramatically the weakness of this monopolistic relationship, a process exacerbated by the identification of Anglicanism with reaction locally and nationally. Henry Bathurst, the Whig Bishop of London, stated in 1832 that 'The greatest threat to the Church arose not so much from a restless spirit of innovation in some, as from an obstinate adherence to antiquated abuses in others.'[12]

From 1830 the Church of England underwent a process of modernization: church-building increased, organization was rationalized and the quality of the clergy was improved respectively by evangelical action, Parliament and the Tractarian movement.

The decision of a leading Tractarian, John Henry Newman, to convert to Roman Catholicism in 1845-6 was unfortunate in its timing. It coincided with the Maynooth question and the growing Irish problem. Was Popery in the ascendancy? Were the Tractarians closet Catholics? Between 1847 and 1851 the Whig government blundered towards the re-establishment of a Catholic hierarchy in England. Papal aggression was feared and resisted but neither Russell nor Queen Victoria professed alarm at the papal bogey. To her the real enemy was within the Church of England. She agreed with a statement made by Thomas Arnold, when headmaster of Rugby, that 'I look upon a Roman Catholic as an enemy in his uniform; I look upon a Tractarian as an enemy disguised as a spy.'

Between 1845 and 1851 people became more conscious of their Protestantism. The Tractarians attained the zenith of their unpopularity and, as a result, an alliance between Low Churchmen and the state was re-established. Convocation began to be used in more positive and less formal ways. The confidence of Anglicanism and the organizational hierarchy of Catholicism had both been restored by 1852.

The 1851 Religious Census pointed to the uncomfortable fact that the dissenting churches commanded the allegiance of nearly half the population of England and Wales. Methodism had been a far more dynamic force than Anglicanism. It had brought religion to areas which the Church of England had neglected, especially the new industrial centres. It had become the dominant religion in Wales. But it was not without its inner tensions, particularly the autocratic attitudes of Jabez Bunting. James Everett led the attack between 1845 and his eventual expulsion in 1849, and his antics dominated much Methodist thinking. People resisted conversion and membership may have declined slightly but, to Bunting, worryingly. The view that 'The world is no proper court of appeal against the decisions of the Church' led to the Methodist Conference being viewed as another 'Star Chamber'. This too was damaging. Everett did not wish to split Methodism only to make the Conference more representative. The public applauded this view and liberal newspapers joined in the national abuse. Conference, however, did not waver. The crisis left the seceders more radical and those who remained more conservative. Wesleyan Methodism had ceased to be a 'movement' and had become a 'denomination'.

From the 1840s there was little difference in growth rates between Wesleyan Methodism and those groups which had seceded – Primitive Methodists, Bible Christians, New Connexion and Free Methodists. Their 'crisis' was similar to that faced by Bunting. Should they act as a conservative or a radical force in society? Certainly the old evangelicalism of the Primitive Methodists still persisted but its conference moved towards conservatism. Fission did not occur because the tension was not between the laity and ministers, as in its Wesleyan counterpart, or between centre and locality. The tension was over whether the Primitives would become a denomination or not. Although they were emerging from their 'ranting' period characterized by evangelical zeal the Primitive Methodists were still able to retain their original constituency among the poor. In 1853 a melancholic Wesleyan said that they were the only denomination to possess the affection and confidence of the poor.

The 1851 Religious Census demonstrated a 'crisis' seen by Horace Mann as far more significant – 5.25 million people failed to attend any church at all. Was society becoming more secular? Was formal religion less important? How can historians explain why a society that was spending more than ever before on church- and chapel-building, on education and tracts and on missionary work in the towns failed to capture such a large number of people? The expanding towns did not have the same traditions of religious observance and attendance as the countryside. The 'crisis' was not just one of confidence and numbers but of appeal and habit.

CONCLUSIONS

Between 1845 and 1851 it is possible to identify a series of 'crises' within Britain. The economy began to show signs of deceleration and changes occurred in both the character and location of some industries. The demographic crisis in Ireland was paralleled in north-eastern Scotland. Social conditions that demanded government action became acute and the dominant *laissez-faire* ideology underwent modification in the area of social reform at the same time as it finally achieved official respectability in economic affairs. 'Crises' were evident in 'high' and 'low' politics with the split in the Conservative party, the Whig-Liberal dilemma, the failure of Chartism and the emergence of legitimate extra-parliamentary pressure groups. The 1851 Religious Census enumerated the depth of the spiritual 'crisis' that ran parallel to a growing sense of secularism. Taken together they constituted a 'general mid-century crisis' in British society and set the agenda for the next half-century.

NOTES

1 On famine in Ireland see R. D. Edwards and T. D. Williams *The Great Famine*, Dublin University Press, 1956, C. Woodham Smith *The Great Hunger*, Hamish Hamilton, 1962 and J. Mokyr *Why Ireland Starved: A Qualitative and Analytical History of the Irish Economy 1800–1850*, Allen & Unwin, 1983 for contrasting approaches. E. M. Crawford (ed.) *The Irish Experience 900–1900: Subsistence Crises and Famine in Ireland*, John Donald, 1989 provides a longer perspective and T. Devine *The Great Highland Famine*, John Donald, 1988 carries the 'great hunger' outside Ireland. D. Fitzpatrick *Irish Emigration 1801–1921*, Economic and Social History Society of Ireland, 1984 asks the pertinent questions briefly. C. O. Grada *The Great Irish Famine*, Macmillan, 1989 provides a brief but essential bibliographical study.

2 On the 'land question' in Ireland see W. E. Vaughan *Landlords and Tenants in Ireland 1848–1904*, Studies in Irish Economic and Social History, 1984 and M. J. Winstanley *Ireland and the Land Question 1800–1923*, Methuen, 1984.

3 D. M. Evans *The Commercial Crisis, 1847–1848*, London, 1849, reprinted Kelly, 1969 is the best contemporary account.

4 P. Mathias *The First Industrial Nation*, 2nd edn, Methuen, 1983, p. 231.

5 E. L. Jones *The Development of English Agriculture 1815–1873*, Macmillan, 1968.

6 J. Clapham *An Economic History of Modern Britain*, Cambridge University Press, 1932, volume 2, p. 12.

7 R. Vaughan *The Age of Great Cities; or, Modern Civilization Viewed in its Relation to Intelligence, Morals and Religion*, 2nd edn, London, 1843, p. 1.

8 Quoted in Countess of Airlie *Lady Palmerston and Her Times*, London, 1922, volume ii, pp. 37–8.

9 W. R. Greg 'The expected reform bill', *Edinburgh Review*, January 1852, quoted in P. Hollis (ed.) *Pressure from Without in Early Victorian England*, Edward Arnold, 1974, pp. 25–6.

10 W. J. Fox *Lectures to the Working Classes*, London, 1849, introduction, quoted in P. Hollis (ed.) op. cit., p. 13.

11 T. Beames *The Rookeries of London*, London, 1852, 2nd edn, reprinted Cass, 1970, p. 26.
12 Quoted in Soloway *Prelates and People: Ecclesiastical Social Thought in England 1783–1852*, Routledge, 1969, p. 247.

Name Index

Subject Index